JACQUELINE KENNEDY ONASSIS

A LIFE BEYOND HER WILDEST DREAMS

DARWIN PORTER & DANFORTH PRINCE

A Special Memorial Edition

JACQUELINE KENNEDY ONASSIS
A LIFE BEYOND HER WILDEST DREAMS

Darwin Porter and Danforth Prince

Manufactured in the United States of America

ISBN 978-1-936003-39-6

Special thanks to the Stanley Mills Haggart Collection,
the WoodrowParrish-Martin Collection, the H. Lee Phillips Collection, the Fredric
and Grace Smithey Collection, and Elsa Maxwell Café Society.

Cover designs by Richard Leeds (Bigwigdesign.com)
Videography and Publicity Trailers by Piotr Kajstura

Distributed in North America, the U.K., and Australia
through National Book Network (www.NBNbooks.com)

2 3 4 5 6 7 8 9 10

THIS BOOK COMMEMORATES THE
20TH ANNIVERSARY OF THE DEATH OF
AN AMERICAN FIRST LADY

JACQUELINE
BOUVIER
KENNEDY
ONASSIS

JULY 28, 1929-MAY 19, 1994

From the Publisher, regarding
Blood Moon's Anniversary Editions

This biography of Jacqueline Kennedy Onassis is the first of a series of special memorial editions commemorating the 20th, 30th, and even the 60th anniversary of the deaths of some of the leading and most enduring icons, male and female, of the 20th Century.

With the passage of time, increasing numbers of post-mortem, behind-the-scenes secrets have been uncovered. These latter-day revelations challenge the image these celebrities presented of themselves to the world. A case in point is Joan Crawford appearing in film clips proclaiming what a wonderful "Mommie Dearest" she was, or James Dean in film shorts promoting car safety.

Despite the glare of publicity that spotlighted these personalities during their lifetimes, they somehow managed to conceal much of their private lives behind a decorative veil of mystery. Today, thanks to different presuppositions about media, libel laws, the *paparazzi*, and the western hemisphere's armies of reporters and their willingness to publish and distribute exposés, such concealment might be impossible.

By now, most of the public knows that among other conquests, John F. Kennedy seduced a number of movie stars. At least they know about Marilyn Monroe. But how many fans are aware of the male movie stars Jacqueline seduced? You'd be surprised.

Drawing from countless sources compiled over many decades, Blood Moon has accumulated amazing and tantalizing information about American icons who until very recently remained enigmatic. In upcoming releases, the glow of Blood Moon's lunar light will shine on their secret loves, their betrayals, their heartbreaks, their triumphs and tragedies, their valiant battles against personal demons, their international adventures, and their inevitable falls.

These anniversary editions will be perceptive, sensitive, and unbiased "warts and all" portrayals, thd kind demanded by Oliver Cromwell when he sat to have his portrait painted.

We will compile these books with no desire to topple any deity from his or her pedestal. Our ultimate aim involves a desire to understand more clearly these iconic personalities within their sociological contexts, since they continue to fascinate us into the 21st Century.

The dust has settled on these figures. The time has come to sweep away the sands of time to see what they concealed. Fasten your seat belts—it's going to be a memorable ride.

Best wishes to all of you, from all of us.

Danforth Prince, President,
Blood Moon Productions

CONTENTS

Thanks for the Memories

This Book Is Dedicated to:

William Walton

Lem Billings

Senator George Smathers

Stanley Mills Haggart

Truman Capote

Peter Lawford

Gore Vidal

Letitia Baldrige

John H. Davis

Roy Cohn

and with Special Thanks to Johnny Meyer

Plus a cast of thousands over the decades,
some of whom did not want to be named

Blood Moon Productions
Award-Winning Entertainment
About How America Interprets its Celebrities

www.BloodMoonProductions.com

Prologue

It was a time of mourning in front of 1040 Fifth Avenue in Manhattan. A candlelit vigil was being staged at the apartment house of Jacqueline Kennedy Onassis. Her more ardent admirers had gathered, along with tourists, the idle curious, and the inevitable reporters and paparazzi. Word had spread that life was ebbing fast for the world's most famous woman.

Inside, Jacqueline Kennedy Onassis, in a bedroom lit by antique lamps, was spending her final hour on earth, slipping in and out of consciousness from a morphine-induced sleep. At her bedside were her final lover, Maurice Tempelsman, along with her beloved children, John Jr. and Caroline.

At 10:15PM, Thursday, May 19, 1994, the attending doctor pronounced her dead at the age of sixty-four—"too young to die."

Someone spread the word to Fifth Avenue. Many fans began to weep, evoking that day in Dallas in November of 1963, when President John F. Kennedy was assassinated.

The following morning, John Jr. appeared on the street, looking composed in a tailored dark blue suit. In what would later be called his finest hour, he addressed the crowd:

"Last night, at around 10:15, my mother passed on. She was surrounded by her friends and family, and her books and people and things she loved. She did it her own way, and on her own terms, and we all feel lucky for that, and now she is in God's hands."

Days later, he revealed to the Kennedy family his mother's final words to him. "Please, promise me you'll give up piloting your own plane. **Please!**"

"I will, mother," he promised. "Trust me. I will."

Jacqueline Kennedy Onassis

Chapter One

Baby Jackie and Black Jack Bouvier

Jackie Grows Up with "The Black Prince"
Her Gambling, Womanizing, Bisexual Father

At the 1934 Southampton Horse Show, **Jackie** stood—both emotionally and physically—between her mother, **Janet Lee Bouvier**, and her father, **Black Jack Bouvier**.	From the beginning of their long and complicated sisterhood, **Lee Bouvier** *(in the carriage)* lived in **Jackie's** shadow.

Torn from the pages of *The Great Gatsby*, Black Jack Bouvier helped define the Roaring Twenties. He was seductive, charming, dangerous, and, in the words of his wife, Janet, "a barnyard rooster."

His legitimate daughters included Jacqueline and Lee Bouvier. His illegitimate twins, and boy and a girl, were sent to Britain.

1

A womanizer, Black Jack was also bisexual, indulging in numerous affairs with both young men and women, often on the same night. He was a hedonist, a rogue, a gambler, a scoundrel, a rascal, a libertine, and a heartbreaker, leading a dissolute life which featured promiscuous sex and other vices he claimed were "not fit to mention in polite company." A moneymaker who dabbled with high risks, he also spent recklessly.

This was the man who functioned as Jackie's role model for her future husbands, John F. Kennedy and Aristotle Onassis. Because of the early examples her father established, she was perhaps able to indulge, or at least overlook, their frequent betrayals and infidelities.

Janet, holding her happy daughter, **Jacqueline**, was unaware of the oncoming Wall Street crash that would mar their lives.

Perhaps Black Jack loved "my darling Jacqueline," too much, at least in the opinion of Janet.

Black Jack himself, *[formally known as John Vernou Bouvier III]*, later recalled that "My daughter, Jacqueline Lee Bouvier, could have chosen a more opportune time to come into the world. She was born on July 28, 1929. In October came the great Wall Street Crash, plunging the world into a depression. I suffered terrible losses that day."

"I was called Black Jack by my friends, because of my dark skin color," he claimed. "My enemies had their names for me. Sometimes, the ladies referred to me as The Black Sheik, claiming that I looked like Rudolph Valentino. I was also called 'The Black Orchid.' My favorite nickname was 'The Black Prince.' When Jackie started going to the movies, she said if I'd gone to Hollywood, I would have given Clark Gable competition. After all, we had the same mustache. Jackie got her good looks from me—or so they say."

"I was a stockbroker, but not a conformist," he said. "A bit of a maverick. My motto came from Martin Luther. 'He who loves not wine, women, and song, is a fool his whole life long.'"

Born in 1891, Black Jack was the oldest son of Major John Vernou Bouvier, Jr. He was one of five children, each of whom would become a future aunt or uncle of Jacqueline Bouvier. These included Black Jack's younger brother, William Sargent Bouvier, nicknamed "Bud;" Black Jack's sister, Edith; and two strawberry blonde twins, Maude and Michelle Bouvier.

Black Jack had graduated from Yale in 1914 at the bottom of his class. His classmate, Tom Collier, later said, "He never opened a book, but practically seduced every virgin who came on the weekends, hoping to pick up Yale under-

---

"Your Relationship with Jackie is Unnatural"

—Janet (Jackie's mother) to Black Jack

graduates in the local taverns."

"No one could believe it. On some nights, he had three or four girls waiting downstairs to be serviced. What a stud! He would bop one and then summon the next. He treated girls something awful, but they flocked to him. We called him 'The Great Lover.' From what I observed of him in the shower, he had one powerful weapon."

Black Jack's Society Seductions
"The Merry Widow" and the Richest Teenager in the World

When the United States entered World War I, Black Jack was commissioned as a 2nd lieutenant in the Army Signal Corps. Black Jack wrote Collier, "While waiting for this dirty little war to end, I'm spending all my time in the smoke-filled, honky-tonk, back alley bars and brothels of the Carolinas."

After the war, he acquired a seat on the New York Stock Exchange.

His friend, Louis Ehret, a wealthy realtor, said, "Jack was reckless with money. He ran up huge gambling debts. What he didn't drink, he pissed away on women. I think he invited half of New York to his apartment at 375 Park Avenue. Women flocked around him like moths to the flame. He even shacked up with Mae Murray, who'd starred in Erich von Stroheim's *The Merry Widow*. Quite a contrast. his dark skin against her powder puff whiteness. One night he went home with Texas Guinan after we visited her speakeasy. He once told me that he'd impregnated at least a dozen women, arranging back alley abortions for them."

"The biggest scandal that circulated about him was that he was seducing his twin sisters, Maude and Michelle," Ehret claimed. "They loved to party as much as he did. Some women wanted both Bud and Jack in their beds at the same time." The reference was to his alcoholic brother, William Sargent Bouvier.

"Bud could drink even more than Black Jack, if that were possible," Ehret said. "The Major eventually cut Bud off, calling him a 'contemptible parasite and dirty nuisance.'"

Black Jack went every day to the Maidstone, the most exclusive country club of East Hampton. If the weather was fair, Black Jack would strip down and sunbathe nude in the courtyard, much to the delight of the society ladies passing by. Some of

Black Jack got to taste the beestung lips of silent screen vamp **Mae Murray**, "the Merry Widow" herself.

them would stop and stare in disbelief. As Kathleen Bouvier wrote, "He never saw any reason to conceal what the good Lord had given him. And by his own reckoning, he had given him just about everything. His seductiveness lay in his aura of unquestionable masculinity. He looked like the concrete realization of a young girl's dreamy fantasy, a glamorous sheik who would whisk her off to his tent in Araby."

One night at a dance at Maidstone, Black Jack met Janet Norton Lee. She was the second of three sisters, the others being Winifred Norton Lee and Marion Norton Lee. Janet could be seen whizzing along the roads of Long Island in her own car. She lived in a big house attended to by servants, and she had spent a year at Sweet Briar College and another year at Vassar.

She bragged that she was "a descendant of the Lees of Maryland," a reference to a rich and prestigious family. Actually, she was descended from Irish immigrants who had fled the potato famine in their home country.

Edie Beale, Jackie's cousin, once revealed a family secret. "Janet wasn't in love with Black Jack. She fell hard for his younger brother, Bud. From what I heard, Bud taught Janet about the birds and the bees. She wanted to marry him, but the Lee family objected to him because he was a notorious alcoholic. So guess what? She married his alcoholic brother, Black Jack instead. You figure it out."

Even so, Bud agreed to be his brother's best man at his wedding to Janet Lee, his former lover, at St. Philomena Church in East Hampton on July 7, 1928. *The East Hampton Star* heralded it as "The Social Event of the Season."

At his wedding reception at the Savoy Plaza Hotel in Manhattan, Black Jack had a fierce argument about finances with his new father-in-law, James Thomas Lee.

Socialite Alexandra Webb, a "friend" of the family, said: "Janet married Black Jack because he was in the Social Register. He married her because her father operated a bank. She was a bitch and he was a bastard, and in the end, both were disillusioned. From such a union emerged Jackie, who inherited all the bad traits of both her mother and her father, but hid it with such charm and grace she enchanted the world."

After their wedding, Black Jack, with Janet, sailed for a five-week honeymoon aboard the *S.S. Aquitania* to Europe.

Janet got a preview of her future life with her new husband. During the crossing, he neglected her shamefully. It was only toward the end of the voyage that she discovered why. In the immediate aftermath of her discovery, she threw a major temper fit, breaking the large wall mirror in their cabin.

By the time they checked into the Ritz Hotel in Paris, some harmony had been restored to their marriage. But their truce lasted for only three nights. That's when he disappeared to the Folies Bergère, later retreating to a seedy hotel on Place Pigalle with three of the shapeliest of the showgirls.

As Cole Porter later claimed, "He also took delight in seducing some of the prettiest of the transvestites at the Carousel. He told me it added spice to his table of delights. 'Variety in the bedroom,' he claimed. 'That's what life is all about. A man gets tired of the same old thing every night.' I knew then that Janet would never be able to contain this man's voracious appetites."

Aboard the *Aquitania*, Black Jack had met a chaperoned sixteen-year-old, Doris Duke, heiress to tobacco millions and in the coming years, the richest woman in the world.

Both of them were very inventive about finding ways to slip away with each other. Even at that young age, Duke was a very independent young woman and often did exactly what she wanted.

After his return to Wall Street, Black Jack boasted to his fellow stockbrokers that, "I deflowered the heiress. The greedy little bitch couldn't get enough of me. We found plenty of places on board the ship for a rendezvous. With a few bribes to the staff, we had any number of compartments open to us for an hour or so. By the time I returned to Janet's bed at night, I was exhausted and went to sleep."

Heiress **Doris Duke** on the dawn of "all those tobacco millions."

Black Jack also told Cole Porter and other friends that he regretted he'd married Janet. "If I had been free, I think I would have wooed and romanced Doris and married her, ending up with control of all those tobacco millions."

Jackie Is Conceived and Parented by Competitive Daredevils

Jackie's mother, Janet Lee Bouvier, was twenty-two years old when she gave birth to Jackie. Friends hailed her as a "daredevil" horseback rider. She later imparted her love of horses to her daughter. In one letter, a classmate described her as "aggressive as hell and intent on marrying a wealthy man."

Jackie grew up in East Hampton in the home of her grandfather, "the Major." On a fourteen-acre estate, he'd built a mansion in the style of an English manor house. He called it Lasata, American Indian for "Place of Peace." It was anything but.

As Jackie grew older, she became a voracious reader. One of her favorite novels was F. Scott Fitzgerald's *The Great Gatsby.* She later claimed that Lasata had been torn directly from the pages of that novel.

Her grandmother was Maude Sargent Bouvier, who indulged her husband, a stern chauvinist and American patriot, a brash and boastful man with a waxed mustache who always dressed in three-piece suits and a high, starched collar.

The Major was called "a *belles lettres* dilettante and a professional curmudgeon behind *pince-nez* glasses."

Jackie later referred to Maude as "a kindly Victorian relic, who turned a blind eye to her husband's mistresses. The Major neglected her and would go for weeks without speaking to her. She lived with heartbreak and witnessed all four of her children get divorced; another had died young. The siblings hated each other, but somehow Maude put up a brave front. She was the glue who held the Bouviers together as a family unit, if indeed such a dysfunctional family could be called a unit. They were more like bickering tribesmen. Lasata was a nightmare place."

In her teens and in riding togs, **Jackie** poses between **Black Jack Bouvier** *(left)* and her grandfather, "The Major," also known as **John Vernou Bouvier, Jr.**

The most devastating critique of the Bouvier family's ancestral pretensions was delivered to the world at large by Truman Capote, who later, after their marriage, became a friend of both Jack and Jackie Kennedy. Like Jackie, Capote was a social butterfly, and he liked gossip even more than she did.

"The Bouviers were *poseurs,*" Capote said in later life after Jackie had dropped him from her list. "They wanted it to appear that they had had breeding, power, and money for centuries. But their geneology was invented. The Major traced his family back to French aristocracy, but they were cabinetmakers. He even created a fake coat-of-arms. It was a total lie. He fooled his own family, including Jackie, who seemed to have adopted the loftiest of Marie Antoinette principles. You know, *noblesse oblige* and all that shit."

"In 1925, the Major had published *Our Forebears,* a work of total fiction," Capote claimed. "In that book, he traced the Bouvier family roots to one François Bouvier, circa 1553, of the ancient house of Fontaine, near Grenoble in the French Alps. This long-ago aristocrat had no connection to the Major's family at all."

"Jackie was descended from cabinetmakers, household maids, ironmongers, tailors, shopkeepers, tavern owners, farmers, and chimney sweepers," Capote charged. "In case you don't know French, 'Bouvier' translates as oxherder, which more or less sums up Jackie's forebears."

Jackie's little sister, Caroline Lee Bouvier, was born on March 3, 1933, the inauguration eve of Franklin D. Roosevelt's first term as president. She would live forever in the shadow of her older sister, Jackie, creating a jealous rivalry that would last until the end of Jackie's life.

It began during childhood and continued throughout Jackie's time in the White House and beyond. Sometimes, the competition involved a battle over men, as in the case of Aristotle Onassis, whom Lee thought might marry her until he proposed instead to Jackie. Lee was also rumored to have had an affair with Jackie's first husband, JFK, as well.

Lee's biographer, Diana DuBois, said, "Lee lived close to the legend, but never became one herself."

After Jackie's birth and throughout her early years, Janet had an uneasy feeling that Black Jack was taking too much interest in his daughter. He insisted on bathing with her in the large marble Bouvier tub in the master bathroom.

Janet was repulsed when she heard her daughter's squeals of delight. "What is he doing to her now?" she repeatedly asked the maid.

His mother, Maude Bouvier, saw nothing objectionable with her son's bathing habits. "It shows how loving my son is to his Jackie." To Maude, Black Jack could do no wrong.

One night, Janet grew suspicious about what was going on in the bedroom. She entered silently and flipped on the light. She pulled back the bed covers to discover a nude Jackie in bed with Black Jack, who had a large erection. She yanked a screaming Jackie from her husband's bed and refused to let him bathe or sleep with Jackie ever again.

Even after that incident, Black Jack continued to worship his daughter. "She practically swooned every time he came home," Janet later said.

Even when Jackie tossed a chocolate cream pie into the face of one of her despised teachers at a school social event, Black Jack never disciplined her. "She's got a free and independent spirit—that's all," he told his mother, Maude. She constantly bragged to her socialite friends, "Jackie is going to grow up to become the female image of my son."

As Jackie grew older, Black Jack called her "Jacks," and he even bragged to her about his sexual exploits. When he visited her at Miss Porter's School in Farmington, Connecticut, they played a special game. Jackie would point to various mothers of her classmates. "Have you had that one, Daddy?"

"Not yet, but check with me next weekend," he'd tell her.

Growing up, Jackie witnessed many fights between Janet and Black Jack. "Often, they were violent," Jackie recalled. "Janet got many a black eye. Sometimes, the fights turned bloody when inanimate objects were used. Father got so awfully drunk that I had to bathe him, mopping up the vomit and urine and changing his bed sheets."

Each of Jackie's parents communicated very different signals. From Janet, she came away with a

Caught hand-holding on camera, **Black Jack** had just emerged from four hours in the woods with **Virginia Kernochan**, his golfing partner. At the Tuxedo Park Riding Academy, a fence-straddling **Janet** *(far right)* seemed oblivious to their affair until this candid photograph was developed.

negative self-image. According to author Tina Santi Flaherty, Jackie was told that her hair was "too frizzy, your size ten feet too big, your shoulders too broad, and your eyes set too wide apart."

In contrast, according to Flaherty, Black Jack told her how to attract men: "To be noticed in a crowd, walk to the center of the room, put on a dazzling smile, and keep your chin up. Don't let your eyes dart around the room. Never act as if you're looking for someone. They should be looking for you. Remember, style is not how rich you are, but a state of mind that puts quality before quantity. That's what makes you a Bouvier."

To Jackie's chagrin, Black Jack and Janet separated in 1936.

After their estrangement, when Black Jack came for her on weekends, she had waited for hours in advance of his arrival. She ran screaming, "Daddy, Daddy" to his car and fell into his arms. In Manhattan, they shared horse-and-buggy rides in Central Park, lunch at Schrafft's, and shopping expeditions on Fifth Avenue.

Following his separation from Janet, Black Jack moved into a two-bedroom apartment at 125 E. 74th Street, where he could date at his pleasure, entertaining a number of very young and beautiful women who succumbed to his charm.

A young broker on Wall Street, Hugh (the same name as Jackie's future stepfather) Brunfield later told an investigative reporter that "for six glorious weeks I was Black Jack's boyfriend. But one weekend when Jackie arrived, he moved me out and rented me a room at the Westbury Hotel. I was dying to meet Jackie, but he wouldn't allow it. He told me I was too effeminate, although he didn't object to that in bed. In bed, he always wanted me to be the woman."

"But, alas, he told me one night that he was no longer going to be my husband. He'd taken up with a 20-year-old female dancer on Broadway, whom he'd met at a party thrown by Cole Porter."

Black Jack teaches Cary Grant How to Walk

"I'm Mad About Black Jack"
—Cole Porter

Years would pass before young Jackie learned that her beloved father also had affairs with men. According to author Edward Klein, "When Jackie was a young girl, she heard her father heap contempt on 'faggots.' The nuns and priests taught her that homosexuality was a sin." Fortunately, Jackie didn't inherit any of her father's prejudices, and she later became a friend and confidant of many homosexuals, including Truman Capote. Klein claimed, "She started to accept the fact that, like homosexuals, she herself was not what most people considered 'normal.' In a way, she was 'almost normal,' just like her gay friends."

Charles Schwartz, in his biography of Cole Porter, revealed that "Some of Cole's most intense affairs were with men from distinguished families. Cole, for instance, was reported to have been very much taken at one time with Black Jack Bouvier."

"I'm just mad about Jack," Cole told his gay friends. Both men had been in the same class at Yale.

Somehow, the Bouvier family became aware of the affair between Black Jack and Cole. "Jack was very bi-," claimed Schwartz. "He joined, from time to time, Cole and actor Monty Woolley during their hunts for working-class males. And not for bridge purposes."

Composer **Cole Porter** expressed his feelings for Black Jack in lyrics—"Mad About the Boy."

Franklyn Ives, an insurance executive in New York, claimed that Black Jack had trouble keeping his fly zipped. One of his favorite Manhattan watering holes was Cerutti's, a gay bar on Madison Avenue. In those days, gay bars were not legal, so many homosexuals invited their gay-friendly women friends to accompany them to the bar so the police would not raid it, which they sometimes did when they found only men drinking at a tavern.

It was here at Cerutti's that Black Jack first encountered Archibald Leach, an entertainer from Britain who would ultimately become the movie legend Cary Grant, according to Ives.

Cary liked to sing Cole Porter songs, including "You're the Top," which for homosexuals had a double meaning not often understood by straight audiences of that day. Ironically, he would end up playing Cole Porter in the movie *Night and Day* (1946) although references to the composer's homosexuality

Black Jack paid **Cary Grant's** rent in return for favors.

could not be presented on the screen. The film's plot had to be almost totally fabricated.

Black Jack and Cary met around the piano where musician Garland Wilson entertained nightly.

When Black Jack met Cary, Cary was living as the lover of George ("Jack") Orry-Kelly, the costume designer, a relationship explored in Marc Eliot's biography, *Cary Grant*. To support himself, Cary was a paid escort, his handsome features and athletic body making him highly desirable as a gigolo. Cary made it clear to all his clients that he was employed just for his "social services but not boudoir duty."

Black Jack, or so it is said, advised Cary about his clothes and even helped him get rid of his lingering British "singsong lilt," as Black Jack called it. "If you want to go to Hollywood you've got to speak like a radio announcer, without any accent at all."

Black Jack later recalled that "I taught Archie how to walk. Before that he walked with acrobatic rubber legs because of his former life as a street acrobat."

When Orry-Kelly kicked Cary out of his apartment, he went to live in a rented room at the NVA Club in the Times Square area. Black Jack paid his rent. Janet became aware of this, and widely distributed the news among her family and friends, hoping to discredit Black Jack.

Cary later dumped Black Jack when Cary took up with Reginald Hammerstein, the younger brother of Oscar Hammerstein II. He was casting a big new musical, *Golden Dawn*, for the autumn. Archie (i.e., Cary) and "Reggie" soon became a frequently spotted-together item in the nightclubs. Black Jack often encountered them, but by then both men had moved on. At one point Black Jack was rumored to be dating a young married couple as part of a *ménage à trois,* socialites from East Hampton.

***

Later in life, Jackie drew up a list of men she'd like to seduce. Cary Grant was included on that list. Her husband, JFK, also found Grant appealing. Sometimes, he'd instruct a White House telephone attendant to connect with him, telephonically, from the Oval Office "Just to hear that impeccable voice."

Once JFK popped the question to Grant. "Are all those tales about you and Black Jack really true?"

"Please don't ask for the truth," Grant said. "I always believed it's wrong to lie to the President of the United States. Let's close the case."

Black Jack Meets His Future Son-in-Law, "A Mick from Boston."

In spite of a failed attempt later at a reconciliation with Janet, the Bouvier's divorce seemed inevitable, eventually transpiring in 1940. Black Jack was ordered to pay $1,050 monthly to support Janet and to maintain their daughters. He was granted visitation rights on weekends.

The support money was difficult for him to raise, as he was involved in various lawsuits for the repayment of loans. In addition, the IRS was in pursuit of him for back taxes.

The divorce was finalized when Jackie was eleven. Two years later, in 1942, Janet would marry Hugh Auchincloss, a wealthy investment banker. He had three children from a previous marriage and would have two more with Janet.

Jackie's new stepfather introduced her to a more lavish lifestyle than she'd ever known. Throughout her high school years, she divided her time between two estates. One was Hammersmith Farm, a 28-room mansion with thirteen fireplaces and views overlooking Narragansett Bay outside Newport, Rhode Island. Most of the farmhands had been drafted, so Jackie had to feed 2,000 chickens a day.

The other estate was Merrywood, lying on forty-six acres fronting the Potomac River in Virginia.

After Hugh Auchincloss became the stepfather of Jackie and Lee in 1942, Black Jack saw less and less of his daughters for a long while. When they were not in school, they were at the Auchincloss estates, either Hammersmith Farm or Merrywood.

Black Jack's drinking became so severe that on three different occasions, he checked himself into a rehabilitation program at the Silver Hill Sanitorium in New Canaan, Connecticut. He was a patient there in 1944, in 1946, and again in 1947. But after each of those sojourns, once he was released, he began to drink again.

One night in Manhattan, during February of 1953, Black Jack met John F. Kennedy. Jackie announced to her father, "This is the man I'm going to marry."

"I hope he doesn't take after his crooked father," Black Jack said.

She later told friends that the two men got along well. "I expected them to talk about politics and sports, but they even talked about other women in front of me," she later lamented.

Even though JFK was a "god damn mick," Black Jack bonded with him and saw him on a number of occasions, even inviting him for lunches at the Stock Exchange Luncheon Club on Wall Street.

One of the most scandalous stories spread by Cole Porter, Black Jack's former lover, was that one night Black Jack and JFK got really drunk and arranged for a showgirl hooker to visit his small apartment. According to Porter, both of them seduced this girl in the same bed. Porter always claimed that more than wanting to have sex with the young woman, Black Jack was motivated by wanting to see his future son-in-law "nude and erect—and in the saddle."

Porter also charged that later, Black Jack was attracted to Lee's first husband, Michael Canfield, whom she'd taken up with after dropping out of Sarah Lawrence College. While working at *Harper's Bazaar,* she had been offered a screen test by the staff at Paramount's New York City office, but ultimately, she turned it down.

Michael Temple Canfield, the adopted son of publisher Cass Canfield, a Marine and a combat veteran, had graduated from Harvard.

Perhaps out of jealousy, Porter later said, "I

After meeting his future son-in-law, **John F. Kennedy**, Black Jack told Cole Porter, "I could go for that cute Mick myself."

don't think Black Jack got to see his other future son-in-law in action, but I'm sure Michael could have dropped his shoes under Black Jack's bed any night. I've known of many closeted, rich, gay homosexual men who 'auditioned' their future sons-in-law by taking them to bed, especially if he were a gigolo marrying into the family fortune."

Janet embarked on a campaign to exclude Black Jack from her older daughter's wedding and from all the festivities surrounding it. A series of pre-ceremony dinner parties were scheduled, and Janet eliminated her former husband from all of these events. Reportedly, his feelings were seriously hurt, which drove him to drink even more. The only time he encountered his daughter was for five minutes at a wedding rehearsal, at which point Janet stayed on the other side of the room and did not speak to him.

"It is the father's role to give the bride away, and I plan to escort her down the aisle," he said loud enough for both Jackie and Janet to hear him.

At Hammersmith Farm, the day of the wedding dawned bright and clear. Janet gave her daughter her rosepoint lace veil, perhaps forgetting that it was the same veil worn at her own (disastrous) wedding to Black Jack.

Jackie detested the gown Janet had purchased for her, and a fashion writer, covering the wedding, seemed to agree, attacking it "as an atrocious mass of tissue silk taffeta, with excessive ornamentation of ruffles, tucks, stitching, and flowers."

For "something blue," she wore a blue garter from Janet.

Black Jack had taken a room at the Viking Hotel in Newport. John E. Davis and Harrington Putnam, married to Black Jack's twin sisters, were sent to retrieve him. They discovered him drunk and naked in bed. "He was cursing Janet, calling her every bitch, slut, whore, cunt, and some other names not in Webster's," according to Putnam.

Janet was alerted and immediately asked her husband, Hugh Auchincloss, in lieu of Black Jack, to walk Jackie down the aisle of St. Mary's Roman Catholic Church. Janet sent word that she'd hired two armed security guards to eject Black Jack if he dared show up at the wedding.

Black Jack was also excluded from the wedding reception at Hammersmith Farm, which attracted some 1,300 guests, many of them drunken Irish politicians from Boston, friends of Ambassador Joseph P. Kennedy.

Later, from her honeymoon in Mexico, Jackie wrote her father, telling him that, "In my mind you symbolically accompanied me down the aisle."

In this 1947 photo, **Jackie** was just about to turn eighteen and become an "independent woman" when she stood with **Black Jack**, dressed in clothes appropriate for post-war Wall Street.

Male friends from Wall Street, fellow stock brokers, often visited Black Jack in his New York City apartment. Sometimes he received them drunk and nude, lying on his couch next to two or three bottles. At other times, he was clad in blue—never white—boxer shorts. These friends reported that he always seemed in a bitter mood and would frequently launch into loud tirades. He was seeing less and less of Jackie and Lee.

"He was very prejudiced," said stockbroker Edward Smythe, "like many WASP men of that day. It was kike this or kike that. He also attacked micks, and had a special hatred for Joseph P. Kennedy, who had been the chairman of Franklin Roosevelt's newly established Securities and Exchange Commission. Kennedy had outlawed some of the various techniques and regulations that had previously allowed Black Jack to profit on the stock market. It was ironic that Kennedy later became Jackie's father-in-law. It wasn't just the Irish. Black Jack called Frenchmen frogs and Italians WOPs."

In contrast to his exclusion from Jackie's wedding, Black Jack did attend Lee's wedding to Michael Canfield on April 18, 1953 at Washington's Holy Trinity Church, and also the reception at Merrywood. But friends later reported that he came away depressed, realizing how luxurious life was at the Auchincloss estate where Hugh could give his daughters far more than he could with his more limited means.

At Merrywood, Black Jack heard the rumor that his son-in-law was actually the bastard son of a married English noblewoman and Prince George, the Duke of Kent, the younger brother of King Edward VIII . *[After a brief and hysterically controversial reign, Edward VIII was "demoted" to Duke of Windsor after abdicating his throne.]*

The Canfields, it was said, had adopted the man who married Lee Bouvier as a means of avoiding a scandal. Later, when Black Jack appraised photos of the legitimate son of the Duke of Kent and compared it to a photograph of his illegitimate son, Michael, he said, "The two boys do look very much alike. It seems the rumors are true."

***

During the final months of his life, Black Jack became a bitter recluse. The summer of 1957 was dying, and so was he. When Jackie heard that he was ill, she cut short her visit to Hyannis Port and flew to his side.

As she told Lee and Janet, he was "very bitter toward me. He claimed that he used to be the man in my life, but ever since my marriage to Jack, I'd come to him only when I needed a favor."

Unknown to Jackie at the time, Black Jack, after a lifetime of alcoholism, had developed cancer of the liver. In agony, he was taken by ambulance to Manhattan's Lenox Hill Hospital on July 27. Tests showed that the cancer had advanced rapidly. There was no hope for him. Jackie visited him in the hospital, but was not told of his cancer.

After her visit, she commuted to Newport, where she spent her birthday (July 28).

On August 3, a call came in that Black Jack was in a coma and was not expected to come out of it. Jackie flew to New York, but it was too late. The former *bon vivant* had died at the age of sixty-six after years of dissipation and chronic alcoholism.

Years later, Jackie lamented not his death, but the fact "that he didn't live three more years to see Jack elected President of the United States and me First Lady."

Jackie took charge of the funeral arrangements and even composed an obituary for publication in *The New York Times.* From one of Black Jack's mistresses, she acquired a photograph of him that she wanted to appear as part of that obituary. "He looked so debonair, so handsome," she said.

She chose St. Patrick's Cathedral as the site of his funeral service, with a burial at the family plot in East Hampton.

Her cousin, Edie Beale, said, "I cried through the service, but Jackie looked very stoic. She didn't shed a tear. In fact, she selected so many summer blossoms like white bachelor buttons that it looked like a June wedding. Eight of Jack's mistresses showed up, heavily veiled. One of these women was overheard telling Jackie, 'After your father made love to me, no other man will ever do.'"

"It was my first experience burying a man I loved." Jackie later said.

In remembering him, Kathleen Bouvier said: "Throughout New York and the Hamptons, his notorious seductions, his cars, and his horses left an incredible impression. After his death, they are like fingerprints in the dust, the lingering last notes of a sonata."

In his will, Black Jack divided his estate equally between Jackie and Lee, giving each of them $80,000. Jackie immediately purchased a sleek white Jaguar sports car as a Christmas present for JFK. She was terribly disappointed when he traded it in for a new Buick. "Politicians can't be seen driving around in a white Jaguar," he told her.

***

After divorcing Hugh Auchincloss in 1976, Janet entered into a third marriage in 1979 to Bingham Morris, an investment broker. He had been her childhood friend. They separated in 1981, but had never divorced at the time of her death.

Janet died of complications arising from Alzheimer's disease on July 22, 1989 in Newport at the age of 81. Her last coherent words to her daughter were, "I didn't give a damn about your being First Lady. It was a real invasion of my privacy."

Jackie directed that her mother's funeral be held at the Trinity Church in Newport, where she was buried next to her second husband, Hugh Auchincloss.

Chapter Two

Jackie in Europe (and Engaged)

"An American Geisha" Auditions Ivy League Beaux

> ### How Jackie Surrendered Her Virginity in a Paris Elevator

In 1947, in Newport, **Jacqueline Bouvier** was named "Debutante of the Year." With her face and flair, she dazzled society at her coming-out party wearing a $59 dollar off-the-rack gown.	After graduating from college, **Jackie**'s first job was as an **"Inquiring Camera Girl"** in Washington. She wanted to pursue "the big fish in the pond," the Senate's most eligible bachelor, John F. Kennedy, or the already-married Richard M. Nixon. Instead, they ended up going after her.

Deep in the 1980s, long after her tenure as First Lady

and at least a decade after the death of her second husband, Jackie Kennedy Onassis recalled to friends, "I will always remember 1947. It was my year, my coming out. I was named Debutante of the Year, signaling to all those handsome *beaux* in the Newport area that I was available for courting and eventually, marriage."

On August 16 of that year, two years after the end of World War II, 300 A-list guests were invited to see 18-year-old Jacqueline Bouvier, wearing a pearl necklace and an off-the-rack white gown, glide down the stairs at her stepfather's Hammersmith Farm Estate outside Newport.

She later said, "My aim was to look fresh and virginal, with the slight suggestion that I was in prime form for deflowering."

That party was followed by a formal dinner and dance at Newport's Clambake Club, where Jackie danced with at least two dozen prospective beaux to the sounds of the Mayer Davis' band. That musical group was often hired for major society events.

Jackie was disappointed that Newport's most famous resident, tobacco heiress Doris Duke, did not respond to her invitation. Partly in jest, Jackie later told fellow debutante Rose Grosvenor, "I shall get even with Duke for that snub by one day seducing her husband." She was referring to Porfirio Rubirosa, the Dominican playboy.

In 1947, her first car, a black Mercury convertible, meant freedom to **Jackie**. "I plan to lure many a beau into the back seat of my car," she boasted, with laughter, to Gore Vidal and others.

Writing under the pseudonym of Cholly Knickerbocker, Igor Cassini, a gossip columnist for the Hearst newspaper syndicate, said: "The Queen of the year for 1947 is Jacqueline Bouvier, the regal brunette with classic features and the daintiness of Dresden porcelain. She has poise, is soft spoken, and intelligent, everything a leading debutante should be. Her background is strictly 'Old Guard.'"

Ironically, Igor was the brother of fashion designer Oleg Cassini, who would become Jackie's favorite designer during her White House Years...and a "sometimes lover."

Igor also informed readers that Jackie was now studying at Vassar, the exclusive college for High Society's daughters. Dorothy Parker had once quipped, "If all the Vassar girls were laid end to end, I wouldn't be surprised."

The college was located outside Poughkeepsie, New York, within an easy commute from Manhattan, allowing Jackie to take the train for visits with Black Jack in his small apartment.

Jackie was clearly the Belle of the Ball—that is, until her younger sister,

Two Guys, Each Named John,
Preface Her Eventual Marriage to Another John

Lee Bouvier, made a late entrance into the club. In contrast to Jackie's virginal white, Lee wore a strapless pink satin gown studded with rhinestones.

She tottered in on a pair of three-inch high heels and had on a pair of long black satin gloves like Rita Hayworth had worn in *Gilda.*

To Jackie, Lee looked like a little girl dressing up in her mother's elegant clothing. But the stag line didn't agree, deserting Jackie to hover around Lee.

Soon, she was dancing with the handsomest beaux, whirling around the danced floor beneath a ceiling studded with tiny blue lights twinkling like the stars above.

After only fifteen minutes of watching Lee upstage her, Jackie made another vow , delivered with a steely determination to Rose Grosvenor, her fellow debutante: "That's the last time Lee will ever do this to me. Never again will the little bitch lure the spotlight away from me."

Two ambitious debs, **the Bouvier sisters** *(Lee is on the right)* set out to lure beaux, but only the marrying kind, and only if they're rich.

In the years to come, Jackie more than honored that vow. Beginning that night in Newport, Lee would forever after live in her older sister's shadow, with a rare exception occurring in 1950, when she was designated as "Debutante of the Year."

After Jackie's debut, her parents agreed to combine their resources and purchase her first car, a black 1947 Mercury convertible. When she posed in front of it, she could have been any attractive housewife from some typical American suburb at the time. She had not yet learned to set off her special look and beauty that one day would electrify the world.

She was extremely proud of her convertible, knowing that it gave her a freedom of movement she'd never enjoyed before. Her stepbrother, Gore Vidal, once went for a ride around Washington, D.C. in her convertible. She told him that she planned to "audition" many a beau in her back seat, "but not go all the way."

"Before she could become the *numero uno femme fatale* in the world, she was still clinging to that outmoded idea that she had to go to her wedding bed a virgin," Gore said. "But I think that in a few short months, she got rid of that outdated idea."

Charles Pearson, a Navy veteran and cohort of John F. Kennedy, told Gore, "The best way to get Jackie is to mix up a batch of lethal martinis and get her really tight. Her inhibitions just fall away. She becomes really hot and doesn't seem to know just how hot she is."

Back at Vassar, Jackie was clearly bored after the excitement of Newport. Her recently published recognition as a debutante did not make her popular—if anything, her fellow classmates resented her.

It didn't help that the gossip columnists had discovered her. Walter Winchell at the time was the most popular columnist in America. He wrote about Jackie's poise, claiming, "What a gal! Blessed with the looks of a fairytale princess, she doesn't know the meaning of the word 'snob'!"

At Vassar, Charlotte Curtis, who later became an editor at *The New York Times,* roomed next to Jackie. "I don't think she liked college, calling it 'that goddam Vassar.' She was smart, a straight A student, though she downplayed her intellect. She told me that she didn't want any beau to find out that she just might be smarter than he was."

After her launch as a debutante, Jackie began to date virtually every weekend. Most of her young beaux were from Ivy League colleges, and she could be seen with them at gala functions at the Waldorf Astoria, the Plaza, or at the St. Regis Hotels in Manhattan.

There, she stayed in the small apartment of her father, Black Jack Bouvier. One weekend, tired of the drabness of his living quarters, she redecorated, charging new furnishings, fabrics, and expensive accessories to his ever diminishing bank account. He was furious, but he ultimately forgave her.

***

One day over lunch at the Plaza, Black Jack asked Jackie about the kind of man she wanted to marry. She told him that men who looked like Greek gods didn't interest her. "I like a man with a funny nose, Clark Gable ears, irregular teeth, a keen intelligence, and a sense of humor. He must also have feet bigger than mine. When I meet a prospective beau, I always look at what size shoe he wears, preferring to see him in a size twelve. Size seventeen, of course, is just too much."

Gore Vidal later gave his appraisal of Jackie during her post-debutante period. "Before she reached twenty, Jackie had perfected the technique of an American Geisha. When I first met her, she spoke in a normal voice. After going without seeing her for several months, I met a very different young woman. I had lunch with her in Washington, and discovered she spoke like the recently emerging starlet, Marilyn Monroe. Her voice...how can I describe it?...came out like a whispering *coo* as if emerging from the throat of a twelve-year-old girl."

"When a man talked to Jackie, she focused all her attention on him, dreamily looking into his eyes. She concentrated with total fascination, as if she were with a celestial version of Abraham Lincoln, returned to Earth to deliver the Gettysburg address. It was, 'Oh, Gore, you are so smart. Oh, Gore, you are truly, truly fabulous.' In addition to praising a man's insights, regardless of how stupid the utterances, she developed the art of flirtation."

"Unless she drifted off," Gore continued, "into some dull marriage, I saw her becoming the mistress of some powerful man, perhaps a future President of the United States. I felt she might hook up with someone like Nelson Rockefeller. He was quite a ladies' man and eventually there would be talk of him running for President. He certainly could afford Jackie. So I saw her becoming a 20th Century Madame de Pompadour, or even a Madame du Barry, but more Pompadour."

As her homosexual friend, Gore would talk about sex with Jackie without threatening her, discussing aspects of it that she would never talk about with a straight man, especially one of her beaux. Once, when the subject of masturbation came up, he admitted that on some occasions, he "jerked off as many as three times a day."

A distant relative and early friend, author **Gore Vidal**, defined Jackie as "an American geisha who speaks like that starlet, Marilyn Monroe."

"About two is all I've ever managed," she said. "Sometimes it provides relief after one of my boyfriends has gotten me all hot and bothered that evening."

"Pass the unsatisfied, unfulfilled studs on to me," he jokingly recommended.

It has been suggested that during her time as a student at Vassar, Jackie had more beaux than any other young woman. But that was not the impression of Betsy Gardner, a student from Syracuse, New York, who wanted a career as a fashion designer. "She never mentioned dating anyone, although I learned later that she did date on weekends. She was so secretive. I once was invited into her room, where I discovered five pictures of her father, whom she called Black Jack. With a nickname like that, he must have been a gambler. Whenever I talked to her, it was 'Black Jack said this,' or 'Black Jack did that.' I hate to say this, but I think she was in love with her father. She was not alone among the girls of Vassar who were in love with their fathers."

Because of the distance involved from Vassar, Jackie visited Hughdie Auchincloss and Janet at Hammersmith Farm at Newport, or at Merrywood in Virginia, only on holidays or else once a month. She privately agreed with Gore that Hughdie was "a stuffed shirt," although spending hours happily locked in his library with his porn collection.

Janet ruled their residences like a tyrant, hiring far more servants than needed. One servant had only one job, and that involved keeping all the toilets sparkling clean. Jackie heard that once, Janet got into fight with a cook in her large kitchen and threatened her with a kitchen knife.

As Jackie confided to Gore, "I think Janet is coming unglued."

Her mother was almost fanatically interested in the young men Jackie was dating, finding all of them unsuitable. Jackie agreed, defining her beaux as "beetle-browed bores."

19

Peter Reed, a college student from Newport, claimed that he took Jackie out on at least ten dates, most often to the Newport Country Club. "I was really horny back then," he later admitted. "But I got nowhere with her in spite of repeated attempts. A rumor surfaced that I was the man who took Jackie's cherry. *It only it were true.* It didn't happen. She was amusing and intelligent, but a bit tight-assed when it came to sex. I got a peck on the cheek when I delivered her to her doorstep—and that was that. In contrast, friends of mine knew her future husband, Jack Kennedy. He was screwing anything that didn't have two heads."

While at Vassar during her freshman year, Jackie dated a number of students from Yale, including Jonathan Isham. "She wasn't really interested in me, not really. I was no more than an escort, taking her to places like the Yale Bowl. Mostly she dated men to sharpen her skills, getting in practice to catch the big fish."

Gore later told a tale about Jackie's dating that seems impossible to believe, although many

WASPS Who Sting: Financier **Hugh Auchincloss** and his new wife, the former **Janet Lee Bouvier**. "Hughdie was not a pretty face, but he had money," Janet claimed.

people in her circle claimed that it was true. If true, that would make Jackie appear pathological.

Even at eighteen, she was a chain smoker, a nasty habit that probably accelerated her relatively early death at the age of 65 in 1994.

"She liked men—and in some cases, adored them," Gore claimed. "But she resented having to turn herself into a geisha, since she was too smart for that. According to Janet's dictates, she had to appear dumb before her men."

"Her precarious financial situation forced her into this subservient position, which she hated. Sometimes, she would sit for an hour or so listening to the inane rantings of some jerk of a date, seemingly hanging onto his every word. Finally, when she could take it no more, she would stub out the glowing ember of her cigarette on the back of his hand. That certainly was a dramatic way to end the relationship."

Ferociously possessive, Black Jack systematically objected to all of Jackie's choices of beaux. He also assumed that his daughter was having sexual intercourse with all the men she dated, applying his own standards of behavior to her. He wrote to her, complaining that he was afraid that he would lose her to some "gink who you think is so romantic because he wears his mother's pearl earrings for dress shirt buttons because he loves her so." He warned Jackie to wait until she was twenty-one before making a serious commitment.

She began avoiding weekends with her father, spending them instead at

Yale. When she grew bored with the men at that university, she switched her allegiance to men from Princeton.

When weekend after weekend passed without her showing up at his apartment, Black Jack wrote a warning to her. "A woman can have wealth and beauty and brains, but without a reputation, she has nothing." He also told her to play hard to get and not give her body to just any boy who comes along.

As her father sank deeper and deeper into alcoholism, he became increasingly unreasonable. When she arrived at his apartment showing off her then fashionable very short "poodle cut"—a look that accentuated her luminous eyes— he was infuriated. He went into a rage, claiming that she had ruined her looks.

On another night at the Waldorf Astoria, at a dance he also attended, Black Jack objected to how close a young man was holding his daughter. He wove his way through the dancing couples to reach her. In his fury, he ripped her pearl

Young, handsome, and promiscuous, **Black Jack Bouvier** was Jackie's "ideal dreamboat." She always kept this photo by her bedside.

necklace from her neck, breaking the strands and sending the beads cascading to the floor. This caused panic among the women nearby, who feared they would slip and fall.

In the aftermath of this incident, both Jackie and Black Jack were ejected from the hotel by security guards.

***

Jackie was known to sustain an ongoing fascination—some said love affair—with Europe. Her fascination for the Continent began with a series of three trips, each quite different from the other two.

In the summer of 1948, Jackie accepted an invitation to tour Europe with two young friends of hers, Judy and Helen Bowdoin, stepdaughters of Edward F. Foley, Jr., Under Secretary of the U.S. Treasury. The third girl was Julia Bissell, of Baltimore. Helen Shearman, Jackie's former Latin teacher at the Holton Arms School, agreed to travel with them as chaperon.

Jackie later admitted, "It was not the way I wanted to travel, but I was so anxious to see Europe, I agreed to go along, chaperon and all. We had only seven weeks, and every day was rigidly scheduled. There were things I wanted to see on my own, but I had to give in to the group's wishes. Fortunately, there were some highlights. Mr. Foley, because of his position, opened many doors for us, beginning in London."

Jackie, along with her party, was invited to the Royal Garden Party at Buckingham Palace, although they did not get to meet King George VI or his Queen Consort, Elizabeth Bowes-Lyon, or even Princess Elizabeth or Princess Margaret. However, Jackie did get to shake the hand of Sir Winston Churchill. In fact, she was so delighted to meet him, she got into the receiving line twice to shake his hand again. When he looked into her eyes, he said, "You're quite pretty. Your face looks familiar."

Holding up the "V" for Victory fingers, **Sir Winston Churchill** wished he were forty years younger when he first met Jackie.

Later, on the French Riviera, while visiting the chic resort of Juan-les-Pins, she met Churchill once again. "You're that pretty girl who got into the line twice to shake my hand at Buckingham Palace, aren't you?" he asked. She took in his flabby body, clad at the time in a loose-fitting bathing suit.

"Shaking the hand of Sir Winston Churchill has been one of the greatest honors of my life," she told him.

"If only I were only forty years younger, I might honor you in another way."

[Jackie had another meeting with Sir Winston in Nassau with her new husband, John F. Kennedy. They were invited aboard a yacht in which Sir Winston was sailing around The Bahamas. "He was very solicitous of me, but didn't recall our former meeting," she said. "Jack wore this white dinner jacket, and Sir Winston mistook him for a waiter and ordered a brandy. Jack dutifully served it from the ship's bar."]

"The schedule of our tour of the Continent was grueling," she recalled, "one of those 'if it's Tuesday, it must be Belgium' tours. There was a motor trip through the Cotswolds, then off to Paris and its Louvre; a dart through the Loire Valley with stopovers in Avignon to see the old papal palace. Then off to Zurich with all those banker gnomes before the beauty of sailing on Lake Lucerne. A stopover in Interlaken to see the Jungfrau. The cathedral of Milan, the Romeo and Juliet romance of Verona, before gliding along in a gondola on the Grand Canal in Venice. The Duomo and the Academy of Florence before two days in Rome—The Colosseum, the Spanish Steps, the Roman Forum, the Villa Borghese. A return to Paris."

"Our final night in Paris, we visited Le Boeuf sur le Toit," Jackie said. "Marlon Brando was in the club that night. I had thrilled to his performance on Broadway in *A Streetcar Named Desire*. I was eager to introduce myself to him, but unfortunately, he was sitting in a booth engaged in commando activities with that black singer, Eartha Kitt." Jackie later admitted, "I was google-eyed."

[Months after she'd left the White House, Brando would become one of Jackie's temporary lovers.]

Back home, she told Black Jack, "I got tired of my traveling companions and bored with my drip-dry blouse and washing out my panties every night in a small sink. The next time will be different. On my own and at my leisure."

***

Jackie did not want to spend her sophomore year back among all the restrictions at Vassar. An opportunity arose when she read about a program called Smith College Junior Year Abroad. Studies, including time at the Sorbonne in Paris, were being offered to young women who qualified. "Having left my soul in Europe, I was eager to return. Naturally, Black Jack opposed it."

Thinking she might not be accepted, as she was not otherwise a Smith College student, she toyed with the idea of becoming a photographer's model. Her experience as a fashion model had been extremely limited, and strictly amateurish. They had included striking appearances at fashion shows in Newport and in East Hampton, where she'd startled audiences by coming out "in the latest gypsy fashion."

Once again, she met opposition from Black Jack, who warned her, "Only whores are fashion models."

Black Jack also lodged strenuous objections to her latest beau, Serge Obolensky, a White Russian prince, age 58, who had fled from St. Petersburg at the time of the Russian Revolution. Considered the best waltzer in New York, he took Jackie out almost every evening—dancing, of course.

Jackie was only nineteen at the time, and Black Jack loudly and frequently asserted that the prince was old enough to be her grandfather.

She reminded her father that his female lovers could well have been among her current classmates at Vassar. She was referring to one in particular—Sally Butler, a strikingly beautiful brunette who evoked the screen

The Russian prince, **Serge Obolensky,** was Vice Chairman of the Board of Hilton Hotels. In 1916, he'd married Catherine Alexandrovna Romanov, daughter of Alexander II of Russia. Later, he married Ava Alice Muriel Astor, daughter of John Jacob Astor IV. In 1943, during World War II, he captured the Italian island of Sardinia with a crew of only three men.

Haute Society, Grand Chic: In 1975, for old time's sake, **Jackie** dances with **Obolensky**, her former beau, just three years before his death.

image of Norma Shearer. Black Jack had proposed marriage, but her parents had violently objected because of Black Jack's age and his reputation as a womanizer and a possible homosexual.

To maintain harmony, Jackie gave up her prince. She began to sink into despair, not wanting to return to Vassar and resenting the control that Black Jack and Janet maintained over her life. She longed for independence. Just as she entered her deepest period of gloom, a letter arrived from Smith College announcing that she'd been accepted for a year of study abroad in various cities of Europe, most notably in Paris at the Sorbonne.

Jackie spent the first six weeks of the program participating in an intensive French language course in Grenoble, in the French Alps, passing with top honors. She also found time to fall in love with twenty-three-year-old Jean Ferran, who had a French father and an Italian mother, who'd emigrated to France from across the mountains in neighboring Italy.

Extraordinarily handsome, with strong legs from mountain climbing, Ferran was a guide. He made a dazzling appearance, standing six feet, two inches, with a muscular build, deep blue eyes, and blondish hair. To her, he looked more German than Mediterranean, but he insisted he was French and Italian, although he spoke perfect German, as she learned later.

Ferran had graduated from the University of Grenoble, and she discovered that he, like herself, was interested in French literature. He introduced her to the works of Jean-Jacques Rousseau and Stendahl, both of whom had lived and written in Grenoble. Through Ferran, she also became acquainted with the lively music and arts scene that flourished in that high-altitude city.

For the first time in her life, she paid the restaurant and tavern bills, as he told her he had very little money.

On weekends, he took her on biking trips or else hiking through the mountains.

Their favorite hangout was La Table Ronde, the oldest café in Grenoble, a favorite of the 18th-century writer and philosopher, Jean-Jacques Rousseau. "I came to adore French fondue," she later said.

When she left Grenoble and returned to Paris, she was befriended by Catherine Grant, from Bristol, England, who had also studied in Grenoble. Jackie shared details of her romantic adventures with Ferran, confessing, "Jean and I experienced French kissing…all over. But I didn't want to get pregnant."

"I was in love," Jackie told Grant. "I even considered marrying Jean and becoming his mountain woman, as ridiculous as that sounds."

"My last night with him was memorable in more ways than one—both good and horrible," Jackie said. "He begged me to surrender my virginity, but I held out. We made love in every other way, though."

"It was dawn when we went for our final walk watching the vendors set up their stands at the place aux Herbes," Jackie said. "I told Jean that I'd fallen in love with him and was prepared to stay in Grenoble with him. I was shocked when he told me that our love affair had—'Like all good things'—come to an end. He confessed that he lived in a small cottage outside of town, on the other side of the Isère River. He told me he had an Italian wife, as well as a boy, age 2, and a girl, age 5. They'd gotten married when they met at the university several years before."

"We kissed goodbye on the square," she told Grant. "It was so romantic, so French, so very heartbreaking."

In Paris, at the Café de Flor, discussing life and love with Grant, Jackie became very upset when her new friend suggested that Ferran might be a gigolo.

"After thinking it over, I think you're probably right. He did suggest to me that he needed money because he'd spent all his time with me and that he had neglected his guide duties. I gave him a hundred dollars. But I don't regret it. It was enchanting while it lasted. Now it's over. It was a learning experience. Actually, for a brief time, it was fun paying a man's bills for a change. Up until then, all my dates had treated me like a hothouse flower. I felt more in charge."

Two weeks later, Jackie's heart had apparently mended. Meeting with Grant for coffee, she said, "As authors have known for centuries, the young heart is a fickle heart. Since I last saw you, I've fallen in love again. My new beau is divine."

***

In Paris, Jackie enrolled at the Sorbonne, the prestigious university noted for its famed school of arts and science, and for its origins stretching back to the Middle Ages. She chose French history and literature as her major field of study.

She did not want to live in a dormitory, but chose to stay instead with an aristocratic but impoverished French family.

In the un-chic side of Paris' otherwise rather chic 16th Arrondissement, Jackie moved into 78 avenue Mozart, lodging with the family of the Comte de Renty, who had died a horrible death in a Nazi concentration camp.

His widow, la comtesse Guyot de Renty, took in American students as boarders, including Susan Coward, whom Jackie had known in the States. She renewed her friendship with Coward and also bonded with Claude de Renty, one of the family's daughters, who was Jackie's age. They would later tour through Germany and Austria together. The countess's 23-year-old daughter, Ghislaine, who had recently been divorced, also shared the apartment with her four-year-old son, Christian, whom Jackie eventually defined as a "terrorist."

From America, Janet sent care packages because there were many shortages in France. Coffee and sugar, plus other canned foodstuffs, were much appreciated in the De Renty household.

Once Gore learned that Jackie was living in Paris, he sarcastically quipped: "She's going to study at the Sorbonne, but she really went to have a good time and to lose her virginity."

For a brief time, Jackie became romantically involved with Ormande de Kay, a young American who wanted to write screenplays. They began to see each other every night, and became patrons of such "literary cafés" as the

Café de Flor and Deux Magots. At La Coupole in Montparnasse, Jackie caught her first glimpse of Albert Camus, one of her favored literary lions.

Ormande and Jackie became quite serious about their relationship. When he had to return to America, Jackie promised to be faithful to him, a vow she would not keep. However, she did resume dating him upon her return to the States.

***

Before her arrival in Paris, Black Jack had warned her not to marry "one of those post-war impoverished counts on the make for an American heiress."

Ignoring his advice, she almost immediately met the young, handsome, and debonair count, Paul de Ganay, who was studying at the Sorbonne with her. He was one of four brothers from a Franco-Argentine family whose story evoked memories of the Rudolph Valentino film, *The Four Horsemen of the Apocalypse.*

Paul was from a wealthy family, not impoverished at all, as Jackie soon learned when he invited her for her first weekend at the elegant Château de Courances, some 36 miles south of Paris.

There, Jackie met Paul's family, and was introduced to some members of French high society. Whereas in Paris, she dined with Paul at the long-enduring French bistro, Brasserie Balthasar, at the château over the coming weeks, Jackie attended balls and parties. "She was an instant success with French society," Paul recalled. "Always surrounded by eligible young men when she entered a room. I tried not to be jealous."

During that winter in Paris, Jackie had other beaux, though she saw Paul frequently. She was involved with him to the degree that she agreed to travel to Madrid with him one Easter, where they stayed together at the Ritz Hotel. From Madrid, he drove her to Toledo. She especially wanted to see the house once occupied by the painter, El Greco.

"Ultimately, Paul and I became friends," she said, "not lovers."

***

Jackie developed another link to French high society, which in many ways turned out to be an even more important liaison than the De Ganay family.

At Vassar, she'd become friends with Jessie Leigh-Hunt Wood, whose father, Henry Leigh-Hunt (1886-1972), had inherited a vast tract of real estate in Las Vegas. Jessie's celebrated mother was the French novelist, poet, and journalist, Louise Lévêque de Vilmorin, nicknamed "Lulu."

A legendary hostess, and muse to, among others, the French composer Francis Poulenc, she was the chatelaine of a château at Verrières-le-Buisson, Essonne, a suburb southwest of Paris, and the heiress to a fortune of her own.

Once Jackie was introduced to Lulu, the elegant *grande dame* found her "enchanting." Soon, Jackie was being invited to her fabulous parties and balls, where deposed post-war kings met with movie moguls from Hollywood, decadent millionaires, and an occasional politician such as the president of France.

Into this mixture Lulu also invited prominent painters, writers, musicians, and ballet dancers.

Prince Jean-Louis de Faucigny-Lucinge claimed that, "Not since the Age of Enlightenment has society found itself so close to artists." Poulenc himself found in her writing "a sort of sensitive impertinence and *libertinage.*"

Many observers claimed that the lessons Jackie learned from Lulu influenced her later decision to invite America's leading artists to the White House when she presided there as First Lady.

At these parties and balls, Jackie was introduced to the cream of international society. Once night, she attended a dinner party that Lulu hosted for Elie de Rothschild and his mistress, Pamela Churchill, who had been married to Randolph Churchill, Sir Winston's son, during World War II.

[The much-married Pamela would later trailblaze her way through the ranks of the very wealthy, thanks partly to her final marriage to a W. Averell Harriman, heir to a railway fortune, her role as a fundraiser for Bill Clinton's Democratic Party, and her eventual designation as U.S.

The celebrated French novelist, **Louise Lévêque de Vilmorin**, nicknamed "Lulu," introduced Jackie to the dazzling world of France's *literati,* plus leading ballet dancers, musicians, and artists.

At the château at **Verrières-le-Buisson**, a suburb of Paris, Lulu presided over gala parties, fabulous balls, and elite dinners for tout France, the members of whom she introduced to impressionable Jackie.

When **Pamela Churchill**, mistress of **Elie de Rothschild**, went to powder her nose, the multi-millionaire made a pass at young Jackie.

27

Ambassador to France.]

When Pamela excused herself "to go powder my nose," the Rothschild heir propositioned Jackie on the terrace.

One night at a ball, she got to dance with Prince Aly Khan. As she later told Susan Coward, "I felt a steel bar pressing against me. Now I know why Rita Hayworth married him after dumping Orson Welles."

Jackie also got to meet Jean Cocteau, the influential and endlessly controversial *enfant terrible* of the postwar arts scene in France, and his lover, the devastatingly handsome French actor, Jean Marais. Cocteau described to her his difficulties in bringing Tennessee Williams' *A Streetcar Named Desire* to the Parisian stage. The two men invited her for a night on the town in Paris when she returned to the Sorbonne, and she gratefully accepted, wondering if she could steal Marais from Cocteau's iron grip.

Bernard Buffet with *oeuvre*, perhaps a self-portrait.

***

Jackie looked forward to every weekend she was invited by Paul to visit Lulu at her château. She began to meet some of the most prestigious figures in France, even some from England.

She'd become enchanted with the work of the French Expressionist painter, Bernard Buffet. A painter whose postwar fame was rivaled only by that of his legendary enemy, Pablo Picasso, Buffet was a modern "anti-abstract" master who had made a colossal fortune from his work by the age of 30 and who, at the age of 71 and the victim of Parkinson's disease, committed suicide in 1999. Jackie was introduced to Buffet and his then-lover, Pierre Bergé, who later left him for a long-term relationship as the companion and business partner of the fashion designer, Yves Saint Laurent.

Buffet, among other achievements, was known for his portraits. He was intrigued by Jackie's face, and asked her if she'd pose for

Businessman and promoter **Pierre Bergé** *(right)* abandoned Buffet to pursue, beginning in 1961, a personal and professional alliance with **Yves Saint-Laurent** *(left)* that eventually defined the fashion designer as one of the most celebrated in the world.

28

him at his studio in Paris. She agreed and attended two sessions as his model.

But when she showed up for the third session, the concierge told her that Monsieur Bergé and Monsieur Buffet had left for an extended trip to Rome. She had not been notified, and she always wondered what happened to her unfinished portrait.

[Although Jackie had been stood up by Buffet, she later became one of his chief defenders. In the 1960s, Buffet's reputation as an artist was seriously attacked, especially by Picasso, who denounced him as a "purveyor of kitsch, a mere faiseur (i.e., routine artisan)."

Buffet would endure a half-century of mockery until a Renaissance of his works occurred during the 21st Century.

"I judged **Jean Anouilh** on his plays, including *Antigone*, and ignored all that gossip about some former Nazi connection," Jackie claimed.

Jackie always maintained that it was Buffet's lightning success and wealth, just after World War II, that turned the art establishment against him. "His paintings sold too well," Jackie said. "Jealous artists like Picasso hated him for that."

She had many arguments with André Malraux about Buffet's merits, maintaining that Malraux had been unduly influenced by Picasso's dour negativity.

Jackie also claimed that Buffet lost many of his homosexual defenders in the art world because later in life, he seemed to switch his sexual orientation and got married.

"Buffet was not appreciated in his homeland," Jackie said, "but was widely praised in such countries as the United States and Japan. I adore his work. If only he'd finished that portrait of me. Damn it all!"]

At one of Lulu's parties, Jackie had an extended conversation with Jean Anouilh, the French dramatist whose 50 years of artistic production ranged from tragic drama to absurdist farce. Fortunately, she'd seen a recent production of his best known work, *Antigone,* which he'd written in 1943 as an politically pertinent adaptation of Sophocles' classic drama. Jackie noted that some of the French guests at Lulu's *soirée* shunned Anouilh, and she later learned that some critics had accused him of being a Nazi sympathizer during the Occupation of France by the Third Reich.

Many critics felt that *Antigone,* which the Vichy government allowed to be performed, was supportive of the Occupation. Perhaps for that reason, Jackie reasoned, he was passed over for the Nobel Prize in Literature in 1962 when she was in the White House.

The French writer and filmmaker René Clair, who had directed silent films, had returned to his native France after World War II. The son of a soap merchant, Clair told Jackie that the films he had made in America were more commercial and mass-market than his personal tastes as an artist would have preferred. He cited *I Married a Witch* (1942) and *It Happened Tomorrow* (1944) as examples. At the time of their first meeting, he asked Jackie if she were an actress. She told him that that had been "my schoolgirl fantasy."

"Your French is beautiful," he told her, "with a lovely, lovely accent. I am going to produce a film, sooner than later, based on Faust's *La beauté du diable (Beauty and the Devil)*. I'd like you to audition for a role in it."

She told him she'd be flattered, but when she called the number he'd given her, he no longer seemed interested. "There went my one chance for stardom," she told Janet. "I assume that Clair would have cast me as the Beauty instead of the Devil."

In spite of her rejection by the director, Jackie continued to follow his career, even when younger Parisian critics attacked him as a representative of *cinéma de qualité,* a pejorative term loosely translated as "the cinematography of old men," dominated by a nostalgia for their younger days.

She wrote him a personal letter of congratulations upon his election to the *Académie française [an organization which regulates the French language by determining standards of acceptable grammar and vocabulary]* in 1960.

In deference to her role as First Lady of the United States, he wrote back. "In all my film career, my greatest mistake was in not casting you as the female star of *Beauty and the Devil.* I will regret it until my dying day."

Filmmaker **René Clair** held out a dazzling prospect to Jackie: "Why not become a French-language movie star?"

The most famous married couple Jackie met through Lulu was Duff Cooper, the 1st Viscount Norwich, along with Lady Diana Cooper, widely acclaimed as "the beauty of the century."

The son of a society doctor, Duff Cooper was a conservative British politician who had loudly opposed then Prime Minister Neville Chamberlain's appeasement policy, as represented by the 1938 Munich Agreement with Adolf Hitler. Hitler and Josef Goebbels consequently labeled Cooper as "one of the three most dangerous warmongers in England."

Under Winston Churchill during World War II, Cooper had served as Minister of Information—read that "Minister of Propaganda." In 1944, at the liberation of France, Duff was named British ambas-

Jackie was always welcome to attend parties and intimate dinners thrown by **Duff and Lady Cooper** at the British Embassy in Paris. The Nazis had considered Duff as one of the three most dangerous men in Britain.

sador to France. He and Lady Diana moved to Paris, where they became immensely popular with the French.

Leaving office in 1947 after he was knighted, he and his stunningly beautiful wife decided to live in France, settling into a villa in Chantilly, within an easy commute from Paris.

When Jackie met Lady Diana, she addressed her as Viscountess Norwich, who responded, "Please, call me Lady Diana. The Viscountess label sounds like a porridge."

The Coopers were enthralled with Jackie's charm and beauty. She became a privileged member of their entourage, invited to their parties and dinners. On several occasions, she visited them on weekends at Chantilly.

One night, sitting alone on her terrace, Lady Diana confided to Jackie, "My beauty is fading. I've had a long reign car-

Without question, **Lady Diana Cooper** was a great beauty, but was she really the most beautiful woman of the 20th Century?

rying the torch as the most beautiful woman born in the 20th Century. But like the sky over our heads, it is twilight time for me."

"I intend to pass on my crown to you. I think you'll go far. You have the potential to become the media darling of the latter part of the 20th Century, following in my footsteps. Of course, a lot will depend on who you marry. It is still a man's world and is likely to remain so—at least for the rest of this century."

"Your forecast of my future, Lady Diana, is a bit beyond my imagination."

"I will not be around to see the end result, but I predict you will lead a life beyond your wildest dreams."

One evening, in Paris, Jackie was surprised when Duff invited her for dinner at Maxim's. She fully expected to see him dining with Lady Diana. But instead, she found Lulu sitting with him in a banquette. When an equivalent invitation was extended to her a second time, she came to realize that her role to some degree was that of a "beard" to conceal the affair between Duff and Lulu.

Once, when Jackie was staying over at the Cooper villa in Chantilly, Lady Diana admitted that she knew of her husband's affairs. "Lulu and his other mistresses may be the flowers, but I am the tree."

It was said that Jackie learned how to handle the womanizing of her future husband, John F. Kennedy, by following Lady Diana's long ago example of how to deal with a marriage to a high-ranking philanderer.

***

Jackie's most prestigious invitation came from Comte Etienne de Beaumont, the society don of Paris. In March of 1949, as a celebration of a return to prosperity after the austerities of France during the Nazi Occupation, he staged a spectacularly glamorous costume ball, *Le Bal des Rois et des Reines,* within his sumptuous mansion in the rue Masseran in the city's very stylish 7th Arrondissement.

In London's Bloomsbury district, the greatest love story was that of **Violet Trefusis** *(left)* and **Vita Sackville-West**, a lifetime saga of lesbian love, cross dressing, bewildered husbands, outraged mothers, and interludes of illicit sex, cruelty, and humiliation. Jackie was intrigued.

Jackie came dressed as Marie Antoinette, mingling with the comtesse de Ganay, who appeared as the Empress Joséphine. Jackie noted that since three of the male guests arrived at the ball outfitted in one way or another as Napoléon, the "empress" had her pick of three potential "husbands."

Many of the most elegant costumed women at the ball wore creations designed by Christian Dior or Jacques Fath. At one point, Jackie stood next to Violet Trefusis, dressed as Queen Victoria. Her companion, poet Vita Sackville-West, came as Voltaire.

[Trefusis was an English writer and socialite who is chiefly remembered for her lesbian affair with Sackville-West. When Trefusis was four years old, her mother, Alice Keppel, became the favorite mistress of Albert Edward (Bertie), the Prince of Wales, who became King Edward VII in 1901. He paid visits to the Keppel household many afternoons, while Keppel's husband, who was aware of the affair, gracefully made himself absent. Trefusis, incidentally, was also the great-aunt of Camilla Parker-Bowles, who later married England's Prince Charles.]

Back in Paris, while still studying at the Sorbonne, Jackie still managed to slip away on most nights for her ritual cocktail hour at the bar of the Ritz Hotel, once patronized by Ernest Hemingway and F. Scott Fitzgerald. She was always accompanied by an ever-changing *beau du jour*, as she called her boyfriends, many from the Sorbonne itself.

After the Ritz Bar, Jackie and her male companion would often have dinner at Chez Allard, her favorite Left Bank bistro. Even on a school night, dinner would be followed by a visit to one of the *boîtes*. Only very rarely did she go to the Folies-Bergère, with a rare exception involving a night when she went to see the black American expatriate performer, Josephine Baker.

Jackie was also intrigued by the seedy side of Paris, especially the world of the *demimonde*. She was taken to Le Carousel on three different occasions, a cabaret that promoted itself as a showcase for the world's most beautiful transvestites.

[Ironically, Le Carousel became one of the favorite Parisian bars of her second husband, Aristotle Onassis.]

As proposed during their inaugural meeting, Jean Cocteau and Jean Marais eventually got around to inviting Jackie for a tour of underground Paris. They landed at La Vie en Rose, patronized mainly by homosexuals who billed it as "The Meat Rack," because of the easy availability of pickups.

When author and filmmaker **Jean Cocteau** met Jackie, he found her enchanting and, days later, invited her, along with his lover, **Jean Marais** *(below)* to tour underground nocturnal Paris with them. "You and Jean are beautiful, and I am not," Cocteau lamented. "My greatest regret in life is in not having been born beautiful."

Some nights, she preferred out-of-the-way restaurants where she could listen to gypsy violinists who had fled from Budapest at the time of the Nazi takeover.

Her favorite jazz club was Le Caveau de la Huchette in the 5th Arrondissment. In another day, it had been frequented by both Robespierre and Jean-Paul Marat, each an essential figure during the bloodshed of the French Revolution. On many an evening, Jackie could be seen gliding down to this deep medieval cellar to hear jazz. One night, she was delighted by a surprise guest appearance of Louis Armstrong.

At one Left Bank *boîte,* Count Paul took Jackie to see the chanteuse, Juliette Greco, who became all the rage in 1950s Paris during that city's "flowering of existentialism." Greco's friends and supporters, Jean-Paul Sartre and his brilliant mistress, Simone de Beauvoir, also attended her opening. Greco appeared on stage clad in what was a very avant-garde statement at the time, a black leotard.

In one of the dimly illuminated booths, Jackie spotted Marlon Brando again. He was no longer with Eartha Kitt. She'd deserted him for the Dominican playboy, Porfirio Rubirosa. Count Paul told her that Brando was now in hot pursuit of Greco herself.

One of her most memorable nights was when Count Paul took her to La Java, a famous old *bal-musette,* a time-honored dance hall where both Edith Piaf and Maurice Chevalier had appeared before they

Cocteau's lover, **Jean Marais**, starring as Xiphares in Racine's *Mithridate*, performed in November of 1952 at the *Comédie française*. In 1950, his legs were voted "the most beautiful in France."

33

became legendary. When the newspapers announced that Piaf would appear in a nostalgic acknowledgement of her early years as an unknown, and then a rising young star, Jackie wanted to go. She'd never heard Piaf sing live before.

"The Little Sparrow" made a spectacular entrance on the arm of her lover, Marlene Dietrich. The German star was dressed in a white tuxedo similar to the one she'd made famous in her 1932 film, *Blonde Venus,* with Cary Grant.

"The Little Sparrow" (**Edith Piaf**, *left*), was in love with tuxedo-clad **Marlene Dietrich** *(right)* when the German *femme fatale* showed up at La Java (a Parisian nightclub) to hear Piaf sing. But did Dietrich really make a pass at Jackie that night?

During the course of the evening, Dietrich spotted Jackie and seemed attracted to her. At one point, she approached Jackie's table and asked Count Paul if she could "borrow" Jackie for a dance.

Jackie later said, "I'd never danced with a woman before. Dietrich held me very close. It was so romantic, but I was not a card-carrying lesbian. Besides, she had Piaf."

[In 1957, during her marriage to JFK, Jackie hinted to her husband that she and Dietrich might have become more intimate that night in Paris than they really were. She did it not only to upset him, but to make him jealous. She'd just learned that both Joseph P. ("Papa Joe") Kennedy and his son JFK (Jack) had, at various times, seduced Dietrich themselves.]

Ever since she'd studied ballet, Jackie had retained her love of the dance. "Instead of a ballerina, I became a balletomane like Gore Vidal."

In Newport, she'd become friends with a fellow debutante, Elizabeth de Cuevas. In Paris, Elizabeth introduced her to her father, George, the Marquis de Cuevas, an impresario who invited Jackie to the Paris Opera.

*[Born in Chile, **George de Cuevas** (Jorge Cuevas Bartholín, 1885 – 1961) was a choreographer and ballet impresario who was best known for the Grand Ballet du Marquis de Cuevas (also known as the Grand Ballet de Monte Carlo, Grand Ballet du Marquis de Cuevas, or later, the de Cuevas Ballet by American theatergoers) that he formed in 1944.]*

The event was the opening of his company's fall season, featuring Rosella Hightower and Tamara Toumanova. Attending a performance were ballet dancers, Margot Fonteyn and Michael Somes. The Marquis introduced the stars to Jackie.

All of them, including Jackie, were invited to a party the Marquis was giving on the Île St-Louis after the performance. Jackie eagerly accepted.

A balletomane, like her friend and distant relation, Gore Vidal, Jackie was more thrilled to meet these ballet legends. In London, she'd seen Somes and Fonteyn dance at the Royal Ballet. She'd also seen Fonteyn dance in 1949 during the Royal Ballet's tour of the United States. Jackie regarded her as one of the greatest of classical ballet dancers, though she seemed rather reserved, perhaps snobbish, when introduced.

In contrast, Somes, Fonteyn's escort for the evening and her sometimes lover, sparked certain fantasies in Jackie, as she'd later reveal. She called him "the most beautiful man animal on the planet."

The guru of American ballet, Lincoln Kirstein, had asserted that Somes was "an absolutely magical creature," and other balletomanes hailed him as "the finest British male dancer of the century."

Jackie had heard that the more experienced Fonteyn had taken the dancer's virginity, even though she was two years younger. Somes had danced in 1938 with Fonteyn, performing in the ballet *Horoscope,* choreographed by Constant Lambert and Frederick Ashton. It was rumored that Ashton had fallen madly in love with Somes. In time, Ashton would choreograph twenty-four more ballets for him to perform.

Tall, dark, and handsome, Somes was the man of Jackie's dreams, even though she'd later admit "I don't normally go for a Greek god."

"God had a talent for creating glorious men," Jackie wrote in her diary about the British ballet dancer, **Michael Somes** *(depicted above).* "Surely, Michael stands as one of His more glorious achievements."

Gore had told her that whenever Fonteyn and Somes performed, there were more Stage Door Johnnies lined up for him than for the ballerina herself. According to Gore, Somes freely dispensed his sexual favors to both men and women when Ashton or Fonteyn didn't have him otherwise occupied in their boudoirs.

When the subject of Ashton came up later that night, Somes told Jackie. "He is my Diaghilev. Before I go on stage, he always tells me, 'Dance like a god.'"

At the party, Jackie virtually monopolized Somes, as Fonteyn was distracted by too many adoring friends. Jackie found that he had a certain bitterness in his voice, a self-castigating edge.

She confided that she, too, had once considered being a ballerina.

When Fonteyn became aware of Jackie moving in on Somes, she came over to investigate.

Somes looked embarrassed. "Jacqueline here tells me she once studied ballet herself."

Fonteyn looked skeptically at Jackie. Then she peered down at her feet. "I'm not sure that ballet slippers come in your size." She turned and walked away.

Before leaving the party, Jackie secretly agreed to meet Somes at the Ritz Bar at seven the following evening. Conveniently, he was staying in a suite at the Ritz, and Fonteyn would be otherwise engaged.

At the bar, she was reported to have found Somes more enchanting than he had been the night before.

But here, a curtain is drawn. She did not immediately speak of the time she spent in Somes' suite at the Ritz.

Years later, at Peter Lawford's beach-fronting home in Santa Monica, she talked to her brother-in-law about her sexual experiences before marriage. She told him that she tried but failed to hold onto her virginity while studying in Paris—"out of fear of pregnancy and not for any moral reasons."

"When I first enrolled in Vassar, I learned that the other girls were trying to become adept at fellatio until they could get that wedding band on their fingers. I held out for a long time in Paris. My night with Michael Somes—I called it my glorious night—I satisfied him with every means at my disposal except number one."

"Marlene Dietrich and I consider fellatio and cunnilingus our two favorite forms of sex," Lawford drunkenly confessed.

"I'd heard that about you, Peter, but I didn't know until now that it was true," she said, to tease him. "Michael told me that if he and I ever had children, our kids would be the most beautiful in the history of humankind."

"Modest fellow, wasn't he?" Peter said.

[Somes would remain the lead male dancer with the Royal Ballet from 1951, the year Jackie met him, until the arrival of Rudolf Nureyev in 1962. In spite of the difference in their ages, the incoming Russian also replaced Somes as Fonteyn's lover.

In a touch of irony, Jackie would eventually compete with her sister, Lee, for the affection of Nureyev as well. "What a tangled web he weaves," Jackie once said about Nureyev's complicated love life.]

Of all the men and women Lulu introduced Jackie to, none stood out in her mind as much as the brilliant and dashing but roguish André Malraux. At one of Lulu's parties, Jackie met this celebrated novelist and art theorist. She'd later proclaim, "André is the most fascinating man I've ever met."

He had been appointed by Charles de Gaulle as his Minister of Information (1945-1946), and later as the first Minister of Cultural Affairs (1959-69). When she met him, Jackie had already read, in French, his novel, *La Condition Humaine (Man's Fate),* which he'd written in 1933, winning the Prix Goncourt.

At the time Jackie became involved with him, Malraux was married to his second wife, Marie-

A young **André Malraux** poses in Saigon with his first wife, **Clara Goldschmidt**, whom he taught to steal Buddhist icons from Cambodian temples

Madeleine Lioux, a concert pianist and the widow of his half-brother, Roland Malraux.

[After Malraux's 1966 divorce from Madeleine, he came to live in Lulu's château at Verrières-le-Buisson, where Jackie had first met him.]

When Lulu observed Malraux's interest in Jackie, Lulu called her aside. "Go for it, darling. André and I had a torrid affair in 1934, but that was so long ago. We emerged the best of friends. Today, he treats me like his mother instead of his passion."

"André didn't speak English very well, but I loved to hear him talk in French," Jackie later said. "He had such an elegant turn of phrase, as when he told me, 'Art is an object lesson for the gods.'"

She also said, "Listening to André makes me feel as if I'm on a raft. It's very exciting, very exhilarating, and very dangerous. I have to hang on for dear life because I don't understand everything he says in his rapid French."

He fascinated her with stories of his adventurous life, as he moved from the literary salons of Paris in the 1920s to colonial Cambodia, and on to Cochin China *[French Cochinchine, the southern region of Vietnam during the French colonial period]*, ending up on the battlefields of Spain during that country's Civil War. A member of the French Resistance during the Nazi occupation of France, Malraux had been captured by the Gestapo, but later escaped.

Sometimes, Lulu was their host, making available one of her upstairs bedrooms for Jackie to meet privately with Malraux. She let them read what became her most famous novel (it was entitled *Madame de...*) before it was published in 1951.

[In 1953, Jackie would see the movie version of Lulu's novel, It became a celebrated film called The Earrings of Madame de... *starring Charles Boyer and Danielle Darrieux, the French actress who had been married to Porfirio Rubirosa.]*

Malraux had his own cultural statement to present as a gift to Jackie. Published in three volumes, it was called *The Psychology of Art (1947-49).*

During Malraux's courtship of Jackie, he took her to several visits to the Louvre. "He made art come alive for me as I'd never seen it before. André is a 20th century Renaissance man."

At one point, they stood for almost an hour in front of Leonardo da Vinci's *Mona Lisa,* the lady with the enigmatic smile who would play such a key role in each of their futures.

To her friends in Paris, Susan Coward and Claude de Renty, Jackie confessed that she regretted that "I did not go all the way with André. I'm still morbidly afraid of getting pregnant, and I refuse to have an abortion if I do. My life would be ruined if I had a child out of wedlock and my chance of a proper marriage dashed. But André and I found many, many other ways to make love. What a man! He's the only Frenchman I've met that I truly wanted to marry."

***

A CIA operative, John Gates, nicknamed "Demi," was another beau who fell in love with Jackie. In America, he had known both of her parents, Black Jack and Janet. Because of that, Jackie often confided in Demi about her difficulties with both parents and their obsessive attempts to control her life.

She claimed that she was well aware of Black Jack's indiscretions, and that Janet had once learned of them as well. They'd sailed on their honeymoon aboard the *Aquitania.* On that honeymoon, Janet realized that Black Jack was not going to be a faithful husband.

He was seen leaving the stateroom of tobacco heiress Doris Duke at three o'clock in the morning. At the casino at Biarritz, he gambled away all his money the first night. Consequently, Janet gathered up her reserve of cash and went to the casino and won it all back before four o'clock the same morning.

Jackie let Demi escort her around to various venues, but she was never as serious about their relationship as he was. "Who wouldn't love Jackie?" he once asked. "I remember that summer night at St-Jean-de-Luz. Gypsy violins were playing; the full moon made her hair lustrous, and she was astonishingly beautiful."

Jackie went on to other beaux, but she and Demi still stayed in touch. When he flew from Madrid to London for the coronation of Queen Elizabeth II in June of 1953, he dined in Mayfair with Jackie. To his astonishment, he learned that she was engaged to John F. Kennedy, whom Demi knew.

He warned her against marrying JFK, confiding that his cousin in New York always lined up an array of beautiful women every time JFK flew into the city. "He's a compulsive womanizer," Demi said. "He never can be true to one woman—it's not his nature."

As he remembered it, she didn't look too surprised, as if she were well aware of that fact. She protested, 'But Jack's the only one pursuing me who has a lot of money.'"

After the coronation, Jackie flew to Paris to do some shopping before taking an Air France flight from Orly Airport to Boston. She occupied a seat near one of the most famous and instantly recognizable pop icons of that era:

"A young girl, sort of prim and proper, had the seat opposite me," Zsa Zsa Gabor recalled. "She rudely kept staring at me throughout most of the flight. She wasn't very attractive and had this kinky hair and bad skin. As the hours dragged on, she finally got up the courage to speak to me. She complimented me on the beauty of my porcelain skin, and had the nerve to ask me how I took care of it. There was no way in hell I was going to give her my beauty secrets."

"Because I was Zsa Zsa, the customs men in Boston cleared me at once—not this ugly little duckling with the pimpled skin. To my surprise, I found Jack *[JFK]* in the waiting room. He rushed to me, hugged me, and lifted

"The little wren with the bad skin soon realized that I'd had Jack before her," claimed **Zsa Zsa Gabor.**

me off the ground. Obviously, he wasn't in back pain that day."

"Oh, *dahlink*," Zsa Zsa said to him. "You seem in the mood for a repeat performance." She was referring to his seduction of her during his previous visit to Hollywood.

"Can't now," Jack told her, "But I'd love to. You'll always be my sweetheart. You know I've always been in love with you."

"At that moment, the Little Wren from the airplane appeared," Zsa Zsa said.

"Zsa Zsa, I want you to meet my *fiancée*, Jacqueline Bouvier. Jackie, this is Zsa Zsa Gabor, the best thing to come out of Hungary since goulash."

"I'm honored, I'm sure," Jackie said in a tiny, almost meek voice.

"Miss Bouvier shot daggers at me," Zsa Zsa claimed. "For the first time, I think she realized that I had been having an affair with her future husband. I told Jack what a beautiful girl he had. I also warned him, 'Don't you corrupt her morals.'"

Jackie looked straight into Zsa Zsa's eyes. With a little smirk, she replied, "He's already been there, done that."

***

Even though Jackie had turned down Demi's proposal, she still maintained a friendship with him. When she was First Lady, she invited him to the White House to a party that she and JFK were hosting for Eugene Black, the head of the World Bank.

Demi noticed that marriage had not changed Jack's ways. "I saw him leave the room with a mother. (I won't name her.) He was gone twenty minutes and returned to the room to reclaim her daughter. He then disappeared with her for another twenty minutes. Jackie could not help from noticing."

One of JFK's best friends, Senator George Smathers of Florida, echoed Demi's claim. "No one was off-limits to Jack—not your wife, your mother, your sister, even your daughters."

***

Jackie's virginity, which she'd protected so ardently, could not be safeguarded forever. She may have wished that it had been André Malraux "who made me a woman," but it was someone quite different.

While still in Paris, Jackie began to date John Marquand, Jr., son of the famous novelist *[John Marquand, Senior]* who developed a reputation as the chronicler of American aristocratic WASPs. Marquand, Senior became first known for his commercially successful stories about the Japanese detective, "Mr. Moto." In 1938, he'd won the Pulitzer Prize for his biography, *The Late George Apley.* At the Shakespeare bookstore on Paris' Left Bank, Marquand, Jr., purchased copies of his father's novels for Jackie to read. She read one or two of them, mainly as a means of better understanding the family dynamic of this new man in her life.

Eventually, they found themselves frequenting a smoky Parisian *boîte* named "L'Elephant Blanc"

Evenings at "The White Elephant" found Jackie lighting one Gauloise after another and downing Grasshoppers *[made from equal parts crème de menthe, crème de cacao, and either fresh cream or vodka, or both, shaken with ice and strained into a chilled cocktail glass],* which that summer was her favorite cocktail.

Seduction was slow in coming. Marquand Jr., told his friends, "Jackie will not go all the way. She'll give me a blow job, but she won't let me screw her in the missionary position."

Perhaps Jackie had too many of those Grasshoppers at the White Elephant, but one night, after escorting her there, Marquand got lucky. In fact, as he later told some male friends, "She was so hot to trot she couldn't wait until I got inside my apartment. I figured I'd better go for it before she changed her mind."

And so he did, as related in Edward Klein's book, *All Too Human, The Love Story of Jack and Jackie Kennedy.* "In the creaky French elevator, Jackie let herself get carried away. She was in Marquand's arms, her skirt bunched above her hips, the backs of her thighs pressed against the decorative open grillwork. When the elevator jolted to a stop, she was no longer a demivierge," *[a term translating as "a "a partial virgin," and indicating a woman who engages in promiscuous sexual activity but who retains her virginity.]*

The elevator had stalled on the second landing. Actually, it was in good working order. Marquand had used the deliberately stalled elevator as a seduction technique on several other young woman he'd previously invited upstairs for a drink.

Jackie later told confidants that she surrendered her virginity "only on my wedding night." That was not true. Jack Kennedy himself confessed to several people, including his brother, Bobby, and to Florida Senator George Smathers, that he and Jackie were having an affair months before their wedding.

According to her gossipy friend, author Truman Capote, "Virginity was something Jackie wanted to get rid of as soon as possible. She knew that her sister had lost hers, and, as the

The famous novelist, John P. Marquand, Sr., didn't want his son, "Junior," using the Marquand name, fearing that readers might be confused. So Marquand, Jr., published his novel, **The Second Happiest Day**, under the nom de plume of "John Phillips." It was marketed by its publisher as "The big novel of today's gilded youth, sated with too much money, jaded because everything is too easy. Here are the reckless loves, the wild gaiety, the bitterness of a new Lost Generation."

Was the book's title inspired by his seduction of Jackie in a Paris elevator? Marquand, Jr., never revealed what his first happiest day was.

older sister, she didn't want to be the last to sample what a man had to offer. If my calculations are correct, she went to bed with at least five guys before Jack sampled the honeypot. Certainly John P. Marquand, Jr., takes the honors as the first in a string of get-lucky beaux."

After their "love-in-the-lift" seduction, Jackie and Marquand Jr., began a passionate affair that lasted until she returned to America.

Janet Auchincloss, Jackie's mother, had trained her daughters "to grow up, look chic, behave yourself, and marry a rich man."

When her mother discovered that Jackie was having an affair with Marquand, she violently objected. "Writers are always poor as church mice."

***

After the initial excitement and novelty wore off, Jackie broke up with Marquand. During her vacation from the Sorbonne, she traveled third class to Austria and for a tour through parts of a devastated post-war Germany. Her companions were her roommates, Susan Coward and Claude de Renty. "I'd never traveled on a train before with chickens and geese."

In Vienna, during the sullen peak of The Cold War, Jackie was arrested by the occupying Russian army, which controlled a sector of the city. Under a hot spotlight, she was brutally grilled for three hours by a fat senior officer of the KGB. She had been arrested for photographing buildings and was suspected of being an American spy. In tears, she was finally let go.

Leaving Vienna, she journeyed to the ruins of Hitler's Bavarian retreat at Berchtesgaden. Later, she visited the site of the former concentration camp at Dachau, where so many prisoners had lost their lives. For weeks afterward, she was haunted in her dreams with visions of gas chambers and torture chambers.

Back in Paris, she reconciled with Marquand Jr., forgetting whatever it was they'd argued about before she left.

***

Jackie and John (Marquand Jr.), as a romantic couple, were seen at fashionable places around Paris, eventually returning to their former haunt, the White Elephant. "I was still in love with John, and he was passionately in love with me," Jackie recalled. "I chose not to listen to mother. After all, I was grown up and wanted to live my own life. Besides, isn't a woman supposed to take a husband for richer or poorer?"

In 1978, Kitty Kelley published a pioneering biography called *Jackie Oh!* that was highly controversial. The public at the time, although fascinated with Jackie, knew virtually nothing of her affairs, only her marriages to John F. Kennedy and later to Aristotle Onassis.

Kelley was the first author to reveal, in published form, an overview of Jackie's first love, John P. Marquand, Jr. In fairness to Kelley, she admitted that

Jackie's reaction to sweaty intimacy might be more "apocryphal than authentic," but as the tale goes, Jackie, upon losing her virginity, said in disappointment, "Oh, is that all there is to it?"

When Kelley's book appeared, Marquand Jr., was ridiculed by his friends, one of whom asked, "Did Jackie have to ask you if you were in yet?" Marquand denied the conquest of Jackie's virginity, but by this time, there were additional links that bound him to his memories of Jackie. He had married Susan Coward, her roommate. Susan's first cousin, Michael Canfield, had become the first husband of Lee Bouvier (later, Radziwill).

"The Kelley story reflected on me a hell of a lot more than it did on Jackie?" Marquand said. "What kind of asshole would make claims on the maidenhead of Jacqueline Bouvier and go around bragging about it? Not only that, but the rumor made me sound less than manly. The story became so prominent that when I was having lunch one day with Jackie I brought it up," Marquand recalled. "She completely dismissed it and asked me to drop the subject."

"It's pure bullshit" she responded. "I don't know where on earth Kelley got such a story. I certainly didn't tell her, and I know you didn't either. It's categorically untrue. But I'm too much of a lady and you're too much of a gentleman to sue. Besides, the press would have a field day with a lawsuit like that. Kelley would sell five million books in hardcover alone."

But apparently, Marquand made up that story about his chivalrous reaction and Jackie's demure response to Kelley's revelations. To his close friends (all male), he told a very different story, claiming that Kelley had been right all along.

Vidal dismissed Marquand Jr., and Jackie's denials: "Jackie did lose her virginity to John in that elevator. He was a friend of mine and he told me the truth."

After the resumption of her affair with Marquand, Jackie returned to America to confront Janet once again. This time her mother slapped her hard on both cheeks, "trying to knock some sense into you."

As Jackie later told her sister, Lee, "Mother never hit me before. She's also withdrawn my allowance. I'm going to have to figure out a way of making money myself."

***

Shortly after her return to America from her tenure (and adventures) in Paris, Jackie enrolled in George Washington University in Washington,

In 1951, after a junior year in Paris, **Jackie** *(first row, center)* was surrounded by lots of men when she earned her bachelor of arts in French literature from George Washington University. "I was hit upon at least once a day, and sometimes a girl can't say no."

D.C. for her final term, seeking and eventually winning a bachelor's degree in French literature. Her dating continued at an accelerated pace, and she made promises to young men she could not possibly keep. As she told her sister, Lee, "I'm weaving such a deceptive web with so many beaux, I feel like Mata Hari."

She somehow resumed her relationship with Ormande de Kay, the young American she had previously dated in Paris, and she became "engaged to be engaged to him." When she slipped off to date other men, she made up some engagement or some project that would make her unavailable to him.

De Kay was with her the day she heard from the editors of *Vogue* that she'd won that magazine's 16th annual *Prix de Paris,* a writing contest open to college seniors. To win the prize, she competed with 1,280 other contestants from 225 colleges. The winner would be offered a one-year contract as a trainee in *Vogue* office, half the time in Paris, the rest in New York. Jackie had won by submitting an essay on fashion, a personal profile, the makeup pages for a mock issue of the magazine, and a personal essay entitled "People I wish I had known."

She'd chosen Sergei Diaghilev, the Russian ballet impresario who'd had an affair with Vaslav Nijinski. She'd become fascinated with Diaghilev once when she'd harbored a young dream of becoming a ballerina, and her awareness of his role in the world of dance had been intensified by her dialogues in Paris with the ballet dancer, Michael Somes.

Another of her choices was Charles Baudelaire, the French poet. She wrote, "He could paint sinfulness with honesty and still believe in something higher." Her final choice was Oscar Wilde, the witty but disgraced Victorian author and man-about-London who had been jailed after a conviction on a charge of homosexuality.

Both Black Jack and Janet urged Jackie not to return to Paris, citing the year she'd already spent abroad. Jackie was ultimately persuaded not to accept the award, but in the end, it was her own decision. After mulling it over for weeks, she announced, "I have decided against a career in fashion."

To reward her decision, both parents offered Jackie a summer tour of Europe. Lee would join her upon her own graduation from Miss Porter's School in Farmington, Connecticut, which Jackie had also attended. Lee would eventually return from Europe to matriculate as an art history major at Sarah Lawrence College.

A week after winning the award, and on a date with De Kay, he told her that the Navy was shipping him to fight in the Korean War. The agreement was that they would wed upon his return.

[Mail deliveries to the front lines in South Korea were hardly efficient. In January of 1952, Jackie wrote a "Dear John" letter to De Kay that he did not receive until mid-April.

She wrote of their "affair of the heart, remembering those romantic walks they'd had together along the banks of the Seine in Paris."

"I want you to be the first to know that I've found the love of my life, the man

43

I want to marry. I am now engaged to wed John F. Kennedy."

De Kay survived the Korean War and returned home. But he didn't see Jackie until May of 1956, when she invited him to a small dinner party at Hickory Hill in Virginia, where she and JFK were living. He found that Jackie was pregnant and expecting a child due in September.

"The talk was all about politics, and I was surprised that Jackie had become the wife of such an ambitious politician. Jack, already a senator, told us that he would seek the Democratic nomination for vice president on a ticket with Adlai Stevenson. Bobby was planning to move to New York and run for Senator from that state. Young Teddy was going to move to Arizona, where he would later challenge Barry Goldwater for his Senate seat."

De Kay had already heard that Jack was a womanizer. "As we boys would say about him, Jack would spawn with any woman who had two legs that twitched."]

***

On June 7, 1951, from the Port of New York, eighteen-year-old Lee Bouvier and twenty-two-year-old Jacqueline Bouvier set out to their first trip to Europe together. It was financed by Hugh Auchincloss after much persuading from Janet, who had been been pestered for months by her daughters to let them go.

Gore Vidal predicted, "It will be a round of men, men, and more men. I'm sure half the eligible bachelors—and some not so eligible—will be lined up to welcome them, presuming wrongly that they are rich debutantes like Barbara Hutton and Doris Duke when they set out to conquer Europe. I expected one of them to land a prince or at least a count." In Lee's case, Gore's prediction would in time come true.

Left on the dock was Michael Canfield, a blonde-haired "beauty of a Harvard man" that Lee had been seriously dating and would ultimately marry. This Harvard University senior had been her most frequent escort, but they also went out with other people. In Lee's case, she was also dating Canfield's stepbrother, Blair Fuller.

Lee and Jackie were armed with letters of introduction, but not a lot of money, forcing them to travel third class aboard Cunard's *Queen Elizabeth*. To their horror, the debutantes found themselves sharing a tiny little compartment in the bowels of the ship with a 90-year-old woman who liked to walk around in the nude.

At night, Lee and Jackie dressed in their Newport gowns and escaped to the first class deck,

When Jackie danced with **Prince Aly Khan**, he'd told her, "I only think of the woman's pleasure when I am in love, and I'm in love with you."

She didn't believe him.

leaping over a large fence and "whizzing down the flight of stairs, leaping over another fence, and finally arriving there." With guilty faces, they spent part of their evenings dodging the ship's officers. Lee later wrote, "I have this fear that Jackie and I will soon be caught in the act. The whistles will blow. The ship will halt while we are condemned."

Nonetheless, every night at sea, they managed to slip into the ballroom. Lee wrote about one dance where Jackie managed to capture the sexy purser whom Lee had been lusting for all day.

Lee ended up with one Iganovich Illiwitz from Persia. "The only thing I could see in the whole room was his nose—and then he tried to point out his family to me. It was the same nose on the same face of every one of them, only it came in all sizes."

Virginia-born **Nancy Astor,** eventually elected a Member of Parliament, was, by some estimates, more regal than the Windsors themselves

Jackie had already warned her about "the sexual quirks" of men from the Middle East. Jackie was already a veteran of an up-close-and-personal encounter on a dance floor with a "very erect" Prince Aly Khan.

Jackie had already been to London, and she made herself Lee's guide to the city where her younger sister would live after her marriage to Prince Stanislas Radziwill.

Through Janet's intervention, and based on a reference from Hugh Auchincloss, one of the most coveted invitations in the U.K. soon after arrived for Jackie and Lee.

It was from Nancy Astor, Viscountess Astor, to Cliveden House, one of the most lavish and stately homes in England. Jackie was thrilled. She had read about it as the meeting place in the 1920s and 30s of the Cliveden Set, a coven of intellectuals.

Although its roots extended deep into the 17th Century, Cliveden House, a Victorian three-story mansion, had been designed by Sir Charles Barry on the banks of the Thames in Buckinghamshire, near London. It had been rebuilt in 1851. Its gracefully sprawling English Palladian design included vast acreages of parks and gardens, and house party guests who included Charlie Chaplin, Winston Churchill, George Bernard Shaw, Franklin D. Roosevelt, T.E. Lawrence (i.e., Lawrence of Arabia), and such authors as Rudyard Kipling, Edith Wharton, and Henry James.

Born in 1879 in Danville, Virginia (USA), to a distinguished family of landowners with roots to the antebellum South, Lady Astor was the survivor of a spectacularly unhappy marriage to a drunkard in Virginia. After their divorce and her subsequent emigration, in 1905, to the U.K., she met and married her second husband, the very wealthy American expatriate, Waldorf Astor. Born in the United States, his father had moved his family to England when Waldorf was twelve and raised him as an English aristocrat.

Eventually, the witty and endlessly controversial Nancy became the first woman to sit as a Member of Parliament in the British House of Commons, despite her birth in America. She still retained her regal beauty and her saucy, piquant wit when Jackie and Lee met her.

One of the most stately of the stately homes of England, **Cliveden House** stands on the banks of the River Thames in Buckinghamshire, outside London. It has been the setting for many a scandal, including a "mini-scandal" instigated by Jackie.

Actually, when the Bouviers met her in 1951, her reputation had become seriously tarnished. Before the war, and publicly supported by her close friend, Joseph P. Kennedy, Sr. *[who had been appointed by President Roosevelt as U.S. ambassador to the Court of St. James's]*, she had wanted to appease Hitler. Astor maintained that Nazism would solve the problems "associated with Communism and the Jews." With deep hatred, her critics on both sides of the Atlantic had publicly denounced her as "Hitler's spokeswoman in Britain."

Ambassador Kennedy, to judge from their correspondence, was also anti-Semite. In one letter, written by Kennedy to Astor, he stated his fear that the "Jew media" of the United States would undermine the stability of the West: "Jewish interests in New York and Los Angeles are already making noises to set a match to the fuse of the world."

In one letter to the ambassador, Lady Astor surmised that "Hitler is no menace. He looks too much like Charlie Chaplin to be taken seriously."

In spite of the Viscountess's unfortunate racial and political opinions, Jackie found Lady Astor a woman of charm and wit. "While you're in England, marry a rich Brit like I did," Lady Astor advised Jackie. "Although I must say, the only thing I like about rich Brits is their money. But if you succeed, I must warn you. The penalty for being rich is to be bored by the same people who used to snub you."

Lady Astor was born in near poverty "because my father had lost his slave labor after the Civil War. It would be wonderful to bring back slavery. But since that is now allowed, I told this group of Negroid students that they should aspire to be servants in the households of the wealthy."

Jackie only smiled at her opinions, each of them increasingly outrageous as their time together wore on.

In her final advice to Jackie, she said, "Regardless of how long you live, never admit to being more than fifty-two."

While Lee was engaged with other guests, Jackie wandered off to inspect some of the rooms. She climbed the stairs, hoping to get a peek into Lady

Astor's bedroom. A door was open onto one of the up-stairs corridors. As she walked by, a man called out to her. She was astonished to find it was Douglas Fairbanks, Jr., a movie star in his own right, and the son of Hollywood's most famous swashbuckler, Douglas Fairbanks, Sr. Fairbanks Jr., invited her in, and she entered his room, where he was adjusting his tie and tuxedo jacket in preparation for dinner that night.

She knew that during World War II, he'd been assigned as a U.S. Navy Reserve to Lord Louis Montbatten's commando staff in Britain. Jackie read that in 1949, he'd been made an Honorary Knight Commander of the Order of the British Empire. A confirmed Anglophile, Fairbanks was a frequent visitor to England after the war.

Douglas Fairbanks, Jr., told Marlene Dietrich, his lover, "During my 'private time' with Miss Jacqueline Bouvier, I wish she had spent more time talking about how wonderful I was and less time trying to get me to reveal secrets about Joan Crawford."

Jackie also knew him to be an ace seducer, having married Joan Crawford when he was only nineteen and having had affairs with everyone from Laurence Olivier to Marlene Dietrich.

What happened at Cliveden in 1951 between Jackie and Fairbanks is not known. Apparently, she didn't confide her encounter to Lee. A servant later reported that Fairbanks closed his bedroom door behind her, and they were alone in his bedroom together for at least half an hour.

She went alone downstairs to the party, and he didn't descend for another half hour.

This secret encounter remains one of the unsolved mysteries of Jackie's life, of which there would be many more in the years to come.

[Douglas Fairbank, Jr. had first met John F. Kennedy in 1940 when Secretary of State Cordell Hull arranged for him to go on a fact-finding tour of South America, ostensibly to investigate the effects of Latin American public opinion of U.S. motion pictures. In actual fact, he had been a spy, sent to gauge how sympathetic these nations were to Nazi ideology. Before going, he enrolled in daily classes at the Berlitz School of Languages in Manhattan to learn at least basic Spanish and Portuguese.

"I sat next to a polite, rather toothy young fellow, about twenty-three years old. He was modest and charmingly impressed to be, as he said, 'in a language class with a movie star.'"

Weeks later, Fairbanks shared adjoining seats with that young man on an airplane returning to the United States from Panama.

From here, we "Fast Forward" the narrative to 1962, when Fairbanks is standing in the Oval Office of The White House with the same man, watching TV coverage of astronaut John Glenn orbiting the Earth.

"How's your Portuguese, Doug?" the man asked.

"Still rusty, Mr. President," he replied.]

Back in London, Janet had arranged for her daughters to attend a party at the home of her friend, Jane du Boulay, who had married a prominent Englishman, Guy de Boulay. During the course of the evening, when the Bouviers told him that they needed to buy a car for the continuation of their tour through Europe, he sold them his Hillman Minx for 500 pounds.

[The Hillman Minx was a series of relatively inexpensive, relatively staid, middle-sized family cars produced by the Japan-based Isuzu Motors under license from a British distributor between the early 1950s and 1964.]

In that car, they embarked on the mandatory tour of the English countryside, stopping in both Oxford and Stratford-upon-Avon before continuing to the Cotswolds.

At Dover, they took the car ferry to the coast of France. From there, they headed for Paris.

***

Paris was Jackie's favorite city. She told Lee that she was tempted to live there permanently and not to return to America, except for holidays. When she got there, she launched herself and her younger sister into a whirlwind of activity, including renewals of former friendships and attendance at fashion shows, museums, the ballet. They also went shopping, although their budget was limited.

Lee was introduced to Jackie's friend, Claude de Renty, and Lee got to see where Jackie had lived in the rue Mozart during her days at the Sorbonne, somehow managing to survive with no heat and scarce hot water.

Claude later recorded her impressions of Jackie and her sister: "Jacqueline was dark, serious, moody, and extremely curious about the world. Lee, blonde and very much the kid sister, appeared perhaps easier to get to know. She was easygoing and affable, but far less profound that Jacqueline. Jacqueline possessed an intensity that Lee clearly lacked."

From Paris, Lee and Jackie drove to Poitiers, 207 miles to the southwest. As a student of French history, Jackie had read a lot about this historic medieval city, the capital of the region of Poitou, an area linked during the Middle Ages to such famous names as Joan of Arc and the Black Prince. Jackie was seeking a reunion with her former beau, Paul de Ganay, who was serving in the French military.

It was a sunny day, and the Bouviers arrived in strapless sundresses, creating quite a stir when they confronted Paul's regiment. His commander asked him, "Are you engaged?"

"To both of them," Paul responded, gallantly.

Jackie's sexual attraction to Paul was a strong as ever, but being with Lee inhibited her movements, of course.

However, Lee was checking out the young men as well, recording in her journal that she encountered "The two best-looking officers this side of Paradise. They wore blue berets and had lovely gold cords twinkling underneath their arms."

***

Driving across the Pyrénées and heading into Spain, Jackie and Lee reached Pamplona in time for the festival of the running of the bulls. Jackie had read about it in one of her favorite novels, Ernest Hemingway's *The Sun Also Rises.*

At the bullfights, the two American beauties nearly caused a riot. Throughout the day, a virtual army of animated young Spaniards had pursued them, but the number of their potential *beaux* eventually narrowed down to five. Obviously, Jackie and Lee weren't enough women to go around, so a fight erupted. The police were called.

Two of the potential suitors were quite ardent. Lee and Jackie had promised to meet them for breakfast the following morning at nine. But they fled from the hotel at six o'clock that morning for the long drive to Madrid.

Dressed in their dark suits, the two young men of Navarre showed up at the hotel only to be informed by the manager that the two *norteamericanas* had left Pamplona at dawn.

Driving into Madrid, the raucously festive, wine-soaked atmosphere of Pamplona during the running of the bulls seemed like a distant world. Under the iron grip of Spain's Fascist dictator, Francisco Franco, the capital of Spain appeared dark and gloomy. As Jackie wrote to Janet, "It was clearly a police state, but we had some exciting invitations, so we decided to make the best of it, if we didn't get arrested as had happened to me in Vienna."

Armed with an invitation, they arrived at the elegant home of the Marqués de Santo Domingo, who showed them his celebrated painting of the Madonna that he claimed was worth millions. He later drove them west to Ávila, where he let them walk along the top of the ancient, once-fortified city walls. He told them that he had the authority to grant that permission, because he owned the walls.

Their next visit was to an elegant country house, El Quexigal, a 16th century former monastery that had once been visited by Philip II. Here, their hosts were the Princes Christian and Alfonso Hohenlohe, who shared their treasures with them, including museum-worthy crown jewels and paintings by Old Masters. Later, as Lee recorded in her journal, after Alfonso put a record on his Victrola, the two princes jitterbugged with Jackie and Lee to the sound of "Wave the Green for Old Tulane."

Later, Jackie took in their collection of Flemish primitives and sat in the chair where Christopher Columbus had plotted his epic sail across the Atlantic to the New World.

Back across the Pyrénées, they stopped over in Provence for a few nights before continuing along the French Riviera "where we did not break the bank at Monte Carlo."

In school, Lee had become fascinated by the Italian Renaissance. She'd written Bernard Berenson, the celebrated expert on Renaissance art, and in response, he had invited Jackie and her to his Villa i Tatti, his Tuscan estate.

When they met him in his garden, he was eighty-six years old, but still sharp of mind. Before talking about Da Vinci or Michelangelo, he gave them some sage advice, "Never marry a man unless he constantly stimulates your mind. Of course, stimulation of the body would be of use, too."

In Italy, **Bernard Berenson**, a leading expert on Renaissance art, survey's Canova's nude statue of Pauline Borghese, Napoléon's sister. The question remains, did Jackie, during her time in Venice, also pose for an artist drawing nude sketches of her?

He'd become rich by authenticating pictures by Old Masters, separating them from the fakes. He then took five percent of the painting's appraised value, which could be a considerable sum.

When he heard they were headed for Rome, he told them to shop the Flea Market there—"perhaps find a genuine Titian that I can authenticate for you for my usual commission."

After visiting Berenson, they drove to the site of their next invitation at Marlia, the former home of Napoléon's sister, Ellsa Baciochi Bonaparte, the Duchess of Lucca. They checked in for a week at the home of Count Pecci-Blunt. Their son, Dino, was half American. He immediately quizzed them about his friend from Boston, John F. Kennedy. The Bouvier sisters had not met him.

Jackie and Lee caused a bit of a scandal when they left early one morning and didn't say goodbye to their hosts. The aging Countess Anna Pecci Blunt was particularly offended, later claiming that the two young visitors "took French leave and had no breeding or manners." Jackie's excuse was that they had to leave early and didn't want to disturb the countess at that hour.

Both sisters wanted their stay in Venice to be leisurely, enough time for Lee to take voice lessons and for Jackie to have a private tutor to improve her sketching. She was fortunate to have a dashing young Venetian artist as her teacher. He was later described as "an American girl's dream of what a handsome, sexy, charming Italian male would look like."

It was later rumored that Jackie posed for nude sketches for the budding artist. Today, those sketches would be worth a fortune, but if they exist at all, they have been lost to history. How could he know that his model would become one of the century's most alluring personalities, not to mention First Lady of America?

So far as it is known, Jackie is America's only First Lady suspected of having posed for nude sketches—or, years later, to be secretly photographed in the nude?

Returning to Paris, Lee and Jackie prepared to go home. They had to sell their Hillman Minx to Harrison Davidson, a young American missionary who planned to drive it to the Sahara desert, after a sea crossing from Spain into Morocco. Lee recorded that he looked "like he'd just escaped from Benny Goodman's String Quartet."

In her journal, Lee wrote: "He wanted our car cheap because every $5 he spent on himself meant one more African child would starve to death. We were slaughtering a whole tribe, but his conscience would let him starve only 206 of them."

***

During their ocean crossing back to America, the sisters compiled a scrapbook of their adventures, with the intention of presenting it to Janet and Hugh Auchincloss, who had financed their trip. Lee did the writing, and Jackie drew the illustrations. The journal was mostly about themselves, not the treasures they'd viewed. "It was our confection to make Mummy smile," Lee claimed.

The scrapbook featured whimsical poems, intricate illustrations, and candid snapshots of themselves. Jackie jokingly said that their scrapbook should be entitled *"Lah De Dahs Across the Pond"* or *"Life Among the Noblesse,"* or even *"Lollygagging in Europe."*

Discovered in an attic years later, the scrapbook, formally entitled *One Special Summer,* was published by Delacorte Press in 1974. It was of interest, for the most part, for the insights it provides about the pre-celebrity lives of two young sisters on the dawn of world fame.

***

With the glitz and glamor of Paris behind her, Jackie returned to Washington, D.C. She didn't want to be trapped in McLean, Virginia, where her mother had married Hughdie and moved Jackie and her sister, Lee Bouvier, into a small mansion, Merrywood.

Jackie could not live very well on the fifty dollars a month that Janet and Hughdie gave her, so she decided to try to find a job, preferably one in journalism.

At Merrywood, she'd met Arthur Krock, the chief of *The New York Times'* Washington Bureau. Privately, Krock was a "media fixer" for the powerful Kennedy clan of Massachusetts. Krock was in close contact with the patriarch, Joseph P. Kennedy, a former movie mogul and bootlegger during Prohibition. He'd been appointed U.S. Ambassador to the Court of St. James's on the eve of World War II, but was recalled by President Franklin D. Roosevelt for his well-publicized efforts to keep the United States out of World War II.

Krock was also a close friend of Frank Waldrop, editor of the now defunct *Washington-Herald.* For reasons of his own, Krock had a policy of hiring "pretty little girls," even if they lacked experience. He'd previously hired two women who happened to be rooming together in Washington, Kathleen ("Kick")

Kennedy, Joseph Kennedy's daughter, who later died in an airplane crash over France in 1948.

He'd also added to his staff her friend, Inga Arvad, a blonde and beautiful Danish journalist.

Nicknamed "Inga-Binga," she'd had a torrid pre-war affair with Kick's brother, John F. Kennedy, whom Inga had nicknamed "Honeysuckle." Before becoming JFK's "hot-to-trot mistress," she had been a companion of Adolf Hitler at the 1936 Olympic Games in Berlin. *[That relationship and its many ironies are more fully explained in the special feature,* JFK and the Nazi Spy, *at the end of this chapter.]*

Although somewhat reluctant, Waldrop hired Jackie as an inquiring photographer, but in a follow-up note to his friend, Krock, he wrote a devastating critique of her physicality:

"I fear you exaggerated the looks of your friend, Miss Jacqueline Bouvier. She is well-groomed, speaking like a Newport debutante, and has perfect manners. But physically, her looks leave much to be desired—no breasts, a bit gawky, feet larger than those of Greta Garbo. Hands more suited to a steelworker, and bad skin, with lots of imperfections on her face. Her wide mouth evokes that of a baby bird waiting for Mama Bird to bring it the worm. She is also skinny, and her oculist has to design a pair of glasses that stretch across the Golden Gate Bridge for its frame to reach both of her widely spaced eyes. She has a certain charm, like that of a puppy, but she also reminds me of a piece of clothing that was put away in a drawer without being properly dried."

Fortunately for Jackie, the young men in Washington didn't agree with Waldrop's assessment of her physical charms.

At first, she turned down dates from what she defined as "The Werewolves of the Fourth Estate." One young editor, who had been rejected by her, called her "No Tits Wonder."

Her job at the *Washington-Herald* involved surveying "average citizens" about their reaction to hot-button, but not particularly threatening, issues of the day. In addition to photographing her subject, she had to ask her interviewee a question and print the answer. One of the first questions she asked some of her subjects was, "If you had a date with Marilyn Monroe, what would you talk about?"

Many evenings, instead of dating, Jackie stayed in her snug little apartment writing a screenplay. Ironically, it centered around one of America's First Ladies, Dolley Madison, the occupant of the White House when it was burned by the British in 1812. Jackie presented a warts-and-all portrait of Dolley, depicting her as a "snuff tobacco addict who was the focus of gay company dancing to violins." *[Of course, "gay" had a different meaning then.]*

She added drama to her plot by exposing an attempt by the British to kidnap Dolley and to bring her back to England to parade her through the streets of London in chains.

Later, Jackie wasn't able to find a film studio interested in her scenario, even though she'd enclosed a glamorous picture of herself with the completed script and a cover letter saying, "I will be willing to play Dolley Madison in my first screen appearance. A possible leading man for me might be Henry Fonda."

Jackie settled into her newspaper job with a lot of other highly competitive young women who were known around the office as underpaid "Tillie the Toilers."

By the spring of 1952, she had her own byline as "The Inquiring Fotographer." Most of her subjects were unknown people, some of them randomly encountered in the supermarket. But on at least two separate occasions, she met famous personalities. She asked Eleanor Roosevelt, "When did you discover that women were not the weaker sex?" the former First Lady chose not to respond. A rising politician from California, Richard Nixon, was asked, "What do you think the future of women in politics might be?"

Jackie wrote a postgraduate screenplay about the life of former First Lady **Dolley Madison**, hoping to star in the biopic.

"By all means, a woman before the end of this century will no doubt be president of the United States," Nixon predicted. But then he asked her not to print that. "I don't want to anger my male constituents," said the future U.S. president to a future First Lady.

Abandoning her hoped-for career as a screenwriter or perhaps a movie star, Jackie reconsidered the viability of newspapermen as potential dates. "I don't plan to marry a

Caught in Jackie's lens, the young senator from Massachusetts was a playboy politician. She had marriage on her mind. He didn't.

reporter, but perhaps through their connections, I might meet a beau who's rich. On her first date with Chicago-born Charles Bartlett, she did just that. In time, he would introduce her to a rising young politician from one of America's richest families. Bartlett had met John F. Kennedy in 1945 after his navy tour of duty had come to an end. They'd been friends ever since. Bartlett would later say, "I became a historical footnote as the man who brought Jack and Jackie together as the 20th Century's most famous couple. But first I tried to score with Jackie myself."

"She was such a darling girl, but there were limits," he later confessed. She was very cute, very sweet, and unsullied—or so I thought at the time. Once night in my car, my hand started traveling north in her long skirt. I got as far as New Hampshire, but Maine had a road block. I never made it to the pot of gold at the end of the rainbow."

She soon dropped Bartlett in favor of John White, who had once worked for the *Times-Herald,* but was now employed by the State Department. "For a woman to attract me, she has to be elfin," he later said. "Jackie fitted that description at the time."

"When I met Jackie through Bartlett, I was moping over a lost love, Kick Kennedy," White said. "Even though she'd found other men, she was still the love of my life. I was in mourning over her death in 1948. Kick and I used to double date with Jack and Inga."

Jackie remembered White as "a literary ex-Marine. His apartment was lined with books. He even had a stack of books by his toilet bowl."

When I first dated her, she was hung up on the poet Sappho from the island of Lesbos," White said. "At first, I thought she was a lesbian herself, since she resisted all of my sexual assaults. But she dropped Sappho and decided she was the reincarnation of Madame Récamier."

"As the new Madame Récamier, I will have my salon in Washington that will become the envy of the world," Jackie told him. "Every night, I will assemble the most celebrated people in America—Robert Frost, Carl Sandburg, Ernest Hemingway, Carson McCullers, Tennessee Williams, Pablo Casals, Walter Lippmann, and Irene Dunne."

"But the week after, she'd forgotten about those goals and had come up with something more obtainable," White said. "She freely admitted that she wanted to marry a rich and powerful man, and be the power behind the throne."

"I prefer him to be American, but I would settle for a British man, perhaps even a Frenchman," she told him. "If a Brit, I would want him to look like Prince Philip."

"I think that later in life, when Jackie was First Lady, one of the reasons she didn't get along with the Queen Elizabeth was because she was jealous that Elizabeth had gotten Philip instead of her," White outrageously claimed.

Jackie was constantly meeting close friends of the Kennedy siblings, but had not met any of them directly. White's best friend was William Walton, a former correspondent for *Time-Life.* In war-torn London, he'd become the best friend of Joseph Kennedy, Jr., JFK's older brother, who later died in a plane crash over France during the summer of 1944.

"Bill" was older than Jackie, and she would sit at his feet, listening to his fascinating stories, including how he and Ernest Hemingway had "liberated" the bar at the Ritz Hotel in Paris in the wake of the Nazis fleeing toward their Fatherland.

"Bill was a darling man," Jackie recalled, "one of the most sophisticated I'd ever met. He made me realize that I needed to marry a man with imagination, but they were hard to find, almost impossible. In the Eisenhower Fifties, the emphasis was on conformity. But I thought having an open mind was what counted."

***

Even though both Bartlett and Jackie had moved on to other partners, they still maintained a friendship. She even attended his wedding to Martha Buck, the daughter of a wealthy tycoon.

Jackie often visited the Bartlett home in Georgetown, where Martha announced one night that she was pregnant. "My husband still seemed interested in Jackie, and I decided something had to be done," Martha said. "I urged Charlie to introduce Jackie to an eligible young man. He just had to get over his fascination with Jackie, who had gone on to other beaux."

Bartlett knew that Jackie had become frustrated in her choice of men, although, unknown to him at the time, she'd been dating the very epitome of a 1950s-era Washington conformist, a stockbroker, no less.

Unaware of that, Bartlett invited only Jackie to a small dinner party that he and Martha hosted at their home in Georgetown. "I decided to play Cupid and introduce Jackie to my dear friend, Jack Kennedy. I'd met him in Palm Beach at a night club right before he declared his candidacy for Congress. Now it was Senator Kennedy, and maybe one day he'd be President Kennedy or at least Vice President Kennedy."

"Jack was a skirt chaser, and I knew that if he wanted to become president, he'd have to find the perfect wife, not some grumpy frump like Bess Truman or some lesbian like Eleanor."

"Jack was a wild thing. He and I used to chase around Washington. When he'd see a pod of beauties, he'd say to me, 'I smell poontang in the air'—crap like that. Before he knocked up half the population of Georgetown, I thought Jackie could settle him down."

"I'd like to report that Jack meeting Jackie was a historic moment, love at first sight, as dramatic as the meeting of Marc Antony when he boarded Cleopatra's barge," Bartlett said. "They did seem to like each other, but it was so very casual. At least, Jack was intrigued enough to walk her out to her car, which was parked outside my house. He told me later that as he walked down the street with Jackie toward her battered old Mustang, he invited her for a drink at this tavern in Georgetown."

"The sound of a barking fox terrier in the back seat of the Mustang ended Jack's possible conquest that night," Bartlett said. "I didn't know it, but Jackie's mysterious beau had accompanied her to my house. Since I didn't know of him, I didn't extend him an invitation. He agreed to wait for her in the back seat, sleeping until our dinner ended. He was then planning to take her to one of the late night clubs in the area."

"When Jack saw that she already had a guy, he fled into the night. He later told me that he went home with two 'young maidenheads,' as he referred to them, that he'd picked up in that same tavern where he'd invited Jackie."

Two days later, I learned the name of this guy that Jackie had been secretly dating," Bartlett said.

The handsome young man, who looked like Robert Redford in 1960, was John Grinnel Wetmore Husted, Jr., three years older than Jackie. He was the son of a banking family from Hartford, Connecticut, spearheaded by John G.W. Husted, Sr., and Helen Armstrong, who were in the Social Register.

"Young John was that stockbroker conformist that Jackie said she never wanted," Bartlett said. "But here she was, locked, presumably, in his arms every night. Later, when I quizzed Jackie about Husted, she told me that he was really 'too immature' for her and that his work as a stockbroker was 'far too tame for me,' her exact words. But she continued to date him for months."

"Later, when Husted and I became friends, and I invited him to my club for a game of tennis, I found out a lot more about him," Bartlett said. "After the game, we stripped down in the locker room and headed for the showers together. At that point, John's attraction to the ladies was on full display."

Husted had attended Oxford University in England before returning to the United States at the outbreak of war in Europe in 1939. He enrolled in St. Paul's School in Concord, New Hampshire, before joining the American Field Service in World War II. After the war, he went to Yale, graduating in 1950.

His parents were friends of Jackie's father, Black Jack Bouvier, and also friends of her stepfather, Hugh D. Auchincloss.

When Jackie was working as an inquiring photographer for the *Times-Herald,* she met Husted at a party in Washington. She found that he was a "wonderful dancer," and that he liked her looks, "especially those high cheek bones, and those sensuous lips, although she was a bit of an ice princess."

"On our first date, I took her to the Dancing Club in Washington," Husted said. "It was filled with debutantes and preppy school boys—very proper, very formal. Jackie fitted right into this atmosphere. She was fun to be with and had a sharp sense of humor."

"On our second date, she complained to me that her limited budget allowance and small salary from the newspaper didn't allow her enough money for the clothing and shoes she needed," Husted said. "I remember walking along on a street with her. She stopped and really wanted these alligator shoes displayed in a window, but couldn't afford them. I felt rotten that I couldn't buy them for her. But just taking her out for dinner nearly bankrupted my own limited budget."

"Sometimes when I was free, I made the rounds with her when she was an inquiring photographer, asking people stupid questions," Husted said. "One question I remembered was, 'Should a married man be forced to wear a wedding band?'"

"One weekend, I took her to meet my mother in Bedford," Husted said. "That was a disaster. My mother hated Jackie on sight, finding her pretentious. Privately, she told me that Jackie was nothing but a gold-digger, although I had no gold at all and only $213 in the bank. Driving back to Washington, Jackie made funny, but sarcastic, remarks about my mother's cooking and home decoration."

"I did better with Jackie's father, Black Jack Bouvier, in New York," Husted said. "At first, he seemed delighted that Jackie was dating 'some man from Wall Street' and might live in New York if we got married. But over a drink, when Jackie was out of the room, he warned me, 'The marriage will never work, but in the meantime, I'm happy for the two of you.'"

"When I met Janet Auchincloss, I thought she was a dreadful woman," Husted claimed. "She obviously didn't approve of me, because I was making only $17,000 a year, hardly enough for Jackie, or so her mother believed. Later,

Jackie told me that Janet wanted her to marry someone at the top of the ladder of success, not someone on the bottom rung trying to climb up."

Janet was very frank in discussing a possible marriage of her oldest daughter. "You wrote in your yearbook that you didn't want to be a typical housewife," Janet said to her daughter. "Picture it: A dull life watching every penny for years to come. Flour up to your elbows. Washing the skid marks out of his underwear. Maybe three or four children running around the house driving you mad."

Jackie told friends that the man she would marry "had to be intelligent, handsome, charming, rich, and filled with an unbounded ambition to succeed, perhaps having homes in Palm Beach, Manhattan, and Beverly Hills. I also want him to have the personal magnetism of Black Jack."

Jackie could be rather blunt at times with her beaux. Before dating Husted, she'd told John D. Ridley, whom she'd gone out with on a few dates, "You're going nowhere—not in the world and not with me. Let's bid *adieu.*"

After only a few dates, Husted claimed that he fell in love with Jackie. He asked to meet her one snowy night at the Westbury Hotel in Washington, where he planned to pop the question. She was two hours late, but when she did show up, "we splurged on cherries jubilee. I finally got up the courage to propose marriage, and she accepted."

"Swallowing a bitter pill," Janet agreed to host an engagement party at Merrywood, with an announcement about the engagement in the newspapers. The night of the party, Husted talked privately with Hughdie, who was drunk. "He was an anti-Semite and hideously ugly, looking like a stern Presbyterian minister," Husted said. "I dreaded having Janet and him as my in-laws."

That was the night that Husted presented Jackie with an engagement ring. Its central sapphire was flanked with two diamonds he'd removed from an old ring of his mother's.

Ralph Gentry, a business associate of Hughdie, was at the party. He recalled, "John and Jackie didn't look like a good match to me. They stayed on opposite ends of the room, talking to their separate coterie of friends, Janet was seriously pissed off, and Hughdie was drunk and didn't seem to give a damn. After all, she wasn't his daughter. I could tell that Jackie wasn't pleased with her choice of a lifetime mate, but was going along with it because it's what debutantes did in those days."

During her engagement to Husted, Jackie was introduced to his first cousin, Helen Chavchavadze, a brunette *divorcée* with two young daughters. Originally a Husted, she had married David Chavchavadze, the son of a Romanoff princess who had been reared in a palace in St. Petersburg. Jackie was fascinated by Helen's life in Europe and her marriage to a real Romanoff prince.

Her future friend, Ben Bradlee, recalled meeting Helen, finding her "totally pretty, well-educated, and interesting, with a feminist mother who believed in freedom and rebellion."

[Jackie and Helen became friends, although not seeing a lot of each other. However, in 1959, when JFK was contemplating a run for the presidency, Jackie invited Helen to a party at their Georgetown home. At the gathering hon-

oring her sister, Lee, Jackie introduced Helen to JFK. "We talked about Russia, and he seemed fascinated by me," Helen recalled.

"I didn't hear anything from Jack until the summer of 1960, when Charles Bartlett, his friend, called me and requested that I come to this party in Georgetown. He told me that Jack Kennedy specifically requested that I come to the party."

"I went and had a reunion with Jack," Helen said. "When I was driving home in my little Volkswagen, I realized I was being followed by a man in a white convertible. When he pulled up beside my Volks, I saw that it was Jack."

"How about following me home?" he yelled to her.

"I accepted," Helen said. "Three hours later, I was in his bed. It was followed by three other secret meetings when Jackie was away."

"One night, I encountered Jack again at a party at the home of the columnist, Joseph Alsop, and his boyfriend," Helen said. "Jack was there, but he was rather cold to me. Months went by, and he became president. Weeks after the Inauguration, Jack showed up at my doorstep unannounced. He was with one of his best friends, Senator George Smathers of Florida, another skirt-chaser. Fortunately, I was in my apartment alone. After drinks, George departed, and Jack and I resumed our affair. I just assumed that the Secret Service was guarding the building."

"After that night, Jackie invited me to several small dinners at the White House, but the President and I never got together alone ever again. In fact, my last invitation from Jackie came only nine days before his assassination. I hoped she never found out that I had betrayed her, but I found Jack just too irresistible."]

In Nantucket in the 1980s, Husted spoke of his long ago love for Jackie. "Back then, I was protecting her reputation and her virginity, claiming that our relationship was very chaste. I didn't exactly tell the truth back then. We made love, but not the type that would get an unmarried girl pregnant."

"I don't want to get too personal here, but Jackie and I went as far as we could back then without going all the way. It was called heavy petting. I don't know what it's called today. Most of these liaisons took place in the back seat of my car. If we pressed them hard enough, most girls give in after they'd dated a boy for a long time. Giving in meant giving a boyfriend a blow-job or masturbating him. Jackie and I had some intensive back seat sessions getting acquainted with each other's anatomies."

"Our engagement came to an end one weekend when I took the train from New York to Washington to see her," Hulsted said. "We had dinner together, but nothing else. At the airport, a kiss on the cheek. I didn't discover it until later, but when she told me goodbye, she'd slipped her engagement ring into my coat pocket."

"When I discovered it on the train, I cried all the way back to Manhattan."

Jackie was too embarrassed to write John a "Dear John" letter, so she asked Hughdie to do it for her. He did as she asked, quoting Husted a familiar refrain from Alfred Lord Tennyson: *"Tis better to have loved and lost than never to have loved at all."*   Hugh added a P.S.—"And I should know."

Husted said, "I felt Jackie and I would have gotten married if it were not for that bitch of a mother of hers. That Janet! She was a tigress. But months later, I found out why Jackie had really called off the wedding. She'd taken up with this whore-mongering, red-haired Irish politician from Boston. There was no way that I, a lowly stockbroker, could compete with Joseph Kennedy's bootleg millions being dispensed rather generously to his son."

Honeysuckle and Inga-Binga
JFK and the Nazi Spy

While working at the *Times-Herald,* Jackie came across the first scandal she'd ever heard about her future husband, John F. Kennedy. It would be the first of many scandals to come.

JFKs scandals with women predated his 1953 marriage to Jackie. And whereas Aristotle Onassis maintained mistresses, and in some cases, boys, using them for adultery during his marriage to Jackie, Ari's philandering was mild compared to what she had experienced during her marriage to Jack Kennedy throughout the 1950s and later during his short term in the Oval House.

In November of 1941, JFK served as an ensign in the U.S. Navy's Office of Naval Intelligence in Washington, D.C. One night at a party, he met Inga Arvad, who later claimed "He took me to bed that very night—three times before dawn broke...I called him 'Honeysuckle.' He nicknamed me 'Inga-Binga.'"

At the age of 15, she'd won the Miss Denmark contest, thanks partly to her thirty-six inch bust and her eighteen-inch waist. Born in 1913, she was four years older than Jack.

In 1936, at the voluptuous age of 23, Inga, by then a journalist focusing on celebrity gossip, had been Adolf Hitler's widely publicized companion at the 1936 Summer Olympics. But between 1941 and 1942, during the darkest years of World War II, she evolved into the mistress of John F. Kennedy.

Prior to her association with Jack, she had been mesmerized by the Führer, writing, for publication, "You immediately like him. He seems lonely. The eyes, showing a kind heart, stare right at you. They sparkle with force." Hitler told her, "You are the perfect example of Nordic beauty."

Inga's youthful liaison with the Reich and its chief mass murderer would follow and plague her until her

Inga Binga Arvad.

death from cancer in 1973 in Nogales, Arizona.

Inga also maintained an affair with Hitler's *Reichsmarschall*, Hermann Göring, whom she described as "very kind, very charming, and insatiable in bed."

She also functioned for a time as the mistress of the notoriously controversial Axel Wenner-Gren, the fabulously wealthy but oft-disgraced Swedish industrialist rumored to have promoted the interests of the Third Reich to, among others, the Duke of Windsor and his scandalous Duchess. Wenner-Gren's mammoth yacht supplied fuel to Nazi U-boats in the North Atlantic.

From the beds of Berlin, the brilliantly multilingual Inga had migrated to the mattresses of Washington, where she got a job as a writer/reporter on the *Washington Times-Herald*. There, she wrote a gossip column documenting the exploits of the movers and shaker in America's capital. Powerful men fell in love with her, including America's best-known financier, Bernard Baruch, who was 71 at the time. A friendship with Kathleen (Kick) Kennedy led to an eventual meeting with JFK.

Her torrid affair with Jack Kennedy captured the attention of Kennedy-hater J. Edgar Hoover at the F.B.I. He told his lover and chief assistant, Clyde Tolson, "The bitch is the Mata Hari of Washington, and that upstart Kennedy brat is fucking her and giving away naval secrets which she's reporting back to Hitler himself."

Hoover called Captain Seymour A.D. Hunter, JFK's superior officer. "Jack Kennedy is revealing naval secrets to some Nazi bitch," Hoover charged.

It was agreed that JFK could not be dismissed or disgraced because of the powerful position of his father. "I'll tell this Kennedy boy that he's going to be transferred to a naval unit at sea. That way, he'll learn no secrets to share with the Nazis. In the meantime, I'll give him a desk job in Charleston, out of harm's way."

Consequently, in January of 1942, JFK was assigned to a station in South Carolina in the frenzied aftermath of the Japanese attack (December 7, 1941) on Pearl Harbor. "Inga came down a few times and I fucked her, but right now I've rounded up three Scarlett O'Haras to fuck," he wrote to his friend, Lem Billings, "So I told Inga to go back to Hitler."

JFK had seemed to know that Hoover's G-men were following him and bugging his rooms. One night in bed with Inga, he addressed the hidden microphones: "Whoever is listening, the next sound you hear will be of me fucking her." He also said, to witnesses, "Hoover's on the take from the Mafia, which pays his heavy gambling debts. With the high cost of dresses and wigs these days, he needs financial assistance from the Mob."

Some Kennedy historians have concluded that the Nazi spy scandal was Hoover's attempt to end the Kennedy dynasty before it had begun.

Chapter Three

The Newport Debutante
& the Senate's Most Eligible Bachelor

Jack & Jackie Get Married!
Their Mexican Honeymoon: A Recipe for Marital Disaster

On September 12, 1953, out in a field, the happy bride, **Jackie** herself, is surrounded by all three Kennedy brothers (from left to right, **Teddy,** standing to her immediate left, **JFK,** and **Bobby**). **Lem Billings** (positioned between the bride and JFK) seems to be coming out of her bridal veil, and Senator **George Smathers** is seated on the ground to the immediate left of the bride. JFK later told Smathers, "I broke a hundred feminine hearts the day I married Jackie."

"With my big, manly hands and Greta Garbo feet, my mother, Janet Auchincloss, told me that it was unlikely that an A-list beau would find me feminine enough to marry," Jackie told Lee Bouvier and others as she recalled her life in the early 1950s. "Mother thought I was too masculine. There were times I didn't know who I hated more—Janet or myself."

"She attacked my love of French culture and criticized me for always reading a book," Jackie said. "She told me that men aren't attracted to brainy women. 'Men want to have all the brains in the family, not the wife,' she said."

"She also told me I had to change—or else. I began to work on my appearance and my clothes. Instead of my usual voice, I developed this whispery voice. I tried to be sexy. I'd gone to see Marilyn Monroe in *Niagara*. Men found her sexy. I felt if I talked like Marilyn, I could interest men. Of course, I could never have her breasts."

Call it Brother Love.
Three handsome Irish-American brothers—*left to right*, **Teddy, Jack, and Bobby**—were destined to fall in love with Jackie. In very different ways, she would love all three of them intimately.

"Charles and Martha Bartlett were dear friends of mine, and they decided that the one man I should marry was John F. Kennedy, even though he was Irish. Black Jack Bouvier, my father, never had much good to say about the Irish, referring to them as 'Micks.' Beginning at a dinner party in the Bartlett home in 1951, I met JFK three times before he became really interested. To him, at first, I was just another debutante from Newport, possibly an easy lay, as he would call it—nothing more."

"At one dinner, the Bartletts hosted, Jack Kennedy disappeared before dessert was served with this beautiful blonde," Jackie recalled. "I didn't think I had a chance with him, though I found him handsome enough. I heard the Kennedys were rich, and that's what every girl in my crowd dreamed about—marrying a rich man."

Jackie didn't record a physical description of JFK when she first met him, but others did. He was six feet tall, weighing only 150 pounds. His ears protruded a bit, and he had tousled reddish brown hair. Like most of the Kennedys, he had flashing white teeth.

He was not a good dresser, wearing baggy clothes. Because of various illnesses, he often had a sickly yellowish hue to his skin.

***

In contrast to JFK's physicality, Jackie was far more turned on by the rugged, masculine charms of the handsome movie actor, Burt Lancaster. Some

"Imagine me marrying a man allergic to horses"

—Jackie Bouvier

aspects of her crush reached the "fantasy fulfilled" level when she met him while sailing aboard the *Queen Mary* to England. It was part of a trip financed by their parents in 1951. Her sister, Lee, was also aboard.

On the sailing's second day, Jackie set out, alone, to explore the ship. She wandered onto a balcony overlooking an open air gymnasium positioned on the starboard side of the sundeck.

A group of young women had gathered to watch two men as they rehearsed various acrobatic routines. Jackie immediately recognized her screen idol, Burt Lancaster, who was working out with his friend, the rather short Nick Cravat. During Lancaster's gig as an acrobat with the Barnum & Bailey Circus, they had performed together.

Both men were headed for Britain, where they would appear in the 1952 release of *The Crimson Pirate,* a swashbuckling film produced by Norman Productions for Warner Brothers. After the film was distributed, critics cited the "splendid and improbable acrobatics from Burt Lancaster and Nick Cravat, just

Nick Cravat *(left)* and the swashbuckling actor, **Burt Lancaster,** rehearsed some of their acrobatics they'd later perform on camera in *The Crimson Pirate*. Jackie, standing on an upper deck aboard the *Queen Mary*, looked down at the pair as they rehearsed and worked out. As she later told her confidant, William Walton, "Marlene Dietrich had Burt booked at night, but he and I managed to slip away for some heavy fondling. You might say I'm 'fondle' of him."

the ticket for bloodthirsty schoolboys." From her perch on the balcony, Jackie got a bird's eye preview of the forthcoming screen action as they rehearsed their routines.

Jackie's biographer, Edward Klein, wrote: "Lancaster was at the peak of his physical prowess, a tall, broad-shouldered Adonis with blue eyes, a toothy grin, and a thick mane of hair. He swung gracefully from one horizontal bar to another, performing twists, flyovers, and somersaults. He landed lightly on his feet and threw open his arms, flashing his legendary smile in the direction of Jackie."

As she later told William Walton, but not her sister, "I was mesmerized by Burt. Janet claimed I could not attract men, but here I was, sailing on the *Queen Mary* with Burt showing great interest in me."

Two hours later, a freshly showered and dressed Lancaster introduced himself to Jackie on deck. "I think we've met before," he told her.

"Not officially," she said. "I'm Jackie Bouvier, your biggest fan."

As they strolled the deck, he told her about the film he and Cravat were rehearsing. "I'm a swashbuckler in the 18th Century in the Caribbean. Nick and I are going to play it for laughs, a sort of spoof of the genre. This is going to be one lusty, gutsy film. Nick and I are going to throw everything into it. I predict it'll take five years off my life."

If Jackie entertained any romantic fantasies about Lancaster, they were crushed that night when she discovered him dining romantically with Marlene Dietrich. The *femme fatale* was showing her age only a bit. She was obviously highly skilled at makeup.

Jackie and Lee were booked into tourist class, although, wearing their best clothes, they frequently slipped into First Class.

Jackie had long heard the rumors that Joseph P. Kennedy, JFK's father *["Papa Joe"]* had had an affair with Dietrich in the 1930s. She wondered if he'd passed Dietrich onto his son, JFK.

Jackie's hopes were raised the next day when she returned to watch Lancaster and Cravat work out. Marlene Dietrich was nowhere to be seen.

As she'd later relate to Walton, "Burt and I managed to slip away to his suite later that afternoon. She confessed that he seduced her "only half way—there was a lot of fondling and groping but not of the type that leads to pregnancy."

Although Lancaster had the rather devouring Dietrich to face at night, he and Jackie did manage to slip away for yet another "fondling interlude." In fact, he enjoyed being with her so much that he invited her to visit him on the island of Ischia in the Bay of Naples, where outdoor filming of *The Crimson Pirate* would begin.

As she relayed to Walton, "I desperately wanted to, but didn't dare." Somehow, she managed to conceal her flirtatious involvement with Lancaster from Lee.

As Jackie recalled, before the end of the transatlantic crossing, she and Lancaster would say their "lip-sucking goodbyes" in one of the ship's utility closets where the crew stored the mops they used for swabbing down the decks.

***

In 1962, during the Cuban Missile Crisis, JFK read *Seven Days in May,* a novel by Fletcher Knebel and Charles W. Bailey II, finishing it in two nights. Its fictional but chilling plot focused on the U.S. military's scheme to overthrow the government. The novel's conception, or so JFK believed, had been influenced by the right-wing anti-Communist political activities of General Edwin A. Walker after he resigned from the military. The believability of the novel's plot was reinforced by the aggressive lobbying of Curtis LeMay, Air Force

Burt Lancaster *(left)* stars with **Kirk Douglas** in a film, *Seven Days in May,* about a military coup against a sitting U.S. president. JFK read the novel and was fascinated that the film was being made, but he never lived to see it.

Chief of Staff, who favored a preventive first strike nuclear option against the Soviet Union.

Based on delicate and highly embarrassing motivations, the Pentagon did not want the film to be made.

But in 1963, JFK had a chance encounter with Kirk Douglas, who was in the pre-production stage of the novel's movie adaptation, with the understanding that the film would co-star himself, Burt Lancaster, and JFK's former sexual conquest, Ava Gardner. Even before it was released, the film—as produced by Joel Productions, an outfit partly owned by Douglas himself, faced fierce opposition from the Pentagon. At the time, Douglas was in Washington for conferences with the novel's co-authors. At a fancy dinner buffet, he met JFK.

[In reference to the novel's plot, JFK said to Douglas, "Who knows? It could have happened during the Cuban Missile Crisis. A lot of military brass wanted all-out war with the Soviets."

At that initial meeting, before bidding Douglas goodbye, JFK requested that a copy of the film be rushed to the White House when it was completed. "I'll show it at a private screening with the Joint Chiefs of Staff."

JFK's endorsement of the movie went even further. While JFK, Jackie, and their children were vacationing in Hyannis Port during July of 1963, the President granted permission for the film's crew to use the White House exterior as a background for the film's opening riot scene that featured supporters of a disarmament treaty brawling with the treaty's opponents. After eight years of tricky negotiations, the U.S., spearheaded by JFK, had signed a test-ban treaty around the same time.

Because of JFK's assassination in November of 1963, the month originally scheduled for the film's distribution, the release of Seven Days in May was delayed until February of 1964.

After seeing it, Jackie sent Lancaster a note, praising his performance.

He wrote back, "Dear Jackie, I have such fond memories of you. My greatest regret in life is not asking you to marry me aboard the Queen Mary."

A decade later, in 1973, Lancaster made yet another film whose plot centered around a U.S. President. Jackie's reaction to that movie would be very different from what it had been for Seven Days in May."

It was entitled Executive Action. Its plot unfolds *in 1963, based on a powerful, right-wing coven of Americans plotting the assassination of President Kennedy because of his liberal stand on Civil Rights and be-*

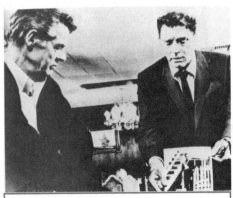

Robert Ryan *(left)* and **Burt Lancaster** star in the political thriller, *Executive Action.*

Released ten years after the assassination in Dallas, its story was inspired by the possibility of a right-wing conspiracy to kill JFK.

Jackie was horrified.

65

cause of his rapprochement with the Soviet Union.

Fearing that the sensitive issues it raised might be problematical for her, Lancaster, a liberal Democrat, wrote Jackie during the production of the film: "We are committed to the project," he wrote. "All the actors are working for Equity minimum. After a good deal of private research, I am convinced there had been a conspiracy and the possibility that Lee Harvey Oswald had been set up as a communist fall-guy. Everything we say in Executive Action *is based on evidence. If I had not been certain that this was the case, I would not be making this film. I was a Kennedy man, and I knew there would be an outcry in some quarters, but I've never worried about what the public thinks. The only thing I took into consideration was the validity of the script."*

Jackie asked William Walton to arrange a private screening of Executive Action. *She did not want to be photographed leaving a movie theater that showcased a film about JFK's assassination.*

After seeing the movie, she opted not to respond to Lancaster's letter. "I was horrified," she told Walton. "At one point during the screening, she let out a loud and terrible gasp," he later said.

She also confided to Arthur Schlesinger, Jr., "The idea that Jack's assassination would be made into a film for public entertainment is appalling to me."]

***

Most of the data about JFK dating Jackie, eventually marrying her, and sharing a Mexican honeymoon with her came from proposals that both Lem Billings and William Walton submitted to publishers but never expanded into published memoirs.

[Whereas Walton had been a confidant of both JFK and Jackie, Billings had been a friend and associate of JFK since their schoolboy days in 1933.]

In 1951, after Jackie's return to Washington from her trip to Europe with Lee, Charles and Martha Bartlett continued their role as matchmakers for JFK and Jackie. Martha later confessed, "I knew that *[my husband]* Charlie and Jackie had once dated. They were still flirtatious with each other. To protect my interests, I wanted to get Jackie married off as soon as possible."

JFK resumed dating Jackie again, although she'd heard that he was also going out with a lot of other women. She knew that he had been sworn in as a U.S. Senator on January 3, 1953, and assigned to room 362 of the Senate Office Building. The office across the hall was occupied by Richard Milhous Nixon, who had been sworn in as Eisenhower's Vice President, the second youngest in history, about two weeks later.

Charles had informed Jackie that Papa Joe's ultimate aim involved his son running for President of the United States. "Actually, Joe Sr., had wanted his oldest son, Joe Jr., to run for President, but, as you know, he died in a plane crash over France during World War II."

One of Jackie's most memorable dates with JFK involved his invitation for her to one of the January, 1953 Inaugural Balls of Dwight D. Eisenhower. Jackie got not only to shake the hand of the President of the United States, but also to be greeted by Mamie Eisenhower. Ironically, although at the time it seemed like just another of those "Beyond My Wildest Dreams" moments, Jackie would replace Mamie as First Lady and *chatelaine* of the White House only eight years later.

On her first visit to Hyannis Port, Jackie was introduced to the Kennedy clan. Its members included JFK's parents, Joe and Rose, along with his younger brothers, Bobby (with his wife, Ethel) and Teddy, and JFK's sisters, Jean, Eunice, and Patricia.

That afternoon (JFK took her boating), she saw him for the first time in a bathing suit. She recorded in her diary: *"Jack is no Burt Lancaster. He has a funny body, skinny, with toothpick legs. His best feature is his handsome face. He is most charming when he smiles. Actually, Bobby seems to show a more romantic interest in me than Jack does. He is even skinnier than Jack, if such a thing is possible. He's married to this aggressive creature, Ethel, who went to college in Harlem of all places. I wonder if she is part mulatto—she doesn't look it. But Harlem!"*

"I have no idea what man Teddy will become, or how he will look in the future, but right now he lusts after me like a lovesick puppydog. It's obvious he has a crush on me. So far, I have avoided being alone with Bobby. I think if I went out alone on a boat with him, he'd rape me. He's rather cute, so I wouldn't put up much of a fight."

During their afternoon together out on the water, JFK saw Jackie for the first time in a bathing suit. She would remember his cruel jab for years to come. "I think I have bigger breasts than you do."

"As a matter of fact, I find your chest rather motherly," she quipped, showing evidence of the caustic wit for which she'd later be famous nationwide. He turned and walked away. She figured that although he could deliver the jabs, he was not too good on the receiving end.

For her first dinner with the Kennedys, Jackie wore a strapless pink cocktail dress. The sisters reminded her of "a gaggle of cackling geese," and they mocked her as "The Debutante."

Ethel asked her, "Do you think you're dining at Buckingham Palace, *Jacque-leeeeen*? The *queeeeeen* wants to be *seeeeeeen*."

Jackie later recorded, "This ugly, catty woman says the most revolting things through her buck teeth."

Both **JFK and Jackie** were beaming on their wedding day at Hammersmith Farm outside Newport, Rhode Island. In the background, their smiles are replicated in the background by **Lem Billings**. Only close friends were invited, 1,200 in all.

The local paper claimed that their wedding "far surpassed the Astor-French wedding of 1934," an event which had been massively covered in the press as a High Society highlight two decades before.

She would later record, "Old Joe was the only one with table manners. The rest of the Kennedys are like pigs. Teddy almost cried when he claimed that Bobby took more than his share of the mashed potatoes."

The next day, she sat with Joe on the veranda watching the Kennedys play touch football. She later said, "He seemed to be evaluating me to see if I were suitable as a potential bride for his son."

Lem Billings, JFK's best friend, a relationship that had begun at Choate in 1933, had arrived that afternoon and joined the football game. He was much stronger and had a more solidly built frame than JFK.

Joe looked at Lem with contempt. "Jack insists on bringing that queer here every summer. He sleeps in Jack's bed, bathes him, whatever. When they deliver the laundry, Lem removes Jack's underwear and personally irons it. I'm not sure, but I think he wipes Jack's ass every time my son takes a crap."

"Do you think there is something unnatural here?" Jackie asked, growing alarmed.

"I don't understand the relationship—slave/master, or whatever," Joe answered. "But people are beginning to talk, accusing Jack of being a homosexual, even though he is widely known as a ladies' man. At thirty-five, it's time for him to settle down with a good wife."

At that point, Ethel came onto the veranda. "Come along, Jackie and join the game. With those clodhoppers of yours, you can kick us a field goal."

After a lot of protesting, Jackie joined in, despite her (accurate) perception that the Kennedys were too rough for her. Bloody noses were frequent. The game soon ended when one of Teddy's beefy friends from school fell on Jackie and broke her left ankle during one of the scrimmages.

After that day, she referred to the Kennedy sisters as the "Rah-Rah Girls" and came up with a subtly disdainful name for Rose, labeling her *Belle Mère*.

"She didn't go over with the Kennedys, except for Joe," Lem recalled, "and he was the one who held the purse strings. He not only condoned the upcoming marriage, he ordained it."

The next day, Jackie, on crutches, was hobbling by the open door to Joe's study. She overheard his conversation with Bobby and JFK. It seemed that they were mulling over what kind of political wife she'd make. She lingered in the hallway, eavesdropping.

JFK expressed doubt about marrying her. Bobby feared that "Jackie is too high class for the average American voter."

Joe assured his sons, "She'll be fine. American women can gravitate to high class broads. Jack, you once told me you'd fallen in love with Grace Kelly and wanted to marry her. Take that other high class broad you're having an affair with, Audrey Hepburn. No tits, like Jackie, but she's high class."

A svelte, brunette competitor:
Audrey Hepburn

"I think I'm still in love with Audrey," JFK said. "I know she's in love with me. Perhaps I should marry her."

"No way," Joe said. "She isn't Catholic, and you can't marry an actress. Can you imagine a U.S. President married to an actress?"

[In 1953, Joe had not anticipated the political rise of actor Ronald Reagan on the arm of a former MGM starlet, Nancy Davis.]

In silence, Jackie slipped out of the hallway. On crutches, she hobbled across the lawn toward the sea. She needed time alone to think most seriously about this strange new world into which she'd stumbled. She felt unwanted, fearing her beau really wanted to be locked in the arms of Audrey Hepburn, not her.

"Visits to Hyannis Port were a disaster for her," Lem said. "The Kennedy girls resented her. Rose flatly told her, 'The American people aren't ready for a political wife like you.'"

Born three weeks before the birth of his cousin, Jackie Bouvier, John H. Davis became her confidant. She felt she could always trust him. He would later write two well-researched books, *The Bouviers, Portrait of an American Family;* and *The Kennedys, Dynasty and Disaster.*

Davis claimed that at first, Jackie didn't take dating JFK seriously. When she heard he wanted one day to run for President, she dismissed that aspiration as "quixotic, chasing windmills across the plains of La Mancha."

"She was rather contemptuous of the Kennedy family," Davis claimed. "I remember her exact words."

"The Kennedy's are terribly bourgeois," she said, "and Jack has all these allergies. Imagine me being married to some man who is allergic to horses."

***

A lot of Jackie's courting took place in the back seat of JFK's car, according to Lem Billings. "He would take Jackie back there to neck," Lem said. "One night, a trooper drove up and got out of his patrol car, shining his flashlight into the back seat. Jack had removed Jackie's bra and was playing with her tits. When the trooper recognized Jack, he apologized and said. 'Carry on, Senator,' before retreating."

"If Jack didn't have sex with Jackie before marriage, I would be amazed," Lem said. "He practically had sex with any woman he wanted. Of course, they were never caught in the act except once or twice."

He might have been referring to an incident as related by author Edward Klein.

The actor, satirist, and comedian, Morton Downey, Jr. grew up next door to the Kennedy compound in Hyannis Port. His father, Morton Downey, Sr. had purchased JFK's used, 1950 two-door Plymouth for his son's nineteenth birthday.

JFK, Jackie, Downey, and Downey's friend, Kennedy loyalist Joey Gargan, attended Papa Joe's screening of *The Winning Team* in the basement of one of the buildings in the Hyannis Port compound. Released in 1952, it starred Doris Day and Ronald Reagan, who interpreted the life of baseball's pitching great, Grover Cleveland Alexander.

[Alchoholism and poor health force a ball-playing legend (as played by Reagan) out of baseball, but because of the tireless efforts of his wife (as played by Doris Day) he gets a chance for redemption and a return to the game he loves and to, as the film's title suggests, The Winning Team.]

After the screening, Joe invited Jackie for a tour of an adjoining room lined with glass-fronted display cases with a collection of dolls from every continent. He told her that he used to invite his mistress, silent screen vamp Gloria Swanson, into this room. "She couldn't get enough," he boasted.

The neighborhood's Wise Guy, Kennedy commentator and TV comic, **Morton Downey Jr.**

On another evening, JFK's new car was under repair in a local garage, so consequently, he asked Downey if he could borrow his old Plymouth to take Jackie to a party at the Wianno Yacht Club in Osterville, a six-mile drive west of Hyannis Port. Downey agreed, with the understanding that he'd be attending the same party, but that he'd get there as a passenger in Gargan's car.

On the way, Downey spotted his car, the used Plymouth, parked on a side road near a ridge.

Downey assumed that JFK was inside, necking with Jackie. He and Gargan parked a distance away and sneaked up on the car. When they reached it, in unison, each of them yelled, "SURPRISE!"

Downey heard Jackie scream through one of the half-open windows. When he aimed his flashlight inside, he discovered that JFK, alarmed by the sudden assault, had bumped his head on the steering wheel. With her panties down, Jackie was lying on her back, her head adjacent to the passenger-side door. Her left leg was slung across the seat back, and her dress was riding above her waist.

JFK, as he pulled up and fastened his trousers, chased the two men down the hill, but they ran and then drove away.

***

In the late spring of 1953, just before his engagement, the *Saturday Evening Post* prepared and ran an article on JFK entitled *THE SENATE'S GAY YOUNG BACHELOR. [Of course, the word "gay" had a different, non-homosexual, connotation back then.]*

"We both liked movies, but our tastes were different back then," Jackie said. "He preferred westerns with John Wayne, even though he was a right-wing Republican. I liked French films, and I preferred Edith Piaf; he liked Irish ballads, particularly 'Danny Boy.'"

"I loved horses; he was allergic to them. He loved hanging out with the Kennedys at Hyannis Port. I detested the place."

"He could be cruel. Right in front of his friend, Lem Billings, he said, "If I had life to live over again, I would have had a loving mother and not some ice queen like Rose; a different father, unlike the bully I was born to, and even a different wife. I'd have been a Protestant instead of a Catholic, and perhaps English rather than Irish."

Jackie ran from the room in tears.

As their marriage date approached, with great reluctance on both sides, Jackie and JFK just seemed to drift toward the altar. The jet fuel for their romance and dating was supplied by Papa Joe himself. He still had great control over his son, and he more or less demanded that he marry Jackie—"and make an honest woman out of her. There are too many rumors about you. The worst is that you're a homosexual. That almost equals a reputation that you'll fuck anything in skirts—age, color, looks not really mattering, just so long as the bitch has a hole to plug at either end."

The inevitable meeting between Rose Kennedy and Janet Auchincloss ended in the disaster that JFK had predicted in front of Jackie. Each of the strong-willed women objected to anything the other proposed about the wedding. "I don't want that old drunk, Black Jack Bouvier, showing up at my son's wedding and disgracing him," Rose said.

"I prefer a quiet wedding—just a few close friends," Janet said.

"Hell, no!" Rose protested. "Joe wants this to be a media event. It'll be covered by the national press. He's already a U.S. Senator, and one day he'll be President of the United States. Now, he's marrying a future First Lady of the Land."

Since the mothers of the newlyweds-to-be could not agree, Joe flew to the Auchincloss home, Merrywood, and confronted Janet. He was used to shouting down some of the most powerful men in the United States, so he got his way. Their meeting was private, but Jackie could hear him shouting.

When he stormed out of the house, Jackie tried to comfort her mother. "This hateful Mick is gauche and venal, a hard-nosed bastard who'll destroy anyone who stands in his way," Janet asserted. "He presented me with a dossier on Black Jack, Hugh, and myself that reads like some horrible magazine exposé. He was very abrasive, very abrupt, quick to anger."

Joe won the battle and the wedding plans were made "his way."

At Van Cleef & Arpels in Manhattan, JFK purchased Jackie's engagement ring—a two-carat, twinned, square cut diamond and emerald band.

On June 23, 1953, JFK's engagement to Jackie was announced on front-pages across the country. A headlined story in the *New York Daily News,* "Senator Loses Bachelorhood to Camera Gal," read: "Hopeful debutantes from Washington to Boston, from Palm Beach to Hollywood, can begin unpacking their hope chests. Those thousands of Boston teenage girls who squealed like

Sinatra fans every time young millionaire John Kennedy campaigned at their high schools will get the bad news this Friday."

On their first weekend after the announcement of their engagement, Jackie, at Hyannis Port, was astonished to find *Life* magazine photographer, Hy Peksin, there to do a photo spread on them. He told her, "I want some leggy cheesecake poses of you. Just make like you're Marilyn Monroe."

"Jack and I had a few romantic moments," Jackie said. But in her diary, she confessed, "He has never yet told me that he loves me. As for his family, they are a pack of barbarians except for Joe."

To celebrate his upcoming marriage, JFK shocked Jackie by announcing he was going without her on a two-week Mediterranean cruise with Senator George Smathers and Torbert H. MacDonald, whom he affectionately nicknamed "Torby." A former college roommate, Torby would soon enter politics, becoming a member of Congress representing Massachusetts.

"I plan to fuck every beauty in every port," JFK told Smathers.

Jackie was very hurt that JFK was abandoning her. She confided in Estelle Parker, a fashion designer in Newport and Palm Beach, "If you marry a Kennedy, you know what to expect," she said. "They treat their women like second class citizens. I don't really want to be the wife of a politician. Also, I know nothing about running a household. I know it's a *cliché*, but I don't know how to boil an egg. It's raw and gooey inside, so I assume it must be boiled for at least thirty minutes. And what do you do if it cracks and all that gooey yellow and other stuff, which looks to me like male semen, runs out?"

Meet the in-laws, **Rose** and **Joe Kennedy, Sr.**

Jackie could barely tolerate Rose, but bonded with Papa Joe. At her first Kennedy family communal meal, Jackie noted that Rose ordered sirloins for Joe and herself, but served hot dogs to the rest of the brood.

While JFK was abroad, womanizing, Jackie, in Newport, was acquiescing to Janet's demands for her wedding gown. "It was being made by a colored woman, Ann Lowe," Jackie said, "but mother didn't want that known."

"Right before the wedding, Lowe's studio was flooded, and Jackie's gown was completely ruined. "Two girls and I worked night and day to make another wedding gown for Jackie," Lowe said. "I was supposed to make at least $700 profit on the gown, but it ended up costing me $2,500."

When Jackie tried on the gown, she detested it, but Janet forced her to wear it anyway. "The only thing I liked about it was the blue garter I wore."

On his return from the Mediterranean cruise, JFK confessed to Smathers, "I'm too fucked out to get it up one more time, even for my bride. I feel I've had enough poontang to last a year. I'm sure you found out that the pussy of a Mediterranean gal tastes like garlic and olive oil."

He got back in time to attend two engagement parties—one thrown by Janet and Hugh Auchincloss at Hammersmith Farm; the other by friends of the Kennedy family, the Harringtons, in their house overlooking the verdant acreage of the Hyannis Port Golf Club.

JFKs wedding gift to his bride was a $10,000 diamond bracelet. Chuck Spalding later remarked, "Jack and Jackie, at least in the press, became one of the most written about romantic couples of the 1950s. Little did they know what was in store for them. Of course, Jack would become one of America's most celebrated and loved presidents,. As for Jackie, a life would unfold for her that was beyond her wildest dreams."

***

In Newport, the morning of September 12, 1953, dawned bright and sunny. Some 3,000 spectators gathered in front of St. Mary's Church. The police had to be called in for crowd control. There was nationwide interest in the marriage, which attracted reporters from New York and Washington. The so-called "gay senator," age 36, was marrying the Newport debutante, age 24.

Some 750 invited guests were crowded into the church. Lee Bouvier Canfield was Jackie's matron of honor, and JFK selected Bobby as his best man, although both George Smathers and Lem Billings had hoped, unsuccessfully, for that official recognition."

Richard Cushing, Bishop of Boston, officiated, and a tenor sang "Ave Maria." An apostolic blessing was transmitted from the Pope in the Vatican. Hugh Auchincloss gave the bride away, as Black Jack Bouvier lay drunk in his suite at Newport's Viking Hotel. Jackie later told Janet, "During the ceremony, I looked into Jack's face. He was very distressed, looking like a prisoner standing before a judge who was issuing a life sentence in prison."

Lem Billings, JFK's dearest and most loyal friend, shed tears. Jackie's eyes met his. She knew he wanted to be in her shoes. After all, she was marrying the only man he'd ever loved…and would ever love.

Chuck Spalding had noted that after the wedding ceremony, and before he left the church, JFK removed his wedding band. "Jack didn't want it to appear that he was out of circulation."

After the wedding, at the reception at Hammersmith Farm, JFK ignored Jackie and worked the room like the aspiring politician he was. After he'd shaken everybody's hand, he was seen in the corner devoting all his attention to a striking blonde who looked like the British actress, Dinah Dors. She had arrived on the arm of a married Wall Street broker, a friend of Joe Kennedy's.

Jackie noticed that JFK and the blonde were drinking champagne. Her tongue darted out and licked the rim of a champagne glass. She then handed the saliva-rimmed glass to JFK, whose tongue also darted out to lick the rim. "The Mating Game," Jackie said to Bobby, who stood by her side. He whispered into her ear, as she later revealed to Walton. He told her, "Don't worry,

Jackie. Whatever happens, I'll always be there by your side, loving you, protecting you."

Leaving the blonde, JFK walked over to them. "It's time for a group photograph," he said. Jackie was directed into a group that included a teary-eyed Lem Billings; an already drunk Teddy; and Bobby, of course, with JFK and Jackie in the middle, flanked by Sargent Shriver, Smathers, and Spalding.

Bobby shocked everybody when he said, "If I weren't married, I would be the one who had just wed Jackie today."

His older brother gave him a sharp side glance, then flashed his soon-to-be-famous smile for the cameraman.

After the Newport wedding, Jackie and JFK flew to New York and checked in for two nights in a honeymoon suite at the Waldorf-Astoria, which Papa Joe had booked for them.

For the first hour and a half within the suite, JFK was on the phone talking to men she didn't know.

Jack and Jackie confronted a wedding cake that had been trucked down from Quincy, Massachusetts, by a Kennedy aide. JFK chose the song, "I Married an Angel" for his first dance with his new bride. But Joe Kennedy, the "orchestrator" of the wedding, almost immediately cut in.

In the bedroom, she prepared herself, putting on a sexy see-through black *négligée* made in Paris.

When he entered the room, he slipped off his clothes and was gone in the bathroom for a long time. She waited impatiently in bed. When he finally emerged, as she confided later to Walton, he was nude and erect.

"He came to bed but didn't kiss me," she claimed. "He plopped down on the bed. He told me, 'I have this awful pain at the base of my spine. You'll have to get on top.' There was sharp jabbing pain that didn't last very long before it was over. He turned over in bed. 'I've got to get some sleep,' he told me. 'It's been one hell of a day. I'm bone tired. See you in the morning, kid.'"

***

Jackie had decided that Acapulco, a port city in Guerrero, on the Pacific Coast of Mexico, would be ideal for their honeymoon. With JFK, she moved into a pink-sided villa owned by Don Miguel Aléman, the President of Mexico and an old associate of Papa Joe's. "The house was like a dream villa, with terraces overlooking the ocean," Jackie recalled later. "It was also staffed by lovely servants."

After the second day in residence here, JFK seemed bored, except when they went dining and dancing at night. He openly flirted with beautiful Mexican *señoritas* who were dancers at the various clubs. During the day, he played tennis, caught a nine-foot sailfish, and studied Spanish from a Berlitz guide-book. Occasionally, he made quick, passionate sex with her, but finished quickly.

On his fourth night in the villa, he revealed to her the contents of a myste-rious alligator bag, which he would frequently take into the bathroom with him.

On that memorable evening, he came clean with her. He reached into the medicine bag and removed a needle. "Don't worry, babe," he said. "I'm not a junkie. But now that you're my wife, you need to know about the shots I have to take. I have Addison's disease."

She was not familiar with the disease, and he explained it to her.

[Named after Dr. Thomas Addison, the British doctor who first described the condition in 1849, Addison's disease is a rare, chronic endocrine disorder in which the adrenal glands do not produce sufficient steroid hormones. Patients suffer from abdominal pain and weakness. Treatment involves replacing the absent hormones with hydrocortisone and fludrocortisone. Victims suffer from muscle weakness, fever, weight loss, anxiety, nausea, vomiting, diarrhea, and headaches, along with night sweats.]

He showed her his penis, which had streaks of vermilion. "This discol-oration comes and goes."

That was not all. He also told her that he suffered from prostatitis, an in-flammation of the prostate gland, which caused him a chronic pelvic pain. He told her that because of his prostatitis, he had intermittent urinary infections. He informed her that when his semen was examined, it was found to contain pus cells. "Sometimes I have to have a prostate massage."

He saved the worst revelation for last: Before the war, he had developed a case of gonorrhea which his doctor, William P. Herbst, was able to cure. But he had also contracted a Chlamydia infection, which he had never cured. He had to explain to her that Chlamydia was a sexually transmitted infection of the ure-thra that causes a white discharge from the penis. He told her that he often ex-perienced a burning sensation during urination, and that sometimes his testicles would swell or else become so tender and sensitive, he could not stand for them to be touched.

She shivered at the bad news when she heard that Chlamydia could be transmitted during vaginal, anal, or oral sex, and that women got it frequently. An infected mother could pass the disease onto her baby during vaginal child-birth.

She asked him if she were in danger having intercourse with him.

"Anything is possible," he answered. "That's why I carry around this medi-cine to prevent something like that from happening."

She later told Walton, "After all those confessions, I could never truly be free of my fear that I'd come down with a venereal disease. Childbirth, I knew, was also a potential problem."

"I felt he should have told me all this before marrying him," she confessed to Walton, "After hearing all that, he still wanted to have sex with me. It was all

I could do to get through it. I was glad it came and went quickly before he fell asleep."

On the following night, he told her that he had to meet with some business associates of the Mexican president.

As the night hours wore on, she drifted around the villa in her *négligée*, standing a long time on the moonlit terrace. Finally, she decided to go to bed.

When he came in, she noticed it was five o'clock in the morning. "It was one tequila night with those guys," he said. "They don't know when to end an evening, and I didn't want to insult them."

It would be years later that she learned he'd spent the night with the screen actress, Merle Oberon. Although older than JFK, she had still retained her porcelain skin and photogenic beauty.

[Once married to the British producer, Alexander Korda, Oberon had starred with Laurence Olivier in one of Jackie's favorite movies, Wuthering Heights. *Jackie was up on Hollywood gossip, and knew that Oberon was a notorious nymphomaniac. She'd even managed to seduce Prince Philip, along with Darryl F. Zanuck, James Cagney, Ronald Colman, Clark Gable, Gary Cooper, David Niven, and Rex Harrison, among a host of other stars.*

In later years, Jackie learned that Oberon had also seduced Teddy Kennedy shortly before the midnight plunge of his car at Chappaquiddick. Teddy was married to Joan at the time. When Oberon asked Teddy if he feared exposure by dating her, he told her, 'The American people will like me whatever I do."

The morning after JFK's return from his long night out was a bit tense.

"Because of my father, I was used to infidelities, but Jack's womanizing hurt me greatly," she said to Walton. "I knew that women didn't find him a great lover. He certainly wasn't. He wanted a quickie and then he was back on the phone talking with some silly politician. When he did have sex with me, he would turn over and go to sleep right away. There I was listening to his snoring and almost crying at my lack of fulfillment as a woman."

After Mexico, JFK and Jackie flew to Los Angeles, where they were the house guests of Marion Davies in Beverly Hills. She had been the mistress of press baron William Randolph Hearst, a former friend of Papa Joe.

They remained in the area for three nights, or at least Jackie did.

Viva Mexico!
Merle Oberon was a major-league diva in London and in Hollywood, and even more of one in Mexico. Here, she appears with **Laurence Olivier** in *Wuthering Heights.*

JFK told her that he had to drive to Palm Springs to meet with some business associates of his father. "Actually, Dad wants me to get in with these guys, because when I run for higher office, we'll have to count on them to put up a lot of money for my campaign."

As Jackie later told Walton, "I actually believed my charming husband. It was years later that I learned that Jack had spent the weekend in Palm Springs with Marilyn Monroe, a rendezvous arranged by either Peter Lawford or Frank Sinatra."

In a rental car, JFK and Jackie drove north to Santa Barbara for a stay at the San Ysidro Ranch and Resort in the foothills of the Santa Ynez mountains. Papa Joe had made the arrangements. It had been one of his hideaways during his long-ago affair with Gloria Swanson.

In Santa Barbara, JFK spent a lot of time talking to associates back East. He frankly admitted he was bored. "As you know," he told Bobby Kennedy and others, "it's the chase that excites me. Once you capture a girl and can have it any time you want, the thrill is gone."

"Jackie is a bit prim and proper in bed," he told Charlie Bartlett. "As you know, I'm really turned on by a big-tit slut who'll do anything in bed you ask."

At the resort, the restaurant manager reported that Jackie and Jack at table hardly evoked romantic newlyweds. He told a reporter, "During the meal, the senator read a copy of the *Atlantic Monthly* he requested from me. He didn't say a word to his bride. Their picture had run in the paper that day, announcing what a happy, gorgeous couple they were. They didn't appear that way to me. They were anything but. While he read, she just stared into space at the ceiling and picked at her food."

JFK seemed bored at the ranch, but the following morning he came up with a solution. He suggested that she fly back to Hyannis Port, and that he'd join her there in a few days. He wanted to fly to San Francisco for a reunion with some of the men who had served with him in the Navy during the war.

Jackie agreed that he could fly to San Francisco, but she demanded he take her along.

***'

In San Francisco, their hosts were Paul B. Fay, Jr., and his wife, Anita Marques. JFK called Fay "Red" because of his striking mane, and the two former naval heroes warmly embraced. Both of them had commanded torpedo boats during the war, and each had been attacked by the Japanese.

Despite his status as a Republican, Fay had backed JFK when he'd run for Congress in 1946. When JFK became president, he would reward Fay by designating him as Under-Secretary of the Navy.

Jackie was amazed at how both men bonded. For the first time on his honeymoon, JFK was laughing, drinking, and having fun. In the White House, she'd refer to Fay as "the court jester." He had become one of the two or three best friends JFK ever had.

He told Jackie, "I married Anita here, but Jack was trying to get me to wed Eunice."

Jackie later claimed, "I was just dumped on Anita, who agreed to show me the Bay area. Paul and Jack went off to the center of town to do whatever they wanted to." She later accused Fay of "hooking Jack up with hookers."

At one point during their trip, JFK confessed to his friend, "I am too old yet too young to be married to anyone."

[In later life, Jackie would come into conflict with Fay because of the revelations published in his 1966 autobiography, The Pleasure of His Company. *This was one of the first biographies focused on the assassinated president.*

He sent Jackie a copy of the galley proofs before publication, and she raised a long list of objections. Actually, she didn't want the manuscript published at all, viewing it as "too invasive not only of Jack's privacy, but of my own."

"It is also filled with vulgarities," she wrote in a letter to Fay. After going over her proposed deletions, he defied her and published the manuscript in its original form. "It was my life with Jack, and she has no right to censor it. I knew Jack better than anyone."

Fay made a shocking revelation in his book, claiming that JFK told him that he was seriously considering not running for President in 1964. "He said he had become discouraged during the Cuban Missile Crisis in having to deal with the fanatical fringe of the nation's top military brass. Jack thought he might support the candidacy of Bobby Kennedy, who surely would have pitted himself against Lyndon B. Johnson."

After Jackie and JFK flew out of San Francisco, heading back East, Fay told his wife, Anita, "There is just too much tension between Jack and Jackie. She's not his kind of woman. He's a wild Irishman, and she still thinks she's a Newport debutante. I predict they'll be talking about divorce in 1954."

Fay's prediction came true.

"Of course, Papa Joe will do anything, pay out anything, to keep her married to Jack," Fay predicted. "Divorce would destroy Jack's chance of moving on to a higher office."

In his 1966 book, Fay remembered sitting next to JFK flying west to Los Angeles aboard Air Force One. "The President looked out at the clouds, gazing wistfully at them," Fay claimed. "'Redhead,' he said to me. 'We travel pretty well. So let's enjoy it. It's not going to last forever.'"

And indeed, it didn't.

JFK referred to **Paul B. Fay, Jr.** *(left)* as "my fuck buddy," a term that dated from their days together in the Navy during World War II, when he and Fay liked to go on "hooker hunts" together. When JFK became President, he made Fay Under-Secretary of the Navy. Jackie dismissed Fay as "the court jester."

Jackie's Married Life: No Magic, and No Fireworks, but Lots of Adultery and Life-Threatening Surgeries

Suicidal, Jackie Submits to Electro-Shock Therapy

During their honeymoon in 1953, **Jack and Jackie** slipped into a photo booth for this candid snapshot. "I never met a gal like Jackie before," the bridegroom proclaimed.	With fears of survival for his son, an aging **Joe Kennedy** accompanies **Jackie** to the hospital of Special Surgery. JFK had undergone a life-threatening operation on his back.

After their honeymoon, JFK and Jackie returned to Washington. She later said, "We lived like gypsies, moving from place to place, including rented homes and in some cases, a hotel."

Their first home together was a 19th-century townhouse at 3321 Dent Place, in Georgetown. Dent Place was filled with a number of buildings that housed student apartments, since Georgetown University was just a short walk away. Often, when she appeared on the street, the male students whistled at her. Janet's diagnosis about her lack of appeal to the male sex seemed more and more ridiculous.

When the lease on the rented house on Dent Place ran out, they moved into a hotel.

In her college yearbook, she had vowed "never to be a housewife." But in her first year of marriage, she found herself fulfilling the definition of that word.

"I tried to cook, but I was awful at it. I even took cooking lessons, but I never mastered the art. I tried to make some brownies, but they turned out like sludge from the dark lagoon. Whatever I cooked I burned. Once, I knocked over a boiling pot and had to be rushed to the hospital to be treated for second degree burns. My skin was purple."

Bored as a housewife, schoolgirl **Jackie** says goodbye to **her new husband** before heading for Georgetown University for postgraduate study.

He's off to the Senate and lunchtime orgies at the Mayflower Hotel.

Sometimes, at dinner, her new husband rejected her cuisine, settling for a Dagwood sandwich or else six grilled hot dogs, followed by five chocolate candy bars.

Her taste in food was remarkably different from that of her husband. She preferred a French cuisine. She claimed, "Jack liked everything with cream and sugar, and even took three heaping spoons of sugar in his coffee. I would try to see that he had an exquisite supper. But he often rejected it, pushing his plate away. He'd say, 'God damn it, Jackie, why can't I have a juicy hamburger?'"

"Jack began to take me out to dinner until he found room in his budget to hire a full-time cook and a maid."

"He was almost never home," she said. "He was always gone, always making speeches somewhere in the country." It was estimated that he made 100 speeches in some 100 cities a year.

Jackie told Charles Bartlett, "It's possible to love a politician without loving

Illusional Nightmare: JFK Gets "Nursed" by Grace Kelly, and Jackie Gets Hit Upon by Lydon Johnson

politics, but it's impossible to marry one without becoming part of his career."

Trying to be "the Senator's housewife," in Georgetown was often a disaster for Jackie. JFK could call from his office at eleven in the morning. "I've invited forty people over for lunch," he'd announce. "What are you serving?" With so little time to prepare meals for such a horde of political cronies, "with their smelly cigars and muddy boots," she would frequently panic.

"A political wife has to entertain a motley group," she said. "They come into your house with their cigarettes or cigars, burning your upholstery and dropping their butts in your French vases. They'll break your Sevrès ashtrays and leave beer bottles and stale midnight pizza on your carpet."

Lem Billings often lived in their house. "Where there's Jack, Lem was not far behind," Jackie said.

Lem himself was astonished to find his dear friend leaving a party in Washington one night with a pretty young woman. It was humiliating for Jackie, but she pretended not to notice. "He was treating Jackie the way old Joe treated Rose," Lem said.

"I was hoping that Jack would settle down when we got back from our honeymoon," Jackie said. "But I soon discovered that Washington's so-called 'gay swinging bachelor' was still swinging. We lived in Georgetown and attended a lot of parties. Jack often humiliated me by leaving with another woman. Lem Billings, his faithful lap dog, would drive me home."

"One night, Lem told me that I'd married a compulsive womanizer—'No one woman can ever satisfy Jack,' were his exact words to me."

"Lem was in the same boat as I was," Jackie said, "and in a way, I felt sorry for him. He lusted after Jack far more than I did, and he was so totally unfulfilled. I once told him, 'Get on with your life. You'll never have Jack, so stop trying. Find some other guy and settle down with him.'"

"That is not possible," Lem told her. "For me, it's Jack or no one."

According to reports, the cronies who most aggressively supported and enabled JFK's sexual exploits included Senator George Smathers of Florida, and a very big man, William Thompson, who stood 6 feet, 4 inches. "He was the original Babe Magnet and known for his endowment," Smathers said. "Bill and I had gone to the University of Florida together, so I knew how women were attracted to him. He rounded up gals for Jack."

Two married playboys, Senator **George Smathers** *(left)* of Florida and his carousing playmate, **JFK**.

In Havana, they indulged "all of our fantasies," Smathers later claimed.

With household help, Jackie was free to follow her own interests. She enrolled in a course on American history at Georgetown's University School of Foreign Affairs. Sometimes, when JFK was scheduled to address the Senate, she would attend and make notes on how he might improve his performance, even rehearsing him in his gestures. Sometimes she helped him write his speeches, even inserting points originally made in French by Voltaire or Talleyrand.

Fellatio in JFK's Senate Offices

On several occasions, Jackie's cook prepared meals for JFK which she took to his Senate office. He preferred to eat lunch in his office and not waste hours chatting with fellow politicians in the Senate Dining Room. His favorite dishes were Boston baked beans and clam chowder, which would be re-heated on an electric hotplate in his office.

One day when she telephoned his office, he told her that his secretary had taken sick and that an "office temp" had replaced her. He asked Jackie if she'd bring his lunch to the office, as she usually did.

Although she told him that she had a class, she realized after she hung up that she had gotten her dates mixed up. Consequently, she opted to bring his lunch to him in the Senate after all. When she telephoned his office, there was no answer. Thinking that the office temp was not yet on duty, she went to the Senate Building anyway and found no one staffing her husband's reception area.

Carrying his lunch, she entered his office without knocking. Almost immediately, she noticed the look of panic on his face. Within a few seconds, she realized that some person was giving him a blow-job from under his desk. At first, she thought it might be Lem Billings.

Apparently, her husband was too far gone to have the aggressor withdraw, and as she looked on, JFK experienced an orgasm.

When the person [the office temp] under the desk realized that Jackie had entered the premises, she rose to her feet in shame and hurriedly ran past her and out the door.

"Jack, you really should hire secretaries with a greater sense of style," were Jackie's first words to him. "That fire engine red sweater and that Kelly green skirt with those hideous brown shoes don't make it."

He rose to his feet and went immediately to his bathroom to clean up. "Thanks for bringing my lunch," he called to her.

When he came back into the room, adjusting the belt in his trousers, he said, "You must have known when you married me: I can never be faithful."

"As I can plainly see," she said. "I'm sorry I can't satisfy all your sexual needs. But I've never been great at blow jobs. I have this gag reflex."

"It's not that," he said. "I can't help myself. It's a compulsion. I will try harder, but I can't make any promises."

"Neither can I," she said, coldly, placing his lunch on his desk. "Enjoy!" Then she stormed out of his office.

[*Peggy Ashe, the office temp, was employed in the Senate Office Building for only two weeks before she was dismissed. Later, in need of money, she tried to sell an exposé of Senator Kennedy to* Confidential *magazine for $500. The magazine rejected her offer. In those relatively demure days of American media, even* Confidential *was gun-shy about printing such salacious material about a popular Senator.*

In her proposal, Ashe claimed that the senator was a "fast shooter and had an average size, uncircumcised penis with a crooked slant to the left."]

After fleeing from JFK's Senate office, Jackie almost literally collided with Lyndon B. Johnson, who was on his way to see JFK about some Senate business. For months, she'd heard complaints, mainly coming through Senator George Smathers, that LBJ was constantly angered by the publicity that media outlets had devoted to JFK.

Smathers quoted LBJ as saying: "Edward R. Murrow should have ME on *Person to Person,* not Jack Kennedy. Who does this young whippersnapper think he is? Sometimes he's so sickly yellow he looks like a Chinaman. He has Addison's Disease, you know. He's never done anything in the Senate, whereas I AM the Senate. He doesn't even know how to fart like I do, a big Texas chili fart."

"How is Jack's back today?" LBJ asked in his Texas drawl.

"He's doing all right for the moment," Jackie said. "Some secretary just performed fellatio on him, so he's in good enough shape for that."

At first, LBJ appeared as if he hadn't heard her correctly. Then he broke into a grin. "You know, honey, if Jack is neglecting you for some other gal, you can always count on me. As you've probably heard, everything grows big in the State of Texas."

She broke away, hurrying along the corridor wanting to flee from the building. How could she have known that within the course of fewer than ten minutes, she'd just had two horrendously embarrassing encounters with both the future President and with the future Vice President of the United States?

She was distant and remote from JFK as they flew from Washington to Hyannis Port for the weekend. Once at the Kennedy compound, he ignored her, spending time huddling with his father. She drifted about, eventually encountering Ethel Kennedy sitting on a veranda. The two women had never liked each other, but that afternoon, they bonded cordially.

"How's married life treating you?" Ethel asked.

"In all honesty, I must admit I've been disappointed," Jackie said. "I expected fireworks."

"In marriage, you don't get fireworks, you get children." Ethel responded.

Always rivals, the New Englander, **JFK**, and the Texan, **LBJ**, became strange, applauding bedfellows for the sake of their beloved Democratic Party.

Nine Years Before His Assassination in Dallas, A Catholic Priest Delivers Last Rites to JFK

"Throughout most of 1954, Jack lived in constant pain," said Lem Billings. In October of that year, he collapsed while walking and could not get up. Help was summoned. After being examined by a doctor in Washington, he was urgently advised to check into the Cornell University Medical Center in Manhattan.

Jackie flew to Manhattan with him, where he was admitted to the hospital for X-rays and preliminary examinations. For ten years, he'd suffered excruciating pain. He had previously, in 1944, endured spinal surgery.

Jackie visited the hospital every day and was mildly perturbed to see that he had hung a cheesecake poster of Marilyn Monroe on the wall of his hospital room. Monroe had posed for a leggy bathing suit shot that emphasized her crotch.

During each of her visits, Jackie had tried to make herself appealing to him, although she feared she couldn't compete with the obvious charms of Miss Monroe. She was staying with her sister-in-law, Jean Kennedy Smith, at her Manhattan apartment. Before visiting JFK, she'd gone to the Helena Rubinstein Beauty Salon on Fifth Avenue. There, she had met "Mr. Kenneth" *[Kenneth Battelle]* who would become her all time favorite hairdresser.

During JFK's hospitalization, Jackie was a devoted, dutiful wife. Lem was even more attentive, helping JFK in and out of bed. He even put on his socks and slippers and spoon fed him.

After extensive examinations, doctors concluded that JFK needed major back surgery, even though the Kennedy family physician, Dr. Sara Jordnal, who was associated at the time with Boston's Lahey Clinc, thought it was too dangerous. Jordnal feared that JFK's wound would not heal properly because of the complications associated with his Addison's disease.

When Jackie was asked, she deferred to her husband's judgment. He told her, "I'd rather risk my life in surgery if it would make me walk again instead of spending my life on crutches. That image of me on crutches would ruin my chance of ever getting elected again to office."

Jackie reminded him that Franklin D. Roosevelt had guided America through the Great Depression and World War II while confined to a wheelchair.

The day of surgery arrived. Both Lem and Jackie were there to kiss him before it began, each realizing that it might be for the last time.

Lem remembered meeting with Joe Kennedy, Sr., the day before the surgery. "Usually, he gave me wide berth, but this time, he held me in his arms," Lem said. He was sobbing. "We're going to lose Jack the way I lost my other son, Joe," he told Lem. "I've called in Father Cavanaugh for last rites."

That night, Lem returned to his apartment and remained awake through most of the night, sobbing. In contrast, Jackie—at least on the surface—seemed to have an iron will, but later confessed, "Inside, I was falling apart, but I felt I had to appear strong."

The chief surgeon, Dr. Phillip Wilson, assisted by three other doctors, performed a "double-fusion" surgery on JFK's spine. It was an extremely delicate operation, and one single mishap could have left the patient paralyzed for life.

When the surgery ended, even though the operation appeared to have been successful, Dr. Jordnal's worst fears came true. A life-threatening infection set in. For three entire weeks, Jackie and Lem visited JFK's bedside twice daily.

JFK didn't want to reveal a direct view of his wound to Jackie. Instead, he asked Lem to inspect it and to "give me the awful truth."

He instructed Lem to pull down his bedcovers, exposing the back side of his nude body. "Is it raw and oozing?" he asked Lem. "Is the fucking wound still open? Is that green pus spewing out of it? How does it smell? Like a shithouse, huh?"

Lem inspected it carefully. "The wound just isn't healing," he reported. "It still looks like a raw piece of meat."

Letters were pouring in from some of the most distinguished men in America—Lyndon B. Johnson, Adlai Stevenson, Bernard Baruch, even Dwight D. Eisenhower.

Eunice Kennedy Shriver in the late 1940s, about the time she was dating Joe McCarthy, until her father squelched it.

Bobby had also flown to New York and was a frequent visitor at the hospital. On December 2, 1954, he reported to his older brother, "You sure missed the bullet in the Senate."

He was referring to the Senate vote, 67 to 22, to censure he notorious Joseph P. McCarthy, chief orchestrator of the communist witch hunt. Papa Joe had once contributed to McCarthy's campaign, and Bobby himself had worked on his investigating Committee as Chief Legal Counsel. Not only that, but Eunice Kennedy had once dated McCarthy to the point that there was even talk of marriage.

When JFK's friend, Chuck Spalding, came to visit, JFK asked him, "Even though I detest some of the shit McCarthy pulled, how can I vote to censure him? Against my wishes, my own brother worked for him. How can I renounce McCarthy when Bobby

Whose reputation will they destroy today? On a witch hunt for "Commie pinkos," Senator **Joseph McCarthy** *(left)* is photographed in a huddle with his chief henchman, the notorious attorney, **Roy Cohn.**

was one of his killer henchmen?"

Charles Bartlett also came to visit JFK, finding him in remarkably good humor. "He was laughing and joking with me, and throwing darts at Marilyn Monroe's poster pussy. He told me that there were about a dozen or so nurses on duty. "I've already had about five of them," he claimed. "Since my back is out, I have to settle for blow jobs."

At a party in Manhattan, Bobby had chatted with Grace Kelly, who had gone to Hollywood to become a movie star. He knew that JFK had dated Kelly when she was working as a model in New York City during the late 1940s, and that Papa Joe was a friend of Grace's father, Jack Kelly.

At the party, Bobby had asked Kelly to visit with her former suitor in the hospital. "He's feeling really lousy and may not live. Please consider it. He'd love to see you."

She willingly agreed, but set her own agenda. She planned to borrow a nurse's uniform and come into his hospital room "to give him a rather invasive medical examination. Yes, a thermometer where the sun don't shine."

The following day, Kelly entered his hospital room. Medicated at the time, he did not immediately recognize her. Striding to his bedside, she ripped the sheet away, exposing his half-erect penis.

"Turn over!" she commanded. Reluctantly, he followed her orders, and she inserted a thermometer into his anus.

As she'd later tell Bobby as well as her friends in Hollywood, "After that business with the thermometer, I ordered him to turn back over. 'Forgive me, but I've got to take a sample of your semen,' I told him. He looked startled, but agreed."

"Do you want me to masturbate into something?" he asked her.

To his surprise, without revealing her identity, she plunged down on his penis, performing an act of fellatio. Finally, after his climax, she raised herself up as he looked down at her. "My God! It's you, Grace! Bobby sent you!"

When Jackie heard about Grace's visit, she said, "I am not amused."

The next day, during her visit to the bedside of her husband, JFK didn't mention Grace Kelly's impersonation of a nurse. Additional rivalries and ongoing conflicts with each other lay in each of the women's futures as First Lady of America and Her Serene Highness, the Princess of Monaco.

At the hospital, JFK's doctors informed Jackie that his wound simply would not heal, and that they were beginning a much more aggressive treatment. Because of his Addison's disease, they opted to surgically insert pellets of corticosteroid hormones directly into his thigh. She was told that that form of treatment would extend his

Cosmo Girl **Grace Kelly**, emerging superstar, in 1955

life for between five and ten more years.

When Lem arrived for a visit the next day, he noticed that the treatment had to some degree bloated his friend's face.

JFK whispered to him, "All these hormone injections are causing my fucking libido to rage out of control."

Eventually, the Cornell physicians decided that JFK might recover better at the Kennedy compound in Palm Beach. He was wheeled out of the hospital on a stretcher. Jackie, along with a private attendant and nurse, transferred with him by ambulance to La Guardia, where they boarded a plane to Florida.

George Smathers called on JFK one day while Jackie had gone shopping for supplies. "I was shocked," he recalled. "He looked like something that had been dug up in the graveyard. He was always a skinny guy, but he must have lost forty pounds. He had to lie on his stomach because of the back pain."

"I've always considered myself Jack's best friend, but there is a limit to how far I would go. He actually asked me to remove this greenish gauze and put on some fresh. I did. But when the gauze came off, I stared into this smelly, pus-laden hole with green stuff oozing out, I nearly threw up. I don't know how Jackie stood it."

Two local doctors in Palm Beach decided that the infection that had developed after the surgery in Manhattan was still not healing. It was determined that he would need more surgery to deal with a situation that was threatening his overall health, and perhaps his life. Consequently, they arranged to have him sent back to the Cornell Medical Center in New York.

On the plane back to New York, Jackie held his hand all the way, looking into his eyes as if sharing the pain. He entered the hospital once again, going into the ward that dealt only with the most difficult of surgeries, those requiring the most advanced treatments.

The night before surgery, Jackie met with Papa Joe. He told her that the chief surgeon had warned him that this second operation was even riskier than the first, and might even be "potentially lethal."

"I gave them permission to go ahead, because I truly believe that Jack will die without it," Joe told Jackie.

That morning, Jackie sat close to Jack, as he held her hand. The pair had never been so close. Very upset, Eunice was there, but trying to be flippant as a means of easing her nervousness. "Jackie," she said. "This is all your fault. It's your cooking that put him here."

No one laughed.

When JFK regained consciousness after the surgery, Joe was away, but Lem and Jackie were by his bedside. The prognosis was that

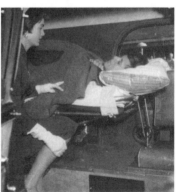

Arriving in Palm Beach in 1954, **JFK** was hoping to recover from dangerous spinal surgery he'd had in New York. Fearing for his life, **Jackie** joined him in the ambulance ride to the Kennedy compound.

the operation had been a success, and that he would heal properly this time, although it would involve a long period of convalescence. Consequently, JFK and Jackie flew together back to Palm Beach.

With time on his hands, JFK grew reckless. Overcoming her disgust at the pus, Jackie had been taught how to bandage his wound, a task she executed every day.

He requested that she secure certain history books about America during its early stages. During the course of his reading, he came up with an idea. "I want to write a book. I'll need you and maybe some others, perhaps Ted Sorensen. I want to call it *Profiles in Courage*. Courage is something I had to have to get through all that surgery."

Profiles in Courage: Who Wrote It?

With Jackie collating the research, often based on historical volumes from the Library of Congress, JFK began to write passages for the book from his bed in Palm Beach, where he continued to recuperate. He couldn't yet sit up, but he could use a writing board, positioning it in any way he could from whatever position that was the least uncomfortable for him at the time.

Profiles in Courage progressed slowly but steadily, as more and more research came in from Jackie. He couldn't work for long periods of time, but she often stayed up way past midnight providing him with the data he needed.

It was Jackie who eventually found a publisher for the book, taking it to Harper Brothers *[later, Harper & Row]*, where she had lunch with Cass Canfield, the company's longtime President and Chairman. Her sister, Lee Bouvier, was married at the time to Michael Canfield, his son. After reading the manuscript, Canfield, with the full cooperation of his company's editorial board, published it.

Knowing that the book might help JFK politically, Papa Joe, out of pocket, launched a major promotional campaign. He even hired young men to buy up copies of *Profiles* at retail outlets around the country, enough to *segué* it into a bestseller.

In 1957, the book would win the Pulitzer Prize. It consisted of eight short biographies, each describing acts of bravery and integrity of eight U.S. Senators. Those who were profiled included John Quincy Adams, Daniel Webster, and Sam Houston of Texas. It became a bestseller, but a controversy still exists because of the widespread belief that most of it was written by speechwriter Ted Sorensen.

Columnist Drew Pearson asserted, "John F. Kennedy was the only man in history that I know who won the Pulitzer Prize for a book that was ghostwritten for him."

Eleanor Roosevelt later stated, "I wish Senator Kennedy had a little less profile and more courage."

Compiled, with JFK's guidance, by a long list of editors, researchers, secretaries, and advisers, the book had clearly been a joint effort. Presumably, Sorensen functioned as its principal writer, in collaboration with Jules Davis, Jackie's Professor of History at Georgetown University, Arthur Schlesinger, Jr., Arthur Holcombe, and James McGregor Burns, all of whom were heavy contributors. The preface was written by Alan Nevins.

At this point, exactly who wrote what part of the book, or how much, might

JFK is seen reviewing a manuscript with speechwriter **Ted Sorensen**, Rumors still persist that it was Sorensen who really wrote *Profiles in Courage*. Jackie later told Gore Vidal, "My own contribution was huge."

never be determined. Certainly, Jackie's contribution might have been awarded with a co-authorship, but other than a brief acknowledgement, such credit was not included in the final product.

Orgies Within JFK's Suite at the Mayflower Hotel

"FDR never wanted to be photographed in a wheelchair, and I don't want to have my picture taken on crutches," JFK announced after a seven-month absence from his responsibilities within the Senate.

Back on duty, he was still under a doctor's care, having selected Janet G. Travell, who would become his chief physician during his occupancy of the Oval Office.

He followed her regimen of non-surgical treatments, which included exercises, along with hot baths, heating pads, and massages. He wore corrective shoes, one of them a quarter-inch higher than the other. It was Travell who introduced him to his famous rocking chair. She recommended that he sleep on a cattle-tail hair mattress She also gave him some disturbing news: "All that life-threatening surgery may have been unnecessary."

Jackie asked the doctor if she could give him a shot of something that would relieve him from constant pain. Travell advised that there was, but that if she used it, her husband would have no sensation below the waist. After advising JFK of this he refused to allow the shot to be administered, telling Jackie, "We can't live with that lack of sensation, now can we?"

During the early summer of 1954, JFK announced his return to the world of politics by throwing an enormous bash for some 400 guests at Hyannis Port. Many Congressmen were invited, along with their wives.

Jackie couldn't tolerate most of the politicians' wives. "They talked about the potty-training of their grandchildren." For reasons of her own, she referred to them as "pigeons."

She discovered that she was pregnant. She protested that their little house on Dent Place was too cramped with a child coming on.

Consequently, on October 15, 1955, JFK and Jackie purchased a historic property in McLean, Virginia, in the vicinity of the Auchincloss family's Merry-wood manse, paying $125,000 for it. Named Hickory Hill, it included both a stable and a swimming pool on its grounds.

Jackie redecorated the house, favoring Wedgwood-blue-and-white-satin upholsteries and antique furniture. Hickory Hill was set on one and a half acres of rolling pastureland close to the Potamac River in Virginia, about a thirty-minute drive from Washington. It had once belonged to General George Mc-Clellan, a commander in the Union Army.

Three months into her pregnancy, she had hardly settled into their new home when she suffered a miscarriage.

JFK did not seem unduly concerned with the mishap, and often didn't return at night to Hickory Hill. Pleading his bad back as the reason, he had rented a suite on the eighth floor of the Mayflower Hotel, infamous for being a convenient venue for off-the-record assignations by U.S. Senators.

Jackie had hoped that JFK's many illnesses would seriously limit his womanizing, but, if anything, they seemed to goad him on. As relayed through Charles Bartlett, JFK said, "I fear I don't have that much time left, and I want to get it while the getting's good."

As Robert Parker, the former *maître d'hotel* of the Senate Dining Room revealed in his 1987 book, *Capitol Hill in Black and White,* JFK operated a virtual bordello at the Mayflower between 1955 and 1959, the debut of his most intense campaigning for the White House. At the time, Parker worked for Harvey's Restaurant.

[Harvey's, a restaurant very close to the Mayflower Hotel, was a favorite venue for JFK's most dangerous enemy, J. Edgar Hoover, who went there almost every day for lunch with his adjunct, Clyde Tolson.] JFK called Harvey's almost nightly with takeaway food orders. "He always seemed to have a party going on," Parker claimed. But whereas Parker diplomatically defined the goings-on as "parties," others interpreted those events as orgies.

Sometimes from his Senate office, JFK would telephone Harvey's and ask for the restaurant's staff to prepare his suite at the Mayflower for an "event." Harvey's staff

For a time, **JFK** and his new bride, **Jackie,** lived at Hickory Hill, a historic residence in Virginia, before selling it to Bobby and Ethel.

Jackie later said, "They're turning our house into a breeding factory. When will those two stop having kids?"

Tempest Storm became America's most fabled stripper, famous for her "Million Dollar Treasure Chest." Both Elvis Presley and JFK enjoyed her ample 44DD charms.

members would stock the bar and deliver *hors d'oeuvres* along with buckets of ice, Many times, a waiter found JFK alone in the suite with only one woman. Most of the women weren't famous, but some of them were media headliners.

One waiter reported having sighted Audrey Hepburn there. Another reported that JFK was "shacked up" with Betty Grable; yet another found him alone in the suite with Marlene Dietrich, who had already sustained an affair with his JFK's father, Papa Joe.

Frank Sinatra was a frequent visitor, and he also provided JFK with "Hollywood hookups."

An "odd couple" pairing sighted at the Mayflower included Tempest Storm, America's Queen of Burlesque, who was performing at the Casino Royale, a District of Columbia cabaret-style strip club that drew politicians. Tempest later claimed that JFK admitted to her that, "Jackie is very cold to me."

Tempest also said, "In my memory, Jack Kennedy's sex drive lived up to his legend. The man just never wore out."

In a confidential discussion with George Smathers, JFK admitted, "I'd rather be screwing Tempest Storm than a dozen Marilyn Monroes. She's got better hygiene than Marilyn, and doesn't let a man leave her bed until he's completely satisfied on all levels. And those tits can't be beat."

Eventually, however, Tempest was stolen away from the arms of JFK, ending up in the bed of Elvis Presley in Las Vegas.

After settling into his marriage to Patricia Kennedy, Peter Lawford, a member at the time of Sinatra's Rat Pack, also bonded with JFK. He, too, supplied him with a bevy of Hollywood beauties and Las Vegas showgirls.

JFK was rather open in his dating dramas, almost flaunting his affairs in front of Jackie. She felt a constant sense of humiliation.

Until she became pregnant again, in May of 1956, she talked about a divorce.

JFK's nemesis at the FBI, J. Edgar Hoover, had

From the Oval Office, JFK used to call **Judy Garland** to hear her sing "Over the Rainbow." At the Mayflower Hotel in Chicago, he had other uses for her golden throat.

already compiled a massive, and growing, file on him. His suite at the Mayflower was staked out. Hoover demanded to know who was coming and going. His voyeurism was titillated when an agent reported that Judy Garland had spent three consecutive nights in JFK's suite.

Hoover also learned that the Massachusetts Senator had staged some orgies within the suite. One FBI informant reported a particularly amazing scene. Prior to the hotly contested Democratic primary of 1956, Senator Estes Kefauver had successfully won the Democratic party's nomination as Vice President on the ticket with Adlai Stevenson, edging out JFK, who had eagerly sought the nomination. To the amazement of the FBI informant, there didn't seem to be any particular bitterness on the part of JFK.

The informant filed a report with the FBI that astonished its chief. "Kefauver and JFK, in front of other guests, were having sex with two prostitutes hired for the night. At one point during intercourse, the Senators switched partners and continued until they were satisfied, lifting themselves off the women, who lay on the carpet, at about the same time. Kefauver and JFK headed toward his bathroom together to wash up."

Sir Winston Finds Jackie Charming
But Doesn't Think JFK Is Presidential Timber

In 1955, JFK had become a member of the Senate Foreign Relations Committee. He invited Jackie along for a two-month tour of Europe. Its itinerary included ten days in Communist-dominated Poland.

In Rome, Pope Pius XII warmly received them, as did Clare Boothe Luce, the American Ambassador to Italy at the time. It was during this trip that Jackie claimed that Madame Ambassador made a lesbian pass at her. She later shared that impression in the historic tapes she recorded for Arthur Schlesinger, Jr., in 1964, in the immediate wake of her husband's assassination.

After Rome, JFK and Jackie flew to Paris, where she had a reunion with her sister, Lee Bouvier Canfield. During the day, Jackie and Lee visited fashion shows and shopped for antiques in off-the-beat locations in Paris. JFK claimed he had "political meetings," but she suspected he was enjoying some of the city's secret pleasures.

One of the most important figures in postwar French politics, Geôrges Bidault, staged a lavish private dinner for them, with Jackie designated as the translator. Bidault later defined her as "a bundle of wisdom and charm."

[During the course of a controversial career that spanned virtually every important development in France's history from the end of World War II until the late 1960s. Bidault functioned, depending on the era and the government empowered at the time, as France's President, Prime Minister, and Foreign Sec-

retary. He was also the controversial director, during the Algerian crisis, of France's shadowy far-right paramilitary, L'Organisation de L'Armée Secrète, and was for a brief time exiled to Brazil before returning to France after being granted amnesty in 1968.]

After their high-level meetings in Paris, JFK and Jackie flew to Nice for a short vacation on the French Riviera. Papa Joe, repeating a pattern he had maintained for decades, had rented a villa on the grounds of the exclusive Hotel du Cap on the Cap d'Antibes.

Aristotle Onassis had anchored his luxurious yacht, the *Christina,* at the nearby port of Cannes. Hearing of their presence, he invited them aboard for a reception he was hosting for Sir Winston Churchill.

Long before she dazzled Charles de Gaulle, Jackie enchanted the controversial politician, **Georges Bidault**, one of the major power brokers of postwar France.

Churchill was unaware that he had met both JFK and Jackie in London on several different occasions when they were younger.

He detested Papa Joe and remembered him unfavorably from the eve of World War II, when he functioned as the U.S. Ambassador to the Court of St. James's. "The son of a bitch wanted us to surrender to Hitler," Churchill told Onassis. "When we desperately needed America's help to prevent a Nazi takeover of all of Western Europe, he did everything he could to prevent the United States from entering the war."

Churchill, however, had heard that Joe's son might become the next President of the United States, despite his status as a Catholic in a largely Protestant nation.

Onassis sent a messenger to the Kennedy's rented villa on Cap d'Antibes, inviting them to come aboard. They were instructed, however, to arrive sharply at 7:15pm and to be off the yacht at 8:15pm. Churchill was steadfast in his wishes to have his dinner served at that time.

In this press photo from 1940, **Joseph P. Kennedy**, U.S. Ambassador to the Court of St. James's, stands beside **Sir Winston Churchill**, who despised him. They bitterly opposed each other on the eve of World War II.

Jackie appeared gorgeously gowned in a Christian Dior outfit of pink satin, and JFK wore a tailored white jacket. The man once known as the "Lion of Britain" seemed enchanted by Jackie and was devoting most of his attention to her. She later claimed that she felt that Churchill didn't consider

JFK as presidential timber and virtually ignored him.

As Onassis' biographer, Peter Evans, later wrote: "Jackie had a withdrawn quality that wasn't shyness and wasn't boredom either. Churchill commented on the way she yielded to her husband rather than be eclipsed by him. He was surprised to hear her speaking fluidly to French guests in their own language. Her accomplishments, as well as her good looks and her youth, were obviously an asset to Kennedy in his public life as well as in his private one."

Onassis himself was mesmerized by her, telling Churchill and his other guests, "There's something damned *willful* about her, something provocative about her. She's got a carnal soul."

Churchill warned Onassis: "Forget it! She's much too young for an old man like you—and especially me. My salad days are but a distant memory."

John F. Kennedy, "The World's Worst Husband"

During their short trip to Poland, JFK strained his back and once again had to appear in public, photographed against his wishes, on crutches. That infuriated him, and he returned to America in a sour mood.

Once again, Jackie announced that she was pregnant, expecting to give birth to yet another child in September of 1956. There was growing talk that JFK would be nominated as the candidate for vice president on the 1956 Democratic ticket with Adlai Stevenson designated as the candidate for president.

The Democrats would face a big challenge from the Republicans. Papa Joe didn't want JFK to run, fearing that Ike would win again in a landslide.

"You and Adlai will go down in defeat," Joe warned. "He's a closeted homosexual, and you're Catholic. And your detractors will insist that it was your religion that caused the Democrats to lose."

Following the beat of his own drummer, JFK campaigned relentlessly throughout the country. He was absent every weekend. Even his friend, George Smathers, pronounced JFK "the world's worst husband."

"As far as Jack is concerned, I might as well be living in Timbuktu!" Jackie asserted, ruefully.

Against her doctor's advice, Jackie was seven months pregnant when she attended the August, 1956 Democratic Nominating Convention in Chicago. Not savvy about politics, Jackie was guided through the event by Josefa Moss, sister of Lyndon B. Johnson, who advised her on what events to attend and what she should say when she got there.

Chicago was experiencing a tremendous heat wave at the time, and at one point, in the

Convention Hall, Jackie fainted. However, she begged her assistant not to tell JFK, fearing that he would send her back east.

Two days later, during the course of Pearl Mesta's raucous champagne party for politico wives at the Blackstone Hotel, she almost fainted once again. Mesta, famous as "the hostess with the mostest," was not impressed with Jackie, defining her as a "beatnik," as members of the Beat Generation were labeled in the 1950s. According to Mesta, "She came to my party without hosiery. Her husband arrived wearing a tuxedo with brown loafers. They are obviously not trained in the social graces. I'll not support a Kennedy."

Jackie remembered these insults when she became First Lady. Mesta, who had been the most sought-after guest and hostess in Washington, did not get invited to one White House party.

At the convention, Jackie did little to conceal her distaste for reporters, especially Maxine Cheshire, the society reporter for the *Washington Post*. When she saw the journalist approaching her, although deep into her pregnancy, she lifted up her skirt and ran toward the exit. She later referred to Cheshire as "my bugbear."

Rather than designating the candidate himself, as he had the legal right to do, Stevenson threw the vice presidential nomination to an open vote on the floor. In spite of frantic backstage maneuvering, JFK lost to Estes Kefauver of Tennessee.

Still acutely distressed at not being on the ticket, JFK had to face the delegates at the convention as ringing endorsements of "Stevenson and Kefauver in 1956" resounded through the hall. It was not until later that he became aware that his brave acceptance of his defeat and his willingness to operate as a team player had elevated his status into that of a hero for the Democrats.

Historian James McGregor Burns wrote: "This was his great moment, the moment when he passed through the political sound barrier to register on the nation's memory. The dramatic race had glued millions to their television sets. Kennedy's near victory and sudden loss—the impression of a clean-but boy who had done his best who was accepting his defeat with a smile—all this struck at people's hearts in living rooms across the nation. In this moment of triumphant defeat, his campaign for the presidency was born."

In a call to his father on the French Riviera, Papa Joe told him, "Hold off until 1960. Then run as President."

These two frumpy dames, each a major Washington insider during their respective heydays, emerged as Jackie's *bêtes noires*. On the left is **Bess Truman**, wife of Harry S Truman, who had little regard for the Kennedys.

On the right is the legendary Washington hostess, **Pearl Mesta**, U.S. Ambassador to Luxembourg (1949-1953), who thought Jackie was a Beatnik.

Out of the public eye, and after his defeat, JFK was enraged, blaming others for his loss of the nomination. Even though Jackie was scheduled to give birth to a child within weeks, he told her that he and Teddy Kennedy were going sailing in the Mediterranean.

Jackie went to stay with Janet in Newport. She told her mother that she was seriously considering a divorce.

Her mother's reaction was violent. "How in hell do you plan to support yourself? You'll never find a husband as rich as the Kennedys. Hang in there. You'll end up with millions. This may be the only chance you'll have, unless you can get Nelson Rockefeller to marry you. At a party, he was overheard telling Jack's friend, George Smathers, that he'd like to fuck you."

Estes Kefauver, the Democratic politician from Tennessee known for wearing coonskin hats, looked like an American Puritan during his anti-pornography campaigns and his pursuit of organized crime.

Privately with JFK, he was a player at some of the orgies within the Mayflower Hotel.

"Perhaps you're right," Jackie responded. "But I just can't see myself spending the rest of my life with Jack Kennedy. It's not going to happen."

"Need I remind you that you're pregnant?" Janet said.

"When I poured out my woes to Janet, she told me that a real woman would be able to satisfy her husband sexually, and would be able to keep him from straying," Jackie later told her sister, Lee.

From Paris, JFK called Jackie, telling her that after a stopover there, he and Teddy would fly to Nice to join Papa Joe at his rented villa on the Côte d'Azur.

Once again, Onassis heard of the Kennedy visit to the South of France, and subsequently, he invited the brothers aboard the *Christina,* where Sir Winston Churchill was once again an honored guest, as before.

Because JFK had come close to winning the vice presidential nomination on the Democratic ticket, Churchill decided to pay him some attention.

He spent two hours onboard talking about politics with JFK, advising him not to conceal his Catholic religion if he ran for president in 1960. "Americans will admire you more if you come out front with it, be proud of it. Have a Profile in Courage—yes, I read your book."

The next day, Senator George Smathers joined Teddy and JFK for a cruise aboard a 42-foot chartered yacht with some unknown women, identified as "party girls."

During the course of the Kennedy brothers cruise, on August 23, 1956, in Newport, Jackie collapsed. She was suffering from severe abdominal cramps. Rushed to the Newport Hospital, it was revealed that she was hemorrhaging. Although attempts were made to save the baby girl, she died before she could draw her first breath.

It had been impossible to call JFK by transatlantic phone, since he claimed that his rented yacht did not have a ship-to-shore radio. Actually, it did.

However, when Jackie woke up, she looked into the eyes of Bobby Kennedy, who was holding her hand. He'd been there for four hours. He leaned over and gently kissed her lips.

"You said you'd be there for me, and you are," she said, softly.

A nurse informed her that her baby had been stillborn. The news had made frontpage headlines in Newport. "I would have named her "Arabella," she told Bobby.

Bobby handled the arrangements for the burial of the infant.

When his yacht chugged into Genoa on August 26, three days after the death of his daughter, JFK learned most of the awful events that had befallen his wife during a phone call to Jackie.

Smathers warned him, "If word of this *[your off-the-record carousing, par-ticularly its co-incidence with the death of your child]* gets out, you can kiss the presidency goodbye."

Two days later, JFK arrived in Newport and rushed to visit Jackie in her hospital bed. JFK didn't seem to take the stillbirth with too much pain. If any-thing, he seemed annoyed. At a dinner party on the evening of his first night back, at Newport's Clambake Club, he appeared in good spirits.

When asked what went wrong, he told some of the other guests, "Jackie probably gave the kid nicotine poisoning. She's like a smoke stack."

Her spirit wasn't lifted the next day when JFK visited her, informing her that "Ethel's dropped another kid, a girl."

Shortly thereafter, JFK left on a campaign tour for the Democratic ticket, knowing that if he didn't, he would not be nominated in 1960.

Jackie told him that she did not want to return to Hickory Hill. "I can't face that nursery I had decorated for our baby."

After she recovered, Jackie flew to New York to visit Lee, who was living apart from her first husband, Michael Canfield. Eventually, Lee's marriage would be annulled.

"I wish I could get my marriage annulled," Jackie told her.

On her first day in New York, there was a call for her from Joe Kennedy. He wanted to meet her the following day for lunch. She knew its purpose involved discussing the rumors swirling around her personal plan to divorce his son.

Papa Joe Makes Jackie an Offer— Or Did He?

At Manhattan's very chic *Le Pavillon*, in the Ritz Tower Hotel, the owner, André Soulé, warmly welcomed Papa Joe and Jackie. In 1941, he'd opened his restaurant in part with Kennedy money.

She was shocked by Joe's condition. Nearly seventy years old, he had deteriorated rapidly in the aftermath of a recent prostatectomy, and he was visibly shaking.

She'd later report to William Walton what Joe talked to her about. He told her he'd heard that she wanted out of the marriage. "If you leave, it will cost Jack the presidency," he said. "Without you, Jack would lose everything he's hoped and dreamed about. He doesn't know what a valuable asset you are."

She told him that she didn't like being the wife of a politician. She also confessed, "I'm not the child-bearing type like Ethel, who's a virtual breeding factory, turning out little Kennedys."

She was unusually frank with him. "I feel your wonderful clan is a bit overpowering for me. Their interests are not my interests. I want to do something else with my life than attend family dinners and play touch football."

"I know how rough it can be if you're not born a Kennedy," he said.

"I also feel locked away every night at Hickory Hill," she said. "Jack is always somewhere else, and he constantly complains about the commute."

"The second problem, I can easily handle," he promised. "I'll arrange for you to move back to Georgetown. As for Hickory Hill, I can sell it to Bobby and Ethel for their ever-expanding brood, but for the same price you paid for it, of course. No profit for you and Jack."

He chose that moment to warn her, "There is danger facing you as a divorced Catholic woman. I suggest you put a divorce out of your mind."

There is great debate about whether he made a financial offer during that luncheon. In her aptly named memoir, *Bitch!*, Lady Mary (May) Sommerville Lawford *[the mother of Jackie's brother-in-law, Peter Lawford]*, claimed, "Old Joe Kennedy offered his daughter-in-law a check for one million dollars. After thinking it over, she shot back, 'Make it tax free and it's a deal.'"

Also within her book, Lady May said, "Jackie Kennedy was a clever girl, such a good business woman."

Time magazine also reported on the one-million dollar offer. Several critics, however, have challenged the story.

When challenged, Jackie never confirmed nor denied it. Once, responding to a question about it from a reporter, she said, "Only one million? Why not twelve million?"

According to rumor, the most controversial aspect of Jackie's discussion during her meeting with Papa Joe was not reported at the time. She allegedly told him that the cost of her staying with JFK would rise to twenty million dollars "if he brings home any venereal disease

Unlike Joan Crawford's daughter, Christina Crawford, Peter Lawford, JFK's brother-in-law, didn't refer to his mother, **Lady May**, as "Mommie Dearest." Instead, he accurately referred to her as **"Mother from Hell."**

from any of his sluts."

Joe agreed, claiming, "If that happens, Jackie, name your price."

Her deep disillusionment with her marriage did not escape media scrutiny. Columnist Drew Pearson, a Kennedy hater, was the first to run an item about it. The news was later picked up by *Time* magazine.

Papa Joe was a man of his word, calling JFK two weeks later with the news he'd rented a house for them in Georgetown at 2808 P Street. They would live there until May of 1957. At that point, Joe found another house for them, this time for purchase. "It dates from 1812," Jackie said, "and it leans to one side and the stairs creak, but it's a sweet little house." It was a three-story brick-built Federal-style house with a rear garden planted with magnolia trees.

Jackie did a lot of the redecorating herself, though she relied a lot on a well-known, high-society and occasionally intimidating decorator, Mrs. Henry Parrish, whose nickname was "Sister." She later described Sister as "a hatchet-faced woman who looks like George Washington."

Jackie filled the house mainly with antiques, later donating some Louis XVI cane dining room chairs to the White House.

In 1957, even in her new home, her marriage continued to deteriorate. JFK could no longer explain the need for a hotel suite since he was living in Georgetown. But he kept that suite anyway, and she heard through gossip more and more stories about the orgies going on there.

One rumor had it that his affair with Marilyn Monroe had continued. On an ironic note, he was also said to be seducing Betty Grable, the big 1940s star that Monroe had replaced at 20th Century Fox.

The night Jackie learned she was pregnant again, she got a full report on JFK's continuing affairs. It became too much for her nervous system. When Jack returned to P Street after one in the morning, she was downstairs, waiting for him, drinking heavily, and dressed only in her slip.

Perhaps their most bitter fight ensued, with accusations going back and forth. At one point, she could no longer handle the pressures of the marriage. Barefoot and dressed only in her slip, she ran out into the street in the heavy rain coming down on P Street.

JFK ran after her. She was screaming so loudly that nearby neighbors turned on their porch lights. Getting herself back into the house, JFK wrapped her in a blanket, gave her a brandy, and called for an emergency long distance limousine. While waiting for its arrival, he phoned Valleyhead, a private psychiatric facility in Carlisle, Massachusetts, a favorite haunt of celebrities having nervous breakdowns.

"When two attendants arrived to escort Jackie out to the ambulance, she screamed at them, "No! NO! I won't let you do this to me. I saw *A Streetcar Named Desire.* They did this to Blanche DuBois. I won't let you do it to me."

Then, she felt the sting of a needle. After that, she remembered only the distant sound of rain as blackness overcame her.

Until the end of her life, Jackie ranked her November, 1963 limousine race through the streets of Dallas as "the most nightmarish ride of my life."

But as she told Janet, William Walton, and others, a transit that was almost as horrible was her transfer to the Valleyhead Psychiatric Clinic for electroshock therapy.

Jackie later claimed, "When I woke up, I realized I had been committed by Jack to a house of crazies, and I was still sane, or at least I thought I was. The place seemed normal enough, like any hospital, but I knew it wasn't. The crazies were probably lurking in the closets, ready to pounce."

Very little is known about the week that Jackie spent at Valleyhead. Not wanting to attract undue attention, JFK did not visit her there. He sent her cousin, John H. Davis, the author, to check on her. He registered at a nearby motel and visited her daily.

Although he was warned not to tell anybody, he did talk to family members. The word spread. Papa Joe warned the Kennedys to keep Jackie's confinement a dark secret. And although JFK himself was not being treated for any psychiatric disorder, he feared that the fallout from his wife's confinement could seriously harm him politically.

In the original draft of his book, *Jacqueline Bouvier: An Intimate Memoir,* Davis included a section about Jackie's confinement at the clinic, but at the last minute, pressure was brought to bear on him to remove the revelations from the final published product, even though Jackie had already been dead for four years when his memoir was published in 1998.

[Joe Kennedy was right in his assumption that revelations associated with electroshock therapy could damage a political career. Around the same time that Jackie was receiving such treatments, so was Thomas Eagleton, a U.S. senator from Missouri from 1968 to 1987. Suffering from nervous exhaustion and depression, the same symptoms attributed to Jackie, he was hospitalized for a while, with disastrous political consequences, at the Mayo Clinic in Rochester, Minnesota,

In 1972, the Democratic nominee for president, George McGovern, selected Eagleton as

It almost had to happen. At some point, Jackie could no longer hold up under the strain of being married to the philandering JFK. Suicidal, she was sent by ambulance to the **Valleyhead Clinic** in Carlisle, Massachusetts, where she underwent electroshock therapy.

100

his vice president to run against Richard Nixon and Spiro Agnew.

In August of 1972, at McGovern's request, Eagleton withdrew from the presidential race and was replaced on the ticket by Kennedy-in-law Sargent Shriver. Weeks previously, Teddy Kennedy had rejected McGovern's offer to run on the ticket with him.]

Joan Mears, a nurse from Boston, was later fired from the clinic for drinking on the job. To retaliate, she tried to sell a story to *Confidential,* but pressure was exerted on the magazine's publisher. It was widely surmised that Joseph Kennedy had bribed the publisher to squelch the scandal.

Mears had been the nurse who had escorted Jackie to a sparsely furnished room at the rear of the clinic. Jackie remembered the walls painted "this sickly green color."

She wasn't certain what she was being prepared for, but Mears greased her temples and checked to confirm that all metal objects, such as jewelry, hairpins, or whatever, were removed from Jackie's body.

Then two doctors and another nurse came in to administer the treatment.

When Sylvia Plath's poignant memoir of her emotional breakdown, *The Bell Jar,* was published in 1967, Jackie read it three times. The treatment described in the novel paralleled her own experience.

[As part of a horrible coincidence, Sylvia herself had been subjected to shock treatments at Valleyhead, with dire consequences, in a series of treatments. In The Bell Jar*, Plath wrote: "Then something bent down and took hold of me and shook me like the end of the world. 'Whee-ee-ee-ee-ee,' it shrilled, through an air crackling with blue light and with each flash a great jolt drubbed me till I thought my bones would break and the sap fly out of me like a split plant."]*

After three separate treatments, Jackie was scheduled for release from Valleyhead on a Sunday morning. JFK asked his close friend, Chuck Spalding, to drive from Washington, D.C., to Carlisle and bring Jackie back to Georgetown. As Spalding remembered it, she spoke hardly a word during the long motor ride back.

He later reported that both of them had hoped to find JFK waiting for them when she returned home. "I remember she searched around for some note, but there was no message. I hated to leave her, fearing she might harm herself, but I had this urgent appointment. I kissed her goodbye on the cheek. She looked forlorn. Being the wife of Jack Kennedy was a tough job for any woman."

Jackie would later reveal to

Jackie was deeply touched when she read **Sylvia Plath**'s *(photo above) The Bell Jar.* Its author had written vividly about her horrible experiences with electroshock therapy at Valleyhead.

Janet and others that coming back to that empty house after what she'd been through caused her to seriously contemplate suicide. "I went into the bathroom and found some of Jack's Gillette blades. I thought I would run a hot bath and get into the tub and cut my wrists and just let them bleed, as I faded away. I don't think the clinic helped me. I felt more depressed after I got back home than I did before I left."

"Having been through two failed pregnancies, I didn't feel loved. I didn't feel life was worth living. Even if Jack became president, imagine the scandal that would be uncovered about his past life, about me. I didn't think I could live through it."

When JFK finally arrived that evening at the Georgetown house at around eight o'clock, she remembered him being more loving than he'd ever been. "Somehow, at least for that night, I thought that life was worth living."

Jackie's friend, Paul Mathias, the New York correspondent for the France-based *Paris-Match,* said, "Jackie was hurt very young in connection with both her father and mother. She never came out of the shock she experienced growing up. I don't think she was born happy. She filled her days as best as she could, but she suffers a lot. From the beginning of her relationship with Jack, she knew about his other women. It pained her a great deal. I have great compassion for her. It sinks into me more and more, just how irreversibly unhappy she is."

[As far as it is known, Jackie contemplated suicide only one more time in her life, and that was in the wake of JFK's assassination in Dallas. That was revealed when Richard McSorley, a Jesuit professor of theology at Georgetown, visited her at Bobby Kennedy's Hickory Hill. She told him, "I don't know how God can take Jack away."

He later said that Jackie had provided a brave front for the nation, but privately, she seemed to have begun to unravel. He recorded details about their series of meetings with Jackie in his diary, for which he would later be severely criticized.

After his first meeting with her, he became her confidant and confessor.

Jackie feared that her mental condition might deteriorate the way Mary Todd Lincoln's did after her husband was assassinated.

During her third meeting with McSorley, she asked him, "Do you think God would separate me from my husband if I killed myself? Wouldn't God understand that I just want to be with him?"

McSorley told her that she had to live for the sake of her children. "Don't mourn the dead, but get on with the living."

He found her not easy to console. She even asked him if he would pray to God to take her life.

"Yes, if you want that. It's not wrong to pray to die."

On their last meeting, she said she was still contemplating suicide, but would not make a rash move without giving it serious thought. If she did kill herself, she said, "I hope my suicide will set off a wave of suicides. I'd like that because I want to see people leave their misery behind. I was happy when

Marilyn Monroe died. She is out of her misery now."

During her phone call to McSorley, she told him that she was much better now because love had entered my life in a way I never expected."

He started to congratulate her, but she interrupted him. "It isn't a love of which the Catholic Church would approve. In fact, the love I'm experiencing now would be called ungodly in the eyes of the Church. I wouldn't even dare to confess it to you."

At that point in her life, she was seeing Bobby Kennedy almost every day.

"Then may God save your eternal soul," the priest told her.

She never called him again.

Her suicide threat of 1964 was not made public until after the priest died in 2002. His private papers were donated to Georgetown University, and his diary was leaked to the press.]

Father McSorley holds John-John in his arms. He urged Jackie not to commit suicide in the aftermath of JFK's assassination, and to live for her children.

At Last: One of Jackie's Babies Is Born Alive

Since JFK didn't like condoms, at least with his wife, and since he did not want her to practice other forms of birth control, it came as little surprise in March of 1957 when Jackie told him she was pregnant again. She had accurately predicted that her father, Black Jack Bouvier, who had died in August of 1957, would not live to see the birth of his grandchild.

The big event occurred three months after her father's death, on November 27, 1957, the day after Thanksgiving, when Jackie gave birth to a baby girl by caesarean. She weighed 7 pounds, 2 ounces. When JFK first saw her, he pronounced her "as robust as a sumo wrestler."

She was named Caroline Bouvier Kennedy, and she became the lone survivor of her immediate family.

Richard Cardinal Cushing of Boston presided over Baby Caroline's christening at St. Patrick's Cathedral in New York.

To free Jackie, and to attend to Baby Caroline's needs, JFK hired a gray-haired British nanny, Maud Shaw. Consequently, Maud's arrival allowed Jackie the freedom to leave for weekend horseback riding in Virginia's hunt country. She also joined JFK on frequent trips to Hyannis Port, where he had acquired a home near that of Papa Joe and Rose, and close to that of his younger brother, Bobby.

Rose told Bobby, in front of Jackie, that "Your intimate embracing and kissing of your sister-in-law is completely improper." However, that did not deter Bobby.

Patricia Kennedy Lawford expressed another, cruder, observation: "Every time Bobby takes Jackie in his arms, he gets a hard-on. It's just a matter of time for those two. Once, when I went boating with them, I told them, 'Get a room!'"

After Caroline's birth, politics dominated Jackie life once again.

In 1958, when JFK entered the race for election to a second six-year term in the U.S. Senate, he did not plan to serve until the end of its tenure. He hoped to be in that post only until his election as President in 1960.

He called on Jackie to help him with his campaign. In Boston's North End, he asked her to address a crowd of 1,000 Italian-Americans. Although her Italian wasn't as good as her French, she went over wonderfully with the prospective voters. Many in the audience thought she was "an Italian woman married to a Mick husband."

Based partly on her knowledge of (and talent for) foreign languages, JFK began to realize what a vote-getter his wife was. Consequently, he organized speaking engagements where at least some of the address was conducted, by Jackie, in Spanish, Italian, or French, as part of JFK's appeal to ethnic minority voters—Puerto Rican, Mexican, Haitian, and Italian—throughout Massachusetts.

During the campaign, an enemy of Jack's became her own enemy. For the first time in her life, she became confrontational with politicians and in some cases, statesmen. One of them was a fellow Democrat, Dean Acheson.

[As United States Secretary of State (1949-1953) during the administration of President Harry S Truman, he played a major role in defining American foreign policy during the Cold War.]

Acheson had told her stepfather, Hugh Auchincloss, something that got back to her: "Joe Kennedy is nothing but a social-climbing bootlegger who is ostracized by Boston Brahmins and had to buy his spoiled brat of a son a seat in Congress."

Jackie's charm didn't work on Acheson, who remained implacably opposed to her husband. As late as April of 1960, he vowed to Truman that he would do everything he could to block the Democratic Party's nomination of JFK as their presidential candidate.

During Jackie's absence, **Maud Shaw** became a second mother to **John-John** and his older sister, **Caroline.** Shaw incurred Jackie's ire after she distributed intimate details about the time she had spent working for her in the White House.

104

Privately, Acheson said, "I don't want Joe Kennedy running the government if his son is elected. Old Joe is a Wall Street wheeler-dealer and a corrupt moneyman whose political mentor was John Francis Fitzgerald. *["Honey Fitz" was the disreputable former Mayor of Boston and the father of the woman Joe eventually married, Rose Fitzgerald Kennedy.]*

As a political wife campaigning for her controversial husband, Jackie had her critics. Mary Tierney, a journalist who worked for the *Boston Herald-Traveler* interpreted her facial gestures as dominated by an "inane smile looking as if it had been fixed in place by a plasterer."

When Jackie flew to Los Angeles with her husband, her beauty did not escape the attention of producers and studio heads. Darryl F. Zanuck was said to have offered her a contract at 20th Century Fox. "She looks more like a movie star than the movie stars I know—and I know all of them."

On election night, when the results came in, JFK and Jackie learned that he'd been re-elected as Senator from Massachusetts by nearly 900,000 votes. She kissed him and congratulated him. "You've just taken a giant step toward becoming President of the United States. They've already begun to chisel your face on Mount Rushmore."

Dean Acheson, Truman's Secretary of State, appeared on the cover of the February, 1949, edition of *Life* magazine. He was one of the leading Democrats opposed to the candidacy of JFK. He publicly referred to Joseph Kennedy, Sr., as a bootlegger and to JFK as a spoiled brat. Privately, he defined Jackie as "a paid concubine."

Like Sinatra and Lawford, JFK Seduces Movie Stars

In 1956, with the national spotlight on the candidate vying for a place on the Democratic ticket, the press began focusing on JFK as never before. There were two issues associated with his campaign that troubled many voters, notably his religion as a Catholic *[with the implication that his loyalty to the Pope would take precedence over his Oath of Office]* and also his youth and inexperience. House Speaker Sam Rayburn referred to him as "that little piss-ant Kennedy."

JFK also feared that news of his Addison's disease might be leaked to the press. Even more compelling, he lived in anxiety that some sex scandal from his past might derail his campaign, especially if J. Edgar Hoover of the F.B.I. turned over even part of the dossier he had compiled about him. Jackie was fully aware of JFK's very real fears.

To close friends like Lem Billings and George Smathers, JFK revealed that his increasing use of cortisone had greatly increased his libido, which had been at a high pitch anyway since he'd been fourteen years old.

"Not only am I hot to trot day and night, but I have occasional feelings of euphoria where I just have to knock off a piece."

In 1956, JFK was seeing a lot of Frank Sinatra and his brother-in-law, Peter Lawford, who were more or less functioning as his pimps. Always intrigued by Hollywood gossip, JFK grilled them for news of their latest Hollywood conquests and the sexual availability of a particular actress. Sometimes, he needed their help in introducing him to a particular star; but on other occasions, he managed it himself.

JFK had long been enamored with the beautiful British actress, Jean Simmons, who was married at the time to the swashbuckling British actor, Stewart Granger.

Ever since JFK had seen Simmons interpret the role of Ophelia in the film version of *Hamlet*, starring Laurence Olivier, he'd found her enchanting. To his male friends, he likened her beauty to that of Elizabeth Taylor.

He'd heard that Howard Hughes, who had placed Simmons under contract at RKO, also lusted after her. As Granger later revealed in his autobiography, *Sparks Fly Upward*, he became so enraged that for a time, he actually plotted to kill Hughes.

As retaliation for thwarting his hopes of seducing her, Hughes got revenge by refusing to release her from her contract with RKO for a co-starring role with Gregory Peck in *Roman Holiday* (1953) at a competing studio. The role went instead to Audrey Hepburn, which made her a star and earned her an Oscar as Best Actress of the Year.

Five years after the Simmons/Granger furor over Howard Hughes and *Roman Holiday*, when JFK learned that Simmons was in Boston, filming scenes from *Home Before Dark*, he opted to pursue the woman he had so long desired.

[Released in 1958, Home Before Dark *focused on Simmons as the conflicted female lead playing Charlotte, a delicate, elegant woman who battles for sanity after her escape from a mental institution.]*

Simmons would later confess to friends, "Jack practically beat down the door to my hotel room until I finally opened it. What I discovered was a man of such charm and grace that it would take a woman far stronger than me to resist him."

Apparently, she told a more limited version to her British husband. Their marriage had already begun to disintegrate, and she would eventually divorce Granger in 1960.

She told him that in Boston, a very attractive

After beating down the door of **Jean Simmons** in her hotel room in Boston, JFK was left with an unresolved question: Did the British actress remind him of Elizabeth Taylor or of Jackie herself?

U.S. Senator was wooing her with flowers and banging on her door. "He had such a lovely smile I nearly let him in."

"What's his name?" Granger demanded.

"He's very important—John F. Kennedy."

"Never heard of him," he said.

"You will," she predicted. "He's going to become the next President of the United States."

When JFK flew again to Los Angeles, he arranged to meet privately with both Simmons (at the Beverly Hills Hotel), and also with Marilyn Monroe, with whom he'd continue his on-again, off-again affair. But he had another younger star in focus as well.

She was twenty-two-year-old Lee Remick, who was six years younger than Jackie, and who had been grotesquely billed as "America's Answer to Brigitte Bardot." She'd caught JFK's attention when he saw her as the sexy, baton-twirling majorette in Elia Kazan's *A Face in the Crowd* (1957). JFK was determined to have her.

He learned that she had married Bill Colleran, a movie director and TV producer, in 1957. For JFK, a married woman was not someone to avoid, but a challenge for him to seduce.

It was made easy for him when he met with Peter Lawford. By a strange coincidence, he discovered that Lawford was having an affair with Remick. Lawford became so smitten with Remick that he confessed to JFK that he was considering divorcing his sister, Patricia, so that he could marry her.

To Lawford's dismay, JFK was spectacularly unsympathetic to his plight: "You and I believe in sharing the wealth. See that Remick is delivered to my suite tomorrow night."

Despite his declaration of love for Remick, Lawford had never been known to disobey an order from JFK. As Lem Billings once said, "When Jack cracked the whip, Peter jumped through the hoop."

In another ironic *segue*, JFK would later learn that Bobby was also having a torrid affair with Remick, who had told him, "I'm bored with my marriage."

Dazzled by the power and prestige of the Kennedy brothers, Remick became a highly visible spokesperson for the Democratic Party, strongly backing JFK. She later told her favorite co-star, Jack Lemmon, "I fucked Jack because he was President of the United States. And I fucked Bobby because I fell in love with him after I fell out of love with Peter."

Appearing on the cover of *Life* in 1960, perky actress **Lee Remick** was involved in a delicate balancing act with the Kennedy clan. She was involved in sexual affairs not only with JFK, but with Bobby Kennedy and brother-in-law Peter Lawford too.

Lemmon later said, "Dear, dear Lee suffered from a lack of self-esteem. By seducing some of the biggest names in America—the Kennedy brothers, Gregory Peck, Peter Lawford, even Frank Sinatra—she felt needed and wanted. But in the end, all these men dropped her. She was used. When she came to realize that, she felt even worse about herself."

***

JFK's next conquest of a movie star occurred not in Hollywood, but in Washington.

The name of Sophia Loren, the luscious Neapolitan beauty, always pops up in the usual round-ups of JFK's move star conquests, including within Mart Martin's *Behind the Bedroom Doors of 201 Famous Women.* Kennedy biographers, including Christopher Andersen, have also published accounts of it.

In 1957, Sophia had rejected a marriage proposal from Cary Grant after they co-starred together in *The Pride and the Passion.* Instead, that same year, she'd married Carlo Ponti, Sr., the pudgy, art-collecting producer or co-producer of such major-league films as Federico Fellini's *La Strada (1954),* Luchino Visconti's *Boccaccio '70 (1962), Marriage Italian Style (1964),* David Lean's *Doctor Zhivago (1965)* and Michelangelo Antonioni's *Blowup (1966).*

La Bella Napoletana, Sophia Loren, attracted the roving eye of JFK, along with half the men in the world. As it turned out, she proved not to be an easy conquest, even when he switched on the fabled Kennedy charm.

[In 1962, Sophia's sister, Anna Maria Villani Scicolone, would wed Romano Mussolini, the youngest son of the Fascist former dictator of Italy, Benito Mussolini. They would produce a spectacularly controversial daughter, Alessandra Mussolini, born in 1962, who became a high-fashion model, a pop singer, an actress, and an Italian politician with a complicated platform that has included advocacy of everything from feminism and gay rights to neo-Fascism.]

Jackie was out of town, in Virginia, when JFK and his highly promiscuous bachelor friend from the U.S. Senate, George Smathers, attended a party at the Italian Embassy in Washington, D.C.

At the party, JFK was dazzled by the entrance of Sophia Loren. He told Smathers, "She's the sexiest doll I've ever seen—those lips, those tits!" Loren was only twenty-four at the time, and a celebrated

Sophia Loren's niece, **Allessandra Scicolone Mussolini,** became one of the most controversial politicians in Italy, a neo-Fascist. Her mother had wed the youngest son of the Italian dictator, Benito Mussolini.

beauty.

According to reports, JFK did not want to approach Loren directly, because a romantic overture would have compromised him in front of his many political enemies at the party. Instead, he asked Smathers to "play the pimp for me."

Consequently, Smathers approached Loren, who was standing with Maxine Cheshire. The Senator from Florida incorrectly assumed that Cheshire was Loren's chaperon, as he was unaware that she was a Society Reporter for the *Washington Post.*

After introducing himself, Smathers pointed out JFK across the crowded room before inviting her to a late night champagne supper at Kennedy's Georgetown residence.

According to author C. David Heymann, Cheshire could see Kennedy through the open doors leading out onto a terrace. "He was impatiently rocking back and forth on his heels."

When Smathers returned to JFK and conveyed the information that Loren had politely rejected his offer, JFK sent Smathers back for another try.

When Loren rejected the second offer, Smathers sized up Cheshire, and then said to Loren, within earshot of Cheshire, "Oh, what the hell...You might as well bring your friend along. We'll make it a foursome."

Again, Loren refused.

When Smathers reported the second rejection to JFK, he flashed anger. "God damn it, I should have known better than to send a boy to do a man's job."

According to Andersen, Smathers later said, "I never saw Jack strike out with anybody if he really wanted to get together with them. He just kept at it until he wore them down. Miss Loren was no exception. She went with Jack, all right, and I understand that they had a wonderful time."

Ms. Loren has neither confirmed nor denied this report.

While still in Washington, JFK launched one more affair before flying away on a political campaign.

***

Pamela Turnure was a Jackie lookalike and a Georgetown debutante. A graduate of the exclusive Mount Vernon Seminary, she was first hired as a receptionist at the Belgian Embassy in D.C. JFK was introduced to her at Nini Auchincloss's wedding.

It was obvious that he was immediately attracted to this strikingly beautiful brunette, with her sparkling green eyes and a slim figure like that of his wife. During conversations with her, he found her bright and well educated. She was said to have been dating Prince Aly Khan, who had previously been married (1949-1953) to screen goddess Rita Hayworth.

JFK soon became a regular late-night visitor to her apartment. The only problem, as it turned out, was that Pamela had a fanatical Catholic as a landlady. Florence Kater recognized JFK and was outraged. So outraged, in fact, that she made it her life's mission to expose the Senator's adulterous affair.

She managed to take a photograph of JFK exiting from Pamela's apartment at three o'clock, during the early morning hours of July 11, 1958. She had copies made and mailed them to every major newspaper, magazine, and TV station in the country. But except for a veiled reference to it in *The Washington Star,* very few, if any, other media published her revelations. Infuriated, Kater then sent the photos and data to J. Edgar Hoover at the F.B.I., who merely added them to his ever-growing dossier on the Senator and future President.

Kater went so far as to place a tape recorder in the air vent funneling into Pamela's bedroom, so that she could record the sounds of her lovemaking with JFK.

Two years later, during the 1960 presidential campaign, when JFK was running for the country's top office and heading the Democratic ticket, Kater would show up at Kennedy rallies with picket signs denouncing him as an adulterer. When JFK flew for a meeting with Harry S Truman in Independence, Missouri, Kater flew on the same plane.

In front of Truman's residence, she picketed the candidate.

She also appealed to Joseph P. Kennedy, who dismissed her as a kook, and she even sent data to Richard Cardinal Cushing in Boston, who advised her to devote her time to other, more worthy causes.

Finally, in 1961, after JFK had been entrenched within the Oval Office, she picketed the White House, even on rainy days.

Jackie, of course, learned about the affair. That's why, in 1961, it came as a surprise to Kennedy insiders and in-the-know media when she designated Pamela as her press secretary.

When her social secretary, Letitia Baldrige, asked her why she had employed the known mistress of her husband, Jackie replied, "That way, I can keep an eye on her."

Pamela Turnure. Why is it that so many women in JFK's entourage look like debutantes?

Chapter Five

Gore Vidal and the JFKs

Confronting the World's Most Famous Couple

Jack and Jackie Reveal Their Secrets to America's Most Cynical Social Historian

Beautiful and mischievous, **Jackie Bouvier** became a chain-smoker for life. She later claimed that her "quasi-relative," author **Gore Vidal**, depicted above on each side of her, taught her to be cynical about men. For years, he was her confidant. She told him amusing tidbits about her life and the Bouviers. "My *mère*, Janet, has this nightmarish fear that I'll marry an Italian."

At a party in Georgetown, in December of 1948, John Galliher, a friend of Gore Vidal's mother, Nina Vidal, introduced the young novelist to Jacqueline Bouvier. "In time, I was a sort of quasi-relative of hers because we had shared a mutual stepfather, Hugh Auchincloss," Gore said.

She had specifically sought an introduction to Gore because he was well known in Washington circles, and she felt he might get her started in journalism or photography, perhaps as an actress, a profession she coveted even more.

Jackie arranged to meet Gore for future lunches. Before she left, Gore claimed to Jackie that Galliher, a rich, bisexual Washingtonian, "came on strong to me. He told me, 'I've gone to bed with your mother, and I'd like to go to bed with you.'"

Galliher later claimed to literary critic Leo Lerman that Nina was "a very earthy, sexy woman. She told me that Gore was a ballet dancer, so I figured he was gay. Not only that, but he was very attractive back then, a very handsome young man."

Nina Vidal, after she divorced Gore's father, Eugene Vidal, married Hugh (Hughdie) Auchincloss, a rich Washington stockbroker. Nina, with

YOU'LL GET

MORE with GORE

In 1960, when Democrat **Gore Vidal** ran for a congressional seat in a mostly Republican district of New York State, his campaign ad was privately mocked by his opponents. They suggested that the "you'll get more" slogan and his hand measurements were falsely referring to the size of his penis.

her eleven-year-old son, Gore, moved into his home, Merrywood, a fifty-acre estate on the south bank of the Potomac River in McLean, Virginia. The house itself was a neo-Georgian brick building evocative of Mount Vernon in design, but not as big.

After Nina divorced Hughdie, he married Janet Bouvier, the mother of Jackie and Lee Bouvier, who subsequently moved into Merrywood to fill the void left by Nina. That's how Gore came to know these soon-to-become famous sisters, who would become better known, of course, as Jackie Kennedy and Lee Radziwill.

"Both sisters were brought up like geishas," Gore claimed. "To get money out of men."

"The relationship between Jackie and Lee was sort of S&M," Gore claimed. "Jackie was the S, Lee the M. Intense rivalry was sometimes combined with sisterly intimacy before their relationship turned sour. Lee was always the loser, Jackie the eternal star."

"I Must Share Jack With Other Women"

—Jackie to Gore

Gore claimed, "I never profited from my relationship with Jackie. In fact, it was the reverse. When she first started out as a reporter in Washington, she claimed she was my sister. She got all kinds of interviews with people by telling them that. She profited a lot more from our relationship than I ever did."

On his years at Merrywood, where he lived, Gore said, "It was a peaceful life, a bit Henry Jamesian, a world of deliberate quietude removed from 20th Century tension. It was a life that gave total security but not much preparation for the real world."

Merrywood had sexual memories for me," Gore recalled. "I was inspired when I came across Hughdie's vast collection of pornography. I first had sex with a girl in the basement of Merrywood. My first sex with a boy was on the white tile floor of one of Merrywood's bathrooms."

"Jackie later told me that it was Hughdie's mammoth cache of porn that taught her about the birds and bees." Gore claimed.

In his 1967 novel, *Washington, D.C.,* Merrywood was used as a setting. He renamed it "Laurel House."

Years later, Gore also wrote about Merrywood in an article for *Look* magazine, referring to its "golden ambience."

By then, John F. Kennedy had not only married Jackie, but was no stranger to Merrywood. During a meal with Gore, he asked, "What's this golden shit you're talking about at Merrywood?" he asked. "It was more like *The Little Foxes.*"

After divorcing Black Jack Bouvier, **Janet Lee Bouvier** married Hugh Auchincloss. Here, she poses for a magazine story entitled "What Jackie Kennedy Has Learned from Her Mother." Jackie ridiculed the article, claiming, "The only thing Janet taught me was how to marry a rich man."

JFK had seen Lillian Hellman's 1941 movie, *The Little Foxes,* starring Bette Davis as a majestic but ruthless bastion of the upper-class *bourgeoisie.* The film dealt with the greed and corruption of a crumbling, financially compromised, Southern family.

An Auchincloss relative told Jackie "Life at Merrywood was all about the sound of slamming doors, great feet thundering up and down the steps, slapping across faces, vile oaths, and Hughdie sitting sort of slumped in the middle of it."

Both Gore Vidal and Jackie grew up at **Merrywood**, Hugh Auchincloss' great estate overlooking the Potomac River.

Gore detested Janet, Jackie's mother. "She didn't belong to the class to which she aspired, and in a sense joined by marrying Hughdie. I think that made her very nervous. There were also rumors that she was Jewish. She wanted to control Jackie. Her obsession was seeing that she wed someone rich. She broke up Jackie's first engagement because the poor guy didn't make enough money."

"Janet was a small woman with a large pigeon bust that neatly balanced low-slung buttocks set atop sandpiper legs," Gore said. "Her sallow face was a great curved nosebeak between small, fierce dark eyes. With me, she was her usual rude, 'poisonivied' self. Jackie certainly didn't inherit her tiny breasts or her looks from her mother."

Between sessions at their respective boarding schools, both Jackie and Gore at different times lived at Merrywood. "Jackie, Lee *[Radziwill]* and I had no money, contrary to what people think. Mr. Auchincloss was very rich. But we were not, and we had to survive out there in the world. That's why I had to work, and why Jackie and Lee had to marry well."

Engaged to JFK, Jackie confided in Gore. "I want more than anything in the world to be married to him. We're having what I call a spasmodic courtship. To be a part of his life as his wife, I'm willing to share him with other women."

Later, when Jackie married John F. Kennedy, then a young congressman, Gore was not surprised.

"Of the available Catholic women in the country, Jackie was about the most glamorous, and the Kennedys were regarded as a big step upward and an on-going victory over the WASPs," Gore said.

When she married JFK, Gore said, "Jackie had been raised to play the modern equivalent of the classic courtesan role. At least, she closed her eyes to Jack's philandering. Their marriage was an 18th Century affair: a practical union on both sides."

Kitty Kelley, Jackie's biographer, said she was attracted to Gore because "He was witty, sexy, brilliant, talented, successful, charming, and an entertaining gossip. Being able to dish the dirt was a criterion for friendship with the Kennedys. They relished famous people who could discourse about their peccadillos."

Gore defined Jack as a better gossip than Jackie, a marvelous repository of information, such as what Marlene Dietrich liked to do in bed, or what Joan Crawford called her vagina. "When I met Jack, he wanted to know the current crop of beauties who slept around," Gore said. "He once asked me about Jean Peters, who was married at the time to Howard Hughes."

"I hear he likes to fuck young male actors, so he must leave Jean alone a lot at night," JFK said. "How about setting up something between Jean and me? I think she's the pretty version of Jackie, with better skin."

In 1956, in Washington, Gore and Jackie saw a lot of each other, often lunching together and, occasionally chatting with Eleanor Roosevelt.

Jackie was a reporter and photographer, but Gore knew that her dream was to become an actress. "She was fascinated by actors and went to bed with a surprising number of them that the public never knew about—I mean more than the usual suspects—William Holden, Marlon Brando, Frank Sinatra, and Warren Beatty."

He once took her to a rehearsal for a teleplay he'd written called *Honor,* part of the *Robert Montgomery Presents* series.

"Jackie was much taken with Dick York, the youthful star," Gore said. "She also flirted with the aging Ralph Bellamy. She later told me she'd rather be a movie star's wife than a senator's wife—'It's so boring.'"

Ironically, it would be Gore himself, not Jackie, who first bedded York.

After they left the rehearsal, Jackie told him, "Jack also loves movie stars, especially if their names are Marlene Dietrich, Joan Crawford, Hedy Lamarr, Marilyn Monroe, June Allyson, Peggy Cummins, Arlene Dahl, Rhonda Fleming, Zsa Zsa Gabor, Susan Hayward, Sonja Henie, Janet Leigh, Jayne Mansfield, Kim Novak, Lee Remick, Jean Simmons, Gene Tierney, and Lana Turner, to get us going. But Old Joe *[Joseph P. Kennedy]* hates actors."

"Well, not all actresses," Gore quipped. "For instance, Gloria Swanson, to name the obvious, but also Dietrich, Crawford, Greta Garbo, Phyllis Haver, Sonja Henie, Constance Bennett, Evelyn Brent, Nancy Carroll, Betty Compson, Viola Dana, and Marion Davies shared with William Randolph Hearst."

Then, Gore continued, provocatively including an accusation about Jackie's husband, "And father and son sometimes seduced the same star—Dietrich, for example, but also ice-skating Henie and the indomitable Joan Crawford," Gore said.

"Oh," Jackie said rather impatiently, "The curse of being married to a Kennedy man."

"In New York a few weeks later, I took her to Downey's, the poor man's Sardi's, a place frequented mostly by out-of-work actors," Gore said. "She first met Paul Newman there, a future lover. She also met Shelley Winters, and John Ireland was there. I told Jackie he had the biggest prick in Hollywood. She was fascinated by that tidbit of information, perhaps planning to date him in her future. Everyone wanted to know who Jackie was. I told them, 'She's a new starlet at Warner's.'"

"After Downey's, I took her to a party at the home of Zachory Scott, who had thrilled her with his devilish looks playing opposite Joan Crawford in *Mildred Pierce,* one of her favorite movies," Gore said. "He was married to Ruth Scott, an actress from Mississippi and longtime friend of William Faulkner, who wrote the play *Requiem for a Nun* for her. When Ruth was out of the room, I noticed Zachory whispering to Jackie in the corner. I thought they were setting up a rendezvous. Why not? Jack played around. Why not

With his pencil mustache, **Zachory Scott** specialized in screen portrayals of duplicitous, spineless cads, most memorably opposite Joan Crawford in *Mildred Pierce.* Jackie learned that on that rare occasion, during his portrayal of that role, he actually went to bed with a woman.

Jackie? She called her affairs 'revenge fucks.'"

"At least three of the actresses at Zachory's party had been bedded by Jack—Gene Tierney, Crawford, and Janet Leigh," Gore claimed. "Jack had already begun his collection of beddable stars that would, in time, outdo those of his father. Jack was the Big Dipper, Joe the Little Dipper."

Back in Washington, I discreetly asked Jackie how it had gone with Scott."

She looked disappointed. "I think he would have preferred going to bed with Jack instead of me."

"The lads of Merrywood," as **Gore Vidal** *(center)* called them, assembled for the wedding of Nini Gore Auchincloss to Newton Steers. **Jack Kennedy** *(shown in profile, standing second from the right in the rear)* also attended.

The only thing Gore remembered about the wedding was that he got to see the penis of the future president when they "shared" a urinal.

***

In 1957, Gore was one of the groomsmen, along with JFK, at the wedding of Gore's half-sister, Nini Gore Auchincloss, to Newton Steers. Nini's stepbrother-in-law was Senator Kennedy. At the wedding, Jackie, in her second trimester of pregnancy, was matron of honor.

The marriage took place in Washington, D.C., at St. John's Church, aptly labeled "the church of the presidents."

[In his 1995 memoir, Palimpsest, *Gore wrote of St. John's: "For over a century, Presidents, on a Sunday, would wander across the avenue that separates the White House from Lafayette Square and its odd little church, whose chaste Puritan tower is topped by an unlikely gold Byzantine dome—metaphor?"]*

"My main memory of the event was sharing a urinal with Jack Kennedy and checking out the penis of the future president of the United States," Gore said. "Of course, a thousand women and his best friend, the very gay Lem Billings, knew what Jack called 'my implement' far better than I did."

In his memoirs, Gore claimed that after the wedding reception at Merrywood, Jackie took the new bride, Nini, upstairs to one of the large bathrooms. "Jackie showed the innocent Nini how to douche post-sex, with one foot in the bathtub, the other on the white tiled floor. There was no bidet."

Jackie had advised Nini to use the white kind of vinegar. "If not properly diluted, you can burn your insides out."

She later joked to Gore, "Can you see Eleanor, Bess, or Mamie lecturing a bride on the finer points of the female douche?"

Later, Gore looked out the window at the wedding party on the lawn. He became aware of an odd curve in the upper vertebrae of JFK's back, just below the neck. Later, Lyndon Johnson would refer to JFK as "that spavined hunchback."

"An odd feeling came over me then," Gore said. "I just knew that one day Jack was going to be President of the United States."

Gore's final memory of that wedding day involved standing next to Teddy Kennedy. "He raised high his champagne glass and then poured its contents over his own handsome, youthful head."

In addition to the wedding reception for Nini, Janet Auchincloss staged another event at Merrywood to celebrate the success of her husband's former stepson, Gore himself. The National Theatre in Washington was presenting his play, *Visit to a Small Planet.*

Even though he didn't like Janet, viewing her as a schemer and a social climber, Gore was honored by the event. He was most conciliatory toward her. But despite Gore's status as the guest of honor, Janet showed utter contempt for him, seating him at the children's table during the dinner that followed the cocktail party.

Later, he and Jackie headed upstairs to look at his former bedroom, which had been hers during her residency there. By the time of Gore's return to Merrywood for the party, Janet was using it as a storage area for linens. The beds were still in the crowded room, to be used in case of an emergency for overflow guests.

In what had previously functioned as his boyhood bedroom, Gore saw once again the twin beds he'd shared with Jimmie Trimble, "the love of my life," a soldier killed on Iwo Jima during World War II. Jackie told him that she and JFK had occupied those same beds when they'd returned from their honeymoon.

"One morning, Jack didn't have a clean shirt, so I gave him one of those Brooks Brothers shirts you left behind," Jackie said. "It fitted him perfectly."

At the party, before going back downstairs, Jackie and Gore talked rather clinically about their mutually shared stepfather. "Nina told me she had sexual problems with him," Gore said. "She claimed Hughdie was incapable of having an erection. To conceive children, Nina had to use a spoon to help matters along."

He later said, "Jackie knew exactly what I meant. I didn't have to explain it to her."

On leaving the room, he noticed an embroidered pillow on Jackie's bed. It read: "Better *nouveau rich* than not rich at all."

In a 1969 article in *Playboy,* Gore said, "I was unaware of Jackie until the Forties. When she was an inquiring photographer in Washington, a budding Brenda Starr, she used her alleged kinship with me to open doors, since I was, pre-Kennedy, the family notable. That got her in to interview everyone from Eleanor Roosevelt to Richard Nixon. At any rate, I certainly knew what her childhood was like, since it was pretty much what I had endured at Merrywood."

In 1956, Gore visited Jack and Jackie at their home in Georgetown. JFK had failed in his bid that year for the Democratic Party's nomination as their

Vice Presidential candidate on the same ticket with Adlai Stevenson.

Gore recalled JFK coming out of the bedroom looking disheveled. "He wore only a bathrobe, and it was open, revealing the family jewels." Gore said. "He was not a shy person. One time at Hyannis Port, he came out of the house wrapped only in a towel. At one point, when he was fixing himself a drink, Jackie and I looked on when the towel fell off him. He walked around for five minutes before putting that towel back on."

Gore remembered another occasion when he was sitting with Jack and Jackie as they read newspaper accounts of Grace Kelly's 1956 wedding to Prince Rainier of Monaco. "It was humiliating for her, but Jack looked over at Jackie, then looked at pictures of the blonde-haired bride, and he said, 'I could have married her.' It was known by the inner circle at the time that he'd had an affair with Grace. From that day forth, Princess Grace became somebody in Jackie's life she could not abide."

Once, during sex, JFK nearly drowned **Hedy Lamarr**, "the most beautiful woman in Europe."

"If you're bisexual, you might have been attracted to Jackie," Gore claimed. "Her body was androgynous, broad-shouldered, flat chested, with long, muscular legs, large hands and feet. The only thing she didn't possess was a cock. She confessed to me that her aim in life was to attract men. As such, she was a subtle, practiced flirt. One day on a boat off the coast of Hyannis Port, her bare leg brushed against my hairy one. She ignited an erotic fire by deliberately rubbing up against me, but nothing came of it."

Gore claimed that he and JFK, from all reports, had much in common sexually, in that each of them was more interested in their own sexual satisfaction than in giving pleasure to a partner.

Hedy Lamarr claimed that JFK liked sex in a hot bathtub with the woman on top. "In an impulsive move, he pushed me backward," she said. "My head was under water, and I felt I was drowning. This caused a vaginal spasm. But he had his orgasm. I never spoke to him after that underwater adventure."

[This revelation was made to Darwin Porter at a party at the apartment of their mutual literary agent, Jay Garon. Garon had signed Lamar as his representative for her tell-all memoir, Ecstacy.*]*

"I can be certain of one thing: He saved the real kinky stuff for his other sexual partners," Gore claimed. "I think that with Jackie, JFK performed the sex act in the old-fashioned way. Unlike another First Lady who would rule the White House in the 1980s, Jackie was not skilled at fellatio, at least that's what Jack told me back in the days when we talked about sex with each other. Rimming was definitely a no-no. From what Jack said, Jackie considered that a disgusting sexual practice. Of course, Jack had his gay friend, Lem Billings, around to perform that act for him."

From The Best Man to Gore's Exile from Camelot

In 1960, Gore had run as the Democratic candidate for Congress in what was identified at the time as the 29th Congressional district of New York State. *[In 1960, the term "29th District" applied to the traditionally Republican enclaves of Columbia, Dutchess, Greene, Schoharie, and Ulster Counties, in southern New York State. Gore at the time lived within that district, at Edgewater, a historically important home on the banks of the Hudson River, in the village of Barrytown, near Rhinebeck.]*

His Republican challenger, J. Ernest Wharton, beat him by a margin of 57% to 43%. Gore received the most votes of any Democrat in half a century, largely because Eleanor Roosevelt, Harry S Truman, Paul Newman, and Joanne Woodward aggressively campaigned for him.

Gore had called Kennedy to tell him, "Eleanor wants Adlai Stevenson to run for a third time, even though he failed twice against Eisenhower. But the best I can do is to get Eleanor to be less hostile to you. She still has bad memories of the feud between Old Joe *[U.S. Ambassador to Great Britain, Joseph P. Kennedy, JFK's father]* and FDR *[Eleanor's husband, Franklin Delano Roosevelt]*."

Eleanor told Gore that in 1941, FDR had invited Joseph Kennedy for a weekend at their estate north of New York City, Hyde Park. "Kennedy was alone with Franklin for no more than ten minutes in his study when I was summoned. Franklin asked Kennedy to step outside. Then he turned to me, his voice shaking, "I never want to see that man again as long as I live. Get him out of here.'"

JFK did arrive in Dutchess County, despite the bad blood associated with his father's visit in 1941. JFK eventually came to Dutchess County to support Gore in his campaign there as a Democrat. A headline in the *Hyde Park Inde-*

John F. Kennedy was still a senator when he came to Hyde Park to campaign for **Gore Vidal** *(left)*, who was running for a seat from the 29th Congressional District in New York. Despite the pain in his back, JFK had flown to the small airport at Hyde Park to deliver a speech promoting Gore.

Eleanor Roosevelt was Gore's supporter and friend. She told JFK that she didn't want him to become president because he'd been pro-McCarthy. She also cited other "deviations from liberalism."

pendent asserted, "KENNEDY STUMPS FOR GORE."

"Vidal has the will and the vigor and he understands the need for action in this changing world," JFK said.

Meeting privately with Gore, JFK told him, "I hope your private life doesn't become an issue in this campaign."

Gore shot back, "I hope *your* private life doesn't become an issue, too."

JFK had not wanted to campaign on location for Gore, figuring his political capital could better be spent elsewhere. "He came at the urging of Jackie," I later learned," Gore said. "I think that was one of the last favors Jackie ever did for me. Our relationship in the early 1960s was soon to head south."

Later, Gore sent both JFK and Jackie his script for his latest play, *The Best Man,* before they eventually saw it on Broadway. One night, as JFK was reading the script, *[whose characters included a womanizing politician named William Russell],* he asked Jackie, "Is Gore writing about me?"

Weeks later, in New York City, on December 6, 1960, with flashbulbs popping, President-elect Kennedy, accompanied by Jackie, entered the Morosco Theatre for a performance of *The Best Man.*

During the performance, when the candidate's sexual promiscuity was mentioned, Charles (Chuck) Spalding, a Kennedy aide, noted that JFK "appeared quite nervous. He gave me a lightning look before sinking lower in his chair."

After the play, Gore dined with Jack and Jackie. "If you had not won the presidency, I would have emigrated," Gore told JFK. "I'm only sorry I won't be in Congress this January to help balance in some small way the powers of darkness gathering there."

JFK's crowded schedule had allowed him only one night in New York before moving on to other venues. When confronted with the choice of which play he'd attend, JFK had opted for a performance of Gore's *The Best Man* rather than *Camelot,* a touch of irony.

In the aftermath of that embarrassing evening, Kennedy told Gore, "When I take office, I'll keep you in mind. The ambassadorship to Mali is open."

***

During the peak of JFK's presidency, in the dying days of the summer of 1961, Jackie invited Gore to visit the president and herself at Hyannis Port. Gore was staying at the time in nearby Provincetown.

On the way, he was stopped by a police car when he tried to enter the Kennedy compound.

He encountered Jackie in a pair of pink Capri pants with a windbreaker, fresh from waterskiing. She was making daiquiris.

When JFK appeared, in chinos and a blue shirt, "He had an odd yellow glint, a manifestation of Addison's disease," Gore said. "He looked older than his photographs."

Jackie told Gore she found the White House claustrophobic. "You're never alone there. You sit in a room and try to write a letter and someone comes in."

Failed presidential candidate George McGovern once called on Gore for lunch. He claimed that when he'd met Jackie, she told him that she overheard "Joe, Jack, and Bobby discussing Jack's career. They spoke of me as if I weren't a person, just a thing, a sort of asset, like Rhode Island."

At the dinner Gore attended in the Kennedy compound in Hyannis Port, Bobby managed only a handshake and a brief hello to Gore. Months before their violent argument at the White House, Bobby contemptuously referred to Gore and others as "Jackie's fag friends."

Over the Kennedy family table in Hyannis Port that night, Gore learned a deadly secret. "Jack and Bobby were preparing to go to war with the Soviet Union if that country ever moved its troops across the border in an attempt to occupy West Berlin."

"It was on that same night that Jackie weighed in with her political opinion. "Yes, it would be better to be Red than dead—not maybe for myself, but for the children." Gore was shocked to learn that Jackie was such a pacifist, that she preferred surrender rather than risking the lives of her family.

"I did learn some tantalizing news from Jackie before I became *persona non grata*," Gore said. "Jackie told me that if Jack had not been assassinated *[in Dallas in November of 1963]*, he would have dumped Lyndon *[Johnson]* as a running mate in the '64 election, and offered the public a Kennedy/Kennedy ticket. The plan was for Bobby to run in 1968 and serve two terms, followed by Teddy *[Edward Kennedy]*, serving two terms beginning in 1976."

During her years in the White House, Jackie also visited Gore in Provincetown in heavy disguise, wearing a blonde wig. But she was nonetheless recognized. He slipped her in to see a local theatrical production of *Mrs. Warren's Profession*. After the performance, he suggested that, while in disguise, both of them should visit the local lesbian bar.

"She seemed fascinated, and she did peek in at all the butches and lipstick lesbians dancing together. But as First Lady, she didn't dare enter."

She later said, "Jack is very sad. He's holed up in Hyannis Port and not meeting his requirement of a new girl every day. So he's reduced to coming to my bed twice a week."

Throughout the 1950s, and up until 1961, when Jack and Jackie took over the White House, they remained friends with Gore. In large part, that was based on Gore's infinite knowledge of Hollywood gossip. When Jackie was out of the room, Jack quizzed Gore endlessly about female stars. In noteworthy contrast, Bobby continued to hold Gore in contempt.

At one point, when Gore and JFK stayed up late drinking, JFK confessed. "I married the wrong sister," referring, of course, to Lee Radziwill. "I guess it was inevitable that Lee and I would eventually crawl between the sheets."

[In the late 1970s, Jackie told her sister-in-law, Joan Kennedy, that she'd learned about Jack's affair with Lee.]

Briefly, during the early months of the Kennedy administration of the White House, Gore was welcome at Camelot. As he admitted, "I was part of the

Kennedy Court. What that meant was that I was called upon for escort duty. 'Gore, dear,' Jackie would call me. 'Please escort Rose to the Metropolitan Opera.' My picture escorting Rose Kennedy would end up on the front page of the *Journal-American*."

"La Divinissima,"
Opera superstar **Maria Callas**, "trashing Jackie."

Gore soon learned how Rose managed to deceive the press. As she was entering the Opera House, a reporter admired her stylish dress. "Where did you get it?" he asked.

"From Klein's bargain basement," she replied.

Gore, however, knew that it was an *haute couture* confection from Balenciaga.

One night in 1961, at the beginning of JFK's presidency, Jackie invited Gore to the White House.

"That night at the White House, I got a little drunk, and my hatred of Bobby spilled over when he demanded that I take my hand off Jackie's shoulder," Gore claimed. "Even before Jack was assassinated, Jackie was hot to trot with her brother-in-law, and *vice versa*. Bobby told Jackie never to invite 'the drunken fag' to the White House again—and she didn't. From that date on, our friendship more or less came to an end, although we'd encounter each other on two or three occasions in the future, including an outing to see *Deep Throat*."

"The feud with Bobby did liberate me as an essayist," he said. "I was free to criticize Bobby in print as harshly as I wanted, even to attack Jackie's future marriage to Onassis. So maybe for my literary reputation and political objectivity, it was perhaps just as well that Bobby and I almost came to blows, so to speak."

***

Gore wasn't around when Jackie married Aristotle Onassis. When a reporter asked his opinion of the union, Gore said, "Highly suitable. The best way to replenish a dwindling bank account."

When Jackie was accused of marrying Onassis for his money, Gore said he understood such transactions. "I was once seduced by an old man of thirty, my absolute cut-off edge, who gave me ten dollars. So I, too, like Jackie, had once been a small player in the commodities' exchange market."

Throughout the course of Jackie's marriage to Onassis, Gore was no longer socializing with her. But he did recall an encounter with opera diva Maria Callas *[the shipping tycoon's longtime mistress]* in Rome. "Maria was getting ready to make *Medea*. And Pasolini was there. But all she wanted to talk about was Jackie. Very funny about her. She talked about the jewelry Ari had presented to Jackie."

"I know those jewels," Callas said. "They're nothing. They're second rate, except the ruby earrings are quite good. I remember those, and I almost took them, but they really weren't right for me. The rest of what he gave her is pure trash. But, of course, Mrs. Kennedy wouldn't know the difference, would she?"

***

For Gore at the White House, Camelot came and went very quickly.

On November 22, 1963, Gore, with his companion, Howard Austen, was in a movie theater in the beach town of Ostia outside Rome. Gore heard a buzz in the audience, with the constant mention of the word "Kennedy."

"Howard and I went outside, where we learned that Jack had been assassinated in Dallas. Immediately, we made plans to fly to Washington."

Later, he was barred from entering the church where JFK's funeral was conducted. "I wanted to use the occasion for a reconciliation with Jackie, but I suspected Bobby's hand barring me, even at the edge of the grave."

"I paid my obeisance to Jack, even though I had to do so at a distance. Howard and I then flew to Hollywood, where we watched the first rough cut of *The Best Man,* a movie which had been inspired in part by the character of Jack."

Gore's novel, *Two Sisters,* was published in 1970. It failed to attract a wide audience, although many people who read it thought it was suggested by Jackie's relationship with Lee Radziwill. The book's character of Marietta Donegal was a devastating caricature of Anaïs Nin. "Despite my protests, Marietta Donegal revealed her not altogether fallen breasts," Gore wrote.

Over the years, it had been reported to Gore that Jackie had told people, "Actually, I don't know Gore Vidal, although, of course, I'm aware that he writes books, which unfortunately, I have not had a chance to read."

In October of 1975, as Gore turned fifty, he shared a chance encounter with Jackie at the Ritz Hotel in London. "Halfway down, the elevator stopped to admit another passenger, a woman in a white trench coat. Our eyes met in mute shock. It was Jackie Kennedy Onassis. Except for two or three occasions when we got together, our friendship never recovered from the night Bobby Kennedy ordered me from the White House in 1961. I did escort her to see Linda Lovelace in *Deep Throat,* but the evening didn't go well. After the screening, she complained of a headache and called off dinner."

In the Ritz elevator, I turned my back on her to discover in the mirror a smudge of ink on my brow. As I used a handkerchief to remove it, the lift opened. In her best Marilyn Monroe voice, she said, 'Bye bye,' and vanished into Piccadilly, where she was mobbed."

Gore's final word on Jackie: "I will forever remember her boyish beauty and the life-enhancing malice that were a great joy to me."

In this 1961 photo, at the insistence of Jackie, **JFK** *(left)* and
Gore Vidal *(center)* attended a horse show, even though
Jackie *(right)* knew her husband was allergic to horses. While
she took in the show, Jack, seething at being there, indulged in
indiscreet gossip behind her back.

Chapter Six

"The Resident White House Queer"
Lem Billings

"The First Friend" Quietly Moves into 1600 Pennsylvania Avenue

Much of the world was at war when this picture of a carefree young **Jack Kennedy** with his constant companion, **Lem Billings** *(right)* was taken in 1940. The setting was the Kennedy compound at Palm Beach. A World War would soon separate the "inseparable companions," who had remained in each other's orbit since 1933.

In snowbound New England, **Lem** straddles his buddy **Jack** for a romp in the snow. Most teen friendships fade with the passing of school semesters, but the bond between these two young men would last "until death do us part."

When Jackie Bouvier started dating John F. Kennedy,

it was inevitable that she'd soon meet Pennsylvania-born Kirk LeMoyne Billings, affectionately known for decades within the Kennedy family as "Lem."

Jack referred to him as "Lemmer," "Leem," or "Moynie." Lem often called his beloved friend either "Ken" or "Kenado-sus."

It is said that Lem fell in love with JFK as they showered together in the Connecticut-based Choate School for Boys in 1933. The bond they formed that year at prep school lasted a lifetime. Jackie once said, "The love between those two lasted even beyond the assassination in Dallas."

As David Michaelis in his book, *Best of Friends,* wrote: "For Lem, Jack was the best thing about life at school. Jack knew how to create the kind of fun that lightened the mood of everyone around him,. His innate gaiety and zest for living challenged even the most caustic, passive members of his class. His high spirits were contagious. For Kennedy, Billings was more than just a partner in school crimes. He was the first intimate friend Kennedy had found outside his family. Lem's passionate readiness to experience the world enhanced Kennedy's cool curiosity. In Billings, Kennedy had a unique ally."

From the very beginning, Lem seemed to want to make Jack his lover. But Jack, at least initially, turned down his sexual advances. However, he did not turn down the offer of friendship.

Friends claimed that Lem had been in love with Jack all his life. On the other hand,

On a summer vacation in 1937, **Jack Kennedy** *(left)* toured Europe with his "best friend for life," **Lem Billings**, his roommate at prep school. Lem was a homosexual in love with Jack.

In France, Lem proposed to Jack that they become "lovers for always" and live together after graduation, but Jack told him, "I'm hopelessly hetero-sexual."

Jack was "in love with Lem being in love with him." Every night at school, Lem even polished Jack's shoes.

As biographer Mart Martin noted, JFK "was the frequent recipient of non-

"Lem Billings is Jack's Other Wife"

—Robert Kennedy

"If you love Jack, you've got to love Lem, too. It's a package deal."

—Jackie

"Of the nine or ten men who were close to the President, I would say that Lem was Number One."

—Eunice Kennedy Shriver

reciprocal fellatio from Lem." But whenever a woman was available, the over-sexed JFK dumped Lem and pursued whichever female he could conquer.

At Hyannis Port, Joe Kennedy didn't like Lem when he arrived for the summer, but he did tolerate him. "He showed up with a battered suitcase and stayed forever." Joe asked Jack, "Oh, my God, must you bring this queen?"

Jack seemed determined, so Joe gave in. When he was in the movie business in Hollywood, Joe had gotten used to being around homosexuals.

"Jack is liable to go and knock up some girl," Joe said, "and then we'll be in the shithouse. You know, the Cardinal preaches against abortion. At least Lem gives Jack some relief. As for Lem, I don't know what he does for relief, and I don't much care. He at least keeps my boy under control."

Lawrence Quirk, in *The Kennedys in Hollywood,* wrote:

"Joe did not want Jack impregnating any of the girls he dated, and he was of the old-fashioned school that held that masturbation was sexually waste-ful, so if Jack allowed Lem to pleasure him, worse things could conceiv-ably happen to anyone as undisciplined, rowdy, tomfoolery-perpetrating, and cynical as Jack was during his teen years and indeed into his twenties."

At one point, Ralph (Rip) Horton was assigned to room with Jack and Lem at Choate, although Lem resented the presence of a third party because he wanted to be alone with Jack. Although Lem tried to keep his love for Jack a secret, it soon became obvious to Horton.

Horton was interviewed by Nigel Hamilton for his book, *JFK's Reckless Youth.* "In Lem, Jack found a slave for life. It was amazing how Lem was abused. He did Jack's laundry. Late at night, he'd run out in the cold weather to buy a pizza. Jack's back was always hurting, and Lem became his unpaid masseur, a job he relished."

While at Choate, Jack and Lem were still virgins, at least with women. Then one day Jack heard through Horton about a whorehouse in New York City's Harlem, where each of them could get laid for only three dollars. Lem was reluctant to join Jack on this quest, but ultimately, Jack persuaded him to go.

First the madam of the whorehouse showed them porno films "to get them in the mood."

For some reason, Jack insisted that both he and Lem should lose their virginity to the same prostitute. Jack went first. Always a quick man on the draw, he was back in only ten minutes.

Lem followed him and gave the prostitute three dollars. But he had another way of getting off. He later confessed in a book proposal he circulated after JFK's death that, "I closed my eyes, thought of Jack, and jerked off."

After that session, Jack became infected with gonor-

Peek-a-Boo!
Guess Who?

rhea, a disease that plagued him for years, according to historian Robert Dallek, who wrote *An Unfinished Life, John F. Kennedy 1917-1963.* JFK managed to get a doctor to supply him with creams and lotions, but because of his rampant promiscuity, he carried some sort of venereal infection for the rest of his life

[JFK, according to doctor's reports, never got rid of venereal disease, because his Addison's disease seemed to fight against the huge doses of antibiotics that he repeatedly ingested. And because of his rampant promiscuity, he constantly re-infected himself. No evidence exists that he told any of his array of sexual partners that he was infected, and, in many cases, he may have infected his partners. He did confess to Jackie about his diseases during their honeymoon.]

***

Over the years, when they were separated, JFK wrote Lem almost pornographic descriptions of his sexual exploits. Sometimes, he also revealed the most embarrassing medical details, as when he wrote to Lem from his hospital bed in London:

> *"Today was the most embarrassing, as a doctor came in just after I had woken up and was reclining with a semi-erection. His plan was to stick his finger under my pickle and have me cough. His plan quickly changed when he drew back the covers and there was JJ. Maher quivering with life."*

Lem and Jack had jointly nicknamed his penis "JJ. Maher." JFK frequently used that reference in subsequent letters to Lem over the years.

In July of 1937, during vacation from their respective studies, Lem experienced the most intimate and romantic period with Jack that he'd ever known or would ever know again. That summer, they went on a tour of Europe together. Jack paid half of Lem's fare but claimed that he expected the money back after Lem graduated from Princeton. Joe agreed to pay for the transport of Jack's Ford convertible as extra baggage aboard the same ship that carried

Lem Billings *(left)* is seen here relaxing on a chaise longue in Palm Beach with his pal, **Jack Kennedy,** during the winter of 1937. Mother Rose Kennedy liked Lem and thanked him for looking after her son and being so protective of him.

Even though Jack loved Lem, he constantly mocked him. After these photo-booth pictures were taken, **Jack** studied them and called **Lem** *'Pithecanthropus Erectus"* (the walking Ape Man), a jab about Lem's high forehead and his clumsiness, including his "simian walk."

them to Le Havre in France, so they could jointly and conveniently tour Europe together. Since Lem had little money, Jack agreed to stay with him in cramped lodgings throughout the course of their trip, usually in rooms without plumbing. "We ate frightful food and slept for forty cents a night."

Before he'd left for Europe, Joe had encouraged Jack to "get laid as often as possible." Jack later claimed, "I can't get to sleep unless I've gotten off. If I go for twenty-four hours without an orgasm, I suffer these crippling migraine headaches." Fortunately, Lem was there night after night to provide relief.

Years later, Lem revealed in a book proposal that whatever hotel they'd checked into would often assign them a single bed, "and I got to hold Jack in my arms all night. It was wonderful. He was very horny, and I took full advantage."

Lem cried when they returned to the States on September 16, 1937. "I was so sorry that the trip was over. I knew in my heart I'd never have Jack all to myself like that ever again."

Jack and Lem endured long separations during the war. After the Japanese attack on Pearl Harbor, both Lem and Jack tried to enlist, but both were at first rejected, Lem because of poor eyesight, Jack because of his chronically bad health. In 1942, Lem joined the Ambulance Corps, which didn't care about his bad eyesight, and saw action in North Africa. Later, through his receipt of a commission in the U.S. Naval Reserve, he got involved in wartime maneuvers in the South Pacific.

Jack was too sickly to qualify for active duty, but he demanded that Joe use his influence to get him into the Navy. He, too, served in the South Pacific, and was commanding his PT 109 torpedo boat when

Lem *(left)* hoists a very young **Teddy Kennedy** with some help from Ted's older brother, **Jack** *(right)*.

a Japanese destroyer split it apart. His heroic rescue of his crew later was used for political advantage when he ran for Congress after the War.

Honorably discharged in 1946, Lem went on to attend Harvard Business School. After his graduation, he held a variety of jobs, including a stint as an executive at Lennen & Newell, a Manhattan-based advertising firm. He invented the 1950s candy drink, "Fizzies," for the company, adding fruit flavor to disguise the sodium citrate taste

(Left to right) **Jack, Teddy, and Lem** were snapped in 1958 at Teddy's wedding. He's examining a wedding gift from one of his ushers, and seems gleeful to have it.

of Bromo Seltzer.

Lem continued in his devotion to Jack, although it was painful to watch him making love to a series of young women. Lem could only dream that Jack's lovemaking be directed at him.

But Jack never deserted Lem, and reserved time every week for them to get together. Their lovemaking became a ritual. Jack would strip completely naked for one of Lem's prolonged massages, which always led to a sexual climax on Jack's part. Lem later told Truman Capote that he "got off by going into the bathroom and jerking off with Jack's semen still in my mouth. At my climax, I swallowed his offering."

Truman Capote later claimed that "Lem at Studio 54 was always bragging about fellating Kennedy in Lincoln's Bedroom."

***

When Jack started dating Jacqueline Bouvier, Lem tried to discourage her from marrying him. He presented a barrage of reasons why Jack would not make a suitable husband. "You're a horsewoman," he told her. "Jack is allergic to horses. He has more allergies than he can count. He breaks out in skin rashes, and some gland on his body is always swollen, often in his throat. He suffers coughing fits and sneezing spasms at the least whiff of dust. He's got a weak stomach—just bland foods, nothing spicy. Spicy dishes make him vomit."

"He wants only milk and butter dishes, demanding New England clam chowder at least twice a day. He drinks three creamy chocolate malts a day. He likes hot chocolate with lots of sugar for breakfast, throughout the day, and at dinner. He consumes a mountain of calories, yet remains a skeleton."

"He's got this asthmatic condition that comes and goes, mostly comes," Lem claimed. "There's something far worse than that. I'm reluctant to tell you. He's had venereal diseases that doctors can't fully cure, and he has to take daily injections. "I think he's infected several women. His doctors told me that if a woman contracts what he has, she might never have children—perhaps a miscarriage. Bobby claims that if a mosquito bites Jack, the insect will die immediately from blood poisoning."

"Jack constantly has high fevers and often experiences these awful seizures where he just collapses on the floor and has to be carried to bed. Sometimes, he just seems to lose it and goes bonkers, running nude out of his bedroom and screaming into the night. Bobby and Teddy, or a house ser-

Dysfunctional trio? Prior to his marriage to **Jackie**, **JFK** (left) looks on as **Lem Billings** hugs his bride-to-be. Although he would always resent the presence of Jackie, Lem on the surface pretended he adored her.

vant, often have to restrain him and carry him back to bed, where sometimes, he has to be tied down."

Jackie not only had Lem to cope with, but also Langdon Marvin, who had been JFK's schoolmate at Harvard. The godson of President Franklin D. Roosevelt, Langdon was sophisticated, witty, and an accomplished athlete, a so-called macho man. He had worked for JFK when he'd run for Congress and was one of his most loyal supporters. Jackie had heard rumors that Langdon procured beautiful young women who were willing to go to bed with her future husband.

Within a short time, Jackie came to realize that both Lem and Langdon were closeted homosexuals, and she suspected that both of them were in love with JFK. A heavy drinker, Langdon one drunken night cornered Jackie at a party. In a bitchy mood, he told her, "The only reason Jack is marrying you is because people are starting to call him a fairy. In this country, if you're not married when you're approaching 40, you're suspect."

She was not startled by his claim, as she'd already heard it from other sources, too.

He also told her the truth about JFK's injured back. "We made up that story that his back injury came from a football mishap at Harvard. We were covering up the fact that he was born with a congenital malformation of his spinal column. He's been a sort of invalid all his life. That's a dark secret that could prove deadly for a career in politics."

"There are some things you might need to know if you're serious about going through with this ridiculous marriage," Langdon told her. "Morning after morning, I've watched him emerge from the bathroom before beginning his daily dress-up ritual. I've often dressed him myself."

"If you haven't already discovered it, he wears an eight-inch wide cloth brace. Not only that, he wears a corset like a woman. His left leg is shorter than his right, and he has to have special shoes made with an orthopedic lift. Honey, you'd be marrying a mess. My advice is, don't do it. If you're looking for a rich beau, why not Nelson Rockefeller? He's handsome and he's rich. I once showered with him in the locker room of a private club. Baby, there's meat there for the poor."

Langdon then confided another morbid secret. "Jack believes he will not live beyond forty. So he takes his pleasure while his candle still burns. That includes lots of women. As he told me, 'I need to get it while the getting's good.' He also claimed that even if he marries, he'll continue to chase after what he calls 'poon.' After

At the Alaska State Fair, **JFK** is seen in this rare picture taken of him campaigning for the presidential elections with his ever-faithful companion, **Langdon Marvin.**

Lem and Marvin competed for attention from JFK, and both of them had opposed his marriage to Jackie. She accused both of them of "wanting Jack for yourselves."

131

all,' he said, 'JJ. Maher has to be satisfied."

"Who in hell is JJ. Maher?" she asked.

"I don't think you're being honest with me," he said. "Surely, knowing Jack, you've met JJ. Maher. Some gals know him for only twenty minutes before he introduces them to JJ."

"Oh, I see."

Langdon had yet another revelation. "Get used to seeing him shooting some mysterious drug into his thighs. I've seen him get dressed hundreds of times. Right in front of me, he shoots that mysterious liquid into his veins."

Later, Jackie told Ted Sorensen, "I discounted half of what Langdon and Lem told me, although some of it may be true. I'll find out, I'm sure. They're not exactly impartial. Frankly, I think either of them would like to be Jack's bride if such a marriage were possible."

When he realized that JFK's marriage to Jackie was inevitable, Lem said, "Both of them came to understand that they were alike, at least in some respects. They had taken rather bad circumstances at birth and made the most of themselves, at least as best as they could. Even their names, Jack and Jackie, are similar. Two halves of a single wheel. They are actors who constantly applaud each other's performance."

Finally, Jackie decided not to allow herself to be swayed by the jealousy of either Lem or Langdon. In 1953, she married the relatively young senator. At the wedding, Bobby was overheard saying to Eunice, "Now Jack has a second wife." He was no doubt cynically referring to Lem as the first one.

***

Fresh from his honeymoon in Mexico, JFK confided to both Langdon and Lem that he had also seduced other women during the trip, continuing to do so when they landed in Los Angeles and later in San Francisco.

"Jackie was new to marriage, and perhaps she thought Jack would settle down after marrying her," Lem said. "Even back in Washington, and I saw this on many a night, she couldn't understand how he would dare disappear from a party with some pretty young thing and leave her humiliated and stranded. You can't say I didn't warn her. I love Jack more than I will ever love anyone, but I have to admit he's a rake. He really doesn't have much sensitivity when it comes to understanding women."

"I knew that Jack and Jackie had similar interests that drew them together, but when I had lunch with Jackie after the marriage, I began to realize that it was their differences that were pulling them apart," Lem claimed. "Almost immediately after marrying him, she became the neglected wife. Jack had many interests and many people in his life. Back in 1933, I tried to monopolize him, but I soon realized how stupid that was."

"I felt that both Jack and Jackie were withdrawn, bitter people, who had become disillusioned by life. Jack covered his disillusionment far better than Jackie, who was a woman of dark moods. You never knew where you stood with that one."

"Jackie told me that she never wanted to confront Jack about his adultery or how he tormented her. As for Jack, he was glad she didn't. He detested confrontation. Both of them constructed a façade to hide his womanizing and family strife. She once told me, 'Jack and I are like icebergs—the public life above water, but the far deeper block of ice submerged.'"

Months later, when Jackie suffered a miscarriage, Lem blamed it on her anguish over Jack's constant womanizing." I visited her several times after her miscarriage. She was morbid and depressed. I asked her where Jack was."

"On the road, I guess," she told him. "I haven't heard from him in three days."

As regards JFK's political career, Lem campaigned vigorously for the man he loved, helping him win both the Wisconsin and West Virginia primaries in 1960. He was also instrumental at the Democratic Convention in luring delegates away from Lyndon B. Johnson.

Beginning in 1961, after Jack became President, Lem was a permanent fixture at the White House, advising Jackie about redecorating, and JFK about how to deal with Russia. He was assigned a permanent bedroom on site.

At the White House, the staff referred to Lem as "First Friend." As Jackie recalled to Democratic Senator George Smathers (Florida), "Just one weekend in my life, I'd like to have my husband to myself, but Lem is always there, bathing and massaging him, even putting on his shoes and socks."

"I never had to have a pass to get into the White House," Lem recalled. "All of the Secret Service men knew who I was."

Some people resented Lem's presence within the White House. That deeply cynical and always provocative distant relative of Jackie's, author Gore Vidal, referred to Lem as "the resident queer."

Historian Herbert S. Parmet claimed, "Lem subordinated his own life to his friend. Members of the President's staff thought of him as a handy old piece of furniture."

Even members of the press learned about Jack's homosexual liaison with Lem, but never printed any stories about it during JFK's presidency. Prior to the late 1960s, homosexuality in print was the love that dared not speak its name. Jack was also protected because the press almost never ran stories about his extramarital affairs.

It was painful and humiliating

Lem Billings was a knave, a courtier, and the court jester during the reincarnation of Camelot. Here, he's seen on the lawn of the White House in 1961. The Secret Service nicknamed him, "First Friend."

for Lem, but Jack forced him to arrange liaisons for him with some of the world's most alluring women. Lem was also assigned the often unpleasant task of getting rid of a woman after Jack was finished with her. Lem didn't try to get rid of Marilyn Monroe. The stakes associated with that particular affair were so high that Jack entrusted the task to his chief troubleshooter, Bobby.

Charlie Bartlett, a Washington correspondent for the *Chattanooga Times*, recalled, "It was a tense time in the Cold War. If the Russians had found out that the President's best friend was a homosexual, it would have been valuable information to them."

Vidal said, "I think Jack felt quite comfortable in the company of homosexuals as long as they were smart enough to hold his interest."

No one questioned Lem's fanatical loyalty to JFK, but friends were often critical of the relationship. Senator Smathers found Lem "childish_and emotionally demanding of JFK. Lem was very jealous, and would throw a hissy fit if he felt that Jack was not paying him enough attention. Lem would almost demand that Jack stop running the country and spend time with him."

"On the other hand, as people betrayed Jack and took advantage of him, he knew he could always count on dependable Lem, even from the first day he moved into the White House," Smathers said.

"He even summoned Lem to take leave from his advertising job in New York and fly to Washington to help Jackie with her renovation of the White House. He had impeccable taste and even advised her on antiques and how to secure them. Jack told me that Lem gave Jackie more self-confidence in her own judgment and helped her get rid of many of her insecurities. Incidentally, I was Jack's best straight friend, Lem his best gay pal."

After a heavy day of renovation in the White House, Lem and Jackie retired for drinks on the Truman Balcony. "It was here that we concluded that neither of us would ever have Jack all to ourselves," Lem recalled. "He needed far more friends than Jackie and me. He got something from everybody—Chuck Spalding, William Walton, Charlie Bartlett, and Ben Bradlee, even the 'Irish Mafia.'"

"He liked to talk over old times in the Navy with Red Fay and made him Under-Secretary of the Navy," Lem said. "Jack liked to pal around with Ray, although I didn't care for him. Sometimes, they would sneak out of the White House to see a movie in a Washington theater, which always pissed off Jackie and the Secret Service. I remember once, they slipped out to see Kirk Douglas in *Spartacus*. Jack wanted women for sex, of course, but he turned to men for companionship. I'm not his only friend who has claimed that."

In the beginning, Jackie had wanted to get rid of Lem, but over a period of months, she came to respect him, especially in his appreciation of the arts and for his knowledge of American antiques. Many of his suggestions for renovating the White House and its choice of furnishings came from him, even though she later took credit for them.

"There was no great love between them," Bartlett said. "They were rivals for Jack's love. Poor Lem was always the third person at what Jackie hoped would be an intimate dinner with her husband. Apparently, Lem never heard the expression, 'Three's a crowd,' but Jack insisted that Lem be there. I don't think Lem ever really liked Jackie, but he did come to respect her. He felt she was more a great mother than a wonderful wife. He thought she did a fine job with Caroline and John Jr."

Lem and Jackie had more in common about art, literature, music, poetry, antiques, and even exquisite food than did Jackie and Jack," Bartlett said. "They also had one incredible bond, and that was their mutual love of the President."

Jackie had told Bartlett that once JFK became President, she felt his need for Lem would fade. The opposite was true. In the White House, he needed his trusted friend more and more, as they mulled over the Soviet Union, the Cuban Missile Crisis, the increasingly troublesome Vietnam, and tensions in Berlin.

"Lem didn't actually make any decisions, or so I believe, but he provided the President with the best listening ear in the country," Bartlett said. "He knew Jack's mind better than anyone, and he was also intimately familiar with every inch of Jack's body, so to speak."

When JFK and Jackie escaped to their country home, Glen Ora, in Middleburg, Virginia, it was Jackie herself who'd invite Lem. She had a reason. JFK also expressed his boredom at staying there, complaining that there was nothing to do.

She wanted to go horseback riding through the countryside and felt guilty at leaving JFK alone with no one to talk to.

While she went riding, Lem endlessly amused Jack as he had since their school days. Jackie noted that Lem and JFK seemed to speak in code, since they had had a longer relationship with each other than Jack had had with any other friend, except his family. He often concealed from Rose, Joe, and Bobby some of his most notorious secret maneuvers.

Lem soon discovered that White House dinners alone with the First Couple weren't peaceful. He recalled their most brutal fight was after the President decided that it would look better if he, a wealthy man, turned over his $100,000 government salary to charity. Jackie protested, claiming that she needed the money for herself and for her children, especially for the provision of clothing. "It's not just to wear on my own back, but John and Caroline need so many things."

But JFK adamantly refused to change his mind about the salary.

After the assassination, Lem did not expect to hear from Jackie again. But she sometimes called him, wanting to talk about Jack. On occasion, she spoke of the assassination and how her life had changed.

She also shared her fear that JFK Jr. might "grow up to be a little faggot, without a strong male role model."

She claimed that one day, she was horrified when she heard her son refer to one of the Secret Service agents as "Daddy."

"I can't have that," she said.

"It's okay," Lem assured her. "He needs a strong male to look up to."

She exploded in rage. "How in hell would you know? You're gay! You don't know a god damn thing about raising a kid." Then she slammed down the phone.

But she called the next day and apologized. "It was just my anxiety talking. I sense something in my little boy. A rebellious streak. His ultimate role model may be what he hears about his father. I think he might grow up to be like Jack in many ways. Like his father, I doubt if he'll ever be faithful to any one woman, at least not for long."

***

Langdon Marvin continued to be intimately involved in JFK's life, although not as closely as Lem. He was a researcher and campaign aide, often described as a "legislative factotum"

He also continued as JFK's pimp, most notoriously supplying the presidential candidate with a hooker an hour or so before he faced Richard Nixon in the first debate in September of 1960. Langdon told Chuck Spalding and others, "I know the exact type Jack likes. Nine beautiful brunettes, followed by an occasional blonde, a sort of Marilyn Monroe clone."

Both Jack and Jackie were concerned with Langdon's notorious pickups in seedy bars in the slum side of Washington. On May 2, 1954, a party was given to celebrate Langdon's 35th birthday.

On that occasion, JFK escorted Jackie to the 1925 F Street Club, a Greek Revival building dating from 1849. *[Laura Gross, a once celebrated Washington hostess, had rented the historic home in the 1920s, entertaining the Washington elite. Until it closed in 1999, the F Street Club entertained not only JFK, but Richard Nixon, Jimmy Carter, Ronald Reagan, George H.W. Bush, Bill Clinton, Fidel Castro, and Nikita Khrushchev.]*

The party's guest of honor showed up with two bandages on his face and a slight limp. Jackie found out later that in a bar, he'd tried to pick up a soldier, who had beaten him severely.

Privately, at the party, she cornered him, suggesting that he should meet some nice young man and settle down. "Some night you're going to meet Mr. Wrong and then it'll be curtains for you. You've got to cut down on the booze. You're destroying yourself." Although he promised to heed her advice, he quickly resumed his dangerous pickups after his body healed from its bruises.

The party was attended by Jackie's stepfather, Hugh Auchincloss. He was deeply offended, not by Langdon, but by JFK himself.

Auchincloss later reported to Janet and others on JFK's behavior, claiming that he had outrageously flirted with Priscilla Johnson, a beautiful young woman who had been a political researcher for JFK.

"A lot of people thought I was a Jackie lookalike," Priscilla later revealed. "If that's what he wanted, the real thing, Jackie herself, was sitting right across from me, trying to divert her eyes from what was going on. I couldn't believe it. With his wife only a few feet away, and with a clear view, he was coming on to me."

JFK never altered his womanizing, and his friend, Langdon, continued his dangerous cruising and heavy drinking. After some drinks, he often made scenes at parties, and once, he struck Lem in the face, perhaps in a jealous rage.

"It was something to see," Gore Vidal claimed, "watching Lem and Langdon vie for the role of resident White House queer. Lem was in control. Langdon was not. On several occasions, JFK had to discipline him. When intoxicated, he often groped hunky members of the Secret Service, a real macho group."

"I never heard the complete story, although that little monster, Truman Capote, spread the scandal," Vidal said. "It was known that the President often got an erection while being massaged. Just ask Sinatra's African-American valet.":

"Apparently, if the bitchy menace, Miss Capote, is to be believed, one night in JFK's bedroom, Langdon was giving the President a massage. Apparently, he chose that moment to take advantage of the President's erection. Jack might have allowed Lem to do that, but he wasn't open to the idea of Langdon doing it."

"From what I heard, he had two members of the Secret Service remove Langdon from the White House. From then on, he was *persona non grata.*"

"I ran into Langdon at a Georgetown bar two months later," Vidal claimed. "He was furious. He had heard that Bobby had posted his picture in the guardhouse of the main gate to the White House, along with pictures of several others who also had been barred from entering the grounds ever again."

According to Vidal, Langdon was outraged. "Year after year, I broke my balls for Jack, and this is how I'm treated. My crime? One night I lost control and did what I've always wanted to do with him. I couldn't help myself. He should have understood that. He always knew how I felt about him."

"Apparently, he allows Lem to do the unspeakable, but he treated me like shit," Langdon claimed. "I should write a book and bring down his Presidency. I think Bobby was behind my getting kicked out. I just know Jack would have forgiven me. Bobby hates me. He always has. I also know plenty of dirt on him, too. I might ruin him if he ever tries to run for President himself."

According to Lem's biographer, author David Pitts: "For Lem, Jack's death in Dallas was the end of the world. It wasn't so much that he never got over it. He didn't want to get over it. By all accounts, it took months for him to resume even the appearance of a normal existence. He just couldn't let go of the man who had been the most important person in his life since he was seventeen years old. Consumed by his memories, he talked about Jack constantly to his friends, and especially to the younger generation of Kennedys for whom he was the repository of so much information about the president in his younger days. For Lem, it was as if John Kennedy was not completely gone. Almost everything he said and did for the rest of his days was somehow connected to Jack."

Since JFK didn't leave any money in his will for Lem, his loyal friend later found himself in dire financial condition. At one point, he approached biographer Lawrence (Larry) Quirk about writing a tell-all book.

Based partly on the discussions they shared regarding the publication of a biography about JFK, Lem developed an intimate relationship with Quirk. As stated by him, "Lem confided in me that theirs was a friendship that included oral sex, with Jack always on the receiving end. Lem believed that this arrangement enabled Jack to sustain his self-delusion that straight men who received oral sex from other males were really only straights looking for sexual release."

After careful thought, even a talk with Jackie, Lem decided to drop the idea. Jackie warned that such a book would not only destroy her friendship with him, but would alienate him forever from the Kennedy family.

After the loss of JFK in 1963, Lem drew very close, even intimately so, to Bobby Kennedy. Jackie felt that Lem was trying to replace Jack with Bobby, as she was doing herself.

Since 1934 Bobby and Lem had always been friends. Drawn together by their mutual sorrow, Lem and Bobby bonded as never before in the years leading up to Bobby's run for presidency in 1968,

Bobby and Lem even took vacations together as they did in 1967 at Waterville, New Hampshire. The year before, at the exclusive Lyford Cay in The Bahamas, they were seen together "in and out of their swimming suits."

A maid found them sleeping together in the nude, but Lem never commented on whether his relationship turned sexual or not. He did say, however, that "Bobby is our best hope for resurrecting Camelot."

Then, according to those who knew him, Lem "went to pieces in the worst way" after Bobby, too, was assassinated in 1968.

In the wake of his father's assassination in 1968, Lem became like a second father to Robert Kennedy, Jr. They were seen together during a trip he took with the boy to Egypt in 1968.

As author David Pitts put it, "They hacked their way through the Columbian bush with machetes, rode llamas across Latin America, confronted poachers in Kenya, sampled ranch life in Mozambique, and navigated a previously unexplored Peruvian River."

"David Kennedy and Christopher Lawford often went with them. "Bobby *[Junior, that is]* got a lot of magnetism from Lem's fixation on him," said Chris.

Somewhere along the way, Lem decided that Bobby Jr. (not JFK Jr.) was the next best shot for carrying the torch of Camelot.

Although he tried to become a surrogate fa-

After JFK's assassination in Dallas, **Lem Billings** seemed to shift his affections to **Bobby Kennedy** *(right)*. Once again, Jackie found herself competing with Lem for the love of a Kennedy brother.

ther to the children of RFK, Lem made all the wrong moves. He turned his apartment into a "candy store" of illegal drugs, with ongoing inventories of pot, cocaine, hash, LSD, even the more dangerous heroin. After 1968, according to Quirk, during the peak of flower power and its socially violent aftermaths, he often plied Robert Kennedy, Jr. and Christopher Lawford (son of Peter Lawford and Patricia Kennedy) with drugs and became a dedicated user himself.

After RFK's assassination, according to Quirk, "These boys developed severe drug habits. Instead of firmly helping them to combat their addictions, Lem joined them and became as big an addict as they were."

Perhaps Bobby Jr. was the second man Lem truly loved. Lem was devoted to him, and they traveled the world together, most visibly in trips to exotic and obscure corners of South America. Through young Bobby, Lem was perhaps reliving some of his school days with Jack. The bedroom next to Lem's in his apartment on the Upper East Side of Manhattan was always referred to as "Bobby's room."

***

John Kennedy was away in Palm Beach with Lem Billings when JFK Jr.— soon to be called "John-John,"—entered the world prematurely, on November 25, 1960, at Georgetown University Hospital, weighing little more than six pounds.

Hearing that John Jr. had been born, Jack and Lem flew back to Washington. John-John was too young and Jackie was too protective of her boy to allow him to spend much time with Lem. Her friend, author Truman Capote, called it "Jackie's homosexual panic."

On occasion, Lem was allowed to take the beautiful, long-haired boy on an outing, such as when they visited Warner Brothers' Jungle Habitat Wildlife Preserve in West Milford, New Jersey, in 1972.

But when Jackie feared that Lem was taking far too much of a sexual interest in John-John, she cut off the relationship.

***

Lem lived to see New York City's Stonewall Riots of 1969 and the advent of the gay revolution, but he never participated. He remained in the closet all his life, and ultimately, he refused to be associated with any book about the Kennedys wherein a publisher would insist that he preview the sexual aspects of his relationships. "I couldn't do that to Jack," Lem said to the literary agent Jay Garon, who politely informed him that without revelations of his sexual relationship with JFK, he could not get "a super advance." Garon, perhaps accurately, feared that without the description of sex, the memoirs would evolve into "just another one of those thousands upon thousands of 'friendship with the Kennedys' books."

Upon his death in 1981, Lem's will specified that his cooperative apartment at 5 East 88th Street in Manhattan be left to RFK Jr. A New York realtor, called in to evaluate its worth, found it piled high, almost to the ceiling, with old newspapers and magazines. He later reported that he also discovered an arsenal of drug paraphernalia. Surprisingly he found scattered human feces on the floors and carpets. Insiders surmised they resulted from Lem's drug and alcohol abuse during his final days.

It was appropriate that Bobby Jr. be designated as the mourner who would deliver Lem's eulogy, and part of it stated, "He felt pain for every one of us, pain that no one else could have the courage to feel. I don't know how we'll carry on without him. In many ways, Lem was a father to me and he was the best friend I will ever have."

Eunice Kennedy Shriver ended the funeral by saying, "I'm sure the good Lord knows that Heaven is Jesus, Lem, Jack, and Bobby loving one another."

Rose Kennedy had a slightly different interpretation after hearing news of Lem's death. "The Good Lord has summoned Lem to Heaven to look after his beloved Jack."

A Merry Christmas

| Rip. | Leem. | Ken. |

In 1935, three "roomies" at Princeton, **Ralph** (Rip) **Horton**, **Lem Billings** (center, identified here as "Leem"), and **JFK** (identified here as "Ken") sent out a joint Christmas card to friends and family. They posed sharing only one tuxedo, with Horton getting the top hat, Lem a giant white bow tie, and Jack the jacket.

The card read, "We're puttin' on our top hats, tyin' up our white tie, and brushin' off our tails."

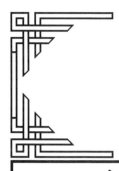

Chapter Seven

Jackie's Road
to the White House

At the Los Angeles Democratic Convention, Marilyn Defines JFK as "Very Penetrating"

Three Kennedys, **Rose** *(left)*, **Jackie** *(center)*, and **John F. Kennedy**, greeted the world on Election Day in November of 1960. Shortly after it was announced that Richard Nixon had been just barely defeated. JFK flew to Palm Beach, where news reached him that his pregnant wife had begun hemorrhaging. The President-Elect returned at once to Washington.

It was a difficult birth. The boy who was later known as "John-John" had emerged into the world prematurely.

Overheard at a Washington reception:

ACTOR RONALD REAGAN: *"Good to see you, Jack—it's been a long time. I hope old Joe is okay. People in Washington tell me you plan to run for President. I'm sort of interested in that job myself."*

SENATOR JOHN F. KENNEDY: *"Unlike you, Ronnie boy, I not only want to be President, I WILL be President!"*

141

In 1960, Jack and Jackie became the most photographed couple in American history.

On January 20, 1960, in the U.S. Senate Caucus Room, JFK declared his run for the presidency. His announcement came as no surprise to the politically savvy.

Jackie falsely assumed that after he announced his bid for the presidency, that his philandering would at least be put on hold until Election Day. She figured that if he made it all the way to the White House, his every action would be under a microscope, and that it wouldn't be possible for him to commit adultery.

Up until then, Frank Sinatra and Peter Lawford had kept him supplied with a bevy of beauties, especially at parties in Las Vegas and Palm Springs.

J. Edgar Hoover's F.B.I. files on JFK had ballooned into several volumes, documenting liaisons which included sexual links with two mulatto hookers in Manhattan and a battalion of showgirls.

The perfect wife of the better candidate poses for *Life's* pre-election- puff piece for the edition of August 24, 1959

He had made at least two trips to pre-Castro Havana to resume his affair with Florence Pritchett Smith, the wife of the aging Earl T. Smith, still the U.S. Ambassador to Cuba.

But even after his announcement to the Senate, JFK added to his list of movie star seductions, picking up glamorous additions who included Sophia Loren, Jean Simmons, and Lee Remick. In Washington, he carried on affairs with both Pamela Turnure and Mary Pinchot Meyer. *[They happened to be roommates.]* Meyer was the beautiful, rebellious, and socially adept ex-wife of a top CIA official.

Even such a womanizer as "Gorgeous George" Smathers warned JFK that he'd better taper off on his "poon-tailing it."

JFK responded, "The American voter doesn't care how many times I get laid."

When he wasn't talking about women to his pals, JFK at Hyannis Port discussed nothing but politics.

As was made clear to Jackie, it was Joe Kennedy, not her husband, who

JFK Pursues Socialites, Strippers, and Sam Giancana's Gun Moll.

was orchestrating the primary campaign. "We're going to sell Jack like corn-flakes," he told her. "However, I'm too controversial. I've got to pull the strings for my puppet." Privately, she was enraged that he referred to Jack as a puppet. Did he plan to run the country if Jack were elected?

Frank Sinatra was an early supporter, flying with Peter Lawford, whom he'd nicknamed "Brother-in- Lawford," to Palm Beach to confer with JFK and Joe. In honor of the candidate, Sinatra even changed the name of his "Rat Pack" to "the Jack Pack."

In Florida, Joe received Lawford and Sinatra in a screened-off area beside his swimming pool, where he lay completely nude on a chaise longue. When they approached him, he was barking orders by phone to Chicago. It appeared that he had "bought" the endorsement and support of Chicago Mayor Richard Daley.

Joe wanted to employ Sinatra as a major-league fundraiser for members of the Hollywood elite. As for his son-in-law, he ordered Lawford to "Keep your god damn mother's mouth shut."

Senator **George Smathers**, known as "Gorgeous George," in his youth, was one of JFK's closest comrades during their "sex hunts" together, even showing up in pre-Castro Havana.

[He was referring to the abrasive and outspoken Lady May Lawford. She'd told columnist Walter Winchell that her daughter-in-law, Patricia Kennedy Lawford, "was a bitch, a real bitch. She has millions, but lets Peter pay all their bills."

Lawford was unsuccessful in persuading Lady May to remain quiet. When JFK flew into Los Angeles for a campaign rally, she rented an elephant and paraded it down Wilshire Boulevard with a large sign, urging voters to support JFK's nemesis, Richard Nixon.]

After he returned to Hollywood from Palm Beach, the first campaign contribution Sinatra sent to Joe was for $25,000 from Marilyn Monroe. More checks from other movie stars would soon follow.

As for Jackie, during the campaign, her private life seemed to have been put into storage. Wherever she went, everybody seemed to be either talking about or working for JFK's campaign.

She witnessed how much her husband depended on Theodore C. Sorensen, who everybody called Ted. The tall, dark, Nebraska-born speechwriter was only slightly older than Jackie, but JFK defined him as "my intellectual blood bank."

Bobby was the campaign's manager and Steve Smith *[JFK's brother-in-law because of Smith's marriage to JFK's sister, Jean]* was in charge of the cam-

Pierre Salinger, press secretary to JFK, warned both Jackie and the President that the injections they were receiving from Dr. Feelgood (Max Jacobson) might be discovered by the press.

paign's logistics and financing.

Jackie got along with Pierre Salinger, the campaign's press secretary. He was of French descent, a *bon viveur*, a gifted pianist, and a war veteran.

Key foreign staffers, along with JFK and Jackie, flew aboard the *Caroline,* a 10-passenger DC-3, a gift from Joe Kennedy. It had been configured with a curtained-off area for sleeping, a small dining area, reclining chairs, and a galley that always had a supply of JFK's favorite food—creamy New England clam chowder with lots of butter.

The airplane became the nerve center of Jack's campaign, where he constantly huddled with "the Irish Mafia," David Powers and Kenneth O'Donnell. While they talked of nothing but politics, Jackie retreated to the back of the plane, where she read the novels of the Beat Generation's Jack Kerouac. *On the Road* was her favorite.

Aboard the *Caroline,* when Jackie wasn't there, the lone stewardess, Janet Des Rosiers, massaged JFK's neck and combed his hair.

JFK's road to the White House was paved with bruising primaries in which Jackie participated in 1959 and during the early part of 1960. Either separately or by JFK's side, she showed up at rallies in New Hampshire, California, and Ohio, concentrating at the beginning mostly on Wisconsin and West Virginia. There were side trips to New Jersey and Rhode Island. The tiniest state was the one most familiar to her because of her deeply entrenched ties to Newport.

The primary in New Hampshire was easily won by JFK, partly because he was from the neighboring state of Massachusetts. The Democrats in New Hampshire interpreted JFK as "one of our own."

But snow-covered Wisconsin and especially coal-mining West Virginia were on the horizon, and at least in the beginning, considerably less welcoming.

The days and nights on the campaign trail became a big blur for Jackie. Sometimes, she

Pete Dye, the famous golfer, lived next door to **Peter Lawford** *(depicted above),* JFK's brother-in-law, in Santa Monica. "It was nothing but *La Dolce Vita,* a goddamn whorehouse when the president came to visit," Dye claimed. "He even hustled my wife and wanted to fly her to Hawaii."

Part of JFK's "Irish Mafia," **Kenneth O'Donnell's** official title was White House Appointments Secretary, but he was the President's political right hand—"troubleshooter, expediter, and devil's advocate." He was known for being blunt. When the President, in his view, steered off course, O'Donnell would say, "Jack, you're full of crap on this one!"

could hardly remember what state she was visiting. "One day," she recalled, "we touched down in seven cities or towns. It's amazing how I survived. Even with all his back pain, Jack seemed to have more stamina that any of us, arising at six in the morning and still shaking hands in some dirty convention hall after midnight. It's amazing we didn't die in a plane crash. He ordered the pilot to fly through thunder and lightning, through hailstorms and blizzards, even piercing Jack the Ripper, London-type fogs."

Ben Bradlee, who joined the campaign on occasion, noticed that "Jackie seemed to pull some invisible shade across her lovely face. She was physically present, but her spirit was somewhere far, far away."

Salinger defined it differently: "Jackie breathes all the political gas in the air, but doesn't inhale."

In March of 1960, JFK was scheduled to fly from Wisconsin back to Washington to face a crucial vote on civil rights legislation before the Senate. By that point, he trusted Jackie enough to make her the star of his campaign, and even, when necessary, to campaign without him. During his absence, brother Teddy agreed to migrate to Jackie's side as they traveled from small town to small town, giving speeches.

It was never proven, but apparently, Teddy, during the campaign, confessed to Jackie that he'd always been in love with her ever since that day she'd arrived on JFK's arm at Hyannis Port.

Apparently, she held him at bay, perhaps suspecting that she would not always be able to control his amorous yearnings.

Still in the early stages of her pregnancy (with what turned out to be John-John), she campaigned with Teddy in snow-covered Wisconsin. Their major challenger was Senator Hubert Humphrey of nearby Minnesota, who was also seeking the Democratic nomination that year.

She was horrified to learn that the American electorate was polarizing into opposing Protestant and Catholic camps. She also felt that Humphrey was "shameless" in his appeal to Protestant voters. There was rampant speculation that if JFK were elected, he'd take his marching orders from the Pope, not from the electorate and the laws of the U.S. Constitution.

Teddy became less visible within the campaign after JFK returned to Wisconsin, having voted for the Civil Rights Legislation in Washington.

One rainy night at some truck stop outside Madison, Wisconsin, both Charles Bartlett and Jackie were stunned when JFK made an astonishing statement. "If the Democrats don't give me the nomination, I'm voting for Nixon."

The second member of JFK's Irish Mafia was **David Powers**, one of the President's favorite storytellers, baseball authorities, political statisticians, and traveling companions. He remained on LBJ's staff for a year after the assassination, then he directed, till 1994, the JFK Library.

When JFK won the Wisconsin primary, narrowly defeating Humphrey by only 106,500 votes, Teddy asserted that it was Jackie who had made the difference. The press differed with Teddy, citing the fact that a large percentage of Wisconsin voters were Catholic, like JFK.

Protestant West Virginia would be their most daunting challenge.

***

On February 7, 1960, taking time out from his hectic campaign schedule, JFK flew to Las Vegas to attend Frank Sinatra's opening at the Sands. While there, he began his second most dangerous romantic liaison, one almost as hazardous as his relationship with Marilyn Monroe.

Judith Campbell Exner at the peak of her allure

Judith Campbell (later, Exner) was so apolitical that when she had been introduced to JFK, she had never heard of him, unaware that he was a candidate for President of the United States. She only knew movie stars like Frank Sinatra or Peter Lawford. "I didn't even know he was married," she later said. "All I knew was that he was gorgeous. After one night of lovemaking, I fell for him."

Sam Giancana, Al Capone's replacement, shared a gun moll with the President of the United States.

As described by Sinatra's valet, George Jacobs, "Judy was the perfect Eisenhower era pinup of the girl next door. That she charged for her wholesomeness was beside the point. Judy would go on to infamy as the fourth corner of a triangle that included Sinatra, Chicago mob boss Sam Giancana, and JFK. But before his son took a bite off the poison apple, the father was there first. Talk about chips off the old block!"

In the late 1950s, when Joe Kennedy had visited Palm Springs, Sinatra had "paid for an expensive gift to him," Judith Campbell herself.

As Judith had matured, admirers defined her as "a little bit of Jackie Kennedy, a little bit of Elizabeth Taylor." She was married to a minor, alcoholic actor in Hollywood films, William Campbell, who was abusive to her.

Actually, through Joe's intervention with the mob, Giancana was helping Kennedy get elected, especially in the "swing state" of Illinois. He provided both union support and campaign money.

As the head of a crime empire, Giancana was held responsible for more than two hundred murders by the year JFK ran for President. He was Chicago's Mafia boss, a successor to Al Capone, dealing in everything from protection rackets to numbers games. Arrested more than seventy times, he had served time in prison, including three times for murder. Johnny Roselli, who represented the Chicago mob on the West Coast, was also involved in an affair with

Judith.

JFK was mesmerized by Judith. Under "ordinary" circumstances, it might have been a one-night stand, but it wasn't. He kept thinking of her. She was shocked on April 6, 1960, when he sent her a plane ticket and money to fly to Washington.

Instead of meeting her in some out-of-the-way hotel, he invited her to dinner at the townhouse he shared with Jackie in Georgetown.

"I learned that Jackie was away," Judith said. "We did it that night in the same bed where he slept with her."

"He told me that Jackie was no good at the oral stuff, and that he had to turn elsewhere for that. He also told me his greatest sexual fantasy was to go to bed with Shirley MacLaine and me at the same time. That never happened."

Judith was summoned again in July of 1960, during the Democratic Nominating Convention in Los Angeles, where his interest in three-ways was blossoming. He arranged a three-way with herself and Marilyn Monroe, Judith later claimed.

Before their coming together, JFK had ordered Sinatra to have Judith made up to look like Elizabeth Taylor. "Marilyn detests Elizabeth, and vice versa, so I know I'll never get those two into bed at the same time," JFK told Lawford. "At my little three way, Marilyn will be real, of course, but instead of Elizabeth, I'll have to settle for Judy, who's merely the mock."

"You'd think that I, America's sex symbol, would be enough for Jack, but he wanted a three-way," lamented **Marilyn Monroe** to her best girlfriend, model Jeanne Carmen.

In time, Judith would evolve into one of JFK's most notorious relationships, even inciting a warning from J. Edgar Hoover, who appeared in the Oval Office to reveal what he knew about this dangerous liaison to both JFK and Bobby.

Judith later admitted she delivered "gobs of money" from California "businessmen" to the Kennedys, and also carried $250,000 in cash from Washington to Giancana in Chicago.

During a period of eighteen months, between 1961 and 1962, she was the President's link to the Mob. In that capacity, she criss-

In a tense meeting, **J. Edgar Hoover** *(center)*, Director of the F.B.I., came to the Oval Office to warn his boss, Attorney General **Robert Kennedy** *(right)*, and **President Kennedy** about the dangers of further involvement with Sam Giancana's mistress, Judith Cambell.

crossed the nation, carrying messages from Washington to Florida, from Chicago to Los Angeles.

Judith also revealed that she carried payoffs, in cash, into the White House from California-based defense contractors wanting government business.

One night during dinner at the White House—Jackie was away, of course—JFK introduced Judith to Bobby. As she told columnist Liz Smith, "He squeezed my shoulder solicitously and asked me if I was OK carrying these messages from Jack and him to Chicago. 'Do you feel comfortable doing it?' Bobby asked me. I told him I did."

Her most memorable moments in the White House came that night after dinner when she retired with the President to his quarters. "Jack stripped down and got into bed, while I went to the bathroom to freshen up a bit. When I came back into the room, all the lights were turned off. I crawled into bed with Jack. To my surprise and shock I found it was Bobby in the bed with me. He was completely naked."

Judith, older, sadder, wiser, and more bitter, poses for a press photo from 1976, during pre-publication promotion of her book, *My Story*, published in 1977.

"I always thought Bobby was the cuter Kennedy, and I was only too glad to have sex with him too," she said. "As we were going at it, Jack, also nude, crawled into bed with us. After Bobby shifted my body to accommodate Jack, the president entered me from the rear. I became the meat in a Kennedy sandwich."

***

The death of Marilyn Monroe on August 5, 1963 had a profound effect on Judith. She feared that Marilyn had been wiped out by either the mob or by friends of the Kennedys, eager to see that they remained in power. "I became afraid for my life. I knew too much. I wanted out."

"When the President called me to come to the White House for another roll in the hay, I didn't let him know that I was leaving him," she said. "I arrived at the White House in the usual way. I don't think Jack suspected a thing."

"When we came together, I told him, 'I can't see you anymore—it's too painful, too dangerous.' Even when I told him that, he still wanted to be intimate with me for one final time. I was still in love with him, as much as that was possible, and it broke my heart to tell him goodbye. I never saw him again after that cold day in Washington."

After that final sexual encounter with JFK, she discovered she'd become pregnant. "Since I knew it was Jack's child, I called him at the White House, not knowing if he'd speak to me. He came to the phone right away."

"When I told Jack I was pregnant and wanted to have his child, he went ballistic," she said. "First he claimed our kid might belong to Sinatra—'Let Ol' Blue Eyes pay for it.' He also claimed that the child might belong to either Sam or Roselli. But the timing wasn't right. I knew he was the father. During sex together, he refused to wear a condom, claiming it deadened the sensation for him."

"I pleaded with him to let me have the child, but he insisted that I have an abortion," she said. "Both of us were devout Catholics, but he demanded I abort our baby. As I always did, I gave in to him."

Finally, JFK said, "Do you think Sam would help us?"

"I realized then I wasn't going to get help from him, and I called Sam. Unlike the President, he was very loving and caring and arranged for me to have the abortion at Chicago's Grant Hospital on January 28, 1963, even though such an operation was illegal. The President's kid was not to be."

The public did not know of the JFK/Judith Campbell link until more than a decade after the President was assassinated.

The goal of the Senate's Church Committee was to investigate the CIA's involvement with organized crime in its effort to have Fidel Castro assassinated.

To her shame and regret, Judith was called upon to testify. Word of her links with JFK and Sam Giancana had become widely discussed throughout Capitol Hill.

Judith appeared before the Church Committee in 1975 with her new husband, golfer Dan Exner, whom she'd married in April of that year.

It was then that Jackie began to learn the details of this bizarre relationship Judith had sustained with JFK. "I knew about Jack's affairs," she told her friends. "I made only one request. Don't humiliate me in public. Don't let an involvement with one of your prostitutes be exposed to the public. Now, with this Judith creature giving testimony of their affair, I felt humiliated. I'd dreaded for so very long that this day would come. Everyone had wanted to keep me in the dark, especially "Butch" and "Sundance" *[i.e., her nicknames for JFK's aides and confidants, Kenneth O'Donnell and David Powers].*

Judith's final words on JFK were spoken shortly before she died at the age of 65 on September 24, 1999, having suffered from breast cancer, and after years of furtively living in fearful anonymity. "I think the Camelot myth should be demystified," she said, "and the Kennedy legend examined for its reality."

***

On the campaign trail in 1960, Jackie dreaded going to West Virginia. To her, it was like a foreign country. She once claimed that the people of West Virginia were "fanatical Christians who handled poisonous snakes, coalminers, and moonshine-drinking rednecks."

Despite Joe's objections, JFK had entered his name into the West Virginia primary. West Virginia was a state that was ninety-five percent Protestant. Jackie became furious when columnist Joseph Alsop wrote, "Kennedy operatives are arriving in West Virginia with bags bulging with greenbacks."

Democratic officials in West Virginia feared that JFK and Jackie represented too much glitz and glamor "to meet the smell test with most West Virginians."

Eunice Kennedy urged the campaign not to allow Jackie a role in West Virginia. "Wait until those hillbillies get a look at this French-speaking, couture-clad, foxhunting gal with her little tiny voice."

"Jackie looked like a movie star, and JFK reminded me of a wealthy, Palm Beach playboy," said Keith Phillips, a campaign volunteer. "And there was that god damn Pope thing."

But as he campaigned in the state with Jackie, Phillips changed his mind. "The crowds seemed pleased with her, the men finding her hot, the women thinking she wore clothes like a princess. Muriel Humphrey was so downhome, she reminded me of a cow chewing her cud in the pasture. She didn't go over well. The public wanted Jackie's glamor, perhaps having tired of ugly Eleanor, 'Plain Jane' Bess, and drunken Mamie with those awful bangs."

Jackie had never been subjected to such close scrutiny from the press. "I felt my every move was being watched and reported on. I attracted a lot of female viewers, especially shoppers. I felt they were more interested in looking at what I was wearing than in Jack's message."

Laura Bergquist covered the Democratic Primaries in 1960 for the then popular *Look* magazine. She shared her somewhat negative appraisal with her readers. "Maybe it was the Irish Mick in JFK, but he neglected Jackie something awful. I don't think he took women seriously, as human beings you work with on a political campaign. I admired Jackie's intelligence, but he was just discovering the asset that she would ultimately become. It took him a while to realize just how valuable she was on the campaign trail. I think she survived all that powerful Kennedy clan by being very private and stubborn, carving out her own existence."

After a few grueling days, Jackie told the press that she'd begun to enjoy campaigning. That was not really true. She found the accommodations uncomfortable and not her style—"more suited for truck drivers sharing a communal shower," she lamented. The greasy food offended her delicate palate.

She said, "You shake hundreds of hands in the afternoon and hundreds more at night. You get so tired you catch yourself laughing and crying at the same time. But you pace yourself and get through it. You just look at it as something you have to do. You knew it would come, and you knew it was worth it."

When she was campaigning, she regretted spending so much time away from Caroline. "The official side of my life takes me away from my daughter a good deal," she said. "If I were to add political duties, I would have practically no time left with my child, with another on the way. My daughter and my soon-to-be-born baby are, of course, my first responsibility."

"I know it's going to be very difficult to raise two children in the middle of all this publicity and attention. I hope my children will be able to lead a normal life when Jack comes to live in the White House, which I know he will, because he's sure to win."

Privately, she told her staff, "This campaign has turned me into a piece of personal property. I don't want that for my children, either my daughter or my newborn. I don't want them to experience life like that."

She said, "I was shocked by the grinding poverty in West Virginia. It was my first exposure to the awful misery Appalachian families endured. The sight of hungry children was horrifying to me. I soon had to drop out, because of my pregnancy, but not before I witnessed a side of America I'd never seen before."

There were mishaps along the way. In an unguarded moment, a photographer snapped a picture of Jackie smoking a cigarette. When it was published, JFK was enraged. He had warned her not to smoke in public, and, in fact, he didn't want her to smoke at all, but she insisted.

On May 10, the day of the West Virginia primary election, Jack and Jackie had flown back to their home in Georgetown. He was despondent. "I'm going to lose the election because of my religion."

To cheer him up, she'd invited his friends, Toni and Ben Bradlee, for dinner.

All through the meal, JFK kept jumping up to call Bobby in Charleston for the latest results. Early returns did not look promising.

"Hoping to distract Jack, I suggested something silly, like going to a movie," Jackie said. "The Bradlees thought that was a good idea, and all of us convinced Jack to go."

As regards their choice of what film to see, JFK and Jackie wanted to see Elizabeth Taylor and Katharine Hepburn battle it out in *Suddenly Last Summer,* based on a play by Tennessee Williams. But when their quartet finally reached the movie theater, the film had already been playing for twenty minutes.

Impulsively, Jackie suggested that their foursome go to an X-rated movie house across the street for a screening of *Private Property,* the story of a slutty wife who seduced every delivery boy or repairman who comes into her home. Amazingly, on the eve of the West Virginia primary, JFK risked getting caught leaving a porno house.

By the time they returned to the Kennedy townhouse, the phone was ringing furiously. Bobby was on the line. "Big Bro!" he shouted. "You're the victor!"

Later that same evening, JFK and his wife boarded the *Caroline* to fly back to West Virginia. Jean Kennedy Smith, JFK's sister, went with them. Jackie remembered running into horrible weather. "At one point, we felt the plane was going to crash. Jean screamed for her husband."

Jackie later shared her memory of JFK's victory celebration in Charlestown with Gore Vidal. "I got a preview that night of how it was going to be during Jack's presidency. His campaign workers more or less shoved me aside. The night belonged to Jack. I ended up sitting in the back seat of our limousine all alone and crying until Jack was ready to fly back to Washington."

***

Next on their agenda was a visit to Louisiana as the guest of Earl Long, the flamboyant governor of Louisiana, who was engaged at the time in an affair with Blaze Starr, the stripper promoted by her managers as "the girl with the fabulous front."

Blaze Starr, who became a notorious stripper beginning in 1950, was born in 1932 as Fannie Belle Fleming in a log cabin in remote West Virginia, fifty miles from the nearest school. She was one of eleven children, and she ran away from home at the age of fourteen. Discovered working in a doughnut shop, she was lured into stripping by Red Snyder, who became her first manager. "I'd never even shown my belly button before."

Stripper **Blaze Starr** found JFK "a voracious lover."

During his tenure as a Senator in Washington, JFK patronized strip clubs and often had affairs with women who caught his eye. One night at a strip joint, he became entranced by Blaze with her red hair and voluptuous (38D-24-37) proportions.

That night, according to her memoirs, he invited her back to his apartment where they had sex. In spite of a bad back, she found him a voracious lover, who couldn't seem to get enough. Senator George Smathers of Florida, who often visited strip joints in Washington with Jack, claimed "the sight of a red-haired pussy used to drive Jack into rapture."

In an interview she gave in 1989, Blaze admitted that she visited Jack's apartment "several more times." Smathers was under the impression that Jack had sex with Blaze on eight different occasions, and had nothing but the highest praise for her as a lover. "She lives up to her name," Jack told Smathers. "The gal is on fire."

Miss Starr had a different appraisal of the flamboyantly corrupt Louisiana governor Earl Long: "Earl is getting so he can't cut the mustard no more!"

Jack would not be the only politician to bed Blaze. In 1959 she was appearing in a strip joint, the Sho-Bar, on Bourbon Street in New Orleans. One night Earl Long, the long-time and spectacularly corrupt governor of Louisiana, escorted by two policemen, came into the club. The brother of the notorious Huey Long of Louisiana, Earl termed himself "the last of the red hot poppas" of politics. When he met Blaze, he was serving his third term as governor.

After the show, Earl came backstage and introduced himself. He stayed around for the second show. At the finale, he shouted to her, "Will you go to dinner with me tonight?"

"Can I trust you?" she shouted back.

"Hell, no!" he yelled at her.

Their affair, launched that night, became the scandal of Louisiana.

When JFK and Jackie arrived in Louisiana during JFK's campaign for President in 1960, Earl invited both of them to the joint where Blaze was stripping. Jack didn't want Jackie tagging along, but she insisted, claiming she'd never been to a strip club before.

After the show, Earl introduced Jack and Jackie to Blaze. Both of the Kennedys knew that Earl was having an affair with the stripper. Blaze later admitted in her 1974 autobiography, "In front of Jackie, I pretended I'd never met Jack before. We pulled it off."

Earl later invited all of them back to the Roosevelt Hotel for a late-night party. Jackie bowed out and returned to her own hotel, but Jack accepted.

"When Earl was elsewhere talking to some of his political cronies, Jack and I slipped away to have a quickie in the closet," Blaze claimed in her memoirs.

Kennedy aide Langdon Marvin estimated that "Jack spent at least twenty minutes in that closet with Blaze while I guarded the door." Later JFK told Marvin that he amused Blaze by telling her that in 1923, President Warren Harding had seduced Nan Britton, a 23-year-old fan whom some observers claimed had been obsessed with Harding since her middle teens, in a broom closet at the White House.

A short time after the Kennedys departed from New Orleans, Earl fell on bad days. Learning of her husband's affair with Ms. Starr, his wife, Blanche Revere Long, managed to have him committed to a mental institution. But since he was still governor, and because the hospital was a state-funded institution, he fired its administration and escaped. "Uncle Earl," as he was called, died in 1960 and never got to see JFK take over the White House.

JFK had become so stimulated during his previous seductions of Blaze that he proposed to his aides that immediately before each of the four upcoming television debates scheduled against Richard Nixon, he needed a stripper—a hired prostitute, that is—delivered to his room.

***

Later, after taking a break at Hyannis Port, Jackie joined the campaign trail, visiting Maine, Delaware, Kentucky, Tennessee, North Carolina, and Pennsylvania.

Many of their campaign stops were disastrous. JFK found that he had little name recognition in some parts of the country. When he landed in Portland, Oregon, there were only three people to greet him, one of whom was Congresswoman Edith Green. With Jackie beside him, he bravely carried on.

In a lilac-colored Chanel suit, she greeted some fishermen at a boatyard. They didn't know who she was, but one of the aromatic men told her she was "one hot tomato."

She had a hard time making small talk, asking them, "Do you ever catch salmon? My favorite dish is salmon tartare."

One night along the Oregon trail, they stopped at a sleazy roadside joint, the 'Er Buck Motel, which catered to hookers. A six-o'clock breakfast was served at Ma's Kitchen next door. Ma's specialty consisted of three eggs fried in lard, three slices of bacon, a slab of ham, one pig sausage, and fried potatoes. Jackie settled for coffee and toast.

At some stopovers, JFK had trouble finding someone whose hand to shake. At one point, he was reduced to approaching motorists at redlights, hurriedly reaching into their car for a handshake and an introduction, with a plea to "vote for me."

During the weeks that followed, Jackie's doctors advised her to leave the campaign trail and to stay at home. She was viewed as particularly vulnerable because of her previous difficult pregnancies.

However, in Georgetown, she worked as much as she could by answering letters, taping television commercials, and giving interviews to newspapers and magazines, and to TV newscasters. She also continued her authorship of a weekly syndicated newspaper column, "Campaign Wife," which was mailed out to potential female supporters.

Her column was chatty, not political. "In these lonely autumn days at Hyannis Port, I follow my husband's campaign with rapt attention. I showed Caroline newspaper pictures of her father receiving an Indian war bonnet."

She was referring to JFK's stopover in Sioux Falls, South Dakota, where the chief of the local Indian tribe placed a feathered headdress on him. He took it off almost immediately, as he refused to be photographed wearing any head gear, even the top hat he was given at his inauguration, although he did put it on briefly. He also refused to be photographed while eating.

At Hyannis Port, she said, "Thank

Straight from makeup, the Democratic candidate for President, **John F. Kennedy** *(top photo, left)*, was lean, tall, suntanned, and dressed in a Savile Row suit. He faced the Republican candidate, Vice President Richard M. Nixon *(top photo, right)*, who sported a suspicious-looking five o'clock shadow and no makeup. When JFK was asked to pose with Nixon, he barely looked at him, turning his face to the camera instead.

Whereas JFK hijacked all the attention, Nixon looked deflated, especially when compared to the "movie star allure" of his opponent.

JFK had just emerged rejuvenated from the bed of a hooker. Nixon had emerged from a bed at Walter Reed Hospital, where he'd injured his leg, with a dreadful knee infection setting in.

Before JFK went onstage, Bobby Kennedy gave his brother some final advice: "Kick him in the balls, Jack!"

God I've escaped all those dreadful chicken dinners where I was forced to sit at the head table wearing a dreadful corsage. I couldn't even smoke a cigarette while listening to some old clodhopper windbag."

She also didn't like a lot of JFK's campaign workers, privately referring to them as "lackeys, jackals, flunkies, and imbeciles."

***

During their early days in Congress, JFK and Nixon had called themselves friends, although their allegiance was to opposing political parties. Joseph Kennedy even contributed money to Nixon's early political campaigns. But before their first televised debate in September, in Chicago, their relationship had turned poisonous. JFK had labeled Nixon "a filthy, lying son of a bitch and a very dangerous man."

To retaliate, Nixon called JFK a "bare-faced liar and a son of a bitch. No, in his case, the son of a rotten bastard who wanted to lick Hitler's asshole." Of course, these stinging evaluations were delivered privately to colleagues and staff members.

JFK's aide, Langdon Marvin, later revealed that half an hour before show-time, JFK demanded that a women be sent to his suite at the Ambassador East Hotel. Their liaison took only 15 minutes. Emerging from his suite after his seduction of the hooker, JFK proclaimed, "I'm ready and raring to face Nixon."

Before the call girl arrived, JFK had relaxed for three hours, listening to recordings by Peggy Lee from the 1940s.

Many listeners who heard the debate on radio, including LBJ, asserted that Nixon had won. But those who saw it on television "watched a young Adonis debate a man with a five o'clock shadow," in the words of one commentator.

In an attempt to correct that impression, during the next three debates, Nixon came onto the stage wearing more pancake makeup than a movie star from the silent screen.

After Chicago, JFK began to draw crowds larger than those associated with any other presidential candidate in history. "My god," said one reporter, "I thought Elvis had hit town." But instead of Elvis, it was Jack Kennedy. Girls screamed after him like a rock star. When he was surrounded by crowds, he often felt hands, both from horny women and gay men, grabbing his crotch.

Paul Douglas, the Democratic senator from Illinois, defined JFK's fan base as "jumpers, shriekers, huggers, lopers, and touchers." A reporter for *Life* magazine called them "gaspers, gogglers, swooners, and collapsers." Senator Stuart Symington noted that everybody wanted "to touch Jack, to feel him, or, in some cases, grope him. Some women seemed to experience orgasm when they put their hands on him."

***

Because of her pregnancy, Jackie did not attend the 1960 Democratic Convention in Los Angeles. Her sister, Lee, did. She was now married to Prince Stanislas (Stas) Radziwill. Every night, she called Jackie to give her a full report, with plenty of gossip thrown in about her errant husband.

At a $100-a-plate fundraising dinner at the Beverly Hilton, JFK was surrounded by the Democratic elite, including Adlai Stevenson and Lyndon Johnson.

He had also invited a number of stars with whom he was alleged to have had affairs, including Angie Dickinson, Janet Leigh, and Rhonda Fleming. His special favorite, Judy Garland, sat next to him in Jackie's place. He met with her later to resume their long-standing affair.

Milton Berle also attended, informing Tony Curtis, "I have the biggest dick in this room. Why can't I get all the dames?"

That summer, JFK found himself pursued by the press as never before. He could no longer be as open and up front about his affairs as before. During the Convention, his secret hideaway was an apartment in a building owned by Jack Haley, who had starred as "the Tin Man" in the 1939 classic, *The Wizard of Oz.*

One night, JFK arranged to meet Marilyn Monroe in that apartment for about two hours. In anticipation of that liaison, he managed to elude his Secret Service detail, something he was able to do even after he become President of the United States.

After he'd seduced Marilyn, he was sneaking out of the building when he encountered three reporters and a photographer waiting outside. Somehow, they'd trailed him to the apartment dwelling. He ran back into the building and— since another photographer was stationed at the rear door— managed to elude his pursuers by precariously navigating his way along and down the building's fire escape on the east side of the structure.

Like the star of a Mack Sennett comedy, he climbed over a neighbor's fence, only to be chased by a bulldog in someone's back yard. Finally, making it to safety, he ran to his waiting limousine with the reporters hot on his trail. Later, he offered the lame excuse that he was only visiting his father.

Right before JFK was nominated to run as president, Harry S Truman resigned as a convention delegate from Missouri. Privately, the crusty former president told his cronies, "I don't want to participate in a convention where the candidate's nomination has been bought and paid for." After saying that, he made a Freudian slip. "I think Joe Kennedy is far too young and inexperienced to be President." Of course, he had meant to refer to "John" Kennedy, not his aging father. Like Roosevelt, Truman genuinely detested the Kennedy patriarch.

To his aides, Johnson continued to express his literal disgust of JFK, continually referring to him as "that spavined hunchback." He also had other epithets, which included "that sickly little shit," or "the scrawny fellow with rickets."

As far as it is known, Johnson was never involved in the plot to steal JFK's medical records from the office of Janet Travell, JFK's doctor. In a heist evocative of the Watergate burglary during Nixon's administration, two hired thieves broke into Travell's office and made off with JFK's medical file. The most tantalizing detail it revealed was that he had Addison's disease.

Amazingly, when John Connally, the governor of Texas, later held a press conference and made this revelation, it received little press coverage.

Ironically, on the morning of November 22, 1963, when JFK and Jackie were getting into the limousine with the governor of Texas, he reminded Connally of that long-ago press conference. "Addison's disease or not, I'm still here."

Early in the campaign, Lady Bird had pleaded with her husband not to relinquish his powerful role as Senate Majority Leader as a prerequisite to accepting the post of Vice Presidential running mate in the 1960 elections. Later, when Clare Boothe Luce asked him why he hadn't heeded his wife's advice, LBJ responded, "L'il darlin', let me tell you. One of every four presidents has died in office. I'm a gamblin' man. I'll pray every day that little shit is shot."

A Kennedy hater, Johnson held JFK in utter contempt, but retained a special loathing for his brother, Bobby, calling him, "a vicious little rattlesnake."

Johnson told his aides, "One day, Jack might sit in the Oval Office behind his desk while some hooker gives him a blow-job, but it will be old Joe Kennedy, that crooked bastard, who will actually be running the country. He'll bring back Prohibition so he can make millions again as a bootlegger and rum runner."

The most outrageous rumor spread across the Convention Hall may not have come from Johnson, but it was nonetheless propagated by his aides. It was widely rumored that JFK and RFK were "a couple of fags." One rumor spread by the Johnson camp involved their possession of candid snapshots of Bobby and Jack dressed as drag queens at a wild late-night gay party in a penthouse along the Strip in Las Vegas. No such photograph ever surfaced.

Jackie was horrified to learn that JFK had selected Johnson as his vice presidential running mate. Her husband had never expressed anything but disdain for the candidate. "I guess he had his reasons," she told Patricia, Eunice, and Rose at Hyannis Port. "The State of Texas comes to mind."

***

Knowing how unpopular he was, and how his close involvement in his son's campaign would be viewed as a liability, Joe directed the scenes from Marion Davies' home in Beverly Hills. He'd known her since his early days in Hollywood when she was the mistress of press baron William Randolph Hearst.

To secure more votes, Joe paid for a hooker to service any delegate who wanted one. Peter Lawford was ordered to round up an armada of prostitutes. He was also requested to round up male hustlers to service female delegates, pending their interest, as well.

Whenever he could spare the time, JFK shacked up with Monroe, among other women. Although she was still married to playwright Arthur Miller, she told JFK, "It's all over between Arthur and me except for the divorce."

So-called well-meaning friends in Los Angeles kept Jackie's phone busy, reporting on all the gossip that Lee didn't already tell her.

"It sounds like a god damn bordello out there," Jackie said.

Her husband had become so brazen in his affair with Monroe that they were seen dining together at Puccini's, a Los Angeles eatery in which Sinatra was a major investor. Peter Lawford, Marilyn's former lover, went along as a "beard."

When JFK excused himself to go to the men's room, accompanied with two Secret Service men, Monroe confided to Lawford, "Last night, Jack was very Presidential, very penetrating. I think I made his back feel better."

When Lawford repeated that quote to his friends, it became one of Monroe's most quoted sayings.

"Jack was out of control," Lawford told Sinatra and several other friends. "By the time dessert was served—cherries jubilee—Jack was finger-fucking Marilyn, who never wore any underwear."

On July 16, on her small TV set in Hyannis Port, Jackie watched as JFK addressed more than 100,000 Democratic delegates assembled into the Los Angeles Coliseum. Only an hour before, he'd been involved with Marilyn Monroe in his hotel suite.

After his speech at the Convention, JFK joined Monroe, Lawford, and other trusted aides for a skinny-dipping party at Lawford's beachfronting home in Santa Monica. "When Marilyn took it all off, all the men's eyes were riveted," Lawford claimed.

The party became so boisterous that irate neighbors called the police. Thirty minutes later, three armed officers burst onto the terrace adjacent to the Lawford family's swimming pool, inaugurating the process of arresting Lawford, JFK, and Monroe. But after one of the officers identified the presidential candidate in the buff, the arrests were called off.

It was reported that Marilyn gave the police "quite a show" before donning a white terrycloth robe. JFK also took his time getting dressed, promising the officers that when he occupied the White House, he'd grant them a Presidential Medal of Honor.

"Wouldn't that have been some photograph," Lawford later told his wife, Patricia. "Jack, Marilyn, and me, with it all hanging out, being herded into a police van and hauled off to the Santa Monica police station?"

Despite plans to return after the party to Boston, JFK delayed his return an extra day for additional time with Marilyn in his Los Angeles hotel suite. According to Peter Lawford, he directed her to "perform every sexual trick she'd ever learned."

***

Before JFK's arrival back at Hyannis Port, Jackie summoned "Mr. Kenneth" to fly from New York to create her now famous bouffant hairdo.

During JFK's absence, she had conducted an hour-long question-and-answer news conference with a select group of reporters on the front veranda of

Joe Kennedy's house. After the press conference, in anticipation of his arrival, she seemed to become angry at her husband, no doubt based on all the reports reaching her about Monroe. She retreated to her bedroom and refused to go to the airport to greet him. Finally, the Kennedy sisters prevailed on her to go. "Otherwise, if you don't show up, it'll fuel rumors," Eunice told her.

Eventually, Jackie acquiesced and with her mother, Janet Auchincloss, was driven to the airport, where she boarded the *Caroline.* Lawford was standing beside JFK as Jackie approached to greet her husband. "There was no kiss, no hug," he later said. "Her first words to her returning husband were, 'Jack, is Marilyn Monroe such a vote getter for you that she'll sweep you into the White House?'"

Later, her husband insisted that she join him in New York for a pre-election parade. In the advanced stages of pregnancy, she feared another miscarriage, another stillborn, or at least a difficult birth. Finally, he overcame her protests.

Back on the campaign trail, this time in New York, she made several stops throughout the city, speaking Spanish in Spanish Harlem, French in the Haitian ghetto in Brooklyn, and Italian in Little Italy. Hearing how well she was going over with Spanish-speaking audiences, Nixon cried foul. "Mrs. Kennedy is taking unfair advantage; after all, Pat doesn't speak Spanish."

The big event that compelled some two million New Yorkers to line the streets was the parade through the "Canyon of Heroes." Both JFK and Jackie occupied tenuous perches above the back seat of a Cadillac convertible.

Fans were so frenzied they almost yanked Jackie from her precarious seat. "They could have caused a miscarriage," she charged to JFK when they returned to their hotel suite.

At one point, the crowds rocked the Cadillac with such force that they almost turned it over. Ironically, many of the fans lining the sidewalks at the time were too young to vote, evoking the crazed bobbysoxers who pursued Frank Sinatra during the early 1940s.

At the end of the parade, JFK turned to Jackie, saying, "That would have been a great time for someone to take a shot at me."

***

On election day, November 8, 1960, Jackie joined JFK in traveling to the West End Library in Boston to vote. Actually, she'd already voted by absentee ballot. Later, she told Ted Sorensen and others, "I voted for only one candidate—and that was Jack." When that remark was heard by others, she angered Democrats seeking lesser offices.

On election night, which Jackie later referred to "as the longest in my life,' she waited for the polls to close on the West Coast. For dinner, she had invited Ben Bradlee, among others. Her friend and confidant, William Walton, also made an appearance, sparking a jealous fit from Lem Billings. Before Walton, Lem had been "Jack's best gay buddy," but to an increasing degree, Walton was becoming very close to JFK as well.

The Kennedy clan had gathered in Hyannis Port to await the returns. "We were all edgy and snapping at each other," Jackie recalled.

At 10:30pm, when early returns indicated that JFK was in the lead over Nixon, Jackie offered her congratulations.

"Don't make me President yet," JFK warned her. "The night is young."

JFK at one point disappeared. As it turned out, he was with his friend, Larry Newman, who had secretly voted for Richard Nixon.

"I couldn't believe it," Newman said. "He was in a neck-and-neck race to become President of the United States, and all he could talk about was fucking women, wondering if his 'poon train' would be derailed when he became President."

Newman lived across from the Kennedy compound. He used to have drinks with JFK at Manhattan's fabled Monkey Bar. He recalled that "Jack flirted with every pretty girl in the bar. I don't think he really wanted to be married, but in politics, he had to be."

While JFK was away on the campaign trail, Newman saw Jackie almost every day. In Hyannis Port, there was local speculation that they might be having an affair, although there is no evidence of that. Perhaps JFK's real reason for visiting Newman on election night involved confirming whether the rumor about his possible affair with Jackie was true. But Jack never brought up the subject, returning within the hour to the Kennedy compound, much to the relief of the Secret Service.

By 11:30pm, "Milhous," as Jackie called Nixon, had surged ahead and was winning. Completely exhausted, almost dangerously tired, JFK went to bed.

It was late the next morning that TV announcers issued a bulletin: Final returns indicated that JFK had plowed ahead by just 115,000 votes out of a total of 70 million cast.

When Bobby heard the news that Nixon had conceded, he immediately asked an aide, "Where's Jackie?" Later, David Powers expressed his amazement that Bobby wanted to tell Jackie the news before alerting JFK that he was President of the United States.

When informed that Jackie had gone for a walk along the beach, a place long deserted by the summer crowds, he ran after her. In the distance, he spotted her kerchief-covered head as seagulls circled overhead. He ran up to her, taking her body, heavy with child, in his arms and kissing her passionately.

"Congratulations! You are the new First Lady. You'll go down in history along with Martha Washington, Abigail Adams, and Ida Saxton."

"Who in hell was Ida Saxton?"

"William McKinley's wife," he answered. "She spent all her time in the White House in bed crotcheting more than 3,500 pairs of slippers."

"Whatever I do as First Lady, I'll top that," she vowed.

Holding her close, he kissed her again, although he could be observed by two Secret Service men. Slowly, he walked with her back to the house. "Don't you think Jack should be awakened and told he's the President?" she asked.

"Might as well," he said. "I don't think we can keep it a secret from him for long. Imagine going to sleep not knowing if you'd become President or not."

Back at the house, Jackie said it would be the thrill of Caroline's life to let her go upstairs and wake up JFK. "Tell him your father is the new President of the United States," she instructed her daughter.

Seated once again in the living room, Jackie told David Powers and Eunice, "All my life I've dreamed of living the life of a storybook princess. As of today, I must live the life of America's Queen."

Two hours later, hung over from lack of sleep, JFK asked Jackie to accompany him to the Hyannis Armory, where a mob had gathered.

She put on a red scoop-neck dress and a string of pearls, but covered them with her purple coat as a means of concealing her pregnancy.

At the Armory, she joked with reporters, "You didn't expect me to show up in sable, now, did you? I, too, can wear the Pat Nixon simple cloth coat that Nixon constantly refers to when he and Pat want to look like one of the 'little people.'"

Jackie not only faced competition from Marilyn Monroe, but from another very sexy star, **Angie Dickinson**. Jackie delivered her appraisal to William Walton: "Marilyn is a sexy tiger; Angie a sex kitten."

JFK's acceptance speech was short, concluding, "So now my wife and I prepare for a new administration and a new baby."

***

At the age of thirty-one, Jackie, the wife of America's 35th President, became the third-youngest First Lady in U.S. history. Both Mrs. Grover Cleveland (Frances Folsom) and Mrs. John Tyler (Julia Gardiner) were only in their twenties.

Jackie told a reporter at Hyannis Port, "It's really frightening to lose your anonymity at my age."

In the aftermath of the election, as JFK was selecting his Cabinet, and making other decisions, Jackie heard a disturbing report that JFK was having an affair with Angie Dickinson, the sweet, sexy, blonde, bright-eyed, and cat-eyed movie actress with the engaging smile. She was two years younger than Jackie and a hell of a lot sexier.

Columnist Joe Alsop told Jackie that Angie had spent three nights in Palm Springs with JFK, presumably at the home of Frank Sinatra, but that was never confirmed.

The closest Angie ever came to suggesting an affair was during an interview with *TV Guide:* "I have always found powerful men attractive—take Frank Sinatra, for instance, or JFK. From the first moment I met Jack, I was hooked, like everybody else. He was the sexiest politician I've ever met. He was the killer type, a devastatingly handsome, charming man—the kind your mother hoped you'd marry."

Once, in 1961, during Jackie's occupancy of the White House, she had left for Virginia. Forgetting something vital, she returned, unannounced, to the White House. It was rumored that during her brief return, before she rapidly exited the building again, she spotted Angie heading for the President's quarters.

In Hyannis Port one morning, after the elections but before they took occupancy of the White House, JFK announced to her that Lyndon and Lady Bird Johnson would be arriving within two hours.

When the new Vice President and America's Second Lady turned up, Jackie stood on the veranda with her husband to shake their hands. Then she went back into the house and retreated upstairs to her bedroom. After his visit with JFK, LBJ announced that he was leaving. Both he and Lady Bird wanted to tell Jackie goodbye, but she refused to come down.

After JFK was elected president, she met often with the Secret Service, sharing her fears with them that her husband might be assassinated or her daughter, or her child to be, kidnapped and held for ransom…or something even worse. "She was almost obsessed with these fears," said agent John Walsh.

***

On November 25, 1960, just 17 days after his father was elected President of the United States, John Fitzgerald Kennedy, Jr., entered the world via caesarean birth. Weighing six pounds, three ounces, he was immediately placed in an incubator. From the moment of his birth, he would spend the rest of his short life in the public spotlight.

[As he was growing up in the White House, he came to be called "John-John," a name he despised. A reporter at the White House had heard JFK calling to his son, "John…John!" Misunderstanding him, the writer had interpreted the child's nickname as "John-John." It soon became a household word across America.]

Although he was out of town during the birth, JFK had flown from Palm Beach to Washington to be by Jackie's side. When he entered her room, she was still a bit hazy from the sedation. She looked up at him and in her whispery voice said, "Jack, I have given birth to a future President of the United States."

Chapter Eight

Jackie & Her Pregnancies

She Blames JFK for Her Miscarriages After He Infects Her with Chlamydia

Dead Kennedys (Arabella and Patrick); Lives Never Lived Caroline and John Jr.: "At Last, I'm Fulfilled as a Woman"

"Mama's Boy," **John F. Kennedy, Jr.**, looks adorable as he's held in the arms of his loving, devoted mother in Palm Beach in 1963. At last, Jackie had given the Kennedy clan the son and heir apparent that had been tacitly demanded of her. Regrettably, the birth of the child that followed John-John would escalate into a heart-breaking tragedy.

During her honeymoon with JFK in Mexico, he had told her that he wanted to have five children—"but never as many as Bobby. I think that before little brother and Ethel give up fucking without birth control, they'll have a dozen or two. They should never have gone to see that movie, *Cheaper* *by the Dozen."*

Don't get too ambitious," she said. "After all, I'm not Ethel cranking out babies like rabbits."

Very privately with his closest friend, Lem Billings, JFK voiced his fear that he might not be capable of fathering a child because of his various diseases. Lem advised him to consult with a Dr. William P. Herbst, a well-known Boston urologist, to have his sperm count tested. The results indicated that he was capable of fathering a child. Even so, in spite of his constant consumption of medications, he still continued to experience a slight burning sensation when urinating. Up until then, no doctor had been able to prescribe medication that relieved him of that pain.

Jack and Jackie Kennedy were doting parents with **Caroline**.

Jackie's problem pregnancies made her feel inadequate. She told Jack, "I can't crank out kids like an Ethel rabbit."

Jackie's gynecologists also warned her that she was "so high strung you might experience difficulty having a baby."

After she'd married JFK, she announced within months that she was pregnant. He was delighted, desperately wanting an heir. Papa Joe had cautioned him, "A politician without a wife and family doesn't go over with voters."

Rose also wanted a grandson. "I want it to be a boy, and I demand that you name him John Fitzgerald Kennedy, Jr."

"Our son, Joseph, died before he could carry on Joe's name and immortalize it as President of the United States. I want you to be President and I want your son, John Jr., to follow in your footsteps to the White House. A father and son as President, as you well know, is not unknown in American history. Remember John Adams and John Quincy Adams? *[John*

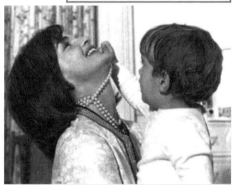

Maybe because the pearls were fake, **Jackie** lets **John-John** use them as playthings. *Faux* or not, these simulated pearls sold at auction for $211,000 in April of 1996, two years after Jackie's death.

As Jackie delivers a stillbirth, JFK Cruises the Mediterranean, with Prostitutes, Aboard a Raucous "Booze and Babes" Tour

164

Quincy Adams, the sixth U.S. President, who served from 1825 to 1829, was the son of Abigail Adams and John Adams, who served as the second U.S. President, holding the office from 1797 to 1801.]

"I know my history, Mother," JFK said. "But I hope my term of office turns out better than John Quincy Adams. He claimed that the four most miserable years of his life was the presidency."

Jackie had told her confidants, including Janet, "If I can deliver that boy that Jack wants, I think I can make him settle down and stop philandering."

She was wrong. During and after her pregnancy, she continued to receive reports that her husband was womanizing as never before.

Three months into her pregnancy, she suffered a miscarriage.

***

She noticed that JFK took trips without her any time he wanted to, and she decided to follow his example. Despondent over both her miscarriage and her failing marriage, in the summer of 1954, she announced to him that she was about to fly to London to see her sister, Lee, who was in an unhappy marriage to Michael Canfield.

JFK objected to her trip, but she packed her luggage and went anyway, staying with Lee at her charming little mews house in Belgravia.

Once in London, Jackie was impressed that Lee, without her husband, had become the darling of the social set. It was obvious that she was also indulging in affairs on the side. Canfield stayed home most nights drinking heavily, while Lee and Jackie went nightclubbing.

Lee's social calendar was full, and Jackie found endless diversions—a yachting trip off Torquay on the Devonshire coast, cocktail parties in Mayfair; lunch at Ascot; a weekend at Blenheim Palace, the ancestral home of Sir Winston Churchill.

Both Jackie and Lee flew to Paris on a shopping expedition. When she returned, Canfield privately sought Jackie's advice. "How can I hold onto Lee?"

Jackie was blunt with him. "Make more money!"

Lee and Jackie bonded over their failed or failing marriages. As Lee's biographer, Diana DuBois wrote: "Jack's never-ending infidelities humiliated Jacqueline, so they were both, albeit for different reasons, unhappily married and childless."

The Canfields had rented a villa during the month of August in Antibes, on the French Riviera, a former haunt of Picasso. Jackie was invited to join them on their vacation, and consequently, she flew with them to Nice. Their mutual friend, an Englishman, Peter Ward, along with his future wife, Claire Baring, also joined them. The two couples and Jackie appeared daily at the chic, cliff-hanging, swimming pool of the Eden Roc Hotel on Cap d'Antibes, the former haunt of F. Scott Fitzgerald and his wife, Zelda.

Ward later revealed that one afternoon, Jackie exclaimed that she had left her husband for good. "Her exact words were, 'I'm not going back to him. Jack doesn't need me. He's had all those other women.'"

In spite of her troubles, Jackie seemed intent on having a good time. She was seen entering the casino at Cannes with Queen Soraya of Iran. Stavros Niarchos, the Greek shipping tycoon, invited her aboard his luxurious yacht. She became friends with the fabulously wealthy Jayne Wrightsman, who was married to the oil and gas millionaire, Charles Wrightsman, famous for their contributions of 18th century French furniture to the New York's Metropolitan Museum. Jackie flew to Venice with Jayne, who became her lifelong friend. The traveling house party often drove to dinner at St-Tropez, a very fashionable fishing village which the French sex goddess, Brigitte Bardot, was about to make even more celebrated.

By mid-August of 1954, JFK had flown to her side. After a night together, they announced that they had reconciled. Apparently, JFK had falsely promised that he was going to give up other women and settle down with her.

But on the very next day, when Jackie and Lee had gone into the Old Town of Nice, JFK showed signs of straying yet again. He soon disappeared with a beautiful brunette model and was gone for two hours. He was back in time to receive his beloved bride, Jackie, who was none the wiser. Or was she?

Whatever their differences, Jackie agreed to fly back with her husband and began life anew at their country home, Hickory Hill.

By January of 1956, Jackie announced she was pregnant again.

"Was your Husband Your Only Sexual Partner?"

—Questions posed to Jackie after the stillbirth of Arabella

Based on her previous miscarriage, Jackie wanted the birth of her first child to be perfect. She'd spent days designing a nursery for her son or daughter at Hickory Hill, although she "just knew it's going to be a little girl." She also dreamed that she'd grow up to be an equestrienne like her mother, so symbolically, Jackie placed a rocking horse in the corner of the room.

Of course, should it be a boy, she could make emergency changes to the nursery, getting rid of the frieze of frolicking pink Easter bunnies and croaking chartreuse frogs and substituting depictions of toy soldiers and sailboats instead.

Her husband with the roving eye shocked her when he informed her that he was leaving for a two-week cruise of the Mediterranean with Senator George Smathers and his youngest brother, Teddy. Smathers would later define the trip as "a Booze-and-Babes" cruise.

She objected, but finally relented, agreeing to pack his luggage. Just to show him that she was aware of what was about to happen, she placed a carton of condoms between his socks and his underwear, in one of his suitcases.

Since she felt lonely and isolated at Hickory Hill after he'd gone, she retreated to her bedroom at Hammersmith Farm, outside Newport, where Janet welcomed her. For the most part, she remained in her room, morbidly depressed and smoking constantly. One morning, she woke up late. It was already eleven o'clock, and the sky was gray and gloomy.

Making her way downstairs, she found the house deserted. A coffee pot was on the stove. As she poured herself a cup, she felt dizzy. Warm blood was running down her leg, spilling out onto the tiled kitchen floor.

She collapsed in pain, screaming for help. Her cries summoned the cook, who was on the back porch. When she spotted Jackie on the floor, she also began screaming. No one answered, so she rushed to the phone and called an ambulance.

Within thirty minutes, Jackie was being hauled into the emergency room of the Newport Hospital. Somewhere along the way, she passed out, and didn't regain consciousness until four hours later.

As Jackie lay in her coma, an incident occurred that was kept out of the press. During her confinement, a crazed young man planted four sticks of dynamite outside her hospital window. Her room was on the ground floor. Before he could detonate the bomb, a gardener spotted him and hit him over the head with a shovel, knocking him out.

The hospital staff did not want the incident reported, and no charges were filed, although the unknown (potential) assassin was hauled away by the police.

What happened to him after that is not known.

Interpreting it as a dangerous and upsetting distraction from the serious medical issues at hand, Jackie was not informed—at least at the time—of the incident, her doctor fearing it could only add to her stress level, which was already far too high.

Still in a daze, she woke up in bed four hours later, feeling great pain. Her insides seemed to be throbbing. Through bleary eyes, she saw JFK's face. No, it wasn't Jack. It was someone who resembled him.

Opening her eyes more fully, she saw Bobby at her bedside. With tears in his eyes, he bent over her and kissed her lips gently. "Thank God you're alive," he said.

"Oh, Bobby," she said, "Thanks for coming. Where's Jack? Where is my baby?"

"It was a little girl," he said. "She's gone to heaven."

She burst into tears, and he held her in his arms, comforting her. Through sobs, she told him, "I was going to call her Arabella." Then she seemed to gasp for breath. "Does Jack know?"

"I'm trying to reach him," he said. "He's at sea. Perhaps off the coast of Elba. There doesn't seem to be a radio on his yacht."

As she started to denounce her husband, Bobby intervened. "Don't condemn him. He can't help being Jack. Besides, you have me, and I'm a better man than my older brother will ever be."

"I believe that, Bobby," she said, reaching for his hand.

[Although Ethel was said to dislike Jackie, she had reportedly been instrumental in sending Bobby to her side in the hospital, asserting, "Jackie is not as tough as she pretends to be."

Ethel, herself in the final stages of another yet pregnancy, thought that Jackie needed Bobby's presence more than she did. "Jack is still whoring around the Riviera," she told her husband, who was already well aware of that.]

As Bobby went outside, as part of an attempt to place yet another call to JFK, Jackie's doctor entered the room.

In polite terms, he told her the details of Arabella's birth, which had been part of an attempt at a caesarean section. There was more bad news. "I hate to tell you this, but I must, as your doctor. We tested your blood. You have Chlamydia."

Before JFK had explained it to her during their honeymoon in Mexico, she had not known what this venereal disease was.

"It's easier to detect in men than in women," the doctor said. "In women, the virus seems to hide in the uterus. It's very dangerous for a pregnant woman to have Chlamydia. The bacteria travels from the cervix through the fallopian tubes, which could lead to a stillbirth."

"How long have I had this horrible disease?" she asked.

"It's hard to say," he said. "For at least two years, I would estimate. The only way to get the disease is through sexual transmission."

"You mean, my husband gave it to me?" she asked.

"I'm not saying that," the doctor said. "Forgive me, I know nothing about your personal life. But you could have picked it up from another sexual partner and passed it on to your husband. You must tell him. He surely has it."

"There were no other sexual partners," she said.

"Then your husband is the culprit."

"In other words, JACK KILLED MY BABY!" she said.

"I wouldn't go that far. There could have been other factors. But you must be treated for this disease. You must eradicate it from your body. Will your husband be arriving? I must talk to him."

"He'll be arriving all right, perhaps in my dreams. Or, in this case, in my nightmares."

***

Based on his respect for an Irish Catholic tradition, Bobby waited three days to allow the infant's spirit time to leave its body. After that, he had Arabella's corpse placed in a miniature coffin at a local funeral home. The label on the coffin did not say "Arabella Kennedy," but "Baby Kennedy Girl."

He watched as her body was lowered into a tiny grave at Newport's St. Columba's Cemetery overlooking Narragansett Bay.

***

While Jackie had been in a hospital recovering from the stillbirth of their daughter, JFK was sailing the Mediterranean with Senator George Smathers and Teddy Kennedy. Along for the ride were at least eight hookers hired for the occasion. The agreement was that, whenever asked, each of the buxom young women would service whichever man requested her services.

In Newport, both RFK and Jackie were distressed that ship-to-shore radio contact could not be established as a means of reaching the seafaring Senator. A photo taken during the cruise surfaced years later. Based on America's then-daunting moral code, had it been published during the mid-1950s, it might have derailed JFK's future as a politician.

The photograph, shot at a distance obviously from the perspective of another boat, depicted JFK sitting on deck while two nude women were swimming off the side of the yacht. Another two women were depicted sitting in a lifeboat immediately above him.

When the photograph surfaced years later, several forensic experts, including Jeff Sedlik, [a Los Angeles-based consultant and testifying forensic expert witness on issues related to photography and imaging] asserted that the photo was authentic, and snapped in August of 1956 during JFK's two-week cruise of the Mediterranean.

Prior to the debut of their cruise, Teddy and JFK had spent two nights in Paris carousing and bedding showgirls who otherwise performed at the fashionable Lido night cabaret. They then flew to Nice, where they joined Smathers. For a while, they stayed at Papa Joe's rented villa on the Côte d'Azur. All three men discussed JFK's future in politics with Joe. Before sailing away again, Teddy lined up a bevy of women to sail with them, paying each of them $500, a considerable sum in the 50s.

When Bobby, in Newport, telephoned Joe, his father informed him that JFK had already sailed away into the azure unknown, and that he was out of range of telephone or radio contact. He estimated that his son's yacht was somewhere offshore from the island of Elba.

Later investigations challenged the claim that there was no ship-to-shore radio. It was reported that Evelyn Lincoln, JFK's secretary, was in radio contact with him. French Maritime law mandated that boats and yachts have an on-board radio.

Allegedly, Lincoln informed JFK that his daughter, Arabella, had been stillborn. Apparently, he had responded that he'd prefer to finish the cruise because at this point, "there is nothing that I can do," and swore her to secrecy.

After learning about his inner-family tragedy, he sailed on. Smathers later claimed to his cronies that JFK sampled all eight of the onboard hookers, but ultimately settled on a preference for "Poppy," a beautiful, golden-haired , large-busted showgirl who danced at the casinos of Monte Carlo, Nice, and Cannes. Her legs were said to rival those of the 1940s movie star, Betty Grable, whose left leg in 1943 was voted "the world's most beautiful."

News of JFK's mysterious lack of availability began to leak. Author Edward Klein quotes one unnamed journalist who attacked the young politician's "terrible obtuseness, his awesome, willful insensitivity that had defined the emotional parameters of his marriage. He had shown what he truly felt—more accurately, what he did not feel. Even after he heard about the stillbirth, he had initially wanted to stay on the boat, to enjoy himself, to relax. He had little apparent regard for Jackie and her anguish."

His not rushing back to comfort Jackie turned out to have been a bad political move. *The Washington Post* headlined a frontpage story—SEN. KENNEDY ON MEDITERRANEAN TRIP UNAWARE HIS WIFE HAS LOST BABY.

By the time the yacht reached Genoa on the Italian Riviera, Smathers spoke bluntly to JFK: "Get your ass to Newport or else you're washed up in politics. Leave the babes to Teddy and me. If you don't justify yourself in the press, American housewives will vote against you in spite of the fact you're one cute fucker, although no match for 'Gorgeous George' here."

JFK arrived in Newport through some difficult transportation connections. He rushed at once to Jackie's hospital room. There, he found his wife heavily medicated. The doctor had already warned him that she was suffering through a deep depression.

Even in her dazed state, she seemed to sense a presence by her side. JFK bent down to place a gentle kiss on his wife's lips.

Still drugged and only half awake, she delivered her first words to her errant husband, "Oh, Bobby, thank God you're back. I need you so. Don't ever leave me!"

Caroline Kennedy

JFK in Sexual Tryst During Jackie's Delivery of "Buttons"

In early November of 1957, Joe Kennedy turned over his apartment at 270 Park Avenue in Manhattan to JFK and Jackie during the final weeks of her latest pregnancy. She had flown to New York because she believed she could get the best medical care available at New York Hospital. After two failed pregnancies, she didn't want to take any chances with her latest delivery. She even gave up smoking,even though her self-restraint would be only temporary. Her sister, Lee, still in a shaky marriage to Michael Canfield, had flown from London to occupy the Park Avenue apartment with JFK and Jackie.

When Jackie entered the hospital in preparation for Caroline's birth, it was rumored that JFK began to pay special attention to Lee. He would later reveal to George Smathers, Charles Bartlett, Lem Billings, and others, that he seduced Lee while Jackie was in the hospital.

Nini Gore Auchincloss later made the claim that Lee had confessed to her that she'd had sexual relations with JFK during that interlude on Park Avenue.

Nini reportedly said, "The bedroom door was open and Jack and Lee were inside. From the living room, Michael could hear them making love. They did it openly, in spite of his presence in the adjoining room."

In the hospital, unaware of what was transpiring within the apartment on Park Avenue, Jackie concentrated on giving birth to a healthy baby. She'd been cured of venereal disease. On November 26, Caroline came into the world, prompting Jackie to define it as "the happiest day of my life."

Janet Auchincloss and JFK had waited impatiently in the waiting room. Janet scolded her son-in-law. "I'm glad you decided to make an appearance for this delivery."

When Jackie recovered consciousness after her anesthesia, her first vision was of her husband coming toward her with Baby Caroline cuddled in his arms.

When he turned the infant over to its mother, she asked him if she could name her Caroline Bouvier Kennedy in honor of her sister, whose full name, at birth, had been Caroline Lee Bouvier.

JFK, who had just emerged that morning from Lee's bed, willingly agreed.

Beautiful and regal in her own right, Princess **Lee Radziwill** lived in the spotlight. But even in that glare, she remained in the perpetual shadow of her more famous older sister.

For years, she reappeared perennially on the list of the world's ten best-dressed women. She found friends and lovers throughout the pantheon of international celebrity.

Lem Billings was their first visitor at the hospital. He later told Jackie, "I really pissed off Jack. He took me to the ward where there were at least a dozen babies. He told me that your daughter, his daughter, was the prettiest and asked me to point her out. I picked what I thought was the prettiest baby. It wasn't Caroline. Now he's not speaking to me."

Jackie was in a bad mood and really didn't want to tolerate Lem that afternoon. She looked at him skeptically: "Too bad that Jack can't impregnate you. You'd like that, wouldn't you?"

Familiar as he was with Jackie's cutting barbs, he chose to ignore her put-down. "Jack was delighted with his daughter, whom he had nicknamed 'Buttons.' He talked about her all the time. He was like a little boy who'd been given this wonderful toy for his birthday. I think Caroline's birth helped stabilize his shaky marriage to Jackie, at least for a month or so. The birth brought them closer together."

Joe Kennedy called immediately and discussed with his son the political advantage of Jackie having given birth, although he had hoped it would be a boy. "If it had been a boy, he might have grown up to become President of the United States one day."

When Lee and others came to visit Jackie, she told them that her own self-esteem as a woman had been restored by this successful birth. She and JFK designated Lee as Caroline's godmother, with Bobby named as the godfather.

After giving birth, Jackie remained in the hospital for two weeks, complaining that she felt too ill at that point to leave.

A hired nurse, Luella Hennessey, tried to teach JFK the fine art of bottle feeding and diaper changing. But when JFK faced Caroline's first smelly potty, he fled. "Let the nanny do it."

He was referring to Caroline's English nanny, Maud Shaw. She would later write a memoir entitled *White House Nanny*. Published in 1964, after her husband's assassination, Jackie read it before publication and, as was her way, wanted to censor it.

Shaw had written, "The moment that Caroline whimpered or dirtied her diaper, Jackie and the Senator would turn the infant over to my care. Mrs. Kennedy refused to breast-feed Caroline. When it came time to feed her, JFK didn't have the patience with her bottle and would immediately hand the baby girl over to me, as if passing on a football."

***

In November of 1960, on the night of the presidential election, Caroline, at least, became a footnote in U.S. history. During JFK's heated race against Richard M. Nixon, votes were still being counted when JFK collapsed into bed at four in the morning.

At 9:30AM the next day, Nixon conceded and JFK was announced as the 35th President of the United States.

With Jackie's permission, Caroline ran into his bedroom. He called out to her from the bathroom, where he was soaking in the tub. "Daddy, daddy," she shouted. "You've won. You're the president!"

He rose suddenly from the tub in joy, giving Caroline her first glimpse of the male anatomy.

As First Child in 1961, Caroline became a media event, in spite of Jackie's attempts to shield her from the press. JFK battled with his wife over this issue, who wanted to keep her locked away from the public eye. In contrast, JFK called in photographers whenever Jackie was away.

As one journalist wrote of the blue-eyed, golden-haired child, "Not since Shirley Temple rode to box office fame in the 1930s has one child received such international coverage as the President's daughter, not even Margaret Truman and her failed attempt to play the piano."

John F. Kennedy, Jr., "The Most Famous Baby in the World,"
"A Future President"

In November of 1960, Jackie was under a great deal of stress, realizing how much smoking alleviated her tensions. But her newborn baby was due in early December, and consequently, she had temporarily given up cigarettes.

Also, in the wake of her husband's electoral defeat of Richard Nixon, she was also jittery about her upcoming move into 1600 Pennsylvania Avenue.

Her friend, the syndicated columnist Igor Cassini *[aka Cholly Knicker-bocker, the brother of her her favorite fashion designer, Oleg Cassini],* came to visit her at her home in Georgetown. He later reported, "She was obsessing about the danger her husband and daughter were facing now that they were preparing to move into the White House. She told me that the Secret Service had informed her how easy it was to kill a President."

"All it takes is a lunatic with a gun," one of the agents had informed her, "providing he's willing to give his life for the President's."

Jackie was also concerned that her children might be kidnapped.

Right before the birth of their baby, JFK had flown to the LBJ ranch in Texas to confer with his new Vice President, Lyndon B. Johnson. After that, JFK had flown to Palm Beach for a brief sojourn with his aging parents.

Back in Washington, he attended Thanksgiving dinner with Jackie and Caroline, along with his faithful companion, Lem Billings.

Jackie was disappointed when her husband informed her that he could not stay in Washington, but instead promised a return in early December for the upcoming birth of their next child. He claimed that he had to meet with political aides in Palm Beach to discuss his transitional government, including recommendations for Cabinet members.

Right after JFK left Washington, Jackie began experiencing labor pains. Even though her baby wasn't due—at least based on the prognosis of his doctors—she suspected that the infant was about to make an appearance.

Evelyn Lincoln called JFK to tell him that Jackie had been rushed to a hospital. 'I'm never there when Jackie needs me," he lamented to his Secret Service.

From Palm Beach, he took the press plane back to Washington. While airborne, he was told at 1:17am on November 27 that he was the father of a newborn baby boy,

To get **Caroline** to adore her baby brother, Jack told her that the boy belonged to her. She became very protective of him, overruling her parents if she felt "something not right for my baby." Lem Billings claimed that Caroline and **John-John** "seemed like twins."

named John Fitzgerald Kennedy, Jr. Delivered by means of a cesarean, the premature baby was slightly underweight, weighing six pounds, three ounces. The infant was experiencing respiratory problems, and was in an incubator, but otherwise seemed healthy.

Arriving at the hospital, JFK was immediately confronted by the Secret Service with news of a crisis. It feared the Jackie might have been the target of an assassination attempt, very similar to the one she'd experienced at Newport in 1956 during the traumatic stillbirth of Arabella. In Newport, she'd been more vulnerable because of her location in a room on the hospital's ground floor. In Georgetown, she was assigned a room on the fifth floor.

JFK was told that a young man had been apprehended at the Georgetown Hospital when he tried to enter an elevator. He was unshaven and wearing scruffy clothing, arousing the suspicions of the Secret Service.

He was apprehended by two agents and was found to be carrying five sticks of dynamite, in circumstances equivalent to the earlier attempt against Jackie in Newport.

The young man was grilled, and the Secret Service called the bomb squad of the U.S. Army. Two officials then arrived to carefully remove and dispose of the dynamite.

JFK learned that the young man lived in Dallas with his mother. *[His father was unknown.]* He revealed nothing of his motivation other than saying, "I hate Kennedy."

As President-elect, JFK then made a major decision. After conferring with his aides, he decided he didn't want to begin his administration with frontpage news about a threatened assassination of his wife and child. He wanted the young man exiled to Dallas under the supervision of a Secret Service agent. The agent was asked to instruct the Dallas police to keep this young man under surveillance as a possible life threatening assassin..

JFK decided not to inform Jackie of this, fearing "She's under enough stress already. Now I want to see my boy."

He was then directed to wherever Jackie was staying, with their child, for a look at his newborn. "What a beautiful baby," he said. "I think I'll name him Abraham Lincoln."

After a few hours of visiting and comforting Jackie, he went to make some urgent phone calls. She asked to be wheeled down the hospital corridor by a nurse to see her son in incubation.

As she was wheeled down the corridor, a photographer jumped out of a broom closet and snapped her picture. She screamed for the Secret Service. One of the agents knocked the photographer to the floor, grabbed his camera, and exposed the film.

By all indications, the man was about to be arrested, but Jackie urged the police not to. "If he's arrested, it will lead off the evening news even if war is declared." At the time, she did not know of the existence or the motivation of the potential dynamiter.

As America's newest First Lady, she made only one statement. "My major effort will be devoted to my children. If Caroline and John turn out badly, nothing I could do in the public eye would have any meaning."

She remained in the hospital for a week. When John Jr. was diagnosed as medically out of danger, he was brought into her room to be with his mother. She protectively cuddled him and received visits from his father at least three times a day. On the second visit, he brought Caroline.

JFK told Jackie that Caroline had been afraid that her mother would give birth to another "daddy's little darling." She seemed relieved that it was revealed that her sibling was a boy—not a girl. JFK told her that John Jr. was her birthday present.

Maud Shaw, the nanny, later claimed that, "For about a year, Caroline referred to the boy as "my baby," and gave me strict orders about what I could do and not do."

From around the world, thousands of gifts poured in, from clothes to toys, but small animals were also shipped. JFK ordered that they be given to centers for needy children.

Jackie was overwhelmed by the thousands of cards and letters addressed to her. She asked to receive only letters from famous people, such as Eleanor Roosevelt. Mrs. Roosevelt pointed out that her children had been considerably older when she and FDR had occupied the White House. "Nonetheless, you and your children will be living in a fish bowl with the entire world staring as you, your boy, your girl, and your husband swim around."

JFK attended John Jr.'s christening on December 8. Jackie dressed him in a lace gown that Rose had had made for JFK in 1917.

When she was well enough to leave the hospital, Jackie was driven by limousine to confer with Mamie Eisenhower at the White House for the traditional meeting of a retiring First Lady welcoming the newly arrived one to show her around.

Mamie had been alerted that a wheelchair would be necessary, with the communication that Jackie had been experiencing periods of dizziness. Mamie balked at that, informing the Secret Service that she would not be the one to push Jackie around the White House in a wheelchair.

After hearing that, Jackie decided to abandon the idea of a wheelchair and that she'd proceed on a walking tour with Mamie unaided. She later claimed that "Eisenhower's wife was very distant, frigidly cold in her greeting. She seemed most anxious to be through with me."

After the tour, during a limousine ride back to Georgetown, Jackie informed her social secretary, Letitia Baldrige, "I'm appalled at the White House. It is so unkempt.

The Belle of the White House, supplanted by Jackie's arrival: **Mamie Eisenhower**

175

Doors needed to be painted. A lot of the wallpaper has yellowed. It looks like an emporium decorated by a wholesale furniture store during a January clearance. I don't want my children to grow up in such an uninviting place. There will be lots of changes when I take over."

That afternoon, she bundled up John Jr. and flew with him to Palm Beach to join Caroline and JFK, who were already there. Perhaps as a preface to the inauguration jitters to come, the family had arranged to spend Christmas together.

In the Kennedy compound Jackie had won the allegiance of a servant, who fed her information about her in-laws, and especially about JFK. Of course, she slipped the servant a hundred dollar bill quite frequently.

To her dismay, she learned that JFK had resumed his affair with Florence Pritchett, the wife of Earl E.T. Smith, the former U.S. ambassador to Cuba. Florence had been an old flame of her husband. Considerably younger than JFK, she'd begun her affair with JFK after his return from World War II. It was rumored that they first made love on the beach between their respective houses. *[Flo, as Jack called her, lived with her parents in a house immediately adjacent to the Kennedy compound.]*

JFK, according to Lem Billings, had wanted to marry her, but Joe had objected, "You can't marry a divorced woman and still be president."

[ALL IN THE FAMILY: Ironically, Flo's husband, Smith himself, had previously dated Janet Auchincloss, Jackie's mother, during the breakup of her marriage to Black Jack Bouvier.]

During his time in Palm Beach, prior to his presidential inauguration, and before Jackie's arrival there for the celebration of Christmas, 1960 she also learned that JFK was carrying on an affair with the 22-year-old Georgetown debutante, Pamela Turnure. Simultaneous with their affair, JFK was urging Jackie to designate Turnure as her Press Secretary.

***

John Kennedy, Jr. moved into the White House in February of 1961 and was given one of the largest rooms in the building. Jackie had already transformed it into his nursery. He'd inherited his sister Caroline's crib, from which Jackie had removed the pink bows and replaced them with blue ones. The contents of his bottle, prepared on a nearby gas stove, was fed to him at six every morning. His morning nap was the south-facing view from the Truman Balcony, which its namesake had added to the White House in 1948. The White House itself was seeing its first resident infant in nearly seventy years.

Overnight, John Jr. had become most famous baby in the world, and he'd grow up to become America's Prince Charming, idolized by millions, especially when the cute little boy attended his father's funeral after the assassination. In 1999, millions more mourned JFK Jr.'s own untimely death in a private plane crash.

But before his tragic death at the age of 39, a glamorous life unfolded for

176

him as the adorable son of the two most glamorous figures ever to inhabit the White House.

Almost from the date of John's birth, there were threats from kidnappers—some real, some unsubstantiated from the "merely deranged." He was assigned a special three-man Secret Service team to protect him.

The Director of the FBI ordered that all these threatening letters be sent to him, so that his agents could investigate each of them separately.

J. Edgar knew that the kidnapping of the most celebrated baby in the world would instantly provoke an international incident, dwarfing the infamy of the Lindbergh baby. "We don't want to be caught asleep when some kidnapper hoists a ladder to Junior's bedroom at the White House and hauls off this precious cargo. Jack Kennedy would have our heads."

From the very beginning, J. Edgar was fascinated by the infant. A spy he had planted within the White House fed him information. He learned that the nannies who changed John Jr.'s diapers nicknamed him "Big Boy." J. Edgar concluded that the boy had inherited his penis from the Bouvier side of his family, not from his father.

J. Edgar's informants picked up and filed the most esoteric and trivial information on the young boy. He didn't like children's theater because he wanted to see dramas "where someone gets their head chopped off." From Moscow, Nikita Khrushchev sent him a Russian puppy named "Pushinka." The boy also loved to visit a snake farm near Camp David where he would let a harmless cobra he named George crawl all over him.

John Jr.'s first attempt at a presidential "assassination" was when the communist dictator Marshall Tito of Yugoslavia was giving a speech at the White House. Playing upstairs on the Truman Balcony, Junior dropped a toy gun, its fall into a maze of television cables caught on camera, causing consternation among the Secret Service.

The kidnapping threats would continue throughout John Jr.'s life, and grew especially heavy during his second year at the New York University School of Law. He refused the FBI's offer of around-the-clock police protection.

A fellow classmate, Baird Jones, told biographer C. David Heymann, "Kidnapping threats were commonplace. I happened to know the people who ran the mailroom at NYU. One day they showed me some of the threatening letters. It was incredible stuff, totally insane. One card stipulated that unless several million dollars changed hands, John would be kidnapped or killed. It surprised me that John was able to go about his business—ride his bike around town, get on the subway—without the slightest hesitation."

Under the Freedom of Information Act, the FBI files on John Jr. have been published, but they are among the most censored ever released by the Bureau. Almost none of them make any sense as the wording, for the most part, has been completely blacked out with a heavy pen. Many contain only the most innocuous words, as the juicy details have been censored.

Throughout JFK Jr.'s FBI file, the word "kidnapping" occurs the most frequently, although there are also references to "abduction."

As informational sources, because of their edits, the files are virtually worthless, and many of the really scandalous have been removed. One document dated October 10, 1996, states: "Supposedly, this was aborted because . . . scheme did not work. . . . was in charge of the plan and for making all the arrangements for the kidnapping. The plan also involved . . . who. . . . After kidnapping Kennedy, he would be taken to. . . . Kennedy would be held there until. . . ."

Patrick Kennedy:
His Death a Foreshadowing of What Was to Come

During the last months of JFK's presidency, the papers headlined the news that Jackie, the First Lady of the land, was pregnant again, after having survived the successful births of both Caroline and John Jr., who was now identified in the press as "John-John," a name he would come to hate.

In August of 1963, Jackie was enjoying a bright, sunny day on Squaw Island, a community less than a mile from the Kennedy Compound at Hyannis Port. *[Squaw Island is part of the Massachusetts mainland, and not an island, as its name would imply.]* JFK had rented Brambletyde, a large, rambling, gray-shingled house, for the summer. A Secret Service command center was installed within a trailer on the grounds.

With two agents of the Secret Service trailing behind, Jackie went for a walk along the seashore, listening to the sound of the seagulls, imagining what JFK was doing in Washington, and wondering what her life would soon be like if her husband ran again for President during the upcoming elections of 1964.

At one point, she became dizzy, tripped, and fell. Something horrible seemed to be happening within her body, which was wracked with a sharp, jabbing pain. She couldn't rise to her feet. She let out a blood-curdling scream, which caused her Secret Service agents, enjoying a smoke, to rush to her side. They virtually had to carry her back into the house.

As the pain continued, she was put to bed. Fortunately, her doctor, John W. Walsh, was vacationing nearby. Within 15 minutes, he was rushed to her rented home. A professor of obstetrics at Georgetown University Medical School, he gave her a quick examination, realizing just how serious her condition was. He asked the Secret Service to summon a helicopter to fly her at once to the military hospital at Otis Air Force Base near Falmouth on Cape Cod.

Within thirty minutes, Jackie, still clutching her stomach, was airborne. A four-room suite had already been prepared for her at Otis by the time she was wheeled in.

After a fifteen-minute examination, three doctors determined that she should have a caesarean at once. The Secret Service sent word to JFK of Jackie's emergency.

Her ordeal on the operating table at Otis was best reconstructed in a novel by Ruth Francisco, a fictionalized account of Jackie's agony, as it appeared in "*The Secret Memoirs of Jacqueline Kennedy Onassis,* published in 2006.

"I go to a frightening purgatory, where disembodied voices swirl around me. Hot lights roast me, and cold instruments prod my body. I push aside the darkness as through murky water, reaching for my baby. I catch glimpses, little fingers, an eye, his lady's slipper bottom, obscured by seaweed, appearing, disappearing, as the ocean respires. The water pitches and tosses me, and I become conscious of its rhythm, its breathing labored and tired. I know breathing is the problem, breathing is the danger. A wave picks me up and throws me against the ocean floor, knocking me out."

A very weak and frail child, Patrick Bouvier Kenedy, was delivered, weighing only four pounds, ten ounces.

The doctors determined that Patrick, based on his not-fully-developed lungs, was suffering from Neonatal Respiratory Disease. He was placed into an incubator.

When Jackie came out of sedation, she was given a full report of her newborn son's distress. Weeks later, she would confide to Janet and a few other close friends her fear that she'd played a part in Patrick's breathing maladies because, in spite of her vows, she had resumed her heavy chain-smoking based on the stress of being First Lady.

She'd later say, "Patrick's death was a horrible foreshadowing of the end of my days with Jack. I lost a husband and a son. All within a period of months."

She had a premonition that Patrick would not survive, and from her hospital bed, she ordered that the infant be baptized at once.

The President was airborne when word reached him about the distress of his son. He was headed for Hyannis Port at the time.

Just before he boarded the plane, he had enjoyed the sexual favors of Mary Pinchot Meyer in the Lincoln Bedroom of the White House. She was the sister of Toni Bradlee, the ex-wife of Ben Bradlee, a high-placed executive of *[and later Executive Editor at]* the *Washington Post.* Meyer herself was the ex-wife of a former official at the CIA, Cord Meyer. Author Nina Burleigh, in her book *A Very Private Woman* wrote that after her divorce from Meyer, Mary became "a well-bred ingenue out looking for fun and getting in trouble along the way." Jackie referred to Mary as "The Jezebel of the White House."

JFK's secretary, Evelyn Lincoln, later claimed that she recorded the number of Meyer's visits to the White House between January of 1962 to November of 1963 as a total of thirty. In fact, she had a romantic encounter with JFK right before he flew to Dallas. She later admitted that in the White House, she had snorted cocaine and smoked pot with the President. Allegations from Timothy Leary, a friend of Meyers, claim her involvement with LSD and hint at her expressed interest in experimenting with it with JFK.

[On October 12, 1964, Mary, at the age of forty-four, was mysteriously shot, dying instantly from a bullet wound fired at close range into the back of her head, and another directly into her heart, during a promenade along a canal-fronting towpath near her Georgetown studio. A soaking wet, disheveled-looking alleged bystander, Raymond Crump, was arrested and charged with her murder, but when he went to court, a jury acquitted him. When Crump came to trial, Judge Howard Corcoran, an appointee of Lyndon B. Johnson, ruled that Mary Pinchot Meyer's private life could not be disclosed in the courtroom. A jury later acquitted him. Mary's murder is still listed as unsolved.]

Years after its grisly conclusion, *The Washington Post* hailed the affair of JFK and **Mary Pinchot Meyer** *(subject of both photos, above)* as *"Midnight in the Garden of Good and Evil* Meets *Camelot."*

Meyer's subsequent unsolved murder has never been solved, nor has her diary, in which she documented details about her affair with the President, ever surfaced.

***

From Boston, a leading pediatrician, Dr. James E. Drorbaugh, was rushed to Otis Air Force Base by helicopter. He examined Patrick thoroughly, and was therefore able to report on his condition to JFK when he arrived at the hospital.

The President's first question stunned the doctor: "Will my son be retarded?" JFK asked. Perhaps he was remembering his younger sister, Rosemary, who had been born mentally retarded and was subsequently sent to an asylum.

The doctor told JFK that Patrick needed to be delivered by helicopter to the Children's Hospital in Boston, which was the best equipped to deal with Patrick's respiratory problem.

JFK agreed, but requested that the infant be taken first to Jackie's hospital room.

With JFK at her side, she held her infant son for ten minutes before he was transferred, by helicopter, to Boston. That was the last time she'd see him alive.

The Boston Globe ran a blaring headline—BABY SPED TO BOSTON. A secondary story said, "Whole World Taken by Littlest Kennedy."

Except for reports on Patrick's condition, other news in America virtually ground to a halt.

Only junior doctors were on duty at the Children's Hospital in Boston that day, as the senior pediatricians were away on vacation.

Dr. Alexander S. Nadas, a pioneer in pediatric cardiology, the finest in the nation, was summoned, although he could not arrive until the next day. In the meantime, Patrick's breathing had grown worse, and far more labored.

In Boston, Dr. Welton M. Gersony remembered JFK as "tanned, calm, cool, and very polite." Once again, the President pressed Dr. Gersony to reveal if the boy would be retarded.

"Right now, Mr. President, we can't possibly know that," the doctor said. "Our aim now is to save his life."

In 1963, the nation was watching the fate of "the littlest Kennedy."

An urgent call came in from Lee Radziwill, who spoke to JFK. She informed him that a Dr. Samuel Z. Levine, a Manhattan pediatrician, had saved the life of her infant, who was also a "preemie," *[a nickname for a premature baby]*.

Secret Service agents located Levine strolling in Manhattan's Central Park and immediately hustled him onto a plane to Boston.

JFK wasn't so polite when he met Dr. Levine. "I'm very impressed with the efficiency of government," the doctor said.

"It's about time you doctors learned that," JFK snapped. "Now get in there and save my boy's life."

At the time, the only treatment that could be recommended was a pressurized device called a hyperbaric chamber, which would increase the oxygen levels in a patient's bloodstream. In most cases, it was used in the treatment of "blue babies"—that is, infants with congenital heart defects that deprived them of adequate amounts of oxygen. On three previous occasions, "preemies" without other recourses had been placed within such chambers, but without success.

Before placing Patrick in the chamber, doctors warned JFK that access to the heightened oxygen levels in the chamber might cause blindness. Without consulting Jackie, JFK decided to take the risk.

[Dr. Drorbaugh later wondered, "Did I do the right think in recommending Patrick for that blue baby chamber?" Medical experts estimate that if Patrick had been born in 2014, under the same conditions, his chance of survival would have been about 95 percent better than it was in 1963.]

The doctors gave a detailed explanation to JFK about Patrick's condition, which was then diagnosed as Hyaline Membrane Disease. *[That malady is referred to today at Respiratory Distress Syndrome.]* He was told that Hyaline referred to a glassy membrane that had formed in Patrick's air sacs, impeding his ability to extract oxygen from inhaled air.

The President was also informed that some 25,000 babies every year were affected with this disease, but he was assured that previous preemies had survived and gone on to great glory, namely Isaac Newton, Albert Einstein, Pablo Picasso, and Sir Winston Churchill.

Lem Billings flew to JFK's side. He remembered, "Jack got down on his knees and prayed like he'd never prayed before for his son to live. He promised that if God would let Patrick live, he'd even give up what he called 'poon.' He also promised that if Patrick's life could be saved, that he would not run for the presidency in 1964."

For an hour, JFK stood at glass partition, looking in at Patrick in his attempt to breathe regularly. Finally, he left to visit Jackie in her hospital room. In the early hours of the morning of Friday, August 8, 1963, he was awakened by a doctor, who told him that his son was dead. Sedated, Jackie was still asleep.

"When his boy died, it almost killed the President," Larry Newman, a Secret Service agent, later said. "He went into a private room and for about an hour, we could hear him crying. It was more like moaning. It was the deepest form of anguish."

In spite of his grief over Patrick's death, JFK was also aware of its political implications. David Powers, his aide, overheard him telling Jackie. "We must not create an atmosphere of sadness at the White House because that would not be good for us, or for anyone—certainly not for the country, and not for the work I have to do."

Author J. Randy Taraborrelli wrote about Jackie sitting alone in the White House nursery that she'd decorated for Patrick: "As days turned into weeks, Jackie fell into a disturbing melancholy, staring off into space, crying unexpectedly, and losing her appetite. No one knew what to say to her to console her, nor did they know how to handle her sudden crying jags and her many questions about her own responsibility in Patrick's death."

Before Patrick was buried, JFK had placed a silver money clip, affixed to a St. Christopher medal, inside his coffin. It had been a gift from Jackie. When she heard what he had done, she asked her secretary, Mary Gallagher, to call Tiffany's and get a replacement as her gift to JFK.

Baby Patrick was the first Kennedy to be buried in the large family plot at Holyhead Cemetery in Brookline, Massachusetts. It had recently been purchased by Joseph Kennedy as a kind of communal Kennedy mausoleum. JFK stood looking at the open grave, just before the coffin, whose color was that of a polished elephant tusk, was lowered into the ground. He put his hand on the coffin. The Secret Service agents saw his tears.

"Farewell, my son," he said softly.

Jackie later had many teary nights fretting over Patrick's unfinished years.

"His precious little life was over before it had begun."

Ghoulish Exhumations
Digging Up the Graves of the Kennedy Infants

James Auchincloss was the half-brother of Jackie. When she married John F. Kennedy in 1953, the young boy carried the wedding train of his half-sister up the aisle. Nicknamed Jamie, he was the son of Janet and Hugh Auchincloss.

At age six, Jamie had visited the White House and got to sit on JFK's desk in the Oval Office. He liked to talk politics with the President.

Janet claimed that "Jamie hero-worshipped Jack. He was so proud of his charismatic brother-in-law.

"It's because of Jack that I've become the first Democrat in the history of the Auchincloss family," Jamie proclaimed.

As Hugh Auchincloss's financial problems intensified, Janet often took out her frustrations on Jamie, treating him unfairly. He was not allowed to know that his father was having money problems.

Relationships between Janet and Jamie were often troubled. He once drove virtually nonstop from Washington to Newport, covering the distance in a then-record eight hours, only to have her attack his sloppy dress. After their confrontation, Jamie immediately got back into his car and drove another eight hours back to Washington.

On that dreadful day in November of 1963, Janet heard the TV blaring with news about the assassination of JFK. She called Jamie at the Brooks School. It was Jamie who spoke first. "Mummy, I think he's dead."

In the emotional days that followed JFK's assassination, Jamie was forced to attend a final funeral that he considered "ghoulish." In the immediate aftermath of her husband's death, Jackie had become obsessed with returning her dead children, both Arabella and Patrick, to positions beside their father's grave.

Jackie insisted that her mother supervise the exhumation of Arabella's coffin. At Newport's St. Columba's Cemetery, Janet witnessed the excavation of Arabella's grave. Janet took the coffin and its rotting contents for temporary storage to her farm at Hammersmith.

Jackie called Cardinal Richard Cushing and asked him to oversee Patrick's disinterment from the Kennedy grave site at Brookline, Massachusetts, the following day.

Subsequently, flying together on the same plane, Caroline, Janet, and Ted Kennedy brought the coffins of Patrick and Arabella to Washington.

Jamie was invited to the funeral, but he was haunted by the coffins of the dead babies. At Arlington National Cemetery, in a December 5, 1963 ceremony scheduled during the dead of night as a means of avoiding the press and photographers, Jamie, along with Jackie, Bobby, and Ted, watched the reburials. Jamie later said, "Jackie needed to do this and she did—at night, in the dark, by the Eternal Flame."

Jamie became interested in photography during his second year at New York City's Columbia University. He didn't know that this relatively harmless hobby would one day lead to his downfall when he was found guilty of taking pictures of nude or semi-nude young boys.

In 2009, Jackie's relative was indicted on 25 counts related to child porn. Within the courtroom of Jackson County (Oregon) circuit judge Mark Shiveley, Auchincloss pleaded guilty to two felony counts for encouraging child sexual abuse. The judge sentenced him to serve thirty days in jail on each count, concurrently, as part of three years of supervised probation. The judge also ordered that Auchincloss be formally registered as a convicted sex offender and that he agree to undergo psychiatric treatment for his affliction. In addition, he was ordered not to have any "unauthorized contact" with minors.

[As early as 1994, the year Jackie died, the family seemed aware of Jamie's sexual proclivities. He did not receive an invitation to Jackie's memorial service.

She was buried at Arlington, next to JFK and near her two babies, Arabella and Patrick.

Jamie had called and asked for an invitation to attend Jackie's burial but was rudely told that he was not invited. "But people know me," he protested to the Auchincloss family. "If I'm not there, it would look bad."

He was told that the family could not prevent him from showing up, but that he would have to stand outside and pay his respects that way.

"Farewell, Jackie," he called out from his position as a family outcast outside the church, as her casket was carried away by pallbearers.]

Partick Kennedy's grave at Arlington

POLICE
MUG SHOT

JACKIE O's
BROTHER
JAILED FOR
KID PORN

184

Chapter Nine

First Lady of Camelot

"I Hate that Name, It Sounds Like a Race Horse"
—Jacqueline Kennedy

Flying on Dr. Feelgood's Speed, Mythmaking Jack & Jackie Are Idolized by Millions

A vision of loveliness in pink satin, First Lady **Jacqueline Kennedy** never looked better than when she appeared at a White House gala on May 11, 1962. She easily dazzled the French culture minister, **André Malraux** *(far left)*, and his jealous wife, concert pianist **Marie-Madeleine Lioux**. Even **JFK** *(right)* looks on with admiration.

"I am the woman who has everything, including the President of the United States."
—Jacqueline Kennedy

185

After their electoral victory, in December of 1960, while JFK and Jackie had retreated to Palm Beach, before the rigors of the inauguration, Clint Hill of the Secret Service informed them of their new code names. JFK would be identified by his security forces as "Lancer" *[how fitting]*, and the First Lady would be known as "Lace."

During their transition into their seats of power, however, the new First Couple almost died.

On December 11, 1960, JFK didn't want to get out of bed to attend Sunday mass at St. Edward's Church in Palm Beach. Jackie insisted that he go because the press and the public would be expecting him. "The world will be watching," she told him.

She had still not recovered from her exhausting tour of the White House conducted by Mamie Eisenhower a few days before JFK's inauguration. Mrs. Eisenhower had not readily made a wheelchair available to her, as she had requested.

Death lurked outside the Kennedy compound. For two hours, a suicide bomber,

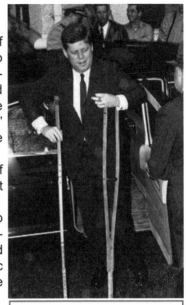

When **President Kennedy** was asked to help dig a hole during a tree-planting ceremony in Ottawa, he seriously injured his back. He had to be flown back to Washington where Dr. Feelgood was waiting to give him injections of "speed."

Richard P. Pavlick, had been waiting with seven sticks of dynamite. As the Secret Servicemen drove the President-elect out of the Kennedy compound's driveway, Pavlick intended to step on the accelerator of his vehicle, plowing his car into JFK's. He expected that the explosion would not only kill himself, but JFK and three Secret Service men too.

At the last minute, Jackie appeared with Caroline to tell JFK goodbye. Their nurse, Luella Hennessey, also appeared, carrying John-John for a goodbye kiss from his father.

As Pavlick later testified, "I just couldn't do it. My aim was to kill Kennedy,

Despite His Injuries and Illnesses,

JFK Transforms the White House into "Poon Heaven"

Jackie Becomes the Most Talked-About Woman in the World

but I couldn't blow up Jackie and her kids, too." According to his later testimony, Pavlick decided to attempt to kill Kennedy later.

His plan was never completed, of course. Three days later, while still plotting an assassination, Pavlick was arrested for drunk driving. The police discovered the plot. He was later charged with attempted murder and, after a trial, sentenced to fourteen years in prison.

When Jackie was informed of the assassination attempt, she said, "My family and I are nothing but sitting ducks in a shooting gallery."

***

In the afternoon, both father and son, Joe and Jack, received their male guests, including some reporters, in the nude. They sunbathed in the screened-off "Bull Pen" near the Kennedy swimming pool. George Smathers sometimes joined them.

Later in the afternoon, JFK would walk along the beach, trailed by the Secret Service, to the home of Earl E.T. Smith, who had been the U.S. ambassador to Cuba.

Perhaps with her husband's knowledge, Florence Pritchett Smith, the wife of the ambassador, sometimes spent two hours with the President-elect before he headed home for dinner with the Kennedy family. Jackie usually stayed in bed, claiming she could not hold down food.

En route to Washington for the inauguration, Jackie had her spirits lifted when Evelyn Lincoln, JFK's secretary, told her that she'd just been voted the "Most Admired Woman in the World," Beating out Queen Elizabeth and all other challengers. Jackie would top that poll every year until 1966.

Their Georgetown house was in disarray, with boxes being sent either into storage or else to the White House. "Pierre Salinger was practically holding press conferences in my bathroom," Jackie later lamented. "I finally told Jack he had to move out while I finished packing."

The President-elect went to live with his gay friend, William Walton.

"I didn't even know he was coming until I heard it announced over the radio," Walton said. "Within minutes, the Secret Service were knocking on my door. When Jack arrived, I offered to give him the master bedroom and sleep in my guest room, but Jack wouldn't hear of it. He shared my bed until he moved to 1600 Pennsylvania Avenue. In the middle of the night, I would wake up and could hardly believe it. Here I was lying in bed with the newly elected President of the United States. Those few precious nights would become the most glorious of my life—and I will say no more."

Arriving at the White House on the first day of their occupancy, Jackie was directed to the Queen's Bedroom because she felt weak. She had to reserve her strength for the evening's festivities. JFK told her that he'd be sleeping across the hallway in the Lincoln Bedroom.

A blizzard was about to hit Washington, and she dreaded inaugural night. Dr. Janet Travell was summoned to give her a Dexedrine, which pepped her up considerably. She warned Travell that she might need another to get through the evening's five inaugural balls.

That morning after riding to the Inauguration with Mamie Eisenhower, Jackie felt that she might get sick in the bitter weather.

She had watched as a bare-headed JFK, the first U.S. President born in the 20th Century, delivered an inspiring Inaugural Address, ending with his message of "Ask not what your country can do for you, but what you can do for your country." She'd later tell him that that speech would go down in the history of oratory, along with Pericles' Funeral Oration and Lincoln's Gettysburg Address. At the inauguration, she got to hear Robert Frost stumble through a poem of his, and Marian Anderson give a belting rendition of "The Star Spangled Banner."

For the Inaugural lunch, the interconnected families gathered—the Lees, the Bouviers, the Kennedys, and the Auchincloss clan, feasting on caviar, shrimp, and lobster.

Joe Kennedy confronted Letitia (Tish) Baldrige, demanding to know who all these people were, since he was picking up the tab.

"They're all a part of your extended family," she told him.

"Okay, I'll fill their bellies today, but don't ever invite this motley crew again," he warned.

Later, at the White House, the mansion overflowed with this extended family. Jackie didn't want to deal with any of them, and she headed up to the Queens Bedroom. She'd need more Dexedrine to get through the night. When cousins tried to come upstairs to inspect the Presidential quarters, they were turned away by the Secret Service.

As one of the worst blizzards in its history hit Washington, Jackie managed to attend only three of the evening's five balls. "Everybody said I looked dazzling," she later claimed, "but I felt like hell."

At the first ball, she was escorted inside by the Entertainment Coordinator, Frank Sinatra. At that time in her life, she detested him, claiming that he was "always pimping for Jack."

Unlike Jackie, JFK wanted to attend every event he could manage, even when he could stay for only a short while.

Jackie later said, "Jack had a little boy's sense of wonder and excitement. He loved greeting all the celebrities who had flown in to wish him well, everybody from Bette Davis to Ethel Merman."

At one point during one of the festivities, she was uncomfortably seated between Lyndon Johnson and Lady Bird. JFK excused himself and sneaked away for about half an hour. Jackie later heard the rumor that during this short interim, he had seduced Angie Dickinson, who was being escorted to the gala by JFK's friend, Red Fay. It might be apocryphal, but Angie was reported to have said, "It was the greatest seven minutes of my life."

Before the end of the third ball, Jackie's energy had faded despite the pep pills, and she asked JFK if she could be excused. He could attend the final two balls on his own, although she suspected he would not be alone for long.

One of Jackie's spies later told her how JFK topped off his pre-dawn morning after retreating from the fifth and final Inaugural Ball. The Secret Service delivered him to Dumbarton Street and the Georgetown home of the gay columnist Joseph Alsop. A group of JFK's most loyal cronies had gathered there for a nightcap with the President-elect.

After the drinks, his brother-in-law, Peter Lawford, took him into the library and introduced him to six Hollywood starlets imported for the occasion. Later, JFK whispered to Lawford, "Instead of *[these lesser]* starlets, if I weren't under such heavy scrutiny, I could have spent the night with Angie Dickinson and Kim Novak."

More and more, as a means of maintaining his sexual appetite, JFK was opting to position himself as the third member in various *ménages à trois.* Lawford had no trouble rounding up various bevies of starlets. "It seemed that every woman in Hollywood wanted to sleep with the handsome, dashing, newly elected President of the United States."

JFK made his selection—one a brunette, another a redhead. He disappeared upstairs with them, heading for Alsop's bedroom, which had just recently been vacated by a Washington pageboy from the Senate. *[Alsop, one of the premier political commentators of his era, freely admitted to his gender preference as a homosexual after an infamous attempt by a Soviet agent to blackmail him, based on an incident in a Moscow hotel room in 1957.]*

"What stamina!" Alsop said to Lawford when he came back into the living room. "On what must have been the longest day of his life, he's still raring to go."

"If you have what he has shot into his blood stream, you'd be up to hear the first rooster crow, too!" Lawford said.

After a round of seductions from some very talented young women, JFK was returned to the White House by the very discreet Secret Service, just as the first streaks of dawn broke through the overcast sky.

It would be the first day of his new Administration.

***

On her first morning in the White House, the sound of hammering woke Jackie up. Carpenters were preparing a pink room for Caroline and a blue nursery for John Jr.

She decided to remain in bed, as she was exhausted and was still recovering from the cesarean birth of her son.

There was a sudden knock on her door before it was thrown open. In barged JFK, accompanied by an aging Harry S Truman. Looking disheveled, she was horrified and pulled a quilt over her exposed breasts.

The former President seemed embarrassed by his intrusion and apologized for disturbing her. "I'm sorry," he said. "Jack and I thought you were up. Please excuse me. Good luck in your new home." Then he quickly departed.

"Thank you, Mr. President," she said to his departing back.

"Catch you later, sweetheart," JFK promised. "How many women have entertained two American presidents at the same time in her boudoir?"

When she did get up, she headed for the bathroom, where she discovered that her toilet overflowed. In an attempt to take a shower, she found that the nozzle ran only cold water.

"The plumbing was last installed during the reign of Rutherford B. Hayes," she later told friends. In the bedroom, she found no bookcases. "Didn't Mamie know how to read? There wasn't even a wastepaper basket."

After coffee, she met with Steve Cotrell, the contractor in charge of some of the structural renovations which had already been inaugurated prior to her arrival at the White House. "I'm going to dread living in this dump," she said. "It's as much a dungeon as Lubyanka. *[a reference to the KGB's notorious prison in Moscow.]*

Jackie's social secretary, **Letitia Baldrige**, was the arbiter of social etiquette. She handled the thousands of invitations directed at the First Lady. "Jackie's usual response was, 'Send Lady Bird instead of me.'"

As she toured the rooms scheduled for additional renovations, she said, "Too much Mamie pink. Everywhere I look, I find bad taste. Oh God, the White House is cold and dreary. I don't think I've seen anything like it, but then, I haven't visited many prisons. I can't bear the thought of moving in. I hate it, hate it, hate it!"

She visited the office of her social secretary, Tish Baldrige, and was horrified at the number of committees, social clubs, and special interest groups requesting her presence. She was invited to attend the National Gallery of Art, where the venue included her presiding over award presentations to America's distinguished women. "There's no way I'm going to stand in line and shake the hands of 4,500 guests."

"Tell Lady Bird to go in my place," Jackie ordered. "The same goes for invitations from the American Red Cross, the Girl Scouts of America, and the Georgia Hogcallers."

"Some school reporters from Vassar, your alma mater, want to interview you," Baldrige said.

"Tell them I'm not well," Jackie said. "Also, I'm not into visiting distant relatives, women's clubs around America, the Dairy Association, or any charity event. Need I go on? I think you get the point."

"I want you to extend a series of invitations to the country's leading poets, dancers, artists, and musicians. Perhaps George Balanchine of the New York City Ballet. Perhaps Margot Fonteyn and Rudolf Nureyev would visit and maybe perform. I'm interested in having Pablo Casals appear. I know he's living in exile in Puerto Rico and that he said he will not perform in any country that recognizes Franco *[Francisco Franco, the Dictator of Spain].* But I think he'll accept an invitation from me."

"One more thing: Lem Billings is always bragging about how he became friends with Greta Garbo on the Riviera. I've always wanted to meet her. Even if she's mostly a recluse, I'm sure she would consider a private invitation to the White House. Set it up. Of course, we'll have to invite Lem, too."

Calling a meeting of the entire White House staff, she presented each of them with a Letter of Agreement for them to sign, in which they would be ordered not to talk about life in the White House or write about it after they left. Of course, in time, many of those agreements would be largely ignored as staff members wrote what it was like inside the White House during the reign of Camelot.

At the end of the first busy day, she retired with JFK to one of the upstairs sitting rooms. He lit a match to an already laid fire. The smoke immediately backed up from the chimney, forcing them to flee to another part of the house.

On Jackie's second day, she continued her march through the rooms of the White House. To her horror, she noted that it was filled with Victorian mirrors. She ordered the staff to remove them. "I detest Victorian mirrors," she said.

She was also alarmed at the parade of tourists through the White House. She immediately cancelled all afternoon tours, claiming that they interfered with her renovations.

Meeting with the housekeeper, she established new rules. "Bath and hand towels were to be changed three times a day. Sheets were to be changed even if JFK and herself had taken only a twenty-minute nap.

She also met with the accountant who kept track of White House expenses. He told her that the Senate had appropriated $50,000 for renovations to their private quarters.

[Within a month of living in the White House, Jackie had spent the entire budget. Through the influence of Senator Smathers, she was able to get the Senate Budget Committee to appropriate another $125,000. That money was quickly absorbed in renovations. She told Tish Baldrige, "Thank God I have some women friends, Jayne Wrightsman and Bunny Mellon, who will donate millions to help me finish the renovations."]

She further strained her budget by bringing in a coven of personal servants—a valet for JFK when Lem Billings wasn't around, a governess for the children, a private masseuse, a press secretary, a social secretary, a hairdresser three or four times a week, with the understanding that "Mr. Kenneth" would be flown in from New York a few hours before any gala or state dinner.

She told her aide, "I have to face my husband's mistress every morning now that he's hired Pamela Turnure as my press secretary."

Meeting with Pamela, she outlined her rules. "I won't pose for photographs. I won't grant interviews until Jack announces he's running for re-election in 1964."

She also made a daily visit to the office of Pierre Salinger, the White House press secretary. She was distressed at the personal items being written about

191

her and her family. "Someone is obviously supplying inside information to *Women's Wear Daily,* all this focus on my wardrobe. My every move seems to be spied on. That dinner for the Shah of Iran and his Empress. That paper even wrote about what food I served on what expensive dishes, even my gown for the evening, contrasting how I stacked up against the Empress.

Her hostility toward the press became so strained that JFK had to warn her, "You've got to suck up more. After all, I plan to run for re-election."

"Jackie was always at war with the press," Salinger said. "I don't understand why. She got a massive amount of favorable copy. Seemingly everybody was writing about her style and grace. In spite of all that, she was constantly pissed off at the press."

Her first dinner party was an informal affair attended by, among others, Franklin D. Roosevelt, Jr. and Joseph Alsop. Composer Leonard Bernstein was the guest of honor.

Both JFK and Jackie were unaware of how the theatrical and very effusive Bernstein traditionally greeted his hosts. Before she knew what was happening, when she reached to shake his hand, he quickly moved in on her, darting his tongue into her mouth.

Standing next to her, JFK was astonished, but decided to handle it with humor. "Don't I get one?"

"You sure do," the famous conductor said, moving in on the new President, whose mouth was soon after invaded by the infamous Bernstein tongue.

The guests gathered around the first couple, drinking champagne and devouring caviar, which Jackie told them was a gift from Nikita Khrushchev.

Unlike Mamie, the new First Lady liked French chefs, jewelry, the cultural elite, lavish dinners, fancy hairdos, beauty, style, high fashion, ballet troupes, Shakespearean actors, jazz musicians, opera singers, Nobel laureates, *et al.*

Just for fun, she'd do something unorthodox, such as throwing a "Twist" party where she twisted with Robert McNamara, U.S. Secretary of Defense. Indiscreetly, she was overhead saying, "I should have married Robert instead of Jack."

***

Jackie's hope that JFK would cut down on his womanizing after his move into the White House was quickly abandoned as reality set in. From reports that reached her, he seemed more dedicated to his adulterous affairs than ever before.

It was said that once JFK took over the White House, he inaugurated a "revolving door policy"—that is, with beautiful young women coming and going.

Even when Jackie was in residence, JFK would slip away to a remote room within the White House for a sexual tryst, especially when he was so well-protected by the Secret Service. According to Senator George Smathers, women "were lining up to fuck the President." Or, as Shirley MacLaine so colorfully phrased it, "Better that he fuck one of us—and not the country."

192

Sometimes, Jackie had long talks with her trusted friend, William Walton, who was frequently at the White House. She confessed that since moving in, she'd confronted JFK only one time about his womanizing. "What is this over-powering need you have for other women?" she asked.

According to Jackie, he looked sheepishly at her and said, "I don't know. I honestly don't know what drives me."

"He sounded like a guilty little boy," she told Walton.

Despite his marriage to Jackie, Jack still remained the capital's most eligible bachelor," Ted Sorensen said, sarcastically.

The men of the Secret Service, nearly all of whom took their responsibilities of protecting the President very seriously, were alarmed at the women he let into the White House without security clearance—elevator operators, hotel maids, hat-check girls, desk clerks, airline stewardesses, showgirls, and an occasional Hollywood star such as Jayne Mansfield. On several different occasions, she was "imported" from the West Coast into the White House just to service JFK.

"It was something else during the so-called 'Reign of Camelot,'" said Traphes Bryant, the kennel-keeper of the White House. *[His memoir,* Dog Days at the White House, The Outrageous Memoirs of the Presidential Kennel Keeper, *evaluated some of the revolving door scandals associated with JFK's tenure. The notorious book was not devoted just to the care and feeding of man's best friend. It was the first book to reveal the numerous affairs of JFK and made the charge that he had an insatiable appetite for women. It is also the original source for a story that's been repeated in countless books: As the revelation goes, Jackie was in the President's bed when she discovered a woman's panties between the sheets. She held up the panties she had found with two fingers in much the same way that she would hold up a dead mouse. She said to the President. "These are not my size."]*

"I had to check with someone in security," Traphes revealed. "I took the elevator to the upper rooms. When the door opened, I saw three nude women running down the corridor. You wouldn't see that when Mr. and Mrs. Herbert Hoover were living here."

"Everyone assigned to the White House, except a spy or two I had, seemed to be doing Jack's bidding...I mean, covering up for him," Jackie claimed. "I heard reports that many of the White House secretaries made themselves available to my husband. His two favorites were nicknamed 'Fiddle' (Priscilla Weir) and 'Faddle' (Jill Cowan)."

"I met Fiddle and Faddle on several occasions," said Smathers. "They were a couple of dogs, but Jack was always hot for them."

"In his own peculiar way, I think Jack loved Jackie," Smathers said. "The other gals were just bimbos going through that revolving door. I can't believe how many women, married or otherwise, were willing to do his bidding, both on the home front and abroad. After all, he was the President of the United States."

During Jackie's first trip away from the White House, as she headed with the children to her country home in Virginia, JFK staged the first of his nude swimming pool parties in the basement of the White House. These parties pleased him so much that they became a frequently scheduled ritual. He got so daring one time that he staged a poolside orgy when Jackie was in residence. A Secret Serviceman, standing at the door leading into the pool area, barred her from entering, which infuriated her. That led to one of her biggest fights with JFK.

"I was often invited when Bobby, Teddy, and Jack were nude, and in the pool with at least five naked women for fun and frolic," Smathers claimed.

"Sometimes, my friend, Lyndon, joined us in these nude frolics in and beside the pool," Smathers said. "He was always proud to show off what he called 'Jumbo.'"

Smathers and others noted that more and more, JFK was moving from one-man, one-woman sex to orgies. Three-ways also became more prevalent. Once when Smathers was with him at the pool, he seduced a young woman and then ordered her to perform fellatio on his aide, David Powers, while he looked on as a *voyeur.*

On many a week, Jackie spent only three nights in the White House. It even became a joke on TV, one comedian signing off with, "Good night, Mrs. Kennedy, wherever you are."

"Jack encouraged her to go away so that he could turn the White House into poontang heaven," Smathers said. "I've known a lot of horndogs in my day, but never any man with Jack's libido. He just couldn't get enough."

Even though she was married at the time *[to a bisexual husband]*, Patricia Kennedy Lawford maintained a pattern of sexual promiscuity that evoked that of her Presidential brother. Smathers estimated she seduced half of the 'hunks' in the Secret Service.

"Most of the guys were straight," the Senator said, "but sometimes, or so I heard, they unzipped for Pat's cocksucking husband, Peter Lawford. After all, he was the President's brother-in-law, and none of the men wanted to lose out on a good job."

"Right in front of my wife, a drunken Eunice one night at a White House party made a play for me. I couldn't believe the audacity of this gal. She was drunk and she groped me. Loud enough for people around her to hear, she said, 'I wonder if it's really as big as they say.'"

Joseph Paolella, of the Secret Service, later claimed, "Our job was to prevent Jackie from walking in on an orgy, or else finding the President in bed, banging one of his bimbos. Mrs. Kennedy knew what he was up to, but didn't want it to be rubbed in her face. At all costs, we were to avoid embarrassing situations."

"The President made it difficult for us when he invited hookers into the White House, especially when Mrs. Kennedy was home. Most of the White House secretaries also seemed only too willing to service the President. Once or twice a week was okay for me, but JFK seemed to need it two or three times a day. I blamed it on the medication Dr. Max Jacobson was shooting into his veins."

Smathers said, "I've shaken the hands of eleven Presidents in my life, including Franklin D. Roosevelt's. Only two of them were faithful to their wives—Harry S Truman and Richard M. Nixon. The rest, at some point or another, especially my good friend, Lyndon, slipped."

[Smathers was wrong about Nixon's fidelity to his wife, Patricia.]

In spite of his womanizing, the handsome and relatively young new President brought a spirit of macho vitality and adventure to the White House, not seen since the days of the Rough Rider himself, Theodore Roosevelt.

Of course, there were times of great tension, including the Bay of Pigs disaster and the Cuban Missile Crisis. "Even Jack kept his libido in check during those tense days when we felt that Washington was going to be blown up," Smathers said.

"During the greatest tensions, Jackie remained loyal to him. He tried to get her to remove herself and the children from the White House, but she steadfastly refused, saying that she'd stand by his side, along with Caroline and John-John, until the atomic blasts blew them into tiny little specks of dust."

Greta Garbo Arrives for Dinner at the White House

In the spring of 1961, Lem Billings flew to France for his vacation, heading for the *Côte d'Azur*. On the French Riviera, at Cannes, a mutual friend introduced him to Greta Garbo, the "retired-from-and-tired-with-the-world" screen goddess.

Over a light lunch, they became fast friends, although "The Sphinx" was usually far more reserved, especially around strangers she had just met. But Lem, thanks to his wit and his charm, warmed and amused her Nordic heart.

He was awed by her fading beauty and her aura of mystery. He'd seen all of her talking pictures.

"Lem amuses me," said the so-called "gloomiest Scandinavian since Hamlet."

Within two days, they'd become fellow travelers, renting a car together and heading east toward the Italian Riviera. For three nights, they lodged at

President Kennedy was unsuccessful in adding the elusive **Greta Garbo** to his list of movie star conquests. He'd had far better luck with Marlene Dietrich.

At a White House dinner, Jackie asked Garbo if she planned a comeback in films.

"So many offers," she answered. "Even the role of Hamlet. Of course, the usual scripts—D.H. Lawrence's *Lady Chatterley's Lover,* Oscar Wilde's *The Picture of Dorian Gray.* Jean Cocteau is working on a script for me, even Orson Welles. Visconti wants me to film Marcel Proust's *Remembrance of Things Past.* I don't know if I'll come back or not."

the chic little town of Portofino, near its colorful harbor. Rex Harrison invited them to his nearby villa for dinner.

After Lem's return to the White House, he fascinated JFK and Jackie with his stories about traveling in Europe with Garbo. Jackie was rather jealous of Lem's friendships. She had always wanted to meet Garbo herself, and, as First Lady, had sent her five separate invitations to the White House, all of which Garbo had rejected.

JFK had had a fascination for Garbo ever since Papa Joe had relayed the details of the affair he had had with her during his Hollywood years.

"If you know Garbo so well, why don't you invite her to the White House so Jack and I can meet her?" Jackie asked.

Lem promised that he would. The next day, he told them that he had talked to Garbo, who had agreed to come to dinner at the White House, but only if it were a small and intimate affair. "I can't stand having a lot of people around me," she'd told him.

Four nights later, Jackie had arranged the schedule so that Garbo would arrive an hour earlier than Lem.

When the White House usher presented Garbo to Jackie, she was surprised by the star's first words: "Imagine the two most famous women in the world coming together in the White House, of all places."

Jackie wanted to escort her on a tour of the private rooms of the White House, including the Oval Office. In the Lincoln Bedroom, Garbo pulled off her shoes and plopped down onto the large bed. Jackie was amazed at how playful she was.

Jackie came up with the idea of a prank she could pull on Lem, who had bragged so often about his friendship with the actress. "I want you to go through the evening pretending you've never met Lem. We'll not tell Jack, so he won't be in on the gag."

"What an amusing idea," Garbo said. "As an actress, I haven't had a role to play in many a year."

When Lem arrived, he joined JFK, Jackie, and Garbo, who were sitting in the private living room in front of the fireplace, having drinks.

"Lem," Jackie said, "I want you to meet our guest of honor for the evening, Miss Greta Garbo. Our dear friend, Lem Billings."

Lem looked at Garbo, then looked in bewilderment at Jackie. "But...but, I don't understand. Greta and I are the dearest of friends. When we vacationed together in France and Italy, she introduced me as her lover."

Garbo cast a skeptical eye at Lem. "I don't know this man," she announced.

"Greta!" He was astounded. "Remember Portofino? We spent our summer vacationing together. We vowed to be friends for life. How could you forget? It was so recent!"

"You poor, dear soul," she answered. "There are so many Garbo impersonators running about. Someone fooled you. Perhaps it was a clever transvestite pretending to be me. I am imitated by so many people."

Throughout the meal, an unsuspecting JFK repeatedly chastised Lem for having invented his tale about a friendship with Garbo. "The next thing I know, you'll tell us that Marlene Dietrich stays with you when she's in New York. That you and your dear friend Katharine Hepburn are lovers."

Trying desperately to jog Garbo's memory, Lem recalled experiences they'd shared and places they'd visited together, even exact dates. "Remember going with me to Chez Tétou at Golfe-Juan? In fact, it was you who suggested it. The world's best bouillabaisse?"

"I never eat bouillabaisse," Garbo said. "I'm allergic to shellfish."

For dessert, you asked for a simple powdered croissant with grandmother's strawberry jam bottled last winter," Lem reminded her.

"I eat grandmother's jam only in Sweden, but it's not something I would order at a seafood restaurant on the Côte d'Azur," Garbo claimed.

Not in on the prank, and with some effort, JFK finally convinced Lem that he'd been tricked by a clever Garbo lookalike. "I can't imagine how you were fooled. No woman has the century's most magnificent female face other than Greta. You really owe her an apology."

At that point, Jackie laughed. The joke had gone on long enough.

"Oh, Lem, darling," Garbo said, rising to kiss him. "My dear boy. Forgive us for teasing you so. How naughty of us." Then she burst into laughter, evoking a pivotal scene from her 1939 film, *Ninotchka.*

Lem later told JFK, "Throughout most of the dinner, I was dying…just dying. It was one of the worst nights of my life. I don't think I'll ever recover."

When Garbo departed after eleven, Lem asked Jackie what she thought of her. She hesitated before answering. "I think she was intoxicated."

Lem noted that JFK stayed with Garbo after dinner longer than he'd ever done with any other visitor to the White House.

Later, Garbo shared details of the evening with her friend, Cecil Beaton, the celebrated photographer who immortalized the nuances of her face. "Did the President ask you to spend the night?"

"I was invited, but I rejected the invitation," she said. "I stayed in a suite he'd booked for me at the Mayflower Hotel. I knew his father intimately a long time ago, and I was happy to meet the President and his First Lady. However, I feared that if I spent the night in the White House, the President might slip into my room. I'm told the young man is often visited by ladies of the night…or should I say, ladies at night? My English…so very poor."

The next morning, Garbo called JFK, who was in the Oval Office. She wanted to thank him for the evening. He told Evelyn Lincoln that he would take her call, the contents of which he'd later share with Lem. At one point, he asked Garbo if she'd slept comfortably at the Mayflower.

"I didn't, actually," she answered. "I was awake for most of the night. I had this horrible nightmare about Mara. All Swedish children know the myth of Mara. On the surface, she is this beautiful woman. But that is a mere façade, a disguise to conceal the evil that lurks in her wicked heart. In my nightmare, she attacked me in my sleep, pouncing on top of me and reaching inside my body to twist and to rip out my heart."

"What a horrible experience," he said. "Could I drop in for lunch?" Could I comfort you and protect you from this dreadful witch?"

"Comfort me?" she said. "Oh, Mr. President, I'm old enough to be your mother."

"Marlene didn't have any objection to my age," he said.

"During the war, that Berlin whore took on half the Allied Army," Garbo said. "I'm more discriminating than that."

"I sometimes like to follow in Dad's footsteps. He told me about his involvement with you *femmes fatales* during his days in Hollywood—first you, then Marlene. I've already been with Marlene. That leaves only you."

"Mr. President, as you well know, the dream, the fantasy, is always better than the reality."

"I think you're missing out on something here," he said. "Like that Mata Hari character you played, you might get me to spill government secrets over pillow talk. You could peddle that information to Khrushchev."

"I must tell you why I am turning down the offer," Garbo said. "You are so divine that I know if I have an intimate encounter with you, I will fall hopelessly in love with you…forever. I can't stand to have my heart broken again. It has been broken so many times in the past. Mr. President, you are an intelligent rogue. Possessing great courage and vision. In some ways, you and I are soul mates, doomed forever to wander the world, our restless hearts knowing no fulfillment. Good morning, you darling man." Then she put down the phone.

***

[In 1963, Garbo was horrified to hear the news that JFK had been assassinated in Dallas. She stayed glued to her television that day, and according to Beaton, sent Jackie, at the White House, a personal letter of condolence:

"Dear Mrs. Kennedy,
I, too, have known the pain of unbearable loss. Though it does not seem possible at the moment, I can only trust that one day, love will re-enter your heart again. One chapter closes, another opens before you. I wish you and your children a long and happy life after you survive this tragedy, and I know you will. Mr. Kennedy suffered the greatest loss of all—an unfinished life."
With my love and respect,
Greta Garbo."]

***

[In 1968, Jackie learned a shocking fact after her marriage to Aristotle Onassis. Before asking Jackie to marry him, he had proposed to Garbo, who had turned him down.

The star later told Beaton, "I think Ari is divine, but he is not to be taken seriously as marriage material. He's like a naughty little boy at times. He amuses himself by pushing people, male and female, into his swimming pool. Not only that, but he seats guests on a barstool aboard his yacht. The stools have been upholstered with the foreskin of whales. Then he asks his guest, 'How does it feel to be sitting on the world's biggest prick?'"]

Dr. Feelgood,
the "Bat Wing and Chicken Blood Doctor"

It was the summer of 1960 in New York, and JFK's close friend, Charles Spalding, of the J. Walter Thompson advertising agency in Manhattan, was feeling rundown. Through Senator Kennedy, he had met Prince Stanislas Radziwill, an exiled Polish prince who would become famous for his marriage to Jackie's sister, Lee Bouvier Canfield. Over drinks, Radziwill heard about Spalding's rundown condition and recommended a visit to Dr. Max Jacobson, who could give him some energy-boosting shots.

The next day, Spalding walked into Dr. Jacobson's waiting room. He later reported that the clients who were waiting there resembled a *Who's Who* of the entertainment industry—they included Zero Mostel, Johnny Mathis, Eddie Fisher, and Alan Jay Lerner. Spalding also reported seeing three "actresses" in there as well. Actually, they were diarist Anaïs Nin, singer Mabel Mercer, and stage and screen star Margaret Leighton.

Later, JFK, who was campaigning in New York City at the time, encountered Spalding, whom he found had been transformed into "a bundle of energy." When he heard that Spalding's bursts of energy had resulted from shots available from Dr. Jacobson, JFK said, "I want some of what you got."

The next day, Spalding, in a call to Dr. Jacobson authorized by JFK, asked that his office be cleared for a visit from the presidential contender. With some reluctance, Jacobson agreed to go to all that trouble, even though it meant rescheduling appointments.

At first, JFK felt the doctor looked like a mad scientist. As he later reported to Spalding. "Big thick glasses, dirty fingernails, a thick German accent, a barrel chest, potbelly, a formidable personality in spite of his disheveled look. His private office was as unkempt as he was."

JFK didn't ask what was being shot into his veins. All he knew was that it worked. "I was suffering severe back pain," he told Spalding, "And low energy.

Dr. Max Jacobson, known as "Dr. Feelgood," may have helped alter America's cultural and political history by treating and drugging JFK, Jackie, Marilyn Monroe, and Elvis Presley, among many others. He accidentally killed his own wife, Nina, with an overdose of his "magic formula."

But after those shots, I became Superman, ready to rape seven Lois Lanes. I had enough energy to fuel a jet."

That visit was the beginning of a doctor/patient relationship that would last until the President's death in November of 1963. JFK even summoned him to Hyannis Port, where he avoided introducing him to Jackie and the Kennedys, but met with him, privately, in a bungalow for more injections.

During their talk, Jacobson could *[and did]* readily drop an impressive list of his patients' names. In addition to Sir Winston Churchill, they had included Marlene Dietrich, Frank Sinatra, Truman Capote, Tennessee Williams, Elvis Presley, Marilyn Monroe, Nelson Rockefeller, Judy Garland, Mickey Mantle, Yul Brynner, and Hedy Lamarr. His patients had nicknamed him, "Dr. Feelgood," or "The Miracle Man."

JFK confessed that he'd already fucked four of Jacobson's clients—"just the females"—and he quickly became dependent on the quack. He even had a code word ("I am Mr. Dunn") he used when he called Feelgood's office. Later, when Jackie became a patient, she was codenamed "Mrs. Dunn."

Surprisingly, even from the beginning, JFK never asked what was being injected into his blood stream. The shots were later revealed to contain amphetamines, animal hormones (often from sheep), bone marrow, enzymes, human placenta, painkillers, steroids, and vitamins.

After he received the injections, JFK felt invigorated, the weakness, pain, and fatigue in his muscles disappearing.

A potential disaster occurred at the Hotel Carlyle in Manhattan. In the spring of 1962, Jacobson was summoned to JFK's suite for more injections. After giving the President his shots, the doctor left the hotel. For about an hour, JFK reported that he was feeling invigorated.

But suddenly, as described by a Secret Service agent, he began to act strangely. "He started running around the room waving his arms. At one point, he stripped off all his clothes." The two agents on duty at the time didn't know how to handle him.

He opened the door and ran naked down the hotel's corridor. Fortunately no one else was in the hallway at that time. The agents captured the nude president and half carried / half dragged him back into his suite.

They had to forcibly hold him down onto the bed and tie his arms. Dr. Lawrence Hatterer, a Manhattan psychiatrist, was summoned to the President's bedside. He told the agents that JFK was experiencing a drug-induced mania, bordering on a psychotic reaction, as an aftereffect of Dr. Feelgood's shots. Dr. Hatterer injected JFK with an anti-psychotic drug, which subdued him.

After that, JFK reportedly drifted off into a deep sleep and didn't wake up until ten o'clock the following morning. One agent reported that when he awakened, the President had no memory of his breakdown.

Within three days, he had resumed his injections from Jacobson.

In the latter days of his presidential campaign, Jacobson flew to JFK's side to inject him with shots before his first debate with Richard Nixon, the Republican challenger who had been Dwight Eisenhower's Vice President. Although that day he'd been suffering bouts of severe back pain, JFK before the camera was young, handsome, and vigorous, in marked contrast to Nixon, who appeared with no makeup, looked pale, and had a five o'clock shadow which some viewers interpreted as sinister.

Throughout the final months of the campaign, JFK continued to receive injections from Jacobson, who sometimes joined him on the trail. Even for a healthy man, the campaign would have been grueling, and JFK depended on Jacobson's injections as a means of boosting his sagging strength.

After the elections, by May of 1961, confronting an exhausting series of foreign trips, JFK began to worry that Jackie was not up to the strain. He told Smathers and Spalding, "Giving birth to John Jr. by cesarean was very difficult for her, and she's never quite recovered. She also suffers great depressions."

JFK asked Jacobson to fly to Palm Beach, where, after receiving his own shots, he introduced him to Jackie. He told Jacobson about his upcoming trips, which included visits to Canada, France, Austria, and England.

In Florida, JFK and Jackie were staying at the elegant home of Charles and Jayne Wrightsman. When an agent of the Secret Service escorted Jacobson to Jackie's bedroom, she complained of her migraine, "one of the worst I've ever had." After a preliminary examination, he asked her "to bare your butt." He injected a shot into her left buttock, the first of many such injections to come.

Before he left her room, she claimed that her migraine had disappeared within five minutes, and she felt in better spirits once again. From that day forth, she became one of his patients.

He was by her side to shoot her up before she flew to Ottawa on her first official visit to a foreign country. JFK didn't fare well in his meeting with Prime Minister John Diefenbaker, but Jackie was a hit with the Canadians. In a red wool suit designed by Oleg Cassini, she reviewed the red-coated Royal Canadian Mounted Police. She was even praised by the Speaker in Parliament for her "beauty, grace, and vivacity. America's First Lady has captured our hearts," he proclaimed.

Disaster came when JFK and Jackie were invited to a tree-planting ceremony on the grounds of Government House in Ottawa. Jackie took a shovel and scooped up only a small bit of dirt, but JFK, in a macho stance, dug into the ground like a ditchdigger. Although he concealed it, he suffered back spasms and agonizing pain. He flew with Jackie back to Washington and had to be secretly lifted off Air Force One onto a stretcher.

Back at the White House, "Mrs. Dunn" put through a call to Jacobson in New York. Arrangements were made for him to fly at once to Washington in a private twin-engine Cessna. He was secretly slipped into the White House to give shots to the stricken President. He later visited Jackie in her bedroom and administered shots to her as well.

It was during the four days he spent in Washington that Jackie made arrangements with him to accompany them on their upcoming State Visits to Paris and Vienna.

The doctor made a discovery while treating the President. He found that—

as procured for him by a Secret Service agent—he'd been taking the highly addictive drug, Demerol. Jacobson asserted that the drug interfered with his amphetamines. Consequently, JFK promised to abandon Demerol. Jackie learned the identity of the agent and fired him.

When Jackie heard that her friend, Truman Capote, was also receiving shots from Jacobson, she put through a call to him. He told her that, once injected, he could go for almost 72 hours without sleep, working at a feverish speed. He also confessed that "after I've been 'shot up,' my libido rages out of control. One night at the Plaza Hotel, even five of New York's best hustlers couldn't satisfy me ."

What Capote didn't tell her was that when coming down from Jacobson's shots, the patient often experienced severe depression, an emotional void, and bouts of paranoid schizophrenia.

***

Reporters were getting suspicious about the Presidential comings and goings of Dr. Feelgood, who had attracted unwanted publicity because of his celebrity clientele. Consequently, whereas JFK wanted him to accompany them to Paris and Vienna, he didn't want reporters to see Jacobson boarding or exiting from Air Force One.

So he had Evelyn Lincoln book a conventional seat to Paris aboard an Air France jet. Paid for by taxpayers, the plane would carry only two passengers, Jacobson and his wife, Nina.

Later, Jacobson complained to Jackie, "With all those flight attendants, and the plane to ourselves, we expected the greatest service of all time. But it turned out to be the worst. The French staff decided to party all the way to Paris. During the flight, some of the staff joined *[or reinstated their memberships in]* the "Mile-High Club," a reference to in-flight seductions in the toilets.

In his unpublished memoirs, Jacobson recalled his time with both JFK and Jackie in Paris and Vienna.

In Paris, after a night in an expensive suite, he was picked up by the Secret Service and delivered to a private château *[a grandly imposing "hotel particulier"]* on the Quai d'Orsay.

After administering shots to JFK before he headed out for a round of appointments, Jacobson waited to be ushered into the Queen's Bedroom.

Jackie was having her hair styled by Alexandre, a celebrated Parisian hairdresser, who was crafting a bouffant hairdo inspired by 18th century antecedents as a means of accentuating her prominent cheekbones. "A beautiful face needs foliage around it," he grandly and poetically announced.

Before she received her injections, Jackie told Jacobson, "In Paris, I'm a bigger star than Jack is."

On the bed were two satin gowns. She was trying to decide which of them to wear for a grand dinner that Charles de Gaulle was hosting for the President and herself that night at the Palace of Versailles.

At one point, Jackie rose to her feet and ordered everybody out of the room, including Alexandre.

When they were alone, she turned to Jacobson and dropped her robe, revealing her nude body. She turned her back to him. "I'm ready for my closeup, Mr. DeMille!" *[She was parroting an iconic phrase from Gloria Swanson's* Sunset Blvd *(1950).]*

Facing Jackie's shapely buttocks, Jacobson injected his "magic elixir" into her left buttock.

The next morning's headlines in Paris would proclaim, "MADAME DE POMPADOUR RETURNS TO VERSAILLES."

In Vienna, Jackie Enchants the Soviet Pig

In Vienna, the Secret Service picked up Jacobson from the very posh Bristol Hotel and delivered him to an elegant private residence in the Viennese suburb of Semmerings. It was within that building, the residence of the American Ambassador to Austria, where JFK would receive Nikita Khrushchev later in the day.

Jacobson visited Jackie's bedroom first and administered her shots before she left to make her appearances for the day.

In JFK's bedroom, Jacobson encountered a President with severe back pain. He recalled how tense he was, anticipating the arrival of the belligerent Soviet dictator. "I feel like shit," JFK confessed. Like Jackie, he dropped his robe, except he still had on his jockey shorts. He pulled them down and lay face down on the bed, inviting Jacobson to administer the shots into his buttocks.

After his long meeting with Khrushchev, JFK reappeared in front of Jacobson two hours later. "It's not going well. We just had a big fight over Berlin, where he virtually threatened to attack America. I need more shots. But first, I've got to take a piss."

The rest of the Summit didn't go well. JFK later claimed that Khrushchev bullied him and even insulted him by referring to him as "The Boy." Ironically, that was the same appellation that Lyndon Johnson used to refer, privately, to JFK.

Jacobson later lamented, "My shots got rid of the President's back pain, but didn't give him the testosterone he needed to stand up to the fat Soviet pig."

When Jackie and JFK were outside the borders of the U.S., Bobby, who had grown increasingly alarmed over the injections they were receiving, slipped into the Lincoln Bedroom and removed five vials of Jacobson's elixirs. He sent them to the FBI lab for analysis.

Larry Newman, a Secret Service agent, was particularly alarmed at the doctor's close link to the President and his First Lady. "He could shoot poison into the President's veins for all we knew. He arrived with this dirty bag of who knows what chemicals. We'd heard that some of his patients had gotten hepatitis from his shots."

Newman went on to denounce Jacobson, defining him as "a batwing and chicken blood doctor. He came and went from the White House like those women who arrived to service the President through the revolving door."

The report from the FBI revealed that the vials contained large dosages of steroids and amphetamines.

When JFK returned from Paris and Vienna, Bobby confronted him and urged him to quit taking the shots. "Hell with that!" JFK shouted at him. "I don't care if his vials contain horse piss. The point is, they work for me."

When Jacobson heard that Bobby was having him investigated by the FBI, he wrote JFK a personal letter, telling him he was going to resign. JFK responded, "Like hell you are! I need you. I can't hold down the job of President without your shots." He then prevailed on Jacobson to stay on, even though JFK and Jackie never paid for any of his services. He donated his time and shots.

At one point, JFK urged Jacobson to relocate into the White House so that he would not have to slip around and administer shots to them in secret. Jacobson turned down that request, claiming, "Some of my 400 other patients would die without my aid."

Senator George Smathers also became concerned with JFK's reliance on Dr. Feelgood. "In Palm Beach, playing golf, he told me he had to have these painkiller injections every six hours. One day on the course, he fell over. We carried him into the locker room and cleared everyone out. He pulled down his pants and dropped his jockey shorts. Then he lay down on his belly on this cot and turned his butt up to me. He instructed me how to use this syringe and a needle about three inches long. In the months to come, I think I saw more of Jack's lilywhite ass cheeks than I did my wife's butt."

Often, Jacobson was able to treat JFK in New York during the President's frequent visits. The Secretary General of the United Nations, Swedish-born Dag Hammarskjöld, had died in a plane crash on September 18, 1961. JFK flew to New York on September 25 to address the U.N.'s General Assembly.

The President hailed Hammarskjöld as "the greatest statesman of our century." Privately, Jackie held him in total disdain, defining him as "a jealous queen."

Her confidant, Adlai Stevenson, fed her information about the bitchy things Hammarsköld had said about her: "Jackie Kennedy is not that beautiful," he had told Stevenson. "We have hundreds of girls in Sweden far more beautiful than her."

He also criticized Jackie for not attending events in her honor. "You can't pick up a newspaper without finding her plastic smile plastered on the front-page. She's treated more like an Empress than a First Lady. All this acclaim for her is not merited."

In Manhattan, Jacobson rushed to JFK's penthouse suite at the Hotel Carlyle, where he administered shots before his speech.

The doctor often experimented with new ingredients within the brews he configured as injections, finding that cells extracted from the livers of baby lambs gave Jackie renewed life. At one point, he experimented with cells extracted from the inner organs of electric eels, injecting them as part of a medley of other compounds into her blood stream.

Jacobson was amazed that in the midst of their various crises, such as Khruschev's threats to blow up America during the Cuban missile confrontation, JFK and Jackie were deeply intrigued by Hollywood gossip about his clients.

They were especially interested in hearing news about Jacobson's patient, Eddie Fisher, and his wife, Elizabeth Taylor.

Jacobson told the First Couple intimate details about what the singer had confessed to him about having had sex with Taylor.

"She likes to strip naked and crawl on the floor on her hands and knees, begging me to enter her from the rear," Fisher had said to Jacobson, who passed his comment on to the President and First Lady.

"She would purr like a sex kitten, begging for more," Fisher had claimed.

Fisher would later sustain an affair with Pamela Turnure, one of JFK's mistresses. Jackie later told Capote, "It was all so incestuous, with everybody doing everybody else."

***

The date was November 3, 1963. In Palm Beach, Jacobson was scheduled to meet with the President for the final time. When he saw them and administered their shots, he discovered that Jackie was tense and apprehensive about their upcoming trip to Texas. "The President seemed in good spirits, particularly after my shots, but I was disappointed that they didn't invite me to fly down with them."

"I'll always remember them standing in the sunlit garden," Jacobson wrote in his unpublished memoir. "Jackie even kissed me on the cheek, and the President shook my hand. He seemed so grateful to me that he looked for a moment like he wanted to embrace me. But he didn't. What a handsome couple! In just days, they would be involved in a tragedy that changed the history of America."

[Although Jacobson's memoirs were submitted to at least fifteen publishers in Manhattan, all of the editors rejected it. The doctor had opted to disclose anecdotes that were far too revealing about his celebrity clients, most of whom were still alive and could have filed libel suits. Nonetheless, the manuscript was read by a number of editors, who leaked spicy details about his claims to the press. At the time, reporters seemed interested only in the drug taking of JFK and Jackie during their time in the White House.

In 1975, the Bureau of Narcotics and Dangerous Drugs seized Jacobson's supply of ingredients. After a review, his medical license was revoked by the New York State Board of Regents.

In the wake of Jackie's death in 1994, her son, John F. Kennedy, Jr., asserted that he fully believed that the doctor's injections had brought on his *mother's lymphoma. His accusation was based on a report from the American Multicenter Cohort's study of 2,500 patients who had been heavy users of amphetamines.]*

"I Am the Man Who Accompanied Jacqueline Kennedy to Paris"

—JFK

"John Kennedy is our President, but Jacqueline is our Movie Star."

—Tish Baldrige

In 1961, Press Secretary Pierre Salinger arrived in Paris, meeting with French journalists and spreading various myths about America's handsome young President and his beautiful First Lady. He made it a special point to relay stories about Jackie's French forebears.

He succeeded beyond his wildest dreams. The French may have chopped off the head of Marie Antoinette, but they were still fascinated by royalty, as represented by Jackie. Before she returned to French soil, television shows had already glorified her presence, her charm, and her grace. She was called the most cultured woman ever to fill the post of America's First Lady.

At Orly Airport, the French President, Charles De Gaulle, and Madame Yvonne de Gaulle, waited on the tarmac to greet America's First Couple.

JFK soon realized that the crowds had turned out for a glimpse of Jackie and not himself.

Walking down the airplane steps, she dazzled in a navy blue silk suit and black velvet pillbox hot.

The screams went up: *"Jacquiii! Jacquiii! Jacquiii!"*

As one reporter said, "Jackie was the Queen of America arriving with her Prince Consort."

The French military greeted them with a 101-gun salute. The *président du Conseil Municipal de Paris* **[i.e., the** *Mayor]* stepped forward to present Jackie with a $4,000 diamond watch. Kennedy aide David Powers privately remarked. "This is the kind of turmoil that will not be equaled until the Second Coming."

The French President had declared the Kennedys arrival in Paris as a national holiday. Escorted by fifty roaring motorcycle policemen, the De Gaulles and the Kennedys were driven into Paris. Along the route, thousands upon thousands of Parisians waved American flags at them. Jackie was seated in a bubbletop Citroën with Yvonne de Gaulle, whom she would later define as, "small and mousy."

For their final ride into Paris, the motorcycle-riding policemen relinquished their positions to the Republican Guard, elegantly costumed equestrian attendants wearing glittering gold helmets topped with red plumes. As they entered Paris through the Porte d'Orléans, the crowds swelled to mammoth size.

Astride their snorting black horses, the Republican Guards led the Kennedys into "The City of Light," as French fighter jets roared overhead.

As America's First Couple arrived in front of the 19th-century façade of the Palais des Affaires Étrangeres, on the Quai d'Orsay, fronting the Seine, Jackie was escorted to the *Chambre de la Reine,* which had last been occupied by Queen Fabiola of Belgium. Within minutes, she was basking in a silver mosaic tub in a bathroom whose walls were layered in mother of pearl.

Within the hour, Alexandre, who had styled the hair of everyone from Greta Garbo to Elizabeth Taylor, arrived to apply the crowning touches for her luncheon date at the Élysée Palace with De Gaulle.

Meanwhile, in the *Chambre du Roi,* JFK was soaking in a gold-plated tub the size of a ping-pong table. He would spend part of his time in Paris soaking in this tub as a means of easing his back pain.

A future President, Lyndon Johnson, would often receive aides while sitting on his toilet outside the Oval Office. In contrast, in Paris, JFK welcomed his aides and some of his visitors while soaking in the tub. He even invited Janet des Rosiers *[the stewardess aboard the Caroline]* into the bathroom. "I'm not bashful," he told her, "but you'll understand why I can't stand up for you."

Later, both JFK and Jackie appeared downstairs, ready to be driven to the Élysée Palace where De Gaulle was hosting a lavish luncheon for them.

For her wardrobe, she had chosen a pale yellow silk suit with a matching hat.

Arriving at the Elysée, the Kennedy limousine was driven through the Grille de Coq where the Republican Guard saluted them with the sound of trumpets and drawn swords. She arrived at the palace bursting with "youth and beauty," in the words of *Le Figaro.* Time later reported, "The radiant young First Lady was the Kennedy who really mattered."

They were welcomed by Nicole Alphand, the wife of Hérvé, the U.S. Ambassador to France. Jackie was surprised when she kissed JFK and hugged him. She didn't know until later that Nicole had been one of his lovers.

JFK had arrived in Paris humiliated by Fidel Castro and the Bay of Pigs disaster. He dreaded flying to Vienna to confront the bellicose Nikita Khrushchev. Aides had warned him that both De Gaulle and the Soviet dictator viewed the United States as an impotent paper tiger.

Both JFK and Jackie were apprehensive about their luncheon with the notoriously chauvinistic De Gaulle. He had little love for U.S. presidents and still harbored hostility toward the policies and behavior of Eisenhower and Franklin Roosevelt during the aftermath of World War II. He also resented NATO, viewing it as an attempt by Britain and the United States to undermine the independence of France.

Seated with Jackie at the head table, he found her enchanting and was astonished at her mastery of the French language.

At one point, Jackie became enraged at the translator. Her husband's dry wit was not being properly presented. She dismissed him and took over herself as the official translator. No one in the history of diplomacy had ever done that.

As David Powers later remarked, Jackie was in essence trying to seduce De Gaulle with her whispery voice.

When not translating between the leaders, she talked with De Gaulle, chatting about everything from Louis XVI to the later Bourbons. "Her knowledge of my homeland and French culture was a glorious surprise," he told the press.

He later told André Malraux that at first, he thought she was like a little girl until she opened her mouth. With perfect manners, she sampled *langouste*, followed by *pâté de foie gras* and *noix de veau Orloff*.

As a gift to De Gaulle, she presented him with an original letter the Marquis de Lafayette had written to George Washington. Her friend, Jayne Wrightsman, had purchased it for $90,000.

She told De Gaulle that she'd named her French poodle "Gaullie."

He would later say, "She is a charming woman, even ravishing, with beautiful hair and dazzling eyes."

Even JFK was impressed with Jackie's performance. He later said, "It would be as if Madame de Gaulle sat next to me and discussed Henry Clay."

[The very influential lawyer, politician, and orator Henry Clay, Sr. (1777-1852) represented Kentucky in both the U.S. House of Representatives (including three terms as its Speaker) and the U.S. Senate. He also served as Secretary of State from 1825 to 1829. He lost his bids for the U.S. presidency in 1824, 1832, and 1844.]

Later in the day, while JFK was meeting privately with the U.S. Ambassador to France, Jackie retreated to her palatial lodgings on the Quai d'Orsay, in preparation for the lavish banquet which De Gaulle had organized for them that evening at the Palace of Versailles.

She needed hours to prepare herself. Alexandre was back on the scene, creating another spectacular bouffant hairdo for her. Her big chignon was topped with a fragile diamond tiara.

She had a choice of two gowns to wear to the palace—one by Oleg Cassini, the other by Hubert de Givenchy. She knew she'd get better press if she wore Givenchy's ivory-colored silk zibeline with a bodice embroidered with silk floss and seed pearls. The skirt was bellshaped, and she wore long white gloves.

Consuelo Crespi, a fashion consultant in Paris working for *Vogue*, would approve the dress but attack Alexandre's hairdo as "not becoming to Mrs. Kennedy."

With flags fluttering and with JFK at her side, Jackie, in an eleven-car motorcade, arrived at what used to be the headquarters and nerve center of the Sun King *[Louis XIV]*. Her arrival was met by a thunderous roar and hundreds of exploding flashbulbs.

At Versailles, De Gaulle descended a pink marble staircase, telling Jackie, "You look as if you just stepped out of a painting by Watteau."

The eyes of the 150 guests assembled in the *Galerie des Glaces* (Hall of

Mirrors) turned and stared as Jackie entered the fabled room on De Gaulle's arm.

Following the banquet, De Gaulle escorted Jackie into the Palace's *Opera Royale*, where they saw a ballet first performed for Louis XV and Madame de Pompadour. The theater was lit with flaming torches.

***

Jackie was thrilled to be back in the city where she'd experienced some of her happiest moments as a student at the Sorbonne.

She had been nervous about meeting Charles de Gaulle, but eager to see his Minister of Culture, André Malraux. The press was unaware that she and Malraux had indulged in some "heavy dating" during her time in Paris. He had always topped her list of the world's most fascinating men. In years gone by, they had reportedly come close to consummating their love affair, but, in Jackie's words, "not gone all the way."

Malraux still seemed all things to Jackie—a romantic adventurer, a daredevil, an eccentric art historian, a hero of both the French Resistance in the early 1940s and the anti-Franco movement during Spain's Civil War in the 1930s.

Privately, Jackie told only her closest friends that she wanted her husband to estab-

It was **Jackie** *(right)*, not Madame **Yvonne de Gaulle** *(left)*, who was the epitome of French style and chic. Some reporters described Madame de Gaulle as "looking like a yard goods saleswoman." In the middle was **JFK** *(left)* confronting an often hostile **De Gaulle**, critical of many U.S. policies.

Very *Louis*, very *ancien régime*:

Two views of two savvy and sophisticated Francophiles outcharming each other at Versailles.

209

lish a cabinet post entitled "Secretary of State for Cultural Affairs," a post occupied with panache, in France, by Malraux himself. She even hinted that she might like to hold down the position herself.

In the years that had passed since her last seeing Malraux, Jackie had had access to at least some of the gossip swirling around him. His claim to have had "metaphysical talks" with Josef Stalin during his visit to Russia in 1934 have been largely discredited, although Malraux insisted that such conversations took place. She'd also heard that he'd run out of money during his visit to Cambodia, and that he had ordered his first wife, Clara Goldschmidt, to steal statues from a Cambodian temple.

When he tried to sell these treasures, he was arrested but later allowed to go free because of his powerful connections within Cambodia's French colonial government.

His claims to have been a close friend of T.E. Lawrence *[a.k.a. Lawrence of Arabia]* went unchallenged because they were frequently sighted and photographed together. Less well-authenticated was the rumor that in the course of one drunken night, Malraux had sodomized him.

Philosopher Raymond Aron wrote that Malraux was "one-third genius, one-third false, and one-third incomprehensible." Journalist Katherine Knorr claimed, "As De Gaulle's pal, Malraux is the court intellectual and occasional buffoon."

While JFK was away, Malraux arrived at Jackie's residence and, as she later told her confidants, "We fell into each other's arms."

When she congratulated him on his new post, he expressed disappointment. "I wanted to be an *homme d'etat* (great statesman) like De Gaulle, but alas, I am only a *ministre d'état.*"

He became her tour guide, escorting her on a very private visit to the Louvre, where they talked about art and she saw recent acquisitions that were new within the vast galleries. Malraux arranged for the room exhibiting the *Mona Lisa (La Giaconda)* to be screened off for her private, up-close viewing.

She was shocked at the condition of that painting, later asserting, "Its pigments were fading, almost disappearing. Some colors had completely gone since Da Vinci's day."

"We have to put a wooden brace on its back to tighten the split that has developed," he told her.

At some point during the viewing, he suggested that he might arrange "the unspeakable"—the transport of the *Mona Lisa* to Washington,

La crème of the French intelligentsia, **André Malraux** also welcomed Jackie to Paris. Jackie had long been captivated by his *La Condition Humaine,* which had won the prestigious Prix Goncourt literary award in 1933 and had elevated Malraux to global attention. She wasn't attracted just to his mind, but had repeatedly called attention to "what a striking figure he is, and how beautifully he speaks."

210

D.C., and New York for viewings by vast numbers of Americans. "I'd be taking a real chance, of course. No ancient painting on wood travels well because of atmospheric changes. It is very fragile, unlike my love and devotion to you, which remain as strong as ever."

The rest of the day was spent touring and lunching with Malraux. Lunch was at La Celle St. Cloud, the former secret hideaway of Mme de Pompadour

Over lunch, Malraux and the First Lady indulged in indiscreet gossip about foreign leaders whom both of them had met. She claimed that the West German leader, Konrad Adenauer, was *un peu gaga [i.e., "a little bit confused."]*. In contrast, she defined the Shah of Iran "a pompous ass." She and Malraux speculated about how the aging Shah sexually handled his much younger wife, Farah Diba.

Jackie also confessed that she despised Queen Frederica of Greece. Years later, Malraux would dedicate his book, *Anti-Memoirs* to Jackie.

Later, they drove, along with the Secret Service, to Malmaison, ten miles from Paris. The house had been purchased by Joséphine, wife of Napoléon, in 1799. It was here that she died in 1814 at the age of 51.

The curator at Malmaison later suggested that Jackie flirted outrageously with the Minister of Culture during their tour. "Why not?" he asked. "He was dark and handsome, and she looked like a porcelain doll. A harmless flirtation. We Frenchmen do that all the time. When America's First Lady toured Malmaison, her smile was charming, but when she looked at André, it revealed a certain carnivorous quality. When Mrs. Kennedy was in the room, André had eyes only for her."

Meanwhile, JFK was addressing 400 members of the press at the Palais de Chaillot. Before TV cameras, he said, "I do not think it altogether inappropriate to introduce myself to this audience. I am the man who accompanied Jacqueline Kennedy to Paris, and I have enjoyed it."

Malraux later described Jackie in his memoirs as *allumeuse ["incandescent, or someone who gives one hope]* and he also suggested that she was *(une femme) qui craque l'allumette [a woman who lights a match and consequently, a fire]*. He ultimately concluded that she was also a *coquette*.

His jealous and musically talented third wife, Marie-Madeleine Lioux, who had not been invited to the lunch at La Celle St. Cloud or on the tour of Malmaison, was more dismissive of Jackie's charms, defining her as "intelligent

During her tour through the Louvre with Malraux, Jackie made an off-hand suggestion. She broached the topic of the international significance of great art. "You should lend us some of your artworks," she suggested to Malraux. "I would love to see Leonardo da Vinci's **Mona Lisa** *(depicted above)* again and show her to the Americans."

He turned to her and smiled. "I'll see what I can do." The "unthinkable" was about to happen.

but superficial."

After the Kennedys flew out of Paris, Malraux met with De Gaulle, telling him, "The wife of the American President is unique."

The senior French statesman agreed that she was, responding, "I can see her in about ten years on the yacht of a Greek petrol millionaire."

De Gaulle's prediction was clairvoyant.

***

[In May of 1962, André Malraux, with Marie-Madeleine Lioux, were enter-tained at the White House by the First Couple. Of the many state dinners Jackie had presided over, she seemed to pay more attention to this than to any of the others.

The first day of Malraux's sojourn in D.C. began when Jackie was sched-uled to meet with a group of visiting foreign students. She instructed her press secretary to tell the group that she was not feeling well.

Within the hour, however, she'd dressed chicly and was seen slipping out the back entrance of the White House to escort Malraux without his wife on a tour of Washington's National Gallery of Art. She appeared in a shocking pink strapless dress revealing a lot of her shapely bare shoulders. As before in Paris, Malraux was awed by her beauty.

During his tour with Jackie, the three paintings that impressed him the most were Rembrandt's Girl with a Broom; *El Greco's* Christ Chasing the Money-lenders from the Temple; *and Domenico Veneziano's* Madonna With Child.

For the dinner she had scheduled at the White House that evening, Jackie had invited luminaries from the art world, including such theatrical personalities as Tennessee Williams, Arthur Miller (who had survived his recent—in 1961—divorce from Marilyn Monroe), and Hollywood director Elia Kazan.

When Miller entered the room, she whispered privately to him, "Our mates are known to stray a bit." She was, of course, referencing Monroe's affair with JFK.

Miller was shocked to be seated by Jackie at the head table. "She was bringing me in out of the cold," he claimed. He was referring to the days when he had been accused of being a Communist by the witch-hunting Senator from Wisconsin, Joseph McCarthy.

Tennessee Williams arrived rather drunk and drugged, although his pow-ers of observation were still sharp and trenchant. "I suspected that Jackie and André have their sexual secrets," he accurately surmised. "I'm sure there has been some hot sex between them, although I have no actual proof. To me, he seemed like one hot Frenchman. I heard that he was once captured by the Gestapo, and that his testicles were tortured, but from the looks of him, I bet those balls were back in working order."

Other guests included the world-renowned choreographer, George Balan-chine, who had arranged for Margot Fonteyn and Rudolf Nureyev to perform a pas de deux at the White House.

Composer Leonard Bernstein showed up, as did critic Edmund Wilson, along with artists such as Andrew Wyeth and Mark Rothko. Novelists and poets included Robert Penn Warren, Archibald MacLeish, Saul Bellow, and Thornton Wilder.

As the party wore on, and as the champagne flowed, Malraux and Jackie seemed to enjoy their own private amusements. She even did a few impressions for him, including one of Queen Elizabeth.

Gore Vidal later said, "Jackie did the world's best impersonation of the Queen, topped only by my own impersonation of Eleanor Roosevelt."

Jackie also invited aviator Charles Lindbergh, who rarely made public appearances.

The dinner at the White House was conducted in two separate rooms, with Madeleine designated as the guest of JFK in the State Dining Room, and with Jackie entertaining Malraux in the Blue Room. As toastmaster, JFK said, "We all want to take part in life's numerous adventures, but Mr. Malraux has left all of us behind."

Jackie asked Lyndon Johnson to give the welcoming speech in the Blue Room. Before that, she'd told Malraux, "Lyndon is an American original, a figure out of Mark Twain. You must meet his Lady Bird and hear her Texas drawl. I call them 'Uncle Cornpone and his Little Pork Chop.'"

Two days after the formal dinner, JFK and Jackie invited Malraux and Madeleine to spend Sunday with them at their private residence, Glen Ora, in Virginia.

Leaving JFK and Madeleine in the house, Malraux and Jackie went horseback riding in the early afternoon, after a light lunch. She said that they would return at four o'clock, but they didn't get back to the house until seven. Their abandoned spouses didn't question them.

Back in Washington, Jackie met privately with Malraux in her private quarters within the White House, demanding that her staff not disturb her during her final moments with France's Minister of Culture. Such privacy led to speculation.

***

On January 8, 1963, Jackie was vacationing in Palm Beach but flew back to Washington to accept the custody of The Mona Lisa. It had been shipped from Paris under heavy guard to the National Gallery in D.C., with the understanding that it would, after a predetermined number of days, move on to the Metropolitan Museum in New York City.

Malraux had returned to Washington for the unveiling. Before her departure from Palm Beach, Jackie had told her secret to JFK. She was pregnant again.

But no one noticed that when she appeared at the National Gallery with diamond earrings, wearing a gown crafted from mauve-colored chiffon embroidered with pearls and crystals.

She was warmly received by Malraux, who seemed to want to be alone with her. She informed him that because of his generous gesture of bringing the Mona Lisa *and* Whistler's Mother *to Washington, she would arrange for the Smithsonian Institution to ship, for exhibition in France, the Hope Diamond as part of an upcoming exhibition of historic French jewelry in Paris. Prior to Jackie's intervention, the Smithsonian had rejected Malraux's request.*

JFK also showed up at the reception to welcome Malraux. The low point of the exhibit came when a paparazzo snapped a picture of him in an intimate conversation with a beautiful young French woman. JFK ordered the Secret Service to confiscate the photographer's camera.

The Da Vinci masterpiece had traveled to America under heavy guard and within atmospherically controlled conditions, aboard the S.S. France. It had arrived at the National Gallery under police escort.

Malraux's address, which had to be translated, went wrong when his microphone went dead. The Culture Minister proclaimed a new heyday for what he defined as "Atlantic culture." Publicly, he had nothing but praise for JFK, although privately, he'd told De Gaulle, "Jack is no FDR."

The big debate that ensued in the National Press was "Who has the better smile, Mona Lisa or Jackie Kennedy?"

Jackie and JFK invited Malraux to visit them at Hyannis Port. When he got there, the First Couple took him boating.

Privately, she said her farewell to him. There is no record of their exchange. With credit to a phrase coined by Marcel Proust, perhaps they shared a "Remembrance of Things Past."

After its display in Manhattan, when the Mona Lisa was shipped back to Paris, Malraux said, "It's sad for Da Vinci's masterpiece to leave America's shores where La Giaconda made so many fans. But I don't feel all that bad, since America has its own Mona Lisa in the face of Jacqueline Kennedy."]

Khrushchev Bullies "Boy Kennedy"
& Cops a Feel of Jackie Under the Table

Air Force One, carrying thirty-five of Jackie's trunks, landed at the Vienna Airport in heavy rain. After being welcomed by Austrian officials, Jackie headed for a rendezvous with Nina Khrushchev, while JFK was driven to the private residence of the American ambassador in the Semmering mountains outside the city.

A chicly dressed Jackie encountered Khrushchev's wife, the cunning, fat, and dowdy Nina, who looked like a bag lady. Later, when asked about her, Jackie said, "She is a very kind woman, the type you'd prefer as your child's babysitter."

JFK's "Summit" with the Soviet dictator quickly degenerated into a *[his words]* disaster.

He told columnist James Reston, "It was the worst day of my life. Khrushchev ridiculed me over the Bay of Pigs disaster in Cuba. The bastard savaged me. He treated me like I was some inexperienced young boy."

When the British Prime Minister, Harold Macmillan, heard that, he said, "Kennedy at last has met a man who is impervious to his charm."

"When JFK returned to Washington, he told Lem Billings, "The son of a bitch threatened me with nuclear war if I did not recognize East Germany's control over West Berlin. When I warned him that a nuclear exchange between the United States and Russia might result in the deaths of seventy million people, he looked at me and said, 'So what?'"

A State dinner had been scheduled for that evening at Schönbrunn Palace, the rococo 1,400-room summer residence of the Austrian Hapsburgs. As JFK and Jackie arrived, the thunderous crowds shouted *"JAC-QUI!!"*

At Schönbrunn, Khrushchev demanded to be seated next to Jackie. He may have dismissed JFK as a statesman, but he was obviously excited by the charm and beauty of his wife. She appeared seductive, creating a sensation in a skintight pink mermaid dress designed by Oleg Cassini. She had awed De Gaulle with her knowledge of French literature, and she tried to impress Khrushchev with her knowledge of Russian literature, talking about the works of Chekhov, Dostoevsky, Tolstoy, and Pushkin.

To her amazement, the dictator seemed unfamiliar with the Russian classics. He launched into telling her how many teachers there were in the Ukraine, as opposed to a much smaller number during the reign of the Czars.

"Oh, Mr. Chairman," Jackie said, demurely. "Don't bore me with statistics."

After dinner, a ballet troupe appeared at their table, throwing flowers. "The dancers are throwing the flowers at YOU, Mr. Chairman," Jackie said.

He shrugged off the compliment. "No, it's for your handsome husband who is being honored. If you want to keep him, don't let him out of your sight. Viennese women are known for being very seductive."

At one point, she informed him that she knew the names of the dogs the Soviets had sent into Outer Space— Belka, Laika, and Strelka. She'd heard

East (in the form of **Nina Khruschev**, *right*) meets West, midway, in Vienna,

(Yes, Jackie won, hands-down, but considering the competition, did she really have to be THAT stylish?)

that one of the dogs had given birth to puppies, and she requested one from him, "The puppy is on its way," he promised.

Two months later, the puppy was delivered to the White House. Jackie made a gift of it to Caroline.

Outside, the roar of voices shouting *JAC-QUI! JAC-QUI!* could be heard in the banqueting hall as she discussed Russian horses and Ukrainian folk dances with Khrushchev.

At one point, Khrushchev was asked if he'd like to pose for a picture with President Kennedy.

"NO!" he said, looking at Jackie, "I'd much rather pose with Mrs. Kennedy."

The next day, some newspapers reported that the seemingly carefree Mrs. Kennedy was intoxicated on Austrian wine. It was also rumored that at one point during the dinner, the Soviet dictator had placed his chubby hand on Jackie's knee, feeling up her dress.

Headlines in Vienna blared: *SMITTEN KHRUSHCHEV IS JACKIE'S HAPPY ESCORT. FIRST LADY WINS KHRUSHCHEV.*

The next day, JFK and Jackie attended a service within Vienna's magnificent Gothic cathedral, St. Stephens. The archbishop of Vienna officiated, and a Mozart hymn was performed by the celebrated Vienna Boy's Choir. A prayer ending the service called for world peace. Leaving the church, whereas JFK remained stoic, Jackie was seen weeping.

During their final meeting, JFK told Khrushchev, "The United States will not abandon West Berlin. It's going to be a damn cold winter."

As JFK and Jackie boarded the plane for London, Khrushchev was known to have told his aides, "Kennedy is a weak boy. The power behind the throne is Mrs. Kennedy. She's the one ruling that god damn country."

***

After Vienna, JFK and Jackie flew to London for a private visit with her sister, Lee Radziwill. The occasion involved the christening of Anna Christina ("Tina"), whose father was Prince Stanislas.

Like Jackie, Lee had experienced a difficult delivery. Tina had been born three months premature, weighing less than three pounds. She had spent three months in an incubator, but had survived against grave odds. Therefore, her christening was an event to be celebrated.

Diplomatic gestures, genuine smiles, and the promise of a puppy from Outer Space characterized the "summit" between **America's First Lady** and the Soviet Dictator, **Nikita Khrushchev.**

On the eve of the christening, JFK and Jackie dined with Queen Elizabeth and Prince Philip in the State Dining Room of Buckingham Palace. In the court circular that described the occasion, Lee and her husband, Prince Stanislas, were listed as "Prince and Princess." In a loud contradiction, however, the London tabloids headlined the news that Her Majesty had never granted a royal license for the Radziwills to use those titles in Britain.

Jackie was not returning immediately to the U.S. She planned to fly with Lee, her sister, to Athens.

Before her departure, JFK warned Secret Service agent, Clint Hill, that "At no point are you to let Mrs. Kennedy cross paths with that bum, Aristotle Onassis."

In London, the Windsors, **Prince Philip** *(left)* and **Queen Elizabeth** *(second from right)* entertain a chicly dressed **Jacqueline** and **JFK**.

Her Majesty liked Jackie more than she did a future First Lady, Nancy Reagan, whom the Queen privately accused of flirting with Philip.

While Jackie toured Greece, JFK retreated to Palm Beach. Once there, he told Senator Smathers, "I am nursing my wounds, getting over my humiliation in Vienna by seducing two White House secretaries, listening to Frank Sinatra records with a little Peggy Lee, and drinking lots of daiquiris. In addition to my bad back, all I have to worry about is an impending nuclear war."

Restoring the White House
"Mrs. Kennedy Thinks She's Marie Antoinette"

After her return from Europe, where "I wowed the masses," Jackie embarked with a fierce determination on her sweeping restoration of the White House. She told JFK and William Walton, "I want to make the White House so grand that Charles de Gaulle will be ashamed of his tacky old Versailles."

J.B. West, the building's Chief Usher, privately told other White House staffers, "I think Mrs. Kennedy thinks she's the reincarnation of Marie Antoinette."

Even before she occupied the White House, Jackie had begun articulating ideas for its transformation, consulting with Sister Parrish (Mrs. Henry Parrish II), and drawing up possible plans.

She learned that there was virtually nothing among the furnishings dating from before 1948. "People come from all over the world to see the White House, and it should be filled with antiques or furnishings owned by former Presidents, something with history attached to it. We're going to begin a restoration. I hate the word 'redecoration.'"

"When Mrs. Kennedy arrived at the White House, she was well versed in its history," said James Roe Ketchum, the building's curator. "She immediately earned our respect."

No sooner was her plan leaked to the press than she faced an assault from Republicans. It seemed that their fear was that Jackie would turn the White House into a monument to Kennedy.

She needed a vast array of contributors and committees to help her carry out her grand scheme,. She hired the decorating firm of the House of Jansen, which previously had restored the Palace of Versailles. The firm's clients included the Duke and Duchess of Windsor.

She also turned to a leading French decorator, Stephane Boudin, and she sought the cooperation of Henry Francis du Pont of the famous chemical family. He was viewed as the leading authority on American antiques. These two strong-willed personalities immediately conflicted, with Jackie forced to serve as mediator.

She also formed committees and set up a White House Restoration Fund as a means of shifting the costs of these financial burdens away from the taxpayers. Collectively, she referred to all these experts and committees she created as "my Politburo."

She also became the supervising housekeeper, issuing almost daily bulletins and memos to the staff. She wanted each of the building's 29 fireplaces ready to be lit at any time of the day or night, and she demanded that all 412 door knobs in the White House be polished weekly.

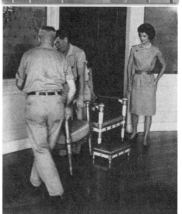

She also brought in her wealthy friend Bunny Mellon, an acclaimed horticulturist, to restore the White House Rose Garden. Today, it is used for press conferences. Jackie later said, "the beauty of the garden even impresses hard-nosed reporters."

For her collection of historic antiques, not everything had to be donated. The White

upper photo: Cover of *Life* magazine, September, 1961

lower photo: Restoring the White House

House had in storage, either in its basement or in a cavernous warehouse in Fort Washington, across the Potomac, in Maryland, a treasure trove of relics. From storage, she rescued many pieces that previous First Ladies had discarded. These included the "Hayes Desk," which Jackie moved into the Oval Office. It had been crafted from timbers salvaged from the mid-19th century three-masted sailing vessel, the *HMS Resolute*, which had been trapped in Arctic ice during an exploratory search commissioned by the Royal Navy, and during which its crew had suffered unimaginable horrors. The desk had been a gift from Queen Victoria to President Rutherford B. Hayes, cementing Anglo-American friendship.

Jackie discovered the White House china that Mary Todd Lincoln had purchased during the early months of the Civil War. On that same day, she turned up James Monroe's gold and silver flatware.

She supervised everything down to minor details, including the banishment of the lighting fixtures in the State Dining Room. She said it deepened the lines in a woman's face. As replacements, she ordered sconces whose candles cast a more forgiving light.

Antique wallpaper was found in a historic Maryland residence, and she ordered craftsmen to painstakingly have it removed and repasted onto the walls of the White House's diplomatic room. The cost: $12,500.

Lacking a budget, she persuaded wealthy donors to contribute, ending up with 160 antique paintings. These included such treasures as a $250,000 portrait of Benjamin Franklin owned by Walter Annenberg, the Philadelphia publisher. Jackie reminded all these donors that they could benefit from a tax deduction.

Truman Capote claimed that Jackie pursued the rich "with gleeful malice. She loaded her various committees and subcommittees with as many wealthy bluebloods as she could find—and then milked them for all they were worth."

By the end of the restoration project, Jackie was no longer the debutante from Newport. She had evolved into an independent-minded woman and had become very assertive. When Arthur Krock *[a three-time Pulitzer Prize winner]* and his wife, Martha Krock *[a society columnist for the Washington Times-Herald]*, were invited to dinner at the White House, Martha got drunk and chastised Jackie for skipping out on several events where the First Lady was to have been honored.

Jackie smiled politely, but the next day, she ordered her social secretary to permanently remove the Krocks from the White House guest list.

Her near decade-long marriage to JFK had experienced its low points. There were times when both of them seemed out of love with the

Paul Mellon with **Bunny Mellon** during the Johnson administration. They were called "the most self-effacing billionaires in the world."

other, a condition accelerated by his constant womanizing.

But as First Lady, Jackie won her husband's respect and maybe even his love. They bonded as never before, becoming true allies, one feeding off the other. One writer claimed that they "fused like two nuclei," sending off explosions of solar energy.

A clever money-raising device involved the publication of a magazine entitled *The White House: A Historic Guide.* It has sold five million copies over a span of time, the money going into the White House Restoration Fund.

For the most part, Jackie's restoration work met with press approval. In the first issue of *Newsweek,* published in 1962, appeared this comment: "Jacqueline Kennedy has made more changes in the White House than any woman in 143 years. This alone entitles her to at least a footnote in history. Her style and influence could easily give her some highly readable paragraphs in the main text of history."

Jackie's chief critic was reporter Maxine Cheshire, who wrote several scalding articles about her for the *Washington Post.* Cheshire exposed the dissension, the arm-twisting used in raising money for the White House restoration, and made several allegations, including that many of Jackie's acquisitions—hailed as genuine American antiques—were actually fakes. She cited such specifics as a desk in the Green Room that had cost $20,000 and hailed as an antique, but which was really a reproduction.

In response to this, JFK telephoned Philip Graham, the publisher of the *Washington Post,* to complain about Cheshire's articles. Graham and JFK had been longtime friends, often going "philandering together." But Graham did not stop the publication of the articles.

"You've reduced Jackie to tears," JFK said to Graham.

At the White House, Jackie was devastated by Cheshire's exposé. She turned to Henry Francis Du Pont, who offered a sympathetic ear. "Cheshire is the most malicious of the harpies," Jackie said. *["Harpies" was Jackie's word for the female members of the Washington Press Corps.]*

On the verge of tears, Jackie said, "That dreadful woman had done what she can to make my life miserable and the lives of my children. I'm trying to do something wonderful, with your help, in restoring the White House, only to have this bitch trash us in the *Post.*"

"The price, my dear, of being in the public eye," Du Pont responded.

***

In 1962, Jackie finally agreed to allow cameras into the White House as part of a guided tour that she would conduct. The program would later be viewed by some 60 million viewers around the world and would win both Emmy and Peabody Awards.

She had worked on the script itself, but often ad-libbed on camera.

Many of her off-the-cuff remarks were not historically accurate. A crew from CBS had to return to the White House to re-record some of her lines.

During the telecast, she claimed that Lincoln had been her favorite president, although she had "the strongest affinity," she said, for Thomas Jefferson.

Jackie carried through on her restoration project, simultaneous with JFK facing one crisis after another—turmoil in the U.S. steel industry, civil rights conflicts in the South, the Bay of Pigs, the construction of the Berlin Wall, and the threat of a nuclear attack from the Soviet Union.

To an increasing degree, she stood up to her husband. Noticing how gloomy he was at the end of a day, she asked him, "Where is all this Irish wit and charm you are said to possess?"

Laura Bergquist, writing for *Look,* claimed, "Mrs. Kennedy is always trying to deflate JFK's ego, and he strikes back, criticizing 'her self-contained privacy,' as he puts it."

As 1963 deepened, Jackie asked her secretary, Mary Gallagher, "Do you think I've done enough as First Lady?"

Gallagher assured her that her many accomplishments guaranteed that she had.

"Good!" Jackie responded. Then she said that she was going to curtail most of her public activities and spend more time with her husband and children.

"Jack desperately wants this child I'm giving birth to," she told Gallagher. "Unlike in my past when I exerted myself too much, I'm going to look after myself. I must succeed in this pregnancy after many failures of the past."

Then she turned and gazed out her office window. "You might say I'm taking the veil."

***

Jackie Kennedy was startled when JFK asked her to go on a goodwill visit to India and Pakistan in March of 1962 without him. She agreed, but with the stipulation that her sister, Lee Radziwill go with her. The crowds in both countries became hysterical, crying out, "*Jackie Ki Jai! Ameriki Rani!*" ("Hail Jackie, Queen of America!")

Jackie drew bigger crowds than Queen Elizabeth during her visit as head of the British Commonwealth. "Nothing else happened in India while Mrs. Kennedy was here," asserted the *Times of India.* "Her presence completely dominated the Indian scene."

She picked up a small fortune in gifts, including necklaces studded with diamonds, rubies, and pearls. Of course, there were the invariable protests, some critics attacking Jackie for wearing high fashion in a poverty-stricken country. Jackie told the press, "I only buy second hand, and everything at the Ritz Thrift Shop."

Her itinerary was planned for her, but she did insist on viewing the erotic carvings of the Black Pagoda of Konarac, especially one of a woman making love "to two violently tumescent men at the same time."

Back in New York, she told Truman Capote, "I'll have to try that position some time."

221

The Newport debutante of 1950, **Lee Radziwill** *(left)* and **Jackie**, the Newport debutante of 1947, were riding high during their state visit to India and Pakistan. These lovely sisters drew far larger crowds than the Queen of England during her visit to the sub-continent.

Chapter Ten

Jackie's Debut as a Fashionista
The First Lady Makes Oleg Cassini a Star

He Returns the Favor by Making Her….
With Papa Joe's Permission

Caught in the act, **Jackie Kennedy,** the new First Lady, was photographed dancing intimately with **Oleg Cassini,** whom she'd dubbed the New Frontier's "Secretary of Style." Rumors of a secret romance between the designer and his favorite fashionista circulated among the Washington press corps.

Oleg Cassini *(left)* is seen chatting with the First Couple. "I do think my social position as a close friend of the Kennedys helped to raise the status and image of American designers throughout the world." He recalled that his most fun night at the White House was when he and JFK got drunk, and Oleg dressed in drag.

In the post-war years, in Palm Beach, Oleg Cassini, the
fashion designer, and his younger brother, Igor Cassini, a gossip columnist, had become friends with Joseph P. Kennedy *["Papa Joe"].* They were often seen playing golf together.

Oleg found Papa Kennedy "mischievous with owlish eyes behind horn-rimmed glasses, with a knowing smile and a puckish sensibility that mocked his very direct manner."

In New York, both men appeared on the arms of stunningly beautiful girls once a week at Joseph's favorite restaurant, La Caravelle. Despite the fact that Joseph was married, he seemed to have no problem being seen in the company of a beautiful woman. But when Oleg started dating Joe's daughter, Eunice, the Kennedy patriarch abruptly put a stop to it. "She's not your type," he told Oleg.

And that was the end of that burgeoning romance.

Oleg and his younger brother, Igor, moved into the world of what was then called café society, a world peopled by playboys such as Porfirio Rubirosa, or heiresses like Woolworth's Barbara Hutton or "Big Tobacco's" Doris Duke.

Igor, later nicknamed café society the "jet set," a term that caught on in the 1950s.

At first, Igor, whose friends called him "Ghigi," became the more famous of the two brothers, writing a gossip column for the Hearst newspapers under the pen name of "Cholly Knickerbocker." It was he who eventually designated Jackie as 1947's Debutante of the Year.

The columnist Liz Smith worked for a while as Igor's journalistic assistant. She defined the Cassini brothers as "a pair of Lotharios," likening them to pirates who slept around.

In 1941, Oleg married the Hollywood beauty, Gene Tierney. Although their marriage survived for twelve stormy years, they had periods of separation.

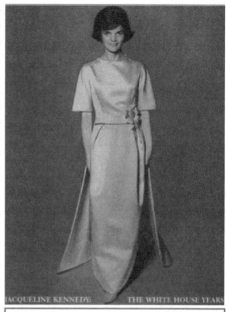

JACQUELINE KENNEDY: THE WHITE HOUSE YEARS

At least some of the credit associated with the image projected by **Jackie** during the Camelot years derives from her aesthetic collaboration with Oleg Cassini.

Here, positioned on the cover of *Jacqueline Kennedy, The White House Years,* the First Lady appears in the white double-satin gown he designed for her to wear to some of JFK's inaugural balls in January of 1961.

"Oleg Cassini's remarkable talent helped Jackie and the New Frontier get off to a magnificent start. Their historic collaboration gave us memorable changes in fashion, and style classics that remain timeless to this day."

—Teddy Kennedy

Right after the war, Tierney informed her estranged husband, who was living elsewhere, that she was carrying on an affair with movie idol Tyrone Power as well as another with "a handsome young congressman from Massachusetts," *[John F. Kennedy]*.

At the outbreak of World World II, Oleg joined the U.S. Coast Guard, but later served in the U.S. Army as a cavalry officer. A bisexual, he was said to have had an affair with actor Victor Mature during the war years, when both of them served in the Coast Guard.

Even though—when deprived of the company of women—they were lovers, back on land they often competed for the attentions of glamorous (female) movie stars.

One drunken night, Mature confessed to him how he destroyed Oleg's once-budding romance with Betty Grable and subsequently took her for himself: "I told her you had syphilis. That's why she dropped you like a hot potato," Mature said. "My exact words were, 'The Cassini family has had it for years. It's the talk of Europe. Everyone knows the Cassinis have syphilis."

Moving through romantic interludes with Gene Tierney (whom he married), Marilyn Monroe, Grace Kelly, and eventually, Jacqueline Kennedy, Oleg, an American fashion designer born to an aristocratic Russian family, was a first-rate "babe magnet."

He developed his reputation designing gowns for Paramount Pictures, but his legacy survives based on his role as the designer for First Lady Jackie Kennedy. He created "The Jackie Look," and his innovative A-line sheath and Empire strapless dress continues to be influential throughout the world of 21st Century High Fashion.

Oleg had designed for stars who included Tierney (his wife); Joan Crawford, Jayne Mansfield, Natalie Wood, Betty Grable, and Marilyn Monroe.

When Christina ("Tina") Cassini was born on November 19, 1948, there was speculation that her actual father might be Howard Hughes, Tyrone Power, producer Charles Feldman, or perhaps JFK.

As Maureen Orth, writing in *Vanity Fair,* said: "Deeply conscious of his romantic image, Oleg Cassini wanted to be seen only with 'top top girls.' Grace

10—Mon., Mar. 20, 1950   ⋆⋆⋆   New York Journal-American

The Smart Set
by Cholly Knickerbocker

Cholly Knickerbocker
Observes: Registered U. S. Patent Office.

Lucius Ordway and Ellen Fraser a Duet;
Dorothy di Frasso Is Here on Business;
Walter Brooks Dating Jeanne Miller

*T*HE GOSSIP MILL: Lucius Ordway, the Palm Beach squire, is escorting Ellen Fraser to all dinner parties. Ellen is one of the best friends of Lucius' estranged wife, Kay Denekla Ordway, who hasn't yet divorced her husband for the simple reason that "Mr. Ordway hasn't asked me for one yet."

The Cassini Brothers: How smart hustlers from Imperial Russia competed for glamour, money, fame, and acknowledgments from "the smart set:"

Above is a typical news flash (March 20, 1950) from the gossipy world of **Cholly** (Igor) **Knickerbocker** (Cassini).

225

Kelly, who fell madly in love with him, was a top top girl, but Marilyn Monroe, he confided to journalist Joe Klein, who ghostwrote his autobiography, was just 'a little polo pony.'"

He had first met Jackie shortly after her marriage to JFK, but he did not become her exclusive couturier until 1961, when she was First Lady. She dubbed him "Secretary of Style."

In 1953, at Manhattan's El Morocco, Oleg was introduced to Jackie. "Even though she just married, she was there with Stanley Mortimer. He was married at the time to Babe Cushing, who would later marry Bill Paley of CBS. As Babe Paley, she would become the world's best dressed woman."

Young love gone awry

Oleg Cassini with 1940s film beauty
Gene Tierney

"I found Jackie charming and envied Jack Kennedy for having married her before I got my chance," Oleg later said. "From the beginning, of my relationship with her, I was flirtatious. At one point, I told her that I was sorry that she'd gotten married and missed out on two catches like Stanley Mortimer and me."

"I was a bit surprised to have discovered Jackie out on a date with Stanley—if that was indeed what it was," Oleg said. "Did Jack give her that much freedom? In those days, it was suspicious for a married man and a married woman to be seen going out together. As for Jack, he spoke to me openly about his affairs, which he did not plan to terminate even though married. The last time I saw him, he told me that even on his honeymoon, he had two other women. I wondered at the time if Jack and Jackie had

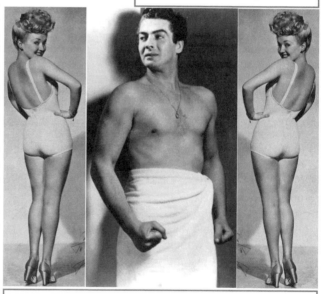

Victor Mature "The King of Beefcake," poses as the meat in a sandwich formed by a double view of **Betty Grable**, the most famous cheesecake of the 1940s.

In a deliberate act of character assassination, Mature later confessed how he sabotaged Oleg's budding romance with her.

what came to be called 'an open marriage.'"

In 1961, Oleg was in Nassau in The Bahamas on a hot date with actress Jill St. John. His male companion was Pat De Cicco, the Hollywood hustler who was once married to heiress Gloria Vanderbilt.

A phone call from Washington came in from the White House with a request. He was told that "Mrs. Kennedy is in a hospital in Georgetown, having given birth to a son. She wants to see some of your sketches in the next few days if you could visit her in her hospital room."

After putting down the phone, Oleg realized that he had no sketches to show her. He didn't even have a sketch pad. After buying supplies, he sat by a swimming pool and feverishly drew sketches of dresses and gowns for the First Lady.

"I had dressed stars before. I decided that Jackie, for all purposes, was being treated like a movie star. In time, she would face so many movie cameras it would have made a hundred *Gone With the Winds.* I was determined, if I became her designer, to have her dominate the social samurai in which she moved so gracefully."

With the first of his rough sketches, he flew from Nassau via New York to Jackie's hospital bed in Georgetown.

For Cassini as an avant-garde designer, there was life before Jackie. Above, two designs by Cassini, *Left* from 1950; *Right*, from 1958.

He landed in Washington with about twenty sketches. When he was ushered into her hospital room, he was disappointed to see her surrounded by sketches from other American designers—(Ferdinando) Sarmi, (Norman) Norell, Andreas of Bergdorf Goodman.

But before that afternoon faded, he had convinced her that she needed only one designer to give her a unified look—"Let's call it 'The Jackie Look.' You don't have to confuse the public by showing up one day in a Dior, the other day in a Chanel."

Jackie's New Frontier Vs. frumpy, judgmental antecedents **Bess Truman** *(left)* with **Mamie Eisenhower**

"Nothing French," she said. "I have strict orders from Joe. Only American designers can be used."

"Then select me," he said. "I'm as American as apple pie."

"You're as American as Russian caviar and French champagne. But you're on."

"Thank you," he said. "I just know you and Jack will usher in an American Versailles at the White House."

"I'm sure you understand," she said. "Right now, the White House looks like a Statler Hotel. I want to transform it, redecorate it, and make it the social and intellectual capital of America, inviting the greatest writers, painters, and musicians, as well as ballet dancers. Only the best French food and wine will be served. Gone forever are the days when Bess Truman ordered that greens with what she called 'fatback' be cooked every day for Harry."

In his memoirs, **Oleg Cassini** proclaimed, "I will not participate in fashionable innuendo and false gossip about **Grace Kelly**. We were in love. We were engaged to be married—no more, no less."

In reference to being in Cannes with Grace during her filming of *To Catch a Thief*, he said, "She was at her most charming and magical at that time."

Jackie told Oleg, "That dowdy, dreadful Mamie, with her bangs, is out the door. I want to bring youth, glamour, taste, and elegance to the White House and to Washington itself. If you're going to be my designer, make sure that no other woman wears your creations. I don't want to see any little fat woman hopping around in the same dress or gown you created for me."

He immediately had an idea. Jackie was no Bess Truman or Eleanor Roosevelt. She was already known for her taste and elegance. "I felt that with the right clothing, I could turn her into a fashion icon of the 20th Century. I began to feel this handsome couple, the most powerful in the world, would go down in history alongside Caesar and Cleopatra, or Napoléon and Josephine. You noticed that I left out Hitler and Eva Braun. Maybe Hitler with Marlene Dietrich could have pulled it off for Germany, not a *hausfrau* like Braun."

When Jackie agreed to endorse Oleg as her fulltime designer, she had already promised to wear a gown designed by Andreas of Bergdorf on the night of the inauguration. But she agreed to wear a design by Oleg at the pre-Inauguration Ball. *[Scheduled for January 19, 1961, at the National Guard Amory in Washington, the gala was staged by Frank Sinatra.]*

Oleg designed a white double satin gown with elbow-length sleeves, a two part bell-shaped skirt, and a princess-shaped bodice. She ended up preferring it to the Bergdorf gown.

The white gown turned out to be ever so appropriate," Oleg said. "On the night of the gala, Washington experienced one of its worst blizzards. Jackie emerged as the glittering Snow Queen."

As snow was falling over Washington, Jackie came into the giant room accompanied by the glitter of emeralds and diamonds on her ears and throat, borrowed from Tiffany's.

Oleg also designed the outfit she wore to the actual Inauguration ceremony, which would be outdoors. His choice for Jackie featured a fawn beige wool coat accessorized with a small sable collar and muff, accompanied by a matching pillbox hat. He was later furious that Halsted was credited with designing her pillbox hat, which Oleg claimed that he'd created.

Igor, Oleg's brother, defined in his column "the little girl look—a flaring, baby doll appearance as adopted by a grown woman."

Joseph Kennedy told Oleg, "Don't bother them at all about the money. Just send me the bill at the end of the year, and I'll pay it. But be discreet. Don't let on about the cost. I don't want to hurt Jack politically."

"When I designed for Jackie," Oleg said, "I was thinking of a hieroglyphic torso—broad shoulders, slim torso, long neck, narrow hips, good carriage, perhaps Cleopatra herself. I called it my 'A-look.' Simplicity plus. I would use the most sumptuous fabrics in the purest interpretations."

After becoming Jackie's exclusive designer, Oleg said his staff had a frantic time. "There must have been an order for a hundred gowns a year. We constructed three mannequins with Jackie's exact measurements, and I also hired a New York model who had Jackie's duplicate figure. I signed on a draper and a cutter. I also had to hire a *première* to research fabrics and colors. I had eight staff designers, and all of them kept busy. Jackie kept calling, 'I've got nothing to wear.' Once I had to rush to Washington just as Air Force One was departing for Paris and on to Vienna to meet Nikita Khrushchev." *[Cassini was referring to the June, 1961, Summit Meeting between JFK and then-Soviet dictator Khruschhev, convened with the express purpose of discussing the future of a divided Berlin.]* "I unloaded her wardrobe right onto the plane. She let me know that every batch of clothing must contain gowns or dresses in her two favorite colors—pistachio and shocking pink. She told me, 'My tastes are simple. I like only the best.'"

"When Jackie arrived at the White House, she had no clothes," Oleg said. "For about ten days, she wouldn't go out. I remember her ask-

Two Cassini Designs worn by Jackie, as exhibited by New York's Metropolitan Museum

229

ing me, 'Can you hurry up, because I have nothing to wear.' The popular idea is that Jackie arrived with hundreds of dresses. The reality was that she'd lived in controlled simplicity. The moment she was in the White House, she was another person. She was suddenly confronted with so many things to do, and she had to play the part."

"After Jack and Jackie moved into the White House, I think he fell in love with her all over again," Oleg said. "Up to then, he'd regarded her as a political liability. His opinion changed when Jack saw her popularity soar. Americans caught 'Jackie Fever.' As First Lady, wearing my clothes, she awed the world, even though she disliked politics. In spite of her youth, she'd found the ideal role as Queen of America, or Princess, if you like. She could be witty, but also decisive and authoritative about getting her way. She was also unpredictable. Whenever I arrived at the White House, I never knew what mood she'd be in."

"As Jackie's designer, I became known as the 'Dr. Feelgood of Couture,'" Oleg said. "I saw such an intimate side of Jackie and got to know her body, perhaps more intimately than did her husband. I even selected panties and brassieres for her. I analyzed every inch of her body and created designs not only to enhance her stunning beauty, but to conceal her flaws. I had the power to envision a Jackie that she wanted to exhibit to the world. Naturally, with such intimate body contact, sexual fantasies arose on both of our parts. It was inevitable that one thing would lead to another. After all, Jackie and I were only human, with both our strengths but also our temptations."

One fashion critic said Cassini's unique designs for Mrs. Kennedy "ushered in a new era of timeless simplicity based on clean lines and crisp forms and opulent and luxurious fabrics."

"If I am America's Queen, as the press calls me, it was Oleg who dressed me for the part."

Throughout America, young girls from age 12 to senior citizens at 80 copied the look of simple, geometric dresses in sumptuous fabrics and pillbox hats with elegant coiffure.

Jackie may have enjoyed worldwide approval and appreciation, but she also aroused jealousy, especially in Ethel Kennedy. At a party in Palm Beach, Truman Capote told Oleg, "Ethel has the mind set of a vulture. She is insanely jealous of Jackie—and not just for her stealing Bobby's love after Jack died. If Jackie throws a big party at the White House, Ethel will throw a lavish shindig at Hickory Hill. Jackie is an obsession with Ethel. She tries to outdo Jackie, but fails miserably. Jackie once told me that Ethel was 'a baby-making machine—wind the bitch up and she becomes pregnant.'"

Sometimes, copying Jackie had disastrous consequences, especially for leopards. She appeared in a leopardskin coat and matching hat, the combined cost of which totaled $3,000, and was photographed for the cover of *Life* magazine. After that, there was such a rush on leopard skin coats that the entire species became endangered.

In later reflections, Igor—as documented in his column—was rather critical of Jackie. "She had always been in love with money, first, and power, a close second. She proved the adage that power corrupts. It corrupted her. Once she became First Lady, she changed—and not for the better."

Although Oleg and JFK were friends, he didn't like Jackie appearing on best-dressed lists. "God damn it," he said. "The New Frontier is going to be sabotaged by a bunch of faggy French couturiers."

Jackie made a promise she didn't plan to keep: "I will even resort to muu-muus if it will save you political embarrassment."

Letitia Baldrige was forced to issue a statement to the press: "Mrs. Kennedy realizes that the clothes she wears are of interest to the public, but she is distressed by the implications of extravagance, or over-emphasis, and the misuse of her name by firms from which she had not bought clothes. For the next four years, Mrs. Kennedy's clothes will be by Oleg Cassini. They will be designed and made in America. She will buy what is necessary, without extravagance—and you will often see her photographed in the same outfit."

The last statement was misleading. As First Lady, Jackie was almost never photographed wearing the same outfit twice, with the exception of that pink Chanel suit that she was wearing that November day in Dallas.

Hubert de Givenchy later claimed that Oleg stole many of his designs and then copied them for Jackie. Letitia Baldrige more or less confirmed that, claiming privately that Jackie and Oleg often took original designs from other couturiers and copied them, taking care to use different colors and different fabrics.

Partly because his father, Joseph Kennedy, was paying for Jackie's wardrobe, the President took little interest in her dress. He did have a few stipulations, however. "Never wear brown. I can't stand brown dresses on a woman. And don't ever wear those Joan Crawford flowery patterns."

Jackie herself insisted that turquoise was a forbidden color. She told Oleg, "It makes me look sallow." Once, when Oleg presented her with a collection of newly designed, specially crafted dresses, she modeled them for JFK, who rejected them: "Hell, send those dresses back. They make you look like a gypsy."

JFK had another demand: He heard that the millinery industry was in trouble. Millions of American women weren't wearing hats anymore. He demanded that Jackie wear headgear—"and be photographed wearing a hat."

For the most part, he ignored her wardrobe and rarely took note of her hairdo. However, one day at the White House, he walked into Jackie's room. "Mr. Kenneth" [Kenneth Battelle; who was cited by Vogue magazine in 1961 as being the celebrity hairdresser that "almost every famous female head in the world has gone or will go to."] had flown in from New York specifically to style Jackie's hair. As the finishing touches were being applied, the President took one look at Jackie's hair-do. "What in hell, Kenneth, are you trying to ruin my political career? Redo that hair-do. She's Jackie Kennedy—not Marie Antoinette at the Court of Versailles."

Jackie acquiesced to her husband's demand. Kenneth restyled her hair, but kept the bouffant. "What he'd done was make my customary bouffant even more pronounced so that I resembled Madame de Pompadour."

She sometimes issued specific instructions to Oleg—"a two-piece summer dress with a straw hat," or "a white dress with black polka dots." Some outfits were rejected outright. Others, such as a red wool hunting jacket, met her approval, but was sent back to be remade with a fabric that "is not so heavy."

Jackie and Lee Radziwill wore the designs of Oleg and created a sensation in India and in Pakistan during her much-publicized visit, Jackie had only one complaint. "I wish I had ordered more wardrobe."

[During their goodwill visit, March 12-21, 1962, Life *magazine estimated that Jackie wore 22 different outfits throughout the course of her trip, in New Delhi alone, changing her clothes 5 times in a single day. According to correspondent Anne Chamberlin, "Her every seam has been the subject of hypnotized attention from the streets of Delhi to the Khyber Pass."]*

***

JFK: *"How would you categorize me? Romantic or erotic?"*
OLEG CASSINI: *"Definitely erotic. In fact, you would be right up there with the greats in history, with Don Juan and Casanova, because you have the physical attributes, but also the charm to seduce. The only thing you lack is time, and, of course, you're married."*
JFK: *"But I can maneuver around those roadblocks."*

When JFK and Jackie moved into the White House, they inaugurated what Robert Frost called "the age of poetry and power." Of course, that era soon came to an abrupt end. Even so, Jackie's sophistication and grace continued to enthrall America and the world.

Oleg became a frequent guest. As Jackie wrote to him, "Every time you come to Washington with designs for me, please plan to stay for dinner. You amuse Jack. The poor President and his wife are so bored in this dreary *Maison Blanche.*"

Sometimes, she complained about JFK to Oleg. "I'm trying to bring culture to the White House. But he doesn't like opera and he dozes off listening to symphonies. The only music he really likes is 'Hail to the Chief.' I want to bring the Bolshoi Ballet to Washington, but he has warned me in advance, 'I don't want my picture taken shaking hands with all those Russian fairies.'"

During Oleg's reign as Jackie's designer, rumors were rampant that they were having an affair. It was commonly spoken about, especially at parties in Palm Beach. Both Igor and Oleg denied such reports, although in later years they confessed that it was true. "For my brother to have admitted to an affair with Jackie would have destroyed his career," Igor said in later years. "Retributions from the powerful Kennedys would have been fierce."

Oleg's "dating" of Jackie came to the attention of Joseph. Oleg recalled sitting out on a terrace with the Kennedy patriarch in Palm Beach, watching the sunset.

"Look, Oleg," he said. "I wouldn't be surprised if you had some ideas about Jackie. If the situation were different, and I was twenty years younger, I'd have some ideas about Jackie, even though she is my daughter-in-law. But the question is: Truth versus perception. The worst thing, to my mind, would be to have the perception but not the reality—that would be silly, a real donkey's game. You understand?"

Oleg later said, "I understood perfectly. He was granting me license to move in on Jackie, but telling me to keep it discreet, which I did, of course. Unlike my brother, Igor, who publishes any rumor he's ever heard, I know what discretion means."

Oleg later said that he more or less began a role as Jackie's escort because JFK was often in horrible back pain, and was in no condition to shake a thousand hands and dance around the floor.

"I took Jackie to parties in New York and Palm Beach," Oleg said. "We had quiet dinners together. She was a very sexy, vibrant woman who needed the love of a man. Jack was too ill to accommodate her. One thing led to another, when you put an oversexed man with a girl who wasn't being serviced."

"I introduced her to my best friend, Porfirio Rubirosa, who told me in the locker room of a golf course that within two months he'd be Jackie's lover. I didn't think he could pull that one off. But then I changed my mind. I never met a woman yet, from Doris Duke to Barbara Hutton, the two richest women in the world, from Marilyn Monroe to Joan Crawford, who didn't take off their panties for Rubi."

"One night, Jackie arrived with Peter Lawford in Palm Beach," Igor said. "I had a small party. Peter excused himself, complaining of a headache. He went to my bedroom to rest, or so he said. He spent three hours there calling people in California. He left me with a huge phone bill. I later mentioned this to Jackie. She said, 'Oh, that's Peter. He makes most of his long distance phone calls from the White House and lets the taxpayer pick up the tab.'"

Oleg also developed a close friendship with JFK. "We would sit for hours and talk about our favorite topic—beautiful women. He was especially intrigued with what made a woman a star, knowing that I had seduced many of them. He was banging Marilyn Monroe at the time. I'd already had her. He'd also banged my former wife, Gene Tierney, who had wanted to marry him."

"I'd hate to have to compete against you for a woman," JFK told Oleg.

Dinners were often informal affairs at the White House, with only a few trusted friends. Charles (Chuck) Spalding was always there, as was JFK's best friend, Lem Billings. "Everybody knew that Lem was gay, but nobody ever said anything," Oleg said. "Whatever relationship existed between Lem and Jack was kept private. But, except for a separation during the war, they had been close buddies in a friendship dating back to their schoolboy days in 1933."

"Lem made me uncomfortable. On several occasions, he propositioned me, but I wasn't interested. I didn't like to be alone with him."

"I never knew what Jack would demand of me," Oleg said. "One night, he asked me to show fellow diners how to do the Twist, which was all the rage. I got up and showed them how. Jackie picked up on it right away, and she and I were wildly dancing the Twist, which I had learned at the Peppermint Lounge in New York. On another occasion, I was asked to teach Jack's friends the Hully-Gully. I had just returned from Paris where that dance was all the rage."

Oleg was such a close friend that he was even invited to the White House for dinner after JFK gave one of the most famous speeches of any American president, warning of the Cuban Missile Crisis and threatening the Soviet Union with a "full retaliatory response."

Oleg later revealed that Jackie in her Pucci pants presided over a meal that included filets of sole Véronique and *canard à l'orange*. "She was the perfect hostess, as always. She tried to be upbeat and cheerful, but the tension was reflected in her voice. It was a difficult evening to live through. But at least we were still alive, waiting for an attack from Soviet missiles."

Oleg had only one criticism of the dinner. The White House steward served a 1959 Pouilly-Fumé. "Here we were facing the end of the world, and the best thing the White House Steward could come up with was a three-year-old wine."

Over a cigar and brandy, JFK told Oleg, "We have twenty chances out of a hundred that we'll be at war with Russia."

Ethel Kennedy was at the dinner. She said, "If this is the end of the world, it's God's will. We're in God's hands now."

"In that case, let's drink a toast to tomorrow," Jackie said.

Everyone clinked glasses around the table, except Ethel, who looked at Jackie as if she were staring down Nikita Khrushchev himself.

***

"After the threat had passed, Jack and I discussed what he might do after he left the White House," Oleg said. "One night, upstairs in the White House, he suggested that he might like to go in with me in the couture business. Perhaps he was joking. He said he could fit the dresses on and off my models, even recommending that I might want to design brassieres and panties. 'I'd be particularly good in taking those garments off the models,' he claimed."

"On a serious note, I told him that I was considering launching a line of men's shirts to get away from the traditional white," Oleg said. "I want to see men walking up and down Fifth Avenue in deep, rich colors—canary yellow, royal purple, navy blue, emerald green, chocolate brown."

"I'll be your model and start wearing them," JFK promised. "When I'm photographed wearing them—it's got to be in color—I can do for colored shirts what Jackie did for the pillbox hat."

Oleg even discussed with JFK the prospect of turning him into the best-dressed man in the world, rivaling the title then held by the Duke of Windsor. "I could make you as important in the world of men's fashion as Jackie is to the women," Oleg promised. He later claimed that "The President was intrigued with my suggestion, which the assassination brought to a horrible ending."

To implement his plan for the President's wardrobe, Oleg suggested getting rid of his socks with holes in them, his frayed shirts, and his baggy, well-worn suits. Shortly before JFK's death, Oleg had launched his campaign to reshape JFK's wardrobe by presenting him with two dozen of the world's most beautiful ties. "Of course, I had to tell him that his nonchalant elegance transcended anything he wore."

"The President and I often discussed my interest in the plight of the North American Indian, but he'd grow bored and switched to more gossipy topics," Oleg said. "We once discussed who had the greater sex appeal—Errol Flynn or Tyrone Power."

JFK stated his belief that the image of Power on the screen was more romantic, whereas the image of Flynn was entirely erotic.

Knowing that Oleg had seduced both Jayne Mansfield and Gina Lollobrigida, JFK asked him which actress had the better breasts. "I've had Jayne, but I never fucked Gina," JFK told him.

"I'd cast my vote for Gina," Oleg said. "She is absolutely erotic in everything she does. There is a quality of sexuality about her every movie. She is Thoroughbred, whereas Jayne is a mere polo pony, like Marilyn Monroe."

Sometimes, JFK and Oleg, for their own amusement, would characterize their friends or enemies as either a bird or a dog. Jackie was a fawn; Joseph Kennedy a wise old owl; Bobby a basset hound; J. Edgar Hoover an old toad; Oleg a Siamese cat; and JFK an Irish setter.

***

The last time Oleg saw JFK was in early November of 1963 at a private dinner party at the home of Jean Kennedy Smith in her Fifth Avenue Apartment in Manhattan. Oleg remembered Adlai Stevenson being there, advising the President not to fly to Dallas. "There's danger there," Stevenson warned. "I was just there, and I felt the hatred."

The President ignored the warning. At the door, Oleg asked him, "Why are you going? America will never have another President as wonderful as you. We can't afford to lose you. Please don't go."

"I feel I must," JFK said. "I also feel I'll be perfectly safe."

On November 22, 1963, Oleg was in his studio when an assistant entered. "Turn on the radio!" he shouted.

Oleg flipped on the radio just in time to hear a bulletin being broadcast out of Dallas. THE PRESIDENT IS DEAD.

"I never really recovered from Jack's death," he later said. "From time to time in the years to come, Jackie and I would have a quiet dinner together, often at her apartment. The dream that we'd dreamed in the glorious days of Camelot had long faded. After Jack's death, our business arrangement came to an end, but we remained friends. But nothing between us was ever the same again."

"I recalled the many nights Jack and I talked about women," Oleg said. "He always asked, 'Does she have *It?*'"

"*He* had *It*. He had it in spades, and we have not seen it since."

One drunken night in Palm Beach, Oleg confessed a secret to Igor, who was not very good at keeping secrets. "I never knew until Jack died, but I was in love with him, not with Jackie."

***

After Camelot had come and gone, *Women's Wear Daily* noted, "There is no doubt that Mrs. Jacqueline Kennedy probably did more to uplift taste in the United States than any woman in the history of our country."

Oleg read an article by journalist Sarah Crichton that he felt accurately conveyed Jackie's legacy with American women.

"She would be the last woman we could idolize. We were not allowed to believe fairy tales any more. Today, no one woman can ever embody all our dreams. But we fell in love with Jackie in a simpler time. When we wanted to grow up to be princesses, she was our princess. And later, when we wanted to be independent, she was independent."

"She made it all look so easy, when for the rest of women, it always seemed so hard—the mothering, the wifing, the beauty routine, the 'stay interesting' thing. We balanced books on our heads, desperate to move like models, but the books always slid. Instead of standing like angels, we looked like chickens. We fussed with Peter Pan collars and bizarre undergarments and Toni home perms that never turned out right."

"And then there was Jackie, with her chiseled collarbones and elegant, clear arms—arms that could juggle babies, dance with giants, rein in large animals. Most women felt so uncomfortable in their skins, but she was radiant in hers."

Cassini's design for Jackie to wear during an audience with the Pope. Basic black and *über*-demure, in silk & wool jersey.

PILLBOX MANIA
Catering to the Jackie craze: Four Jackie lookalikes modeling designs by Oleg Cassini

Chapter Eleven

Jackie Oh! and MM

—The World Knew Them by their Nicknames

"Jackie, I want you to meet Miss Marilyn Monroe"
—Truman Capote

Sharing Poisonous Secrets
Jackie-Oh! in a Face to Face with JFK's Mistress

Truman Capote *(center)* was "The Missing Link" between **Jackie Kennedy** *(left)* and **Marilyn Monroe** *(right)*. During a secret meeting in midtown Manhattan, the gossipy author brought them together for the first time, an event he secretly recorded.

Both Marilyn and JFK, her lover, died while young. Social commentator David Marshall speculated about what might have happened had they lived:

"Her back stooped from osteoporosis, munching carrot sticks and sipping Dom Perignon, Marilyn would sink into her sofa one autumn evening, slide in one of these made-for-TV movies, and smile at just how wrong the filmmakers had gotten it all. Still, she might have mused, 'It made a lovely story.'"

"I never thrilled and throbbed to the manly charms of Jack Kennedy. He's an Irish clunk. Oh, I admit, he has a vulgar appeal—but then, the Kennedys are such a vulgar family!"
—Truman Capote

"I knew Jackie since her days when she was a college student working for Vogue *magazine in New York. I don't know what is wrong with Jackie, except that she is very out in orbit somewhere."*
—Truman Capote

"Talk about 'in orbit.' Truman Capote is one to talk. He was born on Jupiter, emigrated to Mars, got kicked out of Venus, and reached Earth via the Moon one night with the help of Dracula."
—Gore Vidal

"Marilyn Monroe is nothing but a publicity seeker and self-promoter of the most venomous sort. She is a vulgar slut, a part-time lesbian, a full-time nymphomaniac, and a greedy little bitch. She's also unbalanced. From what I hear, there's a serious hygiene problem. She masks the foul odor with Chanel No. 5 when soap and water might better serve her."
—Jackie Kennedy to Lem Billings

Before she died in 1962, **Truman Capote** recalled a talk he'd had with **Marilyn** on the night he took her dancing.

"I told her, 'Why cry over Jack or Bobby? Between the two of them, they can't raise a decent hard-on.'"

"'Oh, Truman,' she chastised me. 'You've always been such a size queen.'"

Truman Capote had been privy to Jackie's early days of romance with the senator from Massachusetts. "From the beginning, Jackie knew that her husband was dating other women. She even knew that he had begun his affair when Marilyn was the most famous movie star in the world and Jack a relatively unknown senator. At times when I saw her she was coming unglued. I don't think she can stand the pressure of being a politician's wife. I think she'll snap."

Her friend, Paul Mathias, said, "Jackie was hurt very young in connection with both her father and mother. She never came out of the shock of growing up. I don't think she was born happy. She fills her days as best as she can, but she suffers a lot. I have great compassion for her. It sinks into me more and more just how irreversibly unhappy she is."

"Jackie hated being a political wife," Capote said. "She had more sophistication than Bess Truman or Mamie Eisenhower. She was naïve in certain respects, shrewd in others. She couldn't tolerate those women. She made fun of their dowdiness and slobbering devotion to their husband's political careers. She detested Lady Bird Johnson. 'They're such pigeons,' she used to tell me."

Truman's Bitchy Putdowns of the Kennedy Men, Especially JFK

Jackie and Truman had long, drawn-out discussions about the affairs of the Kennedy men, including the founding papa, Joseph P. Kennedy, and his relationships with actresses such as Gloria Swanson. "I don't think Jackie realized what she was walking into when she married Jack," Capote said. "He was in constant competition with his old man to see who could nail the most women. Jackie wasn't prepared for quite such blatant womanizing. She hadn't expected to find herself stranded at parties while her husband went off with somebody new."

In her anger one night, Jackie told Capote, "Jack has a miniscule body and a huge head." Capote was far more direct. "All those Kennedy men are the same. They're like dogs, having to stop and pee on every fire hydrant."

"In the 1950s, I used to have dinner with her and Jack when they had this awful old apartment on Park Avenue around 86th Street. But mostly, Jack was out of town, and she and I would have dinner or go to the theater by ourselves. We used to sit around talking until four or five o'clock in the morning. She was sweet, eager, intelligent, not quite sure of herself and hurt, because she knew that he was banging all these other broads. She never said that, but I knew about it rather vaguely."

Truman attended dinner parties with "Jackie and Jack" in the 1950s, during the first years of their marriage. At one such party on Park Avenue, he showed up with Babe Paley, the wife of William Paley, then chairman of the board of CBS.

After dinner, Jackie and Babe left for a brandy in one part of the apartment while the men retired for brandy and cigars in the library. "Some high roller from Texas was recounting his experiences with a $1,500-a-night call girl in Las Vegas," Capote claimed. "He knew her telephone number and her specialties— sucking cock, rim jobs, around the world. He knew how well she did it, how long, how deep, how big a cock she could take, and what she could do with it that nobody else had ever done."

"That's how he talked. It was nauseating, a real stomach-turner. Jack was lapping it up, practically taking notes. He did write some names and numbers on a scrap of paper for future use. Later when he and Jackie were leaving, she asked him what the men had talked about. 'Plain old politics,' he lied to her. But Jackie knew the score. She knew everything!"

"What I don't understand is why everybody said the Kennedys were so sexy," said Capote. "I know a lot about cocks—I've seen an awful lot of them – and if you put all the Kennedys together, you wouldn't have a good one. I used to see Jack when I was staying with Loel and Gloria Guinness in Palm Beach. I had a little guest cottage with its own private beach, and he would come down so he could swim in the nude. He had absolutely nuthin'! Bobby was the same way; I don't know how he had all those children. As for Teddy – forget it! I liked Jack, and I liked many things about Bobby. But I wouldn't have wanted him to be president. He was too vindictive. Teddy is crazy. He's a menace. He's a wild Irish drunk who goes into terrible rages. I'd want anybody to be president before Teddy!"

***

"Marilyn Monroe is a bisexual, hypnotized nymphomaniac, a Mae West caricature."

—Cecil Beaton to Truman Capote

Cecil Beaton, Truman's close friend and fellow homosexual, photographed Marilyn Monroe and shared his impression of the dazzling star with Truman.

"She's bisexual," Beaton told Truman. "Also narcissistic, unkempt, with a hygiene problem, a hypnotized nymphomaniac, as spectacular as the silvery shower of a Vesuvius fountain, an undulating basilisk. Her acting is pure charade, a little girl's caricature of Mae West. She's like two straws in a single soda, running nylons, and drive-in movies for necking—a composite of Alice in Wonderland, Trilby, and a Minsky burlesque queen."

In spite of this appraisal, Capote became one of the few known friends of both Jackie and Marilyn. He was so enchanted by Marilyn that he lobbied for her to appear as Holly Golightly in the film version of his novella, *Breakfast at Tiffany's,* a role she eventually lost to Audrey Hepburn.

He was also privy to her affair with JFK and later, to her affair with Bobby Kennedy. He was around to see her rejected.

In a conversation, Capote listened as a drugged and slightly demented Marilyn shared her dream with him: "Jack told me only last week that he plans to divorce Jackie and marry me. No later than 1964, I will be by his side when he seeks re-election. Imagine me, First Lady of the land. I had ambitions when I was struggling in the early days. With Jack, I will preside over America from 1964 to 1968 as his First Lady. I'll be a very different First Lady from Jackie. I'll be more human, more down to earth. I was the most dreamy starlet to ever arrive in Hollywood. I dreamed of becoming the biggest movie star of all time, bigger than Betty Grable, Lana Turner, and Ava Gardner. That dream came true for me. But in my wildest imagination, I never dreamed I'd become First Lady of the United States."

Coup d'Etat: America's Next First Lady?

MM to Truman: "Jack told me, only last week, that he plans to divorce Jackie and marry me.

Capote learned that Jackie was so upset over her husband's affair with Marilyn that she had checked into to Valleyhead, a private psychiatric clinic in Carlisle,

240

Massachusetts, for electroshock therapy.

In the great tradition of Southern storytellers, Capote was clearly the master. Regrettably, he dined out on more stories than he recorded on paper. There is no doubt that he was aware of many of the secrets of the rich and famous, some of whom he betrayed by writing thinly disguised portraits of them when he published excerpts from his unfinished novel, *Answered Prayers.*

One night in Key West in 1969, Truman told an astonishing story that he claimed would eventually appear as an entire chapter in his upcoming novel. Listening with eager ears were his hosts, Tennessee Williams and his longtime companion, Frank Merlo; James Leo Herlihy (author of *Midnight Cowboy*); and the co-author of this book, Darwin Porter.

All biographers assume that Marilyn Monroe and Jacqueline Kennedy never met face to face, although they occasionally shared the bed of the same man—namely President John F. Kennedy.

Each woman had met the rising young Massachusetts politician in 1951: Marilyn on May 15, Jackie at a different party 12 days earlier.

By the time the Kennedys moved into the White House, the new First Lady was aware of her husband's affairs with other women, including Marilyn. Jackie called it, "the curse of being married to a Kennedy man."

According to Capote, Jackie plotted her revenge. That would come on the night of May 19, 1962. On learning that Peter Lawford had asked Marilyn to fly in from the West Coast and sing "Happy Birthday, Mr. President" to JFK in Washington, Jackie placed a secret call to Marilyn one week before the event. She advised Marilyn to make the song "as sexy as possible because Jack will adore it." Marilyn told her that she thought that was a "great idea," and that designer Jean-Louis was putting the finishing touches on a dress that Marilyn was describing as "just flesh and diamonds."

Appearing late at the televised event, Marilyn walked onto the stage to sing her song. As columnist Dorothy Kilgallen later so aptly put it: "It was like Marilyn Monroe was making love to the President in direct view of 40 million Americans." Jackie wisely had skipped the event to go horseback riding in Virginia.

Although officially, the President had thanked Marilyn for singing "in such a sweet and wholesome way," backstage he was furious, blaming Peter Lawford for the disaster. Meeting privately with Marilyn, JFK whispered to her that their affair was over, even though he invited her back to his suite at the Hotel Carlyle for "a farewell fuck." He warned her never to call the White House

SING TO ME, DARLIN!
Trying to please the Birthday Boy

View of **Marilyn** from behind the scenes at Madison Square Garden, May 19, 1962

again. Belatedly, Marilyn realized that Jackie had tricked her.

Back on the West Coast, Marilyn was fuming and "full of fury," in Peter's words. She phoned him one night to inform him that she was going to call a press conference next week and reveal her long-running affair with the President. She also said that after her press conference, "Mr. President can kiss a second term good-bye."

Peter beseeched her not to, but fully believed she'd do it. He placed a call to Bobby Kennedy, urging him to warn the President. Peter also claimed that Marilyn was growing more and more dependent on drugs, and that she sounded "unhinged."

It is not known how Jackie learned about Marilyn's threat, but apparently she did. Through Peter's help, she placed another call to Marilyn and asked to meet secretly with her at Capote's apartment in Manhattan the following week. The author had agreed to play host at this secret rendezvous.

Marilyn flew in from the West Coast to New York, where she checked into the Hotel Carlyle, earlier site of several secret trysts with the President.

Years later, in Key West in 1969, Capote either was being deliberately vague or did not want his audience to know the exact date of this rendezvous. Obviously it had to have occurred some weekend during June or July of 1962. He did reveal the time of the meeting in his apartment, placing it at around ten o'clock in the evening. He claimed that Marilyn arrived first, looking "camera ready" in a white satin gown with a white sable, even though it was summer. Jackie, according to Truman, arrived twenty minutes later and wore a plain black and severely tailored business suit.

Marilyn sat on a sofa opposite Jackie, who preferred Capote's favorite armchair. "Marilyn oozed charm, but Jackie was distant," he recalled.

After social pleasantries were exchanged, Jackie asked Capote to excuse himself while they conducted private business. He said that he retreated to his bedroom with a drink, and before the evening ended he had a few more. Eventually he drifted off to sleep.

A loud pounding on his bedroom door woke him up at around one-thirty a.m. Opening it, he encountered a hysterical Marilyn, her makeup smeared. She too, or so it appeared, had been drinking heavily. The First Lady had left the apartment.

"It's all over!" Marilyn sobbed to him. As best as he could ascertain, Marilyn had agreed to call off the press conference. She also said that Jackie had forgiven her for her affair with her husband, saying that "only a cadaver can resist Jack when he turns on the charm." Jackie's icy facade had "melted" at some point in the night as she begged

Bitchier than Thou:
Truman Capote

242

Marilyn "not to publicly humiliate me in front of the world." She also pleaded with Marilyn not to make her children victims of a divorce. According to Marilyn, Jackie even spoke of how John-John's face "lights up when his daddy walks into the room."

True to her word, Marilyn, who had only weeks to live, never held that press conference. But through the rest of June and July, Peter reported to Jackie that Marilyn was continuing to make threats against the Kennedys. When Jackie learned that Bobby Kennedy was flying to Los Angeles, she asked him to call on Marilyn to see what kind of trouble she might make for the Kennedys.

Long after Marilyn's death, and long after the assassination of her husband, Jackie told Capote: "Sending Bobby to comfort Marilyn was like sending the most succulent lamb into the wolf's lair. Bobby didn't have a chance. He'd already had an affair, and was still in love with Marilyn."

Marilyn was found dead in her bed early on the morning of August 5, 1962. Murder? Suicide? The debate will go on as long as the public still remembers the star's brief and incandescent, but tragic life.

One of Capote's biographers (who doesn't want his name revealed) tried to track down this story by hiring a private detective. He later refused to answer questions about the date of the alleged meeting between Marilyn and Jackie, even though he was not going to write about it in his biography. He had a policy of not running stories unless he was able to confirm them with some other source, but wanted to keep the detective's report secret in case he wished to write about it in the future.

All that he would confirm was that Marilyn, on a summer night unspecified, left the Hotel Carlyle around 9:30 and was helped into a private limousine, not the hotel's usual car service. Jackie was also in New York that night to attend some charity event, but called and cancelled at the last minute, citing flu-like symptoms.

There were no *paparazzi* to record where the two most famous female icons of the 20th century went on that historic night, which adds veracity to Capote's account, although the Secret Service had to be aware of Jackie's whereabouts. The detective, according to the biographer, concluded that "in all possibility" Capote was telling the truth.

After Capote left that 1969 social gathering in Key West, Tennessee virtually echoed the detective's report. He told his remaining guests that, "I think we have to entertain the possibility that Truman indeed is spilling the beans."

Two months before her death in 1962, Capote dined with Marilyn. "In spite of all the pain she was suffering from both Jack and Bobby Kennedy, she had lost a lot of weight for the film *Something's Got to Give,*" he said. "George Cukor had been set to direct her. There was a new maturity about her. She wasn't so giggly anymore. If she'd lived and held onto her figure, I think she would have looked gorgeous and glamorous for years. Bobby and Jack didn't really kill her, at least in the literal sense."

"They did pay one of her best friends to keep quiet about their affairs with her," Capote claimed. "The friend knew where all the skeletons were. After

Marilyn died, Peter Lawford gave this friend a year-long cruise around the world. For that entire year, no one, not even the police, knew where she was. A cover-up, for sure."

John Cohan

[Years after Marilyn met with Jackie, celebrity psychic to the stars, John Cohan, added a tanta-lizing dimension to the Marilyn/Jackie confrontation in New York. Cohan had been a confidant of Capote's and had 'channeled" psychic readings for him every year.

According to Cohan, the afternoon before the arrival of these two celebrated ladies at his apart-ment, Capote hired a technician to install a hidden microphone and camera. "This was a moment in history I wanted to record for posterity," he said.

Capote told Cohan that he wanted to have the film "to hold over Jackie's head for years to come." Months later, he showed the film of Marilyn inter-acting with Jackie to Cohan.

"Jackie looked very matronly in the film," Cohan said, "but Marilyn pho-tographed beautifully. At one point, Jackie had MM in tears, I recall. It appeared that Marilyn took money from Jackie. Before presenting it to her, Jackie opened a large envelope and showed Marilyn all the cash. She also showed Marilyn pictures of the President tossing darts at a pinup poster of Marilyn on the wall. Before leaving, Jackie, in a surprise move, patted Marilyn's head."

"As years went by, Truman perhaps grew bored with the film…or whatever," Cohan said. "He told me that he sold it to Merv Griffin for a lot of money. He also told me, 'There is just too much out there on Marilyn, and I'm sick and tired of the whole mess.'"]

"The Beautiful Widow & the Rich Frog"

—Capote, discussing Aristotle Onassis

"In Manhattan, Jackie included me among her guests when she seemed to shed her widow's weeds,"Capote said. "She was the most famous woman in the world. Every time she set foot outside her Fifth Avenue apartment, the pa-parazzi were on her ass."

"In October of 1964, she threw this party in honor of John Kenneth Gal-braith, who had been JFK's ambassador to India," Truman said. "Jackie was a dazzling vision in white, wearing a long silk gown and a sleeveless ermine jacket."

"I hung out with Lee Radziwill, Teddy Kennedy, Bunny Mellon, Patricia

Kennedy Lawford, and Theodore Sorensen," Capote said. "At one point, I danced the frug with Jackie to Killer Joe Piro's disco beat. I noticed that Jackie's future husband, Aristotle Onassis, appeared for a few minutes. But I saw him boil with anger when he spotted Jackie dancing with her lover, Bobby Kennedy."

As Kitty Kelley, Jackie's biographer, described the scene, "The guests represented the glittering façade of Camelot, the touch-football games, the parties at Hickory Hill where people were thrown into the swimming pool with their clothes on. They were the beautiful people. They arrived in Cadillac limousines. Their common bond was their idolatry to the memory of John Fitzgerald Kennedy."

More than four years after the assassination of her husband, on December 10, 1967, Jackie attended her first public event since his death, a $500-a-plate dinner for the New York Democratic Party. Accompanying her was brother-in-law, Robert Kennedy.

Behind her back, Capote betrayed her friendship. Unknown to Jackie—at

Family ties, family romances
Bobby and Jackie

Rich, frustrated, competitive, and an enemy of RFK, **Aristotle Onassis** was waiting in the wings.

least at the time—he spread the rumor that, "Jackie is having an affair with Bobby."

"Even though those rumors appear to have been true, it was a dastardly thing to do," said Tennessee. He severely chastised Capote for gossiping about Jackie. "The poor woman has suffered enough. Give her a rest. If she is finding some comfort, even some love with her brother-in-law, she should be left alone to do so. The human heart, and its needs, sometimes follows unorthodox patterns. Of all the people on this earth, you and I, as artists, should know and respect that."

"Ethel must have known about the affair," Capote said. "Everybody in *tout* Washington did. It went on for months and months. But when Bobby decided to run for president in 1968, he had to tell Jackie it had to end between them. With Bobby gone as her lover, Jackie took stock of what was available to her. For years, Aristotle Onassis had pursued her."

"Jackie had warned me that Camelot was on the verge of collapse," Capote said. "She was going to announce her engagement to Ari, the Greek frog with all those ships and an airline."

"The only way I'll get worse press is if I ran off to marry Eddie Fisher," Jackie said.

"I knew about their engagement six months before it became public," Capote said. "Lee Radziwill and I had become close, and she always told me what was going on."

"All those rumors that Jackie was going to run off with Lord Harlech were just a creation of the press," Capote said. "Harlech never pretended to be anything more than a friend, perhaps with an occasional bump in the night. I'm happy for whatever makes Jackie happy—we're great friends. Who can blame Jackie and Lord Harlech, on occasion, for heeding nature's call?"

When Jackie returned to New York after her marriage to Onassis, she met for lunch with Capote.

"I'm sure you've read all those reports about all the fabulous amounts of money I received as part of a pre-nuptial agreement with Ari," she told Capote. "There is no such agreement. It's a god damn lie. I don't have any money. When I got married, my income from the Kennedy estate stopped. So did my widow's pension from the U.S. government."

"I made no premarital agreement with Ari," she said. "I know it's an old Greek custom, but I couldn't do it. I didn't want to barter myself. Except for my personal possessions such as jewelry, I have exactly $5,200 in my bank account. Everything else I charge to Olympic Airlines."

Assassination

JFK and Jackie Fly to Texas for a Date With Destiny
Gunshots from Dallas are Heard Around the World

The Thousand Day Reign of Camelot

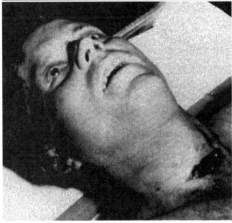 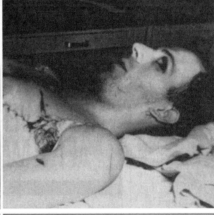

The autopsy photographs released of the slain **John F. Kennedy** are even today the source of raging controversies. By most accounts, the back of JFK's head was blown away by at least one bullet, yet it was alleged that, "acting on orders from the highest levels of government," the autopsy photos were doctored and re-touched.

After being gunned down by Jack Ruby, an event broadcast on nationwide TV, **Lee Harvey Oswald** was rushed to the hospital, where he died. Seen here, sewn together after his autopsy, his body revealed no secrets. Many details about Oswald's role in the assassination died with him.

"God dammit, I hate flying to Texas. I had to practically wring Jackie's neck to get her to go with me. I just hate to go. I have a terrible feeling about going."
—Jack Kennedy to Senator George Smathers

"I didn't want him to go to Texas. I was afraid for him. A lot of people in the South and a hell of a lot of people in Texas hated Jack. They'd like to see him dead, and there are a lot of guns in Texas. Up to the last minute, I begged him not to go. I claimed he could plead illness with his back. He appeared almost fatalistic on our final night together. He told me, 'If God wants me to end my life on Texas soil, then so be it.'"
—LeMoyne Billings

"Both Bobby and Adlai Stevenson warned Jack it was dangerous landing in Texas. But Johnson practically begged him to go to save his own political neck."
—Jackie Kennedy

"If anyone wants to kill Jack or me, it won't be difficult."
—Robert F. Kennedy

The President and Jackie Kennedy, carrying a bouquet of red roses just given to her, land at Dallas' Love Field and begin the transit to their waiting limousine for what was to have been a high-profile but otherwise uneventful ten-mile drive through downtown Dallas.

It would quickly escalate into a ride into the history books.

"I woke up this morning with the strangest feeling. You know how I always feel something in my gut before anyone else has a clue? Well, this morning I felt I was going to become President of the United States before nightfall."
—Lyndon B. Johnson to Lady Bird

"There can be little doubt that the Warren Commission came to the unvoiced conclusion that it might be all for the best if Oswald turned out to be homosexual. That would have the advantage of explaining much even if it explained nothing at all. In 1964, homosexuality was still seen as one of those omnibus infections of the spirit that could lead to God knows what further aberration."
—Norman Mailer

"Don't Go to Dallas, Mr. President."
—Billy Graham

John F. Kennedy had continued his womanizing through most of November of 1963 in New York, Palm Beach, and Washington. In Manhattan, he was introduced to Eva Gabor and invited her back to his hotel suite at the Carlyle. A decade before, a few months before his marriage to Jackie, he had seduced her older sister, Zsa Zsa.

Critics of the President have suggested that he may never have loved Jackie, but used her as a vote-getting "trophy wife."

It's true that JFK and his wife had grappled with his infidelity since their wedding in 1953, and they also had arguments over money, shopping, their in-laws, and even their furnishings and art work. He attacked her drug dependence, but she countercharged that he was "the ultimate druggie in the White House."

Perhaps it was another Kennedy myth, but those close to JFK and Jackie claimed that the President fell in love with her—really in love with her—for the first time in Texas, beginning with the flight there. The recent death of Patrick had brought them together as never before, and he revealed a sensitive side of himself.

They had coped with his venereal disease, and with undisguised bitterness, she had reminded him that he had probably been the source of her infertility and/or difficult childbirths—a miscarriage, a stillbirth, and the most crushing blow of all, the loss of their second son, Patrick.

Each of them had been deeply traumatized by Patrick's death, and each was still somewhat shaken as they prepared, despite repeated warnings, to embark on their intricately scheduled fence-mending trip to San Antonio, Houston, Fort Worth, Dallas, and Austin, which would culminate with a weekend visit with Vice President Lyndon B. Johnson and Lady Bird at their ranch outside Austin.

Johnson had urged the trip, fearing that a split in the Democratic Party might cost the party the Lone Star State in the upcoming elections of 1964. The liberal Texas Senator, Ralph Yarborough, was feuding with both Johnson and the state's conservative governor, John Connally, who was also a Democrat. The party was split in the middle, and Johnson hoped that a visit from JFK and Jackie could bring some much-needed harmony.

At the time of their visit, Texas Democrats were taking a beating on civil rights, as racism was rampant in the state. LBJ had warned JFK that some of the racists were likely to shout NIGGER LOVER at him and post ugly signs.

"I can deal with that," JFK assured him. "Bobby and I get those hate attacks all the time."

Completion of their visit's elaborate itinerary, with so many stopovers, receptions and motorcades, would be grueling to both JFK and Jackie.

At the White House, JFK kissed Caroline and John Jr. goodbye for the final time, the little boy crying out for his daddy and pleading with him to take him to

Texas, too. The First Couple assured the First Son and the First Daughter that they would be back before the week was over.

"Lancer" (JFK) and "Lace" (Jackie) parted from "Lyric" (Caroline) and "Lark" (John Jr.) and flew away. *[Those were the Secret Service's code names for the individual members of the First Family.]*

As JFK, with Jackie, boarded Air Force One at Andrews Air Force Base, he was delivered a telegram from the evangelist, Billy Graham. "Last night, God spoke to me," Graham wrote, "warning me to tell you not to get on that plane. Don't go to Texas today!"

"Hell with that!" JFK said to Jackie and others. "Graham is a preacher, not a prophet. C'mon, Jackie."

The first stop on their complicated itinerary was in San Antonio,

Clint Hill, a Secret Service agent, had been given primary responsibility for guarding Jackie. The agent specifically assigned to JFK was Roy Kellerman, a 48-year-old veteran who had previously protected FDR, Harry Truman, and Dwight Eisenhower. At six feet four, he was an imposing figure, a twenty-three-year veteran with the Service. On the plane en route to San Antonio, he sat with Hill.

As the plane landed, Jackie looked out the window. It was 1:30PM local time. She was told that some spectators, 5,000 in all, had been gathered at the airport since 5AM that morning.

Johnson and Lady Bird, along with Governor John Connally, had arranged themselves at the bottom of the plane's steps to welcome them to Texas. They would meet them at each of their other stops during the course of that trip. Obviously, each greeting was, to some degree, a photo and publicity opportunity and had been arranged that way in advance.

Looking like a Chanel model stepping out from the pages of *Vogue,* Jackie was a vision in taste, wearing a short-sleeved white suit with a narrow black belt and elbow-length white gloves. She wore a black beret to keep her hair in place.

Many of the Kennedys' screaming fans held up signs: *KENNEDY IN '64.*

From the airport, they rode through downtown San Antonio in a custom-made, custom-converted Lincoln Continental whose extra "armor" had increased its weight from 5,215 pounds to a massive 7.800 pounds.

Along the motorcade's route, some 125,000 locals turned out to greet them. The tour ended at the then-new Air Force School of Aerospace Medicine, where JFK gave a warmly received speech.

After the formalities, the San Antonio visit was pronounced a success. The Kennedy/Johnson-with-Connally parties returned to their respective airplanes for the 45-minute flight from San Antonio to Houston.

It wasn't until 2012 that it was revealed that JFK had sex with Jackie during Air Force One's 45-minute flight between San Antonio and Houston. William Manchester, the author of the 1967 book, *The Death of a President,* told author Philip Nobile, who wrote for *Esquire,* that Jackie had described the circumstances, to him, discreetly but directly. Having named him as the assassination's official chronicler, she sat with Manchester for many a daiquiri-fueled hour, revealing intimacies about her life with the President. *[Jackie's relationship with Manchester is more fully described in a subsequent chapter of this book.]*

Manchester asked Nobile not to reveal him as the source of that revelation until his death, which occurred in 2004.

In his book, Manchester suggested intimacies without providing graphic details. For example, he wrote that the First Couple enjoyed "their last hour of serenity" within the small bedroom aboard Air Force One.

After JFK's death, Jackie evolved into a formidable censor, demanding discretion during Manchester's compilation of his book. Ultimately, the dozens of fundamental points they disagreed on involved them in a legal feud, played out in the tabloids.

[Actually, JFK's last hours of serenity with Jackie did not occur within Air Force One, but in Fort Worth in their hotel suite, as part of their final night together. Jackie's ten hours of tapes and notes of her interviews with Manchester have been sealed off from the public in the Kennedy Library, based on her direct and very clear instructions, until 2067.]

As Jackie relayed to Manchester, at JFK's climax she remembered looking up to see a bucolic painting of a French farmhouse. She also recalled the rock-hard mattress that had been installed in the room for his back.

"Their life together now had nearly a full day to run," Manchester wrote. "The tyranny of events and exhaustion would begin to close in when they finished the two-hundred-mile lap to Houston. Privacy was limited aboard the plane, confined to a tiny blue cabin racing 30,000 feet above the tessellated green and brown plains of Central Texas. The President emerged with a fresh shirt."

Following the seduction aboard the aircraft, Jackie had for the first time become a member of the "Mile High club." JFK had long been a charter member.

***

On November 21, 1963, the President's advance security had already arrived in Houston in anticipation of his visit. The Johnson/Connally party had already flown ahead so they could officially greet them when they landed at the airport in Houston. As had been predicted, the turnout was even larger and more enthusiastic than it had been in San Antonio.

Jackie was tired, but upon landing and exchanging greetings with the Veep and with the Governor, she headed for a nearby fence, behind which awaited a crowd of eager fans. Normally, she didn't engage in this kind of person-to-person encounter, but she had agreed to do whatever it took to get JFK re-elected. She followed his example of handshaking.

After more minutes of that than she could endure, she transferred to another Lincoln limousine en route to Houston's Rice Hotel. The vehicle was crowded, with the Governor squeezed in between them. She despised him. After all, he was "the dirty bastard" who had spread the word that JFK had Addison's disease during the 1960 campaign.

In front of their hotel, a huge crowd had gathered. More endless handshaking. Jackie complained to Hill of being tired and wanted some time alone to rest.

Assisted by Mary Gallagher, she slept for an hour, then showered and began to prepare for her delivery of a speech in Spanish at the League of United Latin American Citizens.

She checked her appearance carefully before emerging in a fashionable black cut-velvet dress with long sleeves. She wore a three-strand string of pearls. A hairdresser had ensured that her bouffant was perfectly coiffed.

After the President's speech, she addressed the audience in Spanish, which thrilled them. Shouts of *VIVA JACKIE! VIVA JACKIE!* rang through the large room.

Later, at the Sam Houston Colisseum, JFK paid tribute to Congressman Albert Thomas. After that, they departed for the Houston International Airport, where they boarded Air Force One for the flight to Carswell Air Force Base near Fort Worth.

***

After a fifty-minute flight, JFK and Jackie arrived on the ground at Fort Worth at 11:05PM, to be greeted once again by Lyndon and Lady Bird.

Johnson later said, "I felt like a god damn idiot flying ahead so I'd be able to welcome the Kennedys to every Texas city. But the assholes running this campaign trip insisted, and Lady Bird made me promise to cooperate. If Kennedy fucks with me and drops me from the '64 ticket, he'll experience what it's like to jump into a barrel of Texas rattlesnakes."

Because of the lateness of their arrival, Jackie did not expect a large crowd. But when she and JFK stepped off the plane, thousands of people were present, cheering their arrival. To her surprise, a lot of school children, way past their bedtimes, had also been brought by their parents. It was a particularly riotous crowd, shouting and calling her name, a real Texas welcome.

After thanking and handshaking with the crowd, Jackie joined her husband in yet another Lincoln convertible. Because it was near midnight, the top was raised. They were driven to Fort Worth's Hotel Texas for the night. Outside, another large crowd had formed. The shouting was so loud, the crowd seemed almost hysterical.

After checking into their suite, with separate beds in different rooms if they wanted them, the President spent the last night of his life. It would be memorable for her.

In *The Dark Side of Camelot,* Seymour Hersh wrote, "While frolicking poolside with one of his sexual partners, JFK tore a groin muscle. He had to wear a stiff shoulder-to-groin brace that locked his body in a rigid upright position. It was more constraining than his usual back brace, which he'd continued to wear.

[Although designed to ease his pain, this contraption may ultimately have

led to his death. The two braces made it impossible for him to bend in reflex when he was struck in the neck by a bullet fired the next day in Dallas by Lee Harvey Oswald. The President had remained erect to receive the final and fatal shot.]

After Jackie showered and came into his room in a *négligée,* she found him stripped of braces and lying nude on the bed.

Somehow, the sight of her seemed to sexually arouse him again, as he had been during that commute from San Antonio to Huston aboard Air Force One.

She didn't understand how he could want sex when he was in pain. He'd obviously shot himself with more of Dr. Jacobson's "speed," and he wanted her again. She, too, was aroused.

"I need it again," he told her. He was sensitive that she might not be fully recovered from Patrick's recent birth and death. "I might hurt you."

She wanted to satisfy him. She straddled him, moving her body up and down over him. As he had so many times before, he gave her the orgasm she wanted before he collapsed underneath her, exhausted after time spent on the campaign trail. She put a blanket over him before switching off the light on his nightstand.

In an unguarded moment, several weeks after the assassination, she would share a description of this intimate moment with William Manchester, who would commit it to writing, only to have it locked away, with the understanding that it wouldn't titillate future generations until its release in 2067.

Back in her own bedroom, she was not able to sleep. She wandered about, dreading the upcoming day. Impulsively, she pulled back the draperies and was greeted with a pink neon sign proclaiming BEST RIBS IN TEXAS. That sign would advertise its outrageous claim throughout the night.

JFK was the first to arise, striding forth to the pavement outside the hotel with his Secret Service men, to be greeted by a yelling and screaming crowd calling his name. If there were any disappointment, it involved the fact that the spectators didn't get to see Jackie, who was still in her bedroom, trying to wake up.

Hands waved frantically at JFK as he climbed onto the back of a flatbed truck to address his audience.

Their location in downtown Fort Worth made Kellerman nervous. There were a lot of tall office buildings with open windows fronting the large square. The agent felt that a crazed gunman with a rifle would evaluate JFK as an easy target.

At the beginning of his speech, he said, "There are no faint hearts in Fort Worth," which brought wild cheers.

After his speech, he left the podium and headed back into the hotel, entering its Grand Ballroom, where 2,000 people had purchased tickets for a formal breakfast.

Dozens of people began chanting WHERE'S JACKIE? WHERE'S JACKIE?

JFK sent Hill to her bedroom at 9:10AM and virtually demanded that she appear at once.

In the living room of her suite, Hill noticed that she was already dressed in a pink Chanel suit, with its navy blue collar. When she heard how desperately her husband needed her, she'd put on a pillbox hat and accompanied Hill downstairs.

In the ballroom, she heard the loudest applause of her trip so far. Many men and women stood on their chairs to get a better look at her. Everybody seemed to be commenting on her beauty. A reporter from *The Wall Street Journal* said that Jackie "looked like a woman who jumps out of a cake."

At the microphone, JFK said, "Two years ago, I introduced myself in Paris by saying I was the man who accompanied Mrs. Kennedy to Paris. I am getting somewhat the same sensation as I travel around Texas. Why is it that nobody wonders what Lyndon and I will be wearing?"

By the end of breakfast, both Jackie and JFK concluded that Fort Worth had been an even bigger success for them than San Antonio or Houston.

Jackie followed JFK and Hill back to their suite. The aide, Kenneth O'Donnell, was there to review the day's schedule: "You have just thirty minutes before we fly to Dallas."

Buoyed by the success of her appearance at the breakfast, Jackie said, "If you want me, I'll go anywhere with you on the campaign trail for '64."

"How about California in two weeks?" he asked.

"It's a deal," she said.

He turned to O'Donnell. "You're my witness, Kenny. You heard her."

"I did indeed, Mr. President, and I have found that our First Lady is a woman of her word," O'Donnell said.

"Let's go for it," JFK said. "California here we come."

***

Aboard Air Force One, en route to Dallas, a 13-minute flight from Fort Worth, Kenneth O'Donnell handed JFK a copy of the *Dallas News*, pointing to a black-bordered advertisement that referred to him as "fifty times a fool for signing the Nuclear Test Ban Treaty." It had been paid for by the American Fact-Finding Committee.

E. M. ("Ted") Dealey, publisher of the *Dallas News*, had called JFK "a weak sister. Instead of leading the nation on horseback, the people of Texas think you've been riding Caroline's bicycle." Ironically, a commemorative statue of the publisher's father stood in Dealey Plaza, soon to become one of the world's most infamous public spaces.

JFK handed the newspaper to Jackie. "You know, last night would have been a hell of a night to assassinate a President. I mean it. There was the rain and the night, and we were getting jostled. Suppose a man had a pistol in a briefcase." He mocked pulling the trigger of a gun. "Then he could have dropped both the gun and the briefcase and melted away in the crowd."

She paid no attention to the paper, but complained and worried about how her hair would survive in an open-air limousine instead of a bubble top. She had wanted a bubble top but he'd overruled her. "The people will want to see me."

In yet another early morning newspaper from Dallas, he'd read accusations that he was soft on communism while he allowed his brother, the attorney general, to prosecute loyal Americans. That ad was paid for by the right-wing John Birch Society, who had labeled him a "Communist sympathizer."

"We're heading into nut country today," he told her.

Before disembarking from Air Force One after it winged in for a smooth landing at Dallas' Love Field at 11:30AM, JFK said, "Jackie, it's show time!"

JFK, with his wife, walked down the ramp to a boisterous crowd of supporters and enemies. He managed to read only one ominous-looking sign: *HELP KENNEDY STAMP OUT DEMOCRACY!*

Lyndon and Lady Bird Johnson waited at the bottom of the ramp to welcome them.

This was the fourth time during the course of this trip that they had appeared in advance of a Kennedy arrival to greet them as they descended the steps of their aircraft.

On the surface, at least, the Kennedys and Johnsons were on friendly terms, but privately, when alone with their friends, Lyndon mocked JFK. In contrast, JFK insisted that Lyndon looked like a riverboat gambler. Jackie did him one better: She performed devastating impressions of "Uncle Cornpone and his Little Pork Chop."

Jackie was greeted with calls of her name. The sounds evolved into a chant: *WE WANT JACKIE!*

When she'd heard that the weather had suddenly cleared and turned hotter, she discarded her coat. She squinted her eyes into the sun during her descent of the ramp. She asked O'Donnell, "Do you think we've arrived in Mexico by mistake? It's fucking hot. I'll be drenched in this wool suit."

Following in JFK's footsteps, she headed to the fence, where she was presented with a large bouquet of red roses. The traditional Texas welcome involved the presentation of yellow roses, but florists had run out, so red roses, the symbol of romantic love, had been substi-

Directly in front of **Jackie and JFK**, seated on their respective jump seats, are **Nellie Connally** and her husband, **John Connally**, the Governor of Texas.

A few minutes after this picture was taken, both Governor Connally and JFK would be wounded, either critically or (in the case of JFK) fatally.

tuted instead.

Aide David Powers told O'Donnell, "The President is going to be exposed to half a million people before he sleeps in LBJ's guest room. All it takes is one psycho with a rifle stationed at an office window."

JFK didn't want to look too pretentious and nixed the idea of two Secret Service men riding guard on the back of the limousine. He gave the order, "Keep the Ivy League charlatans off the back of the car." Later, as events in the motorcade began to escalate, Hill would disobey that order.

O'Donnell had protested, "Sir, this is not Kennedy country. We're not in Boston anymore."

"Where did you get that line?" Kennedy quipped. "Sounds like you're ripping off Dorothy from *The Wizard of Oz."*

Jackie was seated on JFK's left in the open-topped convertible's back seat, with Nellie Connally taking the jump seat *[a not-very-comfortable seating platform that can be folded up and out of the way when not in use]* near Jackie, and with her husband, Governor Connally, taking the jump seat near JFK.

Feeling that she was melting in the bright sunlight, Jackie reached for her sunglasses, but JFK warned her to put them back into her purse. "The people of Dallas will want to see your face," he said.

She'd resented riding with the Connallys. Before disembarking, she'd told JFK, "I hate that smug Connally with his petulant, self-indulgent mouth. I just can't bear sitting with him in the limousine listening to him praise himself and put you down."

"Let's be friendly," he had cautioned her. "He may challenge me for the nomination in '64."

The presidential motorcade left Love Field at 11:55AM, heading on its ten-mile downtown run to the Trade Mart, where JFK was to address 2,000 guests. In some places, the wildly cheering crowds fronting their route stood twelve people deep.

They were scheduled, before the day ended, to face another motorcade in Austin, a reception, a dinner at a fund-raiser, climaxed by a helicopter ride to the LBJ Ranch outside Austin.

***

As Franklin D. Roosevelt might have said, November 22, 1963 would be a day in American history that would live in infamy. Almost everyone in the world heard of that day, and would remember it for the rest of their lives. Thousands would come forth with "eyewitness" accounts, even though many of them were nowhere near the motorcade.

Robert Morton, an avid Kennedy fan, even though his wife was a staunch Republican, was also a bird watcher. That morning, he had arrived at Dealey Plaza before anyone else. The route of the motorcade had been published in the newspaper. He decided that the best vantage point to see Jack and Jackie was from a grassy knoll whose summit rose a few feet higher than the pavement of Elm Street.

As he looked around him, no one else had appeared on the knoll. He glanced at his watch. It was 7AM.

In the air, high above the looming bulk of the Texas School Book Depository, he saw a flight of birds winging in, eventually landing on the roof of the building. He prided himself in knowing all the bird species, but didn't recognize this type of bird. They were black but they weren't crows.

He was amazed he couldn't identify the species. The birds didn't stay long. Something must have frightened them. Maybe someone had come onto the roof. In the distance he saw a young man with a rifle pointing down at Elm Street where the motorcade would pass by. He was aiming his rifle at the street.

But he didn't seem to like this stake-out and quickly disappeared inside the building. Morton wondered if this could be a possible assassin. He thought at first that he should report it to the police, but decided against it. He didn't want to appear to be a fool.

As the sun rose higher in the sky, more and more people appeared on the grassy knoll. After seeing that man with a rifle, Morton had become suspicious of everyone. He felt the knoll would be an ideal perch from which to assassinate a president. Three men who stood together looked suspicious. They were obviously from out of town, and were wearing overcoats although the weather hardly called for that. Did one of the overcoats conceal a rifle? It seemed to him that a lot of people in Dallas would like to see Jack Kennedy end his presidency on this particular day.

In the distance he saw the motorcade approaching. He was relieved because he'd grown tired of waiting for it and he was hungry. The three men were still there and hadn't removed their overcoats even in the noon-day sun. Morton moved as far away from them as he could.

The next few minutes would become a blur, although until the end of his life he would attempt to describe what he saw that day to anyone willing to listen to him.

He heard the sound of gunfire but wasn't sure where the shots were coming from. Everything happened so suddenly. Eventually, all he could remember was the sight of those three men in overcoats running from the grassy knoll.

At seventeen, the twisted killer, **Lee Harvey Oswald**, joined the Marines, reading Marxist tracts in his spare time. His fellow soldiers called him "Faggot," "Mrs. Oswald," and "Ozzie Rabbit."

He was court-martialed twice—once for shooting himself in the arm with an illegal gun. He was court-martialed again for pouring a drink over the head of his sergeant.

He later fled to the Soviet Union, where he tried to revoke his U.S. citizenship. The Reds didn't want him, a Moscow psychiatrist diagnosing him as "mentally unstable."

Morton later told his wife, "I think those strange black birds landing on the roof of the Depository was a very bad omen. A very bad omen indeed."

***

On the morning of November 22, in the home of Lee Harvey Oswald, the clock alarm went off exactly at seven o'clock. Oswald's wife, Marina, had risen at 6:30 and was in the kitchen preparing a light breakfast. When she heard the alarm, she assumed that her husband would be getting up to go to work at the Texas School Book Depository, a job he hated. "I'd much rather read books than sell them," he'd told her.

After ten minutes, when he hadn't come into the kitchen, she went to see what was happening, finding him still asleep. He'd been up for most of the night, pacing the floor. She wondered if he were planning to leave her for another woman. He hadn't been very attentive lately.

She shook him awake. He bolted up in bed, looking alarmed. He checked the clock. "Fuck!" he shouted to her. "I overslept. I'll miss my ride to work."

She returned to the kitchen and asked him if he could grab something she had prepared for breakfast.

"Don't have time," he shouted back at her, racing out the door. Through her kitchen window, she watched him go. He was carrying "a package of some sort…in a heavy brown bag. What was it and why would he be taking it to work?"

As it was later discovered, the package contained a mail-order Italian rifle he'd purchased shortly before JFK's arrival in Dallas.

A neighbor, Linnie Mae Randle, was also standing at her kitchen sink and looking out the window as she saw Oswald approach her carport carrying a package. She'd later describe it as "something in a heavy brown bag."

He opened the rear door of her brother's car and put the package in the backseat.

She told her brother, Buell Wesley Frazier, who also worked at the Book Depository, that Oswald had arrived and was waiting for him in the car. Taking a final sip of coffee, Frazier glanced at his watch and got up. He kissed his sister goodbye and hurried outside to the carport. Oswald was already in the passenger's seat.

Getting into the driver's seat, Frazier noticed the brown package resting on the rear seat. "What's that?" he asked.

"Just some curtain rods," Oswald said.

Fearing they would be late for work, Frazier didn't ask any more questions, but he would later wonder why Oswald was taking curtain rods to work. Shouldn't he have left them at home?

Breaking the speed limit, Frazier parked his car about two blocks north of the Depository, the only available space nearby.

Oswald seemed nervous and in a big hurry as he quickly removed the package from the rear seat. Without thanking Frazier for the ride or saying goodbye, he walked rapidly ahead.

All the way to the employee entrance to the Depository, Oswald stayed at least fifty yards ahead of Frazier and never once looked back. Frazier thought that was strange, but then, he had always considered Oswald an oddball.

The last time Frazier ever saw Oswald was the sight of him entering the Depository with that mysterious package.

***

At Dealey Plaza, Abraham Zapruder, a maker of women's garments, was a 58-year-old camera buff who had been born in Russia, and who had come to Dallas via Brooklyn. Unknown to him at the time, this home-movie hobbyist was fated to become a footnote in American history.

He had arrived at a spot on Elm Street, not far from his office, hoping to film the presidential motorcade. The 26.6 seconds of footage he'd later capture—486 frames, without sound—will probably be shown in American history classes three centuries from the day he took it. His images were blurry, but nonetheless vivid. The film was shot in color, Jackie's pink outfit dominating the frames.

Historians still debate exactly what those silent, shaky frames mean. Did Oswald act alone, or were there other shooters?

A.O. Scott, writing in 2013 for *The New York Times*, put it in perspective. "Zapruder can be seen as a pioneer of citizen journalism, a resourceful amateur who caught something crucial that the professional news media somehow missed. Now, everyone with a smartphone is a potential Zapruder."

As amazing as it sounds, at least five eyewitnesses later reported seeing a young man standing at the window of the sixth floor of the Texas School Book Depository with a rifle at "port arms" *[i.e., slung diagonally across his body, with one hand on the barrel and the other hand on the stock.]*

From the Plaza below, a married high school student, Aaron Rowland, directed the attention of his young bride, Barbara, to the man in the window. "See that Secret Service agent stationed there to protect the President?" he said to her.

Robert Edwards and Ronald Fischer had walked to Dealey Plaza from the county auditor's office, where both of them worked. They, too, saw a man stationed with a rifle at the sixth-floor window. Howard T. Brennan, a Dallas pipefitter, looked up at the Hertz billboard *[it displayed the current time and temperature]* atop the Depository. He, too, saw a young man standing motionless in the window. Ironically, none of these eyewitnesses were alarmed at the sight. For whatever reason they had, they did not report the man to any of the policemen stationed within the plaza.

U.S. flags were flapping in the wind as William Greer, the driver of the presidential limousine, turned onto Elm Street heading for Dealey Plaza, a three-acre, triangular shaped park with grass and concrete pergolas. As the limousine neared the Depository, Nellie Connally said to JFK, in one of the most ironic statements made on that fateful day: "Mr. President, you can't say Dallas does-

259

n't love you."

"No, you can't," the President said, waving at the crowds. A rumor spread that Nellie claimed that she heard Jack's promise to his wife. "After last night, there will be no more women—only you. That's one promise I'll keep for the rest of my life."

Jackie is alleged to have responded, "Oh, Jack, if only you meant that."

She had been nervous throughout the ride. Motorcycles from the Dallas police had backfired several times, sounding like gunshots. She became jittery, and would later testify that when she heard the first shot, she thought it was motorcycle backfire.

Jackie was looking directly at her husband, who was on her right, although she'd later claim she was looking to her left. But the Zapruder film shows her looking to her right.

She would always remember a quizzical look on her husband's face. He raised his right hand as if to brush back his tousled chestnut hair. But his hand never reached his head, but fell down limply. When he reached again for the top of his head, it wasn't there. It had been blown off.

[What had happened was this, at least for those who adhere to the "Magic Bullet" theory, which was said to have caused several wounds before exiting. The bullet was later found, almost undamaged, at Parkland Hospital.

The first shot hit JFK in the back, exiting through his neck, where it then hit Connally in the back, exiting his chest, hitting his wrist and then exiting and entering his leg. The seemingly impossible bullet then shot out of Connally's leg and fell onto the limousine's floor.

The second shot missed the limousine, but hit a curbstone, wounding an onlooker, James Tague, who was standing near the overpass.

The third shot was the fatal one, causing a massive wound to the President's head. It entered his skull above and to the right to the bony point—called the occipital protuberance— at the back of his head, where it broke into fragments. The larger fragment shot out of his right temple, the smaller one exiting the right parietal area. Two additional fragments remained in his skull.]

Agent Roy Kellerman, from his position in the limousine's front seat, heard JFK cry out: "My God, I'm hit!"

Connally was the next to cry out, "No, no, no! They're trying to kill all of us!" He slumped over onto Nellie's lap, and she heroically covered his body with hers.

"My God," Jackie screamed. "They've killed Jack! They've killed my husband!"

At this point, JFK's body jerked into the air like a marionette before falling back against the seat. She screamed as her hand scooped up a bloody mess, including part of his brain. His blood cascaded down onto her pink suit.

It was so sudden. Like spurts from some grisly fountain, she had been spewed with blood, brains, and even bone fragments. The vision would haunt her to her grave.

His body lurched forward toward her.

Her next move became the subject of endless speculation. Perhaps in a kind of primeval shock, she jumped up and blindly sprawled across the trunk of the open-topped car.

Accidentally, when she jumped out of her seat, landing face-down on the trunk, she kicked JFK's gun-blasted, bullet-riddled head.

To many viewers of Zapruder's film, it looked like she was trying to escape from the death car.

She would later claim—and agent Hill backed her up on this—that she was trying to retrieve a blob of his brain. To others, it looked as if she were assisting Hill, to help pull him into the car, which had accelerated as Kellerman was demanding that they get to the nearest hospital immediately.

Kellerman's shouts could be heard. "Let's get the fuck out of here! We're hit!"

In the follow-up car, it was Lady Bird who first screamed, "My God, they've shot the President!"

Over the radio, Kellerman sent an urgent message to the follow-up limousine, the one carrying Lyndon and Lady Bird. Agent Rufus Youngblood was aware of what had happened and had hustled the Vice President—who in essence was the President at this moment—to the floor, covering his body with his own.

Without officially being sworn in, Johnson assumed leadership of the Free World while crouched down on the floor of a speeding limousine.

In an almost Herculean effort, Hill had caught up with the speeding car containing the wounded President, landing on the footstand on the car exterior's left side. He grasped a small handrail for balance.

From there, he thrust his body forward onto the trunk and grabbed hold of Jackie. Using all his force, he pushed her back into her seat, where she collapsed. He would later recall the pool of blood and tissue like a vile confetti.

He covered the President's body and that of Jackie with his own body in case there was another (or other) gunman/gunmen. The President lay motionless, a gaping, fist-sized, blood-soaked hole visible in the back of his head. Hill knew, on seeing that, that the Presidential torch had passed to Johnson.

Under his body weight, he heard Jackie's sobbing. "Jack, what have they done to you? I love you!"

[In a memoir, Hill described the sound of the third shot, likening it to "something hard hitting something hollow, like the sound of a melon shattered onto cement." In the same instant, blood, brain matter, and bone fragments exploded from the back of the President's head. His blood, parts of his skull, bits of his brain, were splattered all over me—on my face, my clothes, in my hair."

With Jackie underneath him, and with his right hand, Hill pounded the door frame in his anger and frustration, knowing the President was dead and that the Secret Service had failed him. He knew that although the President might still be breathing, he was technically dead, or at least brain-dead.]

***

Of the 178 witnesses at the scene on that fateful day, 61 claimed the shots came from a grassy knoll in front of the presidential motorcade. Some believed the shots came from the Depository itself. Others stated that they were not certain where the shots originated—"perhaps from several directions."

The official conclusion was that three bullets had been fired within a span of six seconds from a window of the Depository, and that the lone assassin was Lee Harvey Oswald.

The number of rounds of gunfire and the identity of the assassins will no doubt be debated a hundred years from now.

As in the assassination of Abraham Lincoln, conspiracy theories abound.

***

Sirens wailing, the Kennedy motorcade rushed to Parkland Hospital with a moribund President, a comatose Governor, and a shocked-to-her-core First Lady.

Greer, the agent driving, pulled the Lincoln into Parkland's Emergency Entrance at 12:36PM. The staff had been alerted, but in their dumbfounded confusion, they had not hauled out any gurneys *[metal stretchers with wheeled legs]*. Kellerman screamed for two gurneys.

A doctor later reported that if JFK had been anybody else, he would have been pronounced DOA *[Dead on Arrival]*.

From the jump seat, Connally had to be removed before JFK's dying body could be lifted out and rushed into an emergency room.

There was a problem. Jackie held firmly onto the body, JFK's head cradled in her lap. She was refusing to let go, and Hill did not want to use force.

"I'm not going to give him up," she shouted at him. "You know he's dead. Let me alone!"

The agent figured out why she was so stubborn. She didn't want people to see the slain President with part of his head blown off. Consequently, Hill ripped off his jacket and used it to cover JFK's blasted head. "No one will see him now," he assured her.

She released him and he was wheeled down the corridor of the hospital. She followed into the corridor, where no one spoke to her, perhaps because they were so in awe of her presence within this living page of American history.

She sat down on a bench outside the door and began smoking, one cigarette after another.

HAPPIER TIMES

On July 30, 1960, **Lady Bird Johnson** joined **Jackie Kennedy** at her Hyannis Port home, following the nomination of their respective husbands for the 1960 Democratic ticket.

She was still holding a part of the President's brain in her bloody kid glove.

Immediately after he rushed into Parkland Hospital, Lyndon B. Johnson, with a frantic Lady Bird at his side, approached the Secret Service. "Is he dead? *Tell me, God damn it.* Am I the President of the United States?"

Kellerman replied, "We don't know yet. But it appears hopeless."

"Imagine not knowing if I'm the President," Johnson said. "What if Russia launches a nuclear strike?"

Lady Bird, the new First Lady, made her way down what she called "a corridor of silent people" to console the former First Lady, just now dethroned.

She discovered Jackie—"her eyes great wells of sadness"—and told her, "I wish to God there was something I could do, you poor child."

Jackie did not look up and did not respond to the new First Lady.

In the examining room, where nurses had cut off JFK's clothing, he lay nude on the operating table in front of the crowd of people, both from the hospital staff and the Secret Service. No pulse could be detected, but his body seemed to be in the throes of gasping automatically for his final breath. Then a faint heartbeat was discovered.

He was given blood transfusions. Having been told that his blood type was Type O, RH-Positive, he was injected with Type O, RH-Negative *[a medically acceptable practice, Type O, RH-Negative being universally compatible with any other blood type.]* But it didn't really matter at this point.

Drugs were administered in a hopeless attempt to revive him. Even though they knew it was too late, doctors went through the motions of trying to save him. A breathing tube was inserted into his throat, but it didn't work because of his neck wound. Another doctor performed an emergency tracheotomy.

In the corridor, Jackie clung to her fast-fading last hope. She vowed that if her brain-damaged husband lived, she would look after him for the rest of his life, the way Rose Kennedy had cared for Joe after his stroke.

Jackie confronted Dr. M. T. ("Pepper") Jenkins in the corridor. According to the doctor's later testimony, "I noticed that Mrs. Kennedy's hands were cupped in front of her, as she circled around. She was cradling something. As she passed by me, she handed it to me. I took it. It was slimy. I determined it was a big chunk of the President's brain tissue. Long before TV programs were interrupted around the world with a bulletin, I knew that John F. Kennedy had gone to meet his maker."

At this point, Jackie broke away from the doctor and headed for the trauma room, where a burly nurse attempted to block her way. She shoved the nurse aside and came into the room. The nurse chased after her. As she grabbed Jackie's arm, she slapped the nurse really hard. Stunned, she let go.

Dr. George Burkley interceded. "Let Mrs. Kennedy by. She's got a right."

Suddenly, a cardiac pacemaker was wheeled into the room. Dr. William Clark, a neurologist, began to administer a closed-chest cardiac massage, knowing that it was futile. With the compression of JFK's chest, blood gushed from the wound in his skull, dripping into a coagulating pool on the floor, making for a slippery, ghoulish sight.

A priest, Father Oscar Huber, had been delayed by traffic, but was now delivering Last Rites. He placed a white and purple ribbon on JFK's shoulder. The ancient Catholic ritual of Extreme Unction began—*Si capax, ego te albolvo a peccatis tuis. [If possible, I absolve you of your sins.]*

Jackie dropped down onto the bloody, slippery floor, as she heard the final words spoken over JFK's body. "Eternal rest grant unto him, O Lord." Then the priest anointed the President's head with oil.

In a barely understood murmur, Jackie said, "Let perpetual light shine upon him."

After he'd finished, the priest turned to Jackie. "I extend my deepest sympathy and the sympathy of the Church."

She wanted to know—if JFK were dead when the priest had administered the sacrament, would it have had any meaning?

Father Huber responded, as overheard by those crowded into the room, "I believe his soul had not yet left his body, so it was a valid sacrament."

A white sheet was placed over JFK's body. Dr. Robert McClelland reported what happened next:

She approached the corpse and pulled back the sheet. "His mouth is so beautiful." She reached down and planted her final kiss on his lips. "His eyes are open, looking at me for one last time. She kissed his chest, his leg, and even his penis.

Then a Secret Service agent came up and covered the slain President's body again with the sheet. But as Jackie was being led out of the room, she discovered his right foot sticking out from under the sheet. To her, his foot "looked whiter than the sheet." She bent over and kissed it.

In the meantime, a Secret Service agent had ordered a bronze coffin from the local funeral parlor. "The best you have."

Thirty minutes later, the body was placed in the casket. Jackie demanded to see the corpse one final time before flying out of Texas. A nurse helped her remove her bloody kid gloves. She took off her wedding band and placed it on his little finger. "Goodbye, forever, my darling," she said.

***

The pilot of the plane was Air Force Col. James B. Swindal, a veteran of World War II and the postwar Berlin Airlift. He'd become President-Elect Kennedy's personal pilot in 1960. From a portable radio inside the cockpit, he first heard that JFK had been assassinated.

"We were in a sort of bind," he recalled, "because there was no place on Air Force one for a casket, and we sure didn't want to put it in the cargo hold. Back in the rear were seats for stewardesses, Secret Service, and other passengers. So we unbolted these seats—about four rows—and made a space about the size of a couch. I also ordered that the plane be loaded to the limit with fuel to stay aloft for as long as possible in case the assassination was part of a Soviet attack."

***

Back at Parkland, Dr. Earl Rose, the Dallas County Medical Examiner, had unexpectedly arrived on the scene. He informed the Secret Service that a Texas law required that an autopsy be performed on the corpse before the body could be removed from the city limits. Therefore, he had come to claim the body.

"Listen, you god damn son of a bitch," Agent Kellerman said. "Get out of our way or I'll blow your fucking head off. Fuck your local ordinances. This is the President of the United States."

Rose was pushed aside. He could have alerted the Dallas police for a standoff, but chose not to.

Outside the hospital, Jackie refused to ride in front, but demanded to be driven to the airport in a position directly beside the coffin.

The body, within its coffin, was put into a waiting hearse for delivery to Dallas' airport [Love Field], where Lyndon Johnson was impatiently waiting. He was refusing to become airborne unless Jackie was aboard. When the hearse arrived at the side of Air Force One, it was discovered that the casket would not fit through the aircraft's doors until its brass handles were removed, a task the by-now exhausted Secret Service set about with hysterical single-mindedness.

Jackie boarded the aircraft, receiving sympathy from everybody she encountered. She entered the little bedroom where JFK had made love to her.

To her horror, she discovered Johnson sitting on the bed, dictating a letter to his secretary, Marie Fehmer. "Hold in there, little darling," he said, before quickly exiting.

After that, Jackie sat in her seat, smoking a cigarette. Lady Bird came to the rear of the aircraft and asked her if she'd like to change out of her blood-stained clothes.

She refused. "When I return to Washington, I want them to see what they have done." Jackie said.

After Lady Bird had departed, David Powers came and sat down beside Jackie, taking her hand.

"Oh, Dave," she said. "This is the first day of the rest of my life. A life without Jack. I still have my children. I must protect them at all costs."

Johnson had wanted to delay the release of the news about the President's death until Air Force One was airborne. He feared a conspiracy, or perhaps an attack on the United States.

But bulletins were already being flashed around the world. In all its capitals, phones were urgently ringing. One of the most publicized events in the history of America was unfolding, minute by minute.

Within the hour, an industry of conspiracy theories was launched that would lead to some 2,000 books, countless television shows, and endless newspaper articles. The first conspiracy theory that originated was that JFK had been assassinated as part of a communist plot.

265

Near the front of Air Force One, Johnson faced General Godfrey McHugh, JFK's Air Force aide, who urged him to order the pilot to TAKE OFF at once. When Johnson refused, McHugh protested.

"I am the President," Johnson shouted at him. "You'll follow my orders!"

McHugh shot back, "I have only one President. He's lying in the rear in the coffin." Then he stalked away.

Arriving by police escort, a Dallas Judge, Sara T. Hughes, summoned urgently as a player and legal witness to the unfolding dramas and transfers of power, came aboard.

Still in Texas, and still on the ground, the oath of Presidential Office is administered to **Lyndon B. Johnson** by a female Texas judge, with **Lady Bird** *(left)* and a shell-shocked **Jackie** looking on.

Johnson sent an aide to summon Jackie from the rear of the plane. "Mrs. Kennedy, the President wants you to attend the swearing-in ceremony."

At first, she hesitated, but then changed her mind and walked toward the front of the plane. With a rather blank look, she stood to Johnson's left as he was sworn in as the new president of the United States, using JFK's personal Bible, and with Sara Hughes presiding.

After the ceremony, Johnson thanked Jackie and expressed his sympathy.

At 3PM, the plane finally became airborne, after some continuing squabbling as to which legal entity had jurisdiction over the President's body. The former President had been dead for two hours.

Word reached Air Force One that a ferret-faced young man had been arrested after killing a Dallas police officer, J.D. Tippit. Tippit had stopped Lee Harvey Oswald for questioning.

***

On November 22, when the recently slaughtered body of a U.S. President lay in a hastily selected coffin aboard Air Force One, speeding toward Washington, elsewhere in the world, the business of government was grinding on in a perilous way.

Burkett Van Kirk, chief counsel for the Republican minority on the Senate Rules Committee, was hearing damaging evidence from Donald Reynolds, a Washington insurance broker, that Lyndon Johnson and Bobby Baker had accepted payola. Also, reputation-destroying evidence had been provided stating that President Kennedy at the White House had engaged in an extended sexual liaison with a communist spy, who may have been employed by the KGB to learn and then transmit vital U.S. government secrets.

Even Lady Bird Johnson was implicated for accepting gifts she'd selected from a sales catalogue.

The hearing was interrupted when a hysterical secretary burst into the chamber with breaking news out of Dallas. "A Secret Service agent just called from Texas," she shouted. "An assassin blew off Kennedy's head."

The committee members looked at each other in stunned disbelief. It seemed pointless to be investigating the misdeeds of a dead president. Political bases and public opinion had to be attended to, as the power structure in Washington had just become radically unhinged. What did it matter anymore that Lady Bird got a free deluxe stereo and some advertising money for one of her radio stations, and that Lyndon had done some arm twisting to encourage people to come forth with gifts?

The sexual misdeeds of JFK and his communist prostitutes were hardly worth investigating anymore. In fact, to air such charges would probably invoke the condemnation of the American people, who were no doubt about to go into a prolonged state of mourning.

From this moment forth, each of the committee members would be facing the press with only praise for America's slain leader.

***

At the precise moment that JFK was shot in Dallas, an undercover CIA agent in a Paris hotel was presenting former Cuban student radical, Rolando Cubela, with a "poison pen," an actual fountain pen designed for the assassination of Fidel Castro.

Although this sounded like something out of a James Bond movie, the pen, with its syringe full of poison, was to be presented to the Cuban leader with the secret understanding that somehow it could lead to his death when he used it.

Cubela was still trusted by Castro's inner circle and was still allowed to meet with him privately.

Since the details of such a mission have never been made public, it remains a mystery how the poison in the pen could enter Castro's blood stream. Somehow the pen, filled with Black Flag 40, a commercially sold insecticide, was to be used like a hypodermic needle. Was Cubela instructed to jab the point of the pen into Castro's arm or hand? If he had done so, it would surely have been a suicide mission.

THE SURVIVOR: **Fidel Castro**

"The bastard was going to hire his assassins to kill me. Now he's dead, and I'm alive!"

***

267

At his home, Hickory Hill, Robert F. Kennedy had just had a swim in his backyard pool. Ethel had prepared him a tunafish sandwich for lunch.

The phone rang in the hallway. Ethel picked up the receiver. "This is J. Edgar Hoover. I must speak to your husband. Get him at once. At once!"

On the phone, the FBI director was blunt. "The President has been shot in Dallas. I'm told he's either dead or has only moments to live. His brain was splattered everywhere. Lyndon thinks he's next. He suspects a nuclear attack any minute on the United States."

***

Two days after the assassination of President John F. Kennedy, a veteran who'd served with Oswald in the Marine Corps, spoke to a reporter: "One night in a bar he [Oswald] told me that he was going to become the second most famous man in America and would go down in history books."

The former marine claimed, "I chided him. Oh, sure you will. What's your ambition? To become President of the United States? With your record, you can forget that. What a pipe dream."

***

Under darkening skies at Andrews Air Force Base, several thousand U.S. Air Force personnel gathered to honor their slain former Commander-in-Chief at the moment his slain corpse was offloaded from Air Force One. Senators, Congressmen, Cabinet Members, and the extended Kennedy family, along with friends, gathered for this historic event shortly before six that evening. Security was the tightest ever known in Washington.

Attorney General Robert Kennedy, without attracting the attention of the press, bounded up the portable stairwell a second or two after it had been wheeled into place near the front of the aircraft.

The moment he was admitted inside, he rushed along the aisle toward the back of the

One of the most iconic photographs taken in the 20th Century depicts **Jackie**, still in her blood-stained dress, facing a bitter homecoming in Washington. Adjacent to **Bobby**, who's holding her hand, she watches as her slain husband's body is unloaded into a waiting ambulance before it was rushed to Bethesda Hospital for an autopsy.

En route to the hospital, Jackie told Bobby, "The last thing Jack said to me about Lyndon was that he's incapable of telling the truth."

plane, bypassing the newly sworn-in President Johnson, without one word exchanged between them, even though, technically, LBJ was his new boss.

Ignoring everybody aboard the plane, even JFK's closest aides, Bobby headed straight for Jackie and held her tightly in his arms.

Her first words to him were, "Oh, Bobby, I can't believe Jack is gone."

He confirmed that the Dallas police thought they had captured the assassin, Lee Harvey Oswald. "He's a communist."

"Don't tell me," Jackie responded. "A silly little communist." She burst into tears. "That means Jack's death had no meaning. He didn't have the satisfaction of being killed for his championing of civil rights."

Bobby ordered Kennedy aides to block LBJ from coming to the back of the plane, where he had wanted to be photographed disembarking with the slain leader's casket. It was Bobby himself who was shown holding Jackie's hand as they were photographed with Mary Gallagher and Clint Hill as the casket was removed from the plane by a hydraulic lift. A six-man Marine Honor Guard carried it to a waiting Navy ambulance.

Jackie had demanded that only Navy doctors at Bethesda Hospital perform the autopsy. "I didn't want those Texas butchers cutting into Jack," she told Bobby.

Refusing to return to the White House and her children, she asked to travel in the Navy ambulance, sitting beside the casket with Bobby all the way.

At the hospital, while doctors performed the autopsy, she was escorted to the presidential suite on the building's seventeenth floor. With Hill serving as gatekeeper, she received the extended members of the Kennedy clan.

It was 2:45AM when Hill notified her that the autopsy had ended.

The autopsy, both its procedures and its results, are still controversial. Amazingly, no forensic pathologist was present. An unidentified pathologist later studied the evidence, and said, "The JFK medical evidence is so confused and contaminated with false and deceptive information that the only way to truly know the truth about JFK's death would be to exhume the body for a proper autopsy by objective pathologists not under government control and filmed in a public setting, with neutral witnesses."

Perhaps on orders from Robert F. Kennedy, a number of body materials removed from JFK's body and examined at the initial autopsy later disappeared. These include the President's damaged brain, blood smears, organ samples, and certain tissue sections. Allegedly, RFK didn't want this body tissue preserved for display in some museum exhibit. Also, some latter-day historians have surmised that perhaps they didn't want anyone to dissect the body tissues for evidence of either Addison's disease or use of controlled substances by the President. But if, indeed, RFK did order the destruction of this material, he almost had to have the approval of Jackie herself.

[When Ramsey Clark became Attorney General, Jackie called him, requesting that he suppress all autopsy X-rays and photographs of "my husband on that marble slab." Although he at least appeared to respect her wishes, JFK's autopsy photos are available today to anyone who knows how to surf

the Internet.]

Aides Kenneth O'Donnell and David Powers had purchased a mahogany casket at a nearby mortuary since the one from Dallas had been damaged during its frantic transit from Parkland Hospital to Washington, D.C.

At around 3AM, a Kennedy motorcade, followed by a Navy ambulance carrying his body, included Jean Smith, Ethel Kennedy, and Robert McNamara, headed for the White House and arriving at 4:24AM. A U.S. Marine Honor Guard at the Northwest Gate greeted the fallen leader.

Jackie told Bobby, "I departed this place with a young, vibrant husband. This morning, I'm bringing back a corpse."

Still wearing her blood-stained suit, Jackie found her way into the East Room, where the casket rested on a catafalque identical to the one used in the funeral of Abraham Lincoln in 1865 in the wake of his assassination by John Wilkes Booth at the Ford Theater.

Before going upstairs to look in on her children, she met privately with Kenneth O'Donnell. He returned her wedding band, which she'd placed on JFK's finger at Parkland Hospital. "I thought you'd want this back."

She received it gratefully, with a little sob, thanking him.

Some nineteen hours had passed since she'd left the Hotel Texas in Fort Worth. She removed her clothes and took a long, hot bath.

She summoned a White House doctor, who gave her Amytal, thinking that it would make her sleep. Before drifting off, she recalled, "My body was in a state of panic. I didn't think I had enough energy to get through the funeral. I'd never before been called upon to have such resolute willpower. I knew the eyes of the world would be turned upon me, and I was afraid I'd fail them."

She fell into a deep sleep that lasted for only three hours. "At first, I didn't seem to know where I was," she recalled. "Then I felt like the weight of the world had come in on me."

Her children's nanny, Maud Shaw, had already informed Caroline of her father's death, telling her, "Little Patrick needs his father in heaven."

When John Jr. woke up, Jackie had to tell the little boy, "Your daddy is gone."

He looked perturbed. "Did Daddy take his plane with him?" he asked.

"Yes, he flew away in the plane," she answered.

"When is Daddy coming back?" the boy asked.

She did not answer, but clutched him and held him tightly.

"Mom, you're smothering me," he protested.

"There are things I must teach you today," she said, "including how to salute."

***

Lem Billings desperately wanted to see Jackie, but she did not make herself available. Of the many friends and family who gathered, he was the most distraught. Family friend Francis McAdoo claimed, "Lem didn't want to live. He was wrecked for years to come. I don't think he ever recovered. At first, he was stunned and shocked. Then he became morose. He couldn't believe JFK was dead."

As regards Lem, Bobby recalled, "He took it harder than anyone except myself. He was completely devastated. Everything he had lived for seemed pulled out from under him. In the weeks ahead, he practically wandered around in a coma, as I did myself."

In the next few hours, Jackie asked Ted Sorensen to research the funeral of Abraham Lincoln at the Library of Congress. She was hoping for inspiration during the arrangements she was organizing for his burial.

Mary Gallagher helped Jackie with her wardrobe, discovering that she owned only one black dress. It was the same outfit she'd worn in the Senate Building when JFK had announced his intention of running for President.

As it happened, she did not own a pair of black hosiery, so Jackie sent Gallagher to Garfunkel's Department Store to purchase three pairs for her. Rose Kennedy [a veteran observer of many previous funerals] lent Jackie a long black veil.

Like Billings, William Walton, JFK's longtime ally and confidant, was reduced to sobbing. At one point, after hearing the news of Jack's assassination, he became hysterical.

Meeting with Jackie, she evaluated his condition: "Bill, please, pull yourself together. I need you. You've got to help me get through the funeral. Both of us must be strong."

Walton was one of the few people around her whose taste she implicitly trusted. She asked him to be the arbiter of anything connected with the funeral, subject to veto from either Bobby or herself.

She later applauded him for the choices he'd made, except she was shocked when he showed up at the funeral in a tan gabardine suit. "What happened to basic black?" she asked.

"I got caught in the rain with my one black suit, and it was ruined," he told her.

Bunny Mellon, the multi-millionaire horticulturist, was called in to

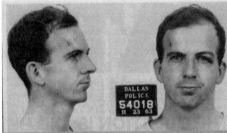

upper photo: Recently beaten by Dallas policemen, a dazed **Lee Harvey Oswald** poses for his mug shot.

lower photo: Detectives wearing Texas style hats hold Oswald firmly in place as he announces, after being formally charged with JFK's murder, "I did not kill anyone. I don't know what this is about."

His role in the assassination of JFK is still hotly debated.

oversee the floral arrangements. Jackie told her that JFK hated "all those purple wreaths and gold ribbons, looking like Harlem or Coney Island."

In the aftermath of that conversation, Mellon went to the White House's Rose Garden and cut white roses, chrysanthemums, two-lipped blue salvias and sphinx Hawthorne branches, using their shapes and colors as inspiration for other floral arrangements to come.

As funeral preparations were being organized, Jackie was notified by Bobby that Oswald had been assassinated in Dallas by someone named Jack Ruby, a Dallas strip club owner. TV cameras were tuned in to the actual event. *[It happened during a publicly televised transfer of Oswald between holding cells.]* Under heavy guard, he was fatally shot in full view of television cameras, who broadcast it around the world, much to the shame and dishonor of the Dallas police department. Shot at 11:21AM, Oswald would die at 1:07PM at Parkland Hospital, where JFK had died two days earlier.

Trembling from the news, and not fully understanding what was going on, Jackie was escorted to the East Room to watch as JFK's casket was transported from the White House to a position beneath the rotunda of the Capitol Building.

The coffin was carried out of the White House through the building's North Portico and placed on a caisson pulled by six white horses. It was the same caisson that had carried the body of Franklin D. Roosevelt in 1945.

Jackie appeared in public holding the hands of Caroline and John Jr. Bobby directed her into a limousine holding Lyndon and Lady Bird Johnson. Together, they rode to the Capitol rotunda, noting hundreds of thousands of mourners and the idle curious linking the edges of windswept Pennsylvania Avenue.

At the Capitol, a Marine military band played a moving rendition of "Hail to the Chief."

Nine military pallbearers removed the flag-draped casket from the caisson and carried the heavy burden up the thirty-six steps to the Rotunda, placing it in a position directly beneath the highest point of the dome. After the eulogies, Jackie and Caroline knelt before the coffin and kissed the flag that covered it. Onlookers were weeping.

"We're going to tell Daddy goodbye," she told Caroline. "We'll kiss the flag, knowing he's inside.

Then Jackie returned to the White House, making final preparations. She had asked that the rotunda be left open to the viewing public through-out the night. Some one-quar-

A State Funeral, modeled on that of Abraham Lincoln, was almost entirely choreographed by the widowed Jackie.

ter of a million people would pass through to view the casket.

The night before the funeral, there had been an intimate dinner at the White House for twelve. Jackie did not attend. Surprisingly, as sometimes happens during wakes, the mood was jovial, at least for a little while. Someone even snatched Ethel's wig and placed it on the head of Robert McNamara, the usually rather dour Secretary of Defense.

The guest list was rather bizarre, having included comedian Phyllis Diller and Aristotle Onassis. Bobby later asked, "Who invited Onassis?" Perhaps to embarrass him, Bobby drew up a semi-legal document in which the Greek shipping tycoon agreed to turn over half of his wealth to the struggling poor of Latin America. To the astonishment of the Attorney General, Onassis signed it. Of course, both of them knew that the document was not enforceable.

The mood became somber when the dinner guests filed into the East Room to pay their final respects. The mood was one of "Good night, sweet prince."

After the guests had departed, Jackie asked Clint Hill to accompany Bobby and herself to the White House's East Room for a viewing of the coffin. The Honor Guard was there, and Hill asked them to turn their back on the coffin for a private viewing of the body. The last time Bobby had viewed JFK, he had been alive. When the coffin was opened, RFK began to cry silently, and tears also fell from Jackie's face too.

She placed two letters, a thin one and a longer one, into JFK's left hand. She'd written a letter to him that took two hours to write. She had also asked Caroline to write her own letter.

She'd selected a blue-gray suit for JFK's burial in the mahogany casket. Because of his massive head wound, a great deal of makeup had been applied to his face. When Jackie first stared at him, she let out a small gasp. "Poor Jack, my darling. It looks like a waxworks from Madame Tussaud's."

Then she turned and asked Hill for a pair of scissors. When he returned with a pair, she cut off a lock of JFK's chestnut hair.

It was Bobby who lowered the casket's lid for the final time. It was 12:46AM.

At the entrance to the East Room, both Bobby and Jackie turned for one final look. She began crying, and he walked her to her bedroom, which he entered, and locked the door behind him.

***

Jackie announced that she wanted her husband's funeral service at Washington's Cathedral church of Saint Matthew the Apostle, the patron saint of civil servants, the seat of the Catholic Archbishop of Washington, even though it wasn't big enough to hold all of the invited guests. (In this decision, out of loyalty to JFK's Catholic origins, she deliberately bypassed the larger [Episcopalian] Cathedral Church of Saint Peter and Saint Paul [i.e. the Washington National Cathedral].

She refused to be driven to the funeral, but planned to walk.

It was a quarter of a mile to the church, but she said she didn't want to be seen "riding in some fat, black Cadillac" behind the horse-drawn coffin.

When Johnson heard this, he, too, agreed to walk along with the procession, even though the Secret Service warned that he could be the victim of an assassin. He refused to listen. "Damn you, pansies. I'm in charge here. I'll walk!"

Éamon De Valera, blind and in his eighties, agreed to walk, too, "in honor of my fellow Irishman." *[De Valera, The New York City-born product of an Irish mother and a Cuban father, was a violently dominant political figure in 20th-Century Irish history. During a political career that spanned more than fifty years, from 1917 to 1973; he served multiple terms as Head of the Irish government, sometimes with fierce opposition from the English. Latter-day evaluations of his life and career have varied, with some historians defining him as devious, divisive, and emotionally unstable.]*

During the procession, De Valera's son was at his side with a hypodermic syringe in case the exertion brought on a heart attack.

Towering over all the other visitors was the stately looking Charles de Gaulle, whose security guards didn't want him to attend the funeral. After their arrival in Washington, they also urged him not to take the walk. He refused their request. "I had to attend the funeral, even though Kennedy and I had had our differences. Frenchman all over my country are crying as if they'd lost one of their own. I'd be impeached if I didn't come."

It isn't known whether Queen Elizabeth would have walked all the way to St. Matthews. She was pregnant and sent Prince Philip instead. He walked in the cortege.

Jackie, Bobby, and Teddy walked behind the horse-drawn funeral caisson holding JFK's casket in a ritual inspired by equivalent symbols during the funeral procession of Abraham Lincoln, less than a century before. It was led by a riderless black horse, its stirrups hanging backward from the saddle. Ironically, the horse was named "Black Jack," the nickname of Jackie's father, Black Jack Bouvier.

A British journalist filed this report: "Jacqueline Kennedy has today given the country the one thing it has always lacked, and that is majesty."

Subdued drumrolls marked the progress of the procession from the sidelines.

At St. Matthews, Jackie was seated up front with John Jr. on one side of her, Caroline on the other. She listened tearfully as Richard Cardinal Cushing delivered Low Mass. He had a hard time with his harsh raspy voice, a by-product of both emphysema and asthma.

In the middle of the service, John Jr. grew restless. In a loud voice, he asked, "Where's my Daddy?"

A Secret Service agent, Robert Foster, took him to the anteroom, where the little boy practiced saluting.

At the end of the service, Luigi Vena, a tenor from Boston, sang "Ave Maria." At the climax, JFK's casket was carried from the front of the church and down the aisle to the sounds of "Hail to the Chief."

Outside the church, a black-veiled Jackie stood rigidly with her children watching the casket being loaded for its transport to Arlington Cemetery. The military rendered a salute to its fallen commander-in-chief.

Jackie leaned down and whispered something in John Jr.'s ear. Thrusting his small shoulders back, he raised his right hand and performed what may be the most famous farewell salute in history.

There are those who say the little boy with his elbow cocked at precisely the right angle, exposing his dimpled knees in short pants and wearing bright red shoes, created a poignancy that made him overnight America's uncrowned prince.

After that, Jackie sent Caroline and her son back to the White House, while she got into a limousine for the ride to Arlington.

A woman and her priest:
The public face of a private moment

As JFK was laid to rest, Air Force jets flew overhead, one of them dipping its wing in a final salute. A Secret Service agent warned Jackie of the upcoming 21-gun salute. They were afraid that the sound would evoke the gunfire of Dallas. She trembled as she listened to seven riflemen each fire three separate volleys in honor of the slain President.

After Jackie was handed a lit torch, she moved toward the gravesite to light the Eternal Flame. The flag that had draped the casket was ceremoniously folded and presented to her.

Sergeant Keith Clark, the Arlington bugler, pointed his instrument in Jackie's direction as he played Taps. He experienced difficulty because of his trembling lips.

***

After her departure from Arlington, Jackie, during the limousine ride back to the White House, told Bobby, "After Arlington, my responsibilities as First Lady are over. I've become a private person again.

That was not quite true. Waiting at the White House to receive her was an array of foreign dignitaries, come to pay their final respects to JFK. Some 220 representatives from 92 countries were at the White House, including ten prime ministers and eight heads of state. Among the guests were Haile Selassie of

Ethiopia; West Berlin's Mayor, Willy Brandt; King Baudouin of Belgium; and Queen Frederica of Greece (whom Jackie despised).

She had a private meeting with De Gaulle. He had been awed by her charm and beauty in Paris. But after the funeral, he met a more determined Jackie, who chastised him for having soured French-American relations.

She went upstairs to meet with Prince Philip, who had gone to present John Jr. with a birthday gift. Ironically, the little boy's birthday was on the day he buried his father.

When she walked in on them, she found the Royal Consort playing with her son on the carpet.

Before Philip, she executed a swift curtsey and turned to John. "Did you make a bow to His Majesty, son!" she asked.

"I did, mother," the little boy said as his nanny entered the room to fetch him.

Jackie sat on the sofa with the Prince. She didn't know if he'd ever heard that he was one of the ten men she'd named as the most desirable in the world from the prospective of a woman.

After sending her regards to the Queen and best wishes for her upcoming pregnancy, she thanked the Prince for coming to the funeral.

At the door, he bent down to kiss her goodbye. As she'd later tell William Walton, "I was shocked. It wasn't a kiss on the cheek, but a real man-to-woman kiss. I think in another life and under different circumstances, we could have been lovers."

After receiving her final dignitary, Jackie turned to Bobby. It was shortly before midnight. "Let's go see our friend," she said.

He notified Clint Hill to get a White House limousine ready.

At Arlington, they could see the Eternal Flame burning in the distance as they walked to the grave site, kneeling before the tombstone for a silent prayer.

At the end, they each stood up and took in the nighttime view of the Potomac and the lights piercing the darkness from the capital's various memorials.

It was time to return to the home she had occupied from 1961 to 1963. She would soon be leaving it.

Journalist Mary McGory would later write, "Mrs. Kennedy held the nation together while she broke its heart."

The End of Camelot

*Don't let it be forgot
That there was once a spot
For one brief shining moment*

That was known as Camelot.

In Washington, Jackie told the story of JFK's assassination over and over again to her closest friends. By so doing, she seemed to be purging herself of that day of horror in Dallas.

"Governor Connally was squealing like a stuck pig," she said time and time again. "Jack died bravely, without making a sound. At his last moment of life, he had this wonderful expression on his face."

In the aftermath of the funeral, Jackie granted an interview to historian Theodore H. White, writing for *Life* magazine. She told him that she and JFK used to lie in bed listening to a recording of the Broadway musical, *Camelot*. White picked up on this angle, and in his article, he likened the Kennedy presidency to Camelot.

A legend was born.

The myth of Camelot, in the view of many, was, historically at least, a flawed image. But ordinary citizens picked up on the epitaph bestowed, and the Camelot

Capturing the heart of a nation. **A star is born.**

myth lasts until this day. It suggests something noble, tragic, magical and mythical.

Jackie told White, "I want to rescue Jack from all those bitter people who are going to write about him in history."

Long after her departure from the White House, bags of mail continued to be delivered to her. Most of them expressed admiration for her or for JFK and offered heartfelt sympathy. Interspersed with these condolences was the occasional hate letter, one woman calling her a BLOOD-STAINED SLUT!

In the waning days of 1963, she had time only to answer those from prominent people. From Paris, André Malraux cabled, "*Nous pensons à vous and nous sommes si tristes.*" [*We're thinking of you, and we are so sad.*]

From London, a message from an unknown man was delivered to her because of its sentiment, "With the death of President Kennedy, every man in the Free World is a Kennedy."

Richard Nixon cabled, "I'm sorry that fate made Jack and me political enemies. I admired him intensely."

She answered Nixon, who had come so close to defeating JFK in the 1960 Presidential elections.

"I knew Jack's death could have been prevented, and I will never cease to torture myself with that. Whoever thought that such a hideous thing could happen in this country? I know how you must feel, so closely missing the greatest prize...and how you must commit all your family's hopes and efforts again. Just one thing I would say to you. If it does not work out as you have hoped for so

long, please be consoled by what you have—your life and your family. We never value Life enough."

Jackie learned that immediately after the assassination, Bobby issued orders that all of Jack's papers were to be moved to the most secure room of the White House and protected 24 hours a day by armed guards. As soon as possible, the hoard would be moved to another (unidentified) location, with strict security.

He also selected trusted aides to review, screen, edit, and in some cases destroy the President's papers and certain tapes. After that process was completed, the documents were shipped to the Kennedy Library, where the most sensitive would be locked up and rigorously guarded for a predefined term of a hundred years.

Jackie heartily approved of how Bobby handled that process.

The widowed Jackie, wearing Rose Kennedy's black veil of mourning, lived her finest hour as she bid farewell to her slain comrade.

Charles de Gaulle, who marched behind her in the funeral procession, later announced, "She gave an example to the world of how to behave."

***

In the weeks following the assassination, Jackie became the most publicized woman on the planet, a media event like nothing any woman in history had ever received. She attracted adoring crowds wherever she went. "I feel like a monument," she told Bobby, "not a woman."

She recalled walking by a newsstand in Georgetown, trailed by a crowd of curiosity seekers. She stopped to notice herself on the covers of a dozen magazines.

"I was no longer Queen of America," she told her friends. "I was now its Pop Princess."

Until 1968, she remained one of the most admired women in the world. The picture of the black-shrouded woman in "widow's weeds" seemed forever etched in the public's mind.

She'd become a widow at the age of 34 and much of her life lay before her, although it would not be a long life.

In the years to come, after her move from Georgetown to Manhattan, she began to damage her pristine image. She got into legal disputes with photographers, such as Ron Galella, and with authors such as William Manchester. These legal disputes tarnished her image. In 1968, she did the unthinkable: She married the

Greek shipping tycoon, Aristotle Onassis, a notorious international celebrity.

Given the Camelot mystique, the public, and even members of her own family, were shocked. The tabloids had a field day. On late-night TV, she became a laughing stock.

***

It wasn't until June 5, 1964, that she was called to testify before the Warren Commission. "I was looking to the left when I heard these terrible noises. You know. And my husband never made a sound. So I turned to the right. And all I remember is seeing my husband. He had this sort of quizzical look on his face, and his hand was up. It must have been his left hand, just as I turned and looked at him, I could see a piece of his skull, and I remembered it as flesh colored. I remember thinking it just looked as if he had a slight headache. No blood or anything. And then he sort of did this *[She raised her hand],* putting his hand to his forehead and fell into my lap, and then I just remember falling on him and saying, 'Oh no, no,' I mean, 'Oh, my God, they have shot my husband,' and 'I love you, Jack.' I remember I was shouting. I just being down in the car with his head in my lap. And it just seemed an eternity. You known, then, there were pictures later of me climbing out the back. But I don't remember that at all."

***

As late as April of 2012, conspiracy theories still swirled about JFK's tragic death. Dr. Cyril Wecht, known for his inquiries into the deaths of Elvis Presley and JonBenet Ramsey, demanded that the President's corpse be exhumed from Arlington and a new autopsy performed. Wecht claimed that he was convinced that a second medical procedure would show that "there had to have been two assassins." He also charged that a second autopsy would reveal a massive cover-up by the Warren Commission.

***

In the aftermath of JFK's assassination, Jackie coasted for several years as the grieving widow of Camelot, trying to rear and educate her children.

As the 1960s came to an end, she fell from her pedestal, becoming the tabloid sensation known worldwide as "Jackie O."

Her marriage to Greek shipping tycoon, Aristotle Onassis, brought her international notoriety and condemnation.

The press interviewed former classmates. "Our nickname for her was "Jacqueline Borgia," said Sheilah Bottoms.

In spite of such criticisms, *Variety* proclaimed her as THE UNDISPUTED TOP FEMME IN THE WORLD.

Her new daughter-in-law, Christina Onassis, labeled her "The Black Widow.

What amazes me is that she survives, while everybody around her drops. She's dangerous. She's deadly. She decimated at least one family, the Kennedys, and now she's after mine."

Some of Jackie's previous comments, which had been ignored by the press, now came back to haunt her. It was reported, for example, that she had called Rose Kennedy "a dinosaur" and a "dimwit."

The always provocative and relentlessly gossipy Truman Capote weighed in, too: "Bunny Mellon remains Jackie's friend only because she is terrified of her. Her secretary, Nancy Tuckerman, is no more than an indentured slave. Jackie may not have seduced the number of men I have, but she's had more than her share."

As the years went by, public opinion continued its campaign to pierce chinks in her armour.

At first, she refused to fly on Onassis' Olympic Airlines "because it reeks of feta cheese," which she loathed.

She demanded a discount at Manhattan's Bonwit Teller because of "all the free publicity I give you."

Other magazines and other biographers continued to amass negative publicity about her.

Ted Sorensen talked to her of the shift in public image that evolved for the most part in 1968 and during the eight years that followed.

But in reference to her armada of fans then abandoning her, "They'll come back," Jackie predicted. "I'll end my life a beloved figure—you wait and see. Right now, I'm going through my Diva period. If Maria Callas can be a diva, watch me go."

Wayne Koestenbaum in *Jackie Under My Skin*, wrote, *"Jackie triumphs because her style is aristocratic. And yet her 'high-class' status is only a vehicle for intangible spiritual victory. Jackie rules and ascends to Nirvana, not just because she's rich and refined, but because we think she deserves to win—because we've thrown out our own id's capital behind her, and imagine that beneath the glamour there rests a sad, grimy alterity, a previous incarnation of sour-smelling muumuus. Jacqueline Borgia will conquer her enemies. You can't refuse such a fairy-tale character destined for victory. She's 'top femme' because she seems not to care. She pretends indifference to fame and supremacy. Meanwhile, she achieves, through her blasé composure, perpetual glory. Her injunction, 'Do not look at me,' means that look we will."*

Chapter Thirteen

History's Most Famous Dress Was a Rip-Off Chanel

A Pink Artifact of Glamor, Splattered Body Parts, Bloodshed, and Tears

Often, **Jackie** as First Lady didn't like to wear the same garment more than once. An exception was a copy of a Chanel pink suit, which was destined to play a role in history. She wore it October 24, 1962 when entertaining the Maharaja and Maharini of Jaipur at the White House.

Months later, on November 22, 1963, blood-stained with her husband's blown-out brains, she wore the suit on the flight back from Dallas aboard Air Force One.

"I looked over my shoulder and saw, in the President's car, a bundle of pink, just like a drift of blossoms, lying on the back seat," said Lady Bird Johnson, recalling the fateful, blood-spattered motorcade that raced through the streets of Dallas on November 22, 1963.

That "drift of blossoms" she referenced was actually the figure of Jacqueline Kennedy, the 34-year-old wife of the slain President, crouching for cover, wearing the rose-colored Chanel suit that became an iconic emblem of the tragedy.

In her book, *Jackie Style,* the fashion expert, Pamela Keogh, wrote: "The outfit is a terrible talisman of American history and heartbreak. But despite symbolizing a very sorrowful moment in our nation's past, it also shows Jackie's stoicism."

As journalist Cathy Horyn wrote, "If there is a single item that captures both the shame and violence that erupted that day, and the glamor and artifice that preceded it, it is Jackie Kennedy's blood-stained pink suit, a tantalizing window on fame and fashion, her allure, and her steely resolve, the things we know about her, and the thing we never quite will."

Fashionista dragon/Nazi collaborator, Jackie-hater, role model for the "you can't be too rich or too thin" crowd, and the woman known for having the best fashion taste in Europe, **Gabrielle Chanel** appears in one of her trademark suits

***

What is the history of this dress?

The infamous pink suit was an exact copy—a knockoff, really—of a Chanel wool *bouclé*, two-piece suit lined with navy blue silk.

The original first appeared on a French model, a Jackie lookalike, in a fashion feature in the September 1, 1961, edition of *Life* magazine. By coincidence, the picture of First Lady Jackie appeared on the cover of that same magazine. Perhaps in flipping through its pages, she discovered the suit and decided to have one made for herself.

The suit was crafted in Manhattan by an expert tailor, Jack Horowicz, who during World War II had been imprisoned in a Polish concentration camp because he was a Jew. Freed by the Allied Armies, he drifted to Munich, where he opened a small shop. "I made dresses or gowns for American Army officers' wives, who were with their husbands stationed with the occupying forces in the area."

In 1952, he emigrated to America, settling in New York, where he became a "finisher" after joining the ILGWU (International Ladies' Garment Workers Union). Highly skilled, he also operated as a sample maker for Oscar de la Renta, working from a base on 39th Street in Manhattan between Broadway and Seventh Avenue, across from Dubrow's Cafeteria.

His son, Michael Horowicz, said, "There was much excitement when my father worked on the First Lady's suit. Jackie ordered it in an East Side boutique one year before her husband's assassination. The finishing work was farmed

A Dress that Will Live in Infamy

out to my father at the De la Renta Shop, and he went about the task in painstaking detail. It was his proud achievement to present it to Jackie, whom he admired greatly."

The original (authentic) Chanel suit had been displayed at Chez Ninon, a Park Avenue salon where Jackie was known as an occasional customer.

Journalist Jane Rudley wrote: "It was routine for Jackie and her sister, Lee Radziwill, to cherry-pick pieces by Givenchy, Chanel, and Pierre Cardin and have them copied relatively on the cheap by their favorite designers, including Oleg Cassini."

Jackie first appeared in the "Chanel-inspired" suit at Camp David in November of 1961 when she wore it to Sunday Mass.

She also was photographed in the suit with her sister Lee in London during March of 1962, when she lunched with Queen Elizabeth II. She wore the suit to greet the President of Algeria at the White House and again on October 24, 1962, when she met the Maharaja of Jaipur and his wife, also at the White House.

Reportedly, for the first time during their marriage, the President took an interest in the wardrobe that Jackie planned for their trip to Dallas. He said, "All those rich Texas broads at our dinners will be showing up in minks and diamonds. I want you to dazzle them by showing them that good taste can be simple but elegant." She complied with his requests.

An aide, Mary Barelli Gallagher, assembled Jackie's wardrobe. "It was feared that it might be raining, so I packed a raincoat in a darker shade of pink for Mrs. Kennedy. But that day in Dallas was bright and sunny, so she left the jacket on Air Force One."

On that horrible day in Dallas, Clint Hill was the Secret Service agent assigned to protect Jackie. He later recalled, "Mrs. Kennedy looked fluorescent against the dark blue of the car carrying the President and the First Lady. She stood out so much in the car because of the color of that suit. It was like the sun just illuminated it."

After the assassination, with part of JFK's brain in her hand, Jackie stood at Parkland Hospital in tears. In that dress, she kissed JFK for a final time before heading, under heavy security, back to Air Force One, where the new president (Lyndon Johnson) refused to be airborne without her.

Aboard Air Force One, flying back to Washington with the slain President's body, Lady Bird asked Jackie if she wanted to change her garment. But Jackie insisted on wearing the blood-soaked Chanel as she stood beside Lyndon Baines Johnson as he was sworn in as the new president.

She told Lady Bird, "Let them see what they've done!"

Later, Lady Bird, in her diary, recorded the event. "Somehow, that was one of the most poignant sights—that immaculate woman, exquisitely dressed, and caked in blood."

One of the most iconic pictures, flashed around the world, was of Jackie wearing that dress and holding the hand of Robert F. Kennedy when she arrived back in Washington aboard Air Force One.

Apparently, Jackie wore the suit all through the night after her return to the White House. The next morning, she gave the suit to her personal maid, Providencia Paredes, who placed it in a dress box. In July of 1964, it was turned over to the National Archives, accompanied with a note from Janet Auchincloss, Jackie's mother. The note read: "Jackie's suit and bag—worn November 22, 1963."

As a means of preserving the historical authenticity of the garment, curators—following standard conservation practices—agreed that the blood stains and other residue would remain, and that the garment would not be washed or cleaned.

Other garments preserved for history include the suit and cloak worn by Abraham Lincoln when he was assassinated. Mrs. Lincoln had given them to a family friend, and the garments remained in that family's custody until the 1950s, when the American Trucking Association raised the money and purchased them as a gift to the National Archives. Other valued garments include Napoléon's death coat and the shoe dropped by Marie Antoinette on her way to the guillotine.

The pillbox pink hat that Halston designed for Jackie has mysteriously disappeared, as have the white gloves she wore that day. But the dress rests in a climate-controlled vault within the National Archives in Maryland.

Jackie's blood-spattered hosiery, folded within a white towel, rests with the suit. Her navy-blue shoes, handbag, and navy-blue blouse are also preserved for posterity.

Technically, Caroline Kennedy owned the outfit and its accessories. But in 2003, she made a gift of them to the National Archives, with the provision that they not be publicly displayed until 2103, a century after the year of her donation, and 140 years after her father's assassination.

Martha Murphy, who is the chief of special access at the archives, said the dress is the only item associated with the assassination that has a restriction. Otherwise, the public can view the suit President Kennedy was wearing at the time of his assassination. Also on view is the rifle used by Lee Harvey Oswald.

"The dress won't see the light of day in my lifetime," said fashion writer Pamela Keogh. "For that, I am grateful. To my mind, there would be something very ghoulish about it being put on display."

Shortly after the assassination, a genuinely ghoulish trend involved the dozens of women who ordered copies of Jackie's suit, as well as copies of her pillbox hat for them to wear at various events. Also, the Chanel knockoff has been copied dozens of times as part of various Hollywood scripts. One of the most recent of these occurred when Minka Kelly wore a version of it in Lee Daniel's film, *The Butler*. Gennifer Goodwin re-created Jackie's pink suit in the TV series *Killing Kennedy,* which aired on *The National Geographic Channel* in November of 2013, marking the 50th anniversary of JFK's assassination.

Caroline's terms will likely be renegotiated by her descendants after her death.

Chapter Fourteen

Bobby Kennedy
The Lancelot in Jackie's Camelot

A Shared Tragedy Evolves Into an Abiding Love

THE LOOK OF LOVE. In the wake of JFK's assassination, **the former First Lady** and **the Attorney General** became lovers. Here, flanked with his wife **Ethel** on one side and with Jackie on the other, one wonders what expression Bobby is returning to Jackie from the threshold of her home in Georgetown.

Bobby Kennedy and Jackie, before the cameras roll at Hyannis Port on May 29, 1964, less than a year after his brother and her husband was assassinated in Dallas.

The program, discussing the late President's spiritual legacy, and filled with tremulous sensitivity, was broadcast from the home of Joseph P. Kennedy.

It was the beginning of a love affair, and it was captured on film by a paparazzo. Just two weeks after Dallas, Jackie, along with Caroline and John-John, moved into the Georgetown home of Averell Harriman, using it as a temporary shelter. Bobby and Ethel came to call.

Only the night before, Jackie had wept for hours, unable to sleep. At Bobby's parting glance, Jackie smiled demurely, a promise of more to come in their relationship. Newsman Ben Bradlee, a close friend, recalled, "Bobby was almost catatonic for several days. It was like he was glued to Jackie. If he left her for a moment, he became jittery, unable to focus on business."

Chuck Spalding added to the post-assassination memory bank. He accompanied Bobby and Jackie to a private hour of mourning alone with the President's coffin the night before the burial. "They were actually conversing with his corpse, both of them...I mean, car-

Family, family, family...The roots of Jackie's allure went deep, as shown by the fascination of Bobby for his sister-in-law in this retro-photo from the early days of the JFK's marriage. From left to right, Teddy, Jackie, JFK, and RFK.

rying on a long conversation. They later told me that they could actually hear Jack's voice speaking to them. It was eerie. Both of them had become unglued."

In one of the most famous pictures ever taken in Washington, Bobby Kennedy was on hand to comfort Jackie when she arrived at the airport with the coffin containing the body of her assassinated husband in 1963. She was still wearing her blood-stained pink Chanel suit, wanting to show the world what "they" had done to Jack.

In the days and weeks ahead, no brother-in-law in Washington political life ever stood by his sister-in-law with such devotion. Along the way, Bobby fell in love with Jackie.

A photograph of Jackie and Bobby walking hand in hand at the president's funeral was flashed around the world.

"The family that fucks together stays together," said Truman Capote mockingly, referring to the post-assassination affair that began between Bobby and Jackie. The author was kept abreast of the affair by his close friend, Jackie's sister, Lee Radziwill.

Before Jackie in the early months of 1964, there had been Lee herself. As author Christopher Andersen claimed, "A decade before the assassination, Lee's first husband, Michael Canfield, had listened in one room while his wife

"Bobby was a father to Jack's children, and a husband to his widow"

—Senator George Smathers

made love to Jack Kennedy in the next.

According to various biographers, Lee herself may have been among the first to get in on the family fun.

Andersen claimed that while Jackie was in the hospital giving birth to Caroline, JFK seduced Lee while her first husband, Michael Canfield, listened to the sounds from his position in the living room outside.

During the early months of 1964, Lee threw two parties for Bobby Kennedy in London. Guests present later claimed that she showed "more than a passing interest in the Attorney General."_

As Capote recalled, "Lee also wanted to sleep with Bobby, and Bobby, like all those Kennedy men, was not one to pass up the opportunity."

By the winter of '64, Jackie and Bobby had become lovers. As revealed in Secret Service files, he was her almost constant companion, either dining in New York at the Four Seasons, tongue kissing at a private club, *L'Interdit,* in Manhattan, or spending long nights either at the 950 Fifth Avenue apartment of Steven and Jean Kennedy Smith, or at her Fifth Avenue apartment.

Coates Redman, who worked for the Peace Corps in Washington and who was a friend of Ethel's, claimed that "Bobby was always rather bedazzled by Jackie, but RFK never intervened to halt the endless humiliation inflicted on the First Lady by her goatish husband. I'd say I'm ninety-nine percent sure they had an affair. You used to go to dinner parties and talk to people who lived near where Jackie lived on N Street just after Jack died. Bobby was constantly there. All hours. And you could see how they had a mad, morbid attraction to each other because they were the two persons most wounded by the President's death."

In the wake of his brother's death, Bobby began spending nearly every evening at Jackie's Georgetown house at 3017 N. Street, which had become Washington's number one tourist attraction. Apparently, they spent hours talking in front of her fireplace. Eventually, he started spending entire nights with Jackie, leaving Ethel alone with the children.

Jackie's close friend, Nancy Dickerson, said, "After Dallas, no one would have believed that Saint Jackie and Saint Bobby were sleeping together, even though they made it obvious. It would have been considered sacrilege. But Jackie and Bobbie were definitely having an affair."

Nancy overstated her conviction that no one would believe it. At the time, Jackie and Bobby were two of the most carefully watched people on earth. Dozens of people learned of their affair, but the press did not report on it. In those days, the press wasn't even writing about the numerous affairs of JFK, including his involvement with the late Marilyn Monroe.

Peter Lawford, Bobby's brother-in-law, was one of the first to break the news. He told his wife, Patricia Kennedy Lawford, that "With Jackie, Bobby is now filling in for Jack *in all departments."*

Jackie and Bobby began to show up everywhere together.

When Jackie flew to New York, the hotel staff at the Carlyle reported that he shared Jackie's suite. She even went with him when he called on Herbert

Hoover in his suite at the Waldorf Towers. It was so obvious to the ex-president that they were in love that he wisely cautioned them that the nation would be shocked to learn of such a liaison.

"Jackie relied on Bobby for everything, and he adored her," said his close friend Chuck Spalding. He was aware that the Kennedy brothers often passed women on to each other. Bobby had "taken over" the affair with Marilyn after the President had broken off the relationship. Even their father, Joseph Kennedy, passed women on to his sons—or vice versa. Marlene Dietrich was an example of such "an exchange."

Capote claimed, "She and Bobby carried on like teenagers, even in public. I used to sit with them at Le Club in New York. They were holding hands, kissing, and dancing as close as two leaves stuck together in a storm. They were lovebirds in every respect. Bobby was crazy about Jackie. Jackie confided to me that Bobby was thinking of ditching Ethel and marrying her."

Not just Capote, but more and more people kept coming upon Jackie with Bobby "sightings." Bruck Balding, an investment counselor on Long Island, found his two famous guests locked in a passionate embrace when he entered his stables one morning.

On a Pepsi corporate jet, with a host of celebrities, Jackie and Bobby flew to Keene, New Hampshire, for a week of skiing. Ethel was not invited. "Bobby hovered over Jackie," Sammy Davis, Jr. claimed. "It was like he owned her. I had a drink with them in their suite late one night. Jackie was dressed in a beautiful silk robe, but Bobby was walking around in his underwear."

The affair continued after Jackie moved to New York into a luxurious apartment on Fifth Avenue. RFK's driver, "Jim," reported that he often dropped his boss off at the apartment at around ten o'clock every evening, picking him up the following morning.

The lovers flew to Palm Beach and the Kennedy compound for a holiday. Socialite Mary Harrington reported that from her third-floor window she could look out onto the Kennedy property. "One morning, I saw Jackie sunbathing on the grass," she said. "She had on a black bikini bottom, but no top. Bobby emerged from the house in white swim trunks and knelt down beside her. He kissed her passionately and fondled her breast with one hand. With the other, he felt between her legs outside her bikini. Later, with a towel thrown around her bare breasts, Jackie disappeared inside the house with Bobby."

Author Gore Vidal, who was distantly related to Jackie, saw the affair in a rather cynical light. "I suspect that the one person Jackie ever loved, if indeed she was capable of such an emotion, was Bobby Kennedy. As Lee *[a reference to her sister, Lee Radziwill]* had gone to bed with Jack, symmetry required her to do so with Bobby."

"Bobby just didn't seem to realize that screwing Jack's widow wasn't going to bring his brother back," said Senator George Smathers. "There's no way that Bobby was going to divorce Ethel."

Russell Gilpatric, a future lover of Jackie's said, "Bobby became the central core of Jackie's life after Jack was killed. She had no brother to turn to.

Bobby had her back and acted *in loco parentis,* including John-John and Caroline in his own family gatherings. Bobby attempted to fill in as father to Jackie's now fatherless offspring. In short order, he was also performing another of Jack's roles."

In the wake of the assassination, Bobby became a surrogate father for John Jr. and Caroline. He played a significant role in their education and, as John Jr. grew older, talked to both children about serious issues such as civil rights.

Biographer Kitty Kelley wrote, "Bobby Kennedy spent more time with his sister-in-law and her children than his own, and Jackie leaned on him for everything. She even considered at one point asking him to adopt Caroline and John-John, feeling she could not raise them by herself. He gave as much as he could, offering her all his love, support, and protection."

Taki Theodoracopulos, the heir to a Greek shipping fortune, became a right-wing journalist and columnist. Back when he called himself "a young, good-for-nothing playboy and professional athlete," he lived with Peter Lawford for a while at the Sherry-Netherland Hotel in New York, but moved out, charging that Kennedy's former brother-in-law was a drunk and a bully.

The exclusive bar at the hotel soon became a rendezvous for cozy *tête-à-têtes* between Jackie and Bobby. Since Taki was often in the bar, he later reported on their romantic liaisons. Lawford had told him that Jackie was sleeping with Bobby. "The press knows about Jack's many affairs when he was in the White House, and they didn't write about them, but Bobby's got them fooled with his altar boy act. He's no more an altar boy than I am."

As Lee's biographer, Diana DuBois, wrote: "Taki's sightings of Jackie and Bobby's *tête-à-têtes* were hardly isolated observations. In the months after Dallas, there many such incidents of hand holding in public and kissing. But so unwilling was the public—and the press—to cock an ear to anything that would diminish the Camelot myth that no one ever wondered if Guinevere and Lancelot were sleeping together now that Arthur was dead."

"Everybody on the inside knew of Bobby's affair with Jackie." said FDR Jr. "They carried on like a pair of lovesick teenagers. People used to see them at Le Club, their torsos stuck together as they danced the night away. I suspect Bobby would like to have dumped Ethel and married Jackie, but there was no way in hell that was going to happen. They were staunch Catholics."

Jackie sent a letter to C. Douglas Dillon, Secretary of the Treasury, telling him that she did not need Secret Service protection during the graveyard shift *[i.e., between 11pm and 7am].* "It is pointless for them to stand in the cold all night outside my apartment building on Fifth Avenue."

Privately, Pierre Salinger, JFK's former Press Secretary, suggested that was because Bobby could come and go during those hours without being identified on the Secret Service logbook.

Perhaps the most romantic moment for Jackie came on Easter weekend in 1964. Ethel took Caroline and John Jr. with her own children on a ski trip to Sun Valley in Idaho. Along with Lee and Stanislas Radziwill, Bobby and Jackie went to Antigua in the Caribbean for a vacation in the sun. With them on the trip was Chuck Spalding.

The Kennedy party were house guests of Paul and Bunny Mellon at the very exclusive Mill Reef Estate, overlooking Half Moon Bay. Jackie liked Antigua so much that Bunny even offered to build her a vacation home on the island.

[Rachel Mellon, the heiress to the Listerine fortune and a fabled horticulturalist, fine arts collector, and designer of the White House Rose Garden, was often the "beard" concealing Jackie's affairs.

Ted Sorensen claimed that Bunny, as she was nicknamed, was the only friend who knew about all of Jackie's affairs, and concealed them from the press.

For hideaways, Jackie often used Bunny's homes in Manhattan, Washington, D.C., her apartment in Paris, or her various vacation retreats on Cape Cod, Antigua, or Nantucket, even her estate at Oak Spring, Virginia, near Upperville, where she entertained Queen Elizabeth and Prince Philip. Jackie favored this retreat for secret trysts with her lovers because Bunny and her husband, Paul Mellon, raised horses here.

As journalist Robert D. McFadden wrote of Bunny Mellon after her death in 2014 at the age of 103, "Like many other fabulously wealthy people, Ms. Mellon lived largely out of the public eye, shielded by lawyers and public relations retainers, unlisted addresses and phone numbers, and retinues to shop and buy tickets."

According to friends, Jackie used Bunny's "barricade of gates against the public" to conceal certain aspects of her private life.

McFadden claimed that Bunny was "fresh-faced, slender, ebullient, radiating confidence, and a dazzling figure in a swirling cotillion or at the taffrail of a steamer.

Jackie trusted her taste explicitly and valued her discretion. "Unlike the rest of us," said Sorensen, "Jackie knew that Bunny wouldn't be writing a tell-all."]

Spalding later said, "Jackie and Bobby were like two school kids in love. They were very close, holding hands, taking long walks on the beach under a moonlit sky. They were always whispering secrets to each other. Bobby and Jackie had separate rooms, but he would slip into her room at night, leaving early in the morning

"Why can't Jack be more discreet like **Bobby**?" **Jackie** had asked, according to William Walton, in 1962 when her husband was to some degree "flinging his affairs in my face." In contrast, Bobby conducted his affairs "like a secret agent operating undercover."

As their affair evolved, Ethel became the neglected wife of Hickory Hill.

before the household rose."

On their own, Bobby and Jackie also visited Sun Valley, and also journeyed to Aspen, Colorado. They went on weekend trips to Vermont. One skier remembered them laughing and hugging each other as they tumbled into a snowbank.

Later that night, in an *après* ski lounge, when there were just a handful of guests, most of whom were drunk, Bobby lay with his head in Jackie's lap, as she combed his bangs with her fingers.

In the summer of 1966, Kenneth McKnight, a former administrator of the Commerce Department during JFK's presidency, recalled keeping an appointment with RFK (then a New York Senator) at his office in Manhattan.

It was scheduled for 8pm, when the staff had gone. He walked down the corridor, where the door to RFK's office was half open.

He heard voices inside and looked in. "Bobby was on the sofa and Jackie was on his lap, planting little kisses on his face and neck. She had her arms wrapped around his neck. Of course, when they saw me, it became all business. I knew Jackie. She introduced me to Bobby. I wanted a job with him. She quickly left."

Sometimes, Jackie complained to William Walton and others that Bobby was too dependent on her, that he was draining her of her strength. "Everyone thinks he's taking care of me, but in essence, I'm looking after him. He became a basket case after Jack was shot. I'm giving him a reason to go on living."

In Manhattan, Bobby and Jackie were often spotted at such hotels as the Algonquin. On a summer day, they often appeared casually, she wearing a blouse and slacks, he in a polo shirt and khaki trousers.

On some occasions, she could be seen with her head on his shoulder, even kissing his neck, as he sipped a vodka and tonic.

Sometimes, in attempts to be discreet, they were seen entering Jean Kennedy Smith's apartment when she and her family were out of town. One doorman remembered them entering at 2am, with Bobby departing the next morning at 10:30AM.

Capote later claimed he received almost daily updates on the Bobby/Jackie romance. He taped a series of interviews in 1976 for film producer Lester Perksy. He called the Bobby/Jackie liaison "the most normal relationship either one ever had. There was nothing morbid about it. It was the coming together of a man and a woman as a result of bereavement and her mental suffering at the hands of her late, lecherous husband. In retrospect, it seems hard to believe that it happened, but it did."

British journalist Peter Evans claimed in his book, *Nemesis*, that both Eunice Shriver and Ethel were aware of Bobby's affair with what Ethel called "the widder."

"Ethel may have been naïve, but she wasn't that naïve," Evans maintained. "In fact, Ethel had reached the same conclusions as Capote about her marriage. Thanks to their children, her husband's Catholicism, and his concern with the Kennedy legacy, she realized that their marriage was largely intact."

Allegedly, Jackie reported the affair to her suitor, Aristotle Onassis. He later told his cohort, Johnny Meyer, "By going public with the details of the senator's affair, I could bury the sucker. But I'd lose Jackie in the process. But can't you just see those headlines?"

Edward Klein, author of *Just Jackie*, said, "There were many who thought that Jackie secretly wanted to replace Jack with Bobby. And it was true that if Bobby could have been divided in two, Jackie might have considered marrying the half that was devoted to her."

When news of Bobby and Jackie first became public, Kennedy defenders wanted to sweep the scandal under the carpet or bury it forever in some deep closet. But FBI and Secret Service reports, released in 2007, more or less confirmed the affair. The Bobby/Jackie liaison was reportedly active between the years 1964 and 1968.

Amazingly, for years RFK had previously enjoyed a reputation somewhat akin to that of a choirboy. But from all reports, Bobby was as much of a sex addict as his brothers, only he was much more discreet and in general he preferred that his women be smarter than Jack or Teddy did. He once told aide David Powers, "Unlike Jack and Teddy, I don't get off on bimbos."

When Bobby began his affair with Jackie, he had previously enjoyed the beds of everyone from singer Rosemary Clooney to Princess Grace Kelly. He'd also seduced two of the same blonde bombshells that his brother had, notably Marilyn Monroe and Jayne Mansfield.

Author C. David Heymann alleged that Jackie's affair with Onassis drove Bobby into the arms of actress Candice Bergen, whom he met in 1965 when she was nineteen. Both Shirley MacLaine and Catherine Deneuve recalled seeing Candice and Bobby together at a party in Paris. Their affair even made the society pages of *Paris-Presse*. Capote alleged that Ethel found out about her husband's sexual tryst with Candice. "They weren't being furtive, they were being rather obvious."

With Ethel and the children left behind at Hickory Hill, RFK's Virginia estate, Jackie and Bobby intensified their love affair during the latter part of 1964. "Bobby and his brother's widow did little to hide their affection for each other," wrote biographer Christopher Andersen. "They continued embracing, kissing, and holding hands."

Classified Secret Service files revealed that the romantic pair were in each other's company several times a week.

Clare Boothe Luce, a long-time friend of Joe Kennedy, Sr., later exclaimed, "Well, of course, everybody knew Jackie and Bobby were involved, if that's the right word for it. At least everyone who knew them was aware of what was going on between them."

Spalding was one of the most intimate members of Bobby's entourage, and a compelling witness to the Jackie/Bobby affair. "Bobby's love for Jackie helped restore her emotional health after that horrible assassination. I really believe that Bobby was happier from 1965 until early 1968 than he ever was in his life. He still loved Ethel and his kids, but he really wanted to marry Jackie, but didn't dare. After all, he planned to run for president. I often went on vacations with Jackie and Bobby. I didn't stand over their bed watching them make love, but I know they often went into a single bedroom at around eleven o'clock at night and didn't emerge until noon of the next day."

In the months ahead, communal sightings of Bobby and Jackie became frequent. Dozens of persons close to both of them reported evidence of their affair. These included socialite Audrey Zauderer (later Audrey de Rosario) who lived at ultra-exclusive Round Hill, a villa compound and resort in Montego Bay, Jamaica. She claimed they were having an affair—"absolutely!"

The family's nanny, Maud Shaw, claimed that Jackie and Bobby had separate bedrooms, but they "kept dodging in and out of each other's boudoir, making no secret of their dalliance."

The German screenwriter, Bernard Hayworth, also on vacation at Round Hill, reported seeing Jackie and Bobby swimming and sunbathing at a secluded cove. "He began massaging her back and kissing her neck," Hayworth claimed. To grant them their privacy, Hayworth turned and left before the action heated up.

Columnist Victor Lasky wrote: *"If the Kennedy dynasty is restored, it will be Ethel Kennedy (with whom she has little affinity) and not Jackie who will occupy the center of the stage. There cannot be two First Ladies in the White House. Yet the fact that she is doomed to be discarded by her brother-in-law should he become president has not deterred Jackie from doing all she can to further Bobby's political fortunes. And because they frequently holidayed together, often without Ethel, there have been rumors that something untoward was going on."*

The New York Times bestselling author, C. David Heymann, has almost made a career out of investigating the private lives of the Kennedys, publishing intimate biographies of Jackie, RFK, and even John F. Kennedy, Jr. and Caroline.

More than any other investigative reporter, he introduced the secret love affair between Jackie and Bobby to the world, even though it was an open secret in Washington in 1964.

The book, *Bobby and Jackie*, is loaded with revelations about their affair, and of Jackie's attempts to learn as much as possible about what Bobby had been up to before their affair was launched.

Jackie even found out about the sex act between Bobby and Marilyn Monroe that had been secretly videotaped in the blonde bombshell's bedroom.

J. Edgar Hoover had called Clark Clifford, former Counsel to the President during JFK's administration, to his office to show him the film and discuss possible fallout from it. No one knew how many copies had been printed.

At a dinner party in New York hosted by *Vogue* editor Diana Vreeland, Jackie confronted Clifford for more details, but he denied any knowledge of the explosive film.

***

After Bobby and Jackie separated as a means of saving his political career, there were other reports that the Kennedy family's youngest brother, Teddy Kennedy, also pursued Jackie, even though she was married at the time to Aristotle Onassis.

"It was no secret that Teddy also had the hots for Jackie," Capote told Bill and Barbara (Babe) Paley at one of their dinner parties at Round Hill, Jamaica. The story was just too fascinating for the guests to keep to themselves. By the time they returned to the States, Washington and New York society was abuzz with the hushed-up whispers.

Whether it was true or not, Capote amplified his story, claiming that on one drunken night at his apartment, Jackie even rated the sexual performances of the three brothers. On her scale of 1 to 10, Bobby got a 9, Jack a 6, and Teddy a 3.

"With Teddy," Jackie allegedly confided, "it was like going to bed with a college freshman. Bobby was the one with the power and the drive. He seduced a woman like he was going after Jimmy Hoffa."

When Capote asked her to describe Jack's performance, she refused. "Just go to any party in New York, Washington, or Hollywood and ask around. You'll get your answer."

When RFK decided to run for President in 1968, he told Jackie he had to end their love affair "because too many eyes would be watching." She understood that the intensity of their love could not continue under these new circumstances. It had been dangerous enough before. "Our love will endure," she told him.

He told her that if he did not win the presidency, "I will come back to you. In the meantime don't run off with Onassis." That was a warning she would not heed.

Other friends claim that it was actually Jackie who broke off their sexual involvement, although their close friendship would continue. Knowing how much he wanted to be President, Jackie told him it would be best for them not to see each other for a while as a means of protecting his political future. She urged him to return to Ethel and his brood.

Peter Lawford claimed that Bobby came to him after the rejection. "He took it really bad. He cried all night and into the next day. I didn't know he was capable of such tears, because he could be pretty stoic."

The actor did not condemn the affair, and later said, "After Jack died, Jackie threatened suicide on more

Here, **Ethel and Bobby Kennedy** appear in public together after Bobby wins the Indiana Primary in 1968.

than one occasion, although she couldn't stand the thought of leaving her children alone in the world. But she came close to killing herself. Her love affair with Bobby may have saved her life."

***

Throughout Bobby's race to the White House, Jackie was seized with nightmares that he might be assassinated. On that dreadful pre-dawn in June of 1968, she learned that lighting had indeed struck twice.

At 3:45AM, she received an urgent call from London, where it was already morning. The news of Bobby's assassination was already being broadcast.

"Jackie!" Lee Radziwill said, urgently. "Bobby's been shot. It just happened."

There was a long silence on the phone, and then a blood-curdling scream. "No, it can't have happened!" Jackie shouted into her receiver. "The only two men I've ever loved. Shot!"

Then she slammed down the phone.

Within minutes, Chuck Spalding was on the phone with an eyewitness account of the slaying of RFK within the kitchens at the Ambassador Hotel.

She demanded that she be flown to Los Angeles at once. En route, she kept repeating, "It can't have happened. It can't have happened."

Spalding met her at the Los Angeles airport. Jackie demanded, "Give it to me straight. No bullshit."

"He's dying," he told her.

She let out a scream like a trapped animal.

In the hospital room, Ethel sat by her husband's side, whispering her love for him into his ear. Getting up when Jackie entered, she embraced her. "I'm so glad you're here." Then she very graciously surrendered the room so that Jackie could spend some time alone with her dying husband.

At 12:45AM on a Thursday morning on June 6, 1968, RFK's doctors approached Jackie and Ethel to tell the widows the grim facts. "There is no brain activity," Dr. Henry Cuneo said. "He's only being kept alive by artificial means. There is no chance ever of recovery."

Ethel ran screaming down the corridor. "I won't do it! I won't kill Bobby!"

With nerves of steel, Jackie confronted the doctor. Very calmly she told Dr. Cuneo, "I am speaking for the family. We want you to disconnect the respirator. I'll sign the consent form."

After the respirator was disconnected, she came into the room. She stood there as RFK breathed on his own for five minutes. Then he stopped. He was dead. It was 1:44AM. Within minutes, bulletins went out around the world.

Robert Francis Kennedy was dead at forty-two years of age.

***

Most of the world, except for his enemies, went into mourning.

At the White House, President Lyndon Johnson was awakened with the news. "I couldn't stand the shit," he said. "But send Air Force One to Los Angeles to bring the body back to New York."

En route East, Teddy sat alone with the casket. Ethel and Jackie were seated next to each other up front, but really had nothing to say.

Once in New York, Jackie placed a call to her trusted friend, Roswell Gilpatric, the Under Secretary of Defense during JFK's administration, "Oh, dear God, please tell me. This is just a bad dream. The dawn will come. I will wake up. Please, please tell me that. When will my nightmare end?"

The burden of yet another assassination—this time of Bobby—became almost too much for Jackie. After the funeral on June 8, 1968, at St. Patrick's Cathedral in New York, Lady Bird Johnson encountered Jackie. "I found myself in front of her and called her name, putting out my hand. She looked at me as if from a great distance, as though I were an apparition. I murmured some words of sorrow and walked on. . . ."

After that funeral, Jackie's anger turned to bitterness. As Heymann wrote, "If she had felt any doubt or obligation to consider the impact of her actions on the political prospects of the remaining Kennedys, they were resolved by the shots that ended Bobby's life. Once again it did not matter who had pulled the trigger, or for what twisted reason."

Chapter Fifteen

The Kennedy Tapes

Jackie's Recorded Dialogues with Arthur Schlesinger, Jr.

Jackie's True Feelings for Friends and "Frenemies"

Her Candid Quotes were Heavily Censored, but Many Leaked Out Anyway

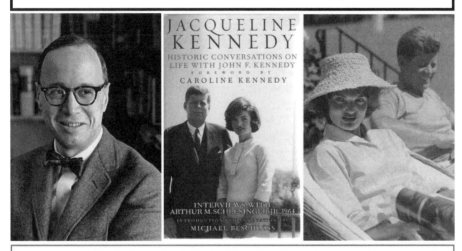

In 1963, **Arthur Schlesinger, Jr.**, *(left)* asked President Kennedy to dictate his own reminiscences for a possible memoir. Although he dictated an occasional memo, and taped hundreds of hours of his White House meetings and phone calls, there were never any introspective "recorded memoirs of my life."

In contrast, in 1964, after her husband's death, Jackie agreed to record seven extended conversations with Schlesinger, ranging from a discussion of JFK's back problems to the quirks of Lyndon Johnson as a running mate. In 2013, an edited version of these conversations *(center photo)* were released to the public.

In the candid snapshot from 1959 *(right photo)*, a straw-hatted **Jackie**, with **Jack** beside her, is seen catching up on her reading.

"I was always a liability to Jack until we got to the White House, and then he came to view me as an asset, telling me I was the most compelling

spouse Washington had ever seen. Before that, I was viewed as a snob from Newport, who had bouffant hair and wore French clothes and hated politics. But he never insisted I change my image and get a little frizzy permanent and be like Pat Nixon."

—Jacqueline Kennedy

JACQUELINE KENNEDY

HISTORIC CONVERSATIONS ON LIFE WITH JOHN F. KENNEDY

FOREWORD BY CAROLINE KENNEDY

INTERVIEWS WITH ARTHUR M. SCHLESINGER, JR., 1964

In September of 2011, Caroline Kennedy released—as audio recordings on CD, accompanied with their transcripts in book form—the interviews her mother gave to the Kennedy family's court historian Arthur Schlesinger, Jr. These historic conversations were recorded early in 1964 in the immediate aftermath of the assassination of John F. Kennedy.

In very candid, sometimes shocking revelations, she shared her memories about "The Reign of Camelot." Although these tapes had been suppressed for forty-seven years, with the Jackie's reported stipulation that they should remain under wraps until 2039, Caroline decided to "prematurely" release them on the 50th anniversary of the assassination of her father.

In the tapes, Jackie does not deliver an overview, or insights about, the assassination. In lieu of that, she was simultaneously involved at the time in a series of detailed conversations with William Manchester, with the understanding that he would be writing a book which would later be entitled *The Death of a President*.

[Whereas the Manchester tapes, whose history is explored in a later chapter of this book, were specifically envisioned as dark, highly emotional source material pertinent to the assassination of JFK, the Schlesinger tapes were envisioned as Jackie's statement about her family's brief reign over Camelot, information she considered pertinent as documentation of Jack's life and accomplishments, with the understanding that Jack himself would never be able to write his memoirs.

And whereas Jackie later regretted that she had talked so candidly to Manchester, and whereas she later sued him to prevent him from publishing secrets she had revealed to him earlier, she had no equivalent discord with the more pliable, more cooperative, Schlesinger, whose interviews, presumably, did not evoke the pain and latter-day trauma of her dialogues with Manchester.

Publishers offered Jackie millions of dollars as an advance, but she refused to write an autobiography or memoir of her own. On the morning after her

"Lady Bird is a hound dog... De Gaulle is an egomaniac... and Martin Luther King is a terrible man"

—Jacqueline Kennedy

death, *The New York Times* reported, "Her silence about her past, especially about the Kennedy years and her marriage to the President, was always something of a mystery."

Beginning on March 2, 1964, the date of Jacqueline's first recorded conversation with Schlesinger, Jackie became the first former First Lady to submit to hours of intensive recorded questioning about her public and private life.

[That Caroline released the Schlesinger tapes before the scheduled time is surprising, because she had previously been perceived as a protective tigress ferociously guarding the gates to Camelot.

In April of 2011, The History Channel was on the verge of broadcasting a TV miniseries about Caroline's parents, and she used her influence to get the $30 million show removed, or at least downgraded, from the national spotlight. Eventually, with a lot of conjecture in the press about who had influenced what, the miniseries was broadcast on another channel (Reelz). Katie Holmes, former wife of Tom Cruise, portrayed Jacqueline, and Greg Kinnear was cast as JFK. Reportedly, Caroline was horrified at the impersonations.

Even before it was cast, the series faced a barrage of attacks. Ted Sorensen, former speech writer for JFK, calling it "character assassination." The series was widely attacked for alleged historical inaccuracies and for presenting an unflattering view of the titular family.

Reviewers in the United States gave the series a mixed reaction, Hank Steuver of the Washington Post *finding it, "All ends up being as harmless as a game of Kennedy paper dolls." Mark Perigard of the* Boston Herald *found it "an absorbing addictive drama, with some authentic performances, but not history."*

Alessandra Stanley of The New York Times *wrote, "There is something wonderfully Kennedyesque about a backroom campaign to discredit a series that claims the Kennedy White House had more than its share of backroom shenanigans." She praised Tom Wilkinson, cast as Joseph P. Kennedy, Sr., portraying his as a "ruthless, tyrannical striver who grasps for power, promoting his sons to establish his rule and cement his legacy."]*

Since Caroline, based on the legal terms associated with the original recordings, was in the power seat, she instructed Schlesinger, a Pulitzer Prize-winning historian, to edit out certain revelations that were "too hot or too personal." But in 2011, since so many editors and technicians had been exposed to the unedited tapes prior to their release, a more complete version of what was on some of those recordings leaked out. Many provide fascinating insights from a First Lady the press had defined as "The most mysterious, fascinating, and feline woman in American political history."

Maureen Dowd, writing in *The New York Times,* said, "Jackie maintains her reputation as JFK's best image wizard, a novelistic observer of history, and the most deliciously original, glamorous, and compelling political spouse we'll ever see."

Another quote emerged, one that had been expunged from the official, Caroline-sanctioned version, something that Jackie revealed about the morning prior to her husband's assassination. Caroline objected to its inclusion in her officially sanctioned version, claiming, "It makes my mother look flighty."

Apparently, Jackie in Fort Worth, Texas, had told JFK about a nightmare she'd experienced the night before their transit to nearby Dallas:

"We were riding in an open-topped car, and I was talking to you. It began to pour, and I realized the rain was really blood. It would drown us if we didn't flee the limousine."

Reportedly, he tried to reassure her. "Don't worry about it. It'll be okay, sweetheart. It'll be fine. You'll see."

At some points during her dialogues with Schlesinger, Jackie was said to have asked him to turn off the recording device whenever he veered too dangerously close into her own affairs. "In the years to come, biographers will no doubt write hundreds of books about me, and I'll leave it up to them to expose my indiscretions. I admit I've had a few, and no doubt will again, because I am a healthy woman with desires. But I will never be what my former friend, Gore Vidal, called profligate."

She later became incensed when she heard rumors that at parties, Vidal was mimicking Truman Capote, another former friend. "Vidal has this whole routine, so I am told, where he does a ten-minute impression of Capote, claiming that I was screwing my big Negro chauffeur while John-John and Caroline were whimpering in the back seat."

Jackie also refused to discuss how she handled her profligate husband's many reported affairs, but it was inevitable that she would eventually be asked about JFK's affair with Marilyn Monroe.

"I knew all about it," she revealed to Schlesinger. "I knew about the affairs with other actresses as well—Marlene Dietrich, Joan Crawford, Gene Tierney, Hedy Lamarr, Lana Turner, Sonja Henie, that ice skater. "Jack knew many, many women, and he broke my heart with his philandering, but sometimes I got even with him."

One of her genuinely startling confessions was that, "I had an arrangement with my husband. I agreed to turn a blind eye if he would be discreet and not flaunt his affairs. On occasion, when he violated our agreement, I pursued my own kind of revenge. I think bitter women call it 'the revenge fuck.'"

Of course, those revelations didn't make it into the final version that was eventually sanctioned and endorsed by Caroline. Nor did Jackie's comments about Marilyn Monroe's notorious rendition at New York City's Madison Square Garden of "Happy Birthday, Mr. President," on the occasion of his birthday in 1962.

"I suspected Marilyn would do something outrageous for the occasion," Jackie said. "That's why I fled to Virginia. I didn't want to be humiliated. Later, I heard that she'd hired my hairdresser, Kenneth Battelle, to style her coiffure somewhat like mine, right down to the bouffant twist with a flip to the left. Many reporters later commented on how similar our 'little girl' voices were."

"I thought Marilyn was doing a send-up to me," she said. "It was as if she were showing millions of Americans on television that she was more desirable than I was. Up to then, most Americans had seen me on television during my televised tour of the White House, where I was respectably clad in a simple linen sheath. Marilyn seemed to be flaunting her sexuality—not only to Jack, but to the world, inviting unfavorable comparisons."

Instead of indiscretions, those who listened to the "officially sanctioned" tapes heard only a flattering portrait of JFK. In a breathy voice, Jackie praised him for his "loyalty, sensitivity, and courage," traits consistent with the Camelot vision she was steering and myth-making for future generations.

She did not reveal that JFK was on drugs and had Addison's disease. However, she did address issues associated with his back pain, including what she claimed was unnecessary surgery performed on him in 1954 that had threatened his life.

She also claimed that her political opinions were identical to those of her husband, a claim that led columnist Dowd to define the recordings as "Memoirs of a Geisha." Historian Michael Beschloss, who wrote an introduction to Caroline's edited compilation of Jackie's recorded conversations, warned that that particular claim by the former First Lady should be taken "with a warehouse of salt."

"I could never conceive of voting for a politician of whom my husband did not approve," Jackie said in the tapes. "I just knew his opinions were going to be the best."

Dowd didn't agree. "The young Jacqueline Kennedy underestimated herself in those dark days of long ago. She had plenty of opinions of her own, tart and tantalizing."

Jackie's interviews were recorded at the dawn of the feminist movement in America. She had not yet transformed herself into a woman who later would give an interview to *Ms.* magazine, claiming that women cannot live through men. When she first arrived at the White House, she admitted, "My relationship with Jack is rather terribly Victorian or Asiatic, perhaps best represented by a Japanese wife."

At the time, according to Dowd, "Jackie considered her main job to be distracting and soothing her husband and making sure the children were in a good mood when the leader of the Free World got home. She did not see herself as an Eleanor Roosevelt, waiting to pester FDR about some pressing political matter."

After listening to the tapes, historian Doris Kearns Goodwin, wife of historian Richard Goodwin, said, that the tapes "certainly don't resemble the Jackie that we knew later on, not the woman who married Onassis, not the woman who became an editor filled with strong opinions. By that time, she had become a different woman."

In the Schlesinger tapes, Jackie does reveal some highly personal details about life in the White House. "The night Jack took the oath, I was recovering from a caesarean section and only made it to the inaugural balls when the White House doctor, Janet Travell, gave me Dexedrine."

She also discussed, briefly, the Cuban missile crisis. "Jack did consider the fear of a possible assassination after his victory over the Russians. He told me,

'If anyone's going to shoot me, this would be the day they should do it.'"

During the peak of the crisis, when she was told that there was a possibility that Soviet nuclear missiles were imminently capable of hitting every major city along America's eastern seaboard, including New York and Washington, she refused to take her children and herself to a relatively safe area, perhaps underground in Colorado. As she reported saying to JFK, "I just want to be with you, and I want to die with you—and the children do too—than live without you."

Puncturing Egos

Here's What the Young Widow Said, on Tape, to Schlesinger, about Some of Her Contemporaries

Martin Luther King, Jr.: "Jack told me of a tape that the FBI had of King when he was in Washington for the Freedom March. He said this to me with no bitterness or anything, how King was calling up all these girls and arranging an orgy at his hotel. I told Jack (that) King was such a phony then. Much later, Bobby revealed to me that some of King's orgies were on tape. It was very painful to learn that he was on tape making fun of Jack's funeral."

Lyndon B. Johnson: "Jack once said to me, 'Oh, God, can you imagine what would happen to this country if Lyndon were president?' I first got along with Lyndon but later turned against him. He'd call me and ask, 'How's my little girl?' I wasn't his girl, little or otherwise. He was a man with an enormous Texas ego. He certainly had his gaucheries, and Bobby hated him. Lady Bird had to put up with a lot."

"Oh well, I think everyone was disappointed because of all the people Jack could have chosen as a running mate, we liked Lyndon the least."

Edward (Teddy) Kennedy: "There was marked difference in style between Jack and his younger brother, Teddy. Jack never—he never said, 'Hi, fella,' or put his fat palm under your armpit, or, you know, any of that sort of business. It was embarrassing to Jack. As is known to half the world, Teddy became one of my 'newspaper romances,' and I'll say no more about that. Arthur, edit out that last line."

Nikita Khrushchev: "It's going to be a cold winter," Jack told me after meeting with Nikita Khrushchev in Vienna. The Soviet dictator was a naked, brutal, and ruthless power who thought he could do what he wanted with Jack. He could be jolly, but underneath, he was very tough."

[In his own memoirs, Khrushchev wrote of Jackie: "Obviously, she was quick of tongue, or, as the Ukrainians say, she has a sharp tongue in her head. Don't mix it up with her: She'll cut you down to size."]

Adlai Stevenson: "I always thought women who were scared of sex loved Adlai. During the campaign, Jack was given a bushel of data about Adlai's homosexuality, including two arrests that J. Edgar Hoover had information about. But Jack refused to let his staff smear Adlai. He did tell me that he thought Adlai had a real 'disease' in not being able to make up his mind." *[Jackie to Schlesinger: "Cut out the gay references."]*

Lady Bird Johnson: "Any time Lyndon would talk, Lady Bird would get out a little notebook—I've never seen a husband and wife so—she was sort of like a trained hunting dog. He'd say something to me as innocent as, 'Does your sister live in London?' Lady Bird would the write down Lee's name and 'London.'"

Indira Gandhi: "In 1961, Jack and I spent a weekend with Prime Minister Nehru and his daughter, Indira, at Hammersmith Farm, the Auchincloss residence at Newport. As a joke, Jack took Nehru on a tour of the great marble mansions of the robber barons, claiming, 'I want you to see how the average American lives.' The joke bombed. Indira was a real prune—bitter, kind of pushy, a horrible woman. I just don't like her a bit. It always looks like she's sucking a lemon."

John Connally: "As you know, the Governor of Texas, John Connally, rode *[in the limousine]* with Jack and me on that fateful day in Dallas. I truly detest him. He had spread the word that Jack had Addison's disease. His last words to Jack were to tell him about a poll in Texas that had him running way ahead of Jack on the ticket. Jack told him, 'That doesn't surprise me.'"

Dwight D. Eisenhower: "The columnist, Joe Alsop, told us that Nixon 'would be the worst president of the United States with the possible exception of Eisenhower.'"

Charles De Gaulle: "He was an egomaniac. In the beginning, he'd been my hero, but he really sunk down. He poisoned *[France's]* relations with Jack and the United States. I named my French poodle after him. Jack used me as a go-between in his difficult talks with De Gaulle. Hubert de Givenchy designed the gown I wore at the state supper at Versailles. Jack told me at one point De Gaulle whispered in his ear, 'Your wife knows more about French history than most French women.' At least I appreciated that."

Franklin D. Roosevelt: "Charlatan is an unfair word. He was a bit of a *poseur*. Jack was cool toward him because of Joe's painful break with FDR in 1941 over intervention in Europe. Jack also resented Eleanor's hostility toward him at the 1960 Democratic convention. To the best of my knowledge, Eleanor was our first lesbian First Lady, although there could have been others. On second thought, strike that last line."

Claire Boothe Luce: "She was so macho she could be a lesbian. In 1955, when she was U.S. ambassador to Italy, she entertained Jack and me at a party for the French Premier, Georges Bidault. I was the interpreter for Jack and him. Clare stood so close when she talked to me, I thought she was coming on to me. The next year, when Joe [Joseph P. Kennedy, Sr.] entertained her at his villa on the French Riviera, she did come on to me in our private cabana. On second thought, strike the last two lines, but leave in my suspicion that she was a lesbian."

Chapter Sixteen

Jackie Vs.
William Manchester
"The Battle of the Book"

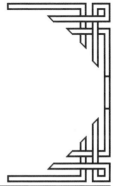

& Jackie's Feud with Ron Gallela
"The Most Co-Dependent Celebrity/Paparazzo Relationship in History"

In the immediate aftermath of JFK's death, his widow, **Jackie Kennedy**, asked **William Manchester** *(left photo)* to write the authorized account of the assassination. Two years later, the ordeal nearly destroyed him, both emotionally and financially. His book was finally published in 1967 and became a bestseller, but only after a bitter year of relentless, headline-generating controversy over the manuscript. It pitted the struggling writer against two of the most powerful and charismatic personalities in America, Bobby Kennedy and Jackie.

Jackie and Bobby may have thought they had won their battle with Manchester, but in the end, it was a personal and public relations nightmare for both of them.

"I thought Manchester's book would be bound in black and put away on dark library shelves."

—Jacqueline Kennedy

Pierre Salinger, JFK's former Press Secretary, called Jackie with the news: "I just heard that Bennett Cerf, at Random House, has contracted for that Jim Bishop guy to write a book about Jack's assassination."

Jackie took the news with a certain sense of horror. "That hack?" she said.

Previously, she had had a feud with Bishop when JFK had practically given him the run of the White House during research for his book, *A Day in the Life of President Kennedy.*

When Bishop was "wandering at leisure," she discovered him going through her wardrobe closet, counting the number of her dresses and gowns, and checking the labels. Later, she discovered Bishop in Caroline's bathroom, watching as her daughter was bathed by her nanny.

"I'm sorry you gave him the run of the White House," Jackie told her husband. "He was a god damn nuisance."

Bishop's previous titles had included *The Day Lincoln Was Shot; The Day Christ Died;* and *The Day Christ Was Born.*

His latest work, *A Day in the Life of President Kennedy,* was in galley form when it was sent to the President in November of 1963. In a touch of irony, JFK took the manuscript with him to read on that fatal trip to Texas. He had not even read the first chapter on the day he was shot.

Midway through his Presidency, **JFK** invited **Jackie** to go sailing on a Coast Guard yawl with him. She was photographed reading a copy of William Manchester's reverential biography of her husband, *Portrait of a President*, published in 1962.

It was Manchester's flattering "first portrait" that prompted her to commission him to write the officially authorized overview of the assassination in Dallas. According to the keepers of Camelot, that was one of her worst mistakes.

In the wake of the assassination, Jackie was not pleased with Bishop's view of her late husband's days in the White House. Nor was she pleased with what he wrote about her.

She was reported to be "mortified" to hear that Bishop would be the first to write about JFK's assassination. For Random House, Bishop had entitled his

"God damn it, you can't tell America I'm a chain-smoker"

—Jackie to Manchester

latest book, *The Day Kennedy Was Shot*. Jackie found the title objectionable and decided to call Cerf at Random House.

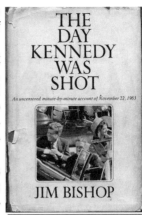

In her call to Random House, Jackie was put through to Cerf immediately. She pressed her case, urging him not to publish Bishop's book. He explained to her that he had already signed the contract. He also told her, "If I turn down the book, every major publisher in New York will want it. It's got 'best-seller' written all over it."

Finally, in desperation, Jackie called Bishop at his home in Florida. She informed him that she was going to authorize her own writer to craft a book on the assassination, and she urged him to bow out.

"There can't be two books on the assassination," she told him.

"Are you kidding?" he answered. "There will probably be more books on this assassination than on the Lincoln shooting."

[Bishop was right. To date, there have been at least 2,000 books published on JFK's assassination, perhaps more.]

"Jim Bishop was nothing but a damn hack," Jackie told William Manchester. "But Jack gave him the run of the White House. When I caught him going through my lingerie drawers, I thought he was a sexual pervert."

Later, Bishop said, "Jackie thinks she can copyright JFK's assassination."

The journalist forged ahead and completed his book in 1968, a year after a competitive book by William Manchester had been published. Bishop's publisher was Funk & Wagnalls, not Random House, as originally choreographed by Cerf. As predicted, Bishop's book became a best-seller.

***

Jackie called around in her search for an author of a book on the assassination, phoning Ted Sorensen first. She asked him if he'd do it, but he turned her down, as he planned to write a book about the span of years he had spent working for, or within the orbit of, JFK.

She got the same negative answer from the Kennedy's family friend, a historian of 20th Century American politics, Arthur Schlesinger, Jr.

She agreed to cooperate with both Sorensen and Schlesinger on their respective books, with the stipulation that they would refer to her only as "Jacqueline" or as "Mrs. Kennedy," never as "Jackie." She also wanted her marriage to JFK to be depicted in loving terms, with no mention of his philandering.

Pierre Salinger suggested she should pitch the idea of a book to William Manchester, whom he agreed to call to see if he'd like to take on this massive research project.

Manchester would later claim that Jackie had "picked me because she felt she could manipulate me."

His first book on JFK had been entitled *Portrait of a President: John F. Kennedy in Profile.* Originally published in 1962, it was described by some critics as an "adoring" account of his first year and a half in the Oval Office.

Manchester had interviewed JFK for his book. "At the end of the day, we'd sit out on the Truman Balcony. He'd smoke a cigar and I'd have a Heineken."

The ex-Marine, a square-jawed, dark-haired, and solidly built man, bonded with the President, who was five years older than he was. Like JFK, Manchester had earned a Purple Heart. *[Whereas Manchester had been wounded during fighting in Okinawa, the president had been wounded during his command of PT-109 in the Solomon Islands of the South Pacific.]*

As a history professor, Manchester had evaluated JFK as "brighter than I was, braver, better-read, handsomer, wittier, and more decisive. The only thing I could do was write better."

The offer to write a book that specifically focused on Kennedy's assassination arrived when Manchester was living with his wife, Judy, and their three children in Middletown, Connecticut. Judy called to him: "Salinger's on the phone."

Getting up, Manchester assumed it was his friend, J.D. Salinger, author of the famous *The Catcher in the Rye.* It turned out to be Pierre Salinger.

"I felt I couldn't turn down Jackie Kennedy, so I finally agreed," Manchester recalled. "So almost overnight, I became a jobless, middle-aged, and highly educated vagrant." As a means of completing such a daunting task, he'd had to resign his teaching post at Wesleyan University.

For the JFK book, he was given only a $36,000 advance. The writing project stretched out over two years, and he ran out of money. After he'd spent the advance, he had to dip into his meager savings.

Early in their negotiations, Jackie and Manchester had agreed that royalties from the book would be donated to the John F. Kennedy Library.

Manchester recalled his first meeting with the former First Lady on April 7, 1964. "She appeared in a black jersey and yellow stretch pants, and I was struck by her camellia beauty. She looked like a woman of twenty-five. I felt I was in the presence of a very great tragic actress. Her instincts were completely feminine, or so I thought at the time. Ultimately, I was to discover the tigress who lurked under her skin. But on that long-ago day, it seemed impossible to think of her burning a bra or denouncing romantic love as counter-revolutionary. She had the quality of feminine helplessness, a kind of submissiveness, to the male animal. A vulnerable person who needed a man to protect her. How I misjudged her!"

Jackie promised to give Manchester her full cooperation, and she agreed to spend ten hours with him tape recording her thoughts on what she called "the nightmare of the century." She was later criticized for this statement, some critics citing World War II and the Holocaust as events far more catastrophic than the Kennedy assassination.

She also instructed her secretary to contact key people within JFK's administration, requesting that they "give full cooperation" to Manchester.

"Jackie withheld nothing during those tapes," Manchester claimed. "Future generations will be tantalized by her revelations. If only Mary Todd Lincoln had made tapes following Lincoln's assassination. Later, Jackie would claim that I kept plowing her with daiquiris to loosen her tongue. She also accused me of taking advantage of her vulnerability."

For his research on the book, Manchester interviewed at least 1,000 people connected with Kennedy or his administration. Only one person, Marina Oswald, widow of the assassin, refused to be interviewed. Over a period of at least two years, he put in one hundred hours of long, tedious work per week to turn out a completed manuscript of 1,201 pages.

Manchester's book was a detailed chronicle of JFK's final days during that fateful November of 1963. Beginning with a reception for him at the White House before his flight to Texas, it traced the motorcade in Dallas, the assassination, Jackie's reaction to seeing her husband's head blown half off, the drama at the hospital, the sad trip back to Washington aboard Air Force One, where LBJ was sworn in as President, and the friction between the JFK camp as it surrendered power to the LBJ cohorts. It also detailed the shooting of the accused assassin, Lee Harvey Oswald, who—while virtually surrounded with Dallas law enforcement officers—encountered a bullet from Jack Ruby, the hot-headed owner of a strip club in Dallas.

Historians who read the galleys of Manchester's book almost universally agreed that Jackie should be pleased with it. Her husband was not only portrayed as a 20th Century King Arthur from Arthurian legend, but LBJ emerged in the traitorous role of Mordred.

[LBJ was mortified by the reference comparing him to Mordred. "Who is this Mordred faggot?" he asked his staff.

In Arthurian legend, Mordred was both the son and nephew of King Arthur, because the king had had sex with his own sister. The prophet and wizard, Merlin, had predicted that King Arthur's own son would one day kill him. When King Arthur heard that, he sent 40 of his baby sons out to sea to die. Only one son, Mordred, survived.

At age 15, Mordred became a knight to King Arthur and was invited to sit at the Round Table.

At age 27, Mordred died. In the Battle of Camiann, King Arthur stabbed Mordred in the stomach, killing him. But at the last second, Mordred crushed the king's head with a sword, mortally wounding him. Merlin's prediction had come true.

LBJ was furious when he learned who Mordred was in the Arthurian legend.

"I don't want to be connected in any way to all this Camelot shit that Jackie likes to perpetuate."]

When he had completed the manuscript, Manchester wrote Jackie, "Though I tried desperately to suppress bias against a certain eminent statesman who always reminded me of somebody in a Grade D movie on the Late Show, the prejudice will show through."

Jackie wrote back, "I don't care. Mr. Lyndon Baines Johnson deserves whatever you can dish out."

She had originally told Manchester, "As far as I'm concerned, you can drop Lyndon in the middle of the shark-infested Atlantic Ocean. But first, put on the heaviest pair of concrete shoes you can find."

Although Manchester had investigated all his personal savings into researching and writing the book, a ray of hope emerged. Gardner ("Mike") Cowles, the publisher of *Look* magazine, then one of the most popular periodicals in America, rivaling *Life,* called with an offer. He would give Manchester $665,000 for the book's exclusive serialization rights.

Calibrated against the currency of the late 1960s, some economists have estimated that amount as equivalent to $5 million of today's currency. Manchester was overjoyed. All his struggles seemed to have been worth it.

"The moment that news was revealed in the press, all hell broke loose," Manchester said. "Jackie Kennedy virtually declared war on me, backed up by an armada called Bobby Kennedy."

***

When Jackie heard of Manchester's offer from *Look,* she exploded. "I will not allow him to cash in on Jack's death. Why would I want to be a party to such a ghoulish thing? It makes me shudder. I must stop him, even if I go to court."

At this point, she had not read the manuscript, which had already been shipped to her. She asked her personal secretary, Pamela Turnure, to read it and to compile a list of objections. Reportedly, Turnure took that assignment very seriously (some said with an almost "missionary zeal") and drew up a long list of objections, recommending that "a ton of personal references" to Jackie and her family be eliminated.

When Manchester was confronted with this, he was furious. "What is a secretary doing, censoring the work of a noted historian?" he asked.

When a copy of the manuscript arrived at the office of Bobby Kennedy, he turned it over to Arthur Schlesinger, Jr., Dick Goodwin, and Justice Department aides Ed Guthman and John Siegenthaler to vet.

Manchester telephoned Jackie, who agreed to see him at Hyannis Port, where she was vacationing with her family. The book, by now entitled *The Death of a President,* was still in galleys. First, she invited him to go boating with her. Quite a distance offshore, she suggested they swim back to land. "She was like a fucking Amazon," he recalled. "With seemingly no effort, she swam ahead, leaving me trying to follow her breathlessly. I practically drowned."

Later, after we'd changed back into our clothing, we had a kind of showdown in her living room. Although she hadn't read my book, she was filled with opinions. I found them unrealistic, unreasonable, actually a bit crazed. Her objections were ridiculous. She seemed scornful of all books on JFK, not just mine. There was a savage look to her. That was not the woman I'd encountered before. To all my objections, she had one response—'JESUS FUCKING

310

CHRIST.'"

She outlined a list of objections, from Turnure, to the Manchester book. She wanted all references to her chain-smoking and drinking removed. She resented that he'd written of her vanity, how she searched her face every morning for the first wrinkles. She also objected to the revelation that she and JFK had slept in separate beds on his final night on earth, although it was revealed that they'd had sex.

She was horrified at a description of JFK's head wound as examined and revealed at the hospital in Dallas. For some reason, she also protested the revelation that she'd removed her wedding ring and put it on JFK's finger, using Vaseline to slip it on.

She also protested the book's revelation that JFK liked to walk around the Lincoln Bedroom in his underwear—or else, on occasion, nude.

Manchester had been told that he could use any material from the ten hours of taping he had previously orchestrated with Jackie. Suddenly, she rescinded permission, refusing to allow him to use any of her revelations. She demanded that all the tapes be sealed until the year 2067 *(i.e. 103 years from the date of their original recording in 1964]*. They remain today, sealed in the Kennedy Library, waiting to tantalize listeners of a future generation.

Manchester also quoted from letters Jackie had written to JFK in the White House while she was cruising with Onassis aboard his yacht. She wanted all mention of those letters removed from his book.

In the weeks ahead, catering to her demands, Manchester made endless revisions until he finally revolted.

"I feel my manuscript, a work of honesty and integrity, was being deluded and eventually wrecked. I finally said I would not tolerate any more revisions. That's when Jackie went after both Harper & Row and *Look* magazine."

Jackie was willing to alienate Manchester's publisher, Harper & Row, which had long been a friend of the Kennedys, having previously published JFK's Pulitzer Prize-winning book, *Profiles in Courage*. The company had also published Bobby's book on his battle against Jimmy Hoffa and the Labor Unions, *The Enemy Within*.

Ironically, during Jackie's threatened lawsuit against them, Harper & Row was represented by Cass Canfield, whose son, Michael, had previously been married to Jackie's sister, Lee Radziwill.

Jackie personally placed a call to Gardner ("Mike") Cowles, the publisher of *Look*. Whereas he agreed to postpone the book's serialization for several months, she demanded that he cancel it completely. He told her that contractually, he could not do that. Furious at his refusal, Jackie hired a top-drawer lawyer, Simon H. Rifkind, to represent her interests.

As a final resort before legal action, Jackie offered to pay Cowles a million dollars not to serialize the book, an offer he spurned.

Following in the footsteps of Manchester, Cowles visited Jackie at Hyannis Port to discuss the *Look* serialization and her objections. "She had hardly offered me tea in her living room at Hyannis before her arguments began. When

I turned down her demand that I abandon the serialization, she called me a bastard and a son of a bitch."

"She became hysterical. Where was that stoic woman who had stood so heroically at Jack's funeral? She even accused me of trying to cause her children great pain. Later, I learned she'd encountered some trouble when she appeared with her children in public."

Whereas Jackie wanted privacy for herself, she was almost fanatical in screening her children from public exposure. She was not always successful. One afternoon, when she went to retrieve John-John from school, a group of boys playing ball on a nearby field chanted at him: "YOUR FATHER'S DEAD! YOUR FATHER'S DEAD!"

The most terrible moment for Jackie occurred when she was leaving her church on All Saints Day in Washington. Suddenly, this crazed woman emerged from the crowd outside, grabbing hold of Caroline. She shouted, "Your mother is a wicked woman. She's already killed three people. She's lied to you. Your father is still alive!"

The Secret Service finally pulled the woman away from Caroline.

"Jackie went overboard to maintain her privacy," Ted Sorensen later admitted. "If a friend so much as mentioned her name to a reporter, she struck that person from her list."

***

Look beat out *Life* for the serialization rights to Manchester's book, paying $665,000, the highest ever paid for a serialization, the equivalent of $5 million in today's currency.

Manchester, who was broke, was delighted, but Jackie wanted the money to go to the Kennedy Library. The author's son, John Manchester, later said, "I think that Jackie Kennedy looked at my father as not being in the same social class as her, and it was part of her notion that he could be pushed around, that he was malleable. When it looked like he was going to get wealthy as a result of all this, she was upset."

All these legal maneuvers caused Manchester to suffer a nervous break-down. He had also drained his bank account.

He told his friends, "I admired Jackie. Now I don't know. The widow is ask-ing me to rewrite history. She wants me to distort the truth. With demands ar-riving every minute, my book is being shredded…ruined, really. I can't believe she's this venomous."

After weeks of legal dispute, a settlement was reached by a battery of lawyers. *Look* went ahead with its serialization, but in the version it printed, 1,621 words had been removed from the 60,000-word manuscript. Jackie also managed to censor many passages from the Manchester book. Ultimately, whatever victory she announced was Pyrrhic, because all the material she found objection-able had already been leaked to newspapers.

Jackie's legal tangles with Manchester generated tabloid headlines and frequently negative reactions. For the first time, she began to lose popularity with the American public.

Even though she claimed she had emerged as the winner, public opinion even-tually shifted against her. Manchester, the un-derdog, emerged as a sympathetic figure, Jackie as the brutal censor destroying his livelihood with her millions and with malice.

Literally thousands of Americans voiced their opinion that "Mrs. Kennedy is trying to trample on the right of Freedom of Speech. She shouldn't do that. It's wrong!"

The New York Times did not sympathize with Jackie. They wrote, "History belongs to everyone, not just the participants. Having made her original decision asking that the book be written, Mrs. Kennedy cannot now es-cape the consequences."

Liz Smith headlined her column JACKIE COMES OFF HER PEDESTAL.

On December 29, 1966, Gallup an-nounced that for the fifth year in a row, Jackie had topped the poll as the most admired and popular person in America. About a month later, on January 31, 1967, a Louis Harris poll revealed that her popularity had nose-dived by 33 percent.

The National Enquirer in a survey of her life from 1963 to 1966, headlined their article

One of the most outrageous satirical magazines ever published was *The Realist*. **Paul Krassner** shocked al-most everyone when he wrote and published an allegorical article based on the (untrue) premise that President Lyndon B. Johnson, aboard Air Force One, returning from Dallas with the body of the slain president, had sexually penetrated the bullet hole wound in the throat of JFK's corpse.

Krassner's trashing of the tragedy infuriated the dead president's sup-porters and strengthened their re-solve to sanitize their authorized version of events associated with the latter days of Camelot.

FROM MOURNER TO SWINGER.

With a spectacular sense of irreverence, the satirist, Paul Krassner published an article, "The Parts That Were Left Out of the Kennedy Book," which imagined, as fiction, censored material far more outrageous than anything that Jackie deleted.

[Krassner's mocking "revelations" were published in The Realist, *a pioneering magazine of social-political-religious criticism and satire. During its brief, controversial heyday, contributors included Lenny Bruce, Ken Kesey, Richard Pryor, Joseph Heller, Woody Allen, Jules Feiffer, Mort Sahl, and Terry Southern. It was intended as a satirical, tongue-in-cheek hybrid incorporating some aspects of* Mad *magazine. Edited and published by Paul Krassner, and flourishing from 1959 until 2001, it was regarded as a milestone in the American underground or countercultural press.*

One of the magazine's most controversial pranks involved the grotesque (and fictional) "revelation" that Lyndon Johnson, aboard Air Force One, had sexually penetrated the bullethole wound in the throat of JFK's corpse.

Krassner, even in his wildest imagination, never believed that someone would seriously believe that that outrageous allegation of presidential necrophilia actually happened. Yet some readers, who should have known better, actually believed—and were enraged by—this libelous satire.

"Now I know why Jackie is protesting some of this material," wrote one reader.

In an attempt to explain why some people believed, word for word, his outrageous "allegory," Krassner said, "My article worked because Jackie had created so much curiosity by censoring the book she authorized. I wrote what was a metaphorical truth about LBJ's personality presented in a literary context. The imagery was so shocking, it broke through the notion that the war in Vietnam was being conducted by sane men."

The Realist, which wasn't realistic at all in regard to the satire it published about JFK's bullet wound, was, incidentally the first magazine to publish conspiracy theories about the assassination itself.]

In yet another irreverent, no-holds-barred satire on Jackie and her censorship, comedian Saul Shapo created a scenario wherein Jackie

Controversy
And Other Essays in Journalism
1950–1975

RosettaBooks

William Manchester

A respected and reputable scholar, **Manchester** managed to remain objective and neutral in his latter-day appraisal of the Jackie controversy in his analysis of *l'affaire Kennedy.*

discovers Marilyn Monroe in her husband's bed after a night spent together in Fort Worth, Texas.

Shapo wrote. "Fully emerged from mourning, Jackie was photographed dancing, skiing, riding in a New Jersey hunt, cruising along the Dalmatian Coast, greeting European nobility, and visiting Acapulco, the West Indies, and Spain."

Although the full extent of Jackie's attack on Lyndon B. Johnson won't be known until the release of the tapes, she was referring to him as "that goddamn Lyndon," to Manchester. To justify her enmity, she cited such incidents as LBJ's refusal to allow Secret Service men to wear their PT-109 ties during his new administration.

Although mention of it did not appear within any of the drafts of Manchester's book, word leaked out that the tapes revealed Jackie as having stated: "Lee Harvey Oswald was just a patsy—part of a larger conspiracy to kill Jack."

Based on what she said, headlines of tomorrow will proclaim: JACKIE KENNEDY BLAMES LBJ AND F.B.I.'S HOOVER FOR HUSBAND'S ASSASSINATION.

"They wanted to bring down Jack," she was reported to have said on the tapes. "Jack was prepared to dump Lyndon on the '64 ticket and run Bobby instead as Vice President. Jack wanted to fire Hoover. Once Lyndon took office, he sent word to Hoover that he could run the F.B.I. 'for life.'"

Later, Bobby warned her that her tape-recorded attack on Johnson might alienate powerful Democrats who could harm his future career in politics.

On January 9, 1967, Jackie was on vacation on the Caribbean island of Antigua, where she was the guest of her billionaire friend, Bunny Mellon. Madame Mellon had generously offered to purchase a scenic plot of land and erect a Caribbean villa for the permanent use of Jackie and her family, but she was turned down.

During that sojourn in Antigua, one afternoon after returning from the beach, Jackie sat down and wrote to LBJ at the White House.

"William Manchester claims that I told him that I objected to you calling me 'honey.' I did not object. Considering some of the names I've been called, 'honey' seems to be the sweetest designation."

LBJ was spectacularly gracious in writing Jackie about the Manchester project. "Lady Bird and I have been distressed to read the press accounts of your unhappiness about the Manchester book. Some of these accounts attribute your concerns to passages in the book which are critical or defamatory of us. If this is so, I want you to know while we deeply appreciate your characteristic kindness and sensitivity, we hope you will not subject yourself to any discomfort or distress on our account."

Gore Vidal reviewed Manchester's book in *The World Journal-Tribune:* "One hopes for once the story will be different—the car swerves, the bullets miss, and the splendid progress continues. But each time, like a recurrent nightmare, the handsome head is shattered."

By 1997, Manchester's accumulated royalties had exceeded the $1 million mark, all of which was donated, as stipulated in the original agreements, to the Kennedy Library.

Manchester himself, in 1977, published a book of essays, *Controversy,* a cadenced and thoughtful retrospective examining the attempts of Jackie and Bobby to censor his book, comparing it, with dry academic rigor, to early conflicts confronted and resolved by historians trying to archive and define complicated moments in American political history.

Book covers for two editions of **Maud Shaw's memoir**. Jackie found the book "an invasion of privacy."

Jackie, The Censor of Books

In addition to her schemes about blocking William Manchester's work, Jackie also threatened writers who were composing other books on JFK. She told Ted Sorensen, "Everybody who's even shaken Jack's hand is trying to write a book about him."

Jackie even took on her young German chef, Annemarie Huste, who had written an article for Weight Watchers. Her actual article did not mention Jackie, but the editor placed on its cover this headline: JACKIE KENNEDY GOURMET CHEF PRESENTS HER WEIGHT WATCHER RECIPES."

At the time, Jackie was trying to "starve myself into a size 8 instead of a size 12." She tried to

By the time *Esquire* published, in June, 1967, this satirical caricature of **Jackie** sleigh-riding with **Eddie Fisher**, her image had gone from that of a heroically grieving widow to that of the international, globe-trotting **Jackie-O**.

316

prevent the article, but it was too late. It was already on the newsstands. In retaliation, Jackie fired Huste.

Jackie was also unable to block publication of Huste's cookbook. Her main objection was that Huste had written that Caroline was a better cook than her mother.

It was also revealed that Jackie had paid Huste only $130 a week. "I am so miserable and depressed, and I miss John-John and Caroline so much," Huste wrote. "I don't think I'll ever be able to work for another family again."

Jackie went so far as to force an agreement from Mr. and Mrs. Quing Non Wong, who had purchased her home at Wexford, in Virginia Hunt Country. Jackie had helped design and furnish the home herself. She sold the house for $225,000 with the stipulation that the Wongs "will not call in *Architectural Digest* the next day."

She also went after Paul Fay's book on JFK, entitled *The Pleasure of His Company.* John Kenneth Galbraith, acting on Jackie's behalf, tried to get Fay to delete "thousands of words" from his text.

Fey had been one of the president's closest friends, and even before censorship, his book was largely a favorable portrait. But for some reason, it offended Jackie, who never spoke to him again. When he sent her a $3,000 check for the Kennedy Library, she returned it.

She enlisted Sol M. Linowitz, the chairman of the board of Xerox, to go to London in an attempt to suppress Maud Shaw's book, *White House Nanny.* She particularly objected to Shaw's claim that she, not Jackie, had told Caroline of JFK's assassination. Linowitz did not succeed.

In her book, Shaw had written that she told Caroline "Your father has been shot. They took him to the hospital, but the doctors couldn't make him better. So your father has gone to look after Patrick. Patrick was so lonely in heaven. He didn't know anybody there. Now he has the best friend anyone could have."

Nothing seemed to shock the tabloid world more than **Eddie Fisher's** marriage to **Elizabeth Taylor** after the death of her (third) husband, Mike Todd.

Fisher had dumped "America's Sweetheart" (Debbie Reynolds) in anticipation of his union with "that evil temptress," La Liz.

But then along came an even more shocking marriage--that of Jaqueline Kennedy to Aristotle Onassis.

Jackie and Eddie Fisher

In 1965, Jackie became notoriously linked in print with crooner Eddie Fisher, who had been married to Elizabeth Taylor. Jackie appeared on the cover of *Esquire* with this quote: "Anyone who is against me will look like a rat—unless I run off with Eddie Fisher."

Jackie was referring to the adoration of her public in her battle with author William Manchester, who had been commissioned by the Kennedy family to write *The Death of a President.* She found the revelations in his book "too personal," and was taking legal action against him.

She was wrong about the public standing steadfastly behind her. Within a few months, their sympathy shifted to the beleaguered author, Manchester himself, who was harassed and threatened with legal action by two charismatic American icons, Bobby Kennedy and Jackie herself.

Actually, unknown to the public, Jackie did meet Eddie Fisher when he was dating Pamela Turnure, who at various periods of her life had been both her girlhood friend and later, her press secretary at the White House. Jackie had been made aware of the rumors that JFK had had an affair with Pamela.

One night, Fisher, in Las Vegas, sat at Frank Sinatra's table, along with Peter Lawford and Joey Bishop. He told these "Rat Packers" that "Pamela made a big mistake during our affair. She fell in love with me. As for Jackie, she told the world that the public would lose respect for her if she ran off with me," Fisher said. "She didn't run off with me, but she sure had the hots for me. The last time Pamela, Jackie, and I had dinner together, our former First Lady couldn't keep her hands off me. She was real touchy, feely that night. If I hadn't been with Pamela, I would have taken her home and plowed her."

Commemorating Camelot (in Bronze)

On her last day in the White House, Jackie placed a plaque in the Lincoln Bedroom. It read: "In this room lived John Fitzgerald Kennedy, with his wife, Jacqueline, during the two years, ten months, and two days he was President of the United States."

When Richard and Patricia Nixon took over the White House, one of their first actions was to order the removal of the plaque.

Jackie and the Paparazzo Fight It Out in Court

Newsweek called him "*Paparazzo Extraordinaire*" and *Time* labeled him "The Godfather of American *Paparazzi* culture." And Jackie Kennedy called him names that were unprintable.

Ron Gallela became the most controversial celebrity photographer in the world.

A Bronx native, son of an Italian immigrant, Galella had been an Air Force photographer during the Korean War. In time, he developed a virtual obsession with Jacqueline Kennedy Onassis, with whom he'd have legal battles. The *New York Post* defined that obsession with her as "the most co-dependent celeb-*paparazzo* relationship ever."

Jackie wasn't the only celebrity Galella tangled with. Marlon Brando, on the night of June 12, 1973, punched Galella in the face outside a restaurant in New York's Chinatown. He broke the paparazzo's jaw and knocked out five of his teeth. Galella sued and his case was settled for $40,000.

Long before the introduction of cellphones, Galella ruled the night during the 1960s and 70s, hiding behind potted plants and leaping out in front of moving cars containing famous people such as Elizabeth Taylor, who once threatened to kill him.

Ever since she moved into her apartment on Manhattan's Fifth Avenue, Galella began to stalk Jackie. He seemed to know every time she stepped out the door. He was waiting there to record the event.

Like Brando, Jackie got violent with a paparazzo only once. Aristotle Onassis, her husband, invited her to the screening of the semi-pornographic Swedish art film, *I Am Curious (Yellow).*

As she was leaving the theater, a photographer (not Galella) snapped her picture. With a quick bit of judo she'd learned somewhere, she flipped him to the street onto his butt.

It is estimated that Galella took 4,000 photographs of Jackie. He never attempted to publish anything that made her look less than attractive. Jackie had gray teeth, and the Galella photos camouflaged that by photographing her in bright light. He also softened the wrinkles around her eyes, and he never caught her smoking or drinking. He followed her to Capri, to Brooklyn Heights, and to Manhattan eateries such as "21," but at his peak he made only $15,000 a year hawking her pictures to the media.

In 2013, he would issue a 400-page book—*Jackie: My Obsession.* His photographs of Jackie were published all over the world, some editors considering them "the most beguiling, glamorous, and dramatic" of her life.

She accused him of tormenting her.

Jackie had a major run-in with Galella in the autumn of 1969. She was riding with John Jr. in Manhattan's Central Park, both of them on bicycles. All of a sudden, Galella leaped from behind a clump of shrubbery, frightening them. The young boy swerved and almost crashed. Only days before, Galella had followed Caroline to Brearley School, which was having a carnival. He pursued the young girl and snapped candid shots of her, frightening her, at least according to Jackie.

In February of 1970, Galella even flew to Athens, where Jackie joined her husband, Ari, on his private island of Skorpios. To reach the island, Galella bribed a local Greek fisherman to take him there. He came

Every time Jackie hit the streets, her stalker, **Ron Gallela**, was there, snapping candid shots of her. He was so relentless in his pursuits that she sued.

ashore, where he found that security was lax. He wandered about, taking forbidden pictures of the compound, though he did not encounter either Ari or Jackie.

When Jackie left for a vacation on Capri, he followed her to that island offshore from Italy's Amalfi coast. Once there, he stalked her along the island's narrow streets as she went on a shopping expedition, attracting crowds of locals and tourists alike.

In clash after clash, week after week, Jackie came to regard Galella as a menace to her life and safety. After one unpleasant conflict with him, she ordered her Secret Service attendant to apprehend him and take him to the nearest NYPD precinct for a booking. Once there, she charged him with harassment and reckless endangerment.

Through her lawyers, she sought an injunction barring him from coming within 200 yards of her Fifth Avenue apartment and within 100 yards from her person or her children.

On another occasion, she asked Ari to intervene with Galella to make him stop.

Ari put his arm around Galella and politely asked him to quit stalking his wife. "Why do you do this to her?"

"You have your job, I have mine." Galella answered.

"She has had so much tragedy in her life," Ari said.

"True, but life goes on, and I'm not deliberately trying to cause her pain," Galella said. "I need to make a living, and the world has hunger for pictures of Jackie and her kids," Galella said. "I'm trying to meet this insatiable demand on the part of the public."

"Don't do it any more," Onassis said.

"You might convince me to give it up if you gave me a job at Olympic Airlines," Galella said.

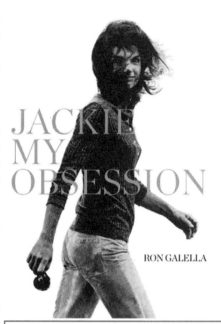

RON GALELLA

Even though she detested Ron Gallela, when he published his book, *Jackie by Obsession*, the photographs it contained were hailed as her most alluring and glamorous. "These were movie star photographs, not First Lady photographs," wrote one critic.

Details of the Gallela vs. Jackie saga were eventually collated into an HBO documentary. Its press and PR material focused on "that brilliant hipster shot" of the former First Lady.

"I will, but it pays only one dollar a week," Onassis said.

In all, there would be two trials against Galella, one in 1972, and another in 1981.

In 1972, Jackie could take it no more and went to court seeking $6 million in damages, although she knew the sum was ridiculous, since Galella didn't have that kind of money.

Ari warned Jackie not to bring Galella to trial, claiming it was bad for her image, making her look vindictive.

Even though she'd suffered a dramatic loss of popularity during her legal maneuvers with William Manchester, she decided to ignore Ari's advice and pursue Galella through the courts anyway.

Infuriated, Galella filed a $1,300,000 countersuit, charging her with assault, false arrest, malicious persecution, and unlawful interference in his work as a *paparazzo*. In her brief, Jackie's lawyers claimed that she lived in "dreaded fear" of leaving her apartment building, where she stated that she was "an absolute prisoner," trying to avoid his lens. She also sued for mental anguish.

In her case against him, Jackie summoned her Secret Service brigade to testify against the photographer. A Federal judge *[incidentally, he'd been appointed by JFK]* ruled in her favor.

In the U.S. District Court in New York City, Federal Judge Irving Ben Cooper dismissed Galella's countersuit. He imposed his demand, forbidding Galella to come within 150 feet of Jackie, or within 225 feet of John Jr. and Caroline, or within 300 feet from her 1040 Fifth Avenue apartment building.

Galella appealed and won a better deal in a higher court, allowing him to come within 25 feet of Jackie, and within 30 feet of her children.

***

Jackie brought a final case against Galella right before Christmas of 1981. Although Galella had been ordered not to come within 25 feet of her, he had defied the court order. On July 21, she emerged from Manhattan's Hollywood Twin Movie Theater on 8th Avenue at 47th Street, where she'd seen the movie adaptation of the Thomas Mann novel, *Death in Venice.*

Out on the sidewalk, she came face to face with Galella. "He was right in my face, only a foot away," she claimed. On the street, she tried to hail a taxi, but he was jumping around her, taking pictures from all angles.

His dance around Jackie began to attract onlookers, and she soon found herself mobbed by people calling out her name.

He followed her to Martha's Vineyard over the Labor Day weekend. She and her companion, Maurice Tempelsman, had gone boating. Galella decided to pursue them in a rented boat of his own. Whether it was true or not, she claimed that his craft nearly crashed into the boat carrying Tempelsman and herself.

After that, Galella followed her to the Winter Garden Theater in Manhattan, where she and Tempelsman were attending a performance of the Twyla Tharp

Dance Company. Galella entered the theater to snap candid shots of Jackie.

In court again, Galella was ordered to pay $10,000 in damages to Jackie and prohibited from ever taking another photograph of her, although he claimed that that ruling violated his First Amendment rights.

The sum total of the financial expenses associated with Jackie's lawsuits exceeded half a million dollars, most of it paid to her lawyers at Paul, Weiss, Rifkind, Wharton, and Garrison. Ari had deposited a $50,000 retainer, but he refused to pay the rest of the legal bill, ordering Jackie to pay it out of her allowance. Finally, Ari's friend, the notorious gay lawyer, Roy Cohn, negotiated the fee down to $235,000.

Jackie's case against Galella finally came to its inglorious end.

Chapter Seventeen

Trashy Novels / Trashy Screenplays:
The Entertainment Industry Exploits Jackie
Enraged, Jackie Demands Censorship

The Eruption of Truman Capote's Feud with Jacqueline Susann.
Her "Fictional Gold-Digging Adventuress" is Inspired by Jackie

The beaded, bare-chested **Irving Mansfield** was **Jacqueline Susann's** agent, and her husband, too, when she wasn't pursuing her deeply secretive lesbian life.	Susann's "little Capon," as she called author **Truman Capote**, engaged with her in poisonous public bitchfests. He warned her, "Don't take on a Southern queen, baby."	A writer named Jacqueline (Susann) wrote a description of her more famous namesake: "**Mrs. Kennedy,** whose eyes are as far apart as New York and Florida, wears sunglasses that would protect her from an atomic blast."

It was gossipy Truman Capote who first alerted Jackie that Jacqueline Susann, although stricken with terminal cancer, was struggling to complete her final novel, *Dolores.*

"From what I hear, it's based on a First Lady whose presidential husband has been assassinated, and on her eventual marriage to one of the richest men in the world, who owns a fleet of oil tankers. I'll give you only three guesses."

Jackie dreaded what Susann would write about her. But in the meantime, with an amused, yet horrified, eye, she watched Capote's own battle as it unfolded with the best-selling pop culture novelist.

***

Capote fought three famous duels in his life—one with Lee Radziwill, one with Gore Vidal, and one with a dying Jacqueline Susann, the author of the megaselling, pill-popping *Valley of the Dolls.*

Some witnesses called it 'The Catfight of the Decade," and it starred two writers—one the brilliant Capote, the other a popular, bestselling hack (Susann).

In New York, in 1967, Capote had attended a screening of Susann's *Valley of the Dolls.* Susann herself had walked out on its premiere, objecting to the way her novel had been adapted to the screen.

Capote had cackled so loudly during the screening that the manager had escorted him out of the theater and refunded his money, asking him not to return.

Donald Windham, Capote's friend and fellow author, said, "As unlikely as it seems, Truman was jealous of Jacqueline Susann. He felt about her as Gore Vidal had felt about him. She had taken over, or at least he felt she had taken over, his place on the bestseller list. She had proven he was not the only person in the world who could get a million dollars worth of free publicity. He was to make cracks about her on various TV shows. I knew this, but it had not occurred to me that he considered her competition, that he coveted her subject matter, and that he thought, 'I could do that better than she could.'"

The feud actually began in 1966, after the release of the Susann novel, *Valley of the Dolls.* Truman took potshots at her on a TV talk show.

Susann heard it, and the next day she told reporters, "I'm flattered that a writer of Capote's standing should regard me as a competitor. However, I don't think authors should castigate one another in public. After all, writing is such a lonely profession."

On the West Coast, Capote continued his attack on Susann's novel. "She doesn't write, she types."

Extremely angered, Susann waited until July of 1969 to strike back, when she appeared on *The Joey Bishop Show.* She'd been trained as an actress, and she was good at impressions, so she did a hilariously funny interpretation of Capote's high, lispy voice. He just happened to be watching the televised show that night, and he swore vengeance.

With a single exception, Vidal and Capote did not agree on anything. But on one subject, they were in harmony: Jacqueline Susann was a bitch. Vidal had never read a Susann novel, but he had encountered her several times in

---

> *"Jacqueline Susann is making you the carnivorous heroine of her latest novel. It's like a warmed over version of* Valley of the Dolls.*"*
> —Truman Capote to Jacqueline Kennedy

various green rooms, where both of them had waited to be called for their respective appearances on nationwide talk shows.

Vidal recalled "her large dark eyes whose thick false lashes resembled a pair of tarantulas in a postcoital state."

Susann had made a dangerous enemy. She was lying in bed with her husband and agent, Irving Mansfield, watching *The Tonight Show* starring Johnny Carson.

Suddenly, Capote was announced. He bounced out onto the set and began to gossip about Susann.

Even though **Truman** *(left)* was a frequent television guest on *The Tonight Show*, starring **Johnny Carson**. "Carson *(right)* is consumed by rage!" the author claimed. "Under the calm surface, there are tornadoes! He can be very mean—there's not an ounce of kindness in that man!"

Carson resented it when the author took control of his wife, Joanne. One afternoon, Carson caught Capote going through her closets, saving what she could safely wear, and tossing out the rest.

"Jackie Susann would be great for the part of Myra Breckinridge instead of Raquel Welch. Jackie is a born transvestite who wears marvelous wigs and sleazy dresses. In essence, she is a truck driver in drag."

There were gasps in bedrooms across America, with those in the in the Mansfield household being among the loudest and tinged with rage. Capote's attack appeared in all the gossip columns the next morning.

Mansfield defended his wife, opting to focus on her wardrobe: "Jackie is one of the best dressed actresses on TV. It's incredible to me that a taped show would not have edited out Capote's slander before it was aired."

Under pressure, Carson claimed that he would give Susann equal time on the air.

Although it had been uttered as a joke, Capote's "truck driver in drag" reference had a certain ring of truth. In a sense, Susann's somewhat harsh, dark features and jet black hair evoked certain masculine attributes.

That morning, Susann, wearing a Chanel suit, sent to the office of the high-profile attorney, Louis Nizer, and urged him to sue Capote for libel.

A shrewd lawyer, Nizer warned Susann that although she might have grounds for libel, it would be an uphill battle, involving enormous attorney's fees. He also informed her that she was on weak ground, because she'd previously mocked him on television as a homosexual, drawing unflattering attention to his own physical attributes.

Nizer told her, "Words are like chemicals. Some combinations fizzle. Others explode. But I don't think we can prove that Capote has actually damaged you in any serious way, certainly in no way for which a court might find damages."

Eventually, she acquiesced to Nizer's advice, expressing regret that, "We can't see this little worm squirm under cross examination."

On September 8, 1969, Susann appeared on Carson's *Tonight Show.* The audience waited; Carson waited; but Susann kept them in suspense. At no point did she even mention Capote's name. Finally, as they were going off the air, Carson, in desperation, asked, "What do you think of Truman?"

"Truman...Truman?" she asked. "I think history will prove he was one of the best presidents we've ever had."

Capote became a formidable enemy, and he did not let up. About two months later, as a joke, he appeared on *Laugh-In* dressed up "like Jackie Susann, in a black leather suit, a truck driver in drag."

When Susann was asked about this by reporters, she responded, "Does an eagle chase a butterfly?"

She didn't clarify which of them was the eagle, but it was widely assumed that she was using the butterfly analogy to describe Capote, since Latinos (pejoratively) refer to homosexuals as *mariposas* (butterflies).

Capote still wouldn't let go. In an interview with *After Dark,* a theatrical magazine in Manhattan, he falsely claimed that Nizer had warned Susann not to press her libel case, because Capote had a secret weapon he was going to use against her. He would assemble a dozen men in drag who resembled Susann. He had already recruited three dark-haired men from a transvestite bar and displayed pictures of them. Amazingly, each of them resembled Susann.

Susann went on the warpath again, demanding that Nizer press a libel case against Capote.

She told Nizer, "Now the little capon has gone too far. I want you to cut off his balls for this—that is, if you can find them. I'll lend you my tweezers."

Responding to Susann's wishes, Nizer wrote a letter of warning to Capote, which elicited yet another attack, phrased in the form of a mock apology.

Capote confronted reporters, "I do apologize to truck drivers everywhere for comparing these fine warriors of the road to Jacqueline Susann. Forgive me, one and all."

He wrote to Nizer. "How pleasant to have a letter from the admirable Mr. Nizer, *even* a scolding one. It is so well written: If only your client, Miss Susann, had your sense of style!"

"I gave merely an aesthetic opinion—a spontaneous observation. Bitchy, yes, malicious, no. I have no malice for your client; on the contrary, I respect her as a very professional person who knows exactly what she's doing and how to do it."

"On the other hand," Capote wrote in his letter, "I suggest you examine a few remarks Miss S. made about me—as recently as an interview three weeks ago in *The Los Angeles Times.* Over and again, she has implied that I am a homosexual (big news!) and a lazybones jealous of her productivity. As far as I am concerned, I couldn't care less if she won the Nobel Prize—so did Pearl Buck."

While all this was going on, Capote reinforced his war machine, enlisting his vast network of gossipy "spies" to supply him with all the lowdown, past and present, on Susann.

He learned that she had launched herself professionally as a lingerie model making $25 a week, and then invented a slanderously pejorative observation about how she lost the job, remarking to anyone who would listen, "Her over-ripe vagina was so large and hairy that it showed through the thin *négligée* fabric she modeled."

He had also heard that Susann had engaged in a number of lesbian affairs, including one with the blonde-haired actress, Carole Landis, when they worked together on Broadway in the 1945 production of *A Lady Says Yes.* In *Valley of the Dolls,* Susann had modeled the character of Jennifer North on Landis, who, in 1948, had committed suicide, in part, at least, because of her failed affair with Rex Harrison.

Privately, Susann had told friends, "How sensual it had been for Carole and me to stroke each other's breasts." Capote leaned that in 1959, Susann had had a brief fling in Paris with the fashion designer Coco Chanel, and that Susann had been rumored to have had a long-running affair with the bisexual Ethel Merman. He added those tidbits and more to his destructive arsenal. Suitably armed, Capote defamed Susann far and wide as he made his gossipy rounds through High Society.

Jackie Kennedy later said, "As a *voyeur,* I watched Truman's drama with that Susann creature unfold. For the first time in my life, I had sympathy for a media event like Elizabeth Taylor. I had once dreamed of being a movie star. They were the kinds of interviews and publicity I might have been subjected to."

The Trashing Of Jackie
And Her Reconfiguration As Pulp Fiction

Even without ever becoming (technically) a movie star, Jackie Kennedy became the unwitting subject of films and novels. One of the most visible of these was *Dolores*, Susann's last novel. It launched Jackie Kennedy as a protagonist in pulp fiction.

Some of the "facsimiles" inspired by Jackie used her real name: others used a fictional name, but made it obvious who the subject was.

Three of the most commercially successful included *The Secret Letters of Marilyn Monroe and Jacqueline Kennedy,* a novel about a fictional "correspondence that might have been," by Wendy Leigh; *The Secret Memoirs of Jacqueline Kennedy Onassis,* a novel by Ruth Francisco; and *The Widow,* a novel by Pierre Rey.

Dolores

An excerpt from *Dolores* appeared first in 1974 in *The Ladies' Home Journal.* When it was published in book form that same year, Jackie was said to have read it in less than an hour, although she denied reading it at all to her friends. Its cover was graced with a pair of beautiful eyes with huge sunglasses raised above them, resting on her forehead.

According to its bareboned plot, after the assassination of her husband, an elegant, universally adored woman, Dolores finds herself strapped for cash, and unable to sustain her extravagant tastes.

She is lonely and unfulfilled as a woman until she meets "a love machine" named Barry. He's great in the boudoir, but lacks the bank account to support her in style. Still in love with him, she must look elsewhere for a rich man to marry.

Unless a reader had been living on Mars in the 1960s, he or she knew who "Dolores" really was. The clue appeared in the book's opening chapter when Dolores disembarks from Air Force One during her final hour as First Lady. Aboard the plane is the body of her dead husband, James T. Ryan, mowed down by an assassin's bullet.

There appears this statement: "She might not be the President's wife anymore, but she would hold on to her newly acquired fame. She loved seeing the crowds that followed her and the Secret Service men in attendance. She would still be entitled to Secret Service men for herself and her children."

During the months that followed, Dolores meets Baron Erick de Savonne, who owns a larger fleet of tankers than Aristotle Onassis, with vast holdings in the Middle East. He lives lavishly and keeps a ballerina who is past her prime.

Even a dummy could figure out that the mistress was not a ballerina, but an opera diva named Maria Callas.

The novel—actually a short novella—ends on a strange note at the Ritz Hotel in Paris shortly after Dolores weds the multi-millionaire.

Thousands upon thousands of hate letters are arriving denouncing her as a gold-digger. The pristine reputation of the grieving widow at the husband's funeral had been shattered. Now, her reputation is being trashed because of her marriage to this "rich beast."

The night before the wedding, Dolores has terrible visions of her wedding night with Erick mauling her. "She could almost feel his lips slobbering on her."

The focal point of this book cover (those mammoth sunglasses) were **Jacqueline Susann's** device for signaling to readers that she was writing a thinly disguised *roman à clef* about Jacqueline Kennedy.

The novel ends suddenly as she lies in her bridal suite wearing a white satin nightgown.

Erick is changing into a gray suit.

"Where are you going?" she asks.

"To my mistress…she's waiting," he tells her, and then he leaves her…untouched.

Presumably, because of the coincidence of her fatal illness and the publication of *Dolores,* the final chapters were written by Susann's friend, columnist Rex Reed.

To combat those rumors, her publisher wrote a note at the beginning of the novel, claiming that Susann not only finished *Dolores* before her death, but that she was able to revise it to her satisfaction. Only the most misinformed of readers actually believed that.

In *Dolores,* Susann described a character she named "Horotio Capon," the painter friend of Dolores' younger sister (who was an obvious reference to Lee Radziwill. Capon is described as "a plumb little man, a blondish pig, who had written a best seller five years ago. He hadn't written anything since, but he was making a career of going on talk shows and attending celebrity parties. He had also turned into a lush."

There was one scene that particularly infuriated Capote as it obviously described an imagined encounter between Norman Mailer and him. Mailer's name was changed to Tom Holt in the novel.

As Susan described it, "Capon clamped his pudgy little hand on Tom Colt's arm and gushed, 'I've read everything you wrote.' His voice squeaked, and he smacked his lips in ecstasy, lowering his eyes. 'My God, but I adore your work. But be careful about getting caught up in the rat race of television. Look what a whore it made of me."

After Susann's death, her husband, Irving Mansfield, aggressively promoted *Dolores,* along with his late wife's other works such as *Valley of the Dolls.* By a coincidence, Jackie happened to wander into the Doubleday Bookstore on Fifth Avenue in Manhattan.

Mansfield was in the store on a promotional tour, hawking Susann novels, especially *Dolores,* of which Jackie was the fictional centerpiece.

As he recalled, "Mrs. Onassis stopped and looked down on my display with utter contempt. She did not look me in the eye. She made an exaggerated gesture as if to hold her nose from the pollution. It was rude and ugly. She turned abruptly and walked out of the store. It was obvious the disdain in which Jackie held my own dearly departed Jackie."

The Widow

Before *The Widow,* published in 1977, Pierre Rey had written *The Greek* (1974), a story about one of the richest, most powerful men in the world. *The Widow* takes off where that novel ended, following "the Widow" through her trials and tribulations, based loosely on Jackie's life. In fact, a Jackie-like image with large sunglasses is depicted on the cover.

In the book, Peggy Baltimore Satrapoulos (read that as "Jackie Kennedy") is the widow of both the assassinated U.S. president and a Greek shipping magnate.

In the first chapter, Rey has *la scandaleuse,* Peggy, entering into a new marriage to a man known as Herman Kallenberg. In one graphic scene, Kallenberg is preparing for his wedding night. He ruminates:

"Until now, Peggy had curiously rejected his advances. As soon as he had brought her to heel, he intended to pay her back for that humiliating refusal as well as for the insane gifts he'd been forced to shower on her. His old anxiety seized him again: How would she react to his tiny phallus? She must know about it for, sadly enough, Kallenberg's penis was as famous as Cleopatra's nose. The Greek (read that as Aristotle Onassis) had been hung like a horse—women tell all kinds of stories. But horses have to die, too, and the Greek's remains had long since provided a meal for the fish!"

Later in the novel, she contemplates marriage to another eccentric, eighty-year-old billionaire Archibald Knight. He has a repulsive habit. Ever since 1925, he has carefully collected his fecal matter and urine until he has collected 18,000 jars labeled with date, time, and weight. The contents of the oldest jars have turned gray. At times, he had discovered that he excreted more than he had ingurgitated.

Some associates at G.P. Putnam's, the publisher of *The Widow,* sent Jackie a copy of the book. In front of her secretary, she tossed it into a wastepaper basket.

Pierre Rey's novel, *The Widow,* traces the tangled life of the most sought-after woman of the century as she fights for a fortune and her future in the world of jet age society.

He named its heroine **Peggy Baltimore Satrapoulos**. Readers were clearly aware of who he was referencing.

The Greek Tycoon

Actor Anthony Quinn, growing up impoverished in Mexico, "wanted to be Napoléon, Michelangelo, Shakespeare, Martin Luther King, Jr., Picasso, and Jack Dempsey, all rolled into one."

What he never dreamed of being was Aristotle Onassis, until he was offered the title role in *The Greek Tycoon* (a character named Theo Tomasis) on the screen. Released in 1978, it co-starred Jacqueline Bisset as Liz Cassidy, obviously based on Jackie Kennedy. Bisset played the beautiful widow of an assassinated president of the United States.

In the movie, the Greek had first met Liz when she was married to President Cassidy (played by James Franciscus), who starred as the charismatic senator from Massachusetts.

A private screening was scheduled for Jackie, who renounced the film as "the trash version of my life, obviously inspired by the lurid pages of a Harold Robbins novel. "Why did the producers bother to use fictional names?" she asked staff members. "Guess who is the humble Greek peasant who rises to become a mogul, owning oil tankers, Mediterranean islands, and airlines. And who might be the handsome blonde

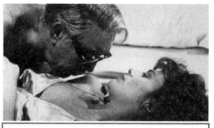

Starring **Anthony Quinn** as Onassis, and yet another **Jacqueline (Bisset)** as Jackie, *The Greek Tycoon* was a frothy, tepid fabrication loosely based on the life and romantic adventures of the late President's widow.

James Cassidy, who is elected President of the United States? And his widow, Liz Cassidy, who survives him to hook up with the Greek tycoon? And what imagination did it require for the writer *[Morton S. Fine]* to have the president appoint his brother as Attorney General? Surely that couldn't have been Bobby?"

The film opened at the time the public had begun to tire of so-called jet set movies. The heyday of such films as *The Carpetbaggers* were the 1960s. Writing in *The New York Times,* Vincent Canby evaluated *The Greek Tycoon* "as witless as it is gutless. It recalls a sort of newspaper journalism you don't see much anymore—the Sunday supplement recapitulation of a famous murder, divorce, or other scandals put together from the morgue clips. It's the literature of vultures."

Variety denounced the picture (which had been produced on a bare-boned budget of $6.5 million) as "trash, opulent, and vulgar." *Time Out London* called the move "glossy travesty. Upmarket exploitation pics tend to make it on the merest meal of money, sex, and scandal, and this effort just reeks."

"I understand Quinn walked off with a million dollars—and that was good for him," Jackie said.

Until the release of *The Greek Tycoon,* Quinn had considered himself a friend of the Kennedys and a political backer.

A year later, on a hot day on the French Riviera, Quinn and his wife were dining in a seafront restaurant in Cannes, enjoying the bouillabaisse.

As Quinn looked up from his table, he spotted Jackie entering the restaurant, accompanied by an unidentified male friend.

She walked right by his table, their eyes not meeting, although he'd waved at her, hoping she would stop by. With a nod of recognition, she passed by, heading for her own table.

For Jackie, Anthony Quinn no longer existed.

She did not tell her associates that although Bisset was voted as the most beautiful actress in the world, "I hope I look better than that. She should stick to that wet T-shirt."

[She was referring to Bisset's celebrated underwater scenes in the movie, The Deep *(1977).]*

Jackie Onassis was dead before Bisset once again portrayed her on the screen. This time, it was as part of a 2003 teleplay called *America's Prince: The John F. Kennedy, Jr. Story."*

The Secret Letters

of Marilyn Monroe and Jacqueline Kennedy; a Novel

Reviewed as "an audacious example of epistolary eavesdropping," Wendy Leigh's novel, *Secret Letters,* envision an imagined, artfully contrived, and purely fictional private correspondence between Marilyn Monroe and Jackie. Leigh has Marilyn writing to Jackie on July 9, 1962, shortly before the star's death. Marilyn confesses her love for Jack at their first meeting on May 15, 1951 at the home of her lover, producer Charles Feldman.

Marilyn writes: "When Jack focused those eyes on you, you really felt it. First he stared at your left eye, then at your right. Each eye at a time, never together. I felt like he was raping me with his eyes. I blushed from head to foot: A real flush. All over my body."

Marilyn Monroe did not actually write these (fictional) letters to Mrs. Kennedy, but perhaps she should have.

Two legends—the much-respected wife and the sexy mistress—come together as friends in this novel. Readers know, of course, that they'll inevitably clash.

"We had sex that same evening, at a bungalow he rented for us at the Beverly Hills Hotel. Jack had magic for me. That night and always. He was a cute guy who set me on fire and that when I woke up in his arms, I felt safer, more special than I ever had before. I've had so many men, stronger, sexier, taller, and bigger than Jack. But no one ever reached into my heart, body, and soul like he did."

Jack's Widow

In *Jack's Widow,* a "fictional" 2006 novel by Eve Pollard, the writer even explored the inner workings of Jackie's marriage to Onassis.

In this book, clearly advertised as a work of fiction, Jackie's marriage to Onassis was described as the romantic adventures of a woman who *"went from a Greek god to a goddamn Greek,"* and with the slogan, *"When his life ended* [a reference to the assassination of JFK], *hers had only just begun."*

Avon, its publisher, ran a disclaimer: "While many of the characters portrayed here have some counterparts in the life and times of Jackie Kennedy Onassis, the characterization, dates of events, time frame, and incidents presented are totally the products of the author's imagination."

Within the pages of *Jack's Widow*, the heroine's honeymoon, at least, had gone well. "The sex had been exciting," Pollard wrote. "Jackie was enthused by Ari's zest for lovemaking and the extraordinary nights of courtship had taught them both a great deal about what pleased the other."

But the marriage soon turns sour. "As if he were fighting to obliterate the world's resentment, he demanded to be given more caresses, more kisses, more sensual thrills and excitement," Pollard wrote. "He was insatiable and made love to her frequently and often quite roughly. She was desperate. Now not only did the whole world think she had married a monster—on occasion, she was starting to agree with them."

Although defined as "total trash" by Jackie herself, the novel got a few good reviews. *Kirkus* asserted, "Pollard supplies morsels of Camelot lore that will satisfy fans hungry to learn the regal widow's secrets." *USA Today* found *Jack's Widow* "laced with enough facts about Jackie and John F. Kennedy that the reader stars to think it's all true."

Romance writer **Eve Pollard** expressed in a fictional format a tantalizing tale of what might have been, entangling the image of the widowed Jackie into a scandalously juicy thriller.

Near the end of the novel, Jackie discovers a Fabergé picture frame enameled in translucent apple green and gold. "What a gift," she says. "It must have cost a fortune." When she examines the card that came with it, she realizes it was intended for Maria Callas but delivered to her by mistake. Now she knew the truth. During her entire marriage to her, Ari had continued his affair with the opera diva, in spite of his denials.

In an evocative moment, Pollard wrote, "She would make love to a husband who she was sure had betrayed her. She had done it before."

Ironically, way back in 1969, during an era that journalistically, at least, might be defined as "more innocent," Pollard had written a mainstream, conventional, relatively short (159 pages) and rather staid biography of the former First Lady—entitled *Jackie*—in which she stuck to the facts.

The Secret (Fictional) Memoirs Of Jacqueline Kennedy Onassis

Also published in 2006, *The Secret Memoirs of Jacqueline Kennedy Onassis* was a novel by Ruth Francisco. The writer re-imagines Jackie's feelings and thoughts between the lines of recorded history. Although fiction, much of it rings true, even to so-called experts who have devoted years to exploring Jackie's life. Some of the scenes would shock the faint of heart. For example, Francisco as a novelist can intrude into secrets of the boudoir.

The novel contained graphic depictions of Jackie having sex, including on her wedding night.

Ironically, Francisco's depiction of her, as fiction, may have been historically accurate. Jackie is seen on her wedding night, sitting up in bed "perfumed and powdered, her body trembling with anticipation, her heart fluttering like a butterfly."

JFK enters the bedroom from the bathroom. "I need you on top, baby," he says to Jackie. "He lies on his back and pulls me on top, his penis, cool and sharp, stabbing into me. He jogs my pelvis up and down like a milk shake, his eyes squeezed shut, wheezing, *ahhh*, squeezing my buttocks. His muscles tense, vibrating, then collapses."

That's it for her, as she's left panting and unsatisfied with a fierce ache inside her. "Disappointment settles of me like a hunter's net. He taps my thigh. 'I'm beat, kid. Let's get some sleep.'"

In yet another sex scene, Francisco depicted Jackie in the bathroom, brushing her hair in the mirror.

She writes, "Jack wants sex on demand, anytime during the day or night, without kisses or affection. He just comes up to me from behind, lifts my nightie, and enters me. He hugs and puffs for a minute or two. My hips bang against the sink, hurting—His oozy sweat smells vaguely chemical from the drugs he takes. I study his face in the mirror, twisted and red, and try to see the man I fell in love with. I see only anger and frustration and an anonymous violence that alarms me. As if I weren't there at all."

Jackie once famously said, "I want to live my life, not record it."

To some degree, **Ruth Francisco**, in a "fictional" format, might have done the job for her. Rather brilliant in its concept, her provocative novel about Jackie goes where a biographer can't, exploring and articulating some of her unspoken passions and emotions.

These fictional accounts coincide with what many women who had had brief sexual encounters with JFK had claimed.

In May of 2004, in *Vanity Fair,* journalist Salley Bedell reported that "Jackie Kennedy found sex with Kennedy unsatisfying because he goes too fast and then falls asleep."

She was quoting from Jackie's friend, Dr. Frank Finnerty, who advised her that sex could be more enjoyable if she and Jack engaged in foreplay.

"I may be the first person who ever talked to her in this way," Dr. Finnerty claimed. "The sex got better, but the President continued his womanizing. But Jackie no longer had reason to believe that their difficulties with sexual intimacy had been her fault."

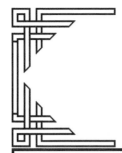

Chapter Eighteen

America's Queen Vs.
The Literati

Competitive Bitchfests: Jackie is Repeatedly Embarrassed by
Norman Mailer, Gore Vidal, & Truman Capote

NORMAN MAILER *(left)* said: "The first time I met Jackie Kennedy, she gave me a hard-on. But later, I began to see a darker side of, especially after I referred to her, in print, as 'The Wild Witch of the East.' She thought of herself as Madame de Pompadour, a real royal phony."

GORE VIDAL *(center)* said: "After frequently defending JFK's policies on television, I became known as an unrewarded apologist." One night William Walton, in front of Jackie at the White House, asked Vidal, "Why don't you ask Jack for something? You'll probably get it." That would have been, of course, a payoff for not writing about Jack's health."

"The only job I want is Jack's," Vidal responded to Walton, as Jackie listened.

"Then, without being asked," Gore later wrote, I was put on the President's Advisory Council on the Arts. I made it a point never to attend a meeting or reply to a letter. I didn't believe that any government as philistine and corrupt as ours should involve itself in the arts in any way."

TRUMAN CAPOTE *(right)* said: "I met Jackie in the mid-1950s, when we became friends. She was married to this relatively unknown senator from Massachusetts. Jack liked me and used to call me from the White House. He bragged that his phone operators could track me down anywhere, even at a gay leather bar in the Village. One night at a party at Babe Paley's house, I bragged about how intimate I was with Jackie, so intimate that she'd sometimes invite me into her bedroom as she was dressing for the evening. That indiscretion was repeated to her, and it was enough to cause her to drop me, as she had so many other people who had been close to her."

After Jackie spent time with Gore Vidal in Washington,

she realized that he was compulsively competitive with both Truman Capote and Norman Mailer. All three of these young novelists had vied with each other in the late 1940s to see which of them would emerge on top as the novelist of the decade—Capote because of his *Other Voices, Other Rooms;* Vidal because of his *The City and the Pillar* and *Williwaw;* and Mailer because of his novel about World War II, *The Naked and the Dead.*

When **Jackie** wasn't feuding with **Norman Mailer**, she often encountered him socially, as in this scene from October 3, 1978, in New York City.

"Sometimes, he could be sane, but often, he behaved like a psychotic," she claimed. "Like many other artists, he had a very dark side. A kinder description would be 'creative malady.'"

Jackie had read all four books, deciding that *The Naked and the Dead* was the best novel to emerge from the mayhem and bloodshed of World War II. Vidal had a different opinion. "I never read all of it…just couldn't get through it. But I thought it was a clever, admirably executed fake. It was artificial plumes on an eagle's wings."

Vidal confided to Jackie that Mailer had interpreted his novel, *The City and the Pillar,* as "disgusting—two fags getting it on and one killing the other."

Vidal said he came face to face with Mailer in 1952 at the Manhattan apartment of the actress, Milly Brower, who lived on 4ᵗʰ Avenue.

"I went over to Mailer and extended my hand," Vidal told Jackie. "To piss him off, I said. 'I see I'm better looking than you are.'"

"But you can't get the women I can," Mailer shot back. "Not that you would know what to do with one if you caught her."

"From what I hear," Vidal told Mailer, "we're both sexual marauders, so at least we have something in common."

As a devotee of literature, Jackie wanted to get to know famous American novelists. What she didn't want was a personal involvement in their petty feuds. Increasingly, she found herself a virtual sounding board as one author attacked another in front of her. In time, however, she would develop her own, intensely personal, feuds with each of these novelists.

Mailer Physically Assaults Gore Vidal: Jackie, a Witness, is Horrified.

First, there was Norman Mailer. Her relationship with him began peacefully enough.

When John F. Kennedy was running for president in 1960, Mailer wrote Jackie and requested an interview at their compound in Hyannis Port. Eager to meet Mailer herself, she asked her husband to agree to the interview, which would eventually appear in *Esquire* magazine.

Everyone at the compound that day was wearing casual sportswear, but Mailer showed up in a formal black suit more appropriate for a funeral. As he admitted himself, "I was sweating like a goat."

In her soothing yellow-and-white living room, Jackie asked him to take off his jacket while she poured him iced verbena tea with a sprig of fresh mint.

As Jackie offered Mailer his tea, she provocatively said, "Perhaps you'd like something stronger."

He knew that she was aware that during the previous month at Provincetown, he'd been arrested on a charge of drunkenness and rude and disorderly conduct.

She introduced him to her fellow guests, including Arthur Schlesinger, Jr.; Prince Stanislas Radziwill; Peter Maas of the *Saturday Evening Post;* and Pierre Salinger, press secretary to JFK.

Jackie was obviously pregnant, and Mailer sensed that although she wanted no part of a political campaign, she was still trying to be the dutiful wife. He later described her mood as one of "quiet desperation."

Mailer was impressed by the young presidential candidate, although originally, he'd considered him too conservative. "He won my heart by praising my less successful novel, *Deer Park,"* Mailer recalled. "Everybody I met had good words for *The Naked and the Dead.* But *Deer Park!* He was my kind of guy!"

Later, when she was alone with JFK, Jackie gave her own review of *The Deer Park.* "The novel is a documentation on the oversexed imagination of the American male."

Prior to Mailer's arrival at Hyannis Port, the Democrats had released what became a celebrated campaign poster. It featured a swarthy, scowling Richard Nixon with the tag line, "Would you buy a used car from this man?"

Before the debut of his own dialogue with JFK, Mailer interjected an unexpected and unpleasant surprise by showing his hosts the Republican party's response to the Democrat's campaign poster.

Mailer read it to JFK in front of Jackie: It proclaimed, "If you bought a used car from Jack Kennedy, you would trust him and you would buy the car, and then after you'd bought the car, he'd drop by to pay a visit and see that it was working. And then he'd seduce your wife."

"I really don't know what that ad means," JFK said.

Before Mailer, Jackie had never been written about by such a hawk-eyed novelist, who noted such details as her "surprisingly thin but not unfeverish calves." This was no female reporter asking the standard questions put to the wife of a political candidate. "There was an air of self-indulgence about her, subtle but precise," he wrote. "She disappeared at least half a dozen times.

One was certain she liked time to compose herself."

Although he was sexually attracted to her, he did not lose his keen powers of observation, commenting on "her elusiveness and concealed cruelty."

He wrote: "Jackie Kennedy was a cat, narrow and wild, and her fur was being rubbed every which way. Over tea, I noted something droll and hard that came into her eyes as if she were a very naughty eight-year-old indeed. There was something quite remote in her. Nice willed, not chilly, not directed at anyone in particular, but distant, detached. She had a keen sense of laughter, but it revolved around the absurdities of the world. She was not unlike a soldier who had been up at the front for two weeks. There was a hint of gone laughter. I liked Jackie Kennedy. She was not at all stuffy. She had perhaps a touch of that artful madness which suggests future drama."

Mailer also focused his sharp perception on JFK as well, writing that his most characteristic quality "was the remote and private air of a man who has traversed some lonely terrain of experience, of loss and gain, of nearness to death, which leaves him isolated from the mass of others."

He wrote of JFK's "Dozen faces, with his appearance changing with the mood. He would seem at one moment older than his age, forty-eight or fifty, a tall, slim, sunburned professor with a pleasant weathered face not particularly handsome. Five minutes later, talking to the press on his lawn, his appearance would have gone through a metamorphosis., He would look again like a movie star, his coloring vivid, his manner rich, his gestures strong and quick, alive with that concentration of vitality a successful actor always seems to radiate."

When **Norman Mailer** introduced Jackie to his wife, **Adele Morales**, a Spanish-Peruvian artist, the future First Lady bonded with her and engaged in intense discussions about art. Later, Mailer accused his wife of having lesbian tendencies and of wanting to seduce Jackie.

Mailer and Adele were photographed (above) on December 21, 1960, just after their appearance together in court, where she had refused to sign a complaint against him. He'd been arrested on charges of stabbing her, puncturing her cardiac sac. Miraculously, she survived.

The interview at Hyannis Port had been scheduled as a two-day event. Jackie suggested that on the following day, Mailer might want to show up with his second wife, Adele Morales (Mailer), a Spanish-Peruvian painter. Mailer had met the sensual beauty just after she'd broken up with Jack Kerouac. Before Adele's arrival at Hyannis Port, Mailer had warned Jackie, "She has elemental and primitive qualities."

Jackie bonded with Adele, finding a mutual appreciation for art. Jackie later learned that she'd taken some very esoteric art appreciation courses.

The day went well, and as a quartet, Jackie, Adele, Mailer, and JFK formed a warm camaraderie over lunch, although JFK, the campaigner, was interrupted frequently by phone calls.

[In 1960, Jackie was shocked to read in The New York Times *that Mailer had stabbed Adele with a pen knife, and that she'd survived. At a Saturday night party at their home, she had denigrated his work and denounced him as an inadequate lover.*

He loudly responded by accusing her of having had a lesbian affair. At their party, an argument ensued, and he pulled out a two-and-a-half inch pen knife and stabbed her in the upper abdomen and again in her back. One of the wounds was close to her heart. Her cardiac sac had been punctured by the knife.

As Adele lay on the kitchen floor, one of the male guests at their party tried to help her. Mailer snarled, "Get away from her. Let the bitch die."

That following Monday, Mailer appeared on the Mike Wallace TV show, announcing his intention to run for Mayor of New York. Later on the show, when he (and the show's viewers) were confronted with questions about the stabbing, Mailer claimed that he had done it "to relieve Adele of her cancer."

Eventually, Mailer turned himself in to the police. A psychiatrist issued a report that he was having an acute paranoid breakdown and delusional thinking. He was diagnosed as both "homicidal and suicidal."

In a hearing before a judge, Mailer was sentenced to the psychiatric ward at Bellevue.

Later, Mailer pleaded guilty to a reduced charge of assault and was given a suspended sentence. Morales made a physical recovery and divorced Mailer in 1962.]

***

When Mailer and Adele departed from Hyannis Port later that afternoon, Jackie felt assured that the magazine article he'd submit to his editors would have positive effects for JFK during the election.

When Jackie read Mailer's article entitled *"Superman Comes to the Supermart,"* after it appeared in *Esquire* in November of 1960, she sent him a handwritten letter praising the piece. Thus began a sometimes turbulent relationship that would stretch out over many years.

He responded to Jackie, perhaps with a touch of egomania, "I think my piece had more effect than any other single work of mine, and I think this is due as much to its meretriciousness as to its merits. I think my calling JFK 'the Existential Hero' was a matter of great historical moment. My article added the one ingredient Kennedy had not been able to find for the stew—it made him seem exciting. It made the election appear important. Around New York there was a turn in sentiment: One could feel it. Kennedy had glamor. Until now, of course, you have always provided glamor for him."

***

Mailer later admitted he'd made a mistake when he wrote Jackie to announce that in the near future he planned to write a biography of the Marquis de Sade, hoping to reveal "the strange honor of the man." He believed, in error, that as a student of French literature, she would appreciate both the project and his role as its creator.

She did not respond to his letter. When *Esquire* assigned him to write an article about Jackie, she refused his request for an interview.

He was reduced to writing an impressionistic overview of her instead. It was very critical, and he referred to her as "The Wild Witch of the East." He even attacked her "cultural timidity" in her choice of the writers and artists she invited to the White House. "Her guest list," Mailer wrote, "should include Allen Ginsberg, William Burroughs, and Norman Mailer himself."

"What we need and what she could offer us was much more complex than the public image of a Madame de Pompadour in a tea-dance dress. Would the Kennedys be no more intelligent than the near past, had they not learned America was not to be saved by Madison Avenue, that no method could work which induced nausea faster than the pills we push to carry it away."

To conclude, Mailer denounced Jackie as "a royal phony."

[Ironically, John F. Kennedy, Jr. would eventually hire Mailer to report on and analyze the 1996 Republican and Democratic conventions for publication in his magazine, George.*]*

In 1962, at a Manhattan cocktail party, Jackie was introduced to Mailer's third wife, Lady Jeanne Campbell, the voluptuous, bright, and beautiful daughter of the roguish Ian Campbell, the 11th Duke of Argyll. Lady Jeanne was widely famous as the favorite granddaughter of the British press baron, William Maxwell Aitken (Lord Beaverbrook).

[Behind a very polite mask, Jackie had reason to dislike both Mailer and his newest wife: Whereas Norman had written an unflattering magazine article about her; Jackie's husband, between 1955 and 1959, had reportedly had an on-again, off-again affair with Lady Jeanne.

Before taking up with JFK, Jeanne had been the lover of Henry Luce, the founder of Time/Life, Inc. In 1961, she'd ditched Luce for Mailer.

Jeanne and Mailer were frequently quarreling partners in one of the most turbulent "literary marriages" of the 20th Century. He was known to have dangled her by the ankles from a second-story window. When she read the unflattering portrait of herself in his novel, An American Dream, she publicly defined it as "the hate book of all time."

In her own memoirs, she wrote: "Norman and I fought so much we could empty a room quicker than any couple in New York. Even the hosts would put

AN UNLIKELY SPITFIRE who aged with dignity: **Lady Jeanne Campbell**, legendary for having sustained affairs with JFK, Nikita Khrushchev, Henry Luce, Fidel Castro, and a turbulent marriage to literary bad boy, Norman Mailer.

on their hats and coats and leave."]

Before leaving that cocktail party in Manhattan, a drunken Mailer crudely confronted Jackie with the threat, "Tell Kennedy that if he fucks my wife again, I'll see to it that he's singing soprano in the choir."

In November of 1963, for *The Evening Standard* in London, Lady Jeanne, as a journalist, reported on JFK's funeral.

[Lady Jeanne lives in legend, along with Marilyn Monroe, as the only woman—so far as it is known—who had sexual liaisons with John F. Kennedy, Fidel Castro, and Nikita Khrushchev. Marilyn was introduced to Nikita on his one-time visit to Hollywood, where he was hosted by 20th Century Fox. Later, Lady Jeanne interviewed Castro in Havana and Nikita in Moscow. "Powerful men were interested in my mother because she was intelligent," Cusi Cram, Jeanne's daughter, later claimed.]

***

In addition to her own frequently embarrassing relationship with Mailer, Jackie became almost obsessed with how he antagonized, and tangled with, Gore Vidal. Early in her relationship with Vidal, before she drifted away from him, he gave her firsthand information about his competitive and upsetting exchanges with the controversial Mailer.

Jackie found herself in a difficult role, as, for a while, at least, she functioned as a kind of sounding board for Mailer's feuds with both Capote and Vidal.

Early in her relationship with Mailer, she accused him of "deliberate cruelty." It was her response to Mailer's observation, in print, of what he had defined as a "concealed cruelty" of her own. As she told Vidal, "Blanche DuBois in *A Streetcar Named Desire* insisted that deliberate cruelty was the one thing she could not forgive."

Jackie was referring to Mailer's published (and highly unflattering) review of her famous guided tour of the White House, which had been broadcast on TV on Valentine's day of 1962 to an audience of 46 million viewers.

In *Esquire,* Mailer wrote, "The voice was a quiet parody of the sort of voice one hears on the radio late at night, dropped softly into the ear by girls who sell soft mattresses, depilatories, or creams to brighten the skin. She moved like a wooden horse and looked like a starlet who will never learn to act. The show was silly, ill advised, pointless, empty, dull, and obsequious to the most slavish tastes in American life."

After that, although she wanted to drop Mailer from her address book, her ability to do that somehow eluded her.

"Over the years, I encountered him frequently, especially when I became an editor in New York. We were always showing up at the same parties. There was no way to avoid him."

Because of her pregnancy, Jackie did not attend the 1960 Democratic convention in Los Angeles. But Vidal spoke to Jackie on the phone, delivering "delicious tidbits" to her. He did tell her that he had run into Mailer at the convention.

"He came up to me and started yelling at me," Vidal said, "saying, 'I hate you! You're too successful!'"

Jackie was eager for gossip about any of the famous names Vidal had met at the Convention. He revealed that he had been assigned to a dining table hosted by Charlton Heston, with whom he'd worked in Rome during the filming of *Ben-Hur*. "He introduced me to his friends, Gary Cooper and Bing Crosby. Later that night, I attended this party hosted by Tony Curtis and Janet Leigh."

In his overview of the event, as delivered to Jackie, Vidal avoided revealing one tidbit of scandal: He'd gotten drunk at the party and had indiscreetly confronted Leigh, asking her, "So how was Jack Kennedy in bed?"

***

Still mourning the assassination *[June 6, 1968]* of Bobby Kennedy, Jackie did not attend the Democratic National convention *[August 26-29, 1968]* in Chicago. But she avidly watched it on television, especially the soon-to-be-notorious confrontation between Vidal and William Buckley, Jr.

Pierre Salinger spoke to Jackie about what Vidal had told him about Mailer.

"Mailer was real cozy with that right-wing creep, William Buckley. In fact, he was brown-nosing the fascist. Does that mean he's gone over to the enemy?"

***

Jackie seemed fascinated by Vidal's points of view about Mailer. "Each time he speaks, he must become more bold, more loud, put on a brighter motley and shake more foolish balls. He certainly knows how to advertise himself. He called *Life* a dirty magazine and said Eisenhower was 'a bit of a woman.' Who knows what outrageous things he'll say tomorrow?"

Even though they were out of physical touch, Vidal continued to send Jackie his essays and, in one instance, a critical appraisal he wrote about Mailer.

"There has been from Henry Miller to Norman Mailer to Charles Manson a logical progression. The Miller-Mailer-Manson, or M3 for short, has been conditioned to think of women as, at best, breeders of sons; at worst, objects to be poked, humiliated, killed."

When Mailer read that, he admitted, "Something blew inside my brain."

Gore also mailed Jackie his 1971 review of Mailer's latest book, *Prisoner of Sex,* his response to the women's liberation movement:

"Mailer's essential arguments boil down to stating that masturbation is bad and so is contraception because the whole point of sex between man and woman is conception. Well, that's what the Bible says, too. He links homosexuality with evil. He claims that the man who gives in to his homosexual drives

is consorting with the enemy. Worse, not only does he betray a moral weakness by not fighting those drives, but he is a coward for not daring to enter into competition with other Alpha males for toothsome females."

As the years went by, Jackie tried to avoid both Mailer and Vidal whenever she could. In 1965, the director, Harold Clurman, escorted her to a production of *Tartuffe* at the Washington Square Theater in Greenwich Village, New York City.

Norman Podhoretz, the editor of the magazine *Commentary,* invited Jackie and Clurman to an après-theater dinner party at his home. The "little Jewish boy from Brooklyn, as Podhoretz satirically defined himself, was enjoying the trappings of celebrity, money, and success.

Jackie agreed to be a guest, with the stipulation "that Norman Mailer will not be there."

Two days later, Mailer commented on his explusion from "the Queen of America's Court."

"I guess Jackie still hasn't forgiven me for writing that terrible review of her White House tour," he said.

After the dinner party, Jackie herself became the subject of another bad review, this time from Podhoretz's wife, Midge Decter. "Jackie Kennedy is the world's oldest sixteen-year-old."

***

In mid-November of 1971, Jackie learned that Vidal and Mailer were scheduled for a joint appearance together on *The Dick Cavett Show.* Although she had another engagement, she cancelled it to stay home to watch the telecast.

In language uncharacteristic of Jackie, she once said, "**Janet Flanner** is one tough old broad, but I adore her *Letters from Paris.*"

She later heard that when Mailer and Vidal came together in the waiting room before going on the air, Mailer, using an assault technique lifted directly from the rough-and-tumble of a soccer field, opted to "headbutt" his rival, causing Vidal pain. A few moments later, Mailer was overheard announcing that he planned, after facing the TV audience, to "smash the fucking teahouse," whatever that meant.

Also waiting to go on was Janet Flanner, the celebrated Paris correspondent for *The New Yorker.* Mailer's behavior shocked her. Jackie had always been a faithful reader of her insightful and widely read "Letters from Paris" column.

Homoeroticism Among the Beat Generation
Gay shenanigans *On the Road*
with **Jack Kerouac and Neal Cassady**

Flanner and Vidal had already discussed Mailer's threat with Cavett before Mailer was introduced. When Mailer came out in front of the TV cameras and refused to shake Gore's hand, Cavett asked him why.

"I have to smell Vidal's works from time to time, and that has made me an expert on intellectual pollution. He has a weak and shameless intellect. The contents of his stomach are no more interesting than the contents of the stomach of an intellectual cow."

In response, the audience booed. Mailer briefly tried to win them back, pleading for understanding. "I've had to face cowards like Vidal, who kicked me in the nuts." Although that remark drew some short-lived applause, Mailer went downhill from that point on.

Mailer then accused Vidal of publicly bragging "about what you did to Kerouac."

"Well, he didn't die," Vidal answered.

The audience was baffled. Mailer was referring to Vidal's widely gossiped-about claim that he had had anal sex with Kerouac, which—in Mailer's opinion—had led to Kerouac's drinking himself to death. After the show, Mailer explained to Flanner what he had wanted to say, but couldn't. "When Vidal fucked Kerouac in the ass, he took the steel out of his *cojones*."

During the program, Cavett was clearly siding with Vidal, provoking Mailer into asking him, "Why don't you look at your question sheet and ask a question?"

"Why don't you fold it five ways and put it where the sun don't shine?" Cavett shot back.

After sitting through the show, Jackie later gave her own review: "I'd grant it five stars. It's real entertainment, the best thing on TV this year."

***

Mailer greatly offended Jackie again with his 1973 biography of Marilyn Monroe, entitled *Marilyn, a Biography.* In the final chapter of the controversial book, Mailer suggested that agents of the FBI and CIA ordered the murder of Marilyn based on the implications of her affair with Robert F. Kennedy, who had few friends in either of the agencies.

Her former husband, Arthur Miller, delayed his response until the 1987 publication of his memoirs, *Timebends.* In it, he scathingly wrote: "Mailer was himself in drag, acting out his own Hollywood fantasies of fame and sex unlimited and power." Miller's editor removed the last line: "Mailer obviously wanted to be Marilyn himself."

***

It would be six years before Vidal encountered Mailer again. The occasion, in 1977, was at a chic Manhattan party given by socialite Lally Weymouth, the daughter of Katharine Graham, the publisher of *The Washington Post.* The party was in honor of Princess Margaret, who telephoned shortly before her scheduled arrival that she was suffering jet lag after her flight from London and that she wanted to go to bed.

Weymouth quickly shifted the theme of her party, morphing it into an event to honor Jackie instead.

Both Mailer and Vidal attended the event, in its early stages staying separated and on opposite sides of the room.

As chicly dressed Jackie entered on the arm of journalist Peter Hamill, all eyes focused on her. She was greeted by an array of celebrities who included author William Styron, Marella Agnelli, Jerry Brown, John Kenneth Galbraith, columnist Joseph Alsop, Gay Talese, William Paley, Barbara Walters, Lillian Hellman, Sam Spiegel, and Susan Sontag.

Appearing unexpectedly, almost from out of nowhere, Mailer stood before Jackie, monopolizing her time.

Aware of their former friendship, Weymouth, in her role as hostess, went over and asked Vidal if he'd like her to escort him over to greet Jackie.

"No way!" Vidal said. "I'll stay here in my corner. She knows where to find me if she wants to talk to me."

He looked over at Jackie's side of the room, where Mailer was talking to her rapidly, "as if fired up about something." When she moved on to another conversation with someone else, Mailer, with a glass of gin and tonic, headed over to Vidal.

Jackie had told Mailer that she rarely saw Vidal, except for a movie date, since Bobby Kennedy had thrown him out of the White House in 1961. Mailer came up to Vidal, who remained seated on a sofa. Jackie glided over to within ten feet of these two antagonists to hear what was going on, even though she seemed absorbed in what Alsop, JFK's gay friend, was saying.

"You look like an old Jew," Mailer said.

Vidal responded, "Norman, you *are* an old Jew."

After he said that, Mailer tossed his gin and tonic into Vidal's face and then threw the glass at him too. It hit Vidal on the mouth, causing his lower lip to bleed. For a few moments, Vidal blacked out.

When he regained consciousness, the first person he noticed was Jackie standing nearby, surveying the scene. After delivering one long, stern look, she turned on her heels and moved away.

Mailer later told her, "I was going to fist him, but first I used an old street fighter's trick of blinding your opponent."

Mailer then grabbed Vidal by the arm, trying to force him to rise to his feet. Vidal tried to fight Mailer off. Both of them struggled with each other, ripping the other's jacket.

As the hostess, Weymouth rushed to the scene, but was asked by others of her guests not to interfere.

She later apologized to Jackie "for this outrage. I thought I was inviting civilized people to my party. What if Princess Margaret had been here? Mailer and Vidal are behaving like two drunken sailors in a bar."

"Oh, Lally," Jackie said. "You couldn't buy such entertainment as this."

Finally, Howard Austen, Vidal's long-time companion, pulled Mailer off Vidal. Mailer stumbled back, falling against Max Palevsky, who stumbled and spilled his champagne onto Weymouth's gown.

In the meantime, Sam Spiegel, the Austria-born film producer, rushed to Mailer's side, urging him to once again attack Vidal. At this point, super-agent Sue Mengers rushed to Vidal's side, wiping the blood off his lip with her delicate lace handkerchief.

Mailer shouted at Vidal, "Listen, you faggot, get up and come out on the street and fight with me like a man."

Austen volunteered that he'd fight him instead.

Mailer looked with contempt at Austen. "A nine-year-old pansy could beat the shit out of you, you little asshole."

Mort Jankow, another guest, later said, "I think the Vidal/ Mailer fight ranks as one of the great moments in modern American literature."

About a year later, in 1978, Vidal and Mailer came together once again, this time at a party following the National Book Awards. Mailer staggered into the reception area drunk, and became instantly enraged the moment he spotted Vidal.

"Without warning, he blindsided Vidal, knocking him back onto the buffet table," said an editor, one of the other guests.

Vidal straightened himself up and turned to Mailer with a slight smirk: "Well Norman, once again words fail you."

"Capote's a Ballsy Little Guy."

—Norman Mailer

"He Should Know... I Seduced Him."

—Truman Capote

During the time that Jackie was still on speaking terms with Truman Capote, Gore Vidal, and Norman Mailer, each of them conveyed their opinions of their rivals to her.

One afternoon in the summer of 1971, Capote invited Jackie for lunch at the Plaza Hotel in Manhattan. Invariably, the subject of Mailer and Vidal came up. "Out of all those people who began publishing when I did, right after the war, there are only three left that anybody knows about—Gore Vidal, Norman Mailer, and me," Capote told Jackie.

"There has to be some 'X' factor, some extra dimension that has kept us going," Capote continued. "Really successful people are like vampires: you can't kill them unless you drive a stake though their hearts. The only one who can destroy a really strong and talented writer is himself."

A month later at a party in Manhattan for authors, publishers, and editors, Jackie encountered Norman Mailer. At one point, he spoke to her about Capote. "Truman and I never became great friends. But we never became enemies like Vidal and myself. Truman and I were neighbors when we both lived in Brooklyn. One afternoon, we strolled into an Irish bar on Montague Street for a long talk. He came in wearing a lavender gabardine cape."

"I thought, 'My god, I've walked into this drunken den of sour male virtue with a beautiful little faggot prince. I figured that the bar flies would pick a fight with me but they didn't. If I looked, walked, talked, and acted like Truman, I'd die of adrenaline overflow.' He was just being himself, and he didn't give a flying fuck what others thought of him."

"Both Jackie and Mailer respected Capote as a writer, claiming that he wrote some of the best and most evocative sentences of his generation. "A Marxist might look at *Breakfast at Tiffany's* and think it's a charlotte russe," Mailer said. "But it captured a capsule of time of life in New York."

"I once in print claimed that Capote is a ballsy little guy," Mailer said, "but he always exaggerated. He rewrote my line, changing ballsy to the bravest man in New York. He had no right to tamper with my simple little quote. I wrote to him and said, 'Come on, Truman. You may be a ballsy little guy, but you're not the bravest in New York. There are guys waiting in line in New York to be the bravest."

"Of course, there was a kind of bravery there," Mailer admitted. "I saw that first hand when we were both booked on *The David Susskind Show* with Dorothy Parker. I wasn't that experienced in facing the TV camera. At first, I did all the talking, but when Susskind turned to Truman, he went to the races. Once the audience got used to that voice of his, he had them laughing hysterically."

"The next day, my friends called me, and all of them claimed that Truman had KO'd me," Mailer said. "There he was, a little faggot in gaudy colors being exactly who he was and getting the audience to laugh with him, not at him. He didn't lower his voice. He didn't keep his wrist from limping. I was floundering all over the place with these huge philosophical and long speeches, and he was zinging me with one *bon mot* after another."

Like Jackie, Mailer was also impressed with Truman's *In Cold Blood,* and he found inspiration to write his own "non-fiction novel," *Armies of the Night* about his involvement in protests against the Vietnam War.

For the movie version of Truman Capote's *In Cold Blood*, the two stars posed for *Life* magazine with the author, who looked like a prisoner himself, on a lonely road in Kansas. **Scott Wilson** *(left)* was cast in the role of mass murderer Richard Hickock, with **Robert Blake** (right) playing Perry Smith.

"Going to Kansas to research *In Cold Blood* was the best thing that ever happened to Truman," Mailer said. "It made him more macho, and that meant a great deal to him. In fact, to be more masculine was more important to him than to any other gay guy I knew. He didn't want to be perceived as a homosexual."

"In Kansas, he met all these macho types, and some of their testosterone got implanted in our little faggot."

"But, alas, as the years went on, Truman got fatter instead of leaner and meaner, like Gary Cooper. Then he did the unforgivable: He became boring. Before that, he considered bores the curse of the earth, and then he became one himself. He had all these opinions, especially about crime, that no one gave a rat's fart about. Not only that, as he aged, he began to look like J. Edgar Hoover . Of course, he despised drag queen Nellie Hoover, who kept a burgeoning FBI file on Truman, or so I heard."

The killers described in Truman's "nonfiction novel" were **Richard Hickock** *(left)* and **Perry Smith** *(right)*, who massacred four members of the Clutter family one bleak night in Western Kansas.

During the research for *In Cold Blood,* Capote fell in love with Smith when he was incarcerated and awaiting execution.

"Hoover keeps a fat file on everybody in public life," Jackie said. "I'd love to read what his boys have dug up on me."

At a party the following year, Jackie encountered Leonora Hornblow, wife of Arthur Hornblow, Jr., the novelist and friend of Capote's. At this party, Jackie heard some astonishing gossip. Truman confided to the Hornblows that one night, he'd seduced Norman Mailer.

When he heard that, my husband got up and walked out of the room." Leonora told Jackie. "Arthur just couldn't believe it, and didn't want to hear another of Truman's lies. He claimed that there was no man he couldn't seduce. Norman Mailer? I wouldn't believe that if I saw it happening here on the carpet!"

When Vidal heard Capote's boast about having seduced Norman Mailer, he said to Jackie, "He's such a liar, but on every other Thursday, he tells the truth. I mean, the mutt seduced John Garfield and Errol Flynn, and he gave Humphrey Bogart a blow-job on the set of *Beat the Devil.* Did he seduce Mailer, perhaps? James Baldwin once told me that Mailer confessed to him one night that he was a closeted homosexual, but that he had consciously chosen to go the other way. Baldwin also claimed that Mailer viewed the American Negro male as a walking phallic symbol."

"I also remember meeting one of Mailer's wives at a party in Manhattan one night—I don't remember which one," Vidal said. "She confided in me that Mailer came home late one night, and she asked him where he'd been. 'Guess what?' he said to her. 'I just fucked a black drag queen.' The way I figure it, if it's a full moon, Mailer and Capote are likely to do *anything.*"

"Truman Lost His Crown as Society's Mascot"

—Norman Mailer

Jackie turned down Truman Capote's invitation to his Black and White costume ball, scheduled with fanfare at Manhattan's Plaza Hotel for the evening of November 28, 1966 and hailed as the Party of the Century. Ostensibly, it was because it was uncomfortably close to the anniversary date (November 22, 1963) of JFK's assassination.

But the day after the party, she made many calls, including one to Lee Radziwill, to find out what she had missed.

Capote had been warned by Babe Paley not to invite Mailer to the party, which had been conceived to celebrate the release of Capote's *In Cold Blood*. "I hear he's very disruptive when he gets drunk and sometimes picks a fight," Babe said.

As it turned out, Babe was correct in her prediction of future violence from Mailer. After only an hour of heavy drinking at the costume ball, he became belligerent.

Editor Norman Podhoretz was close at hand when Mailer got into a rather violent argument about the Vietnam War with McGeorge Bundy, who worked at the White House.

"They had ugly words, Podhoretz said, "most of them coming from Mailer. It got so rough that Mailer invited Bundy to step outside to duke it out with their fists."

Bundy told Mailer, "You are very silly, acting like a naughty little boy."

In Mailer's view, "Bundy pissed me off by pretending to have superior knowledge. He told me I didn't know much about Vietnam and the war, that all I knew was how to protest. I was brave that night, because I was drunk. He looked in better shape than me. Hell, I was roaring mad, and I wanted to kill him. He didn't take up my challenge, and walked away."

"At that point, Lillian Hellman butted her fat dyke ass into the fray, as she always took the side of the person who had the most clout," Mailer claimed.

"Mailer, how dare you threaten Mr. Bundy," Hellman scolded.

"Get lost, bitch," Mailer said. "I don't give a damn whether you wrote *The Little Foxes* or not."

A fellow guest, William Buckley, Jr., was also at the ball. He said, "Mailer was challenging everybody to a fight that night, not just Bundy."

Hellman faded away, soon to be replaced by the former star of *The Little Foxes,* Tallulah Bankhead, who detested Mailer. "Oh, you're the young man who doesn't know how to spell fuck," were Tallulah's first words to him.

[In The Naked and the Dead, *Mailer's publisher, in a misguided fit of prudery, had insisted he substitute the word "fug" for "fuck."]*

"I was real proud the next day," Mailer said. "*Women's Wear Daily* awarded me the worst dressed man at the ball. I showed up in a dirty gabardine raincoat with my black tie. At any rate, I saw Mia Farrow there. I understood why Frank

Sinatra, a child molester, liked to fuck her. All in all, I had to hand it to Truman. He pulled off a grand ball. I don't think I've ever went to anything grander, even if the cowards I challenged there were afraid to fight me. The ball was better than any of Truman's books."

"I know I said Truman was a ballsy guy, and I meant it at the time," Mailer said to Jackie. "But as time went on, those balls got swollen at a certain point, and he just lost it. He became very different in the end. He should never have tried to be the mascot of café society. He thought being society's darling was a great triumph. But it turned out to be the cause of his failure and decline."

Jackie didn't need Mailer's analysis of Capote's downfall, as she had a front row seat to the oncoming disaster, thanks to reports from Lee Radziwill, who had been his friend for so long.

"Truman became devoured by his social life," Jackie claimed to her sister. "By his beautiful so-called swans. I was never that close to him to be one of his swans. In many cases, those swans were ugly ducklings, but beautifully attired and groomed. He was wasting his creativity hanging out with the likes of Babe Paley."

"He should never have started that unfinished novel, *Answered Prayers,*" Jackie said to Lee. "Naturally, I didn't appreciate his unflattering references to me. Of course, café society—or what's left of it—tossed him to the sharks. What in hell did he expect, having publicized those horrible caricatures of his friends at the time? Naturally, you had to drop him when he tried to drag you into that lawsuit with Gore Vidal."

"Truman was unrealistic," Jackie said. "He told me he was going to expose his society friends, but he didn't anticipate their reactions. I warned him that his friends would be friends no more."

"I'm such a powerful figure," he had told Jackie, "that they wouldn't dare not accept my phone calls."

"But suddenly, when *Esquire* came out, Truman was not longer the amusing trinket who had entertained them. Now, he was entertaining the public with their foibles and their very dark secrets."

"With drink and drugs devouring his body like a cannibal, I just knew he would never finish *Answered Prayers,*" Jackie said. "He lied to me and told me it was almost ready to send to Random House, which it wasn't. The book had died within him a decade earlier, and he hadn't buried it yet. He said that the novel would seal his position as the Proust of the 20th Century."

"I'm comparing myself to Proust to you because you're about the only person I know who's actually read him," he said to Jackie.

"He burned his bridges and then looked back in nostalgia," Jackie said to Bennett Cerf. "He faced the more tranquil oasis on the other side of the river bank. But he could neither swim nor take a boat to it. It was too late for such a crossing. He couldn't swim over to that bank because he'd be washed away by the raging current. Truman drowned in his own excesses."

Chapter Nineteen

Jackie's Taste for A-List Movie Stars

After Dates with Sinatra and Brando, She Awards Top Honors to William Holden

Jacques Lowe, JFK's personal photographer, shared a close-up of the private lives of President Kennedy and his First Lady. "They pretty much led separate lives. Jack was jumping in bed every night with some woman, but it wasn't always Jackie. As an Irishman, he viewed women as saints or whores. You have fun with your mistress, sex with your wife for procreation."

Senator George Smathers said, "Don't feel sorry for Jackie because she was married to 'Roto-Rooter.' She may have had a *wham, bam, thank you, ma'am*, type of husband, who was a very selfish lover. But she received in one week more propositions from men, some of whom sent pictures of their erections, than either Elizabeth Taylor or Marilyn Monroe. Of course, I'm guessing at that. Jackie was very selective, but she enjoyed many liaisons as Bathsheba knew David."

Revelations about Jackie's affairs continued into the 21st Century. *The New York Daily News* waited until June 25, 2009 before headlining her affair with Marlon Brando. The public had first learned of the affair in Darwin Porter's biography, *Brando Unzipped,* published in 2005. Many readers insisted that it was unrealistic to expect American icons, such as Jackie, to be held to conventional standards.

"It's just too damn bad," wrote Kerry Chilham. "Jackie was a human being with the inevitable marital conflicts and sex drives."

A distant relative of the Roosevelt family, who preferred to remain anonymous, wrote, "Former Presidents of the United States—and yes, that includes our dearly beloved Franklin Roosevelt and even his wife, Eleanor—have been involved in sexual dalliances. It began with our founding father, that hustler and whoremonger, George Washington, and even went on to include our two gay presidents, Abraham Lincoln and James Buchanan."

Tracy Connor, a staff writer for *The New York Daily News,* wrote, "The Queen of Camelot was heart-wrenchingly aware of the sexual affairs of President John Kennedy during his years in the White House."

She may have been pained by his flagrant philandering, but, as has been revealed in countless articles over the decades, she was no stay-at-home wife. She had her own flings, affairs, romances, and one-night stands, especially with a select few of her favorite movie stars. Most of them were fleeting passions, dispensed like the last rose of summer.

Aboard a yacht in New York Harbor, **Jackie** was caught in a gust of wind. Her whole life had seemed like a hurricane.

"Jackie liked men—maybe not as much as I do, and she did not lead a monastic life," said her former confidant, Gore Vidal. "She was pretty good at concealing her affairs, but she had her share. There was one thing that Jackie, JFK, and I shared in common: All three of us were priapic."

As tabloid stories touted Jackie's romances, many outraged readers expressed their disbelief—"Oh, no, not Jackie!'" Many were still trapped back in the days of the grieving Camelot widow, forgetting that she had married Aristotle Onassis for financial gain instead of love.

Other readers were more sophisticated, including Maressa Brown who wrote: "Although we thought 'Poor Jackie,' upon considering Jack's cheating dog behavior, she was no innocent flower herself. In an attempt to get back at her husband, she had affairs with the likes of actor William Holden, among others."

Super agent Swifty Lazar said, "When it came to movie stars, Jackie didn't go for Sunny Tufts, Lawrence Tierney, Dane Clark, or Brad Dexter, those B-minus stars. She went for the big box office attractions. She certainly had good taste."

In the text that follows, Jackie's conquests are presented in alphabetical order

---

Her "Casting Couch" Included Paul Newman and Gregory Peck,

But presidential hopeful Howard Hughes received a resounding "NO!"

Warren Beatty:
"The Sexiest Man Alive"

In some quarters, Jacqueline Kennedy was considered "The Most Desirable Woman in the World," and actor Warren Beatty was hailed as "The Sexiest Man Alive." Ironically, that same title would later be bestowed on her son, JFK Jr.

Their relationship got off to a rough start. According to rumors, Warren was a bit hard to get.

Of course, at the time, he had virtually every woman at his feet, with gay men left to dream about what might have been.

Warren's reputation had reached the White House. His sister, Shirley MacLaine, had told reporters that "Sex is Warren's hobby." Joan Collins had confided to friends, "Three, four, five times a day, every day, was not unusual for him, and he was able to accept phone calls at the same time."

After a screening of *Bonnie and Clyde*, Jackie told Lee Radziwill and Truman Capote, "There's no way in hell that **Warren Beatty** can be impotent. Some day, I'll have to conduct my own personal investigation. Hopefully, neither of you will have beaten me to him."

The homosexual playwright William Inge had fallen madly in love with Warren Beatty and fashioned two screen properties for him, *Splendor in the Grass* (1961) and *All Fall Down* (1962). Natalie Wood fell in love with him during the filming of *Splendor.*

Both those young stars came together on the rebound. "Warren was depressed because his sweetheart was in England," Natalie said, "and I was devastated over the end of my marriage." *[Her references were to Joan Collins and Robert Wagner.]* She also claimed that "Warren and I spent hours ruminating and analyzing each other's problems."

"Yeah, right," said the jealous Inge. "I'm sure they did when they took time off from fucking."

After her stunning, Oscar-winning performance in the Tennessee Williams' drama, *A Streetcar Named Desire* (1951), Vivien Leigh decided once again to interpret one of the playwright's *grandes dames* on the screen. She agreed to star in *The Roman Spring of Mrs. Stone* (1961) cast (or was it miscast?) opposite Warren as the Italian gigolo. Vivien told her lover, Jack Merivale, "I think he's had some casting couch sessions with Tennessee."

The German actress and chanteuse, Lotte Lenya, befriended Vivien during the shoot, and became her confidante. "At first she disliked Warren intensely, really didn't care for him at all, but he exerted a powerful charm and ended up seducing her."

Jackie saw all three of these films and decided that Warren was the most exciting actor to come along in a decade. When she was told that the film, *PT*

109 had not yet been cast, and consequently, she suggested that Warren would be perfect cast as a young JFK during his career in the Navy. "He'd be charismatic in the role—and oh, so handsome, just like Jack."

JFK gave Jackie some disappointing news: "I've already promised the role to Frank Sinatra."

"Oh, he's a little Italian sausage," Jackie protested. "You're an Irish Catholic. Sinatra would probably get that dreary Angie Dickinson to play me."

"Sorry, sweetheart, but the story ends years before I met you."

When Sinatra turned it down, JFK was open to the idea of Warren appearing as him on the screen. He sent Pierre Salinger, his press secretary, to Hollywood "to feel Warren out. Watch out, Pierre, that he doesn't seduce you," JFK jokingly warned.

After he received it, Beatty said, undiplomatically, "It's one of the worst scripts I've been offered this year. Very poorly written. I don't want to disgrace myself by appearing in it."

Peter Lawford brought Salinger and Warren together at his home. Salinger had heard reports that Warren was "all mixed up."

"Quite the contrary," Salinger claimed. "I found him intelligent, very personable, and thought he'd photograph very handsomely as a young Navy lieutenant."

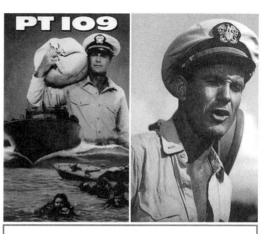

Jackie wanted Warren Beatty to play her husband as a naval lieutenant during World War II in the movie, *PT 109*.

She didn't get her wish. The role went to **Cliff Robertson** *(depicted in both photos, above)* instead. In spite of high hopes, the picture was a failure.

In April of 1943, **Jack Kennedy** *(standing in photo, above)* was sent to the Pacific as commander of a patrol torpedo boat. One night, his boat was sliced in half by a Japanese destroyer. Two of his crewmen were killed.

With the survivors, Jack towed one of his badly injured comrades to safety by clutching the strap of the fellow's life jacket in his teeth and swimming the breaststroke for five hours to reach an island.

Halfway through his discussion with Warren in Hollywood, Salinger thought it was a "done deal," that Warren would definitely accept the movie role of JFK in PT 109. "Then he delivered a bombshell."

"I loathe Bryan Foy and under no circumstances can I work with him," Warren said.

Salinger's heart sank. Foy happened to be the producer of PT 109.

Salinger brought the bad news back to Washington. Warren wouldn't do the picture. Finally, JFK and Salinger suggested Cliff Robertson, who was then thirty-six years old.

Jackie was furious when she heard of this. "I don't know who in hell Robertson is, and I don't want to know. Invite Warren for dinner at the White House. I'll sit next to him. Before the evening is over, he'll definitely agree to play Jack. I can be very persuasive."

Amazingly, and to Jackie's frustration, Warren refused to take any more calls from the White House.

Jack Warner, head of the studio set to release *PT 109*, wanted to cater to the wishes of the White House. He called Warren and told him that JFK wanted him to fly to Washington "to soak up some atmosphere." Arrogantly, Warren sent word back to the president. "Come to Los Angeles and soak up some atmosphere. We have a lot of hot babes here. I'll introduce you around."

Salinger couldn't reach Warren, so Jackie said, "I'll have my social secretary put through a call to him. He'll definitely talk to me."

But Warren did not accept her call, which infuriated her. "The better looking they are, the more arrogant they are," she told her secretary. Even a personal handwritten note from Jackie on White House stationery went unanswered.

Within a period of a year (1962), Warren was offered seventy-five scripts, including *PT 109*. His rejection caused ripples that extended deep into the power structures of both Hollywood and Washington. The actor allegedly told the press, "If the President wants me to play him, tell him to come to Hollywood himself." Later, that remark was cited as an example of Warren's "narcissistic behavior."

After *PT 109*—starring Robertson—opened and flopped, JFK encountered Warren at a social gathering. "You sure made the right decision on that one," the President told the actor.

But although his post-production banter had been friendly with JFK, it was a lot less so with the President's brother. When Warren encountered Robert Kennedy in an elevator, all that the attorney general said to him, was "You're the guy that turned

What do Candice Bergen, Leslie Caron, Cher, Julie Christie, Jane Fonda, Anjelica Huston, Bianca Jagger, Diane Keaton, Madonna, Mary Tyler Moore, Vanessa Redgrave, Diana Ross, Jean Seberg, Carly Simon, Barbra Streisand, and Elizabeth Taylor have in common with Jackie Kennedy? Answer: **WARREN BEATTY!**

355

down my brother in *PT 109*." No further words were exchanged. Warren later issued a statement, denying the quotation attributed to him. "Even as a joke, I never said it, never thought it. Actually, I don't believe there is any actor who wouldn't be pleased at being considered for the role of President Kennedy as a young man. I turned down the script for the simple reason I did not feel I was right for the part."

***

The aging Lothario didn't enter Jackie's life until the late 1970s when Warren was no longer celebrating "The Sweet Bird of Youth."

By then, the former First Lady had gone through two husbands, was working as an editor at Doubleday, and lived in a luxurious apartment on Fifth Avenue.

It was to this apartment, on December 20, 1978, that Jackie decided to invite a list of celebrities who included Andy Warhol and Bob Colacello of *Interview* magazine.

Warhol later claimed that "Jackie was mad as hell when Warren showed up with Diane Keaton on his arm. I suspect Jackie had planned to seduce him that night, and Keaton was needed like a third arm."

When Warren called Jackie the next day for a date, she accepted. Their dates were casual, but confidants of Jackie claimed they usually ended "with a roll in the hay." *[Since Jackie and Warren were not seen out together, it was assumed that their times with each other were conducted as part of private dinners at her apartment.]*

"Jackie was not serious about Warren," Truman Capote claimed. "She was using him like a plaything. She was attracted to him just for his looks, not his brain. In fact, she told me he can't even formulate a complete sentence at one time."

When Warren was interviewed on *Entertainment Tonight* in 1997, the host asked him if he were sleeping with Jackie. Beatty denied it, but was not convincing in his denial.

The relationship ended one night after an intimate party at Jackie's apartment. Warren was in the corner talking to about four or five male guests. One of Jackie's woman friends overheard his conversation. She went to Jackie and told her that "Warren is bragging about having gone to bed with you."

Jackie walked over to Warren and asked to see him alone. As she started to confront him, she noticed Colacello nearby. She quickly shut up and walked away. She didn't want her private conversation with Warren reported in *Interview* magazine.

She liked to think she was the most discreet person on earth, and she couldn't tolerate Warren gossiping about their sexual trysts.

After that, Jackie was no longer available to receive Warren's calls. "Let him go back to Joan Collins, whoever in the hell that is," she told Capote.

One afternoon at Doubleday, Jackie's secretary presented her with a just-published list of the rumored sexual liaisons of Warren. It included the usual suspects, such as Jane Fonda, Vanessa Redgrave, Barbra Streisand, and Natalie Wood. But what horrified Jackie was her own name on the list, followed by Lee Radziwill and Christina Onassis.

"I don't like sharing men with my former daughter-in-law and my sister. Of course, it's not incest, but . . . ."

She never finished her sentence.

Marlon Brando, Jackie's First Seduction After JFK

"I could have been a contender!" Marlon Brando might have said, had he continued pursuing Jackie after his inaugural fling with her in 1964.

"She's the most famous woman in the world, and I'm the most famous—and the best—actor, so we would have made the perfect couple."

Jackie had long admired Brando, especially his "sexy performance" in Tennessee Williams' *A Streetcar Named Desire*, and during the depths of her depression in the months following JFK's assassination, she was eager to meet him. That happened during the period when Marlon's best friend, George Englund, the writer, producer, and director *[he'd helmed Marlon in* The Ugly American *(1963)]*, was dating Jackie's sister, Lee Radziwill.

A double date was arranged, as revealed in Englund's memoir about Marlon, *The Way It's Never Been Done Before*. "There were Secret Service inside and outside the Averill Harriman House in Georgetown," Englund wrote. "We felt like college boys calling on our dates. We were shown into the living room and there were two of America's prettiest people. Jackie and Lee rose to greet us."

A shirtless **Marlon Brando** appears in his most celebrated role, that of the brutish Stanley Kowalski in Tennessee Williams' *A Streetcar Named Desire*.

When her closest confidants inquired about Jackie's time with Brando, she said, "I have enjoyed all of his performances."

About three months after the assassination of JFK, George Englund, a close friend and partner of Marlon Brando, was separated from his wife, Cloris Leachman, and spending a lot of time with Jackie's sister, Lee.

Lee had invited Englund to visit her and Jackie in Washington, and she asked him to bring Marlon along for the visit. The two sisters were staying at the home of the former U.S. Ambassador to both Great Britain and the Soviet Union, Averell Harriman, who had lent Jackie his home as a refuge following the assassination of her husband in Dallas.

At the house, guarded by the Secret Service, Englund introduced "the two best known people in America," Mrs. Kennedy and Marlon Brando. Fueled by martinis, Marlon told them about his travels in the South Pacific during the filming of *Mutiny on the Bounty* (1962) and discussed his work on behalf of Native Americans.

In turn, Jackie demonstrated how Jawaharlal Nehru *[Prime Minister of India, 1947-1964]* taught her how to stand on her head to meditate. Although a bit tipsy, Marlon followed suit. He would continue the practice throughout the next three weeks. Finally, complaining of headaches, he gave up head stands.

Jackie suggested that all four of them go to her favorite French restaurant in Washington, the Jockey Club. It was the evening of January 29, 1964. At the restaurant, the party was ushered to the most private table. But nonetheless, someone spotted the quartet and tipped off the press. Within half an hour, paparazzi and reporters descended in record numbers to cover Jackie's first social appearance since the funeral of JFK.

Abandoning hope of having dinner in privacy, the quartet fled through the restaurant's kitchen door.

Back at Jackie's temporary home, and still hungry because they had to skip dinner, Marlon went into the kitchen and prepared some omelets for them. Jackie, Lee, and Englund sat in her living room, going over the recent, traumatic events in Dallas.

Once the omelets had been consumed, Jackie turned down the lights in the living room and put on Wayne Newton's rendition of "Danke Schoen." Englund and Lee began to dance and neck, and they were soon joined by Marlon and Jackie.

To the sound of the soft music, Jackie danced close to Marlon "pressing her thighs against me." As Lee and Englund wandered off, Marlon—as described in the first draft of his memoirs, joined Jackie on the sofa, where, they began to make out passionately.

"From all I'd read and heard about her, Jacqueline Kennedy seemed coquettish and sensual but not particularly sexual," Marlon wrote in the first draft of his 1999 autobiography, *Songs My Mother Taught Me.*

Joe Fox, a friend of Jackie's and an editor at Random House, prevailed upon Marlon to cut that sequence out of what was eventually published.

"If anything, I pictured Jackie as more voyeur than player," Marlon wrote. "She kept waiting for me to try to get her into bed. When I failed to make a move, she took matters into her own hands and popped the magic question, 'Would you like to spend the night?' And I said, 'I thought you'd never ask.'"

"Some people thought Jackie was more of a voyeur than a practitioner—that she liked to watch," claimed Gore Vidal in his memoirs. "I'm not at all convinced of that. She and Jack both loved gossip and could go on talking endlessly about other people's sex lives, but I always got the distinct impression that she was very interested in sex the same way that Jack was very interested in sex. It was a game for them, and they both played it."

Some published accounts have asserted that Marlon had had too much to drink that night and turned down Jackie's invitation for sex. Because of his drunken state, according to these claims, he feared he'd be impotent and would damage his reputation as one of the world's greatest lovers.

He denied these reports to his best pal Carlo Fiore. "I have never been circumcised, and my noble tool has performed its duties through thick and thin and without fail. Jackie was the recipient of my skill in the boudoir. Proof of that was when she called me three weeks later and invited me for a repeat performance."

After Marlon departed from her home the following morning, she told him, "It was good to know that I have not forgotten how to laugh and be happy."

Jackie's friend, Franklin D. Roosevelt, Jr., claimed that Jackie was "enchanted" by Marlon and found him "extremely attractive." Chuck Spalding, another close observer of the Jackie scene, said, "Like half the other women on the planet, Jackie found Marlon Brando completely irresistible."

She followed up her seduction with a thank you letter to Marlon, claiming that "I found the omelets wonderful and the conversation even more wonderful." She asked him not to tell anyone, but invited him to join her for a secret weekend in New York away from the prying eyes of the press. In Manhattan she had checked into the Hotel Carlyle, where JFK had enjoyed trysts with Marilyn Monroe, among others.

The second seduction took place at a small apartment on Manhattan's swanky Sutton Place, which belonged to some unknown friend of Jackie's.

In that section of his memoirs never published, Marlon wrote of her "boyish hips and her muscular frame. I'm not sure she knew what she was doing sexually, but she did it well."

He later told Fiore, "In some ways it was like fucking a very beautiful boy, and you know how I like to do that."

In his infamous 1956 interview with Truman Capote, Marlon had admitted that he had "gone to bed with lots of men. I'm not gay. These men are attracted to me, and I was doing them a favor."

After his two brief episodes with Jackie, Marlon, back in Hollywood, wrote her a letter in which he proposed marriage. He claimed that his own marriage to Movita Castenada, the Mexican actress, survived in name only. "I can easily get a divorce," he wrote her. In the letter he promised that he could provide privacy from the press and comfort for Jackie and her children on an island in the South Pacific.

Jackie found his proposal "amusing" and filed it with some 2,000 other offers she'd received, including one from a Greek shipping magnate that looked the most promising, at least in terms of financial gain.

In 1974, after Jackie had become Mrs. Aristotle Onassis, Marlon had a violent run-in with Ron Galella, America's most notorious paparazzo, breaking Galella's jaw and knocking out some of his teeth. Galella was known to all tabloid readers for his constant harassment of Jackie. After his release from the hospital, Galella sued Marlon for half-a-million dollars. The lawsuit was settled out of court for $40,000.

Jackie reportedly was "thrilled that Marlon was still out there, looking out for me."

William Holden: Jackie's "Golden Boy"

When Jackie married Senator John F. Kennedy on September 12, 1953, at St. Mary's Catholic Church in Newport, Rhode Island, it seemed unlikely that the paths of this seemingly happy couple would ever cross with those of Audrey Hepburn and William Holden

But both Jack and Jackie were products of an era when devoted movie-goers developed crushes on their favorite stars. Jackie told her sister, Lee Radziwill, that she'd become enchanted with William Holden ever since she saw him portray a beautiful, tormented boxer, Joe Bonaparte, in the 1939 film version of the stage sensation *Golden Boy*. "He exudes masculinity," Jackie claimed.

Likewise, when JFK saw *Roman Holiday* (1953), he told his aide, David Powers, "All little boys jerk off at night dreaming of a fairy princess. When I saw Audrey, I knew at once that she was that fairy princess with whom I could live happily ever after. Unfortunately for me, somewhere along the way, reality set in, and I made the most politically acceptable marriage I could."

From the very beginning, Jackie had been aware of JFK's womanizing, but she did little about it. However, by 1956, she became furious when he did not visit her bedside during the stillbirth of her daughter.

When he made *Picnic* in 1955, **William Holden** told its producers, "I'm too damn old and too conservative to do a striptease."

When Jackie met him two years later, she disagreed. "He was so very sweet, so classy," she told producer Charles Feldman. "Thanks for letting us use your house. Incidentally, did you see that movie, *Love in the Afternoon*, with Bill and Audrey Hepburn?"

Later, she was informed that he had been "shacked up at the time *[of her stillbirth]* with some bimbo."

She wanted revenge and would wait until the opportunity arose.

That came in January of 1957 when she went with her friend, William Walton, a gay artist and former journalist, on a ten-day trip to California. As President, JFK would later appoint Walton to head the White House Fine Arts Commission.

Producer Charles Feldman invited Jackie to a party at his home in Beverly Hills' Coldwater Canyon. It was here that she first met Holden, who had long been her screen idol.

Holden became a household word in 1939 when he starred opposite Barbara Stanwyck in *Golden Boy*. During production of that movie, he also be-

360

came bisexual Stanwyck's lover.

Holden had already appeared in such classics as *Sunset Blvd.* (1950) and *Born Yesterday* (1950), and later, he'd win an Oscar for his role in *Stalag 17* (1953).

Although he suffered from alcoholism and clinical depression, he managed to conduct affairs with such luminaries as Grace Kelly.

Jackie was immediately captivated by him. He'd always been one of her screen idols. Up close and personal, he was even more charming, the archetypical macho American male, with a strong open face and a disarming smile.

Regrettably, at least from Jackie's point of view, Holden was at the Feldman party with his wife, actress Brenda Marshall, whom he'd married in 1941 and with whom he had two sons. When Brenda went out on the terrace to talk with friends, Jackie seized the opportunity to speak privately with Holden.

Jackie told Holden that she was staying at a cottage on the grounds of the Beverly Hills Hotel and suggested that "it would be marvelous if we could go horseback riding in the morning. It's no one's business but our own."

As author C. David Heymann so accurately pointed out, "Jackie would regard Jack's wanderings as an inevitable feature of upper-class wedlock. Also, she would respond with several affairs of her own."

Holden not only showed up for horseback riding, but launched a week-long affair with Jackie. She did not want to be seen entering the Beverly Hills Hotel with such a famous actor, so Feldman agreed to give them the use of his house during the day.

After Jackie had flown out of Los Angeles, Holden during a drunken evening with Feldman, said, "I had to teach Jackie how to suck cock. She told me that Jack had never insisted on that. At first she was very reluctant, but once she got the rhythm of it she couldn't get enough of it. If she goes back to Washington and works her magic with Kennedy, he will owe me one."

Jackie later told Capote, "I've gone to bed with men who have had a problem with hygiene. Not so Bill Holden. He was a compulsive bather before and after sex. He told me he took four showers a day."

Jackie later told Lee Radziwill, "William Holden reminds me of Black Jack. I don't mean in looks. They both love the bottle and adventure. And they're both reckless in love. Regrettably, they both were Republicans."

Jackie also revealed to both her sister and to Capote that she'd confessed her affair with Holden to her husband after her return to him in Washington. She revealed all to JFK, even saying, "Unlike some men I know, William Holden is not a selfish lover. He's very skilled under the sheets."

JFK's reaction is not known. From all reports, he clearly interpreted Jackie's behavior and its subsequent confession for what it was: Payback time.

Although the story may be apocryphal, JFK became so excited by his wife's confession that he seduced her on the carpet of their home.

All that love-making after Holden seemed to have paid off. Jackie announced to JFK in April of 1957 that she was pregnant again. This time she would see the child to term, giving birth to Caroline.

In 1959, when Holden took up residence in Switzerland as a means of avoiding US income taxes, he became the object of public vituperation. Even the future U.S. Attorney General, Robert F. Kennedy, cited Holden as an example of "the rich who pervert our tax laws," and RFK's wife, Ethel, publicly referred to Holden as "a traitor."

Holden confessed how he eventually got even with RFK. "I had Jackie Kennedy," he claimed, "while she was married to Jack. She had long told friends that she thought I was the sexiest man in Hollywood. Word got back to little Bobby, and he was seriously pissed off at me. Later, I learned the fucker was also getting into Jackie's pants."

Letitia Baldrige was photographed with **the First Lady** in 1963.

She later said, "Jackie dazzled heads of state with her knowledge of foreign languages. She knew how to make conversation with princes, ambassadors, and potentates of all kinds. She completely made over the tired, frumpy White House. She was a completely disciplined creature. If she put on two pounds, she would eat nothing the next day. She watched the scale with the rigor of a diamond merchant counting the carats. She set about the task of becoming the most gracious First Lady in the history of America."

***

Although it wasn't widely known at the time, Jackie's affair with Holden continued on and off until 1965, when they drifted apart. The setting for their secret trysts was most often New York.

Several friends knew of Jackie's affair with Holden. They included artist William Walton, Director of the White House Fine Arts Commission; author Truman Capote; and Letitia Baldrige, the etiquette maven who at the time was Jackie's Social Secretary.

As Jackie's assistant, Baldrige was often the person who arranged for Jackie's rendezvous with Holden. The two women had known each other since their days at Vassar, and Jackie affectionately called her "Tish."

The First Lady trusted Baldrige, knowing she was the epitome of discretion. It was only after Jackie's death that Baldrige spoke of the affair, and that was only after she had learned that Jackie had confessed the affair to author William Manchester. Her "confession" *[as discussed in another chapter of this book]* was locked away at the Kennedy Library for future generations to ponder.

"Mrs. Kennedy was in love with Bill—he didn't want me to call him Mr. Holden—for a very, very long time," Baldrige claimed.

When Jackie's gossipy, treacherous friend, Truman Capote, learned about Jackie's fascination with Holden, he filled her in on what he called "the dirt." He knew that Jackie had seen all of his movies, including *Sunset Blvd.* (1950); *Born Yesterday* (1950); *Stalag 17* (1953); *Sabrina* (1954, and co-starring Audrey Hepburn); and two movies with Grace Kelly—*The Country Girl* (1954) and *The Bridges of Toko-Ri* (1955).

Capote informed Jackie of Holden's past seductions of beautiful women, including Grace Kelly, Audrey Hepburn, Barbara Stanwyck, Gail Russell, Shelley Winters, Lucille Ball, and Dorothy Lamour.

"After Holden seduced her, I know that Jackie became mad about the boy," Capote claimed. "I envied her. I was also mad about the boy myself. She told me that 'He was totally into women and gave of himself completely. She claimed that he was sensitive to a woman's needs and didn't just take a woman selfishly as a means of satisfying his libido. I think that was a subtle dig at her husband."

"If she had any complaint about Holden at all, it was that he treated her like a goddess. I remember her exact words. She said that 'Bill handles me like his special angel—never the whore. It's a wonderful feeling, but at times, I'm slightly embarrassed by being placed on a pedestal.'"

"The only thing that upset me was when Mrs. Kennedy would cancel an important engagement I had set up for her and rush off for a secret rendezvous with Bill," Baldrige said.

"I don't care how important the person or group was. Mrs. Kennedy fled when Bill called unexpectedly and wanted to get together, as he was passing through New York, rarely Washington," Baldrige said. "At the last minute, I'd have to get her mother, Janet, to fill in for her, even, on occasion, Rose Kennedy."

Although she left her job at the White House six months before JFK was assassinated, Baldrige remained Jackie's loyal friend and ally. Even after her departure, The First Lady used her "for special arrangements," and they spoke to each other at least once or twice a week.

Eventually, Baldrige wrote three books that capitalized on her brief but shining White House career, but they were of a vanilla nature that didn't alarm Jackie. "It was my moment in history, and I knew I was part of something incredible," Baldrige told the press.

Privately, she confessed, "I knew every time a mouse ran across the floor of the Oval Office—yes, about the President's womanizing and all that. I was also privy to Mrs. Kennedy's love affairs. However, none of that good stuff got into my books, which were mostly about menus, etiquette, or recipes. I deliver only a few minor 'shockers,' such as Mrs. Kennedy calling Helen Thomas and other White House newswomen 'the Harpies.'"

To an increasing degree, Jackie turned to Walton as her confidant, especially when Capote began to spend most of his time with her sister, Lee Radziwill.

Walton was a gay man, and she felt she could confide her sexual secrets to him. Some nineteen years older than Jackie, he was frequently her escort, and he was adept at arranging for Jackie to slip away and meet with Holden, "covering her tracks," as he told his close friends.

Gregarious, intelligent, and sophisticated, Walton became particularly close when he helped her redecorate the White House. He was such a good friend that Jackie invited him as a guest to the Kennedy's first Thanksgiving dinner (November, 1961) in the White House.

"A lot of people didn't know it, but Mrs. Kennedy had this wild, romantic streak in her," Walton said. "She would always come back after visiting Holden with a gleam in her eye. I think she was truly in love with him, even though aware of his personal problems—and those included alcoholism and his ever-constant depression."

"One time, she sounded like a romance writer when she told me that the most exciting moments in her life occurred when Bill was making love to her, and his face was right over hers, and he looked deeply into her eyes," Walton said. "As I recall, she said, 'He makes me feel like a real woman, unlike some of the cads I have known.'"

"Jackie had only one regret about keeping her affair with Holden a secret," Walton said. "She often wondered how word could be leaked to Princess Grace in Monaco. She had heard that Grace had fallen madly in love with Bill when they'd worked together in pictures. Jackie was very competitive with Grace, knowing that she'd slept with the President. Maybe she was seeking some sort of revenge by sleeping with Holden, hoping to make Grace jealous."

Walton also added a footnote to American history. Holden's best friend was Ronald Reagan. Through that connection, Jackie secretly became acquainted with the future two-term American President of the 1980s.

"Sometimes, Reagan helped arrange meetings between Jackie and Holden," Walton claimed. "I don't mean to imply that Reagan was a pimp. I prefer to call him a discreet facilitator. Reagan attended a few private dinners between Jackie and Holden, always disappearing after dessert was served."

Even though she'd long ago lost touch with him, Jackie continued to have a special crush on Holden. When she was free to pursue a possible marriage to him, she decided it was too late. Descriptions of his alcoholism had reached her, filling her with despair. "Such a waste of a life from such a talented and charming man," she said.

Through Capote and other friends, she kept up with him and was horrified as he descended deeper and deeper into alcoholism. "If I had married Bill instead of Jack, I could have saved him," she told Capote. From a friend in Rome, the author had learned that the actor had been charged with drunk driving and manslaughter in Italy.

His Ferrari had crashed into a small Fiat on the *autostrada*. The driver of the Fiat was killed instantly. Holden was pronounced guilty in an Italian court, but got off easy. The judge gave him an eight-month suspended jail sentence after he'd settled $80,000 on the victim's widow.

In his unpublished memoir of his years as a confidant of both JFK and Jackie, Walton said that she had told him that it was then-President Reagan who called her on November 16, 1981, from the White House, to report to her that Holden had been found dead in Hollywood.

The actor had been drinking heavily and fell, hitting his head on a coffee table. He lapsed into a coma and never regained consciousness. Several days passed before his body was discovered. Normally, his maid came in five days a week, but she had retired, and Holden had not yet hired a replacement.

As Jackie reported Reagan's conversation with her, the President said, "Bill was beloved by millions, but died alone."

Through tears, Jackie said, "Mr. President, you and I may stand on different political fronts, but we do share something in common. Both of us loved Bill. He spent a good part of his life trying to rescue endangered animals in Africa. But it was Bill himself who was an endangered species—a nice guy."

In the film, *Sabrina* (distributed in the U.K. as *Sabrina Fair*), **William Holden** fell in love with **Audrey Hepburn** both on and off the screen. But when he shared a "deadly secret" with her, she broke off their affair.

[Weeks later, Jackie gasped in horror when she learned the gruesome details of the discovery of Holden's body. On November 16, 1981, when Bill Martin, the manager of Holden's apartment building, became alarmed when the actor hadn't been seen in many days. He let himself into Holden's apartment with a passkey. As an autopsy later revealed, "The body was in an advanced state of decomposition, with maggots present and a large amount of putrefaction present, as evidenced by the tissue separation and blisters with fluid present. It is theorized that he probably started vomiting blood, and possibly lacerated the lower portion of his esophagus. He apparently had been dead for days. The alcohol level in his bloodstream was 2.2.

Coroner Dr. Thomas Noguchi concluded that Holden at first did not comprehend the seriousness of his injury, even though a phone was just inches from his head. Apparently, he'd tried to stop the bleeding but then passed out from the loss of blood. It was estimated that he was dead within 15 minutes of his fall.]

JFK's Love Affair With Audrey Hepburn
Love, Infidelity, Politics, and the Movies

Shortly after the April, 1953 wedding of her sister, Lee Bouvier Radziwill, to Michael Canfield, Jackie, the roving reporter with a camera, interviewed Senator John F. Kennedy in Washington. Across the hall she also interviewed Richard Nixon, the Vice President of the United States.

After her eventual marriage to JFK, Jackie revealed to him that his future opponent for the office of President "had made a pass at me. The pass was not intercepted."

Senator Kennedy told Jackie how much he admired the Veep and that he'd contributed $1,000 to Nixon's campaign in 1950 when he'd run a smear campaign against Democratic Senator Helen Gahagan Douglas ("she's as pink as her underwear"). But despite its auspicious beginning, the Nixon/JFK friendship, tenuous even at its best, would not endure for very long.

JFK called Jackie the next day and invited her out on a date for dancing at the Blue Room in Washington, D.C.'s Shoreham Hotel. She bought a new gown for the occasion, but when he came to pick her up she was disappointed to see that he'd brought along his buddy, David Powers, as a kind of chaperone.

Powers, part of JFK's "Irish Mafia," helped the young naval veteran win his first election to Congress and then served as his personal aide and confidant throughout his short presidency,

After that night, JFK began to date Jackie, and she learned to get by without flowers, gifts, or love letters. He also had a strict rule, "No touching in public, there are photographers everywhere."

Meeting with David after work, JFK told him that he'd fallen in love with Jackie. He produced four pictures of Jackie and himself which had been snapped by an automatic camera in a photo booth in a penny arcade, "I could tell from the adoring look on each of their faces that they were in love."

Later in life, David said, "My friend Jack was full of surprises. Take the night he arrived late at my apartment in Boston."

JFK had come to him to talk over "a very pressing matter. I'm in real trouble."

David thought he'd been caught up in some scandal, no doubt having impregnated a married woman.

Sitting with a drink in David's living room, JFK said, "I'm in love with Jackie. But I'm also in love with Audrey Hepburn." He carried a picture of her which he pulled out of his wallet and showed to David.

Hepburn's face had been world famous since her appearance with Gregory Peck in *Roman Holiday* (1952).

The knockout *gamine* looked and behaved like a Princess in the picture and also in real life.

"I'm having a very secret affair with her," JFK told David.

"I'll say this for you, you sure do have good taste in women," David told him.

"Pencil thin and doe eyed, that Hepburn was some dish," David said. "She was ravishingly beautiful. Throughout her life she would appear as the epitome of class but without the snobbery. She was real. Jackie—and I loved the gal dearly—was much more pretentious."

"Audrey dazzled us the first time she walked into Senator Kennedy's office," said JFK's secretary at the time, Mary Gallagher. "With her black-and-white dress, with a long-stemmed scarlet red umbrella, she was impressive.

She had the grace of a swan, the movement of a gazelle."

"Believe it or not, Jack's staff didn't know he was having a torrid affair with Audrey," David said. "Remember this was the Fifties. The image of a movie star and a handsome United States Senator, much less a future President, was not in everybody's mind back then. It would have sounded too far-fetched. Audrey escaped detection on the radar screen, even though she was seen leaving his Georgetown residence at three or four o'clock in the morning."

"All of us on Jack's staff knew that he was dating Jackie—not just dating her, but in love with her," Gallagher said. "Believe it or not, we didn't think anything was going on between Audrey and Jack. How naïve we were back in those days."

When Joseph Kennedy heard of Jack's "two loves," he called him to Hyannis Port for a face-to-face, father-son talk. "You want to be President one day, don't you?"

"You know that father," JFK said.

"Then it's got to be Jackie, even though her father—that Black Jack faggot—is a complete shit. Hepburn is a cute little piece," his father continued. "But she's foreign born. She's not Catholic. She's about to make a movie with William Holden and Humphrey Bogart. At least one of them will end up fucking her. I'm putting my money on Holden. Take my advice. Audrey for fucking, Jackie for marriage."

Joe Senior was right. By the time "Jack & Jackie" announced their engagement, Audrey had returned to Hollywood to star in *Sabrina*. When the cameras weren't on her, she was indeed maintaining a torrid affair with Holden.

Jackie, who loved gossip, heard about the Holden/Hepburn affair. At one point, Holden planned to leave his actress wife, Brenda (Ardis) Marshall, to marry Audrey. Audrey had even predicted, "I think we could have beautiful babies together."

But he was forced to tell her the truth. He'd had a vasectomy after the birth of the second of his two sons. He could have no more children. She was devastated, as she desperately wanted to have children. Finally, even though she was in love with Holden, she told him she couldn't marry him. This time, Holden was devastated.

"After Audrey refused to marry me," Holden said, "I fucked my way around the world. My goal was to screw a girl in every country I visited. I'd had practice being a whore. When I was a young actor starting in Hollywood, I used to service actresses who were older than me." *[He was referring to Barbara Stanwyck.]* "I'm a whore. All actors are whores. We sell our bodies to the highest bidders."

Audrey was very sad to learn about the marriage of Jack with Jackie. "It could have been me," she told Gregory Peck. "I know that Jack in his heart was in love with me and wanted me to be his wife. He was forced to choose Jackie for political reasons, for his career."

Two gay authors, both friends of Jackie's, weighed in with their views of the marriage.

"Jackie was always a 'cash 'n carry' kinda gal," said Capote.

"Jackie married Jack for the money," said Gore Vidal. "There weren't that many other openings for her. Actually, if she hadn't married Jack, she would have married someone else with money, although it wasn't likely she would have gotten someone as exciting as Jack as part of the bargain. When given a choice of glory or money, most people choose glory. But not Jackie. She also wound up with plenty of the latter, of course, but she didn't need that like she needed to be rich."

What the world didn't know at the time—and what Jackie later found out—her husband's affair with Audrey continued on and off until the year of his death (1963).

The whole world seemingly remembers Marilyn Monroe singing her erotic version "Happy Birthday, Mr. President" on May 29, 1962, only months before she was murdered.

But far fewer people know that it was Audrey, another movie queen and a former lover of JFK, who sang the final "Happy Birthday, Mr. President" to him a year later, on May 29, 1963.

Hepburn had been invited to the White House to sing "Happy Birthday" on the occasion of JFK's forty-sixth year on Earth, which would be his final one. Her rendition—presented in front of a very private gathering of cronies—resulted in enthusiastic applause.

Afterward, she stood with singer Eddie Fisher in a receiving line to greet the president. "I knew they had been lovers, and the President seemed genuinely pleased to see her again," Fisher said. "Had Audrey pleased Joseph Kennedy as a prospect for marriage, she, not Jackie, would have been the First Lady of the land."

"Kennedy's face lit up like a Christmas tree, when he came up close and personal with Audrey, who looked lovely," Fisher said. "He whispered something in her ear. I suspect it was an invitation for their final fuck—for old time's sake, you know."

Jackie had her own surprise planned for the day of JFK's birthday that year. Even though it was raining, she had organized a cruise down the Potomac aboard the presidential yacht *Sequoia*. Bobby and Teddy Kennedy were obvious choices on the guest list, as was the ever-faithful Lem Billings. David Niven and Hjordis, his wife, were among the surprise guests. *[After Niven's return*

It was **Audrey Hepburn**, not Marilyn Monroe, who sang "Happy Birthday, Mr. President" to him during the last year (1963) of his life.

Here, Miss Hepburn is depicted as Eliza Doolittle in *My Fair Lady* (1964), as costumed by Cecil Beaton.

to Hollywood, he said, "I think that Lem Billings would eat Kennedy's shit if he asked him to."]

Jackie may have been a bit impish in having invited the Nivens on board the cruise. She'd learned that her husband was having an affair with Hjordis. Audrey, however, was definitely not included on her guest list.

"If I'd invited all of Jack's lovers, the *Sequoia* would have sunk into the Potomac," Jackie said later.

Capote, a friend of both Jackie and Audrey, told the actress that "Jackie is very jealous of you. There are those who say that you out-Jackie Jackie herself."

Before JFK even boarded the *Sequoia* that afternoon, rumor had it that he had already deflowered Audrey in the Lincoln bedroom.

Even though her dignity might have been trampled upon during at least some of these events, Audrey retained an affectionate memory of the President, and always spoke with nostalgia of "what might have been."

***

On Friday, November 22, 1963, Audrey was on the verge of a nervous breakdown during the filming *My Fair Lady* in Los Angeles, where daytime temperatures hovered between 110 and 118 degrees Fahrenheit. She'd been in bed for three days under a doctor's care, and had just returned to work. George Cukor, the film's director, was on the set discussing a scene with Audrey when a grip's portable radio brought news of the assassination of John F. Kennedy.

"I was too shaken to make the announcement or tell the crew," Cukor later said. "I asked Audrey if she'd do it. I knew how close she'd been to the President."

Putting up a brave front while holding back tears, she said, "I'll do it." She was trembling as she took the microphone and announced to the cast and crew, "The President is dead. Shall we have two minutes of silence to pray or do whatever you think is appropriate? May God have mercy on us all."

Months after JFK was assassinated, in one of Audrey's rare instances of immodesty, she spoke about the President to her closest friend, the French actress Capucine.

"I adored him. I think I made a big mistake in not marrying him. My greatest role should have been First Lady. Many members of the press claim that I have more grace, style, and flair than Jackie herself."

Audrey carried a picture of JFK around with her for years. She had cut Jackie out of the photograph and in its place, imposed a picture of herself instead.

Howard Hughes; Bisexual, the Aviator Flies After Both Jack & Jackie

For a very rich and very decadent bisexual like the fabled aviator and movie mogul, Howard Hughes, the amorous pursuit of both a husband and his wife is not all that unusual. Howard, during different eras, pursued both a young John F. Kennedy during his visit to Hollywood in 1940, and, much later, after the assassination of her husband, an older Jacqueline Kennedy.

The story begins just before the outbreak of World War II, when JFK, loaded with references and addresses from his famous father, arrived in Hollywood and met actor Robert Stack, who became his best friend.

Between other romances, Howard had become smitten with Robert and invited him to go sailing one Sunday afternoon. The young actor asked if he could bring a friend from Boston. Howard reluctantly agreed, thinking it might be one of Robert's young starlet girlfriends. In those days the extraordinarily handsome actor was making the rounds, seducing "a starlet a minute," as he put it. Howard would have preferred to enjoy the actor's charms alone but agreed to play host to whomever Robert opted to bring along for their weekend sail to Catalina.

Even though she was carrying on an illicit affair with her brother-in-law, Robert Kennedy, it is believed that Jackie gave serious attention to an offer of marriage from **Howard Hughes**, the billionaire aviation and movie mogul.

He wanted to run for president, and he wanted her to hit the campaign trail with him, knowing they would attract record crowds. But before she'd accept his proposal of marriage, she made her highest ever demand on his bank account.

On the deck of the rented *Sea Queen*, Howard was introduced to the young John F. Kennedy, who was dressed like a sailor, all in whites. "He's Ambassador Kennedy's son," Robert said, introducing the young newcomer, who was twenty-three years old and a recent graduate of Harvard. He'd just published a book, *Why England Slept*, which had been ghost-written for him.

Howard detested the young man's father, Joseph Kennedy, their feud stemming from the time the liquor dealer had been a power broker in Hollywood. On a few occasions, both men had seduced the same women, notably actresses Constance Bennett and Nancy Carroll.

When Howard later thanked Robert for inviting the young man for the weekend, Robert knew Howard was smitten. John soon became "Jack." Howard confided to Robert, "He has the most perfect blue eyes I've ever seen on a man."

The moment Jack flashed his soon-to-be-famous smile at Howard, the tall, thin, very rich Texan bonded with the New Englander, with his natural charm and grace. It was as if Howard had waited all his life to meet the perfect Prince Charming. The only problem was that the gleam in this young man's eyes was not directed at Howard, but at every beautiful woman in Hollywood. Over dinner that night, Jack told Howard that, "I want to fuck every woman in Hollywood." He called it "celebrity poontang."

A lifelong lover of gossip, Jack admired and was intrigued with Howard and was eager for anything he might reveal about the many legendary stars he'd seduced. During his sojourn in Hollywood, Jack wanted to use Howard as his role model. "You're the swordsman out here," Jack told Howard. "No doubt about that. Even Dad admits it's true—and he's bedded a few beauties, not just Gloria Swanson. I'm the new boy in town and I want to follow in your footsteps."

Previously, Robert had amused Howard by telling him that Jack, although he'd just arrived in Hollywood, had already orchestrated a total of eight seductions, each time with a different woman.

Robert Stack formed an immediate friendship with young John F. Kennedy when he first arrived in Hollywood.

Stack said, "Jack was the only man in Tinseltown better looking than me, and all the hot tamales on the West Coast took notice. He really needed a date book. I've known him to have sex in the afternoon with a woman, sex at cocktail time, sex after dinner, and even a sleepover after midnight, each with a different woman."

"I've known many of the great Hollywood stars, and only a few of them seemed to hold the attraction for women that Jack does," Robert said. He noted that even before his handsome friend entered politics, he'd just look at a woman and she'd "tumble."

"Unlike me, Jack had completely versatile taste in women—blondes, brunettes, redheads, young ones, mature ones, gals with large breasts, gals with lemons for breast," Robert said. "Regardless of the girl, he always insisted on shapely legs."

Aboard his yacht, Howard seemed voyeuristically eager for details about young Jack's string of conquests.

Before they reached Catalina Island, Robert realized that both Howard and Jack were experienced sailors "born to ride the waves." "The men quickly bonded," he claimed. Robert said that he never informed Jack about Howard's homosexual streak. "I figured Jack could take care of himself. Many gays had come onto him."

Somehow Howard and Jack struck a harmonious note with each other, especially during discussions of their sexual conquests. Robert later admitted he felt left out. At that point the only woman that both Howard and Jack had each had some form of sexual contact with was Marlene Dietrich. "That didn't surprise me, since Marlene did anything in pants or skirts, although she never got around to me," Robert said.

On Catalina Island, Jack wandered off for about five hours," Robert said, "so Howard and I just assumed he'd gotten lucky. We know for a fact that he boarded another yacht in the harbor. The following Sunday we went for a nude swim. I couldn't help but notice that Howard checking out Jack's equipment. Of course, Howard himself had all of us beat."

Robert said that he wasn't surprised when another invitation for another weekend was extended by Howard. "This time I was excluded, and it was all right with me. I got mixed up with Howard in the first place because I thought he was going to advance my career. But by 1940 I'd come to realize that Howard wasn't going to do a god damn thing for me. He just wanted Hollywood's handsomest boy—namely me—to hang out with him."

"Jack told me he was going to Palm Springs for the weekend with Howard," Robert continued. I didn't warn Jack not to go. Why shouldn't he go? He dropped a bomb on me when he told me that Howard had convinced him that he should pursue a career as a motion picture star, even though the ambassador, his father, wanted him to go into politics one day. Two days before Jack left to join Howard in Palm Springs, I noticed that he kept looking at himself in every mirror he passed. I think every good-looking guy and beautiful gal in the world dreams of becoming a movie star. Why should Jack be an exception? He said, 'I can just hear his dad shouting at me: No Kennedy becomes a movie star.'"

The details of that weekend in Palm Springs remain sketchy. The only source for what happened was Stack, who wasn't even there. He later reported that he "learned a little bit from Jack and not a lot more from Howard himself."

Howard had obviously set up the weekend to impress Jack. He seemed to bask in the flow of Jack's admiration for him. Jack had been bragging about his conquests to Howard, but the older man wanted to show the younger one that he too could round up two "hot dates" for the weekend.

After the Palm Springs weekend, Howard continued his hopeless pursuit of Jack, who'd soon be heading back to the East Coast. Howard didn't get to see Jack in action, but he did take him to the private studios of a tall black masseur, who called himself "Nobu." During the war years, Nobu, from some unknown country, was famous in Hollywood for his thorough massages, which involved masturbating his clients, both male and female, to the "mother of all climaxes." His patrons included Errol Flynn, Lana Turner, Paulette Goddard, Joan Crawford, and Howard himself.

Although it later became fashionable for certain masseurs in New York and California to give massages that involved sexual climaxes, in Nobu's time no one did that except prostitutes hired for that purpose.

Jack told Robert that Howard took him to be worked over by the "magic hands" of Nobu. Both men lay nude on separate beds in Nobu's studio while sensual music played. "I got this big erection," Jack later confided to Robert. "By the time he was finished with me, I was splattering the ceiling. I've never seen anything like it. He really knows how to touch the right spots."

Although Nobu may have been a peak experience in Jack's life, other masseurs have reported that he always got an erection when being massaged, even by a man. Frank Sinatra's valet, George Jacobs, wrote in his memoirs, that he gave Jack a massage in Palm Springs when he was the guest of his boss. "By the time I rolled him *[meaning Jack]* over to do his trunk and thighs, he had an enormous erection."

From all reports, Howard never got to experience Jack's erection first hand. Robert speculated that Howard made one attempt and failed to win Jack over. Such an occurrence may have happened during Jack's final weekend on the West Coast before his return to the East Coast. This time Jack was picked up and delivered to a beach house in Santa Monica which was owned by Marion Davies.

"I knew Jack was looking forward to it," Robert said.

"I fully anticipated that he'd arranged to have Rita Hayworth, Lana Turner, and Betty Grable there. To Jack's disappointment, when he got to Santa Monica, he found that he was the only invited guest."

"I don't know exactly what happened that weekend because Jack never told me everything," Robert said. "And Howard abruptly changed the subject a week later when I inquired."

"The following Monday morning, when I was telling Jack good-bye, he told me that he never wanted 'to see Howard Hughes again—that guy's too much of a creep for me.'"

***

A blaze of gunfire on November 22, 1963 in Dallas, Texas, Howard Hughes' home state, ended the reign of Camelot. Howard was sitting with his pimp, Johnny Meyer, discussing plans when news came over his television set that President John F. Kennedy had been shot in a motorcade. The extent of his wounds was not immediately known.

Before his own death, Meyer had shopped a tell-all book about his former employer. As part of its sales proposal, he claimed that in the immediate wake of the assassination, Howard dropped all of his plans and stayed glued to the television for the next eighteen hours without sleep.

"I knew that bossman had known young Jack Kennedy years before," Meyer claimed in his book proposal. "I also knew that Howard hated old man Kennedy and wasn't a particular admirer of the 'left wing' politics of his son. Yet he stayed glued to that set like he'd lost his best friend. I just didn't get it. It was weeks before I learned the full extent of bossman's scheme. He wasn't mourning the slain president. He was planning to replace him!"

In the year of Kennedy's death, Howard refused to face business emergencies. He either postponed decisions or ignored them completely. "There were more than brush fires to put out," Meyer said. "There were bonfires. Everybody on the planet was suing Howard, sometimes successfully."

The spring of 1963 had gone badly for Howard. On February 11, 1963, he had refused to appear for deposition in a TWA lawsuit. On May 13 of that same year, a Federal judge in New York had awarded TWA a default judgment for Howard's refusal to show up. He was ordered to pay his own airline

$135,000,000 in damages and sell his own stock. "That was a bitter pill for Howard to swallow," Meyer said.

"I think Howard was lusting for other worlds to conquer, but he hadn't made up his mind what those worlds would be," Meyer said. "By 1967, he would channel his fading energy into acquiring the Desert Inn Hotel and Casino in Las Vegas, the first step on the road to building an empire in Las Vegas and becoming King of the Desert."

In the aftermath of Kennedy's assassination, Howard began to develop a dream that was far greater than Las Vegas. In September of 1960, he'd turned fifty-five, and with his gray hair and declining health had begun to refer to himself as middle aged, even though he hated the term. "Who in the fuck decided that a man in his fifties is middle aged?" he once asked Meyer. "How many men do you know who are a hundred years old?"

When he got cleaned up and dressed, **Howard Hughes** looked respectable enough to consider running for president. From his delusional mind, he made a bid for an unbeatable electoral accessory: THE WIDOW JACKIE

As November faded into a bleak Christmas of 1963, Howard began to take stock of himself. He'd conquered many fields—more or less successfully—including aviation and motion pictures. Satellites his company manufactured were orbiting the planet, bringing *I Love Lucy* into homes in Bombay and Sydney. TWA was flying passengers across the globe. But three years before Kennedy's assassination, Howard had lost control of TWA.

"One time he turned to me and I'd never seen such a pathetic look on his face," Meyer said. "Normally when I looked into his eyes, I saw a feudal baron of immense power staring back at me. Even though we'd been asshole buddies for years, and I knew all his secrets, those blazing eyes of his sent shivers through me. Howard scared the shit out of me, he was so vindictive. I never wanted to cross him. I like eating too well, as one look at me will quickly reveal. He'd already turned on his business manager, Noah Dietrich, and made him the enemy. I knew he could do that to me as well."

"He seemed obsessed with Kennedy's assassination and couldn't wipe it from his mind," Meyer claimed. "I don't know how he got it, but he'd obtained a copy of the Zapruder film, which he watched endlessly. He must have seen it a thousand times. He wasn't just watching a home movie, but studying it with the eyes of a cobra."

A Dallas-based manufacturer of women's garments, Abraham Zapruder just happened to be shooting a home video recording of Kennedy's Dallas motorcade at the precise moment of the assassination. Had he not done so, the actual assassination would not have been captured on film. Zapruder sold his historic film to *Time Life* for $50,000, although Howard thought that it was worth at least two million—"maybe more"—he confided to Meyer.

"He was watching it for some clue, although I didn't know what at the time," Meyer said. "At first I thought he was seeking some clue as to who shot Kennedy. But he had something else on his mind."

"Mrs. Kennedy is being portrayed in the press as the grieving widow," Howard told Meyer one day after viewing the Zapruder film for at least three playbacks in a row. "But I see something else there. This woman is a 'me-first' type gal. She's a survivor."

In the weeks to come, Howard ordered Meyer to gather up all the information he could about those HUGHES FOR PRESIDENT clubs that had sprung up across the country in the wake of his August, 1947 testimony in front of Senator Ralph Owen Brewster's Senate committee. Although they had virtually disappeared, Howard instructed Meyer to "reactivate them—money is no object."

Howard's plan began to reveal itself to Meyer more fully. Howard had more or less assumed that Lyndon B. Johnson, a fellow Texan, would seek and win the presidency in 1964. "Howard announced to me that he was going to run for president in 1968 on the Democratic ticket even though he was an arch-conservative," Meyer said. "He wasn't a Democrat. Neither was he a Republican. Politically, Howard lived in limbo land."

The way Howard saw it, his chief competitors for the 1968 Democratic Presidential nomination would include Lyndon B. Johnson and Robert Kennedy. Richard Nixon, he surmised, would seek the nomination on the Republican ticket.

"Howard felt he could eliminate Nixon by offering him bribes," Meyer said. "He believed that Nixon was such a crook that he'd accept any bribe. Once Howard had him where he wanted him, he'd release news of Nixon's dirty deeds to the press, which would destroy his political career and cost him the election."

"But how do you plan to knock out Bobby Kennedy and LBJ?" Meyer asked Howard.

"Howard looked at me for an astonishing moment, then said, 'I plan to marry Mrs. Kennedy!' You could have knocked me over with a feather. At first I thought he was joking, but when I saw that steely look in his eyes, I knew he was determined."

"My surprise wasn't over," Meyer claimed. "Later that day, he told me that I was to be the go-between in negotiating a marriage between Mrs. Kennedy and himself. It was to be a marriage of convenience. I was to contact Mrs. Kennedy and offer her ten million dollars if she'd marry Howard and campaign for him in the 1968 election. For her cooperation, he would also set up separate trust funds for her children, John F. Kennedy, Jr. and Caroline Kennedy."

"Tell Mrs. Kennedy that I'll reinstate her in the White House," Howard said. "She can return in triumph, and I'll promise to give her unlimited power for a First Lady. I understand that dame loves power."

"I'll pay for the next goddamn redecoration of the White House—if that's what it takes to please her," Howard told Meyer. "That's not all. I'll even call that shithead Oleg Cassini, whom I hate, and tell him that Mrs. Kennedy will have *carte blanche* to order clothes from him, as many outfits as she wants even if it's three gowns a day. Tell her I'll also open charge accounts—the ceiling's the limit—at both Tiffany's and Cartier. I'll also provide 24-hour-a-day security guards for her and her kids."

Meyer said that he made at least eight attempts to get in touch with Mrs. Kennedy, via hand-delivered courier and by telephone, as he'd easily obtained her private number. "She would not answer my letters, nor take my calls," Meyer said. "Someone else always answered the phone at her house. Sometimes it was a man, but more often a woman. One time, the voice on the other end sounded like Bobby Kennedy."

"It must have been three o'clock in the morning in Washington, D.C., when Mrs. Kennedy finally returned my call," Meyer said. "I was in bed with, of all people, *[the tap-dancing Big Band era star]* Ann Miller. I had lured Ann to my bed with three pieces of incredibly expensive jewelry that Howard had originally given Ava Gardner and that she'd thrown back at me, telling me to return the jewelry to Howard. I never did. I presented the gems to Ann, who seemed willing to give me a night of pleasure for the stones. I don't mean to imply that Ann was a hooker. But, unlike Ava, she respected the value of Howard's baubles."

"Mrs. Kennedy's voice came over the phone wires," Meyer said. "I would have recognized that little girl voice anywhere. 'Mr. Meyer,' she said. 'This is Jacqueline Kennedy. I've received your latest letter and would like for you to fly to Washington Tuesday night to meet with me. I'm at least willing to hear what Mr. Hughes has to say.' She proceeded to give me instructions on how to reach her. After doing that, she gently put down the phone."

"I could swear she was drunk," Meyer told Ann.

The next morning, he informed Howard of the news, and "Bossman seemed elated. His plan to take over the White House, and ultimately the nation—maybe the world—was about to be launched. I'm not exaggerating when I say world. Howard believed that the man who controlled the White House in 1968 could ultimately control the world. He even had a plan to wipe out the Soviet Union in a sudden, unexpected missile attack. 'With Russia out of the way, no one will stop me,' he told me."

Meyer flew to Washington and at the pre-designated hour appeared at Mrs. Kennedy's Georgetown dwelling, finding her alone in her house. "She even answered the door herself," Meyer said. "She asked me if I wanted tea but I requested a drink instead. I was trembling all over. I mean, here I was in the presence of the most famous woman on the planet. In terms of fame, she ranked up there with Helen of Troy, Catherine the Great, and Cleopatra."

Meyer recalled that he sat on a sofa facing Mrs. Kennedy, who occupied a winged armchair, positioning her legs in a typical "debutante pose—all prim and proper."

"I tossed out Howard's offer to her even though I knew I was treating her like a hooker," Meyer said. "She didn't seem shocked—nor even surprised."

"In that little girl voice, almost a whisper, she finally said, 'I thought it was something like that.' I remember her leaning back in her chair and saying, 'You go back to your Mr. Hughes and tell him I'll accept his proposal of marriage, but not for ten million. I put a higher price tag on myself than that. Tell him my price tag is fifty million. Also my attorneys will set up trust funds for each of my children. Enough money to give each of them a lavish lifestyle, if that's what they want, for the rest of their lives. I like the offer of 24-hour security protection. But the Hughes Tool Company will have to agree in contract to offer that protection not only for the rest of my life but for the rest of the lives of both John and Caroline.'"

"Of course, Mrs. Kennedy," Meyer said, "I'll take that counter-offer back to Mr. Hughes."

He then remembered Mrs. Kennedy leaning forward in her chair. In almost a whisper she said, "There is one final thing, Mr. Meyer. A delicate issue. Mr. Hughes will have to agree, and put it in contract form, that marriage to me will not entail conjugal visits."

"That hit me like a lead balloon," Meyer claimed. "But I told her I'd also convey that request to Howard. Frankly, I think Howard would have accepted the offer. He wanted to marry Mrs. Kennedy to gain political power unlike anything he'd ever known. He wasn't marrying her to get some pussy, although with her brunette hair and good looks, I think she could have gotten a rise out of bossman. But his libido was pretty much shut down by 1964."

Meyer flew back to the West Coast, conveying the astonishing news to Howard. "The financial terms didn't bother him at all," Meyer claimed. "Bossman knew he'd have to pay many more millions to get into the White House, and he seemed prepared to do that. He said he was going to delay for three weeks a formal response to Mrs. Kennedy, which he was going to deliver in person, meeting her at a secluded cottage on Martha's Vineyard, which I was to rent and secure for him. I went ahead with plans for the Martha's Vineyard rendezvous, but it never came off."

At this point, Meyer hesitated in his remembrance, claiming that what he was about to reveal was so shocking that "it defies believability."

"Howard delivered his answer to me in about three weeks, more or less, but it wasn't the message that Mrs. Kennedy was waiting to hear," Meyer said.

"He had concluded that he could not run for president because of one thing: He'd have to shake the hands of half the male and female population of America, if not the world."

"In the years to come, I'll have to shake all those slimy paws," he said. "Some of whom will have just emerged from the toilet after wiping their ass and not washing their hands. The germs will surely kill me. I can't make the run. I have to thank Mrs. Kennedy for her acceptance, but withdraw the offer. I can't go through with it!"

"Frankly," Meyer said, "even though bossman instructed me to, I didn't have the balls to write or call Mrs. Kennedy with the turndown. It was too goddamn embarrassing. But perhaps my visit to Mrs. Kennedy jarred her into a new reality. I'd heard that she'd been drinking heavily, was in a deep depression, and was carrying on an affair with her brother-in-law after her husband's assassination. At least, I got her thinking in the right direction. Another rich man, but not Howard Hughes, lay in that gal's future."

***

Meyer did not appear again in Jackie Kennedy's life until after she married Aristotle Onassis. When Hughes was finished with Meyer, he hired himself out to Ari as a "spy, cover-up, flunky, procurer, asshole-wiper, whatever you want," Meyer said. "I'd do everything but rim jobs, although in spirit I do those too."

To Meyer's surprise, one of his jobs involved spying on Jackie after her marriage to "The Greek."

Years after their initial encounter, when Meyer came face to face with Jackie again, no mention was made of their earlier negotiations. At first she was cold and distant with him until he learned how to break through to her. He soon found out that she loved indiscreet gossip, and since Meyer was more informed about the secrets of the nation's personalities than Walter Winchell, Hedda Hopper, and Louella Parsons, she slowly began to let down her guard.

One day he relayed to her the latest gossip about two of her dearest friends, Truman Capote and Bobby Kennedy, who lived in the same New York City apartment complex near the United Nations.

One night a drunken Capote had encountered Bobby in the elevator and propositioned him, asking him if he could give him a blow-job. At first Meyer thought Jackie would respond coldly. But she smiled, lit a cigarette, leaned back and said, "If I know Bobby, he accepted. I hear Capote has mastered the art. I was never good at that."

From that moment on, Jackie accepted Meyer into her good graces, often inviting him for a private luncheon. Sometimes she had special requests: "Tell me all you know about Lyndon Johnson's mistress."

One afternoon after Jackie's second marriage, Ari sent Meyer with her on a shopping expedition to Athens. They lunched together in a little out-of-the-way Turkish restaurant.

"I know Ari has hired you to spy on me," she said. "But since we've become *confidants*, why don't you tell me the most hideous secret you've ever learned about Ari."

At first reluctant to do so, Meyer was eventu-

One night, **Peter Lawford** confessed to JFK a sexual problem he was having with the president's sister, Patricia. "I go to bed with her—after all, she's my wife, and she's into it—but I can't get it up for her. I'm not impotent, because I did fine with two call girls the night before."

"I have the same problem with Jackie," JFK confessed. "Alas, the curse of married life. Why does society make us take wives?"

378

ally won over by her charm.

"Ever since he was a boy and raped by a Turkish lieutenant in his native land, he discovered he has a gay streak in him," Meyer claimed. "But with a very perverted twist. He has a boy stashed in an apartment in Paris, another one in Athens. They are only kids. I've met both of them. They're each in their late teens. Ari likes to beat them severely before sodomizing them."

She looked startled. "Sometimes," she said, "it's better not to know everything."

Peter Lawford, Jackie's Errant Brother-in-Law

Jackie had long resented her actor brother-in-law, Peter Lawford, knowing that he was her husband's Hollywood pimp, lining up movie stars or wannabee actresses for JFK to seduce. She also knew that Peter had been the "go between" for JFK during his sexual trysts with Marilyn Monroe.

Peter had wed JFK's sister, Patricia Kennedy, and Jackie was well aware that the unhappily married couple were never faithful to each other throughout the course of their ill-fated union.

Since his heyday during Camelot, Peter, according to biographer Lawrence Quirk, has frequently been vilified as a "playboy, opportunist, bisexual, nymphomaniac, drug addict, alcoholic, and pernicious sycophant to both Frank Sinatra and the Kennedys." But despite those extremes, Quirk nonetheless, from personal encounters, remembered him as a kind and gentle man.

In his biography, *A Woman Named Jackie,* C. David Heymann wrote that "Peter provided JFK with every imaginable amenity from dates with actresses and showgirls to a California safehouse where Kennedy could carry out his West Coast assignations. Peter often acted as a 'beard' for JFK, distracting the press and providing a convenient front for Jackie's benefit."

"I detest Peter Lawford," Jackie had told her friend, William Walton, in 1962. "He's nothing but Jack's pimp."

But by the summer of 1966, she'd softened her position on Peter. This time, she told Walton, "Up to now, I've been blaming Peter for Jack's womanizing, and that's

In Honolulu, **Peter Lawford and Jackie** are seen disembarking with their children for a "family vacation" that became the source of international rumors.

Was she actually having an affair with her former brother-in-law, the White House pimp for her late husband?

wrong. Ultimately, it was Jack who was responsible. Of course, Peter did his bidding, but what else could he do? I, of all people, know how difficult it was to say 'no' to Jack, especially when he became President."

She decided to call Peter with an invitation to go on a vacation with her in Hawaii. At the time, he did not know that she wanted to use him to make her boyfriend, architect John Carl Warnecke, jealous and perhaps goad him into a proposal of marriage. He, too, would be enjoying a holiday in Hawaii with her. "I'll divide my time between them," she told Walton.

Peter was already divorced from Patricia when he and Jackie agreed to fly to Hawaii together. Even so, he felt there might be some negative publicity if he became too intimately linked with the former First Lady.

He asked his best friend and business manager, Milton Ebbins, if the trip would be all right, fearing that it might generate bad publicity. "Why not?" Ebbins asked. "Mrs. Kennedy will be traveling with her children, Caroline and John-John, and you'll be with Christopher and Sydney. Just call it a family affair."

"Yeah," Peter said, "but I was afraid that the press might view it as an affair, forgetting about the kids. I already rejected Jackie's sister, but I don't think I could turn down the lady herself if she came on to me."

"Don't flatter yourself," Ebbins said. "Take the trip. It'll be fun."

Peter always claimed that Lee Radziwill had made a play for him in the early 60s when they were taking a stroll through Hyde Park in London. He said that he had turned her down "because I had too much respect for her husband."

From gossip, Lana Turner, Peter's former lover, heard that he would soon fly to Honolulu with Jackie. Lana took a dim view. "If Lee Radziwill wanted him, Mrs. Kennedy might also want Peter. After all, sisters sometimes go for the same guy. I hear Jackie has a high libido. I can personally vouch for the libido of John Kennedy. I, of all the stars in Hollywood, knew what a strong sex drive he had."

Flying out of New York on June 6, Jackie arrived in San Francisco with her children, where she rendezvoused with Peter, his son Christopher, and his daughter Sydney for the ongoing flight to Hawaii.

At the Honolulu Airport, Jackie's arrival was greeted like that reserved for a head of state. Some five thousand spectators showed up to see her, along with Peter and their children.

Outside the airport, Pat Lam, from Hawaii's Department of Transportation, showed up to put two *leis* around Jackie's neck, which seemed embarrass her. But her actual emotions were hidden behind a pair of wraparound sunglasses. As the trade winds blew through her hair, a local band played the "Hawaiian War Chant" as a hula troupe swung their hips.

Eager to flee, Jackie waved hello and disappeared inside a Lincoln Continental.

She was driven to an elegant home on fashionable Kahala Beach, a mile from Diamond Head. She was paying $3,000 a month to the owner of the house, Senator Peter Dominick of Colorado. Incidentally, he was a Republican.

A *paparazzo* snapped the arrival of this Kennedy/Lawford party departing from their plane in Honolulu. Patricia Kennedy Lawford (Peter's ex-wife) had given permission for Peter to take their sons to Hawaii, but Ebbins hadn't informed her that Jackie would be along.

When Patricia found out, Ebbins claimed she wasn't just boiling mad, she was livid. She'd told friends that she'd long suspected that Peter "had this thing for Jackie." Rather sarcastically, Patricia added, "And you know Jackie. She's the girl who can't say no."

The so-called "Hawaiian honeymoon" of Jackie and Peter lasted for seven weeks. To keep up appearances, Jackie technically lived in her rented ocean-front house. Peter's hideaway cottage on the grounds of the Hilton was just down the beach.

In Hawaii, Peter perfected the famous cigarette routine that Bette Davis and Paul Henreid did so well in *Now, Voyager* (1942). Over cocktails in the Hilton bar, he was seen placing two cigarettes between his lips, lighting each of them, and then handing one to Jackie.

Writing for a local paper, reporter Gwen Holson tracked every public move she could of Peter and Jackie. She was hoping to sell a *exposé* to a national magazine. "Throughout their vacation," Holson said, "Peter acted like Jackie's gallant husband. He took her everywhere, and he behaved like a father to her children. Lawford was very familiar with Hawaii, and he became Mrs. Kennedy's tour guide. He introduced her to all his friends, and they were great as a couple, dazzling everyone."

"Lawford even threw this big garden party for Mrs. Kennedy at the Kahala Hilton. *Tout* Honolulu turned out to greet her. Everybody wore their finest clothing, and we expected Mrs. Kennedy to turn up in an Oleg Cassini original. She arrived in a light beach shift with sandals."

"In front of everybody, Lawford hovered over Mrs. Kennedy, even taking her hand to guide her over to the next group of friends to show her off. Unlike that whispery Marilyn Monroe voice she used on camera, Mrs. Kennedy spoke in a normal voice."

"I know that Jackie spent a lot of time at the beachfront house Lawford had rented on Oahu. I paid a servant one hundred dollars for the lowdown. She virtually confirmed on the Bible that Mrs. Kennedy and Lawford slept together. Today, it would be front page tabloid news, but back then no respectable paper wanted to touch it."

"But rumors were flying over Honolulu, and I think many mainland newspapers made veiled references to reports of an affair between Lawford and Mrs. Kennedy. We now know that Jackie slept with Bobby. Why not Lawford?"

Peter, at this point in his life, was deeply troubled, and reportedly, Jackie rallied to his side. He was worried, now that he was cut off from the Kennedy clan, that he would not be offered any more film roles, at least good ones. He admitted to Jackie and to others that he had been too imperial when he was the president's brother-in-law and had made a lot of enemies, including Frank Sinatra. He also feared that he could not provide for his children in a style worthy of patterns already established by the Kennedys, and that his kids would lose respect for him.

"I'm going to find a life after the Kennedys, and I'm sure you will too," Jackie said that in front of other guests, as if she wanted other people to believe it. Few did. After his separation from the Kennedy connection, everything went down-hill for Peter.

In Hawaii, Peter got to know Jackie as never before. Such prolonged intimacy between the two of them would never be repeated. In the future, Jackie would, to an increasing degree, withdraw more and more from Peter, based perhaps on burnout after their Hawaiian holiday and on his growing dependencies on liquor and drugs..

"Jackie wasn't completely honest about herself," Peter said. "She doctored up her family background. She told social fibs to avoid having to make appearances. She would tell the press practically anything to get them off her back. She obviously had known about Jack's affairs. She told me she knew. She said she once caught him in the act."

When author Truman Capote heard about a possible Peter/Jackie affair, he said, "I'm not at all surprised. Jackie, dear heart that she is, believed in the revenge fuck. She'd always known that Peter supplied Hollywood actresses to Jack. By fucking Peter, she was probably getting even with Jack, even though his bullet-riddled body was in the grave."

Years later, when funds were running so low he could hardly pay his rent, Peter sold the story of his role as his brother-in-law's pimp to a tabloid. In the article, he claimed that JFK would examine women "like he was admiring some fine China."

Commenting on his marriage to Patricia, he said, "I always felt that her love for her father took precedence in a funny way over her love for me. She worshipped him."

On the day of their departure from Hawaii, Jackie didn't want to create another scene at the airport, so she kissed Peter goodbye in the privacy of her rented home. He didn't know it at the time, but for the most part, their intimate relationship had come and gone with the trade winds.

On vacation in Hawaii, architect **John Carl Warnecke** proved a better lover for Jackie than a bodyguard for her children. After an underwater accident, Caroline ended up on crutches and John Jr. fell into a campfire and later had to have skin grafted onto his buttocks.

John Carl Warnecke, the Architect of Love

Within two hours of Peter's departure, John Carl Warnecke had arrived on her doorstep and into her arms. When Jackie returned to the U.S. mainland, she shared information about some of her Hawaiian adventures with her friend, William Walton.

Later in life, Walton tried to understand the nature of her romantic attachment to Warnecke. "She knew that he was, like Jack, a womanizer. In fact, he had quite a reputation with women. He also appealed to her artistic sense, as he was a man of impeccable taste. They could talk for hours about art and architecture."

"He had an artistic vision that she very much appreciated. Yet there was a sense of mystery and danger about him. She told me she also found him very sexy. He was also a charismatic figure like Jack. When Warnecke walked into a crowded room, people noticed him. If Jackie was on his arm, they practically formed a circle around the couple."

Warnecke was in Hawaii as part of his contracted commitment to redesign the state's administrative centerpiece, the Hawaiian State Capitol. *[Completed in 1969 in the "Hawaiian international" style (an adaptation of the Bauhaus style), it was designed through a collaboration between John Carl Warnecke and Associates and Belt, Lemon and Lo (aka Architects Hawaii, Ltd.)]*

At first, the trip had gone smoothly, until two accidents marred, to some degree, the holiday. On a sharp piece of coral reef, Caroline suffered a deep cut on her left foot while swimming in front of their rented home. Warnecke rushed her to the local hospital, where her wound required six stitches. She was next seen at the Kamehameha Day Parade on crutches.

Caroline's accident was followed by something more serious. John Jr. had gone on a camping trip to Kapuna Beach on the island of Hawaii. At one point, he lost his footing and fell backward into a pit of burning coals. Screaming with pain, he used his right arm to push himself upward.

That led to first and second degree burns on his hand and forearm.

John Walsh, Jackie's Secret Service agent, rushed him to a hospital. His buttocks were also severely burned, and in time he would need a plastic surgeon, Dr. Eldon Dykes, to restore his skin. The blisters and severely burned sections of his skin had to be surgically removed.

In spite of the disasters that had befallen her children, Jackie decided to stay another month in Hawaii. She and her charges moved into one of the buildings on the eight-acre Koko Head estate owned by Henry J. Kaiser. *[Kaiser and his wife were also in residence at the time, occupying the estate's main house.]*

Kaiser, an American industrialist, was famous for launching Liberty Ships during World War II. After the war, he formed Kaiser Aluminum and Kaiser Steel. The tycoon would die in 1967—the year after Jackie's occupancy of his estate—at the age of 85.

The Kaisers often entertained John Jr. and Caroline, taking them to beaches and on tours, even to the Pacific Coast League baseball games. For the most part, Jackie was involved with Warnecke, who would fly by helicopter to the estate whenever he wasn't otherwise busy with plans for the Hawaiian state capitol.

Apparently, Mr. Kaiser did not approve of Jackie's romantic attachment to Warnecke, and he placed a call to Bobby Kennedy on the U.S. Mainland, hoping that he might intervene.

"Take it from me," he told Bobby. "John Warnecke, that whoremonger, is not an appropriate beau for Jackie. I know you will want to protect her reputation."

Bobby listened carefully, because the Kaisers and the Kennedys had long been friends.

Walton later said "Bobby called Jackie and gave her a talking to. She did not tell me what Bobby told her, but her relationship with Warnecke soon came to its painful end."

Warnecke wanted to show Jackie the sights of Hawaii. Once, on a trip to Maui, they took off together without John Walsh, her Secret Service agent. He also flew her to the "Big Island," as Hawaii is called, and they spent the night together in Laurance Rockefeller's guest cottage on Parker Ranch.

He even took her trekking into the Kauai Mountains, where locals often went to hunt wild boar. He also knew the secluded beaches of the islands, where the paparazzi would not intrude.

For him, the highlight of the trip came when he brought her to his own five-bedroom home on Black Point, off Diamond Head Road. He pointed out the master bedroom she'd share with him when they got married. She also selected the bedrooms for Caroline and for John Jr.

During her stay, Jackie made rough drawings of how she'd redecorate, like she did in the White House.

She was overheard telling a servant, "If I didn't know better, I would swear that Bess Truman or perhaps Mamie Eisenhower decorated this house."

Warnecke had hoped that Jackie would set a date for their upcoming wedding. But she did not, holding him off. She needed to think more about it, she informed him.

During a final visit with the Kaisers, she told them, "It is not at all certain that John and I will be married. He has promised great privacy for me and my children, an escape from the world if I live with him in Hawaii. He has even gotten a promise from the local newspapers like the *Star-Bulletin* and the *Honolulu Advertiser* that they will not allow their photographers and reporters to harass me."

"But I'm not so sure," she continued. "I never intended to use Greta Garbo as my role model. After all, it was Garbo, not me, who said, "I *vant* to be *alone.*"

[For more information on the outcome of Jackie's interlude with John Warnecke, refer to chapter 20.]

Love Triangle
John Warnecke, Jackie, and Ella Raines

Lem Billings, a noted homosexual, was JFK's best and most enduring friend. But occasionally, he also bonded with women, and at one point considered marriage to two of them.

First came JFK's "favorite" sister, Kathleen Kennedy, nick-named "Kick," who became a special friend to Lem. He dated her in the 1930s before she moved to England. Privately, he told friends that "Kick reminds me of Jack in drag. They look alike. She has the same self-deprecating humor and Irish wit." During the most intense period of their dating, Lem, at JFK's urging, proposed marriage to her.

Aware of his gender preference, she handled his offer gently, reminding him, "Lem, you and I both know you're not the marrying kind."

Lem was greatly saddened when he learned that Kick, during a vacation in the South of France, had died in an airplane crash near Cannes on May 13, 1948. Sharing the twin-engine De Havilland Dove with her was Lord Peter Fitzwilliam, a 37-year-old British lord, whom she'd married.

Lem's next platonic girlfriend was the sultry brunette movie actress, Ella Raines, a sensitive but tough-talking babe, who had migrated from Wisconsin to Hollywood and into the bed of film director Howard Hawkes.. He had attempted, with the help of Charles Boyer, to transform her into a film star to rival Joan Bennett.

Although noted for her work in film noir and in Westerns, she never made it to superstardom, but mostly worked as a back-up beauty for bigger stars like George Sanders, Randolph Scott, and Charles Laughton. Her career was finally reduced to appearances in Republic Pictures cheapies.

Ella and Lem developed an intense friend-ship, but she discouraged talk of marriage.

One night in the mid-1960s, Lem introduced her to John Carl Warnecke, who at the time was also having an affair with Jackie. He was en-tranced by Ella. According to Lem, their affair began the night he introduced them.

"I did some fancy stepping to keep Jackie from finding out about them, because I knew she would never forgive me, viewing it as a betrayal," Lem said.

Three views of **Ella Raines**, lower photo: with **John Wayne** in *Tall in the Saddle;* and *(middle)* on cover of LIFE magazine in 1944. Unknown to either women, both Ella and Jackie competed for the boudoir adoration of architect John Carl Warnecke. Sometimes, he managed to visit the beds of both of "my goddesses," as he called them, on the same day.

"Ella's affair with John lasted only about eighteen months, but she was rhapsodic in her praise of him as a lover," Lem claimed. "She told me he was hung like a donkey and could go all night—lucky Ella, lucky Jackie."

Paul Newman
Jackie Claims His Penis
Was Identical to JFK's

Before he'd even met Jackie Kennedy, Paul Newman had campaigned vigorously for JFK, contributing both his money and his time.

In the wake of JFK's assassination, during the 1964 presidential campaign, Paul decided to throw his political support behind Lyndon B. Johnson. He later told Lem Billings, "I am sadly disappointed. I thought Johnson would de-escalate the war in Vietnam. From this day on, I've become leary of politicians."

In 1968, after the assassination of Bobby Kennedy in Los Angeles, **Paul Newman** was among the first to successfully get a phone call through to Jackie to express his condolences. "I want to come to you and hold you, and tell you it'll be okay. You'll go on."

She later told Lem Billings, "I think Paul wanted to come and live with me. For how long, I don't know. I got the feeling he wanted to replace Bobby in my life."

But as time would tell, he did not have that fear about First Ladies.

Every straight or bisexual male has his fantasy woman. For Paul Newman, he still considered Elizabeth Taylor one of the most enchanting women of her time. But, as he'd once told intimate friends, "Jacqueline Kennedy is the most desirable woman on the planet. Our Helen of Troy."

In 1968, after her brother-in-law, Robert F. Kennedy, announced that he was going to run against Eugene McCarthy for the Democratic nomination for president, she placed a discreet call to Newman, who was backing McCarthy.

He was thrilled to be speaking to her and hearing that famous voice that in some way reminded him of Marilyn Monroe. He agreed to meet her in the bar of the Hotel Carlyle in Manhattan—the same hotel where John F. Kennedy had had sexual trysts with Monroe.

The sale of her home in Georgetown in Washington, DC, had allowed her to purchase a Fifth Avenue apartment, but despite that, she chose to meet him at the Carlyle Hotel, perhaps as some kind of symbolic assertion of her independence.

Of his many involvements with famous personalities, Newman's short-lived link with Jackie is clouded in the most mystery and the subject of the most speculation. A doorman reported that he arrived at the pre-designated time of eight o'clock in the evening, and was seen leaving the following morning around 8:30, hailing a taxi and quickly disappearing. He wore dark sunglasses and a hat. The sunglasses were familiar; the hat was not. Even so, the staff at the Carlyle recognized him and spread the word. The story was too good, too hot, to keep to one's self.

Susan Strasberg claimed that within days, the rumor was making the rounds at Downey's Restaurant, sometimes known among hipster New Yorkers as "the poor man's Sardi's," where it quickly spread through the grapevine to Washington and on to Hollywood.

The only recognizable name who spoke openly about the night Newman spent with Jackie in her hotel suite was Truman Capote, her treacherous friend. In Tennessee Williams' New York apartment, Capote claimed that Jackie had confessed to him "only some of the details of that night."

Capote asserted to many of his friends that one night he and Jackie, drunk on champagne, named the three movie stars they'd most like to seduce. For Capote, the size of their appendages seemed to dominate his selection of John Ireland, Steve Cochran, and Rock Hudson.

As her most-desirable sexual candidates of choice, Jackie named Marlon Brando, William Holden, and Paul Newman, claiming, "I've already attained two-thirds of my goal." At that time, she was referring to Brando and Holden, not Newman, whom she was yet to meet.

Newman loomed in Jackie's future, and when Capote found out that they had finally met within her apartment, "I was all ears when she wanted to talk about it."

"When she'd had enough champagne, Jackie often would become outrageous, not the 'steel butterfly' so often depicted on camera," Capote claimed.

One night at a White House gala, when she'd had more than her share of the bubbly, Jackie took off her shoes and danced and flirted with every handsome man in attendance, much to the annoyance of her husband, who hawkeyed her every move. Perhaps she was paying him back for his own sexual trysts with his women *du jour*.

Even JFK had told associates that "Jackie is known for developing crushes, like on Warren Beatty. But she's very fickle. They don't last long. She becomes bored quickly."

That night Newman met Jackie, he encountered a very different woman from the brave but beleaguered widow he'd read about in the press. Sitting opposite him was a flirtatious and attractive woman with a mischievous gleam in her eyes, not the grieving widow of a slain American president.

In a secluded corner of the bar at the Carlyle, Jackie, in dark sunglasses, greeted him. He kissed her on both cheeks. She casually pointed to a man in a dark business suit sitting a few tables away. She told him that he was a member of the Secret Service assigned to guard her. "He's also my lover," she allegedly told Newman. If he were shocked, he masked it effectively. He even assumed that she might be joking because it was unbelievable that she'd be this frank with him.

Upon his arrival, he'd presented her with a porcelain rose, which was investment enough for him, even though he'd heard she would spend as much as $100,000 on an antique snuff box.

From what Capote learned, Newman spent a good part of the evening hearing about the Kennedys. Jackie was very supportive of Bobby, and urged Newman to switch the allegiance he'd developed to Eugene McCarthy.

One speculation she may have shared with Newman that night was her belief that her husband, had he managed to dodge the assassin's bullet, would not have been re-elected. "His indiscretions had become so plentiful, so well known, that they would have made headlines during the campaign and would have destroyed him."

Alone in the hotel suite with Newman, she is alleged to have repeated her standard selling points with Newman, as she did to anybody she was hoping to "win over to our side." She spent at least an hour extolling the virtues of Bobby Kennedy. Allegedly, she asserted that she personally knew McCarthy, but that she believed that he was a one-issue candidate, and that his political obsession revolved solely around "the war." She reportedly expressed it as, "that God damn Vietnam War."

She went on to warn Newman that there were other issues associated with the upcoming race, including the War on Poverty. "Bobby can offer hope to the downtrodden that McCarthy can't. Bobby is a candidate whose stand on the issues, not just the war, is all-encompassing. He can save this nation from itself. That is, if he can save himself from an assassin's bullet. They've already killed one Kennedy in this country. They might strike again." Supposedly, she never revealed who "they" were.

The most provocative shared indiscretion of the evening, if Capote is to be believed, is that Jackie confided to Newman that she'd never been able to satisfy her husband sexually. "Perhaps I can change that state of affairs with you tonight," she may have told him.

After their one night together at the Hotel Carlyle in New York, there is no evidence that Jackie and the actor ever connected sexually again. Lem Billings asked Jackie why not. "He was always on your fantasy list of actors to seduce."

She startled him with her confession. "It was the most amazing thing," she said. "Paul and Jack have an identical penis. It was like getting seduced by my husband all over again. It was eerie."

At least for one night, Jackie may have convinced Newman to switch his political alliance. But in the sober light of morning, after his departure from the Carlyle, he remained in McCarthy's camp. He later told Tony Perkins, "I faced more temptation that night than Antony when he met Cleopatra."

Of course, when Bobby Kennedy was assassinated in Los Angeles in June of 1968—allegedly by Sirhan Sirhan, although rampant speculation about the assassination remains—Newman's support of Jackie's brother-in-law as a candidate became a moot issue.

Howl!, a scandal sheet emanating from New York City's East Village that flourished for only two months during hippiedom's "Dawning of the Age of Aquarius," was the only newspaper, if that's what it could be called, that carried the rumor. The headline, as were all that short-lived paper's headlines, was blunt and to the point: PAUL NEWMAN FUCKS JACKIE O.

***

Jackie and Paul Newman may not have always agreed on politics, but both of them found each other compatible as friends. Jackie was one of the first to call and express her sympathy to Paul when his son, Scott Newman, was found dead.

During dinner one night, Jackie told Newman, "I read a quote about you from Janet Leigh. She said, 'Paul makes you respond to him. That is the basis of his sexual appeal.' Is that true?"

"You'll have to answer that yourself," he told her, raising an eyebrow. "After all, you're qualified to do so."

"*Touchée*," she murmured.

"When Janet and I made *Harper* (1966) together, I stole a gimmick from Bobby Kennedy. For my character of Lew Harper, I borrowed Bobby's technique of listening to people without actually facing them."

"Bobby always referred to that as 'The Sideways Approach,'" she said.

Rather flirtatious with her, he said, "I hope he didn't do everything sideways."

"Not at all," she said. "During sex, he was on top, with his eyes boring into mine."

Gregory Peck, "The Handsomest Man in the World"

"Gregory Peck is the ultimate movie star. You know, there's nobody handsomer or more gentle or more romantic on the screen, I think. For all ages."
—Liza Minnelli

Gregory Peck failed his first screen test, as his features were considered "too large and irregular." He ultimately prevailed, of course, even though his left ear was larger than the right, he was hailed in the movie magazines of Hollywood's Golden Age as "The Handsomest Man in the World."

In time, Peck would celebrate his triumphs, but later plunge to the depths of heartbreak, feeling the pain of what he viewed as "my many failures." Yet he always bounced back, never more gloriously than when he played Atticus Finch in *To Kill a Mockingbird*.

As Hollywood actors go, Peck was known to cheat on the two women he'd marry over the course of his life, but only rarely.

He famously seduced Ingrid Bergman when

What did **Gregory Peck** and JFK have in common? Both had seduced Marilyn Monroe

he co-starred with her in *Spellbound* (1945), and he'd also seduced Ann Todd, his co-star in *The Paradine Case* (1947). His really sleazy affair was with Barbara Payton (*Only the Valiant; 1952*), who later became a drug-addicted, alcoholic prostitute in Las Vegas and other towns.

Peck had long been a supporter of JFK, and on occasion, Jackie had written him a note of gratitude. Ironically, she had invited Peck to a White House dinner scheduled for December 10, 1963. Of course, those bullets in Dallas ended all plans for that gala dinner.

Jackie detested fund raising, but, out of devotion to Bobby Kennedy when he was seeking the presidency in 1968, she worked the phones, soliciting donations for his campaign. One call was placed to Peck. He not only graciously accepted it, but made a $10,000 contribution.

During his subsequent visit to New York, Peck invited Jackie for dinner at "21." She accepted, even though it meant canceling another engagement.

Over dinner, he expressed some of his fears about surviving in the New Hollywood. "All in all, I'm sort of old fashioned, and my name is not Tab, Rory, Rock, or Rip. I'm considering a name change to 'Boulder.'"

"Perhaps you could change it to Whip? Jackie said, teasing him. "How about Lash?"

After the assassination, Peck narrated a film, *Years of Lightning, Days of Drums,* for the United States Information Agency. In it, he praised JFK for such accomplishments as the Peace Corps, the Alliance for Progress *[a ten-year, multibillion-dollar aid program for Latin America],* civil rights, and the Space Program.

According to reports, Peck went home with Jackie that night after dinner at "21." Later, he accepted an invitation from her to go horseback riding in Virginia. Both were avid equestrians. Peck owned "Different Class," the thoroughbred Steeplechase racehorse. It had been favored to win the 1968 Grand National, but came in third.

They may have talked about religion, as both Peck and Jackie were Roman Catholics. He confessed that he had once seriously considered the priesthood. He did not always adhere to Catholic doctrine, however, not agreeing with the church's stand on homosexuality, abortion, and the ordination of women.

[In spite of his contributions to Bobby's campaign, President Lyndon Johnson, one of Bobby's most bitter adversaries, honored Peck in 1969 with a Presidential Medal of Freedom, the nation's highest civilian honor. Jackie cabled her congratulations, but did not attend the ceremony.

At the time of Peck's weekend with Jackie, he was married to the French journalist, Véronique Passani. In 1953, after traveling to Rome from her base in Paris, Passani had interviewed the actor during his filming of Roman Holiday *with Audrey Hepburn.]*

Jackie may have quizzed Peck about Marilyn Monroe, since she knew he was originally envisioned as her co-star in what became her last picture, the unfinished *Let's Make Love* (1960). Peck and Monroe were said to have had a brief fling.

However, when her husband, Arthur Miller, rewrote the script, Peck's role was greatly diminished while Marilyn's was lengthened. After reading the revised script, Peck dropped out of the cast. He was replaced with the French actor/singer Yves Montand, with whom Marilyn had yet another affair.

As Jackie later told William Walton, "Gregory didn't stick around long enough for it to be called an affair. Perhaps a *passion de passage* would be a more accurate term. I'd definitely consider him marriage material if I hadn't made too many other promises."

Columnist Earl Wilson wasn't exactly subtle when he inserted the following blind item in his syndicated column: "What Hollywood matinee idol is said to have made a famous widow *Spellbound* on his trip to New York? *The Man in the Grey Flannel Suit* obviously had *The World in His Arms* when he spent the night at her apartment, leaving at *Twelve O'Clock High.* Perhaps he knew her as *David* came to know *Bathsheba,* and no doubt he made a *Gentleman's Agreement* not to reveal the (*Macomber*) affair. The question is, did this *Designing Woman* experience *Moby Dick?*"

Arnold Schwarzenegger: Jackie's "Crush" on the Governator

A young Arnold Schwarzenegger, an aspiring Austrian bodybuilder, was first mesmerized by Jackie Kennedy, then First Lady of America, at the 1961 Summit Meeting in Vienna between the United States and the Soviet Union. He'd entered Vienna eager to join the throngs amassed to see America's exciting new President and his glamorous First Lady.

Arnold's mother, Aurelia Jadrny, a brunette, was relieved when she discovered Jackie's picture pinned up on her son's bedroom wall, along with an array of male bodybuilders in the briefest of posing straps. Up to then, she had expressed her fear to her husband, Gustav Schwarzenegger, once defined as "an Austrian version of Cary Grant," that their son was a homosexual. "He covered his bedroom walls with pictures of nude men," she protested.

Years would go by before Arnold actually met Jackie, and that was in 1976, after he'd completed

When Jackie first met body-builder **Arnold Schwarzenegger**, she came face to face with a man with a perfectly muscled body and a fierce ambition. She never suspected that he'd become a member of the Kennedy clan—and a Republican at that.

On his wedding day (April 16, 1986) to Maria Schriver, Jackie said, "That goes to show you what Austrian charm, talent, and sheer bravado can do for you."

the filming of his movie, *Pumping Iron.*

In Manhattan, Jackie made a sudden appearance at Elaine's, the fashionable East Side restaurant, where a party was being hosted in Arnold's honor as a means of promoting his movie. No one expected her, and her mere presence at such an unlikely event caused a stir. Arnold appeared somewhat tongue-tied when he was introduced to her.

Of course, his press agent didn't miss the opportunity to have a paparazzo snap a photo of them together. It then appeared in newspapers across the country. One reporter even suggested that that photograph transformed Arnold into an overnight celebrity.

Jackie warmly embraced Arnold and kissed him, then moved on to greet such illustrious guests as the aging movie star, Paulette Goddard, former wife of Charlie Chaplin, and Andy Warhol. At the time, Jackie was an editor at Viking Press.

When asked what he thought of Jackie, Arnold gave an unusual reply: "She likes very much where I came from."

Barbara Walters was there, telling Jackie that when she touched Arnold's arm, she was amazed at how soft it was.

"That soft arm, as you call it, can turn into a very threatening machine," Jackie warned Walters.

Despite its designation as a movie about bodybuilding, the premiere attracted some of New York's most coveted *glitterati*, including Paul Simon, Tom Wolfe, Mikhail Baryshnikov, and Carly Simon.

Jackie later saw *Pumping Iron* at a private screening, and delivered her own review: "Many people wrongly consider bodybuilders grotesque, and accuse them of being gay because of the tortuous demands and long hours spent on their bodies to make a Mr. Olympia or Mr. Universe. But Mr. Schwarzenegger has shown in this film that musclemen are deeply motivated to train their bodies, but they are also men with the same fears, ambitions, and desires of men with less physical attributes."

It was reported that the director/producer George Butler wanted to use Jackie's evaluation for publicity purposes, but she refused to grant permission.

Almost overnight, Arnold burst onto the scene, evolving from a "gym rat" into a figure pursued by high society. Even Diana Vreeland *[the fashion mogul who influenced* Harper's Bazaar, Vogue, *and later, the fashion collection at New York's Metropolitan Museum of Art]* told Jackie, "The boy is charming—just charming. That accent is utterly divine."

Jackie, along with Patricia Kennedy Lawford, attended a party for Arnold hosted by Fiat heiress Delphina Ratazzi. Once again, Warhol appeared, as did Charlotte Curtis *[a top-tier columnist for The New York Times, and eventually a celebrity in her own right]* and a host of other media headliners.

By that time, Arnold had hired a publicist who made the claim that "Jackie is begging" to be permitted to edit Arnold's next book, following the publication of *Arnold: The Education of a Bodybuilder* in 1977.

Jackie's friends were amazed. "Did I hear that right?" asked Vreeland.

"Jackie wants to edit a book about Arnold's bodybuilding and run pictures of him in revealing posing straps."

So far as it is known, Jackie's crush on Arnold never went beyond her wildest dreams.

***

Arnold—originally billed as Arnold Strong after his arrival in the America in the 1970s—was a 30-year-old bodybuilder when he met Maria Shriver, a 21-year-old *ingénue.* Arnold himself defined it as "instant chemistry," after he spotted Maria at a 1977 tennis-related charity event in New York.

Politically, they were worlds apart: He was a staunch Republican and she was a Kennedy Democrat, part of a political dynasty.

When Jackie heard that Arnold was dating her relative, Maria Shriver, she was mildly shocked. She told Truman Capote, who bruited it around town. "I would think that Arnold was too much man for Maria, who is so sweet." She went on to say, "Arnold will fit right into the Kennedy family, whose men have always sought their sexual pleasures outside the beds of their wives."

After Arnold became the biggest movie star in the world, revelations about his past were exposed in the tabloids. It was learned that Arnold's father, Gustav Schwarzenegger, with his "Hitler-style mustache," had been a member of the Nazi party. Arnold himself had been a great friend of the disgraced Kurt Waldheim, former U.N. chief who participated in Nazi atrocities during World War II.

In 1992, *Spy Magazine* reported that in the 70s, Arnold "enjoyed playing and giving away recordings of Hitler's speeches." During the filming of his 1977 *Pumping Iron,* he was rumored to have said on camera that he "admired" Hitler, although the director wisely removed that controversial footage from the film's final cut.

Columnist Bob Herbert in *The New York Times* stated the case for the opposition: "He may once have admired Hitler for whatever reasons, but, I'm sure if you asked Arnold Schwarzenegger whom he admires most, the honest answer would be *'Ah-nold!'* Welcome to the world of undiluted narcissism. The man has spent a lifetime pirouetting in front of cameras and mirrors, contemplating his navel and every other part of his once-buff bod. Adoration is the thing. In the mad, mad, world of Hollywood stardom, the undiluted narcissist doesn't have to worry about what to say. Image is everything."

Jackie was awed by the rapid rise of Arnold as the world's number one movie star, particularly after the release of his most famous role, *Conan the Barbarian,* in the "sword-and-sorcery/adventure film" released in 1982. She watched in amazement as the seven-time winner of the *Mr. Olympia* contest dominated the action movie genre. "He has not just real muscle, but box office muscle," Jackie said.

She attended the wedding of Maria and Arnold at the church of St. Francis Xavier at Hyannis Port. Ronald Reagan cabled his congratulations (at the union) and his regrets (about not being able to attend the ceremony). Jackie showed up in a smart navy blue suit with a white triangular inset. The crowd that gathered outside the church gave her the loudest cheers.

Both Jack and Bobby Kennedy had been altar boys at this church. When Jackie spotted Arnold and Maria together at the altar, she told Arnold's mother, Aurelia *[who wore a violet suit under a mink coat]*, "Maria is certainly one lucky young woman."

Jackie's children, John Jr. and Caroline, also attended the wedding, and Maria's father, Sargent Shriver, gave the bride away.

Even Jackie was impressed with the wedding cake, weighing 425 pounds and towering seven feet high with eight tiers. Arnold danced the first waltz with his bride to the sound of Peter Duchin's seven-piece band. Another dance was with Jackie, who seemed to "melt into his muscled arms," in the words of one of the wedding arrangers from the Robert Isabell Company in New York.

He also noted that Jackie took delight in eating a *Mozart Kugeln,* a chocolate confection filled with marzipan, said to be Arnold's favorite treat. "In addition to those muscles, Arnold knows what's good," Jackie told her fellow guests at her table, which, like the others at this lavish ceremony, was draped in rose-colored linen with a basket of flowers that included Queen Anne's Lace.

Kurt Waldheim, the disgraced politician from Austria, did not show, but cabled his regrets.

Instead, Arnold proposed a toast to honor Waldheim, saying, "My friends don't want me to mention Kurt's name, because of all the recent Nazi stuff and the U.N. controversy, but I love him and Maria does, too, and so thank you, Kurt."

Reporters noted that Jackie "turned visibly pale at the toast." Later, she told Teddy Kennedy and others, "I don't know why Arnold doesn't want to distance himself from an accused Nazi. His association with Waldheim can only harm him."

Arnold told reporters for *People* magazine and *The New York Daily News,* "Kurt has just had a bad press."

One reporter shot back, "So did Adolf!"

In the wake of the wedding, Waldheim was elected President of Austria, winning 54 percent of the vote. That didn't please Elie Wiesel, the Nobel Peace Laureate, who said, "Waldheim's election by the people of Austria is a stain on that country and all of mankind." Posters advertising Arnold's support of Waldheim had been plastered across Austria during the weeks prior to the elections there.

In 1976, Arnold posed in the nude for the celebrated photographer, Francesco Scavullo for a *Cosmopolitan* centerfold. "He was nude and most

At the posthumous sale of many of Jackie's most personal possessions, Arnold Schwarzenegger showed up to purchase this **Norman Rockwell portrait of JFK.** "My kids have Kennedy blood in them," he said.

cooperative, very charming and a delight to photograph. But after seeing the nudes, he seemed to feel they were too personal, as they depicted his genitalia. He changed his mind and asked that the pictures not be published. I put them in a bank vault and gave him my solemn promise that I would never publish them."

Jackie's friend, William Walton, claimed that she made an effort to obtain copies of these photographs, but he did not know if she succeeded or not.

The photos of Arnold that appeared in the 1977 edition of *Cosmopolitan* followed the example set by an earlier centerfold, Burt Reynolds. No views of genitalia were shown. The "full monty," as the English say, had been artfully concealed.

In 1978, Arnold again posed nude for the talented homosexual photographer, Robert Mapplethorpe, the pictures becoming a hot seller in the gay porn world. "I have absolutely no hang-ups about the fag business," Arnold said.

One hot summer afternoon, following his marriage to Maria, Arnold and Jackie both attended a pool party at Hyannis Port. They were seen engrossed in conversation about art. Later, Arnold confessed, "I like hanging out with successful people. If you hang out around low foreheads, it means you are a low forehead yourself."

Arnold talked to Jackie about how much he liked to paint late at night after the members of his household had gone to sleep. He would retreat to his office upstairs, light a fire, and play soft music. Sometimes, he painted until two or three o'clock in the morning. He told her that once, he painted a bucolic scene of the Austrian countryside of his youth. It featured snow-covered mountains looming in the background. "For the cows, I colored them blue or purple," he said. "If you make the cow its true color, it's boring."

More than one biographer has suggested that both Jackie and Teddy Kennedy tried to influence Arnold to switch from the Republican Party to the Democratic side.

Maria told her family, "Don't look at him as a Republican. Look at him as the man I love. And if that doesn't work, look at him as someone who can squash you."

***

Both Maria and Arnold were said to have been greatly saddened at Jackie's untimely death in 1994.

In 1996, still a Republican, Arnold issued a warning to his party: "You're going to lose until you become a party of inclusion, that you love the foreigner that comes in with no money as much as a gay person, as a lesbian, as anyone else."

That year, he appeared at a Jackie Onassis auction of personal possessions, spending $750 on memorabilia. He purchased items which included JFK's golf clubs plus a portrait of the President by Norman Rockwell, plus dozens of other items. "I was a big fan of Jack Kennedy and Mrs. Onassis, and

I think it would be great for the kids to know where part of their blood comes from."

Jackie, of course, did not live to see Arnold successfully run for governor of California. Although she predicted that he would never be faithful to one woman, she perhaps would still have been horrified at all the publicity surrounding his breakup with one of her favorite relatives, Maria. Surely she would have been mortified to hear that he'd fathered a love child with the family's housekeeper.

Perhaps what would have offended Jackie the most were the stories that came out during his race for Sacramento. Newspaper after newspaper compared Arnold's womanizing to that of JFK.

During his race for the governor, Arnold was accused of sexual harassment and was labeled "Governor Groper" in the press. At least 16 women came forward describing his previous episodes of sexual misconduct during the filming of his movies.

On the set of *Terminator 2,* one female crew member claimed he walked over to her and pulled out her breasts, exposing them. Another alleged when she went to his trailer to summon him onto the set, she discovered him performing oral sex on a woman. He looked up at the script girl, telling her, "eating is not cheating."

He told *Esquire* magazine, "When you see a blonde with great tits and a great ass, you say to yourself, 'Hey, she must be stupid or must have nothing else to offer, which is the case many times.'"

Finally, Arnold called a press conference, admitting "I behaved badly sometimes."

Frank Sinatra: Jackie and the Boudoir Singer

"Even in the pre-JFK years, Jackie had more men per square inch than any woman I've ever known."
—Letitia Baldrige, longtime friend and social secretary

"The Kennedy media image that shielded Jack's peccadilloes also protected Jackie, and neither one could divorce the other while in the White House. 'We are like two ice-

Past differences aside, but with many future dramas to come, **Jackie** and **Frank Sinatra** were most gracious to each other during the Inaugural Ball in January of 1961.

bergs,' Jackie said, 'the public life above the water, the private life submerged.'"
—Dr. David Eisenbach, political historian

During his 1960 campaign for president, JFK, in Jackie's opinion, was seeing too much of Frank Sinatra. She voiced her suspicion to Peter Lawford that "Sinatra seems like an endless wagon train hauling young women to Jack,"

Whenever possible, Jack took time off from the campaign to party with Frank, sometimes in Las Vegas and sometimes in Palm Springs. Party time meant available women, and Jackie knew that.

She was particularly furious about his dangerous liaison with Judith Campbell Exner, who had been introduced to JFK by Frank. Jackie was enraged when she learned that Exner had "slept over" with JFK at their Georgetown home when Jackie was out of town.

Behind JFK's back, Frank called him "Chicky Boy." Somehow Jackie found out about that nickname and used it to taunt her husband when she discovered yet another of his infidelities, many of which had been orchestrated by Frank himself. She referred to the young women that Frank set up for JFK seductions as "lollipops."

JFK asked Frank to organize the roster of entertainers slated to perform at his 1961 inauguration. Frank gladly accepted and later claimed that the gig was the highlight of his life.

During the frenzied weeks he spent arranging the events, Frank was on the phone day and night, getting commitments from an impressive array of leading stars, each of whom promised to perform, onstage, at the President's inauguration. Ella Fitzgerald was willing to fly in from Australia, and Shirley MacLaine agreed to wing in from Tokyo. Frank located Gene Kelly in Switzerland, where he was shacked up with a male ski instructor. Sidney Poitier flew back from Paris. Ethel Merman got permission to leave her Broadway show, *Gypsy*, for a single performance in D.C. Frank even got Eleanor Roosevelt to agree to show up, although she really would rather have seen Adlai Stevenson as president instead.

Joey Bishop signed on as master of ceremonies, and Leonard Bernstein agreed to conduct an orchestral rendition of "Stars and Stripes Forever."

Frank brought his girlfriend, Juliet Prowse, although he planned to devote most of the evening to Jackie herself. Be-

Frank Sinatra *(left)* and **President Kennedy** during the reign of Camelot. Frank felt he should be named "Secretary of Bimbo Procurement."

Jackie disagreed, referring to the crooner as "The White House pimp."

397

cause of their interracial marriage, Sammy Davis and Mai Britt were not on the guest list, but Kennedy loyalists Janet Leigh (one of JFK's mistresses) and Tony Curtis were invited, as were Bette Davis, Jimmy Durante, Mahalia Jackson, Harry Belafonte, Milton Berle, and Nat King Cole.

In one of the most embarrassing moments during his organizing of the event, Peter Lawford had to confront Sammy Davis, Jr., and Frank with the bad news: Bobby Kennedy didn't want Sammy to perform with the other stars.

"Bobby feels he's too controversial," Peter explained." He turned to Sammy. "This planning to marry a blonde Swedish actress is a bit much even for the liberal Democrats to take," Peter said. "Bobby is afraid we'll lose our Democratic base because of Sammy. They might even vote Republican next time."

At first, Frank balked, threatening to walk out the door, but Sammy urged him to stay on. "It's not the first time that this darkie was shown the back exit," Sammy said.

Dean Martin called Frank, "I'm too busy on this shit movie in Hollywood to come. By the way, who won the election? I was drunk that night."

The pre-inaugural gala of January, 1961 was "the biggest night of my life," Jackie said. She was about to become the First Lady of the land. Elegantly attired and coiffed, she was escorted up the steps of the National Guard Armory in Washington, D.C.

As host of the proceedings, a tuxedo-clad Frank was her escort. At *The Washington Post* an editor saw this picture and asked, "Where is JFK?" A reporter replied, "He's probably in a broom closet somewhere, fucking Angie Dickinson."

At the time, Jackie held Frank and his Rat Pack, whose members included Peter Lawford, in disdain, claiming that the Kennedy family was merely star struck. "The Rat Pack is the wrong image for you, Jack," she told her husband. She was credited with eliminating the presence of the Rat Pack during JFK's quest for the presidency.

Even though he had escorted her into the ballroom, Jackie kept Frank "at arm's length." Later, she changed her mind about him. "Once you melted his protective façade, he was one of the most sensitive men I ever met, so unlike Jack."

Finally, the inauguration got underway in spite of Washington's worst snowstorm. John F. Kennedy was the epitome of youth, and surely no First Lady had ever looked as glamorous as Jackie that night—not Martha Washington, Mary Todd Lincoln, and certainly not Mrs. Calvin Coolidge or Bess Truman.

Arriving at the National Guard Armory, Jack and Jackie were treated like the newly crowned King and Queen of the World, despite the snowdrifts blowing across Washington.

Frank opened that gala with his hit song, "That Old Black Magic." Except for this performance, the lyrics were changed to "That Old Jack magic."

"It wasn't Black Magic, it wasn't Jack magic, it was Jackie magic," Frank said. "I literally came under her spell, and before my life ends, I'll be god damn if I'm not going to get her."

Back in Hollywood, Frank, over drinks, discussed the inauguration with Lawford. "I was speechless when Jackie emerged from that limousine with that bouffant hairdo. I wanted her just for myself and to hell with Jack. She wore a long white gown—the women reporters called it 'organza'—along with sparkling jewels. She literally left me speechless. I got a hard-on. Fortunately, I was able to conceal it as I escorted her up the steps to the armory, thanks to my heavy duty jockstrap."

One evening during the early weeks of his presidency, based on JFK having told Jackie that he wanted to dine alone with her, she was expecting a romantic evening. But when she came in for dinner, she discovered Frank with Jack, discussing women. The moment she entered the room, they abruptly changed the subject.

It turned out that JFK had created what he called "a dynamite idea for a film," and he wanted Frank to star in it, playing himself as president. The plot involved a Texas-based *coup d'état* and a plot to forcibly remove a sitting president from his office.

Ironically, after JFK's own assassination in 1963, that half-formulated idea became a central point in many of those claims about how Lyndon B. Johnson had engineered the assassination of JFK, as a means of elevating himself to the status of president.

In later years, Jackie and Frank discussed JFK's premonitions about how he was going to die in Dallas.

In April of 1961, some malicious person, no doubt a Republican within the F.B.I., sent Jackie an anonymous letter which asserted that the Bureau had learned that *Confidential* magazine had affidavits from two mulatto prostitutes in New York stating that Jack and Frank, from within a suite at the Hotel Carlyle, had had sex with both of them. The anonymous letter went on to assert that the magazine would soonafter release the story to the world at large.

Without alerting her husband, Jackie placed a call to Frank himself for verification. At first he denied it, but then he relented, admitting the story's validity after he learned that the report was about to be printed.

"You created this mess. Now get rid of it!" Jackie reportedly admonished Frank. Then she slammed down the phone. It is believed that Frank then called Joe Kennedy, who had gotten him involved in the campaign in the first place, and persuaded Joe to buy off the magazine for $50,000. The story was never run.

Jackie later told Peter Lawford, "My call to Sinatra may have saved Jack's presidency in its early stage."

This same unknown informant within the F.B.I. also sent Jackie a detailed report from Belden Katelman, who was identified only as a Las Vegas investor. In the report, Jackie read that Frank and JFK had shared a suite at the Sands during the campaign and that Peter Lawford had also arrived for a visit. "Showgirls from all over were seen running in and out of the Senator's suite at all hours of the day and night," the report alleged.

After he was elected president, JFK often called Frank just to talk to him.

The President was especially interested in hearing about the latest young movie stars, especially those Frank had already seduced.

One night over an after-dinner drink, Jack told his brother-in-law, Peter Lawford, "I should really invite Frank to the White House. Throw something special as a means of thanking him for all he did for me in the campaign."

"That's impossible," Peter said. "Jackie hates Frank."

"The next time Jackie goes horseback riding in Middleburg, ask Frank to come and see us," JFK said.

Peter called Frank that very night and found him elated by the invitation. Two weeks later he flew to Washington where a limousine was waiting to drive him to the less-frequently used southwest gate of the White House as a means of avoiding photographers.

Peter later whispered to JFK, "I think Frank wanted us to send Air Force One to fly him here from California."

"People don't get what they want in life," JFK said, "except for me."

JFK himself escorted Frank on a personalized tour of the private rooms of the White House. The tour ended with Bloody Marys on the Truman Balcony.

The next day, Teddy Kennedy and both Patricia and Peter Lawford accompanied Frank on a private Kennedy plane to Hyannis Port where they went boating on a yacht.

After his arrival in Washington, Frank hooked up with the President for a sail on the Potomac, this time aboard the Kennedy yacht, the *Honey Fitz*.

Before they had a falling out, JFK would lavishly entertain Frank, in league with other celebrities who included both Judy Garland and Audrey Hepburn, at Washington's Mayflower Hotel, where he maintained a suite. Jackie was never invited, but she was made aware that Frank often arranged the presentation of beautiful starlets for the president to sample.

As a senator, JFK had used the Mayflower Hotel, in the words of one observer who worked in the White House, as "his personal Playboy mansion."

In 1962 Marilyn Monroe called Jackie at the White House, and, surprisingly, the First Lady took the call. The two women would meet months later within Truman Capote's New York apartment. On their initial call, Marilyn urged Jackie to step aside and divorce her husband so she could marry him.

Jackie later told Peter, "Marilyn really must have been on something. Welcome to reality, something she obviously doesn't know anything about."

She was furious that Marilyn would have the audacity to actually call her. "The woman has no shame," she told her secretary. "I know she calls Jack at the White House. But phoning me is unforgivable. I blame Frank Sinatra for all of this."

Through Peter, Jackie sent word to Frank that "you are no longer welcome at the White House."

Years would go by before they made up. The flare-up with Frank occurred at the same time that Bobby Kennedy began to go after some of Frank's mob associates, including Sam Giancana, Johnny Roselli, and Mickey Cohen. Ultimately, it was Bobby who warned Jackie to steer clear of Frank.

On March 16, 1974, Peter Duchin, the pianist and band leader, brought Jackie and Frank together again after a long alienation.

In an interview with Duchin, Sarah Bradford, author of *America's Queen*, claimed that as a friend of both Jackie and Frank, Duchin managed to convince them to bury their hatchets.

In the wake of their reconciliation, Frank invited her to attend his concert in Providence, Rhode Island. Claiming "that sounds like fun," she accepted. He sent his plane to pick her up.

Accompanied by Peter and Cheray Duchin, Jackie flew to Rhode Island, where she hooked up with Frank after the show. They then flew on his private plane back to New York where a limo waited to whisk them into Manhattan for a late dinner.

Reportedly, at the end of the meal, Jackie told Duchin, "I don't think Frank is my type."

"Nothing happened," Duchin told Bradford. "I think either she would have told me or Frank would have told me."

Perhaps Duchin's impression is right. Nothing happened on that particular night. Their brief fling would occur later.

One night in Manhattan, Fiat czar Gianni Agnelli, the richest man in Italy, arranged to have dinner with Frank. "We Italians must stick together,"

"The Rake of the Riviera," as Agnelli was called, had what he termed "a monkey curiosity about gossip." Pamela Harriman had once kept him amused about what was going on in London and Paris, but Frank was the best source for the peccadilloes of Hollywood scandal. Over the course of their dinner, Agnelli revealed a scandal of his own: While Jackie Kennedy had been married to the President, he had asked her to seek a divorce and marry him.

Jackie had met Agnelli when she went on a holiday—during the presidential administration of her husband—to Ravello, Italy, to visit her sister, Lee Radziwill. The two-week holiday stretched on for a month.

Wild stories began in Washington and spread to Los Angeles. One report claimed that the CIA had received on order to retrieve Jackie's diaphragm from the White House and have it sent by plane to Ravello.

Agnelli told Frank, "I was in love with Jackie. But we decided to view our relationship as a summer romance."

"You've got me excited," Frank said.

When Frank Sinatra had dinner with his friend, the Fiat czar, **Gianni Agnelli**, the singer learned that he'd seduced Jackie years before, when she was First Lady.

"Maybe she was addicted to Italian salami," Frank joked. "I'm next. She'll probably want a steady diet of it when I finish with her."

[For more information on the Jackie/Agnelli affair, see the following chapter.]

"Up to now, Jackie has disliked me very much because she knew I pimped for her husband. But now, you've convinced me that this babe can be had."

In 1974, Frank called Jackie and invited her for a performance at the Uris Theatre in New York. She accepted the invitation. To the awe of the audience, he sat in the center of the theater with Jackie, listening to his opening act of Ella Fitzgerald and Count Basie. At intermission he excused himself and left to perform. During his performance on stage, his seat was occupied by a member of the Secret Service.

After his performance, the romantic pair had a late night dinner at the 21 Club in Manhattan. He was in a playful mood and over dinner, he joked with her.

"After Jack died, you were quoted as saying that you'd have the respect of the American people, just so long as you didn't run off to marry Eddie Fisher. Why didn't you say Frank Sinatra instead of Eddie?"

"I figured he needed the publicity and you didn't," Jackie shot back.

Before their final brandy of the evening, she offered an editorial proposal: "Frank, you must write your memoirs. I'll volunteer to be your editor."

"There are just too many things I've done in my life that I'm not proud of," he told her.

"Perhaps we can skip over the really horrible ones and tell a tantalizing story at the same time," she responded.

"Perhaps. Let's you and I sleep on it."

"Is that an offer?"

In separate limousines, they left 21 Club for the Hotel Carlyle for a sexual tryst. Ironically, this was the same hotel where her husband had had several sexual encounters with Marilyn Monroe.

Jackie must have been impressed with Frank's performance, because he was invited back for "a second show." This was not to be the beginning of a long-running affair. They would not be alone together until almost another year had passed.

Many Jackie watchers felt that that time at the Carlyle marked the end of the Jackie/Sinatra affair.

Not so. In J. Randy Taraborrelli's *Sinatra: Behind the Legend*, he reports another sexual tryst between Jackie and Frank, this one occurring at the singer's suite within New York City's Waldorf Towers in 1975.

Several sources, including Sammy Davis Jr., confirmed that afterward, claiming that Jackie and Frank "connected" on rare occasions, Frank bragged about his conquest of the former First Lady. One source, an employee of Frank's, told Taraborrelli that he dropped Jackie off at the Waldorf and picked her up there the following morning. According to the book, Ethel Kennedy may have been instrumental in convincing Jackie not to accept any more of Frank's calls.

When Truman Capote asked Jackie about the rumors that linked her, romantically, to Sinatra, Jackie jokingly said, "I should have stuck with Eddie Fisher."

Capote told Jackie, "I don't know how you could let Frank get away. He let me feel it one night, and I'm a good judge of cocks, having seen enough of them in my day. If I were you, I would still be swinging on it. Of course, it wasn't as big as that of Porfirio Rubirosa, who seduced your sister-in-law, Pat Kennedy."

Frank met Jackie one final time in New York. It was in 1994, at 21 Club, when Jackie was an editor for Doubleday. Spotting her, he asked the maître d' to invite her to his table. She accepted.

Without mentioning their shared past with each other, she urged him once again to write his memoirs.

"As I've said before, I can never do that," he told her. "Too many secrets. But for you, I'll think about it one more time."

She had long ago forgiven him for sharing Judith Campbell Exner with President Kennedy, and for the role he played in bringing Marilyn Monroe back into JFK's life. At the end of the dinner, as she got up to leave, he kissed her, on the lips, goodbye.

The next morning he sent her a bouquet of exquisite flowers and a bottle "of the most expensive perfume in New York." He wrote: "You are America's Queen. I can't write those memoirs. God bless you, always. Love, Frank."

He knew her days on this Earth had grown short, and when he heard of her death he wept bitter tears. "I could have loved her. She could have loved me. The saddest words are always what might have been."

At Jackie's funeral, on May 24, 1994, Frank sent two dozen red roses but didn't show up.

GLORIA SWANSON TO JACKIE:
"I HAD ARI FIRST, DEARIE!"

Jackie encountered silent screen vamp **Gloria Swanson** *(photo below)* at a party, decades after her heyday. For years, Jackie had been hearing stories about Swanson's long-running affair in Hollywood during the late 1920s with her deceased father-in-law, Joseph P. Kennedy. Virtually unknown to the world, Swanson had also had an affair with Aristotle Onassis.

At the party, Swanson provocatively told Jackie, "I got to Ari first, dearie. In fact, Ari sent Johnny Meyer to meet with me recently. He's heard talk that I might write my memoirs, and he doesn't want me to mention our affair."

"I told Meyer that I was surprised Ari thought I would want to rake up our long-ago friendship at this point. I also told him to tell Ari that his 'injunction' is a compliment to my memory but an insult to my integrity."

What Swanson didn't tell Jackie was that Meyer had arrived at her swank apartment in New York with $250,000 in cash to offer her for the removal of Ari's name from her upcoming memoirs. She refused the money. "Great stars have great pride," she said, using the famous line of Norma Desmond in *Sunset Blvd.*

"I got her to agree not to mention you, and I saved you a quarter million," Meyer later told Ari. "Sounds like bonus time to me."

HOW MARILYN TRIED TO KILL BOBBY KENNEDY
AND WHAT JACKIE SAID ABOUT IT AFTERWARD

As First Lady, Jackie immediately became suspicious of David Powers, who had been Jack's longtime aide and intimate friend. She believed that Powers was concealing the facts associated with Jack's obsession with having his "daily dose of sex."

After JFK was assassinated, Powers wrote a book, *Johnny, We Hardly Knew Ye,* in which he claimed that every time Jackie left Washington, he and the president dined together. Then the president, according to Powers, said his prayers like a good Catholic and went to bed alone. When Jackie read this, she said, "What a piece of fiction!"

Infuriated over Jack's sexual conquests, Jackie often left the White House in a huff. But she had a spy (or spies), who told her what went on during her absence.

She was especially concerned whether Marilyn ever visited the White House in disguise. Her friends at the Hotel Carlyle in New York said that on occasion, Marilyn had arrived disguised in a brunette wig, hiding behind large sunglasses, the kind that Jackie herself was often photographed wearing.

When Jackie read a play, *The Best Man,* written by her distant relative, Gore Vidal, she knew at once that the character of William Russell had been based on her husband. In the play, the womanizing character wonders how, after he becomes president, he'll be able to sneak women into the White House.

In an impudent mood, Vidal gave copies of the play to both Jack and Jackie. Each of them read it in bed. Jackie asked her husband if the character of William Russell reminded him of anyone in politics. "Not at all," Jack said. "It's pure fiction."

At one point before the election of 1960, Jackie confronted Bobby, warning him that her husband's affair with Marilyn might jeopardize his chance of ever occupying the Oval Office. "I think if the American public knew that their future president was cheating on his wife and humiliating his family, those same people would not vote for Jack."

Jackie was aware that Bobby knew the details of Jack's affair with Monroe, but he never revealed any of them to Jackie.

But in 1965, in the midst of his own affair with Jackie, Bobby did tell her that on the last day he saw Marilyn, only hours before her death, she had become a candidate for a padded cell. He confessed that in the midst of a violent argument, she'd taken a butcher knife and tried to stab him in the chest. He overpowered her, knocking her to the floor and wrestling the knife from her hand.

"Marilyn may have died at a convenient time," Jackie said. "She could have brought down the Kennedy House of Cards."

Chapter Twenty

Jackie's Lovers,
Listed in Alphabetical Order
Friends and Flings— What's Love Got to Do With It?

JFK Orders Paternity Test on Caroline and John, Jr.

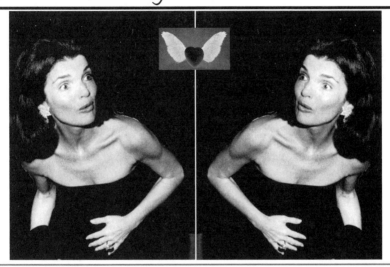

Although **Jackie**, on occasion, sometimes dated—or at least slept with—men her junior, she admitted to her confidants that, "I'm often drawn to older men, sophisticated men, men of the world, men of experience." Perhaps by coincidence, many of these men were rich, earning for her a reputation as a gold-digger.

At various galas, parties, and openings, mostly in Manhattan, Jackie most often arrived with an escort. Only on very rare occasions did she arrive alone somewhere.

During the course of her life, she apparently received solicitations from three U.S. Presidents, namely Lyndon B. Johnson, Richard M. Nixon, and Gerald Ford. Often, presidential hopefuls, including Adlai Stevenson and George McGovern, dated her, hoping that lightning would strike twice—a reference to her role in JFK's winning of the presidency, of course. Perhaps these men hoped that Jackie wanted to be First Lady a second time.

In 1994, as Jackie Kennedy Onassis was dying of cancer in her Fifth Avenue apartment in Manhattan, she summoned Nancy Tuckerman to her side. The woman had for years been her most devoted female friend.

Tuckerman had been Jackie's White House social secretary. Originally, they had met when they'd roomed together at Miss Porter's School in Farmington, Connecticut.

For her farewell to life, Jackie was getting her documents in order. One of her primary concerns involved destroying letters written to her by lovers or wannabee beaux over the decades, from when she was married to either JFK or Aristotle Onassis, but mostly from her years as a twice-widowed American icon. Many of the letters were quite passionate, and Jackie didn't want them published after she was gone.

In his book, *Farewell Jackie. A Portrait of Her Final Days,* Edward Klein wrote about the letter burning. "There was a passionate letter from the writer, John Marquand, Jr., Jackie's first great love." *[He was alleged to have taken her virginity in a Paris elevator.]* "Another letter, equally ardent, came from Rear Admiral Guérin, the French naval attaché during the Kennedy administration. There had been rumors that Jackie and the dashing French admiral were carrying on an affair. The rumors were true, and the letter went into the fire. Ditto a love note from Gianni Agnelli."

After the death of Aristotle Onassis, Jackie tried to change her public image from that of a gold-digger to a working woman and single mom when she became an editor in New York. The antagonistic press once again became her ally.

Gore Vidal, however, remained cynical about her. "She didn't let her part-time employment cramp her style. No one could keep up with the men who came and went in her life. One night it might be Peter Duchin, the musician, or perhaps the scenic designer Oliver Smith, maybe Peter Beard, the photographer and writer, even Carl Killingsworth, the so-called King of CNBC. Brendan Gill wrote for *The New Yorker* for 60 years, and Jackie was seen on his arm. Of course, many of her dates were gay."

She was, on occasion, escorted by Thomas Hoving, director of the Metro-

> *"In the years immediately after Onassis' death, Jackie's name was linked as usual to a number of men, some of them lovers, some just friends. Even the occasional one-night stand. Jackie moved with the times, doing exactly as she pleased in matters of sex."*
>
> —Sarah Bradford, biographer

politan Museum of Art in New York. She also went out with Karl Katz, a museum director and conceptualist.

For a brief time, there was rampant speculation that she might wed Senator George McGovern, who'd run unsuccessfully against Richard Nixon for president. Several gossip columnists speculated that he was ready to divorce his wife, Eleanor, to marry Jackie. Vidal claimed, "From what I heard, George took her out on five different occasions. I doubt if sex entered the picture—but who knows for sure?"

No sooner was McGovern out of the picture than Jackie was seen in the arms of Alejandro Orfila, the dashing Argentine ambassador to the United States and the General Secretary of the Organization of American States.

At a gala at the Kennedy Center, Jackie swept into the Bicentennial Ball with Orfila. Nelson Rockefeller was there. He told friends at his table, "Jackie looks like the Queen of the United States, being restored to her throne after years of exile with Onassis."

That very night, Jackie bestowed love and kisses on Henry Kissinger, Teddy Kennedy, Rose Kennedy, and President Gerald Ford. Ford was overheard complimenting her, "If only you'd met me when I was a male model on the cover of *Cosmopolitan.*"

She jokingly told him, "To my knowledge, you're the only president who was a male model. If Ronald Reagan makes it to the White House, he'd challenge your claim. After all, he used to pose for beefcake."

The dancers made room for Jackie and her handsome beau, Orfila, forming a circle around them on the dance floor. Rockefeller somewhat snidely suggested, "I think Jackie has ambitions to become the next Evita Perón."

Whereas she was seen in public with all these escorts, with some, of course, she had a more intimate relationship than with others. What was not known at the time was that she was slipping around for very rare sexual trysts with Frank Sinatra during the time he spent in New York. It was also rumored that Jackie had had an affair with Dean Martin, Sinatra's fellow Rat Packer.

Actually, what happened was this: Sinatra's flight into New York was delayed because of bad weather. He called Dean Martin at the Plaza Hotel and asked him if he'd take Jackie, with his apologies, out to dinner.

Later, Martin and Jackie were seen dining together at the Plaza in the Oak Room. Columnist Earl Wilson appeared and spotted them. He just assumed Martin and Jackie were having an affair. He asked his companions, "Is there a former lover of Shirley MacLaine's that Jackie hasn't tried to seduce? Perhaps she's getting back at Shirley ever since JFK asked Peter Lawford if Shirley had red pussy hair."

Both Sinatra and Martin were said to have become intimate with MacLaine during the making of the 1958 hit, *Some Came Running.* However, Martin later said, "I love her, but her oars aren't touching the water these days."

Jackie was also known for stealing Journalist Peter Hamill, MacLaine's boy friend of seven years, from her.

There was speculation in the press as to why Jackie and MacLaine were attracted to the same type of man. Parallels were also drawn between MacLaine and her marriage to producer Steve Parker and Jackie's marriage to Onassis.

MacLaine had told the press, "I don't have to worry about my husband growing tired of me because I never see him."

Likewise, Jackie's marriage to Onassis was characterized by long absences. At one point, he called her whenever he planned to fly into New York, thereby allowing her ample opportunity to wing her way off to Paris, or wherever.

One aggressive newspaper reporter from the *New York Daily News* asked Jackie, "What do you think of Shirley MacLaine?"

She snapped, "Check with Martin Rackin."

Rackin was a producer who'd made a dishy comment about the actress. "Shirley MacLaine is a disaster, a fucking ovary with a propeller, who leaves a trail of blood wherever she goes. A half-assed chorus girl, a pseudo-intellectual who thinks she knows everything; wears clothes from the ladies of the Good Christ Church Bazaar."

Jackie may have gotten the ultimate revenge on MacLaine. She eventually seduced her younger brother, Warren Beatty.

***

After her departure from the White House, when Jackie was still living in Georgetown in Washington, she invited Margot Fonteyn to spend a weekend with her. Onstage, the British *prima ballerina* had danced frequently with Jackie's intimate friend, Rudolf Nureyev.

Recalling her weekend, Fonteyn later told friends that she was surprised at how candid Jackie had been with her. "She told me that she knew that her husband, President Kennedy, had been a womanizer. She also said that he had suspected her of having had numerous affairs, too."

"Behind my back, Jack had paternity tests performed on both John Jr. and Caroline," Jackie told Fonteyn. "Apparently, the results pleased him. They proved that my children came from his seed."

Charles Addams
Jackie As a Manifestation of Morticia

In 1966, between marriages, Jackie had a momentary fling with Charles Addams, the cartoonist known for his darkly humorous and macabre characters, some of which included the Addams family.

Friends speculated that Jackie was just trying to make Bobby Kennedy jealous, but it appears that she found Addams an amusing companion and competent lover. "His sense of humor is different from that of anybody I know," she said. "And I adore his artwork."

His fans didn't know that in private, Addams was known as a lady killer, making A-list conquests who ranged from Joan Fontaine to Greta Garbo.

His biographer defined him as "a well-dressed, courtly man with silvery back-combed hair and a gentle manner."

Seventeen years older than Jackie, the New Jersey born cartoonist was a distant descendant of U.S. presidents John Adams and John Quincy Adams, despite the different spellings of their names. He had always been artistically inclined, "drawing with a happy vengeance," according to his biographer.

In Westfield, New Jersey, a spooky house on Dudley Avenue *[the police once caught him breaking into it]* became the inspiration for the Addams Family manse in his cartoons.

"Roguish and a bit crazy, but utterly fascinating," was how Joan Fontaine described cartoonist **Charles Addams**: "I took up with him, though I feared that Greta Garbo was a tough act to follow. The last person I expected him to be involved with was Mrs. Kennedy."

Jackie found Addams very social and debonair, but eccentric. He told her that his first job in 1933 involved working in the layout department of *True Detective* magazine. He had to retouch photos of corpses, removing the blood stains.

He also told her that he found the inspiration for his cartoon character, Morticia Addams, in his first wife, Barbara Jean Day, in 1942.

Jackie found Addams' previous marriages fascinating, especially when he told her that in 1954, he'd married another "Morticia look-alike" in the form of Barbara Barb. "She was a lawyer, a very clever fox, who tricked me into giving away all my legal rights to the TV and film franchise for the Addams Family. She also took out an insurance policy on me for $100,000. I consulted my lawyer, who told me to see Barbara Stanwyck in *Double Indemnity* (1944)*,* in which Babs plots to murder her husband for his insurance money. I immediately divorced my second wife in 1956."

Addams often escorted Jackie to the movies or the theater, where she complained that people were always staring at her. He told her to let her hair down instead piling it up into a towering bouffant, and he also advised her not to wear large sunglasses in darkened theaters because that only drew attention to her. "Follow my advice and people won't notice you so much," he said.

The first time Addams visited Jackie's apartment, she told him, "I can't trust my servants. I think all of them are writing books about me. They always try to eavesdrop on my conversations, and I suspect they are going through my garbage."

"Jackie was an enigma never solved," Addams told his friend, the columnist Doris Lilly, former lover of Ronald Reagan. "She once left me a handwritten note. Out of curiosity, I took it to the best handwriting analyst in New York. It was not signed, so he didn't know it had been written by Jackie. He carefully analyzed it. Later, he told me, "You sent me the script of an egomaniac."

Addams had first met Jackie during the summer of 1964, when she was still recovering from the trauma of JFK's assassination that previous November in Dallas.

James Fosburgh, director of the Special Committee for White House paintings, once invited Jackie and Addams to spend a weekend with him at his country home in Westchester County.

A fellow guest included Kitty Carlisle Hart, who had been married to the playwright Moss Hart.

"All of us tried to show Jackie a good time, since she'd suffered through so much," Hart said. "To my amazement, Charlie was showing a romantic interest in her. I didn't think she would respond to him, but she did. An unlikely couple, they seemed captivated by each other."

"Each of us had separate bedrooms, but it became obvious that Charlie was slipping into Jackie's boudoir at night," Hart claimed. "The next afternoon, we played a silly game around the swimming pool."

"Instead of our present careers, the point of the game was to reveal what we would have preferred to be. Charlie said he wanted to be Harry James, the leader of a big band, married to Betty Grable. I wanted to be the world's leading movie star, a rival of Katharine Hepburn. Jackie surprised all of us, announcing that she would have preferred being born a falcon."

"Jackie and I later, in private, had a heart-to-heart talk if you can forgive the pun," Hart said. "I had lost Moss, and she had lost Jack. We talked

Often as zany as his Addams Family cartoons, **Charles Addams** *(upper left)* is seen wearing the armored head of the headless "soldier" standing behind him.

Anjelica Huston *(upper right)* played Morticia in a later movie adaptation. In the bottom photograph, Gomez and Morticia were played by **John Austin** and **Carolyn Jones** in the popular 1964-66 TV series.

Jackie told her relative, John H. Davis, "I had no desire to become Charles' next Morticia. I would have had to wear my hair down."

about the adjustments a widow has to make. We shared our grief. I was shocked when she gave me a very graphic description of that day in Dallas."

"She described the horror of seeing the President's brain blown away, pieces of it falling onto her," Hart said. "She was filled with regrets. She felt if she'd moved in a different direction, she might have prevented it. She even claimed that she wished that she'd taken the bullets for him."

"It was ghastly hearing her talk," Hart said, "but I knew she needed to unburden herself. I was glad to see her moving on with Charlie. After all, she still had most of her life to live. She began to date Charlie, to the surprise of all of us."

Jackie was seen leaving Addam's apartment in Greenwich Village, and she also slipped away with her Secret Service for weekend visits to his home at Sagaponack, Long Island.

The affair ended abruptly when Addams bragged to friends, including George Plimpton, about how well Jackie performed in bed. "Seducing her is like living a fairy tale," he told his friends.

One night at the Restaurant "21" in Manhattan, Addams was dining with his friend, Doris Lilly.

"He could not stop bragging about Jackie and his involvement with her," Lilly later said, although she didn't write about it in her column. "I felt he was being indiscreet. Since they moved in somewhat the same circles, I feared word would get back to Jackie."

"In a coincidence of the type found in a Charles Dickens novel, Jackie, with some escort I didn't recognize, entered 21 that night," Lilly claimed. "The *maître d'* was directing her right by our table. Charlie spotted her and stood up to welcome her warmly, extending his hand. She stared straight through him as if he were an apparition."

When Jackie was out of hearing distance, Addams sat down and said to Lilly: "What a bitch!" What a god damn fucking bitch!"

That marked the end of their affair.

Gianni Agnelli
Jackie and the Uncrowned King of Italy

Jackie Kennedy had long been impressed with Gianni Agnelli, the czar who ran Fiat during the jet age. She once called him "the godfather of the male style," and was said to have envied Pamela Harriman when she became his mistress.

Many *fashionistas* hailed Agnelli as one of the most stylish men of the 20th Century. Men in the West copied—or tried to—his casual elegance and inventive style. *Esquire* magazine named Agnelli one of the five best-dressed men in the history of the world.

Agnelli's own favorite appellation was "The Uncrowned King of Italy." He also liked being called "the James Bond of *vroom.*"

He was also nicknamed *L'avvocato* ("Lawyer") because he had a law degree, but never practiced. In France, because of his promiscuity, he was known as "the Rake of the Riviera".

Not just women, but other playboys such as Gunther Sachs and Porfirio Rubirosa were also attracted to him and his world of private jets "flying anywhere," martinis in heavy glasses, secluded coves along the Adriatic, and his pick of his era's most desirable women. They included not just Pamela, but big-bosomed Anita Ekberg; the beautiful Linda Christian *[wife of Tyrone Power]*; and the French actress, Danielle Darrieux, former wife of Rubirosa.

Agnelli never wore the same outfit twice, usually showing up in the latest bespoke suit created by Caraceni, with a Battistoni shirt.

While President Kennedy remained behind at the White House, **Jackie** *(far left)* was vacationing along Italy's Amalfi Coast with Fiat czar, **Gianni Agnelli** *(far right)*, hailed by *fashionistas* as "the most elegant man on Earth." On those moonlit nights, and in spite of his wife being present, love was in the air between "Jackie and Gianni." Regrettably, it attracted the attention of the world press.

When Jackie got to know him, she often wrote down some of his comments. "To be a man of elegance, you should be interested in everything—art, design, cars, sports—all things to express beauty."

When Agnelli appeared with the top two buttons of his shirt unfastened and his tie askew, it was not by accident, but a deliberate attempt to create his own artful style without formality. He defined it as "casual grace."

He was a tall man, very fit and slender, with wide-set eyes. He was intelligent, witty, charismatic, sophisticated, a man of the world, the personification of Continental elegance. When he walked into a room, everyone took notice. Whenever he was around, there was a sense of excitement in the air, as if something big was about to happen.

"He was an icon," said Pamela Harriman. "I can just picture him skiing on the face of a Swiss mountain at Gstaad, with a cigarette dangling from his lips, perhaps jumping nude from his yacht off the coast of Sardinia in August."

The press called him "unflappable, punctilious, nonchalant—at all times an aristocrat." Robert Rabensteiner, fashion editor of *l'Uomo Vogue,* claimed, "His life was his art. It was a beautiful life, and he lived it uniquely."

In August of 1962, during the peak of JFK's brief regime in the White

House, Lee Radziwill and Prince Stanislas rented the elegant Villa Episcopi at Ravello, along the Amalfi Coast south of Naples. It was a 900-year-old, 12-room palazzo overlooking the Bay of Salerno.

Jackie was invited to bring Caroline and to join fellow house guests, including Gianni and Marella Agnelli, Benno Graziani *[the celebrity photographer for Paris-Match]* and his wife, Nicole, and C.L. Sulzberger. *[Cyrus Leo Sulzberger II (1912 – 1993) was The New York Times' lead foreign correspondent throughout the 1940s and 1950s, and a member of the family that owned that newspaper.]*

JFK was reluctant to let Jackie go, but since the Radziwills would be there, and since Caroline would go along, he finally agreed, even though he had always been suspicious of Agnelli.

Sulzberger would record details about the gathering in his book, *The Last of the Giants,* published in 1970. In it, he stated, "Jackie was a strange girl and also strange looking, but quite lovely in spite of the fact her eyes were too far apart. She is a good athlete, swims, water-skis, and dances as well and has a fine figure. She has an odd habit of halting constantly as she talks, a kind of pause rather than a stutter, so sometimes you think she's through saying something when she isn't."

"I didn't have the impression that she was particularly brilliant, despite her reputation for being so, or that she was unusually cultivated. Speaks good French and some Italian. A rather typical society girl, but sweet, exceptionally fond of Caroline, and somehow on the whole, unspoiled."

He later recalled to friends, "To say that Jackie and Gianni were mesmerized by each other would be putting it mildly. They were enchanted, in spite of her sister and Gianni's wife being with us. Jackie and Gianni, those two lovebirds, managed to slip away for several trips together."

Agnelli's wife, Marella, *[Marella Caracciolo dei Principi di Castagneto)* was a discreet noblewoman and a well-known fabric designer. She managed to excuse herself whenever she wasn't needed or her husband preferred to be alone with Jackie.

At one point, Edoardo Agnelli, who had been born to the couple seven months after their marriage in 1954, showed up. He had been born in New York, making him an American citizen. Jackie soon discovered that he had no plan to become a Fiat czar in the footsteps of his father. He was interested in mysticism, and, at Princeton University, he had studied religion.

[In 2000, about six years after Jackie's death, Edoardo committed suicide by jumping off a bridge in Turin, the city where Fiat was headquartered; where his father had been born; and where, he would die.]

Agnelli arranged various excursions with Jackie in his 82-foot yacht. They even went so far as Naples to dine with an old Neapolitan count and his young mistress.

Trailed by the paparazzi on their every outing, Jackie and Agnelli walked through the ancient streets of Ravello, having a Campari at a café opening onto the Piazza del Duomo.

One moonlit night, on the deck of Agnelli's yacht, they danced barefoot to the sounds of a mandolin band. There were strolls along the beach after midnight.

As *Vanity Fair* claimed, "The tam-tam of international gossip worked with full rhythm; the paparazzi shot one photo after another, while the fantasies of the reporters went crazy. Jackie and Agnelli were often photographed on his blue sailing ship, or having drinks on one of the hotel terraces in Ravello, always at each other's side."

In the White House, JFK had been sent one photo too many of his wife with Agnelli, one of them picturing the two of them swimming together. JFK cabled her—"MORE CAROLINE, LESS GIANNI."

Before flying home, the "love story" of "Jackie and Gianni" had captured the curiosity—but not necessarily the approval—of the world.

Much of America was outraged, especially women. One group, Concerned Citizens of America, threatened to picket the White House after Jackie's return.

She was sent a cable "Would you not better serve the nation and the President by returning to his side? We have honored you greatly with the position of First Lady of our land, and we only ask that you not violate the dignity of that title."

Jackie's response? She was photographed the following night dancing the Twist with the Duca di Sangro at a night club, The Pirate's Den. Columnist Drew Pearson wrote: "How can a man handle the problems of a nation when he can't handle his wife? She's off dancing wearing a red blouse, red slacks, and red shoes with some aristocrat until four in the morning. Doesn't she have enough respect for her husband to be a good wife?"

Jackie and Agnelli received even more attention when they sailed over to Capri. Jackie already knew some expatriates on the island. Her first greeter was a Texan, Robert Hornstein, the heir to the Puss 'n Boots cat food fortune. She knew him only slightly.

Notorious, and much sought-after on Capri for his scandalous *La Dolce Vita* parties, he greeted Jackie with a gift of a dozen of the most expensive and beautiful silk scarves made in Italy.

On Capri, flamboyantly dressed in loose-fitting, purple-colored cotton pants and red *espadrilles,* he showed up at the pier to greet her. He welcomed her to the island and also invited her to his villa on the Via Tragara, "the Park Avenue" of Capri. In the garden behind his villa was the most exclusive nightclub on that very fashionable island.

Jackie had requested to meet Princess Irene Galitzine, who was sometimes compared to a Russian version of Coco Chanel, and who operated exclusive fashion boutiques in Florence and Rome. The most celebrated fashion designer on the Italian scene, she had created "Palazzo pajamas," which had become the virtual uniform of the international set.

On Capri, the paparazzi stalked them. Agnelli, with Jackie on his arm, escorted her to the Galitzine's rented Medici villa.

Ushered into the designer's bathroom, Jackie ordered a vodka after making a selection of palazzo pajamas, choosing a design in lime green Thai silk. After that stiff drink, she made a spectacular appearance at dinner.

Later, she and Agnelli went to Horstein's nightclub, where she danced the Twist and the Cha-Cha before departing aboard the Agnelli yacht for the return trip. They sailed against the backdrop of a pre-dawn sky. It was rumored that on this romantic ride, Agnelli proposed to Jackie, claiming he would divorce Marella and urging her to divorce JFK. She didn't give him an answer, but agreed to go below with him for what is known as a "farewell fuck."

***

[Jackie's friend, Robert Horstein, fell on bad days.

Semiramis Zurlo, a voluptuous, melodramatic sculptor of Ottoman descent, told Vanity Fair: *"Bob was a professional snob, loving flashy names and titles. Sexually, though, he preferred local fishermen and sailors, but only the really hot ones. One time, as a joke, Joan Crawford worked as a waitress for him at his club. Many guests thought she was just an impersonator.*

Zorlu said, "Horstein was alleged to have bit off a local boy's penis during a wild, alcoholic-fueled night. To keep his parents from going to the police, he gave them his villa. After that, he disappeared from the island and was never seen again."

Dr. Christiaan Barnard
Jackie Gave Him Her Heart

A classically handsome heart surgeon from South Africa, Christiaan Barnard had long intrigued Jackie. Seven years older than her, she had first heard of him in 1950 when he did postgraduate work on a two-year scholarship in cardiothoracic surgery at the University of Minnesota in Minneapolis, studying under open-heart surgery pioneer Walt Lillehei.

One of Jackie's college classmates, Sarah Hagan, had dated the surgeon and had fallen in love with him, sending Jackie a picture.

Born into genteel poverty, the son of a wilderness missionary, Barnard possessed touseled good looks, a ready wit, and a genius for thoracic surgery.

Jackie once listed **Dr. Christiaan Barnard** as "one of the most desirable men in the world." Of course, she revised that list from time to time.

When she finally met him, he stole her heart.

Short of money in Minneapolis, Barnard had mowed lawns, delivered news-papers, and washed cars. He'd seen *Gone With the Wind* (1939), and, like Scarlett O'Hara in the movie, he vowed never to go hungry again. He told friends that if he couldn't make lots of money in the medical profession, he'd marry an heiress. Although he did make money in surgery, he also married an heiress.

Like the rest of the world, Jackie heard of Barnard once again on December 3, 1967, when he performed the first heart transplant on a human. He would later confide to Jackie that he had first experimented by transplanting hearts into fifty dogs. "For a dying man to make a decision for a heart transplant is not a difficult choice," he once told her. "If a lion chases you to the bank of a river filled with crocodiles, you will leap into the water, convinced that you can swim to the other bank before the reptiles devour you. At least you have a chance at life, which is what one of my heart transplants provides."

[The history-making event occurred when Denise Darvall, a 25-year-old woman, was brought into the hospital following a car crash. Her heart was still beating, but her brain no longer functioned. At the moment of her death, Barnard removed her heart and surgically installed it into the chest of Louis B. Washkansky, 55, a businessman suffering from end-stage coronary artery dis-ease. The patient survived for only eighteen days, dying from pneumonia that overwhelmed his weakened system. Today, inprovements in anti-rejection drugs have made the procedure almost routine.]

The surgeon had ignited a firestorm in South Africa when it was revealed that he'd transplanted the heart of a white woman into the chest of a black man. Later, he infuriated some white South Africans when he publicly supported Nelson Mandela as South Africa's first post-apartheid president.

Almost overnight, Barnard was propelled into the jet set. When he arrived in New York, Jackie was among the first to call him with congratula-tions. He invited her out to dinner. Thus began a series of shared evenings.

She told friends such as Truman Capote, "Christiaan is my dream man. Utterly charming. A great conversationalist."

She learned that sudden fame had taken a toll on his personal life. In 1948, he'd married Aletta Gertruida Louw, a nurse, divorcing her in 1969.

He broke with his second wife, Johannes-burg socialite Barbara Zoeliner, in 1982 after twelve years of marriage.

His final marriage was to a 24-year-old model, Karin Setzkorn, daughter of a multi-mil-lionaire. His friends warned Barnard, then in his

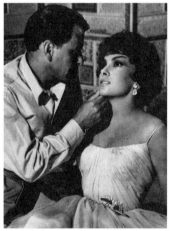

In the movie, *Never So Few,* **Frank Sinatra** is paying special attention to the Italian sexbomb, **Gina Lollobrigida,** but she, like Jackie, gave her heart to Dr. Barnard.

late 60s, about the dangers of marrying a young woman. "It may prove fatal," said his fellow surgeon, Dr. Denton Cooley.

Barnard replied, "Well, if she dies, I'll get a younger one."

Even though Jackie took extreme precautions for secrecy while they dated, word leaked out that Barnard had spent a weekend with her in her Fifth Avenue apartment.

Apparently, he and Jackie had discussed the downside of international fame. His point of view, as expressed to others, differed from Jackie's: "Any man—or woman, for that matter—who says he doesn't like applause and recognition is either a fool or a liar. Success gives you the courage to go on and do even more."

On the other hand, she complained about the exposure of her affairs. "I want less publicity, I should date men who are not household names. I can't even go out with a man before the boys of the press have me marrying him. Everyone I date is rumored to be my next husband."

Jackie was spotted dining in Manhattan with Barnard at both The Sign of the Dove and at Jimmy Weston's. At the latter restaurant, they encountered Frank Sinatra, who joined their table. A waiter later claimed that the singer sat with them for three hours.

The surgeon had seen only one of Sinatra's films, *Never So Few.* Released in 1959, it starred Gina Lollobrigida, an actress rivaling Sophia Loren as Italy's reigning sex symbol. The picture also starred Steve McQueen and Peter Lawford.

"How dumb I was," Jackie later told Lawford. "Christiaan spent a lot of time grilling Frank about Lollobrigida."

"I gave my heart to Christiaan," she said to Lawford, "but he returned it."

Within weeks, she read in the gossip columns that Barnard was having a torrid affair with Lollobrigida.

As Jackie related to Lawford, "What is it with me? Sex symbols give me so much competition! First, Marilyn Monroe competing for Jack; now Gina Lollobrigida putting designs on Christiaan."

Jackie's romance with the surgeon fizzled out soon after it began. However, the two stayed in touch over the years.

In 1985, long after the termination of their brief fling, he sent her a carton of Glycel, an expensive "anti-aging" skin cream. Apparently, it didn't work, and was forced off the market by the U.S. Food and Drug Administration. Noting that Jackie was concerned with wrinkles, he also suggested she visit the Clinique La Prairie in Montreux, Switzerland, a spa and wellness center with which he was associated as a research advisor. She graciously rejected his suggestion.

In later life, during Jackie's tenure as an editor within Manhattan's publishing community, he wrote novels and sent her his manuscripts for her comments and consideration. Although she praised his skill as a novelist, she privately told her senior editors, "Christiaan's skills as a writer will never equal his medical achievements."

Barnard survived Jackie, dying in September of 2001 in Cyprus. The first reports claimed that he died of a heart attack, but an autopsy showed that his death was caused by a severe asthma attack. Plagued by arthritis, he had retired from surgery in 1983. When he died, he was set to embark on a promotional tour for his latest book, *50 Ways to a Healthy Heart.*

His daughter, Deidre Visser, told the press, "My father could stand being alone, but he could not stand loneliness. The man belonged to the world."

André Meyer
Jackie and "The Picasso of Banking"

The French-born Wall Street investment banker, André Benoit Mathieu Meyer, was in love with Jackie, but there was a problem: She was not in love with him. Another thing: Born in 1898, he was thirty years older than she was.

Launching his banking career at the age of sixteen in the Paris Bourse (Stock Exchange), he rose with lightning speed in the industry, enjoying a decades-long association with the famous firm of Lazard Frères. When the Nazis took over France, Meyer fled to the West.

But he returned after the war and became, in the words of David Rockefeller, "the most creative financial genius of our time, launching such innovations as automobile financing. The media labeled him, "the Picasso of banking."

In the United States, he was soon drawn into the orbit of Joseph P. Kennedy and later, into the entourages of Jackie and JFK. He became their financial advisor. Over the years, he was a lifelong friend to Jackie, although he wanted more out of the relationship than friendship. But she held him at bay. Once she introduced him to Lyndon B. Johnson, who was impressed. Later, during Johnson's presidency, he often called on Meyer for advice.

Jackie was drawn to Meyer not just for his financial wisdom, but for their shared interest in art. She was dazzled by the paintings in his private collection, which included works by Paul Cézanne, Pablo Picasso, Claude Monet, and Marc Chagall.

David Rockefeller claimed that André Meyer was the first financier for Jackie. "He could take a one million dollar investment of hers and turn it into five million. He had the Midas touch."

Jolie Gabor, mother of the three celebrated Gabor sisters, including Zsa Zsa, claimed that André Meyer liked to bring all his mistresses together at the same party. "None of us could compete with Jackie, however."

In time, he amassed one of the finest collections of 19th Century European art in private hands. She vacationed with him at his retreat in Crans-sur-Sierre in the Valais region of Switzerland.

When she was First Lady, and upgrading the furnishings at the White House, Jackie got Meyer to donate a $50,000 Savonnerie carpet. When she later wanted an apartment in Manhattan, he secured for her a spectacular 15-room, five-bedroom apartment on the 15th floor at 1040 Fifth Avenue at 85th Street.

She paid $250,000, which was a great bargain even back then. He arranged for her to stay in a suite at the Carlyle while $125,000 of renovations were completed. Later, when raising money for the Kennedy Library, she got him to contribute $250,000.

When Jackie was in love with Bobby Kennedy, she wanted to spend every evening with him. Of course, that was not possible, so she often called Meyer to escort her to various events—a Broadway play, the opera or ballet, the latest art exhibition.

Meyer maintained a lavish residence within the Carlyle, and Jackie often attended his cocktail parties. As Meyer's biographer, Cary Reich, claimed, "Jackie constantly toyed with Meyer. What drove him to distraction was her breathless, little-girl-lost manner in which she addressed him. It was, 'Oh, André, what should I do?'"

"Women flocked around Meyer," said Jolie Gabor, a friend of his. "He often gave parties inviting many of the women who had been his mistresses. But the moment Jackie walked into the room, he had no time for us. He ignored his other guests and devoted all his attention hovering over Jackie, catering to her every wish. Naturally, we were jealous. But which of us could compete with the great Jackie Kennedy?"

"With her, you never knew if she'd snatch your husband away," Gabor said. "When I visited with my young husband, I made sure he was in chains before I let him go inside. Jackie was skilled at stealing other women's husbands, at least for a momentary diversion. I was glad that my dear Zsa Zsa made love to her husband. It served Jackie right."

Meyer became the chief fundraiser for the Kennedy Library and later managed its $60 million endowment. He also grew very close to Bobby Kennedy, who appointed him manager of the various trust funds established by his father, Joseph P. Kennedy.

When Meyer learned that Jackie intended to marry Aristotle Onassis, he repeatedly urged her not to. "He has great charm and intelligence," Meyer told her. "But he is rough, yacht or no yacht. He will not make you happy. And then there is his reputation, casually casting Maria Callas and your own sister overboard. There are rumors—more than rumors, actually—about his homosexuality. Did you know that he maintains a pretty young boy installed in an apartment in Paris, and another in Athens, to provide some diversion and variety in his sex life when he tires of women? How very Greek of him."

Word reached Jackie that Meyer had died in Lausanne, Switzerland, on

September 9, 1979. Gianni Agnelli, another of Jackie's beaux, was at his bedside. Agnelli later told her, "André's last words to me were, 'Make sure Jackie's all right.'"

He died fretting about a former First Lady who, largely because of his investments, had millions.

Years later, Dr. Henry Lax, a Swiss-born doctor who operated out of an office on Park Avenue, claimed that Jackie had once admitted to him that she'd had a one-night fling with Meyer.

"She told me it was not very satisfactory, and she had no desire to continue it," he said. "Even so, André had much that attracted Jackie to a man—money, power, and the dignity of age."

Peter Cook
"I Loved Cuckolding JFK"

After Jackie's death in 1994, London's *Daily Mail* broke the story that Jackie and Peter Cook, the English actor, satirist, writer, and comedian—described as "the finest comic talent of his generation" and "the funniest man ever born"—had had an affair.

The news brought an avalanche of mail from readers, including this comment from Stephen Harris of Totnes, Devon: "So basically, Jackie was cheating on John Kennedy with Peter Cook. Peter was cheating on his girlfriend, Wendy Snowden, with Jackie. JFK was cheating on Jackie with just about every skirt in Washington. All the while, Bobby Kennedy was in the company of Lee Remick. (No doubt Ethel was at home looking after his brood.) If you take away the music, the 60s generation was altogether a pretty pathetic bunch. Red arrow me if you like, but anybody looking at the 'norms' of modern society and wondering where it all began to go wrong, need look no further than the 1960s."

One of Jackie's classmates, Deborah James, once wrote: "Peter Cook was about eight years younger than Jackie. She always had this thing for the English schoolboy look, varying it by dating older men."

Before she'd been introduced to Cook, Jackie had been amused by his satire, which usually pro-

"All of us were part of the British invasion," claimed TV host David Frost. "Our inside joke was that **Peter Cook** invaded Mrs. Kennedy." Cook is pictured above *(left)* with his partner, **Dudley Moore.**

moted as anti-establishment comedy. She'd seen a tape of his performance at the Edinburgh Festival impersonating Britain's Prime Minister, Harold Macmillan. Cook was part of a four-man troupe, "Beyond the Fringe." Its other members included Dudley Moore, who would go on to major stardom, Alan Bennett, and Jonathan Miller.

Through channels, Jackie extended an invitation to Cook to perform at the White House. But he very arrogantly turned her down, asserting, "We're not some fucking traveling cabaret troupe." He sent word to Jackie that if she wanted to see his group, she could do so on Broadway.

Surprisingly, Jackie was not insulted. During one of her visits with JFK to New York in 1962, they went to see *Beyond the Fringe.*

After the curtain came down, the President and Jackie went backstage to congratulate the group. JFK wandered off somewhere. Bennett later claimed, "Jackie went into a huddle with Peter. She was all over him. Stroking his arm, laughing at his humor. At one point, she was heard telling Peter, 'Oh, you're so naughty,' responding to something he'd whispered into her ear. I later learned from Peter that they had a fling. In New York, he escorted her to a party or two while JFK went back to Washington."

Jackie was known to have made an appearance one night at Cook's apartment in Manhattan's Greenwich Village, where he lived with his future wife, Wendy Snowden, whom he eventually married in 1963. Cook and Snowden's fellow guests included model Jean Shrimpton, and actors Terence Stamp and Albert Finney, each a talented actor and designated participants in that era's "British invasion."

Journalist Glenys Roberts claimed, "When he first met Jackie, Cook had not yet become the predatory satyr that he was in later life. He was a handsome, romantic lad with floppy hair and a slender figure."

When members of his entourage asked Cook about the rumors of a fling with Jackie, he told them, "I put the double knight's move on her."

It didn't take Snowden long to hear about Cook's fixation on Jackie. At this stage in their marriage, Jackie and JFK had drifted apart because of his numerous affairs. "According to her contemporaries, she was by no means the virginal bride suggested by her squeaky little voice, pillbox hats, and prim Fifties frocks," wrote Roberts. "Because of her unsatisfactory marriage, she had a reputation as something of a scalp-hunter."

Snowden went to Puerto Rico for a brief vacation, but returned unexpectedly. Upon her return to the apartment she shared, she was told by Cook's chef that "Peter is at that new Manhattan club, Strollers. Jackie Kennedy is there tonight, I heard."

"Peter went into a panic seeing me," Wendy said. "He introduced me to Jackie. She was tall and slender, with thick black hair and a vermillion mouth, immaculately groomed in an expensive black dress with a diamond pin. She had a little girlish laugh."

There was speculation that Jackie abruptly ended her affair with Cook when their relationship became too public.

She would see him one final time on Broadway when she and Lee Radziwill attended one of his performances of his show, *Good Evening.* As he confided to his wife at the time, Judy Huxtable, an actress and model, "I began an affair with Lee."

The *Daily Mail* also claimed that Cook had an affair with Lee. If so, this would not be the first time that the sisters had become sexually engaged with the same men. The others had included John F. Kennedy and Aristotle Onassis, among others.

Cook was reported to have become even more promiscuous in the years that followed. Following the collapse of his marriage to Snowden, he developed a standard and oft-repeated phrase which he communicated to any of "the birds" who flirted with him, "I am cheating on my wife with other girls, but I could fit you in if you want it."

After the collapse of his marriage to Snowden in 1971, Cook became "a bloated bloke," as described by the London press. One reporter asserted, "He was knee deep in unopened bills and empty liquor bottles."

He would marry two more times before his death on January 9, 1995, outliving Jackie by only one year.

In the years after his death, a minor planet *[20468 Petercook, in the main asteroid belt]*, was named after him.

"Jackie Kennedy and a planet—not bad for a little Devonshire lad, the son of a colonial civil servant," said TV host Davis Frost.

Robert D. L. Gardiner
and the Purloined Cigarette Lighter

In March of 1966, Jackie met Robert David Lion Gardiner, the New York socialite, at a dinner party at the apartment of Lady Jeanne Campbell on Fifth Avenue in Manhattan.

He was there with his wife, Eunice Baile Oates, a former British model many years his junior. While his wife conversed elsewhere, Gardiner seemed very impressed with Jackie "despite the vacant look on her face."

Her fascination with Gardiner stemmed from the fact that he, along with his niece, Alexandra Gardiner Creel Goelet, owned Gardiner's Island, one of the largest privately owned islands in the world. He called himself "the 16th Lord of the Manor."

Robert David Lion Gardiner with his wife, **Eunice**. "You don't just accuse the former First Lady, Mrs. Kennedy, of being a thief."

Jackie was most curious about how he came to own such a valuable piece of property. *[Gardiner's Island, part of East Hampton, New York, in eastern Suffolk County, is located in Gardiner's Bay, between the two peninsulas stretching eastward from the eastern end of Long Island. It is the only American real estate still intact as part of an original royal grant from the English Crown.]* Gardiner's ancestor, Lion Gardiner, an English settler, purchased it from the Montaukett Indians in 1639. According to Gardiner, "He traded the island for one large dog, one gun, some powder and shot, some rum and several blankets, worth in all about five pounds sterling."

Gardiner referred to the Fords, the Du Ponts, the Rockefellers, and later, to the Hollywood tycoons who purchased property on Long Island as "the nouveaux riche."

Before the dinner party ended, Gardiner had invited Jackie to stay with him at his sumptuous East Hampton estate. He promised to take her to Gardiner's Island on his boat, showing her around its 27 miles of coastline and introducing her to its 3,350 acres of forests, streams, and buildings, some of which dated from the 17th Century.

Little is known about what occurred during Jackie's private visit to Gardiner's home in East Hampton when his wife was away. There was a lot of speculation linking the two of them. He may have revealed his romantic fixation on her—or perhaps not. He later wrote praising her "high cheekbones and striking looks, with her dark hair, which she obviously inherited from my friend and her father, Black Jack Bouvier."

That weekend, during a tour of the island, he told her fascinating stories of its origins, beginning when his family received a charter from King Charles I of England. "It is rumored that Captain Kidd buried his treasure on the island," he told Jackie. "We're still looking for it." He also revealed that former First Lady, Julia Gardiner, the wife of President John Tyler, had been born on the island. "She used to be called 'The Rose of Long Island.'"

[Young Julia Gardiner, the wife of aging John Tyler, was First Lady only from 1844 to 1845. Tyler married her during his term as President, at a ceremony in the White House. A coquette who had spurned his previous offers of marriage, she was a buxom, dark-eyed beauty who had attracted dozens of male suitors. Like Jackie, she was accused of being an outrageous flirt.

Julia Gardiner married the widowed President, John Tyler, and ruled over Washington society during their short reign in 1844-45. Like Jackie in another century, "The Rose of Long Island" completely refurbished the drab White House, but, unlike Jackie, used her family's fortune to do so.

She met President Tyler in 1842, and he was said to have been mesmerized by her, although thirty years her senior, and still in mourning for his dead first wife, Letitia.

After Julia's father was eviscerated by an ex-

plosion on the deck of the Princeton *in 1844, Julia decided she needed a man in her life. At twenty-four, she became the youngest First Lady up to that time to occupy the White House.*

She traveled about in a four-horse carriage and set about to refurbish the White House with her family's money. She had garish new livery made for the staff, and she selected a dozen female companions to accompany her as "ladies-in-waiting." The press dubbed them "The Vestal Virgins."

For her Grand Finale Ball, the most lavish in the history of the White House, she ordered "oceans of French champagne" and danced with nearly every ambassador from the nations of Europe.

That night, she introduced the polka to Washington, and got the Marine Band to play "Hail to the Chief" for the first time, a tradition that continues to this day. She was such a skilled dancer that a New York publisher printed "The Julia Waltzes" so that the masses might dance to her favorite tunes.

After retirement, John Tyler, then in his 70s, continued to sire children, ending up with a brood of fifteen.

In later life, Julia fell on bad days financially, but insisted on being addressed as "Mrs. Ex-Presidentress."

Reading about Julia's financial woes, Jackie vowed she'd never let that happen to her.

FUN FACT: Julia bore Tyler seven of his children. When Tyler was born, George Washington was President. When Julia and John Tyler's youngest daughter, Mary, died, Harry S Truman was President. The combined lifespans of John Tyler and his youngest daughter, Mary, represent a span of thirty-two presidents, or more than 150 years.]

***

Jackie's closest friends referred to her fling with Gardiner as "a passing fancy" or "the whim of a moment." Whatever it was called, it ended badly.

After a dinner with Gardiner at his East Hampton home, he and Jackie retired to his oak-paneled library for a French cognac and an espresso.

According to Gardiner's later defamations, Jackie reached into her purse and removed a cigarette from a package. Spotting a gold cigarette lighter on a pink marble-topped table, she picked it up and lit her own cigarette.

The lighter belonged to Gardiner's wife, Eunice Bailey Oates. To Gardiner's astonishment, Jackie snapped open her purse and put the gold lighter inside.

He wanted to say something, but did not want it to appear that he was accusing Jackie of stealing the lighter. He thought she might have chucked the lighter into her purse without thinking. So he decided to "smoke her out." He went to his humidor, positioned near the fireplace, and removed a cigar, cutting off its tip. He turned and looked for the lighter. "Have you seen my wife's lighter? It's usually here on the coffee table."

She looked around the room. "Well, she must have taken it tonight. It doesn't seem to be here. I don't have a clue as to where she left it."

"I thought I saw you use it," he said.

"Never," she answered. "I carry around my own lighter. It's made of gold...perhaps that's why you were confused."

Gardiner later asked his friends, "What was I to do? Search her purse like that of a common thief? After all, she is one of the world's most celebrated figures, a former First Lady who should be treated with respect."

The following morning, Jackie returned to Manhattan. Before her departure, over breakfast, she lit her cigarette with a silver lighter she carried in her purse.

On the evening after her departure, Gardiner had a drink with the novelist, William Styron and some of his other friends. He told them about the incident. The story was too tantalizing for them to keep it to themselves.

The rumor soon spread from East Hampton to Manhattan. When it hit the party circuit, the story was that Gardiner was accusing Jackie of kleptomania, evoking a similar charge made against actress Hedy Lamarr, one of JFK's former lovers.

After Jackie married Aristotle Onassis, his lawyer, Roy Cohn, told him that Gardiner was still spreading the story of Jackie's alleged theft two years before. "People are gossiping about Jackie something awful," Cohn claimed.

Onassis asked Jackie what she knew about the lighter.

"Nothing," she said. "I always carry my own lighter."

"Then the son of a bitch is lying," Onassis said. He called Cohn the next morning. "Write that Gardiner a letter threatening him with a multi-million dollar lawsuit if he doesn't stop libeling my wife." Then he paused. "But just in case he's telling the truth, enclose a check for $5,000. Don't admit to anything. Just say, if you're so desperate for a god damn cigarette lighter, go buy yourself one at Tiffany's and shut your fucking mouth about Jackie, you lying son of a bitch."

Gardiner's gold cigarette lighter didn't resurface until after Jackie's death in 1994. Caroline Kennedy, probably unaware of its origin, put it up for auction at Sotheby's in Manhattan, along with other Jackie possessions.

The Marques de Garrigues
"I Would Have Posed Nude for Goya"

—Jackie

Antonio Garrigues y Díaz-Cañabate, the Marques of Garrigues, had supported Franco's Nationalist forces, using sabotage and propaganda, during Spain's Civil War in the late 1930s. He had befriended the young and very handsome Joseph P. Kennedy, Jr., during the Kennedy brother's involvement in the conflicts of war-torn Spain.

Throughout most of the war, the Marquis had opted to live in Madrid during the time when it was controlled by Revolutionary forces opposed to Franco. Garrigues had worked as a spy, an undercover "Fifth Columnist," secretly working to advance Franco's (fascist) agenda through propaganda distributed at night. In the brochures he secretly published and distributed, he urged the people of Madrid to change their allegiance away from the monarchy and to support the fascist forces of Franco—or else risk having Madrid bombed out of existence.

AS POSH AS IT GETS:
Antonio Garrigues y Diaz-Cañabate *(left)* with **Queen Sofia** and **Juan Carlos** of Spain, chat with **JFK** *(right)* at the White House

Garrigues toured the battered city streets of Madrid with Joe Jr., distributing subversive literature. When men from the local militia stopped him, Garrigues claimed that he was merely showing Madrid to a foreign friend.

When JFK, Joseph's younger brother, became President, Franco appointed Garrigues as the Spanish ambassador to Washington, thinking that his long-ago link with the Kennedys might help in some way to relieve tension between his repressive dictatorship and the United States.

A frequent visitor to the White House, Garrigues interpreted Jackie as "the century's most enchanting woman." Reacting to that, she became highly susceptible to his charms.

Even after the assassination of her husband, Jackie stayed on good terms with the Ambassador. As reporter Michael Mullan, wrote, "She dropped in on him as she dashed between continents."

In January of 1966, she stayed with Garrigues in Rome, where he had become Spain's Ambassador to the Vatican. It was he who introduced Jackie to Roman nobility, escorting her to parties, lavish dinners, and accompanying her during her shopping sprees through Rome's exclusive boutiques.

She called on Princess Irene Galitzine, one of Italy's leading fashion designers and socialites. After Garrigues arranged for Jackie's private visit to the Vatican, he took her to Princess Galitzine's exclusive salon, where the designer agreed to

The Duchess of Alba was said to have posed for Goya's notorious **The Naked Maja**. Jackie told Garrigues that if Goya were still around, she would have posed for an equivalent portrait.

426

have her staff work overtime making an elegant yet restrained black dress for her upcoming audience with the Pope.

Because Jackie was seen so frequently around Rome with Garrigues, the tabloid press wrote that she was planning to marry her Spanish host, a sixty-two-year old widower with eight children.

***

As a lark, Jackie flew to Spain to attend the annual *feria* in Seville, a six-day, post-Lenten fiesta of parties and bullfighting. She was the guest of the Duke and Duchess of Alba. Garrigues accompanied her as her escort.

As in Rome, there was rampant speculation in the Spanish press that Garrigues was set to become her third husband.

After her return to Madrid, he arranged a private dinner, unknown to the press, for himself and Jackie with King Juan Carlos.

Rumors about the impending marriage of Jackie to Garrigues became so prevalent that Angier Biddle Duke, the then-U.S. Ambassador to Spain who had previously been JFK's White House Chief of Protocol, summoned a press conference in Madrid on April 20, 1966. "On behalf of Mrs. Kennedy," he announced, "I wish to make it crystal clear and completely understood that there is no basis to rumors of an engagement to the Marques de Garrigues."

Garrigues made no statement at all, and some commentators seemed to think he was enjoying the rumors swirling around about Jackie and himself.

Right before she flew out of Spain, Garrigues proposed marriage to Jackie. Ever so graciously, she rejected his offer. "Spain is one of the most fascinating countries in the world," she told her suitor. "But it is not for me. You already have a Duchess of Alba. You don't need another. Of course, if Goya were still around, I might become his second *Naked Maja.* I'm sure he would have done a painting of me that would hang in the Prado for centuries to come."

Roswell Gilpatric
Jackie is Cited, in Court, as "The Other Woman"

In the early 1960s, those heady days of Camelot in the White House, Roswell Gilpatric was cast as Sir Lancelot, as suggested by the Washington Press Corps. The publisher of *The Washington Post,* Katharine Graham, claimed that "Jackie was doing to Jack Kennedy what Guinevere did to King Arthur."

Madelin Gilpatric, the third wife of Roswell, once said, "I wish the First Lady would stop chasing after my husband."

Gilpatric, 23 years older than Jackie, was already in his 50s when he became seriously involved with Jackie. When she had to bow out of JFK's campaign for the presidency in 1960, Gilpatric flew to her side to comfort her. She was pregnant at the time with John Jr.

Although hardly a household name today, Yale graduate Roswell Leavitt Gilpatric, a prominent New York corporate attorney, later became a high-placed official in JFK's administration.

He had been a childhood friend of Nelson Rockefeller. In the White House, JFK used to question Gilpatric about Rockefeller's womanizing, asking how such a prominent politician

A high-powered New York corporate attorney, **Roswell Gilpatric** had been Undersecretary of the Air Force during the presidency of Dwight Eisenhower. Of Jackie's many beaux, he surfaced near the top and stood by her when she needed him the most.

managed to get away with it. That was ironic. The President was getting away with "it" on a far more epic scale than Rockefeller.

Gilpatric was a towering figure during the Kennedy years in the White House. He not only managed to seduce the First Lady, but he became a trusted adviser to the President too. Previously, under Dwight D. Eisenhower, he'd been Undersecretary of the Air Force.

Kennedy appointed him Undersecretary of Defense in 1961 because he considered his boss, Robert McNamara, "Too inexperienced in the ways of Washington." Gilpatric was also a trusted adviser to JFK during the Cuban Missile Crisis. He urged the President to follow a course of limited action, resisting the call of the hawks to bomb Cuba out of existence.

In most cases, however, he'd been a staunch Cold Warrior, part of Operation Mongoose, launching dirty tricks against Fidel Castro in Havana.

He also argued for major U.S. involvement in Vietnam as a means of thwarting a complete communist takeover.

JFK's longtime aide, Ted Sorensen, once wrote: "Gilpatric, whom the president calls 'Ros,' made himself an indispensable figure in the Kennedy administration."

Jackie came to view Gilpatric as such a supportive friend that she relied on him more and more. Of course, she was aware that he would never be faithful to a mistress or girl friend, as he was known in Washington circles as a ladykiller, although his conquests, in his own estimation, never equaled those of his boss, John F. Kennedy.

JFK became aware of Jackie's romantic attraction to Gilpatric. "I don't understand it," he told Bobby Kennedy and others in the White House. "He's not that handsome. Perhaps it's the father image thing."

One evening, in front of her guests at the White House, Jackie defended Gilpatric's appeal. "I think he's one of the most attractive men in Washington. Men just can't understand why women find him sexy. I find men over sixty sometimes more attractive than younger ones. General Maxwell Taylor is a marvelous example, keeping himself lean and fit. Many of Jack's classmates have let themselves go and look awful. General Taylor is over sixty, plays tennis, and keeps fit, as does Ros."

She got to know Gilpatric in the privacy of Camp David when she was seven months pregnant and JFK was in California checking out military installations and Marilyn Monroe. After spending quiet, restful hours with Gilpatric, Jackie wrote: "I loved our time in Maryland so very much. It made me happy for a whole week."

As she neared childbirth, Jackie wrote from Hyannis Port, thanking Gilpatric for his recent visit there. "It was so thoughtful of you to write me about my baby. It was such a happy time being with you, and I thank you so much for coming to see me, as you did at Camp David. And now that I don't have all those ladies' lunches to go to, I hope I can come and see you and Madelin some time in May or June."

That invitation never came from Madelin, who had long been jealous of Jackie because of the attention being heaped upon her husband. *[Madelin's marriage to the five-times-married Gilpatric eventually ended in divorce.]*

In 1963, just weeks before JFK's assassination, Gilpatric came to visit Jackie, telling her that he planned to resign his government post and resume his law practice in Manhattan.

She later wrote him: "I feel sorry for whomever succeeds you, and I will never really like them—no matter who they turn out to be. They will always live in your shadow, and no one else will be able to walk in your shoes." The letter was effusive in praise of him, expressing the sadness his leaving would cause her.

"Please don't worry, my darling," he wrote back. "You'll never get rid of me. If you ever need me, I'll come running."

He predicted that "there will be many happy moments between us, not only in New York, but elsewhere."

His prediction came true.

During her first visit to New York after Gilpatric had moved there, reporters and photographers followed Jackie, thinking she was dating him. She shocked the press when they discovered that her escort was actor Kevin McCarthy, a long-time friend of Montgomery Clift.

However, the very next night, Gilpatric was seen escorting her to the chic Colony Restaurant in Manhattan.

In November of 1963, Gilpatric was devastated by news about JFK's assassination in Dallas. He was waiting at the White House for a private visit with Jackie when she returned from that fatal trip, devastated, in her blood-stained pink suit.

In March of 1968, after Gilpatric turned sixty-one, Jackie invited him as her escort for a trip to the Mayan ruins of the Yucatán, in Mexico. The paparazzi was on her tail, and reporters were filing stories that Gilpatric, already married, would soon be her next husband.

Annoyed at the massive press coverage, she told him, "I've given up. From now on, I can't concern myself with what the press says about me. I'm like a public commodity. Let them have their fun at my expense. To hell with the bastards!"

Both Gilpatric and Jackie found Mexico romantic, especially on warm moonlit nights. A paparazzo managed to take a picture of them kissing. Hand in hand, they scaled the pyramids and went on horseback rides at night along the beach. During the day, they explored the ruins of Chichén Itzá.

Gilpatrick continued to deny rumors of their affair, although reporters bribed room service waiters and maids, who claimed that Gilpatric was sleeping in Jackie's bed in her suite at night.

"Mrs. Kennedy has long been drawn to intellectual companions," he told the press. "She is a person in her own right. She doesn't like the peephole publicity of *Women's Wear Daily*. But she knows that she is a public figure of interest to the world. She prepares herself to meet the press. Before we landed in Mexico, the plane had to circle around until she was camera ready to face the mass of photographers."

Publicly, he stated: "Mrs. Kennedy has long had a tremendous interest in visiting the Yucatán. She had read a lot about the Mayans and has been fascinated by pre-Columbian art."

Writing in *Women's Wear Daily,* Agnes Ash said: "There was a lot of public smooching and hand-holding in full view of the press. Jackie was all over the place. At one point, she jumped into a stream, fully dressed. John Walsh, her Secret Service agent, had to go in after her. Another time, she climbed one of the Mayan pyramids and posed like the Queen of England opening Ascot."

In general, the Mexican press was lavish in its praise of Jackie, and their favorable reports were broadcast widely, both in Spanish and in translation. The American media, however, had for the most part been banned by Jackie from accompanying her, with the noteworthy exception of Ash. But after her latest article, Jackie turned on her, too.

After that article appeared, Jackie tried to get Ash removed from the traveling press corps. Mexican police threatened Ash that she might end up in a local jail. At one point, the phone service in her hotel room was cut off.

Jackie called Rose Kennedy at Hyannis Port, asking her to use her influence with John Fairchild, the editorial director of *Women's Wear Daily,* to suppress Ash's articles on Jackie in Mexico. Fairchild turned down the requests, running the articles intact.

In the middle of her trip, Jackie received news that Bobby Kennedy had announced that he would seek the Democratic nomination for President in the 1968 race. When queried by reporters, Jackie said, "I'll always be with him with all my heart. I shall always back him."

Gilpatric reported that Jackie was deeply concerned about Bobby's run for the presidency. "She didn't want him in the race. She told me that the same thing that happened to Jack might also befall Bobby. She feared for his life."

"There is so much hatred in America," she said. "In fact, more people hated Bobby than hated Jack. I repeatedly warned Bobby not to run, but he told me he's not afraid. He seems fatalistic."

Although Bobby had dismissed Jackie's fears for his safety, her concerns were prophetic. Gilpatric was by her side in Mexico when she received an urgent call from J. Edgar Hoover of the F.B.I. He had tracked her down.

Very bluntly, he told her that Bobby, after delivering his victory speech, had been shot in the kitchen of the Ambassador Hotel in Los Angeles, and that he was still alive, but barely.

In response, she screamed into the phone. When she slammed down the receiver, she turned to Gilpatric, who held her in his arms. "It's happening again. They're killing Kennedys."

Back in New York, Gilpatric was by Jackie's side at New York's Kennedy Airport when he placed her aboard a private jet belonging to IBM's Thomas Watson for her flight to Los Angeles to be by the bedside of the dying Bobby Kennedy.

***

After Bobby's funeral, Jackie was seen with a number of escorts, including gay author Truman Capote. She was also seen with William Walton, a correspondent for *Time* magazine. A bachelor, he had been a paratrooper in World War II, where he was a friend of Ernest Hemingway. Like Jackie, Walton was obsessed with celebrities, and he invited "the big names" to his galas. She was also drawn to his landscape paintings, particularly of old Cape Cod.

Another escort was Godfrey McHugh, an Air Force major a decade older than her. A world traveler and the survivor of dozens of military missions, he enthralled her with stories of his exploits around the world. As a bachelor, he was a popular guest on the dinner party circuit.

On at least three occasions, Robert McNamara, JFK's Secretary of Defense, was seen escorting Jackie to various events. John Kenneth Galbraith, the economist, was also a reliable escort, as were Franklin D. Roosevelt and Arthur Schlesinger, Jr.

Charles (Chuck) Spalding, one of the Kennedy family's oldest friends, also took Jackie out, as did Michael Forrestal, who had flown with

Jackie is seen out on the town with her close friend and confidant, **William Walton**. She admired his taste in art, and he liked her choice of Husband Number One.

As Walton told his gay friends, "Jack can put his shoes under my bed any time."

431

Jackie and Lord Harlech to Cambodia and Thailand.

Jackie was perhaps avoiding seeing so much of Gilpatric at this time, because she didn't want to get involved in his divorce proceedings from Madelin.

When Madelin Gilpatric filed for divorce, she claimed in her petition that "My husband's sycophantic devotion to Mrs. Kennedy broke up my marriage. I won't go into the sordid details except to suggest that my husband and the former First Lady were very, very close. It was a particularly warm, intense, and long-standing relationship."

Somehow, Jackie managed to juggle all these escorts. At the same time, she more or less escaped notice by the press that she was being pursued by Aristotle Onassis. Gilpatric later said, "Perhaps the boys of the press didn't catch on to what was going on in spite of the rumors. That's because no one believed the gossip."

When asked about Jackie's marriage to Onassis, Gilpatric said, "She once told me that she felt she could count on him. It was an attribute she looked for in all her friends."

Having suffered through the publication of nude photos of herself *[snapped with the collusion of her husband on Skorpios]*, Jackie endured yet another personal embarrassment in 1970. Love letters she'd written to Gilpatric had been stored in his vault. But according to Gilpatric, someone who knew the combination to his safe at Cravath, Swaine & Moore stole the letters and made them public. Charles Hamilton, the Manhattan autograph dealer, was auctioning them to the public. The contents of the letters were subsequently leaked to the press.

Onassis, who by then had then already been married to Jackie for two years, was said to be devastated by one of the "Dear Ros" letters Jackie had written while aboard his yacht, the *Christina* , during their honeymoon.

He told Johnny Meyer, his aide, "What a fool I've been, a god damn fool. I now know what a calculating woman Jackie is, coldhearted and shallow."

"Dear Ros,
I would have told you before I left—but then, everything happened so much more quickly than I had planned. I saw somewhere what you said and I was very touched—Dear Ros—I hope you know all you were and all you will ever be to me.
With my love,
Jackie."

Biographer Christopher Andersen said, "Ari was mortified. He behaved as if his manhood had been dealt a deathblow. He did not particularly mind being characterized as a voracious cretin, a barbarian at the gates, or even a crook. But he could not bear the idea of being publicly cuckolded—not by the woman who was spending his millions with abandon. He was convinced that the whole world was laughing at him."

Actually, Onassis could hardly castigate Jackie for her letter to Gilpatric, because he had by then resumed his long-standing love affair with opera diva

Maria Callas.

Under subpoena from the court, the love letters from Jackie to Gilpatric were seized and eventually returned to him as his personal property.

***

Suffering from prostate cancer, Gilpatric died on March 15, 1996, two years after Jackie's death. .

Right before his passing, he finally admitted to his closest friends that in spite of his frequent denials over the years, he and Jackie had been lovers.

"I was devoted to her—madly in love, so to speak. She had strong feelings for me, too. I was going to divorce my wife to marry her."

"The highlight of my affair with her was that trip to Mexico. I had never had such a romantic experience with any woman. She was so incredibly free and open with me, completely giving of herself. That's why her marriage to Onassis came as such a shock to me, although I concealed my pain."

"Even though Jackie is gone, gone, I am just as much in love with her today as I ever was. We'll meet again on some distant shore, I just know."

John Glenn
Did the Astronaut Send Jackie Into Orbit?

Truman Capote claimed that Jackie's love affair with astronaut John Glenn took place inside her head. "Call it an escapade of the imagination, a mind fuck like she had with Robert McNamara or General Maxwell Taylor, even Henry Kissinger, though what she wanted with that fat slob I'll never know."

Glenn became the first American to orbit the Earth aboard *Friendship 7* on February 20, 1962, when Jackie was First Lady. She stayed glued to her television, eager for news of his history-making flight into space. He was aloft for nearly five hours, landing safely. He became the first American to orbit the Earth and the fifth person to reach Outer Space.

Overnight, Glenn became a national hero, designated as the centerpiece of a ticker-tape parade in New York that evoked Charles Lindbergh's historic flight to Paris aboard *The Spirit of St. Louis.*

JFK and Jackie entertained Glenn at the White House, Jackie praising him for his courage.

She raved about Glenn to C.L. Sulzberger, foreign affairs columnist for *The New York Times.* "He is the most controlled person on Earth. He would be a fine ambassador to Moscow."

She told her friends, "John is the kind of man a girl should marry—what a guy, so strong, so brave, so masculine, so handsome. He's like that football hero in college we fantasized about."

The astronaut bonded so well with the Kennedys that he became a personal friend of Jackie, Bobby, and JFK. On February 23, 1962, JFK flew with him to Florida, attending a parade at Cape Canaveral Air Force Station, where he awarded Glenn a NASA service medal.

JFK described, to Jackie and others, his intention of using Glenn to his political advantage, as he had been the most visible player associated with the success of Kennedy's space program. At the time, the Americans and their scientific savvy were behind the Soviets, who had sent Yuri Gagarin into space as early as April, 1961.

Vice President Lyndon Johnson also recognized Glenn's political value. "He is one of those good old clean-cut American boys—war hero, churchgoer, family man, small town values. He could produce a lot of votes for the Democrats. If only he were a Negro."

The New Frontier's leaders gathered at least once a month at Bobby's Hickory Hill, which had once been owned by Jack and Jackie. During the summer of 1962, Bobby and Ethel staged an outdoor dinner and dance for Patricia Kennedy Lawford and her husband, actor Peter Lawford.

It was a riotous party that ended up with some fully clothed guests getting thrown into the swimming pool. Glenn became such a frequent visitor that one reporter claimed, "Hickory Hill has become his *lunching* pad ever since he got back from Outer Space."

JFK wanted Jackie in Washington to greet the arriving President of Ecuador, who had cabled that he was especially interested in "meeting America's glamorous First Lady." Jackie turned JFK down, claiming she had another engagement. JFK called his mother, Rose, and asked her to fill in for Jackie. He announced to the press that the First Lady was ill.

Astronaut **John Glenn** was featured on the cover of *Life* magazine on February 2, 1962, when he became the first person to orbit the Earth.

He also sent First Lady Jackie into orbit. She confided to friends that he was her dreamboat, but how far into Outer Space her relationship with him went remains as mysterious as the dark side of the moon.

However, photographs appeared in newspapers the next day, showing her water-skiing at Hyannis Port in a strapless bathing suit with her "handsome hunk," John Glenn. JFK was furious.

In July, 1963, *The New York Daily News* ran this item:

"Star athletes, including the Kennedy family and John Glenn, teamed up today to stage a dazzling three-hour water show in Lewis Bay. The undisputed star was Jacqueline Kennedy wearing a skin-tight, one-piece black-and-white bathing suit and then a flaming pink one. Jackie was in the pink number when she skied in tandem with a grinning spaceman, Col. John Glenn. Both wore mono-skis and put on a show for a flotilla of boats."

In Washington, Jackie's attraction for Glenn did not go unnoticed. There were rumors of an affair, although no smoking gun was ever found. Senator George Smathers, a Democrat from Florida and one of JFK's closest friends, claimed, "I think it was just an affair of the heart, not of the groin, but one can never be sure in these matters."

Glenn was such a family friend that he was in Los Angeles with Bobby in 1968 when he was assassinated. He was later one of the pallbearers at Bobby's funeral.

Teddy Kennedy had told Jackie that he wanted to run for the nation's top office in the 1976 presidential race. However, the drowning accident of Mary Jo Kopechne on July 18, 1969, in a car that he was driving put an end to that dream. The scandal from the island of Chappaquiddick practically overshadowed the coverage of the United States putting a man on the moon.

With Teddy out of the race, Jackie suggested that Glenn might be the ideal candidate to seek the Democratic nomination for president. In 1974, he'd already been elected Senator from Ohio.

"As a senator, he'd be in a perfect position to run for president," Jackie said. "Being a national hero would also help. Better that than a peanut farmer from Georgia."

In anticipation of the 1976 elections, Glenn was listed as one of the Democratic candidates for the vice-president under a ticket spearheaded by Jimmy Carter, but he lost to Walter Mondale. In 1984, he attempted to be nominated as the Democratic party's candidate for president, but lost once again to Mondale, who eventually lost the election to a Republican, Ronald Reagan.

Although Glenn on occasion, escorted by a widowed Jackie to public events, the nature of their relationship has remained a mystery. Glenn was born in 1921, and he ever plans to write about the nature of his friendship with Jackie, especially if they ever became intimate, he had better get to work on the tell-all manuscript.

Pete Hamill
How Jackie Stole Shirley MacLaine's Boyfriend

Truman Capote, Jackie's duplicitous friend, indiscreetly told his high society friends that Jackie had grown tired of older men dominating her life. "She has millions of her own money, and she earned it the hard way—by sleeping with Onassis until he got tired of her and went back to hearing Maria Callas hit the high note in bed."

He also claimed that "For a few times in her life, Jackie wanted to be the one in charge, the one with the purse strings. It was at this time that Jackie shopped for a younger stud. Along came Peter Hamill, who certainly knew his way around a woman's boudoir. After seven years of shacking up with Shirley MacLaine, he must have learned all the maneuvers in *Kama Sutra*."

Columnist Earl Wilson wrote, "Jackie Onassis is captivated by Peter Hamill. He is handsome in a rugged, masculine way. He has the toughness of one of those newspaper reporters in a 1930s movie at Warner Brothers. He is very bright and possesses a kind of personal magnetism. Of all of Jackie's many conquests, he would rank up there at the top as a babe magnet. She also admires Hamill's mind and his endless battles waged in the New York tabloids against social injustice. He is a friend of the working man, and a very, very special friend of Jackie O's."

A famous New York columnist, **Peter Hamill**, once wrote a novel called *Loving Women*.

He was just the man for that challenge. Just ask Shirley MacLaine or Jackie Kennedy.

Hamill started dating Jackie right before Christmas of 1976. Before that, he'd been with Shirley MacLaine, who had been a supporter of the Kennedys, including Jackie.

The musician, Peter Duchin, remembered taking Jackie to Shirley's Broadway opening of her show, *One Woman at the Palace*. He accompanied Jackie backstage to congratulate the star. All that goodwill changed when Jackie started dating Hamill.

Six years younger than Jackie, Hamill is an American journalist, columnist, and novelist. He came to Jackie's attention when he became one of the four men who disarmed Sirhan Sirhan in Los Angeles after he'd shot Robert F. Kennedy.

Hamill had been editor of the *New York Post* and also of the New York *Daily News*. Jackie admired his columns, calling them "the work of a testosterone-fueled maverick."

His columns sought to capture the unique flavor of New York City's politics and sports, with a particular focus on crime in the city.

Some critics referred to Jackie and Hamill as "the odd couple," and wondered how a relationship between the two of them developed.

In 1968, the body of the assassinated Robert F. Kennedy had been flown from Los Angeles to New York aboard Air Force One.

After a funeral at Saint Patrick's Cathedral in Manhattan, *[during which Jackie snubbed Lady Bird Johnson]*, she rode in a 12-car funeral train that carried the coffin to Washington for burial at the Arlington National Cemetery, site of JFK's tomb.

Previously, Hamill may have believed the image of Jackie as the Ice Queen. On the train, he was accompanied by his longtime girlfriend, Shirley. She later said, "Jackie was very regal, as only she can be, with this marvelous sense of anticipatory dignity. She was always able, somehow, to anticipate when the train was going to lurch or when it would bump, and queenlike, take hold of something so that when the bump came, she wasn't disturbed or dislodged."

Years later, Shirley would be sounding a more discordant note about Jackie.

A friend of Hamill's, who did not want to be named, claimed that "Pete and Shirley were on the verge of breaking up before he started dating Jackie. I gathered from Pete that he wanted to marry Shirley, but she kept turning him down. I can't read his mind, but I think he has a better chance of becoming Jackie's husband."

During the time, Shirley was involved with Hamill, she was in a "trans-Pacific open marriage to Steve Parker, the Tokyo-based producer. He'd been her husband since 1954, but the couple preferred to remain in different parts of the world.

An outrageously dressed **Shirley MacLaine** had something to cry out about. Her nemesis, Jackie Kennedy, not only seduced her boyfriend, Peter Hamill, but her brother, Warren Beatty, too.

When he'd first started dating Jackie, Hamill said, "I like her and I think she likes me. There's nothing clandestine about it. It doesn't alter my relationship with Shirley—things are still the same between us. She knows I'm taking Jackie out."

That doesn't seem to be true. Close friends of both women often commented on their rivalry and jealousy of each other.

After hearing Hamill's comment, Helen Gaillet, a photographer, said, "Ha! They should ask Shirley how she feels about Jackie. Our former First Lady runs through men like she runs through clothes."

In Manhattan, Jackie and Hamill were seen everywhere, often popping in at P.J. Clarke's late at night for a hamburger. They were also seen at such high-profile places as Elaine's, where they were given the best table in the house.

A waiter at the Top of the Tower Restaurant *[in the Beekman Tower Hotel, in Manhattan at First Avenue and East 49th Street]* reported seeing them holding hands and looking into each other's eyes "as if tomorrow belonged to them. He made her laugh. They were obviously sexually attracted to each other."

People magazine once assessed the Jackie/Hamill coupling:

"Money aside, the burning question remains about Mrs. O. How's her love life? The answer enigmatic, as always. Currently standing out from a pedigreed but lackluster cast of escorts is New York's biographer of the underclass, columnist Pete Hamill. He and Jackie are just pals, says Pete—an assessment her friends wholeheartedly endorse. 'He's fun for her to go out with,' says one. 'But the chances of her marrying him are slim.' She does telephone Hamill at his office, though, and if he's out, leaves the hard-to-ignore message: 'Tell him Mrs. Onassis called, please.'"

437

One night at P.J. Clarke's, Frank Sinatra spotted Jackie eating hamburgers with Hamill. He later told Sammy Davis, Jr. and Dean Martin, "Jackie definitely has the hots for Pete. But I don't think they'll get married. Pete doesn't have enough dough for a high-class dame like Jackie."

[Hamill had always been a great fan of Sinatra and once wrote a book about him called Why Sinatra Matters. *Hamill concluded that "Sinatra's audience at the beginning was primarily female; it ended up primarily male. He helped humans trained to silence—or emotional numbness—to express some of their deepest emotions."*

At one time, Sinatra proposed that Hamill might ghostwrite his autobiography. Aware that such a book would immediately become a best-seller, Hamill agreed, but on one condition—that Sinatra come clean about his women, his link to politicians, and his connections to the Mob. Sinatra agreed to the first two conditions, but balked at the final requirement. "I don't want someone knocking on my fucking door late at night," he told Hamill.]

On a few occasions, Hamill escorted Jackie to his favorite bar, the seedy Lions Head in Greenwich Village. Called "the writer's bar," it was the venue where Dylan Thomas drank himself to death.

Author Lindsay Van Gelder spotted Jackie and Hamill at a private screening of the film, *Welcome to L.A.* (1977) at the MGM Building in Manhattan. "In her breathless little voice, she was whispering sweet nothings in his ear and flirting outrageously. Her eyelashes were fluttering."

Long a Kennedy supporter, Hamill had experienced an outrage when Jackie married Aristotle Onassis in 1968. At the time, he was a columnist for the *New York Post*. He vented his rage in a 1971 column, which later became notorious.

> *"Many marriages are put together the same way as the Jackie/Ari deal, although the brutally commercial nature of the contract is often disguised with romantic notions about love and time. Some women can be bought with a guarantee of ham and eggs in the morning and a roof over their head; others with a mink coat on the anniversary of the sealing of the contract. Ari bought one of the few reigning international objects, the unapproachable widow of a slain prince, buying her the way another might buy a Lear jet or a Velásquez. But understanding Jackie Kennedy is a more complicated matter. For part of her adult life she was hidden behind the Kennedy publicity machine; she spent another crucial part, after the murder of her husband, enshrined as some national object of veneration.*

> *"She was not, of course, the victim of that veneration; she encouraged it, indulged it, created the desire for more knowledge by cultivating the image of her aloofness. The price of an art object increases in direct ratio to its rarity.*

> *"It is outrageous to think that someone will spend $120,000 a year on clothing in a world where so few people have more than the clothes on their*

back. It is obscene that a woman would have more money in a month to use on applying paste to her face and spray to her hair than the average citizens of Latin America could earn in 100 years."

After submitting the column, Hamill almost immediately retracted it, submitting another more vanilla version. "I was just too vicious to Jackie," he later said.

But although the column was killed, it was filed away in the morgue at *The Post.* By the time Hamill started dating "The Widow Jackie" in 1976, he was writing for the *Post's* rival and competitor, the *New York Daily News.*

Suddenly and unexpectedly, after Hamill's departure from the *Post,* Rupert Murdoch, its owner, perhaps in an act of vengeance, *[and certainly as a means of boosting circulation]* ordered that Hamill's 1971 column be printed, under the teasing headline: *WHO WROTE THIS?*

Press baron **Rupert Murdoch** betrayed Peter Hamill by publishing an outdated column of his wherein he labeled Jackie a courtesan for marrying Onassis.

For four days running, excerpts from his (original) column ran on Page Six of the *Post.*

Finally, on the fifth day, the *Post* featured a picture of Jackie and Hamill dating. The caption read: "In 1971, Pete Hamill wrote of Jackie Onassis that it looked as if no courtesan ever sold herself for more. He didn't approve of her marriage to Ari, you see. Times change, and so do Pete's opinions, and now, the gossips are saying that Mrs. Onassis, 48, will make Hamill, 42, her third mate."

Hamill exploded in fury, feeling he'd been double-crossed. He immediately called Jackie and explained the situation, blaming everything on Murdoch. She seemed to forgive him, but he may have sensed a coolness from her.

There was a suspicion that Jackie never really forgave Hamill for his 1971 "retracted but published anyway" opinion. For appearances' sake, she showed up on November 17, 1977 at his publication party, celebrating the release of his novel, *Flesh and Blood,* a book that dealt with the controversial theme of mother-son incest. The party was held at O'Neal's Ballroom, across from Lincoln Center. Guests noticed that Hamill was seen chatting briefly with Jackie, but for the most part, they remained in opposite corners.

She didn't stay long, and she was escorted out by Denis Hamill, Peter's younger brother. He hailed her a taxi. Later, he said, "A date with Jackie is like taking out a big, bright red fire engine."

Hamill still shared weekends with Jackie, Caroline, and John Jr. There were trips to Hyannis Port, where he was with her on the day Elvis Presley died. He flew to Memphis, inviting Caroline to go with him, so she could write her own story. He was also instrumental in getting her a job at the *Daily News.*

Jackie showed up at the 1977 premiere of *The Turning Point,* starring Shirley MacLaine and Anne Bancroft and directed by Herbert Ross. At the premiere, Jackie and Shirley gave each other wide berth.

Ironically, Ross would marry Lee Radziwill in 1988. Shirley didn't like the younger Bouvier sister either, often doing an imitation of her pretentious manner behind her back.

Writing for *The New York Times,* Alex Witchel interviewed Hamill in 1994, the year of Jackie's death. "This is a man from a bygone era, before bodies required preservation like works of art. But he's far from unattractive. He says he has had romances with Shirley MacLaine and Jacqueline Kennedy Onassis, but turns a little bit pale at the prospect of a rehash. 'I'm a happily married man,' he says, reaching for a cigarette. 'Only a cad would talk about his life that way.'"

Peter Davis

It Wasn't Meant to Last

After breaking with Hamill, Jackie became a cougar *[a woman with an eye for younger men]* before the term was invented. She took up with director Peter Davis, who was about eight years her junior.

She'd been impressed with his TV documentary on FDR, a series consisting of 26 episodes. For the documentary, he'd interviewed members of the Roosevelt clan, their friends and enemies, and whatever cabinet members were still alive from that era.

At one time, Davis had been married to the novelist Johanna Mankiewicz. Her father, Herman J. Mankiewicz, had written *Citizen Kane* with Orson Welles. Johanna's brother, Frank Mankiewicz, had been Bobby Kennedy's press secretary.

Davis won an Oscar for his documentary, *Hearts and Minds,* about the U.S. military presence in Vietnam.

Davis and Jackie were spotted together at such events as the Robert F. Kennedy Celebrity Tennis Tournament in Forest Hills (Queens, NY). Ronald Capil, a reporter, sat near them. "Instead of watching the game, Jackie was whispering in

An older Jackie, perhaps tiring of aging men, became a cougar when she chased after the younger **Peter Davis,** a documentary filmmaker.

He turned out such award-winning movies as *Hearts & Minds*, a film that was critical of the U.S. presence in war-torn Vietnam.

his ear. They huddled close together, holding hands."

The next week, Davis was seen aboard a chartered plane with Jackie flying to Hyannis Port. A week later, she was seen driving him to the airport in Caroline's red BMW. At the airport, she kissed him goodbye.

No one had a video camera or a tape recorder in Jackie's bedroom, but observers concluded that they were having an affair. They were seen all over Manhattan, and Davis was spotted coming and going from her Fifth Avenue apartment.

Richard Merryman, correspondent for *Life,* once invited Davis to a party at his brownstone in Greenwich Village. He asked his host if he could bring a date, "I nearly fell over," Merryman later claimed. "His date was Jackie Onassis."

Merryman also commented on Hamill's affair with Jackie. "It was never meant to end in marriage—and both parties knew that. For Peter, it was a momentous event that comes only once this time around. It was quite wonderful for him as long as it lasted. But from the beginning, it had an expiration date on it. He took it as it unfolded. When it was over, he expressed gratitude for having known a goddess, an icon, and such an imposing person, however briefly."

The literary and film agent, Swifty Lazar, later said, "After Onassis and a lot of other men, Jackie was discovering the delight of young flesh. Why not? She was still beautiful, worth millions, and had the intoxicating aroma of being the most famous woman on the planet, the former wife of a slain American hero."

Davis was not made to last, However. In a touch of irony, Jackie's next affair was launched with Shirley MacLaine's younger brother—none other than Warren Beatty, that "walking streak of sex from Hollywood."

David Ormsby-Gore (5th Baron Harlech)
His Offer to Make Her Lady Harlech

Lord Harlech (David Ormsby-Gore) was JFK's alltime favorite foreign minister. He told Jackie and others, "I trust David as much as I would a member of my own cabinet."

During JFK's reign, Lord Harlech, Britain's ambassador to the United States, played golf with the President at Palm Beach or went sailing with him off the coast of Hyannis Port. When JFK was out of Washington, Harlech was often Jackie's escort for an evening.

With JFK in the White House, Lord Harlech became practically a resident himself, supplying the President with Cuban cigars, which were otherwise banned to Americans. He played a major role in the Cuban Missile Crisis, and he also helped to promote the first ever Test Ban Treaty with the Soviet Union. Jackie later praised "David's influence on Jack. He urged Jack to act like a statesman rather than a politician."

In the late 1930s, Lord Harlech had been known as David Ormsby-Gore, before he was raised to the peerage after the death of his father, William Ormsby-Gore, 4th Baron of Harlech. David had bonded with a young Jack Kennedy when he studied in Britain during the ambassadorship (1938-1940) of his father, Joseph P. Kennedy, Sr., at the Court of St. James's.

Lord Harlech's close friend, the celebrated photographer, Cecil Beaton, defined Jackie's appearance as "somewhat Negroid." But **Lord Harlech**, as can clearly be seen in this picture, was enchanted by her.

The press, however, was premature in hailing the former First Lady as the next Lady Harlech.

That early bonding carried over into JFK's term in the White House, when Lord Harlech was the British Ambassador to Washington, D.C. JFK's sister, Kathleen Kennedy, had married a first cousin of Lord Harlech, Billy Cavendish, *[aka Lord Hartington]*, heir to the Duke of Devonshire. JFK's beloved "Kick," as he called her, had died in an airplane crash over France in 1948.

Jackie told friends, "David might be a British Lord, but he's far from stuffy. During his years in the White House, Jack adored him. Both of them had had reputations as playboys when they were young. David likes fast cars, racing, and jazz. He's very indulgent toward his five children. Some of them are hippies."

Jackie had met Harlech's younger daughter, Alice, who had been engaged to Eric Clapton in 1969. They had lived together for five years but never married. She later died of a heroin overdose in 1995. Another daughter, June, had an affair with Mick Jagger in the 1960s. The Rolling Stones' song, "Lady Jane," was said to be about her.

A son, Julian, had become a male model in London. Harlech told Jackie, "God knows what kind of modeling he's doing. I hope it's not in his birthday suit." In 1974, Julian fatally shot himself.

After JFK's assassination, Jackie received thousands upon thousands of letters from around the world. But her secretary knew to bring her Lord Harlech's. In his sympathy note, he wrote: "Jack was the most charming, considerate, and loyal friend I have ever had. I mourn him as if he were my own brother."

Arthur Schlesinger, Jr., said, "David has a nice urbanity and a rather sardonic view of people and events." Economist John Kenneith Galbraith said, "David has *savoir-faire*, the savviness and wisdom that Harold Macmillan had 25 years ago."

Ted Sorensen once asked Jackie, "Why Lord Harlech? You have your pick of all the eligible men in the world, even royalty if you wish."

"I like him because he likes to wear lilac shirts and purple ties," she said.

Lord Harlech escorted her to one of his favorite restaurants in Manhattan, Trader Vic's at the Plaza Hotel. On another occasion, they flew to Atlanta to visit the Georgia plantation of John Jay Whitney, former ambassador to Great Britain. Harlech embraced "Jock," his longtime friend, telling Jackie that Jock had once been engaged to the formidable Tallulah Bankhead.

Lord Harlech was with Jackie in fun-loving moments, but also during times of tragedy. He stood at her side during the funeral of the slain Bobby Kennedy. He'd been one of the pallbearers.

She also told friends such as Martha Bartlett, "I do not plan to marry David. Cuddling up to him is like cuddling up to an encyclopedia."

Reportedly, Lee Radziwill said, "Lord Harlech is far too unattractive a man for Jackie to marry." She made that statement just months before her sister married Aristotle Onassis.

To challenge rumors of a torrid romance with Jackie, Lord Harlech confronted the press, "Mrs. Kennedy and I have been close friends for thirteen years, but there is no truth to the story of a romance between us. I deny it flatly."

In England, Lord Harlech, who had been noted for occasionally driving on Britain's motorways at 140 mph in his Gordon-Keeble, took Jackie for a visit to his inherited 400-acre estate, Woodhill, at Oswestry in Shropshire. *[The Gordon-Keeble was a high-performance, problem-plagued sports car made in England between 1963 and 1967. Only 100 of them were ever assembled before the company went bankrupt. Ninety of them are registered today as highly collectible, highly esoteric examples of a terribly stylish dream gone bust.]*

She also dined with him at his posh flat in London's Kensington district. Princess Margaret was his guest one night as she had wanted to meet and to chat with Jackie in a private setting.

Not all of Lord Harlech's friends were impressed with Jackie's look. The photographer and art director, Cecil Beaton, recorded his impressions of her in his diary, defining her as "an over-life-size caricature of herself. Huge baseball players' shoulders and haunches, big boyish hands and feet; very dark, beautiful, receptive eyes. A somewhat Negroid appearance, the suspicion of a mustache, and very dark hair."

Jackie did not like Lord Harlech's role as Britain's national film censor, as, in theory, at least *[and unless it involved something to do with the assassination of JFK]* she opposed censorship of media. Harlech responded that he was the most lenient film censor in British history, and that he'd ordered only a few minor cuts from the film version of James Joyce's *Ulysses* and the movie adaptation of the notoriously pornographic novel, *Fanny Hill.*

In 1967, Jackie flew to Ireland with John Jr. and Caroline, wanting them to see the homeland of their ancestors. Their father had been wildly popular in Ireland.

Lord Harlech flew in from London as her escort.

Arriving in Dublin, her hawknosed escort faced banner headlines—JACKIE: FROM FIRST LADY TO LADY HARLECH.

For her family holiday, Jackie had rented a spacious Georgian home near

Waterford. When she'd flown into Shannon, she'd been mobbed by her admirers and by curiosity seekers. Her husband had been a beloved hero in Ireland.

On the way to her rented residence, the road was lined with well-wishers. At Waterford, in her rented Georgian residence, the servants formally lined up in the entry hall to greet her. "It looked like a Royal reception," she later recalled.

She wrote to friends back in New York. "Can you imagine? Forty-nine bedrooms and only one bathroom."

While in Ireland, Jackie went with her children to Dungastown, ancestral home of the Kennedys. She also visited the Waterford Glass Factory, purchasing chandeliers for the Kennedy Center.

She was seen with Lord Harlech at a state dinner in her honor at Dublin Castle, where she emerged in a bright green, full-length gown of chiffon wearing a white ermine stole, a fashion plate to delight the Irish paparazzi.

Lord Harlech took her to the Irish Sweepstakes, to a performance of the Dunhill Players, and to Toomey's Irish pub. He even went shopping with her for Irish tweed riding habits, and he spent the Fourth of July watching John Jr. attempt to play Gaelic football.

In Ireland, Jackie went swimming but nearly drowned in the rip tide roaring along the Irish coastline. She later wrote: "The water was so cold that one could not hold one's fingers together. I am a very good swimmer and can swim for miles and hours, but the combination of the current and cold were something I had never known. There was no one in sight to yell to."

"I was becoming exhausted, swallowing water and being swept more out to sea. Suddenly, I felt this great porpoise at my side. It was Mr. Walsh *[John F.M. Walsh]* of the Secret Service. He set his shoulder against me and together we made it back to the spit of land. Then I sat on the beach coughing up sea water for half an hour while he found a poor itinerant and borrowed a blanket for me."

Jackie would make one more high profile trip with Lord Harlech, as their relationship became tabloid fodder.

***

In Washington, Robert McNamara defined Jackie's upcoming visit to Cambodia as a good will tour, hoping that she'd charm that country's ruler, Prince Norodom Sihanouk, who had severed relations with the United States because of the war in neighboring Vietnam.

After JFK was assassinated, Prince Sihanouk had gone on the air in a nationwide broadcast. "We must thank the divine protection after causing the complete destruction of Cambodia's enemies."

The speculation about the upcoming marriage of Lord Harlech to Jackie accelerated when she flew with him to Cambodia to visit the ruins of Angkor Wat.

On the arm of Lord Harlech, Jackie created a sensation at the airport at Phnom Penh, Cambodia's largest city and capital.

Little girls had sprinkled the red carpet with rose and jasmine petals. Walking along the carpet, Jackie looked sensational in an emerald green mini-skirt and short white gloves. The prince received her under a canopy-covered golden throne.

She spoke to the people of Cambodia in French. "President Kennedy would have wished to visit Cambodia. He would have been attracted to the vitality of the Khmer people, a quality he showed in himself and which he so admired in others. By your warm greeting today, you have shown that you recognize his dedication to peace and understanding among all people."

Prince Norodom Sihanouk of Cambodia seemed to take delight in the assassination of John F. Kennedy, defining him as "the enemy of our people." He nonetheless staged a royal welcome for Jackie and her new lover, Lord Harlech.

The prince had staged a gala dinner for Jackie and the British Lord at his official residence, the Chamcar Mon Palace, built on the banks of the Mekong River during the French colonial occupation of Cambodia. With the prince, she stood on his panoramic terrace watching a parade of caparisoned sacred white elephants.

The next night found Lord Harlech and Jackie in Angkor, where they visited the ruins of a lost civilization. With her lover guiding her, Jackie took off her shoes and wandered barefoot "into this living history book." Her way was lit with hundreds of candles and spotlights.

Although the prince appeared to be mesmerized by Jackie's appearance, he did not soften his negative opinion of America. In Angkor, he held a press conference. "America did not come to Asia to help the yellow people!" he charged. "They came to exploit Asia as a neo-colonial power. America's criminal aggression against Vietnam is a threat to our own country."

In the city of Sihanoukville, Jackie stood on a flag-festooned platform to dedicate Avenue J.F. Kennedy. A problem that day involved Lord Harlech's attempt to usher Jackie into a black Lincoln convertible. She covered her face in horror, the vehicle evoking the one where she'd taken her last ride with JFK in Dallas.

Ultimately, overcoming her horror, Jackie got into that limousine, whereupon Sihanouk, also a passenger, directed the chauffeur to drive them past the wreckage of a downed American airplane. He turned to her, saying, "You Americans have killed many people."

***

After her visit to Cambodia, many countries in the area were inviting her to be their guest. She chose neighboring Thailand, where she expected a reception that wasn't plagued with political overtones like her visit to Cambodia.

King Bhumibo and Queen Sirikit, often called "The Jackie of the Far East," housed them in the Royal Palace in Bangkok and threw a gala reception for them. It included a performance of Thailand's Royal Ballet.

Lord Harlech had escorted Jackie to the celebrated Temple of the Emerald Buddha, and accompanied her on a shopping trip the next day.

Although pressure for her to do so was intense, Jackie turned down an invitation to visit U.S. troops fighting in Vietnam. The press was almost unanimous in its denunciation of her decision, claiming that it would have been a great morale builder for the soldiers. She also politely rejected a visit to Manila, and was consequently criticized in the local papers for not flying to the capital of an important U.S. ally.

***

In 1968, after hearing of her marriage to Onassis, Lord Harlech, with a slight quiver in his voice, said, "Mrs. Kennedy has been a very close friend for fourteen years. I hope she will be very happy."

In contrast, Coco Chanel, on the same day, expressed a very different point of view. "Everyone knew she was not cut out for dignity. You must not ask a woman with a touch of vulgarity to spend the rest of her life over a corpse."

When Lord Harlech had wed Pamela Colin in 1969, a year after Jackie's wedding to Onassis, she had told the British press, "If Jackie had wanted David, he was hers for the asking."

At one point, Lord Harlech had told his friend, Lord Jenkins of Hillhead: "Marriage to Jackie would not have worked. To begin with, I'm not wealthy enough to support her in the style that she would want. It would also have been like having a sixth child. Jackie requires the kind of adoration that a child asks for. She demands constant attention day and night. Also, like the legendary Marilyn Monroe, she is never on time. I would have spent half of the rest of my life waiting for her to show up."

President Kennedy once said that he trusted **Lord Harlech** as much as any member of his Cabinet. But was that trust misplaced? The baron coveted JFK's beautiful wife.

***

In the years before he died,

after denying it for most of his life, Lord Harlech finally admitted to his friends in England that he'd had an affair with Jackie. "The press was on to something," he said. "Jackie and I were secret lovers. We were thrown together for many nights, and love was bound to blossom."

He recalled one time when he'd flown to Boston to attend the annual meeting of the Kennedy School of Government at Harvard, where he was a trustee. "Jackie and I shared a double suite at the Ritz-Carlton with connecting doors. One morning a room service waiter, delivering us an early breakfast, caught me in bed, jaybird naked, with Jackie."

Lord Harlech would die in a car crash in western England at the age of 66 on January 26, 1985. Ironically, the first Lady Harlech, Sylvia Thomas, eighteen years before *[in 1967]* had also died in a car crash.

With Teddy Kennedy as her escort, Jackie had attended Lord Harlech's funeral in the tiny 12th-century parish church at Llanfihangely-Traethau (St. Michael's on the Beaches) in northwestern Wales. She created a sensation in this remote part of Britain. She told the press, "My husband and Lord Harlech shared a sense of history and a joy in politics. They both thought of public life as the greatest and most honorable adventure. Teddy called Lord Harlech the most intelligent man he had ever known."

Fighting back tears, Jackie was escorted out of the graveyard that flanked the modest church.

One reporter from London described Jackie's appearance at the church as "the weeping black widow," which must have embarrassed the present Lady Harlech, Pamela Colin. The appearance of the paparazzi had disrupted the funeral.

A few days later, when Lady Harlech was planning a quiet, post-burial memorial service in honor of her late husband, she received a note from Jackie, asking if she could attend. In reply, Lady Harlech wrote: "Quite honestly, Jackie, I don't want to see a Kennedy at this memorial service. Because I've gone to great trouble to do this for David, I don't want this to turn into a three-ring circus that you made at his funeral, attracting all those reporters and photographers."

Jackie told friends she was extremely insulted and did not want to speak of Lord Harlech ever again. "I've had to learn to bury the past and live for today."

She did speak of Lord Harlech again on her deathbed in 1994. She told Bunny Mellon and others, "I truly loved the baron. When he proposed, I was swayed by the modest lifestyle he could offer me in Britain. That changed my mind, and I married Ari instead. My stupid mistake has haunted me for years. If only I had said yes, I'm sure I would have been much happier."

Adnan Khashoggi
Jackie in a Billionaire Sultan's Harem?

It might be assumed that Jackie's interest in Adnan Khashoggi stemmed from the fact that in the early 1980s, he was considered one of the richest men in the world, sitting on a mountain of cash that totaled about $40 billion in U.S. dollars.

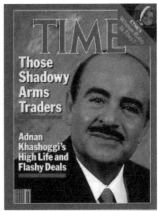

Born to a Turkish family of Syrian ancestry in 1935, he was educated in universities in Ohio and California, but abandoned his studies to seek his fortune—and that's what he found.

Khashoggi was somewhat ostracized from Saudi society, criticized for his "flamboyant lifestyle" and "Western ways." He was also attacked for making money off Saudi weapons deals.

In the 1980s, the era of flamboyant lifestyles, Jackie was often seen being escorted by the fabulously wealthy **Adnan Khashoggi**.

Bebe Rebozo, Richard Nixon's best friend, frequently sailed aboard Khashoggi's yacht, *Nabilia,* the largest in the world. Reportedly, Jackie once went aboard on a secret excursion. In 1983, she'd attended a screening of the James Bond film, *Never Say Never Again*, starring Sean Connery. The *Nabilia* was featured as one of the locales in the movie.

Ultimately, he became too exposed, too hot, and too controversial for her to handle.

In spite of his shady dealings, Jackie seemed attracted to Khashoggi's money and lavish lifestyle. During a visit to Spain, she made a clandestine visit to his lavish estate at the chic resort of Marbella, along Andalusia's Costa del Sol.

He had constructed one of the most ostentatious villas along the resort-studded coastline, throwing extravagant parties that attracted movie stars, politicians, and celebrities famous for being famous.

[In 1985, celebrity chronicler Robin Leach claimed that a five-day birthday party thrown by Khashoggi in Vienna for his oldest son was the most extravagant in European history.]

In 1980, Khashoggi told Jackie that it cost him $250,000 a day just to maintain his lifestyle.

"Do you you actually mean 'per day?'" she queried.

In Manhattan, Khashoggi was seen escorting Jackie to premieres, elegant dinners, or to galleries and the theater.

During Ronald Reagan's second term, Khashoggi was implicated in the Iran-Contra scandal as a key middleman in the arms-for-hostages exchange. That had led to his arrest in Switzerland, where he was accused of concealing funds.

He was held in a Swiss jail for three months before being extradited to the United States, where he was released on bail and later acquitted.

In 1990, a Federal jury in Manhattan again acquitted Khashoggi from charges of racketeering and fraud.

By this time he'd become too controversial for Jackie to be seen with, although she continued to read about him and keep abreast of his activities. In *Vanity Fair,* she read an article about him written by Dominick Dunne. "Lavish villas, perfumed *houris [voluptuously beautiful maidens],* costume balls, fabulous deals with foreign powers, and Oriental potentates—Adnan Khashoggi's life was a 1980s remake of *The Thousand and One Nights."* Dunne also revealed that he'd been forced to sell his fabulous yacht to Donald Trump for "a mere trifle of $30 million."

"He understood high visibility better than the most shameless Hollywood press agent, and he made himself one of the most famous names of our times," Dunne wrote.

Jackie was dead before his financial empire began to crumble. But once, when asked, she said, "Adnan dared dream dreams that no one else dared to dream."

John Kriza
Jackie Falls for "Billy the Kid"

Long before the arrival of Rudolf Nureyev on America's shores in the 1960s, John Kriza was hailed as the sexiest dancer in ballet.

Gore Vidal had been attracted to him after seeing him perform the title role in the 1938 version of *Billy the Kid. [With avant-garde choreography by Eugene Loring and music by Aaron Copland, it was the most electrifying dance composition America had seen till then.]* Kriza created gasps in the audience, especially among females and homosexuals, when he appeared on stage as the notorious outlaw, wearing a brief white bikini and leather chaps. The dance stunned audiences, and became the most acclaimed and controversial dance within his repertoire.

Two balletomanes, Gore Vidal and Jackie Kennedy, competed for the passions of ballet superstar **John Kriza**, famous for dancing the title role of *Billy the Kid,* and depicted in both photos, above.

Kriza mesmerized even larger audiences when he performed a key role in Jerome Robbins' *Fancy Free* (1944) on Broadway, playing a sailor on shore leave, setting out to sample the sights and diversions of New York. *Fancy Free* was later adapted into a movie musical, *On the Town* (1949), with Frank Sinatra cast in Kriza's stage role.

In time, Kriza would work for all the major choreographers, not just Loring, but Jerome Robbins, George Balanchine, Agnes de Mille, Léonide Massine, and Antony Tudor.

Vidal later recalled, "As the leading balletomane of New York, I pursued dancers from the dance after the curtain went down. It was a glorious time. I didn't dare fall in love with John Kriza, because the competition for him was too stiff. But we had great fun while it lasted."

In his memoirs, Vidal wrote, "Many men and women fell in love with Johnny, who responded wholeheartedly in an absent-minded way. He had a large car that he called Florestan, and together, we drove down the east coast of Florida, receiving the homage of balletomanes in their beachside houses."

Born in Illinois, the scion of blue collar Czech immigrants, Kriza was associated with the American Ballet Theater from 1940 to 1966.

"Johnny was about the sexiest thing that ever wore a pair of tights," Vidal told Tennessee Williams.

His infatuation did not evolve into a grand passion, although they continued to have sex together for a number of years. His ballet company toured America.

Vidal said, "Johnny had at least three boyfriends in every major city, often young husbands. He had a beautiful body and was worshipped by his fans. He also attracted equal numbers of female fans because he was bisexual."

On several occasions, Vidal escorted Jackie Kennedy, a fellow balletomane, to performances. One night, he invited her to see Kriza perform as Billy the Kid.

"I'd been to the theater with Jackie before," Vidal said. "But when Kriza pranced out onto that stage, her eyes lit up. She seemed mesmerized by him. After the curtain went down, she practically begged me to take her backstage to meet Johnny. Since I was used to sharing him, I didn't feel any particular threat from Jackie."

"Backstage, Johnny seemed enchanted by Jackie. I knew it was incumbent on me to be their pimp. I invited both of them for lunch that Saturday afternoon at my apartment."

"They showed up for lunch, but I might as well not have existed," Vidal recalled. "Those two had eyes only for each other. I'd never seen Jackie so flirtatious, and she was a notorious flirt. They were really turning each other on."

"I did the honorable thing any good host would do," he said. "After the luncheon, I lied and said I had an appointment. Actually, I had nothing to do, but wandered off to see Bette Davis in what many fans interpreted as her worst picture. I loved Bette in it. Instead of *All About Eve,* I still think Bette in *Beyond the Forest* was Mother Goddamn at her best. I would later write two movie scripts for her, *The Catered Affair* and *Scapegoat,* but I fell in love with Bette on the screen that day. Of course, Bette off the screen was a different matter."

"In the movie house, I got lucky and picked up a handsome male secretary to one of the justices of the Supreme Court," Vidal said. "I won't 'out' the justice, but his secretary told me he often allowed His Honor to perform fellatio on him, claiming 'It's part of the job, I guess.'"

"When I got home at around ten o'clock that evening, having had a divine time, Johnny and Jackie had gone. She had graciously written me a note thanking me for my hospitality. I'm sure she had a lot to thank Johnny for, too."

"When she became First Lady, Jackie invited Johnny to perform at the White House. Later, he danced for Nikita Khrushchev in the Kremlin."

"The world lost a superb specimen of manhood when Johnny drowned in 1975 in a freak accident in the Gulf of Mexico, near Naples, Florida."

Robert Lowell
An Obsession With Jackie Lands Him in the Mental Ward of a Hospital

Poetry-loving Jackie had long admired the works of the Boston Brahmin, Robert Traill Spence Lowell IV. When he learned of her interest, he sent her an anthology of his latest poems, along with an edition of Plutarch's *Lives.* After reading them, she turned them over to Bobby Kennedy, her fellow poetry lover.

A correspondence between Jackie and Lowell followed. They eventually met in 1962 when she invited him to the White House to meet André Malraux, France's minister of culture.

Jackie and Lowell bonded that night, and in the coming years, he became one of her escorts.

Both Lowell and Jackie shared a mutual friend, *politico* Blair Clair, who also had been one of JFK's best friends.

"Robert seemed captivated by her, his initial attraction turning in time into a sort of obsession," Clair claimed.

Lowell had roots buried deep in New England, his ancestors having come over on the *Mayflower.* He had descended from such towering historical figures as William Samuel Johnson, a signer of the U.S. Constitution, and Jonathan Edwards, the Calvinist, North

When Jackie started dating poet **Robert Lowell**, she didn't know that his best friends had nicknamed him "Cal," short for Caligula, the notorious and debauched Roman emperor.

When she finally broke off from him, the words spewing forth from his mouth were anything but poetic.

451

American theologian.

Lowell labeled himself "thick-witted, narcissistic, and thuggish," and was defiantly proud that his friends had nicknamed him "Cal" after the notoriously debauched Roman emperor, Caligula.

His previous wife had been Jean Stafford, a novelist who was celebrated in her day. The poet, Anthony Hecht, had called that coupling "tormented and tormenting." At the time that Jackie became involved with Lowell, he was married to his second wife, Elizabeth Hardwick, the literary critic. *The New York Times* characterized that marriage as "restless and emotionally harrowing."

Lowell lived on the West side of Manhattan. In a note to him, written when she was living on Fifth Avenue, Jackie wrote that she was pleased to "have a friend across Central Park." That reference became the title of his next poem.

Both Lowell and Jackie began to be seen in Manhattan at the Café des Artistes, and she was embarrassed when a *paparazzo* from *Women's Wear Daily* snapped their picture, and the two of them appeared on the cover of the December 1, 1965 edition of that publication. They were also caught on camera leaving the theater on the opening night of *Hogan's Goat*, a play by William Alfred.

She reacted in horror when word reached her that Lowell was telling his friends that he planned to divorce Hardwick and marry Jackie. Those rumors reached the gossip columns.

Jackie was far more attracted to Lowell's mind and his talent, but he kept pressing for a sexual relationship with her. It appears that she gave in on occasion, but perhaps her heart wasn't in it. She wanted to maintain his friendship, but she had no intention of becoming his third wife.

His obsession with her seemed to grow stronger. She'd also heard that he was ingesting a lot of lithium and was a manic-depressive. He'd had a history of going in and out of mental hospitals. It was rumored that his obsession with Jackie triggered another of his manic-depressive spins.

When she heard he was recuperating in McLean Hospital in Boston, she wrote him a loving note. Not calling attention to his condition, she said, "It is wise to go away for a time on a vacation. All of us need that from time to time." She avoided mentioning that his vacation happened to be unfolding within a mental hospital.

"Jackie obviously did not consider Lowell husband material," Clair claimed. "But she adored his poetry, and she encouraged a friendship between Lowell and Bobby. Before he ran for President, Jackie was secretly trying to educate Bobby, expand his horizons, so to speak, the same way she had tried to make Jack more cultured. Jack was my roommate at Harvard, and he was more interested in pulchritude than in Plutarch."

Lowell asked Bobby to read Juvenal and Cato, and he also gave him a biography of Alexander the Great.

In February of 1966, Jackie's former lover, Rudolf Nureyev, invited her to an intimate party at the Russian Tea Room, prompting her to invite Lowell as her escort. In the aftermath of that event, Jackie dropped him from her list of acceptable escorts.

During dinner, one of the guests mentioned that Sidney Kaye, owner of the Russian Tea Room, was Jewish.

One of Nureyev's guests reported, "That seemed to set off a tirade in Lowell. He started raging that, 'If I had wanted Jewish food, I would have gone to a deli.' He went on and on, sounding more like Goebbels all the time."

"After his ranting, Jackie stood up and abruptly excused herself. She raced toward the front, where she hailed a taxi. To my knowledge, she never saw this anti-Semitic poet ever again."

Jackie was very disappointed to learn that Lowell, who bitterly opposed the war in Vietnam, was supporting Senator Eugene McCarthy, instead of Bobby, for the Democratic nomination for President in 1968.

However, when Bobby was assassinated in Los Angeles, Lowell wrote a poem about the slain leader and sent it to Jackie. Arthur Schlesinger, Jr., later said, "It was the most beautiful poem ever written about Bobby."

Mike Nichols & Richard de Combray
Was There Carnal Knowledge of Jackie?

When Berlin-born Mikhail Igorevich Peschkowsky, otherwise known as Mike Nichols, was directing Elizabeth Taylor and Richard Burton in *Who's Afraid of Virginia Woolf?*, released in 1966, he shut down production to return to New York for a date with Jackie.

Upon his return, Taylor snidely remarked, "He looks like the cat who swallowed the canary."

Jackie, who opposed film censorship, learned from Nichols that he was defying Hollywood standards in this film adaptation of a controversial Broadway play by Edward Albee. Reportedly, he'd told her that his film would contain "thirteen god damns, three bastards, seven buggers, four screws, four sons-of-bitches or SOBs, and twelve variations of Christ's name taken in vain, as in Jesus H. Christ. There would also be references to scrotums and one reference to 'a right ball.'"

Upon the film's release, critic Stanley Hoffman wrote that when Burton delivered his famous line about "hump the hostess," old-fashioned Hollywood censorship came to an end.

Another of Nichol's controversial films was his 1971 *Carnal Knowledge*. Starring Jack Nicholson and Ann-Margret, it made frequent casual and

Director **Mike Nichols** and **Jackie Kennedy** formed a mutual admiration society, perhaps a lot more.

blunt depictions of sexual intercourse. Aside from his films, what most impressed Jackie about Nichols was that he was a third cousin twice removed of Albert Einstein.

Jackie had long felt that Nichols was a major talent, and that his 1968 *The Graduate,* starring Dustin Hoffman and Anne Bancroft, was one of her favorite movies. She had seen it twice.

"He certainly deserved his Oscar as a director," she'd told Andy Warhol. Three years younger than Jackie, Nichols was introduced to her at a party her sister, Lee Radziwill, gave "to brighten up Jackie's life."

Reportedly, Nichols found her mesmerizing. She entered the party in a stunning white silk Yves Saint Laurent gown with a white mink jacket. Her escort for the night was the very rich and very famous politician, businessman, and railroad heir, Averell Harriman. She would later tell Radziwill, "I find Mike enchanting."

The guests lined up to greet her. They included men who had chased after her—and some of those who had caught her—Franklin D. Roosevelt, Jr., Adlai Stevenson, and Bobby Kennedy. She was also greeted by Sammy Davis, Jr., who sloppily wet kissed her on the lips. Later, she turned to her friend, Bunny Mellon, "After exchanging body fluids with Sammy, does that mean I'll have what he has?"

At the party, she had a reunion with Pierre Salinger, who had been JFK's press secretary. The highlight of the evening was when Maurice Chevalier sang just to her.

Nichols could not help but notice that Bobby, without Ethel, hovered over Jackie as if she were his personal possession.

Jackie gave Nichols her phone number, and he called her the following morning and asked her out on a date. At the time, he was also dating feminist Gloria Steinem.

Presumably, Nichols was between marriages. Beginning with his marriage to Patricia Scott in 1957, he would wed four times, the last and most successful beginning in 1988 with ABC World News anchor Diane Sawyer.

When Jackie got to know Nichols, she found they had many common interests other than their love of film and theater. Both of them liked to go horseback riding. In Connecticut, Nichols was a noted horse breeder on a farm he owned. He imported top quality Arabian horses from Poland, later selling the animals at record-setting prices.

In 1976, Nichols collaborated with other breeders through their shared involvement with an auction at Bridgewater, Connecticut. The sale generated nearly a million dollars and was attended by Jackie herself, along with Candice Bergen and Warren Beatty, whom Jackie once defined as "my dream man."

During the next few weeks, Jackie was spotted dining with Nichols at Sardi's, followed by dancing at Arthur's, the then-most fashionable night club in Manhattan, owned by Sybil Burton in the wake of her divorce from Richard Burton. He had succumbed to the charms of Elizabeth Taylor when they'd filmed *Cleopatra* together in Rome.

A former lover of Burton, actress Susan Strasberg, daughter of Lee Strasberg of the Actors Studio, was there to watch Nichols enter with Jackie. She later reported, "They looked very much in love, holding hands and seemingly charmed by each other."

On another night, Nichols and Jackie were seen dining at La Grenouille, the fashionable French restaurant in Manhattan, with actor Alan Arkin and his wife.

With Nichols as her escort, Jackie also paid a surprise visit to Coney Island with her children. He purchased Nathan's famous hot dogs for the brood. Jackie showed up in Coney Island wearing a Royal blue miniskirt whose hem was positioned five provocative inches above her knee.

Sometimes, Nichols accompanied Jackie on shopping trips. One afternoon at Bergdorf Goodman's, a crowd, mostly women, formed a circle around Jackie. "Taking you somewhere is like dating the Statue of Liberty," Nichols told her. "My God, you're a national monument!"

"That I am," she said. "But isn't it fun?"

Nichols also appreciated Jackie's sharp wit. They took the elevator to an upper floor. When they got off, he asked her, "Did you see Billy Baldwin?"

"I did, indeed," she said. "I almost stepped on him."

[Baldwin, of course was the dean of American interior decorators, and had been hired, on occasion, by Jackie as well as by Nichols himself. Other clients included Cole Porter, Paul Mellon, and Diana Vreeland.

He and Jackie had once discussed the possibility of publishing a book on decorating. He told her that in the 1930s, all the leading decorators were women—Marian Hall, Rose Cumming, Elsie de Wolfe, and Diane Tate. "Their tastes were based on 18th-century concepts," he told her. "Today, most of the major decorators happen to be men, and you're looking at the best of them."

Jackie claimed, "The only person who admired **Billy Baldwin's** taste as a decorator was Billy himself."

Jackie continued her friendship with Nichols even when they dated other partners. He was around when Maurice Tempelsman became her main escort. At one time, Nichols introduced Jackie to the rather dashing Richard de Combray. When she was an editor at Doubleday, she worked with Combray on his novel, *Goodbye Europe,* published in 1983.

At one point at a dinner, Combray invited both Nichols and Tempelsman, who blended cordially. A surprise guest that evening was Claudette Colbert, who had flown in from her home in Barbados.

Author **Richard de Combray**, a bisexual, violated one of Jackie's basic rules: You don't kiss and tell.

Jackie had introduced herself previously to Colbert one afternoon when both of them had lunched at Mortimer's, a tony East Side hangout. Spotting Colbert as the aging actress was leaving the restaurant, Jackie had jumped up and asked the restaurant's owner, Glenn Bernbaum, "Wasn't that Claudette Colbert?"

He assured her that it was.

Jackie rushed out onto the sidewalk, "Miss Colbert," she said. "I'm Jacqueline Onassis, and I have long admired your work."

Bernbaum claimed that Colbert appeared honored to have been so greeted by Jackie.

Once the celebrity-obsessed Jackie confided to Nichols that she had once stalked "the ever so mysterious Greta Garbo on the sidewalks of Manhattan. "I followed her for about ten blocks before she eluded me. When I became First Lady, I invited her to the White House, and she accepted my invitation."

Claudette Colbert— Jackie had to chase her down the street.

The much-married Nichols was not always available as an escort for Jackie. Sometimes, when he was directing a picture or otherwise engaged, she'd call another escort. For some reason, in February of 1978, she attended the Seventh Regiment Armory on Park Avenue in honor of the posthumous publication of the James Jones novel, *Whistle.*

Jackie showed up on the arm of Walter Cronkite and greeted a distinguished array of guests—Lauren Bacall, Woody Allen, Theodore White, super agent Swifty Lazar, Art Buchwald, and such novelists as William Styron and Irwin Shaw.

Andy Warhol greeted Jackie. He'd been talking to Lee Radziwill and her lover, Peter Tufo. To his astonishment, he noticed that Radziwill quickly exited the party with Tufo, heading for the elevator and never once coming face to face with or greeting her sister.

When **Andy Warhol** escorted Jackie to the Brooklyn Museum for an exhibition of Egyptian art, the first question she asked was, "What's Elizabeth Taylor really like?"

The other person who avoided Jackie was her rival for men, Shirley MacLaine, who made an ostentatious show of immediately (and loudly) heading for the buffet table. In a voice that Jackie could clearly hear, she said, "God, I'm starved!"

Combray once talked to Nichols about the fallout from dating Jackie. "We had lunch one afternoon alone. A *paparazzo* snapped our picture as we were leaving this restaurant, and we ended up on the front-page of the tabloids. The next day, the reporters were calling me, asking me when Jackie and I were getting hitched. I told them we were working on a book."

Lee Radziwill avoiding her sister, Jackie, at a Manhattan party.

"Everything got distorted," he said. "I came to realize, as surely you must have, that you can't merely have lunch alone with the most famous woman on the planet without attracting a hell of a lot of attention. With all this publicity, my relationship with Jackie was damaged, through no fault of my own. She didn't welcome all this publicity about us."

Perhaps Combray was not being completely honest about his relationship with Jackie. She didn't blame him for reckless press speculation.

Apparently, they did become romantically involved one weekend, and he bragged about it to some of his close friends, Word got back to her. She had a pattern of dropping any beau who boasted about seducing her.

Gore Vidal later said, "I understood men who bedded Jackie and wanted to present it as a feather in their cap. I would be like a gay man bedding Tom Cruise, Paul Newman, Robert Redford, or one of those heartthrobs. Of course, as you're hanging out in a gay bar, you'd want to brag about your conquests, perfectly understandable."

Combray was a bisexual. His December 13, 2013 obituary in *The New York Times* asserted that he was survived by Miles Morgan, his life partner of 59 years, and also by a former wife, Natalie Hough de Combray.

Nichols remained Jackie's friend throughout her life, even appearing at her funeral to read a passage from the Bible right before opera diva Jessye Norman sang "Ave Maria."

Frank Richardson
The War of the Roses

A year after Jackie's death, she came very close to being named "the other woman" in a sensational 1995 divorce played out in the tabloids and in court. The notorious divorce between Frank and Nancy Richardson was, years later, nicknamed "The War of the Roses."

The battle in court was said to have inspired the 1989 movie, *The War of the Roses,* starring Michael Douglas in a plot about a warring couple who could not agree on a property settlement.

Journalist Alex Novak later wrote that at one point, Nancy alleged that her husband might have had an affair with Jackie. Whereas her actual name was not mentioned in court, lawyers used an oft-repeated, veiled reference to "a towering figure." The one woman named was Federal Court Judge Kimba Wood.

To bolster her charges of infidelity, Nancy had found the secret diaries of her husband.

In his diary, Richardson wrote about his feelings for the mystery woman, presumably Jackie. "I was intoxicated by her body."

Nancy claimed that her estranged husband's diary contained "puerile musings about where he and his lover went, how they felt when they touched, and how they made love."

If a sexual tryst between Richardson and Jackie actually occurred, it would have been at his 53-acre Long Island estate opening onto Oyster Bay Cove. Here, he maintained a 50-room mansion with a swimming pool and tennis courts. According to a servant whose information was paid for by a tabloid reporter, Jackie made at least three visits to Richardson's fully staffed stable, one of the best in the region. She went horseback riding, her favorite sport.

In court, Richardson denied having had an affair with Judge Wood and also disputed his affair with "that other woman," (aka Jackie). At the time, Richardson's net worth was estimated at around $160 million. In the final divorce settlement, the court awarded Nancy $80 million. In the wake of that, Richardson ran off with a *Playboy* bunny.

At one point, Jackie was said to have been interested in Napier House, a residence owned by Nancy,

In his diary, **Frank Richardson** described a mystery woman whose body he found "intoxicating."

Only the timing of Jackie's death saved her from being named as "the other woman" in a bitter divorce dispute.

who had put it on the market for $1.3 million. The house at Sag Harbor, on Long Island, had once been owned by the U.S.'s 21st President, Chester A. Arthur, who occupied the White House from 1881 to 1885. The building later became a funeral parlor.

Jackie was fascinated by this obscure president and later claimed that his life and legacy had inspired her to upgrade the furnishing and décor of the White House.

Mike Douglas and **Kathleen Turner** in *The War of the Roses.*

Arthur once told the press, "I may be president of the United States, but my private life is nobody's god damn business."

The widower president was the first to employ a valet, who looked after his 100 suits. "Arthur was the first president to bring men's fashion to the office," Jackie said.

In addition to being America's best dressed president, he rode around in a lavish carriage with gold lace curtains.

Like Jackie, he had detested the White House décor and its dilapidated furnishings. He set out to renovate the building. To raise money for his project, he began to empty the White House of its furnishings. On the front lawn, he staged a yard sale, attracting hundreds of prospective buyers. He even auctioned off a pair of old trousers once owned by Abraham Lincoln. He also personally auctioned off a hat worn by John Quincy Adams.

When he was challenged on this sale by critics, who claimed that these relics should be donated to museums, he responded in anger: "To hell with that! I need money for new furniture. Hell, if the British hadn't burned them, I would have auctioned off Dolley Madison's bloomers, even with skid marks."

Felix Rohatyn
Jackie's "Felix the Cat"

Journalist Richard Wilner wrote: "In December of 1975, Felix Rohatyn was King of New York. Presidents and potentates took his calls. Cabbies, believing the 47-year-old bank titan had saved the financial life of New York, refused to accept his money, driving him around Manhattan for free."

Only a year older than Jackie, Vienna-born Rohatyn was an investment banker famed for preventing New York from going bankrupt. At the time he became the city's financial adviser, NYC was $11 billion in debt.

Rohatyn, was a partner associated with the prestigious international banking firm, Lazard Frères. *[Another partner was André Meyer.]* Rohatyn was also a long-term financial adviser to the Democratic Party, and in time *[from 1997 to 2000]* served as U.S. ambassador to France during the Clinton administration.

Rohatyn, with Meyer, sometimes double-dated, Meyer escorting Jackie and Rohatyn escorting his steady girlfriend, Hélène Gaillet de Barcza, a renowned photographer. This arrangement often began with Sunday dinners at Meyer's apartment within the Hotel Carlyle in Manhattan.

Gaillet, in her capacity as the eight-year mistress of Rohatyn, shared a penthouse with him at the Hotel Alrae in Manhattan. *[Originally built in 1927 on a quiet stretch of East 64th Street, the Alrae, after extensive renovations, evolved into the very posh Plaza Athenée Hotel in 1987.]*

At a low point in their relationship, she flew to Paris for an exhibition of her photographs. Upon her return, she found that Rohatyn had moved all his possessions from their penthouse.

Jackie and Rohatyn began serious dating in 1976. As he became involved with Jackie, he had

> **"Felix the Cat" Rohatyn** was not only a financial genius, but a ladykiller. Once again, Jackie found herself competing with Shirley MacLaine for the affections of a man.

to dump Gaillet. She did not mourn in silence, telling the press, "Ms. Onassis uses men and discards them the way she does one of her summer dresses. I cannot believe how she betrayed me. I viewed her as a friend."

"When she is ready to move on to another man, she calls and leaves a message with their secretary. 'Tell Mister Whoever not to call Mrs. Onassis again.' Even though she is middle aged, she is still attractive. Being one of the most famous women in the world certainly adds to her allure."

Gaillet told William D. Cohan, author of *The Last Tycoons,* "I wasn't in love with Felix. He was not in love with me. It was not even a great affair. It was just something that was happening. But in a sense, I enjoyed having an affair with him, because we always had dinners, at which time the most interesting part was the conversation."

After their breakup, Gaillet discovered that Rohatyn was a real Romeo, perhaps dating both Shirley MacLaine (Jackie's longtime rival), and Barbara Walters, on the side. Not only that, but he'd taken a mistress, Elizabeth Vagliano, whom he would eventually marry in 1979 when his divorce from his first wife, Jeannette Streit, was finalized.

Rohatyn allegedly was never faithful to any one woman. One report had his partner, André Meyer, arriving at Rohatyn's office at Lazard Frères and discovering that the door was locked. He yelled out in a voice loud enough for the entire office to hear: "Felix, why don't you go to a hotel room like the rest of our partners?"

Office rumor had it that Rohatyn was locked away for a daytime tryst with Shirley MacLaine at the time. But that was never proven.

Gaillet and Rohatyn had flown to Skorpios, Onassis' private island in Greece, to offer comfort to Onassis following the death of his son, Alexander, in a plane crash. She remembered Onassis driving to meet them at the island's landing strip, positioned on a high plateau. "He took us on a tour of his island, and we went to the beach with him, even did some gardening, anything to distract him from the loss of his son. He was in deep mourning. Five days later, Jackie flew in with Sir John Russell, the British ambassador to Spain. All of us, including Jackie, tried desperately to bring some solace to poor Ari."

During Rohatyn's dating of Jackie, finances were often discussed, especially her own. But she was also concerned with her mother, Janet. When Hugh Auchincloss had died, he was going broke. He'd been forced to sell Merrywood, his palatial estate in Virginia, and he even had to put Hammersmith Farm, outside Newport, on the market, selling it to a group of investors.

In the wake of her 1976 divorce from Auchincloss, in 1979, Janet had married banker Bingham Morris, separating from him two years later, although they never divorced.

Jackie felt her mother's financial position was precarious. Rohatyn suggested that Jackie set up a $1 million trust fund for her, which she did.

In 1976, Rohatyn accompanied Jackie to the Democratic Nominating Convention at Madison Square Garden. She was there to show her support for Sargent Shriver, who wanted to be the Vice Presidential nominee. But the candidate, Jimmy Carter, supported Walter Mondale as his running mate instead. Jackie told friends, "I will not campaign for Carter. I simply can't abide this peanut farmer."

During the convention, in the VIP box above the main floor, she sat between Ted Kennedy and Rohatyn. She was overheard making fun of Carter, "You know, he looks like Howdy Doody."

She also mocked Rosalynn Carter. America's upcoming First Lady would be called "the Steel Magnolia" and compared unfavorably to Jackie.

After hearing her voice, Jackie turned to Rohatyn, batting her eyelashes and assuming a Scarlett O'Hara accent, "*Fiddle-de-dee*, Lady Bird is just gonna love this Georgia peach with her corn syrup-and-pancake voice."

When Jackie stopped dating Rohatyn, they still stayed in touch. She knew he wanted to become Secretary of the Treasury, a dream that was subsequently thwarted by twelve years of Republicans in the White House.

During the 1992 presidential campaign, he did not fully understand what was coming, backing Ross Perot over Bill Clinton for President, and thereby demolishing his chances of becoming an appointee in the new Clinton Administration. *[In compensation, and partly because of his financial support and his status as a life-long Democrat, he was eventually appointed U.S. Ambassador to France (1997-2000) during Clinton's second administration.]*

Jackie told her associates, including Ted Kennedy and Arthur Schlesinger, Jr., "Felix knows how to handle finances, and he certainly can date A-list women, but when it comes to politics, he is tone deaf."

Franklin D. Roosevelt, Jr.
Jackie and the President's Son

Their parents, Franklin D. Roosevelt and Joseph P. Kennedy, became enemies, but their respective sons, Franklin D. Roosevelt, Jr., and John F. Kennedy, bonded and became lifelong friends.

The young men had much in common, as each had been a Naval officer during World War II. Both men had at one time been a congressman, FDR Jr. representing the 20th congressional district of New York from 1949 to 1955. He got to know JFK so well, he often went out on double dates with him.

FDR Jr. was married at the time to Ethel du Pont of the famous family of industrialists. JFK was dating a young model in New York, Grace Kelly, who at the time had some vague plan about becoming a movie actress.

Born in 1914, FDR Jr., was the fifth child of Franklin and Eleanor Roosevelt. Although not associated with the scandals that frequently engulfed his older brothers, James and Elliott, FDR, Jr. was in frequent trouble with the police, usually for traffic violations such as driving while intoxicated.

Kelly would migrate to Hollywood, and the Du Pont heiress and FDR Jr., would soon divorce. He later introduced JFK to his second wife, Suzanne Perrin.

JFK campaigned for FDR Jr., in 1954 when he ran for governor of New York, although he lost to a Republican, Jacob Javits. It was at this time that JFK introduced Roosevelt to his new bride, Jackie Bouvier Kennedy.

She got to know FDR Jr. much better when he campaigned for her husband in the 1960 West Virginia primary, where he was seeking the Democratic nomination for President, competing against Senator Hubert Humphrey of Minnesota. Often, when JFK was overscheduled, he asked Roosevelt and Jackie to make an appearance for him. When he became President, JFK designated Roosevelt as Under-Secretary of Commerce and chairman of the President's Appalachian Regional Commission.

Franklin D. Roosevelt, Jr. is pictured with his illustrious mother, **Eleanor Roosevelt,** who always beat out Jackie in influential polls gauging the popularity of First Ladies.

During her years in the White House, Jackie and Roosevelt became close friends, seeing each other with or without JFK. The President later told his best friend, Lem Billings, "I think Jackie has a crush on Franklin. At times, when she gets angry with me for cheating on her, I think she would have preferred that he had become president, following in his father's footsteps, so she could have been his First Lady instead of mine."

In 1963, and in need of a vacation, Jackie decided to accept an invitation extended by Aristotle Onassis for a tour of the Greek islands aboard his luxury yacht, *Christina,* named after his daughter. The invitation was extended through her sister, Lee Radziwill, who was having an affair with Onassis, the shipping tycoon, at the time.

JFK only reluctantly agreed to let Jackie go. Although it was clearly understood that Lee would be aboard, he also insisted that Jackie invite FDR Jr. and his wife, Suzanne.

"How cheeky," Jackie said, using a British expression. "Jack thinks I need both my sister and Franklin, even his wife, as chaperon. He's the one who should have a chaperon."

She flew into Athens with the Roosevelts. Although Onassis had given them the use of *Christina,* he agreed, for a time, at least, to remain in the background, knowing that he was a controversial figure for the First Lady to be seen with.

Both the Roosevelts and Jackie were impressed with the luxury of the *Christina,* a former Canadian frigate that had been converted into Onassis' personal seagoing statement. It employed 60 servants and two chefs, as well as a masseuse and two hairdressers on call 24 hours a day.

When Jackie came aboard, she found that Onassis had decorated the vessel with pink and white gladioli and red and yellow roses.

She wandered at leisure throughout the yacht. Its bar stools were upholstered with skin harvested from the scrotums of whales. Its (working) fireplaces had mantels crafted from lapis lazuli, and its bathroom fixtures were plated with gold. Onassis assigned her the stateroom which Sir Winston Churchill and Greta Garbo had occupied during (separate) and previous cruises.

As devised by the *Christina's* captain, Costas Anastassiadis, an itinerary was presented to Jackie. First stop, the island of Lesbos, the former abode of Sappho. That announcement was followed with the usual lesbian jokes.

The captain later sailed his VIP guests to the island of Crete, where all of them went aboard for sightseeing.

When the *Christina* docked in Turkey at Izmir *[aka Smyrna, Onassis' birthplace]*, she sent word to ask the Greek tycoon to join their party. He accepted her invitation to appear aboard his own yacht, but kept a low profile, avoiding any opportunity that might allow paparazzi to snap his picture with "the President's Lady."

Onassis catered to Jackie's every wish, hosting lavish dinner parties on shore at every port, including Ithaca, where they anchored. She often danced with either Roosevelt or with Onassis on deck under a starry night.

Suzanne noted that Jackie flirted with both her husband and her host. But she didn't think that Jackie was having an affair with Onassis because at the time, he was involved with Lee Radziwill, when not chasing after Maria Callas.

Roosevelt and Onassis often stayed up late at night, drinking after Jackie and Suzanne had gone to bed. One night, Onassis shocked Roosevelt by asserting, "Every Greek man worth his salt has a wife, a mistress, and a beautiful young boy with a tender ass on the side—it is our custom."

A *paparazzo* hired a boat and sailed close to the *Christina,* snapping a picture of Jackie sunbathing in a bikini on deck. When JFK was told that the photo had appeared on the front page of practically every newspaper in the world, he was furious. He fired off a telegram that ordered Jackie to return to Washington.

Jackie ignored the protests, even when they were delivered from the floor of Congress. Representative Oliver Bolton, Republican Congressmen from the eastern suburbs of Cleveland *[Ohio]*, attacked the First Lady for "her demonstration of indiscretion accepting the lavish hospitality of a notorious shipping tycoon who had defrauded the American public and been investigated by the FBI."

"If Mrs. Kennedy wants to go gallivanting all over Europe, why not see America first?" Bolton asked. "She's never visited the great attractions of the United States. She should see them first instead of publicizing the glories of the Greek islands."

When the yacht docked in Istanbul, Onassis presented Jackie with a ruby-and-diamond necklace worth

Oliver Bolton, Republican Congressman from Ohio's 11th District, in office from 1963-1965

about $75,000. Lee Radziwill got what she later described to Truman Capote as "three dinky little bracelets that Caroline wouldn't even accept as gifts at her own birthday party."

Johnny Meyer, who had been the pimp for Howard Hughes, and who later agreed to work for Onassis, revealed that Jackie and Roosevelt went off together on a sightseeing tour of their own to visit some ruins outside Istanbul. "Ari asked me to tag along as their bodyguard," Meyer claimed. "He recommended that they stop off at one of his favorite inns, where the chef had been ordered to prepare a Greek feast for them of his favorite dishes."

After drinking the wine and eating a good meal, Jackie complained of the heat. She said she'd had too much to drink.

"I arranged for them to have a siesta upstairs in two of the best rooms at the inn," Meyer claimed. "At around five o'clock, I came for them to drive them back to Istanbul. I discovered that Roosevelt's room was empty. I didn't want to call attention to it, but it was obvious when I came for Jackie that the son of a famous president was in the room with her."

"On the way back to Istanbul, I saw them holding hands. I knew he'd made love to her that afternoon."

***

"The next months passed quickly, and then came Jack's flight to Texas, accompanied by Jackie," Roosevelt said. "To me, his term seemed just like it had begun, and then with some gunshots, it was all over. I joined many others to offer Jackie all the loving support I could."

He called on Jackie every day, although he felt he was making Bobby jealous. "After Jack was killed, Bobby seemed to take possession of her."

One night, FDR Jr. invited Jackie to a small dinner party at his home. Since it was late, he drove her back to her residence in Georgetown.

Even though it was late at night, some thirty curious people were gathered outside her home, hoping to see her coming or going.

Seeing the crowd, she burst into tears. "I can't stand these people any more," she told Roosevelt. "They're like locusts swarming around me, devouring me. I'm going mad. I can't go anywhere without being stalked."

Roosevelt stormed out of his car and chased the people away, threatening to call the police and have them arrested. Then he disappeared inside the house with Jackie at around one o'clock in the morning.

A Jackie "stalker" later reported that Roosevelt left her house at nine o'clock the following morning. It is not known what excuse he used to tell his wife, who must have been jealous of Jackie, as Ethel was of her because of Jackie's close ties to Bobby.

In Manhattan during October of 1964, Roosevelt recalled escorting Jackie to Richard Burton's suite at the Plaza Hotel. Burton had been there talking to Bobby Kennedy, who had become his good friend.

Later, Roosevelt confided to Senator George Smathers [a Democrat from

Florida] details about what took place there, claiming that Burton had already consumed too many Irish whiskies before they arrived.

"After about an hour, he became very indiscreet," Roosevelt told his friends. "He even urged Bobby to divorce Ethel and marry Jackie, and make an honest woman out of her. He went on and on. Jackie wanted him to shut up, so she begged him to recite something from Shakespeare. That did the trick."

When Gore Vidal later heard about this intimate cocktail party at The Plaza, he snidely remarked, "Jackie had something in common with Bobby, Burton, and Roosevelt. On occasion, she'd seduced all three of them, especially Bobby."

Eleanor Roosevelt

Her Death and Jackie's Role at Her Memorial Service

An early-morning call came in from FDR Jr. to Jackie at the White House. His voice was grim. "Mother has passed on. It would mean so much to all of us if you and the President could come to her funeral."

The date was November 7, 1962. Eleanor Roosevelt, the greatest First Lady in the history of the Republic, had died.

Jackie burst into tears. Recovering, she promised Roosevelt that she and the President would journey to Hyde Park for the funeral.

In the past, the Kennedys had had their differences with the Roosevelts. FDR had ended up "detesting" Joseph P. Kennedy after he'd failed as Ambassador to the Court of St. James's on the eve of World War II. As late as 1960, even after JFK won the Democratic nomination, Eleanor had stubbornly backed his competitor, Adlai Stevenson, until the cause was lost.

But Eleanor was a Democrat to her aging toenails, and she disliked Richard Nixon. Consequently, the Democratic Party could always count on its battle-hardened diva, even as she neared the end of her life.

When JFK was inaugurated as President, Mrs. Roosevelt, the beloved duenna of the Democrats, attended with other First Ladies, going back as far as Edith Wilson. Bess Truman and Mamie Eisenhower were there, as were Lady Bird Johnson, Patricia Nixon, and Betty Ford.

Jackie learned that Eleanor had specifically requested a "small, simple service in a plain pine coffin covered with a blanket of

Their relationship was complicated and strained:
Eleanor Roosevelt with **JFK**

pine boughs." She wanted to keep her funeral private.

Even though he was juggling some of the darkest moments of the Cuban Missile Crisis, with ample evidence that America was in imminent danger of a nuclear attack, JFK attended the service, along with Jackie. Former President Harry S Truman showed up, as did Dwight D. Eisenhower, along with a future President, Lyndon B. Johnson.

The service was held at FDR's St. James' Church in Hyde Park, a hundred miles north of New York City. FDR Jr. welcomed Jackie and warmly embraced her. He invited her to lunch at his home next door to his mother's Val-Kill Cottage.

After the service, Jackie sat on a sofa smoking a cigarette and wearing a dark mink hat. She watched JFK talking with Eisenhower and Truman.

Bess called Harry to come at once to attend to some perceived problem. On the way out, Harry informed Jackie that Eleanor Roosevelt was actually "the First Lady of the World." Jackie viewed that as a put-down, since she'd heard that Truman had called her "the White House mannequin" a dismissive reference to her stylish wardrobe.

Friends close to Jackie said that attending Eleanor's funeral gave Jackie many ideas for a state funeral in case JFK ever died in office, perhaps the victim of an assassin's bullet.

Before 1962, only five presidents had been given state funerals. Ted Sorensen advised Jackie that she should leave some instructions for her own funeral if she should die during her tenure in the White House.

He told her that American First Ladies were rarely commemorated. Mary Todd Lincoln was the rare First Lady whose death had been officially sanctioned with flags flying at half mast.

"From my reading of history, I noted that most First Ladies were dispatched with little more than prayers and flowers in small towns across America," Sorensen said. "Eleanor's funeral was the first time that three presidents had ever attended such an event."

Eisenhower had almost canceled at the last minute. [In 1952, there had been talk of nominating Eleanor to run against Ike for President.]

As transport to the funeral, JFK and Jackie had flown aboard the new Air Force One, making its maiden voyage. The following year, she'd also be on that plane as it flew JFK's corpse back from Dallas.

After hugging and kissing FDR Jr. goodbye, JFK and Jackie departed from Hyde Park. On their way out, their limousine passed a protester holding up a sign—WE'RE GLAD YOU'RE GONE, ELEANOR. The Hyde Park police were in the process of arresting him.

Back in Washington, Jackie wrote to her mother, Janet Auchincloss: "After attending Eleanor's funeral, I am convinced that, God forbid, if Jack ever died in office, the American public will need some official display of our mourning. It should not be a quiet, private funeral, but a major event to rally the nation in its hour of grief—a kind of group therapy to heal our wounds. The only shame will be for those of his enemies who do not join the jeremiad."

Adlai Stevenson
"Jackie Is the Temptress of Her Age"

"Jack so obviously demanded from a woman a relationship between a man and a woman where a man would be the leader and a woman be his wife and look up to him as a man. With Adlai, you could have another relationship where—you know, he'd sort of be sweet and you could talk. I always thought women who were scared of sex loved Adlai."
—Jacqueline Kennedy in *Historic Taped Conversations (1964)*

In the early evening of the night before Jackie boarded that morning flight to Texas with JFK, she received an urgent call from Adlai Stevenson. The President had selected him as the U.S. Ambassador to the United Nations. Since she was busy, she told a White House staff member, "Tell Adlai I'll get back to him in the morning before I leave."

The messenger returned. "The ambassador says it's urgent that he speak to you, a matter of life or death."

After a preliminary greeting, Stevenson got right to the point. "You must convince our President not to go to Dallas. The *Dallas Morning News* is running an editorial that will stir up hatred against the President. I was recently in Dallas. I was pelted with eggs and spat upon by hate mongers."

"Oh, Adlai," she said. "I'm sure everything will be all right. There will be tight security."

"But as the President has often told us, 'If someone wants to trade his life for mine, he can do it.'"

"I appreciate your concern," she said, "but I trust my husband. He wouldn't let me fly with him if he felt we'd be in danger."

"Very well," he said. "I'll pray that both of you return to Washington safely. But I must warn you a final time: You're flying into hostile rattlesnake country."

"Good night, Adlai, and thank you for your concern."

Her rejection of his warning angered Stevenson. The following night, he expressed his concern to Katharine Graham,

Adlai Stevenson never gave up in his desire to become President, even after he lost to Dwight Eisenhower in 1952 and 1956.

Like Martin Luther King, Jr., Stevenson had a dream. He fancied that if he could persuade Jackie to marry him, he might sail into the White House based on her popularity as a "second-time" First Lady.

publisher of *The Washington Post.* At that dinner, he also called Jackie "a royal tease. The temptress of her age."

After her return to Washington from Dallas, Jackie would often tell friends and associates about that late night panic call from Stevenson. "If only I'd listened to him."

***

Until the assassination, Jackie always maintained a superficial relationship with Adlai. Occasionally, they talked, as when he called her after attending the birthday gala for JFK at Madison Square Garden in May of 1962. Stevenson saw Marilyn Monroe singing "Happy Birthday, Mr. President" while wearing what he called "only skin and beads."

He phoned Jackie the next day to report on the evening. He described the party he'd attended after the gala. It had been hosted by Arthur Krim, president of United Artists. "I never got to dance with Miss Monroe," he said to Jackie. "Bobby Kennedy put up strong defenses around her. He was dodging round her like a moth around the flame. The President stayed on the other side of the room, surrounded by an array of admirers."

Although Jackie on several occasions denied her political involvements in policy issues during her husband's administration, JFK often used her charm as a political buffer "to soothe ruffled feathers" in his words.

Such was the case during the Cuban Missile Crisis when he ordered Jackie to share a private dinner with Stevenson. He had aroused Stevenson's fury when his aides leaked word that Stevenson endorsed a policy of capitulation to the Soviets.

Jackie apparently succeeded brilliantly in her assignment, and won over Stevenson with her charm assault. She later reported, "We talked art and literature—not politics, and he seemed to enjoy being in my company."

At the 1956 Democratic Nominating Convention, JFK had wanted Stevenson to designate him as his vice presidential running mate. At the convention, Jackie was seated with both Bobby and Teddy Kennedy, as well as with Jean Kennedy Smith, Sargent Shriver, and Ted Sorensen.

All of JFK's backers were terribly disappointed when Stevenson decided to let the delegates select his running mate for him. The convention voted for Estes Kefauver, the coonskin-cap wearing senator from Tennessee.

As surprising as it sounds, Stevenson wanted to be nominated once again as the Democratic candidate for president in 1960, despite having previously lost (twice) to Dwight D. Eisenhower. The thinking of his backers, including Eleanor Roosevelt, was that Eisenhower had been too popular to beat. Richard Nixon, however, seemed a vulnerable candidate who did not benefit from Ike's wide and popular appeal. At the convention, Stevenson's candidacy went down in defeat.

[The Democrats were opposed to giving Stevenson a chance for a third run for President. Other than JFK, the candidate to beat was Lyndon B. John-

son.]

Following JFK's assassination in 1963, Johnson, the new president, grew increasingly alarmed by his growing unpopularity resulting from the Vietnam War. He called his trusted aides to decide which other candidate might oppose him if he ran for re-election in 1968. Eugene McCarthy and Bobby Kennedy were each interpreted as formidable challengers. The name Adlai Stevenson also came up.

"Can you believe it?" Johnson asked his cronies. "This faggot *[a reference to Stevenson]* has come up with this crazy scheme that he should run once again for president. He has told his closest aides that if he can get the widow Kennedy to marry him, he'll have yet another chance to run for President in 1968, this time on her skirttails."

As commented upon by Johnson, Stevenson had begun to woo Jackie right after the assassination.

Stevenson had launched his pursuit of Jackie even before her move to New York. In 1964, at her Georgetown residence, he wrote her, "Please be merciful and indulge an old man and let me know when you are in New York."

When she eventually moved to New York, Stevenson sent another note to welcome her. "I hope you can find some peace here—I haven't! And I will give you none—until you set aside an evening for me—alone!"

He began to invite her on trips, beginning with a day trip to Washington in a special plane that would return her back to New York later that evening. He even invited her to Spain for the *Feria* in Seville. She did not accept. He asked her, "How can you see the world save in the tender care of a safe, old chaperon like me?"

Paul Mathias, the New York correspondent for *Paris-Match,* summed up how Adlai Stevenson fitted into Jackie's life after the assassination. "She not only perfected the art of the tease, she invented it. She was Miss Narcissist, perpetually searching mirrors for every wrinkle or strand of prematurely gray hair. She didn't worry about growing old, she worried about looking old."

"Within eighteen months after the assassination, she had at least two dozen of the world's most brilliant and important men dangling like marionettes, dancing at her fingertips. Most of them were very married, very old, or very queer."

Most in-the-know Washingtonians included Stevenson in the latter category.

Stevenson wasn't the only political bigwig arriving at Jackie's new Fifth Avenue apartment. Other *politico* guests included the President himself, Lyndon Johnson, and Senator (later Vice President) Hubert Humphrey. Even Haile Selassie of Ethiopia and King Hassan II of Morocco came by to pay their respects. Rudolf Nureyev also was a frequent visitor.

After their first dinner together in New York, Jackie sent Stevenson a watercolor she'd painted of the Sphinx, one with her face emblazoned on the monument itself. She wrote, "A Sphinx is rather what I feel like when I go out with you—as it all seems so responsible—and it is really the most marvelous 'cover.'"

That watercolor was followed by an invitation from Stevenson for Jackie and Lee Radziwill to have lunch with him at the United Nations. The luncheon was followed with another note from Jackie: "We had the most exhilarating time. Lee, that fickle creature, came there adoring the Greek ambassador but left in love with Dr. Ralph Bunche!"

Johnson had always held Stevenson in contempt. For reasons of his own, he seemed upset by Stevenson dating Jackie. He called her one morning and chatted casually. He didn't seem to want to say that Stevenson was gay, but he hoped to send a signal. "Jackie, I hate to tell you this, but I have it on good authority that Stevenson squats to piss."

He'd made the call after seeing a picture in the morning paper of Stevenson escorting Jackie to the ballet in Manhattan.

Stevenson's son, Adlai Jr., seemed impressed with Jackie. "She needed someone like my father to go to the theater and other cultural events to escape the Kennedy tribe. He didn't play touch football. She was a wonderful, sensitive woman who needed to escape. My father was cultivated, a man of the world, gentle, sophisticated."

Stevenson seemed to believe that the way to win Jackie's heart involved courting her children. When Caroline enrolled at the School of the Convent of the Sacred Heart in New York City, Stevenson escorted both Jackie and her daughter there. On some occasions, he picked up both John Jr. and Caroline and took them to an ice cream parlor, followed that evening with a private dinner with Jackie.

For about six weeks, he became a kind of surrogate father. Once, he took Caroline and John Jr., on a ferryboat ride to show them the Statue of Liberty. He even escorted them one summer to Coney Island, where they were seen enjoying the rides and eating Nathan's famous hot dogs.

Often, in the evening, he would escort Jackie to the theater.

"I'm alarmed by Adlai's growing romantic interest in me," Jackie told friends. As author C. David Heymann revealed, "The more he saw of her, the more attracted he became. When she sensed that he had developed a romantic attachment, she retreated, sending him a series of playful but off-putting notes."

The end of the relationship came when Stevenson, at Jackie's Fifth Avenue apartment, proposed marriage to her. Stressing what a wonderful father he would be to Caroline and John Jr., he finally accepted the fact that she had no sexual interest in him at all. Not giving up, he proposed that they could have a *mariage blanc,* a strictly platonic union, not a sexual one. He tried to win her over by claiming, "The two of us can continue to carry out Jack's work that he wasn't allowed to finish."

What Jackie knew at the time, but Stevenson didn't, was that Bobby was considering challenging Johnson for the Democratic nomination for President at the 1968 convention. Of course, Jackie would throw her considerable support behind Bobby.

It was all over between Stevenson and Jackie.

Pierre Trudeau

Jackie and the Young and Swinging Prime Minister

Ten years older than Jackie, Pierre Trudeau began his career as a lawyer and activist in Québec province. Later, he joined the Liberal Party of Canada, becoming in time Minister of Justice. "Reason before passion," was his personal motto.

In April of 1968, the year Jackie married Aristotle Onassis, Trudeau was elected Prime Minister. T h e press defined him as "Canada's swinging young bachelor," inviting comparisons to the lifestyle of John F. Kennedy's womanizing.

In January of 1970, Trudeau shocked Canada by showing up at the celebration of Manitoba's Centennial with Barbra Streisand. Tall, handsome, and unmarried, he gave off a youthful aura even though he was fifty years old. He'd met Streisand a year earlier at the premiere of *Funny Girl* in London. Although often in different cities, they continued their romance. He made a series of weekend flights to New York to date the singing star.

Pierre Trudeau, the Prime Minister of Canada, was hailed as that country's answer to JFK.

The romance heated up, especially when Streisand flew to Ottawa to complete the shooting of her latest film, *The Owl and the Pussycat* (1970). Speculation was rampant that she was about to become the First Lady of Canada. In a TV interview, Trudeau was asked about his relationship with the star. "None of your business," he snapped.

Streisand was reported to be contemplating how she could maintain a career in Hollywood and function as First Lady of Canada at the same time. In 1977, years after the end of her affair with Trudeau, she gave an interview to *Playboy.* "I'd have to learn how to speak French, and I could only do movies in Canada. I would campaign for Pierre and get involved in all his causes—abortion rights or whatever."

Perhaps unknown to Streisand, Trudeau was secretly dating two other women when she wasn't around. One was the 21-year-old Margaret Sinclair. The other was Jackie, who, though married to Onassis, was more or less living separately from him at the time.

Teddy Kennedy was a friend of Trudeau. Once in New York, he asked Jackie to have a private dinner for Trudeau, who had expressed a strong desire to meet her. No record exists of what went on that night, other than what is obvious: Jackie and Trudeau became instant friends.

Unlike Streisand, Jackie could speak French to him. A series of private dates occurred with Jackie. It was all very secretive. On two different occasions, they spent weekends in Virginia going horseback riding. "I'm seriously considering divorcing Ari and marrying Pierre," Jackie told Truman Capote and other friends. "I have to admit that the idea of becoming another First Lady intrigues me. First Lady of the United States, First Lady of Canada. That leaves out only Mexico. If I can pull that off, I would have First Ladied myself across the entire North American continent. I'd certainly be the first woman to have achieved that."

At the time, Jackie viewed Streisand as her major competition. She resented the star for outrageously flirting with JFK on May 17, 1963 at the White House. Her first words to the President had been, "You're a doll!"

"How long have you been singing?" JFK had asked her.

"About as long as you've been President," she quipped.

From reports reaching Jackie, if her husband had invited Streisand to sleep over

Pierre Trudeau is seen here on a date with the Brooklyn diva, **Barbra Streisand**. What she might not have known was that he was also offering Jackie a chance at becoming First Lady of Canada.

Both Barbra and Jackie lost out when **Trudeau** wed a very young **Margaret Sinclair**. Later, Teddy Kennedy reinforced his family's link to the Trudeaus by launching an affair with Canada's First Lady.

with him in the Lincoln Bedroom, she would have accepted.

"I like Pierre's lovemaking and I like his politics," she told Patricia Kennedy Lawford, Ted Sorensen, and Senator George Smathers during a yachting trip off the coast of Cape Cod. "Streisand is a Jew and Pierre is Catholic. With Pierre and me, there would be no religious issues."

Although by now Onassis had returned to his mistress, Maria Callas, in Paris, Jackie did not immediately accept Trudeau's proposal of marriage.

"Pierre has an old-fashioned gallantry," Jackie told Patricia and her other friends, who later gossiped about the affair. "He knows how to please a woman, especially in the boudoir. He's also very intelligent and, like Jack, well informed on world affairs. His personality is warm and charming. He believes in moonlit walks in rose-scented gardens. And like me, he has a taste for French cuisine. What do I admire about him the most? He has this amazing informality. During some of the hottest days last summer in Canada, he addressed Parliament in a pair of sandals. He also wears bikini underwear with the imprint of a tiger across his crotch."

While waiting for Jackie and Streisand to make up their minds, Trudeau, in an impulsive move, on March 4, 1971, married Margaret Sinclair at St. Stephen's Catholic Church in North Vancouver.

Within three months, he knew he'd made the wrong decision. They were incompatible, and his busy schedule left little

UP IN THE AIR: **Margot Kidder** as Lois Lane flies high with **Christopher Reeve** in *Superman II*. When she returned to earth, Pierre Trudeau became her lover.

time for her. He also learned that she was suffering from bipolar depression.

Yet he would not divorce her until 1980. Although he no longer secretly dated Streisand, he was rumored to have slipped around about six or seven times during the 1970s for rendezvous with Jackie.

As Christopher Andersen wrote in his book, *Barbra: The Way She Is,* "Canada's nonconformist First Lady would quickly prove to be something of a loose cannon. At one point, she decided to break away from her domineering husband and the pressures of her being First Lady by joining the Rolling Stones on tour. As a result, the prime minister found himself in the awkward position of having to defend his young wife's erratic behavior on the floor of Parliament. Even so, the union produced three sons."

To complicate matters, Teddy Kennedy confessed to Jackie that he had become romantically involved with Margaret, Trudeau's wife.

William Hofer, who spent ten years on Teddy's staff, later penned a memoir, *The Senator.* In it he wrote about his boss's affair with Canada's First Lady.

"One Friday, when Joan Kennedy had been away for the week, George Dalton asked me to drive to the National Airport in Washington to meet Margaret Trudeau. I waited for her at the gate, recognized her instantly, and introduced myself. During the drive to McLean, Virginia, I realized she had planned to spend the entire weekend with the Senator, and I felt decidedly uncomfortable. Whatever understanding the Senator and his wife had about their marriage was not my business, but there were children around."

Although they stopped dating, Jackie continued on occasion to speak to Trudeau on the phone. In 1984, he told her he had become involved with the Canadian actress, Margot Kidder, who is best known for her role as Lois Lane in the 1981 film, *Superman II.*

Reportedly, Jackie later regretted not having married Trudeau.

Months before her own death, Trudeau sent Jackie a copy of his memoirs, which later became a best-seller. "You'll be happy to learn," he wrote, "that I did not put you in it. If I had, it would have been my most glorious chapter. But sometimes, a man must keep his most precious secrets secret. The forbidden romance is always made more enticing than the one played out in public."

José Luís de Vilallonga
Jackie and the Don Juan of 20th Century Spain

Jackie had such a brief fling with the Spanish Grandee, José Luís de Vilallonga, Marquess of Castelbell, that her romance escaped the attention of her other biographers.

Renowned for his indolent air and lanky elegance, he sailed the world on the finest yachts, rubbing shoulders with Aristotle Onassis in Athens, going to the racetrack in Paris with the Rothschilds, or swimming laps in the swimming pool of the Kennedys at their Palm Beach compound. Joseph P. Kennedy, Sr., introduced Vilallonga to JFK and to Jackie.

As Vilallonga later told Truman Capote, "The moment I laid eyes on Jackie, I knew I had to have her."

Tall and handsome, he was already a familiar face to Jackie because he'd co-starred in one of her favorite movies, Truman Capote's *Breakfast at Tiffany's,* which had starred Audrey Hepburn as Holly Golightly. Vilallonga interpreted the character of José de Silva Pereira, the dashing millionaire from Brazil who wants to marry Holly.

José Luís de Vilallonga as he appeared in *Breakfast at Tiffany's*, cast as the Brazilian lover of the character played by **Audrey Hepburn**, Holly Golightly. Vilallonga had a taste for exceptionally beautiful women, numbering not only Audrey, but Jackie among his conquests.

When JFK had to leave Palm Beach and fly back to Washington, Jackie stayed on for another week. She spent a lot of time in the company of Vilallonga, including rendezvous during two separate dinners within his rented villa.

When he was introduced to her, he had immediately attracted her attention by saying, "Like Helen of Troy, your name will live down through the ages. In your time, you will surely topple empires the way Cleopatra did."

As Jackie later told Capote, "No man had ever said that to me before. Surely, he was exaggerating."

"No, my dear," Capote responded. "He speaks only the truth."

Nine years older than Jackie, Vilallonga seemed to have had enough experiences to fill a century or two. She was utterly fascinated hearing about this colorful background. He was not modest in discussions about his past.

To toughen up his sixteen-year-old son, his father, Salvador de Vilallonga y de Cárcer, forced him to join the National Execution Platoon, fatally shooting captured Revolutionary soldiers opposed to the Fascist dictator, Francisco Franco.

"I shot at least one young man a day," he confided to Jackie. "On arguably my finest day, I executed eight young men in the prime of their lives. All these murders made me very confused."

It is not known why Jackie would be attracted to such a man, although both Capote and Audrey Hepburn claimed, "José could literally charm the pants off you."

Perhaps Jackie could forgive Vilallonga because he was only a teenager under the stern control of his autocratic father. Later, he was placed on Franco's enemy list, especially after the publication of his novel, an anti-Franco indictment entitled *The Ramblas End in the Sea* (*Las Ramblas terminan en el mar; 1954*). He was barred from re-entering Spain and was sentenced *in absentia* on a charge of sedition. He told Jackie that the combined total of all his various sentences would define a jail term spanning more than three centuries.

Jackie requested something from him. She wanted to be left out of his string of autobiographies that eventually totaled four. In these volumes, he wrote about his numerous affairs. In Lisbon, before she emigrated to America, Magda Gabor, sister of Zsa Zsa and Eva, had maintained a torrid romance with him.

Villalonga didn't write about all his affairs, claiming it would take ten volumes of documentation and description. "When I lived in Argentina after the war, I didn't claim I was regularly seducing Evita Perón, based on fear that I might be wiped out."

Vilallonga's first marriage (1945-1972) evolved into an international scandal. His wife was the Honorable Essylt-Priscilla Scott-Ellis, the wealthy daughter of Thomas Scott-Ellis, 8th Baron Howard de Walden, one of the richest peers in England. Vilallonga's father had opposed the marriage, claiming that when his daughter-in-law, this former debutante nicknamed "Pip," had joined Franco's forces during the Spanish Civil War, she'd seduced half of the entire National Army of Spain.

After 27 years of marriage, and after Vilallonga had spent his wife's inheritance and sold off her valuable art collection to finance his lavish spending sprees, he filed for divorce.

Forced to find a job, and from a location in Paris, he edited the Spanish version of *Playboy* and also wrote a racy column entitled "Letters from Paris" for the soft-porn scandal weekly, *Interviú*.

After Franco died, Vilallonga returned to Spain, befriending King Juan Carlos and later writing a biography of the monarch.

In a drunken interview given to *Paris-Match* in Paris during the late 1970s, Vilallonga boasted that during the filming of *Breakfast at Tiffany's*, "Audrey couldn't get enough of me. Truman Capote told me I had the most magnificent penis he'd ever seen, and he'd seen a lot of them. Mrs. Kennedy told me that she didn't know how thrilling sex could be until I seduced her one moonlit night in Palm Beach so long ago."

His boasting was viewed as so outrageous that his comments were not published.

Upon his death at the age of 98 in 2007, Jackie was long gone. His obituary in *The London Telegraph* defined him as "a playboy, a wastrel, a fortune hunter, and a bit-part actor."

Vilallonga wrote his own epitaph: *HERE LIES THE DON JUAN OF THE 20TH CENTURY. AT LEAST HIS LOVERS KNOW WHERE HE'S SLEEPING TONIGHT.*

Andrei Voznesensky
Jackie's "Pervert" Russian Poet

When the great Russian poet, Andrei Voznesensky, arrived in the United States for the first time in 1963, he told a reporter, "There are four people I want to meet in America—Marilyn Monroe, Jacqueline Kennedy, Arthur Miller, and Allen Ginsberg."

When his host, Stephen Miller, asked him privately why those four Americans interested him, he replied secretly: "The women to satisfy my Russian cock, the men to fuel my ever-expanding mind."

The famous Russian poet, **Andrei Voznesensky**, as he looked in his later, post-Jackie period.

During his tour of America, the poet functioned as a sort of "unofficial Kremlin cultural envoy," according to *The New York Times.*

Voznesensky helped lift Russian literature out of its state of fear and virtual "serfdom" under Josef Stalin. Nonetheless, the poet frequently got into trouble with Soviet authorities.

Raymond Anderson, writing in *The New York Times,* said his "poetry epitomized the setbacks, gains, and hopes of the post-Stalin decades in Russia. His hundreds of subtle, ironic, and innovative verses reflecting alternating periods of calm and stress as the Communist Party's rule stabilized, weakened, and then, in 1991, quickly disintegrated."

Anderson also wrote: "Creating poetry at a troubling time in Russian history, Voznesensky, like Boris Pasternak, became a persistent foe of literary censorship, and he urged

*I am Goya
of the bare field, by the enemy's
beak gouged
till the craters of my eyes gape
I am grief
I am the tongue
of war, the embers of cities
on the snows of the year 1941
I am hunger
I am the gullet
of a woman hanged whose body
like a bell
tolled over a blank square
I am Goya*

Andrei Voznensensky

the Soviet leadership to end all controls over fiction. But he endeavored to avoid a public collision with the authorities that might have forced him into exile or even doomed him to prison camp."

Before flying to America, Nikita Khrushchev had put Voznesensky on the best-seller list by denouncing him. Born in Moscow in 1933, the son of a professor of engineering, Voznesensky was invited to this event, hosted by the ruling Communist Party, in December of 1962. The Soviet Dictator addressed the gathering, making scathing remarks about Voznesensky. "Just look at this new Boris Paster-

The younger and impassioned **Voznesensky** as he looked when he—how shall we say this diplomatically—helped cultivate Jackie's taste for Russian caviar.

nak! You want to get a foreign passport tomorrow? You want it? And then go away, go the dogs. Go, there! Let starving wild dogs feed on your wasted flesh! I brand you before the world as a pervert."

The poet later said, "Because of this attack, I became more popular than the Beatles."

In Washington, one of Jackie's sometimes lovers, the American poet, Robert Lowell, introduced her to Voznesensky, telling her that "He is one of the greatest living poets in any language." It was Lowell who had also introduced Jackie to some of his works, including "The Triangular Pear," "I Am Goya," and "First Frost." W.H. Auden had translated many of the Russian's poems into English.

Jackie later told Lowell and others that, "I adore his mind and his poetry. I am particularly enthralled by the eccentricity of his metaphors."

After meeting him, she invited him to dinner at the White House. She entertained him there within Kennedy family's private quarters. The president was out of Washington at the time.

Voznesensky was also invited for a "sleepover" in the Lincoln Bedroom. It was Lowell himself, who could get rather miffed at Jackie from time to time, who spread the rumor that Jackie and Voznesensky had had a fling. "What would Abe have thought?" Lowell asked his friends.

That year, Voznesensky went on a tour of the United States, performing to sold-out crowds, reading his poetry in stadiums, concert halls, and university auditoriums.

When Bobby Kennedy was assassinated in Los Angeles in 1968, Voznesensky hastily wrote a poem about his death and sent it to Jackie. But he first had it published in a Moscow newspaper. That reduced the possibility that he might be accused of evading censorship or having an unauthorized contact with a foreigner.

The link between Jackie and the poet might have fallen under the radar screen had it not been for Gore Vidal. In 1987, along with Gregory Peck, Graham Greene, and Norman Mailer, he attended a peace conference in Moscow, where he gave a speech on the origins of the Cold War.

At a reception, he talked to Pierre Trudeau, Yoko Ono, and the economist, John Kenneth Galbraith, who introduced Vidal to Voznesensky.

In his memoirs, Vidal wrote: "This great charmer, Russia's best poet, knew that I knew that (Top Secret) he had fucked Mme Onassis. So every time he could get me to one side, he would ask, wistfully, for news of *her*. Which I gave as best I could."

Later that night, Voznesensky introduced Vidal to Mikhail Gorbachev, who described his recent meeting with President Ronald Reagan. "Your President wanted to know whether, if we are invaded from Mars, would Russia and the United States stand together as allies against the aliens from Outer Space?"

John Carl Warnecke
Lighting an Eternal Flame Under Jackie

Architect John Carl Warnecke is best known today for designing the John F. Kennedy Eternal Flame Memorial Gravesite at Arlington National Cemetery.

His link with the assassinated President dates back to 1941, when he attended Stanford University with a young JFK, who was briefly auditing courses there. Their friendship continued when they attended Harvard, Warnecke studying under Walter Gropius.

The two future lovers of Jackie were a study in contrast. While in California, JFK was thin and sickly, recovering from an illness. Warnecke stood six feet three inches and weighed 215 pounds. He was called "dynamite" when he played football for Stanford at the Rose Bowl. JFK must have looked on in envy.

By the time of the Kennedy administration, Warnecke's reputation as a world class architect had grown immensely. He had designed notable monuments and buildings in both the Modernist and Bauhaus styles, and was an early proponent of contextual architecture.

When he became President, JFK called

Arguably, the noted architect, **John Carl Warnecke**, became the most serious candidate for Jackie's hand in marriage. He fell in love with her, or so he said, when he first danced with her at the British Embassy in Washington during her tenure as First Lady.

upon Warnecke to save the historic buildings surrounding Washington, D.C.'s Lafayette Square, which were in danger of being demolished.

That appointment brought him into contact with Jackie. In February of 1962, Jackie lobbied the General Services Administration to stop the demolition at Lafayette Square. Warnecke later asserted, "I fell madly in love with Jackie when I danced with her at the British Embassy. In October of 1962, with Jackie's endorsement, his plan for a revitalized Lafayette Square was approved.

In March of 1963, in an ominous foreboding of what was to come later that year, JFK and Warnecke visited the President's future grave site at Arlington.

Jackie and Warnecke began to see each other frequently. Since he was working with her on plans for Lafayette Square, no one in the press hinted at any romance occurring between them. "She was full of spirit and a delight to be with," he later said. "She was also as inquisitive as hell, and she showed great interest in my architectural designs."

"The first time I showed her my

John Carl Warnecke *(left figure in top photo)* discussed his architectural plans for Lafayette Square in Washington with **the President**.

He also won the approval of **Jackie** *(lower photo)* with his vast concept for saving the square from demolition. Unknown to JFK at the time, Warnecke had other "designs" for Jackie.

designs for the square, she was thrilled, or so she said," he claimed. "Ironically, she was wearing the same pink Chanel dress suit that she would wear to Dallas on the day of John's assassination. Over a period of months, we saw a lot of each other, more than I could ever have dreamed. One thing led to another. I was free as a bird, having divorced my wife, Grace Cushing, two years earlier."

Guarded by the Secret Service, Jackie once paid a visit to Warnecke at his elegant townhouse on Russian Hill overlooking San Francisco Bay. She also went horseback riding with him one weekend on his 300-acre estate on the Russian River, forty miles north of San Francisco. She was also seen making frequent visits to his townhouse in Georgetown in Washington, D.C.

Robin Duke, the wife of JFK's chief of protocol, later said, "It was obvious that Jackie was very taken with Warnecke. He was an imposing figure of a man and extraordinarily seductive to women. He was also worth millions, or so we thought at the time."

Warnecke later credited Jackie with having saved Lafayette Square from demolition. After that project was wrapped, he became more or less the unofficial architect for the Kennedy family, rejuvenating Teddy's home at Hyannis Port and making vast improvements to Bobby's estate, Hickory Hill, in Virginia.

Tabloid speculation about **John** (the architect) and **Jackie**

Jackie began to invite him to private parties at the White House. "All of us were aware of Jack's womanizing and his neglect of Jackie," Warnecke said. "That worked to my advantage. I always knew when he was going to be out of town. At those times, I visited Jackie frequently. I still don't know to this day if she were in love with me, or was just getting even with Jack for running off with some other dame and leaving her alone at the White House."

After the President was assassinated in November of 1963, Jackie chose Warnecke to design the President's tomb at Arlington. She told him that she wanted an eternal flame at the gravesite. Both he and Jackie agreed that the monument should be simple. Work proceeded under tight secrecy.

Warnecke set about this project, consulting architects, sculptors, painters, landscape architects, stonemasons, calligraphers, and liturgical experts, even meeting with the sculptor Isamu Noguchi.

Finally, in a memo to Jackie, he wrote: "This particular hillside, this flame, this man, and this point in history must be synthesized in one statement that has a distinctive character of its own. We must avoid elements that in later decades might become superficial and detract from the deeds of the man."

On the rainy morning of March 15, 1967, JFK's gravesite was officially opened with little fanfare. The 20-minute ceremony was attended by Lyndon B. Johnson and Jackie.

At this time, according to reports, Jackie was so romantically involved with Warnecke that she was contemplating marriage.

To author Edward Klein, Warnecke recalled the first time he made love to Jackie, at Hyannis Port when Caroline and John Jr. were away. "It was like an explosion. I remember saying to myself, 'What am I doing here? What's happening?' A lot has been written about Jackie being cold. The image is all wrong. There is nothing inhibited or cold about her. All those aspects that made Jackie so delightful—her sense of fun and joy—were also part of her lovemaking."

Jackie and Warnecke had a secret love nest for their trysts, a romantic cottage on Bunny Mellon's property on Cape Cod, a twenty-minute drive from Hyannis Port.

One weekend, Jackie took Warnecke to visit her mother at Hammersmith

Farm outside Newport. "I admired Janet. She was still very attractive, a woman with real sparkle and spirit. I don't think she ever abused Jackie—that was just gossip. She led me upstairs to show me the bed where President Kennedy stayed when he came to visit. 'I want you to get used to sleeping in this bed during your stay with us. It will come in handy when you marry my daughter.' Janet definitely was urging Jackie to accept my proposal of marriage."

After his visit, Janet told her friends, "John is in love with my daughter, and I think it's time for her to contemplate marriage again. All in all, Jack is gone. Unlike Jack, John would be a faithful husband to my daughter."

Early in 1964, Jackie was said to have abandoned her widow's mourning when she threw a party at Manhattan's Sign of the Dove restaurant for John Kenneth Galbraith.

Manhattan society showed up, some of her friends winging in from Palm Beach. Gianni Agnelli flew in from Turin, and figures from the *demimonde* appeared, including Andy Warhol escorting his doomed superstar, Edie Sedgwick.

Jackie had hired "Killer Joe" Piro and his Rock 'n Roll Crazies, and she danced the frug and the jerk with Warnecke. She introduced him to guests as "my *very* special friend, John Carl Warnecke."

During the summer of 1966, Jackie spent time with Warnecke in Hawaii, dividing her time with her former brother-in-law, Peter Lawford. Both Jackie and Lawford had brought along their children.

But before the end of the year, Jackie's relationship with Warnecke came to an abrupt end.

One night he called her from San Francisco. Up to then, she was under the impression that he was a multi-millionaire. On that night, he gave her the bad news, reporting that he was overdrawn at the bank to the tune of a million dollars. She didn't know that anyone could be overdrawn at any bank for a million dollars.

"While I've been with you, all those months working on Lafayette Square, Jack's grave site, the time in Hawaii, I have not been attending to business."

She feared what was coming. He asked her for two million dollars as a means of getting him over his financial predicament. All her life, she had been reared to accept money from men, not to lend men money. She became cold and distant on the phone, rejecting his request.

In 1994, Warnecke, the brilliant third-generation California architect, read that Jackie was dying of cancer in Manhattan. He sent her a Valentine card. Its message was simple: "I still love you."

This rare photo of **The First Lady** in a bathing suit was taken in 1962 during the peak of the Reign of Camelot. Gianni Agnelli was courting Jackie, even though both of them were married. JFK, for appearance's sake, was demanding that Jackie return at once to the White House.

She had other plans, extending her vacation.

Chapter Twenty-One

Jackie Vs. "Rubber Hosa" and The World's Richest Woman

Wife-Swapping Among the Rich, the Powerful, and the Well-Endowed: Jack and Jackie and Rubi and Odile

Left photo above: The first First Lady that the tobacco heiress, **Doris Duke,** ever met was Eleanor Roosevelt who, for some reason, invited her to a West Virginia homestead to visit 500 poor refugee miners. In a full-length mink coat, adorned with diamonds, Duke met the underfed and struggling class. Young children asked for her autograph, thinking she was a movie star.

As First Ladies go, the beautifully dressed **Jackie Kennedy** was more to Duke's liking. One night in Newport, Duke confessed to Jackie, "I must be the last woman in Newport your husband hasn't seduced." She could say that about JFK, but not about Aristotle Onassis. Duke had gotten to Ari long before Jackie.

Right photo above: **Doris Duke** and her controversial but studly husband, **Porfirio Rubirosa** were photographed nightclubbing together at Manhattan's El Morocco. Their marriage lasted only a year, but even after their divorce, Duke often sent a plane to fetch him, "whenever I needed it really bad."

What Duke might never have known is that Jackie had a brief interlude with him in Palm Beach.

483

The patriarch Joseph ("Papa Joe")

was the first within the Kennedy clan to meet and befriend Porfirio Rubirosa, the Dominican diplomat, polo player, and henchman of the notoriously bloodthirsty dictator, Rafael Trujillo.

Joseph had already become friends with the Cassini brothers, both Igor, who wrote a Hearst gossip column under the pen name of "Cholly Knickerbocker," and his older brother, Oleg, who would in time become Jackie's official fashion designer when she was First Lady.

Igor had married Charlene Stafford Wrightsman, the younger daughter of Charles B. Wrightsman, the oil baron and don of New York and Palm Beach society. The Wrightsman estate adjoined the Kennedy compound.

In time, both Oleg and Igor became regular golf partners of Joseph, who introduced them to his sporting son, JFK.

Rubi, as he was nicknamed, became a family friend of both the Kennedys and the Cassini brothers. The playboy became especially close to Oleg.

Perhaps too close, according to gossip bruited around Palm Beach society. Igor privately confirmed rumors that his older brother, Oleg, occasionally gave in to his bisexual impulses and fellated Rubi, who was most generous in dropping his jockstrap for his beloved friend.

Here, **Doris Duke** is seen as she appeared on her wedding day in Paris in 1947. Moments before the ceremony, she had her lawyers coerce Rubi into signing a prenuptial agreement.

Angered at having to do that, he smoked a cigarette throughout the marriage ceremony.

Unique in celebrity autobiography, Oleg described Rubirosa's penis in graphic detail in his book, *In My Own Fashion,* published in 1987.

"Porfirio was an apotheosis, the ultimate playboy, a strange combination—one of the few Don Juans I've ever met who was a man's man *and* a ladies' man. Rubi was an athlete—he played polo and boxed—but he also had the gift of knowing how to talk to women. He was of medium height, well muscled but trim, with rugged good looks…and, of course, he had the most remarkable piece of equipment; he was known for it. A common joke when dining out in those days was to refer to a sixteen-inch pepper mill as 'The Rubirosa.' His

---

Porfirio Rubirosa: The Priapic Dominican Playboy

"Rubi's Monster looks like Yul Brynner in a black turtleneck sweater."
—Jerome Zerbe, society photographer

---

nickname was *Toujours Prêt [always ready]*."

Oleg seemed to have intimate knowledge of Rubi's equipment. He wrote: "There was another, rather exceptional secret about Rubi that directly involved his reputation as a lover and as a man. He suffered from a rare sexual malaise: priapism. He was in an almost constant state of arousal, but unable to be satisfied. He achieved orgasm very rarely, and then only after hours of struggle. He knew that thing of his was a potential meal ticket, and he actually trained to keep it in peak condition. He did exercises. He would drink each day a potion called *pago-pago,* which he said came from the bark of a certain tree in the Dominican Republic; he believed it guaranteed his performance. He claimed to be able to think himself from semitumescence to full sail."

Igor claimed that his brother first became familiar with Rubi's penis one night when Rubi placed a bet with Oleg. The playboy said he could balance a chair with a telephone book on his full erection. Oleg claimed that was impossible. According to Igor, Rubi won the bet that night, and consequently, Oleg practiced the art of deep throating.

Rubi's fourth wife, Barbara Hutton, the Woolworth heiress, seemed to echo those sentiments. "Rubi is the ultimate sorcerer, capable of transforming the most ordinary evening into something of magic. He is priapic, indefatigable, grotesquely proportioned."

Rubi's third wife, tobacco heiress Doris Duke, defined it as "the most magnificent penis I've ever seen," and she'd seen a lot of them.

When JFK married Jackie in 1953, he introduced her to Rubi as part of their first visit to Palm Beach as a married couple.

Rubirosa had a goal that involved marrying the two richest women in the world. After his divorce from Doris Duke, the world's richest woman, he married the Woolworth heiress, **Barbara Hutton**, the world's second-richest.

Their marriage hardly survived the wedding night, but the divorce settlement was mammoth.

In one of the most famous celebrity shots of 1953, **Zsa Zsa Gabor** holds up a wedding picture of Barbara Hutton at the time of her marriage to Porfirio Rubirosa.

"He attacked me and gave me a black eye when I turned down his proposal," she told the assembled reporters. "He's not used to being rejected by women. He admitted to me that he's marrying Hutton for her money. He needs a rich purse to pay off his gambling debts. The marriage will last as long as an ice cream cone dropped on the streets of Las Vegas during a heat wave."

Jackie, who married JFK the same year, followed the scandal with avid interest.

485

"I found Rubi charming and sophisticated," Jackie later told her millionaire friend, Bunny Mellon. "Be careful he doesn't go after you. He's known for seducing women, especially if they're rich. He has an aura of mystery about him, but also one of danger. I think he could charm any woman except a lesbian."

Jackie, however, didn't tell Mellon what actually happened when she was seated next to Rubi at a dinner hosted by Joseph at the Kennedy compound.

Rubi was known for taking a very direct approach with women. Like JFK himself, it didn't matter if the woman were married, even if she were married to a friend.

Midway through the dinner, between courses, he reached under the table for her delicate hand. Very gently, but firmly, he placed it directly on his semi-erect penis.

She later told Igor Cassini, "I didn't know that men's appendages came in that size. I maintained my self-control. I hope I didn't register shock on my face. When the right moment came, I withdrew my hand."

As far as it is known, Jackie made only one other comment about Rubi's legendary anatomy. "Seeing is believing," she told Truman Capote.

"Been there, done that," he responded.

In her diary, she wrote: "Rubi, as he is called, is not a tall man, yet he appears a towering figure. He is not traditionally handsome, but has a kind of Latino beauty—call it rugged good looks. *Confidential* magazine calls him the 'Ding Dong Daddy.' He has a high forehead, is well muscled, with thick lips, high cheekbones, and curly black hair. He seems to evoke a macho camaraderie. Perhaps the Spanish word *tiguerismo* would best describe him. His wardrobe rivals the Duke of Windsor's. I know what should be engraved on his tombstone: *HERE LIES THE WORLD'S MOST EXPENSIVE MALE PUTO."*

***

When Rubi met Odile Bérard, she was only nineteen, the daughter of a well-known physician in Lyon, France. She had launched herself as an actress under the name "Odile Rodin."

Rubirosa's fifth and final marriage was to the French actress, **Odile Rodin**. Despite its turbulence, it was the playboy's most successful, culminating a lifetime of seductions that had ranged from Evita Perón to Jackie herself.

Society had already gossiped about JFK's affair with Rubi's wife.

Although she did not find him particularly handsome, he was mesmerized by her, attracted to her fresh look and her blondish hair, blue eyes, and freckles.

He wanted her to become his fifth wife, and after a whirlwind courtship, she agreed. She traveled with Rubi to Havana, "the wildest city on earth," during its decadent heyday under Cuban dictator Fulgencio Batista. During their visit, there were rumblings in the hills that the guerilla fighter, Fidel Castro, was organizing a revolution.

Rubi had been appointed as Ambassador to Cuba by the Dominican dictator, Rafael Trujillo, his mentor, protector, and employer.

It was in Havana, in 1958, that JFK, although married to Jackie, was indulging in a tour of that city's notorious bordellos, accompanied by his friend, Senator George Smathers, a Democrat from Florida.

Rubi openly bragged to JFK and others that Odile had been the first woman to cure him of his priapism. "I'm now having orgasms like a sixteen-year-old boy jerking off."

Later, JFK told Teddy Kennedy, Smathers, and Chuck Spalding what Rubi had claimed. "This gal sure must have some sexual technique," JFK said. "Wait until Frank Sinatra hears about her."

When Rubi married Odile in 1956, JFK was very impressed, showering attention on her. Jackie did not like her, and warned her husband to stay away.

"I'm sure Rubi wouldn't mind," he said, as if to provoke Jackie. "With me, he has always believed in share and share alike."

Patricia Kennedy and Peter Lawford celebrate their marriage on April 24, 1954, in New York. It would become one of the most unsuccessful marriages in Hollywood. Peter pimped for JFK, finding plenty of stars or starlets left over for himself. Patricia, too, was adulterous.

Peter Lawford *(left)* was photographed with **JFK** sailing off the coast of Hyannis Port during the first year of his presidency.

When he saw this photo, JFK told Peter, "God damn it, it looks like I'm listening to your advice...from you of all people."

Lem Billings, JFK's closest friend, said, "I've never seen Jackie lose her composure with another woman—except when she's around Odile. She was incredibly jealous of her, fearing she was younger and prettier. Jack really set Jackie off. When Odile was around, he had eyes only for Odile. Jackie and I always suffered together. Neither of us were getting enough from Jack."

"Every time I turned around, Odile and Rubi were popping up," Jackie told Billings. "They were thrilled when Jack won the White House in 1960. I guess Rubi figured he could come and go at the headquarters of power around the world."

On New Year's Eve, right before the JFK's inauguration during January of 1961, a major A-list party was staged in Palm Beach.

JFK attended the gala with Jackie, and Rubi showed up with Odile. The two couples were considered the most glamorous in Palm Beach.

During the reign of Camelot, **Frank Sinatra** and Peter Lawford vied for the role of *numero uno* White House pimp. It was a tie.

Jackie in the boudoir loomed in each of their futures.

However, the next morning, Jackie was enraged when she picked up the Palm Beach newspapers. She'd been pushed to the side by the press, who preferred to run a photo of the newly elected president "Twisting" with the young and beautiful Odile. There was no equivalent shot of Jackie dancing with Rubi.

***

On September 24, 1961, Frank Sinatra, along with Patricia Lawford, flew to Hyannis Port aboard Kennedy's plane. With them were Rubi, Odile, and Teddy Kennedy. Disembarking from the Caroline at New Bedford, Frank emerged from the plane with a champagne glass. He ordered cabbies to drive the party to the Kennedy compound, fifty-three miles away.

When they got there, the presidential flag indicated that JFK was already in residence. Jackie had chosen not to come. At Joe Kennedy's house, Peter Lawford was already waiting, and Rose had ordered that the dinner table be set for twenty-six guests.

The following day the party cruised aboard the *Honey Fitz*. Sinatra entertained the party with anecdotes about his recent audience with Pope John XXIII.

"All your friends in Chicago are Italian, too," Peter quipped. His flippant remark was met with an icy stare from Frank.

Jackie was none too happy that Odile had been invited on the yachting trip. Friends had gossiped to her that Odile was having an affair with JFK.

At that point, the White House was trying to distance itself from Frank. Some spin story had to be put out to the press. Supposedly, Frank was in Hyannis Port to work out an agreement with Joe Kennedy about a souvenir recording of the inaugural gala.

When news of that cruise reached the world, President Kennedy was attacked for "hanging out with such unsavory characters as Frank Sinatra, who never met a Mafia boss he didn't like, and Porfirio Rubirosa, the one-time son-in-law of the notorious dictator Rafael Trujillo of the Dominican Republic." One paper even called Rubi "a sleazy international gigolo," referring to his marriages to Doris Duke and Barbara Hutton. Others suspected that he might, acting on orders from Trujillo, have been involved in a strategic murder or two.

The cruise off the coast of Cape Cod lasted only four hours. When it ended, Teddy invited Frank, Peter, and Odile, among others, to go on a tour of the local pubs. Odile said that she was tired and wanted to remain aboard the yacht to catch up on her sleep. JFK also decided to stay behind on the yacht, claiming that he had a lot of papers to read. Rubi said he didn't feel well, and Patricia claimed she'd gotten too much sun on the cruise, and both of them excused themselves from the pub crawl, and disappeared for points unknown on shore.

The next day, Frank asked Rubi how he'd spent the day. In whispered tones, the playboy claimed, "I had a pleasant day fucking Ambassador Kennedy's daughter."

When JFK heard that his sister had been seduced by Rubi, he bluntly asked her, "Is it as big as they say?" His sister refused to answer, but her husband, Peter Lawford, claimed he already knew Rubi's exact measurements.

A member of the staff called Jackie and told her that JFK had had an affair with Odile. Within a day, Jackie, too, arrived on the scene.

During the course of that assemblage, when Rubi and JFK were having a drink on the veranda at Hyannis Port, Jackie was in an upstairs bedroom with the window open, She could clearly hear their voices as they discussed the women they had shared in common. Marilyn Monroe was the first on the list, followed by Joan Crawford, Zsa Zsa Gabor, Lana Turner, Ava Gardner, Susan Hayward, and Jayne Mansfield.

As Jackie later told Igor Cassini, "Jack tactfully left out his seduction of Rubi's wife, Odile, and Rubi tactfully forgot to mention his seduction of Jack's sister, Patricia. Rubi, however, did admit to seducing Athina ("Tina") Onassis, wife of Aristotle Onassis." *[At the time of her death in 1974, Tina was officially designated, thanks to her birth as the unhappy daughter of Greek shipping*

TIna Livanos Onassis Niarchos Blandford

Long before Jackie appeared in his life, Aristotle Onassis, then 40, had married 17-year-old Tina Livanos, daughter of the wealthy shipowner, Stavros Livanos.

Maria Callas, Ari's later mistress, claimed, "It was motivated by business reasons with shadows of child molestation." The wedding took place in 1946 at the Greek Orthodox Cathedral of Saint Trias in Manhattan.

Ari's marriage to the slim, blonde, beautiful, and unstable Tina would be riddled with adulteries, but it would produce two children, Alexander and Christina.

magnate Stavros Livanos, followed by an astonishing set of very wealthy but spectacularly unhappy marriages, as Athina Livanos Onassis Blandford (or Spencer-Churchill) Niarchos.]

***

"Eventually, payback time came for Jackie in Palm Beach," Igor said, enigmatically.

Joe Acquaotta was a driver working the night shift for the Esplanade Limousine Service in Palm Beach. One night, his dispatcher received a call that a passenger needed retrieving in front of the Biltmore Hotel.

Upon his arrival there, Acquaotta noticed a man and woman in the shadows. They were holding hands. When Acquaotto drove up, the man reached for the woman and kissed her passionately. It was almost four o'clock in the morning. She seemed reluctant to break away, but after she managed to loosen herself from his grip, he called her back for a final lingering farewell kiss.

"When she got into the back of my taxi, I saw that it was Mrs. Kennedy," Acquaotta said. "The Kennedys often used our limousine service, and I recognized her at once."

"I said, 'Good morning, Mrs. Kennedy.' At first she didn't answer. Then she snapped back, 'I'm not Mrs. Kennedy.'"

"That was such a ridiculous lie," Acquaotta said. "She was the most photographed face in America. I didn't take her to the Kennedy compound as I usually did. Instead, I delivered her to the oceanfront home of Colonel C. Michael Paul. As I later learned in the papers, that's where she and the President were staying, instead of in the Kennedy compound. I read that JFK had gone to Miami for the weekend and may have gone on a boating trip to the Florida Keys without her, with his good friend and fellow womanizer, Senator George Smathers."

"When I pulled up at the Paul home, she gave me a ten dollar bill for a six-dollar ride. I said 'Good night, Mrs. Kennedy.' She just glared at me and rushed inside the gate."

Later, Acquaotta figured out who the man in the shadows was. It was published in the Palm Beach papers that Rubirosa was occupying a suite at the Biltmore."

In spite of the two romantic couples—Jack and Jackie and Rubi and Odile—more or less switching partners, they were welcomed at the White House until the end of the Kennedy era.

In fact, Odile and Rubi were among the last guests JFK and Jackie entertained together before flying to Dallas in November of 1963.

***

On January 5, 1965, Oleg, in Paris, called Jackie to describe a recent tragedy. Rubi, at the age of 56, had died early that morning when his Ferrari 250

GT had crashed into a chestnut tree after an all-night celebration at Jimmy's nightclub, in honor of winning the *Coupe de France* Polo Cup.

She wanted to know the details. Oleg revealed that he had been with Rubi only an hour before the fatal crash. "He was deeply troubled. He'd just had a bitter fight with Odile. She'd gone out with some other man. All of us at the club were celebrating and drinking champagne from the Championship Cup."

"I looked into Rubi's face. His eyes were dead. The celebration had gone from him—and I knew it involved more than Odile."

"He'd pleaded with me to go away somewhere else, but I begged off, because I had an early morning appointment."

"He poured out his troubles to me—they involved more than Odile: He was in a horrible financial situation and feared he'd have to sell his house."

"It's not the same," Rubi said. "Odile has become impossible."

"He begged me to come home with him and drink until the dawn, but I just couldn't," Oleg said. "Then he confessed what no man likes to confess to another:"

"Standing before you is the world's greatest lover," Rubi said. "But I can't get a god damn erection any more."

"We embraced," Oleg said.

"Please, Oleg, *mon vieux,* come and stay with me."

"I kissed him goodbye, then quickly departed," Oleg said. "Two hours later, I received a call at my suite at the George V. Within an hour of leaving Jimmy's, Rubi, driving at high speed, killed himself. He could hold his liquor. I think he deliberately crashed his car. He knew that the sexual revolution was coming, and he wasn't going to be part of it. From the look in his eyes that early morning at the club, I knew that he knew that the concept of an old-fashioned playboy in a tailored tuxedo holding an exquisitely gowned beauty like Zsa Zsa Gabor in his arms was as dated as Clark Gable."

Jackie didn't say anything for a long time. Then she spoke softly. "It's a terrible thing to live long enough to face the day you go out of style. I desperately hope it doesn't happen to us. Good morning, darling Oleg. Bless Rubi wherever he is right now...on a journey perhaps." Then she put down the phone."

How Elvis Presley Got Involved

Ever since the tobacco heiress, Doris Duke, had become the third wife of Porfirio Rubirosa, Jackie had been fascinated by the exploits of "the richest girl in the world." Her mother, Janet Auchincloss, had once said, "In some ways, Doris had been a role model for Jackie. She envied Doris being born to all that wealth, and wished she'd had a father who, unlike Black Jack Bouvier, might have left her a vast fortune.

Jackie and Doris had more in common than sharing Rubi's magnificent penis. Black Jack Bouvier had taken Duke's virginity when she was only sixteen.

In later life, Jackie and Duke became friends. The tobacco heiress was a friend of Aristotle Onassis, with whom she'd also had an affair.

Jackie had made several visits to Duke's estates in Somerville, New Jersey, and in Newport, Rhode Island.

Jackie always claimed that if she had been born rich, she never would have to be beholden to some man, notably Jack Kennedy or Aristotle Onassis.

Jackie did agree to lend her name and support to the Doris Duke Newport Restoration Foundation, aimed at preserving and restoring colonial structures and homes in the area.

"Apparently, Jackie and Duke avoided two subjects—Rubi and Black Jack," said Truman Capote.

As Duke's biographer, Stephanie Mansfield, wrote: "Jackie was drawn to the super-rich Doris the way she was drawn to Bunny Mellon and Jayne Wrightsman. Jackie and Doris were friendly, if not close friends. Doris had reportedly loaned her the use of a plane to fly between Washington and Newport on occasion, and Doris's cousin, Angier Biddle Duke, served as the Kennedy's Chief of Protocol at the White House."

One night, Duke invited Jackie, along with Lady Bird Johnson and "all the Rockefellers," for a lavish dinner at her Somerville (New Jersey) estate. She called Jackie and told her that she wanted her to come, but didn't want the Secret Service. When Jackie responded that she couldn't come without the Secret Service, Doris relented and allowed them onto her property.

Duke told Truman Capote that her party in honor of Jackie, Lady Bird, and the Rockefellers was so boring that she'd asked them to leave as soon as dinner was over. Capote relayed Doris's words and point of view to Jackie with a certain relish and glee.

Jackie once again admitted to friends that the only reason she kept Capote in her life was as a means of keeping her abreast of the latest gossip. He was also a font of information about Duke.

From Duke's estate in Hawaii, Capote provided Jackie with even more tantalizing gossip.

Doris Duke developed a fixation on **Elvis Presley** after seeing him shirtless in a movie, *Flaming Star* (1960). She was said to have seen all of his movies, some more than once.

To Truman Capote, she collectively summarized all the plots of his films: "A Southern boy beats up a guy and then sings to him."

When they came together, she was a ripe 55, Elvis a mere 32.

Truman reported that in Hawaii, Duke had entertained both Elvis Presley and himself at a private dinner with the full realization that they represented an "odd couple" of mismatched guests. Unknown to the world, Doris, 55, had developed a romantic fixation on Elvis, 32. They both belonged to the Self-Realization Fellowship *[an organization dedicated to enhancing awareness about the possibility of attaining a direct personal experience of God]* in Los Angeles. Each of them maintained a loose allegiance to the same fashionable guru *[the Paramahansa Yoganandi],* and both of them adored black soul music.

What Truman didn't tell Jackie was that he had discussed her with Elvis. "She's my closest friend, and she has a secret crush on you," Capote told Elvis. "I can arrange for you to have a rendezvous with Jackie if you want to fuck her."

To Jackie, Capote presented a very different scenario, claiming that Elvis had told him that he was the one with the crush on Jackie. "If you'd like to meet him, I can set up a rendezvous for the two of you."

"The idea, of course, is absurd, although I have a certain interest in him," Jackie said. "Elvis is, after all, an American original. I found him very sexy in the 50s, although he doesn't sing my kind of music."

There were rumors that Capote actually did arrange for Elvis to meet Jackie—at least that's what he claimed. He'd managed to pull off a meeting between Jackie and Marilyn Monroe, so why not Elvis?

Even President Richard Nixon could not turn down Elvis' request to visit him in the Oval Office. The singer had that kind of awesome popularity at the time.

***

In June of 1973, Onassis invited Duke, Jackie, and John Jr. to sail in the Caribbean, stopping first at a resort long associated with the Rockefellers *[Caneel Bay, on St. John in the U.S. Virgin Islands]* before cruising on to Haiti.

Doris was with Leon Amar, her swarthy young Moroccan decorator, twenty-seven years her junior. Jackie was surprised that she'd taken Amar as a lover. She had worked with him on the restoration of the White House.

Amar later claimed that "Doris was green with jealousy of Jackie, though they remained friends on the surface. She sometimes tried to dress like Jackie, although the former First Lady was younger and far more beautiful. One time, they showed up wearing the same clothes—black tops, identical tan slacks, and voodoo medallions from Haiti along with Hermès scarves on their head and Gucci loafers."

Also on board was Ibrahim ("Bobby") Farrah, a young Lebanese dancer who was giving Duke private lessons. She urged Farrah to instruct Jackie in Middle Eastern dance.

Farrah later said, "Doris was fascinated by Jackie and wanted to know what made her tick. I don't think she ever found out. Jackie was very mysterious. She'd had all these incredible experiences but told very little about herself. Ari liked Doris because both of them considered themselves connoisseurs of art, but I felt Jackie knew more about art than the two of them."

Both Farrah and Amar observed close at hand that the marriage of Jackie and Onassis was becoming unglued. At one point, Onassis left the *Christina,* taking a flight from Port-au-Prince to Paris. A rumor spread that he was flying for a rendezvous with his mistress, the opera diva, Maria Callas.

493

After Onassis returned and at dinner aboard the *Christina,* he asked Jackie in front of his fellow guests if she'd agree to obtain a Haitian divorce.

"If you'll divorce me in Port-au-Prince, it'll kill those rumors that you married me for my money," Onassis told her. "A week after the divorce, I'll remarry you. That will show the bastards who spread tall tales about you being a gold-digger."

Jackie said nothing, but rose from her chair and returned to her cabin.

During the day, the guests noticed how John Jr., amused himself. The *Christina* was well stocked, and rickety old boats filled with Haitians often surrounded the yacht begging for money or food. John Jr. would toss them cartons of cigarettes or bottles of wine. On a few occasions, he threw some of Onassis' clothes and shoes overboard.

Of course, Jackie returned to New York without divorcing Onassis. She didn't believe him when he promised he'd remarry her. "I wasn't falling for that line," she told Bunny Mellon and others. "I took a vow 'till death do us part,' and I'm living up to that."

Chapter Twenty-Two

Capote Vs. "Jackie Oh! and La Principessa"

The Tormented Saga of Capote's Lost Friendship With America's Most Famous Sisters

The two fashion plates of Camelot, **Jackie** *(left)* and her sister, **Lee Radziwill,** popularized "the Jackie look," walking the streets in their well-tailored suits made with the best of fabrics and, as always, those white gloves.

The older sister had to ignore or at least forgive Lee for sleeping with both of her husbands.

Author **Truman Capote** became a some-times confidant of Jackie's and intimate friends with Lee. But, as each sister painfully learned, gossipy Capote was not anyone to keep secrets, at least not for long. Either in his writings or on television, he ended up exposing both sisters with rather vicious caricatures.

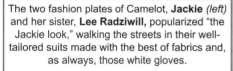

Truman Capote, the controversial novelist, first met Jackie at a party in New York City during her brief stint in the late 1940s (prior to her marriage to JFK) working for *Vogue*. The writer and the student found each other amusing. Capote later claimed that at the time of their inaugural meeting,

Jackie was considering the pursuit of three possible careers: As a fashion editor or perhaps a photographer's model; the pursuit of Hollywood stardom; and finally, or marriage to a rich and famous man. "Obviously, she went for the third choice," Capote said.

When he'd first met Jackie, she complimented him on his novel, *Other Voices, Other Rooms*. "That won me over to her side," he said. "In those days, I divided people into two groups—those who had read my novel and those who had not."

Capote's friendship with Jackie survived her marriage to John Kennedy.

At first, it would seem that the Congressman from Massachusetts and the author from Alabama would have little in common: Capote feared that the more macho Kennedy might be put off by his gayness. Not at all. JFK and Capote struck a common ground: Both were interested in gossip, the more salacious, the better.

Jackie and JFK were avid movie fans, and Capote always had plenty to tell about the private lives of the stars. They could ask him a question such as, "Is Cary Grant really gay?" Capote would paint a detailed picture, including naming Grant's male lovers—and not just Randolph Scott.

Two bathing beauties of 1935 **Jackie** *(left)* and her younger sister, **Lee**, each showing hints of the beauty they'd each later be famous for.

When JFK became president, Jackie invited Capote on several occasions to the White House. Even when she couldn't see Capote, she often called him.

To her surprise, so did the President. He told Jackie, "Sometimes, when I want to forget the Cuban Missile Crisis, I call Cary Grant just to hear the sound of his voice. Or I might call Judy Garland and ask her to sing 'Over the Rainbow' for me. Or else, I'll call Truman just to hear the latest and most outrageous stories such as Fred Astaire getting caught in a sex act with a ten-year-old boy."

The President would often test the efficiency of White House telephone operators who bragged that they could get anybody in the world on the phone. JFK tested them one boring afternoon.

"Get me Truman Capote."

Within fifteen minutes, the operators had traced him to Palm Beach, where he was the guest of Gloria Guinness, who had an unlisted phone number.

In New York, during February of 1964, about three months after the as-

"For Lee Radziwill, 'The Divine Jackie' is a Tough Act to Follow"

—Truman Capote

sassination of her husband in Dallas, Jackie maintained a busy calendar but often managed to fit in Truman.

One weekend in Manhattan, she checked into the Carlyle, the deluxe hotel where JFK had staged so many of his sexual trysts, including one with Lana Turner.

Jackie's schedule for that Saturday read: "Breakfast with Irwin Shaw; lunch with Truman Capote, dinner with Pamela Harriman, and evening with Bobby Kennedy. Scheduled visit with Bobby to see the ailing Herbert Hoover at the Waldorf Astoria."

Bennett Cerf, Capote's publisher at Random House, claimed that Jackie often visited Capote when he lived in an apartment at the United Nations Plaza. Bobby Kennedy also maintained an apartment in the same building.

By that time, Capote knew Jackie so well, he provided her with a set of keys to his apartment. One afternoon, when he came home, he found her beside the large window in his living room working on a sketch. "It was the second anniversary of her husband's death, and she was still in deep mourning."

"We stayed up and talked until five o'clock that morning, when she left with the Secret Service. In the meantime, we killed off a few bottles of champagne."

"I helped her on with her coat, a Balenciaga. But I noticed she carried a Chanel handbag. I chastised her for that because Coco, that reformed Nazi, had attacked Jackie as 'the worst dresser on any continent.' What a stupid, ridiculous statement."

When Gore Vidal heard about Jackie's visit to Capote's apartment, he sarcastically remarked: "I'm sure Jackie first visited Bobby Kennedy to get fucked, then drifted upstairs to see Capote for some *après sex* girl talk."

Stephen Smith, the New York businessman who married Jean Kennedy, once said, "Jackie was very fond of gay men and liked being with them. In many ways, she found them more devoted to her than straight men or other women, who were likely to be jealous."

"1968, the year Jackie had expected Bobby Kennedy to be elected president, was the last complete year of my friendship with Jackie," Capote said. "I often went with her on shopping sprees. She was a world class shopper. Once, she spent $150,000 in one store, charging everything to Ari *[Aristotle Onassis]*"

"She would barge into a store with me and order anything she fancied without asking the price. We went to a Valentino show in Paris, and she practically bought the entire collection."

"At the United Nations Plaza, I gave a party for her," he said. "Lee came, but my dog in the bedroom chewed up her sable coat. Lee exploded but Jackie soothed her. 'Go tomorrow morning and buy another one and charge it to Ari,' Jackie said. 'He'd love to pay for it.'"

***

Capote's friendship with both Lee and Jackie began to fizzle in 1965 after his *La Côte Basque* was published in *Esquire* magazine. In it, Capote's character of Lady Coolbirth evaluates the patrons at Henri Soulé's renowned restaurant, La Côte Basque, on East 55th Street in Manhattan.

Truman later admitted "that Lady Coolbirth is me! Her conversation is precisely the kind I might have had."

In *La Côte Basque,* Lady Coolbirth (aka Capote himself) observes Lee dining at table with her sister. "If I were a man, I'd fall for Lee myself," Lady Coolbirth claims. "She's marvelously made, like a Tanagra figurine."

Jackie was described as "very photogenic, but the effect is a little unrefined, exaggerated."

***

Princess Lee Radziwill first met Truman Capote at a chic dinner party in New York in the late 1950s. These two celebrities had grown up in different worlds, but "a spark was ignited between us," Truman later recalled. "Lee reminded me of Holly Golightly in *Breakfast at Tiffany's.*"

His fanciful stories amused her as they were told with the wit and charm that he'd put on paper in his published works. From the beginning, she recognized his tendency to exaggerate, which she defined as a *"folie d'imagination."*

Lee recognized that Truman's ticket into the world of the rich and famous was "because he had a talent to amuse."

Michael Tree, a Britisher whose wit was once compared to that of Oscar Wilde, said, "Capote is the rich man's Pekingese."

Lee put it differently: "Truman knew that everyone expected so much of him. He had to entertain them, though at times it became exhausting for him."

From that dinner on, a friendship slowly developed, beginning as a social diversion that would in time turn into a serious friendship. Each of them became the other's confidant, sharing potentially "dangerous" secrets about their private lives. In the months and years to come, they would travel together to exotic locales.

Initially, Jackie resented her sister's burgeoning friendship with Capote, as she regarded him as one of her special confidants. Jackie didn't want Capote carrying tales between the two sisters and reporting to the world at large the indiscreet remarks one sister might make about the other.

Lee was married to a Polish prince, Stanislas Radziwill, a naturalized British subject, which meant he had renounced all claims, past and future, to his title. Lee, however, insisted on being addressed as "Princess" anyway.

Stas Radziwill *(left)* with **Oleg Cassini** in 1963, discussing their favorite subject: the indiscretions of his wife Lee and Jackie Kennedy.

Apparently, Stas, as he was known, let her wander around the world on her own and seemed to overlook her infidelities, which Truman learned a lot about.

He soon began to consider himself one of Jackie's intimate friends, but, as she told her intimates, "Whereas I always know to keep him at arm's length, Lee seems to be taking him to her bosom."

On February 9, 1962, Truman wrote Cecil Beaton. "Had lunch with Princess Lee Radziwill. My God, how jealous she is of Jackie. I never knew. Understand her marriage is all but *finito*."

During the summer of 1966, Truman flew to Lisbon and was driven south to the little port and tourist resort of Setúbal, where Lee was vacationing with Stas and her children.

The French actress, Leslie Caron, was also vacationing there. "Lee and Truman were like two birds of a feather flocking together," Caron recalled. "Although very different, they seemed to share the same vision about many things. Truman liked to tell naughty stories that were fascinating in a bizarre kind of way."

On another occasion, Truman and Lee sailed together along the Dalmation coast of Yugoslavia aboard the luxurious yacht of the Fiat heir, Gianni Agnelli.

They also flew to Morocco, where they were driven through the northern outskirts of the Sahara to the deluxe Hotel Gazelle d'Or in Taroudant, where both of them relished the rose water baths.

It was in Morocco that Truman suggested a career change for Lee. He began to tell people, "I'm in love with Lee Radziwill."

As Cecil Beaton explained, "I'm sure he did not mean that in a sexual way. But he was awed by Lee's fame, her connections, her wit, and style. Instead of saying, 'I'm in love with her,' he should have said, "I'm charmed by her.' That would be more accurate."

"We had so many differences I didn't think he could go on imagining that he was in love with me," Lee said. "We had cozy times that were brotherly and sisterly. The whole point of our relationship was that Truman had this grand passion for me. I knew he loved and adored me, as I did him."

Truman pushed me into acting," she said. "I did not have a burning desire for it."

The suggestion that she become an actress occurred while they were sitting under a palm tree in the Sahara as part of their trip to Morocco. "You could completely divorce yourself from Jackie and her image if you became an actress—perhaps a movie star. Jackie herself once told me she'd dreamed at one time of becoming a movie star instead of a political wife."

He even named what he thought would be the perfect vehicle for Lee to launch her stage career, Philip Barry's *The Philadelphia Story,* the brilliant but talky tale of a society girl who yearns for a down-to-earth romance and is torn between her ex-husband and a fast-talking reporter who falls in love with her. Both of them had seen the 1940 George Cukor film that starred Cary Grant, Katharine Hepburn, and James Stewart. They'd also seen its lackluster 1956 remake, a Hollywood musical *(High Society)* starring Grace Kelly, Frank Sinatra, and Bing Crosby. It had been Grace's last acting role before she married a real prince, unlike Lee's second marriage to "Prince" Stanislas Radziwill.

The leading female character within *The Philadelphia Story's* original theatrical version, Tracy Lord, a high-spirited *divorcée*, eventually returns to her ex-husband after her fleeting romance with a newspaperman.

Perhaps motivated by the desire to keep her co-dependent on him and his vision, Truman had carefully planned the structure and phases of his persuasive efforts, having included within his luggage a copy of the Barry play. Staying up late that night to read it, Lee, the next morning, did not think it was the right vehicle for her. "I feel absolutely *nothing* in common with the character of Tracy Lord. She has none of the feelings I understand, of sadness, of despair, or of knowing loss."

Capote, however, could be very convincing, and he still had enough clout to get her cast in the lead in a revival of the play scheduled to open in Chicago for a month-long run beginning on June 20, 1967.

Truman was able to get Lee cast in the lead because the Kennedys—after JFK's assassination in Dallas and before RFK's downfall in Los Angeles—were still perceived as America's Royal Family.

When Truman pitched the idea of casting Lee to the producers in Chicago, they recognized that she had no experience, but felt she'd be able to pull off the role because her personal history and well-heeled background seemed to have paralleled—as a form of type casting—the fictional life of Tracy Lord herself.

"Let's face it," one of the producers said. "It's a play about an attractive, spoiled, ultra-privileged, Eastern Seaboard post-debutante. Of course, we'd have preferred Jackie herself for bigger box office."

Once she flew back to London, Lee became totally committed to the role, taking it most seriously, even hiring an acting coach. At one point, she rented an empty London theater as a means of getting the feeling of actually appearing on stage during rehearsals.

She also took three trips to Paris to meet with designer Yves Saint Laurent, who was creating a spectacular stage wardrobe for her, in a production deliberately accessorized (some said over-accessorized) with many costume changes. Lee seemed to sense that most of the women in the audience would be coming to gape at her gowns more than at any drama unfolding on stage.

The backers of the play in Chicago wanted to advertise her name as "Princess Lee Radziwill," but she adamantly refused, ordering them instead to bill her as "Lee Bouvier."

To his closest friend, Cecil Beaton, Capote tried to explain why he was thrusting Lee so forcefully onto the stage. "Hopefully to make a name for herself."

"When they were growing up, Lee was the pretty one, getting all the compliments. Jackie was viewed as that bookworm in the corner. But then the spotlight shifted. Jackie became one of the most beloved women in the world thanks to her marriage to JFK. Forevermore, Lee was destined to live in Jackie's long shadow, and she resented it. Lee once lamented to me, 'I've done nothing and Jackie is virtually the Queen of America.'"

Then, to Beaton, Truman made a ridiculous confession: "Ours is the story of Pygmalion. I will make her a work of art, shaping her destiny, molding it, perfecting it, the way a sculptor applies the chisel to a marble statue. She's an extraordinary girl who will create an identity of her own, and eventually surpass her older sister, who may—just may—spend the rest of her life in widow's weeds attending memorials to John F. Kennedy."

Many disappointing months later, Truman was the first to admit that his forecast to Beaton had been spectacularly wrong.

Before her marriage, Jackie had briefly entertained an ambition about becoming an actress herself, and consequently, she could hardly criticize Lee about her decision to appear on stage in *The Philadelphia Story*. Knowing that Truman was behind Lee's move, Jackie chastised him instead: "If Lee falls on her face—and she is likely to—I will be ridiculed in the press more than she is. I think you're luring her into a potential trap."

But to Lee, Jackie sounded a different note, as she listened to her younger sister tell her that "Noël Coward is giving me tips as an actress. In addition to Truman, Rudi *[A reference to their mutual friend, Rudolf Nureyev]* is also advising me. George Masters is flying in from Hollywood to do my makeup, Kenneth from New York to style my hair, gowns by Yves Saint Laurent."

In Chicago, the director, Sidney Breese, jokingly asked Truman, "When you introduce me to the Princess, am I supposed to curtsy?"

Robert Thomson, who had been cast in the play as Tracy Lord's father, said, "At first, I didn't recognize the figure of that little man sitting in shadows in the back row of the Ivanhoe. He had on a fedora, pulled down to conceal his face. Someone told me that was Truman Capote overseeing our rehearsals."

"That guy knew acting talent, I'm sure, but he seemed blind where Lee was concerned," Thomson claimed. "After he made himself known to the cast, he sat closer to the stage. He would applaud virtually every time Lee let out a fart—I'm speaking symbolically here. In that squeaky little voice, he'd proclaim, 'Oh, Lee, that was wonderful, I mean really, really wonderful. You're perfect, oh so right. *Yesss, yessss,* and *yessss* again. You're such a dear. You're going to wow them.'"

German-born John Ericson, who was seven years older than Lee, was cast as her handsome leading man. She'd seen him play a pianist in love

John Ericson had a great body and didn't mind showing it off to magazine photographers. On more than one occasion, he even flashed "the full Monty."

After starring opposite Elizabeth Taylor and Grace Kelly, he was assigned Lee Radziwill as a leading lady. He was not impressed.

with Elizabeth Taylor in the soap opera, *Rhapsody,* in 1954. She'd also gone to see Grace Kelly in *Green Fire,* also in 1954, in which Ericson played her no-good brother.

Ericson was not impressed with Lee. "The play was just put on to take advantage of her famous name. I've never worked with anyone as unprofessional as she was. At one point, I became so exasperated with her I told her, 'You've got a lot to learn about acting.' Brother, did that piss her off, but it was true. I shouldn't say this, but I found the Princess a real airhead. Behind her back, the rest of the cast, all professionals, were saying, 'Come and see the freak show staged by Truman Capote in perhaps some gay mischief scheme."

Jackie turned down Truman's invitation to fly to the opening night at the Ivanhoe Theater in Chicago. As Truman cattily remarked, "Jackie has decided, conveniently so, to be out of the country."

When opening night came, Jackie was with her son, John Jr., and Caroline in Waterford, Ireland, on a private holiday. They were the guests of Murray and Charlotte McDonnell and their eight children at their Regency mansion. However, Jackie sent Lee a cable with good wishes on her opening night, and she arranged for a small Battersea enamel gift box, originally made in the 1700s, to be delivered as a gift to Lee's dressing room.

Right before opening night, George Masters, Hollywood's leading makeup artist, flew in to "put a face on the Princess." He got off to a bad start, mocking the gown she was wearing from Yves Saint Laurent. It was in shocking pink, purple, and chartreuse. "Even the gaudy Supremes wouldn't wear this drag," he told her.

Later he told the director, Breese, "Capote didn't ask himself a basic question: 'Can the Princess act?'"

To complicate matters, Zsa Zsa Gabor arrived at the Ambassador East Hotel, where Lee and Truman were staying in separate suites. She was going to appear in a play after Lee had closed in hers. Zsa Zsa requested the best suite in the house, only to be told that it had been booked by Aristotle Onassis for Lee.

In the lobby, Zsa Zsa threw a fit, demanding that the manager evacuate Lee to make room for her. Truman was called and he rushed down to the lobby to confront Zsa Zsa.

"Let Lee have her moment in the sun," he told Zsa Zsa. "You're already established as one of the world's greatest actresses, but she wants this chance to escape from Jackie's shadow. I'll move out of my suite

Aristotle Onassis had booked the best suite in Chicago for his mistress, Lee Radziwill, but **Zsa Zsa Gabor** arrived in town and demanded it for herself.

To the rescue came Truman Capote, who "song and danced" himself into the Hungarian diva's graces, giving her his bed instead.

and make room for you. It's as good as Lee's suite."

Zsa Zsa seemed flattered and agreed. He escorted her back to his suite. She later recalled, "Before he packed his clothing, he insisted on doing a number of dances for me, to the music coming from his phonograph. At one point, he danced, singing he was 'going to wash that man right out of my hair' from *South Pacific.* I knew the song well. Once, George Sanders was going to star in that play, and he sang it endlessly around the house."

In a call to Jackie, Capote delighted in tantalizing her with this anecdote about Zsa Zsa, since he knew that Jackie resented Zsa Zsa for having once seduced JFK.

***

Before opening night, Lee was a nervous wreck. Throughout the ordeal, Truman had nursed her through nights of nervousness, fatigue, and insomnia. She later praised "his friendship, his loyalty, and his caring when I needed bolstering."

Reporters from all over the world were flying in for what Lee claimed "Was to see me face a massacre."

The big draw, of course, was Jackie, since word had leaked that she would make a surprise appearance. Every journalist wanted to learn about Jackie's reaction to her sister's debut on the stage.

Truman said, "We never expected all this attention, all the press scrutiny, all the famous names such as Rudolf Nureyev and Margot Fonteyn booking seats." Even though he said that, surely he wasn't that naïve. At the time, Lee Radziwill was one of the most talked-about women in the world, with the power to fill up a small neighborhood theater on Chicago's seedy North Side.

On opening night, Lee waited, "a mass of nerves," for Masters to show up to do her makeup. The stage hands claimed that he showed up drunk and fell down backstage, spilling the contents of his makeup kit. "Hell, there goes the face of Princess Radziwill."

When she ascertained his condition, she asked an assistant to do her face.

The critics were more or less unanimous in their evaluation that A STAR IS NOT BORN.

Critic Chauncey Howell, who had flown in from New York, wrote: "Miss Radziwill delivered her first lines in an unmistakable Miss Porter's lockjaw. She looked gorgeous but seemed ill at ease. The acting was amateurish, stock company level. Her performance stayed at consistently wooden levels. Even though she can't act, she is gosawful beautiful."

Instead of doing a tomahawk job on Lee, two reviewers were kind, as if searching for something nice to say. One critic even acknowledged her for knowing her lines. The critic for the *Chicago Sun-Times* claimed that Lee "laid an egg—but a golden one."

Erika Slezak, one of the supporting actors, said, "Lee's famous friends were flying to Chicago. But the regular audience was coming for only one reason.

They hoped to see a carbon copy of Jackie on stage. They were sorely disappointed."

Everyone wondered, "Will Jackie show up in the audience?"

"I once asked Lee about Jackie," Slezak claimed. "The hairs on Lee's arms stood up."

Truman did not give up so easily. During any free time available to him in Chicago, he worked on the script for a teleplay of John van Druten's romantic comedy, *The Voice of the Turtle*. It had been made into a movie with Ronald Reagan playing a lonely soldier who falls in love with Eleanor Parker.

Lee got her own revenge on Chicago. When she confronted a reporter in New York, she said, "What did it matter? Chicago is merely a small, out-of-the-way town."

Lee's Acting Staggers Onward

"Truman, You're Subjecting My Sister to Ridicule"
—Jackie Kennedy

"Jackie Is Such a Cow"
—Truman to Columnist Liz Smith

By the end of the run of *The Philadelphia Story,* Truman had completed a rough draft of his teleplay, *Voice of the Turtle*. He delivered it to TV producer David Susskind, who telephoned him two days later with the intention of rejecting it. But in a conversation that managed to both reject one teleplay and hold out the promise of another, Susskind discussed how intrigued he was with the idea of "casting Jackie's sister in a play. But instead of *Turtle* as the appropriate vehicle, I'd like to see her star in a remake of Gene Tierney's *Laura*. I'm sure you've seen it. With Lee, we could get top actors to play the Clifton Webb and Dana Andrews roles."

After a call to Lee, who voiced her approval of the idea, Capote, in haste, wrote a new version, suitable for television, of the classic film, *Laura,* the 1944 *film noir* that had originally been directed by Otto Preminger.

Laura had been one of Jackie's favorite films, even though Tierney had once been the mistress of JFK. She'd wanted him to

When Gore Vidal saw this picture, he wrote: **"Hell's Angels: Lee Radziwill and Truman Capote**, having just received instructions from the Lord of the Flies, gleefully surface to do his work."

marry her, but he turned her down. Reportedly, Jacked looked more kindly on Tierney than on other movie stars with whom JFK had been intimate.

"Gene is so tragic," Jackie had told Lem Billings. "Her child born handicapped. I honestly would prefer losing a child, as I did Patrick *[1963]* to having one that was handicapped."

Susskind had reservations about Lee, telling Truman, "She's not a good actress, but maybe in the small box of TV, she'll glimmer and gloss."

Truman submitted a two-hour "movie of the week" adaptation of *Laura,* for which he was paid $50,000. Rehearsals began in London during the autumn of 1968.

On a $600,000 budget, Susskind was able to hire some of the most famous stars of the 1960s, including George Sanders, Farley Granger, Arlene Francis, and Robert Stack. Later, Susskind told Truman, "I made a mistake hiring these veterans. They were so good, they showed up Lee's inadequacies."

As it turned out, none of the performers, except for Lee, liked the script. Rewrites were ordered, but Truman refused to do them.

Lee began to falter. She was considered so bad that Susskind considered replacing her.

Lee alienated Granger after a necking scene with Stack. Not knowing that her mike was on, she said, "Farley kisses well, but you are so much better."

Stack was heard to respond, "That's because I'm not gay."

As Granger remembered it, "We tried to make a Princess look like an actress, and we failed. From the beginning, we knew it was a vanity project, compliments of one Truman Capote."

Granger hung out every night with "my drinking buddy," Arlene Francis. Out of courtesy, he invited Lee to dinner one evening. "She spent the evening lambasting Truman for not showing up for rehearsals. Later that night, we tried in vain to reach him by phone. No answer. I think he'd planted a spy on the set, and he knew that a disaster was imminent."

The director finished taping *Laura* on October 26, 1967, with a TV premiere set for January 24. In December, Susskind threw a preview party, inviting Jackie, who didn't show. Many famous guests, in-

Robert Stack in 1960. During rehearsals, he amused Lee with tales of the days back in 1940 when he and a JFK went on "celebrity poontang" hunts in Hollywood.

George Sanders observed Lee's attempts at acting. "I'm used to bad actresses, darling," he told the producer. "After all, I was married to Zsa Zsa Gabor."

Arlene Francis recalled, "I was delighted that Radziwill couldn't act. Susskind enlarged my role to fill up the slack."

cluding the likes of Ingrid Bergman and Johnny Carson, did attend. Bergman and Carson left after only fifteen minutes.

"As my guests saw the film, I watched Truman's face," Susskind said. "His droopy, sad look said it all. He realized that promoting *Laura* for the Princess was a big mistake—initially, his mistake, and then my mistake for listening to him."

Steven M. L. Aronson, the publisher and author, said, "Truman thought *Laura* would soar and take off—a private jet. Such a fiasco that vehicle turned out to be—like an unmechanized wheelchair tethered to the ground."

For the TV premiere, Lee and Stas invited Jackie and her children, Caroline and John Jr., to their apartment in New York. Jackie was most gracious and rather reserved, though complimentary, at the end. John and Caroline were surprised to see their aunt "making love to Robert Stack and Farley Granger on the screen."

Late that night, Jackie called Truman and accused him of subjecting Lee to ridicule. "People are mocking her and making horrible fun—and it's all your fault, some weird game you were playing!"

Before he could respond, she slammed down the phone.

The TV reviews were more hostile than those generated by the Chicago critics. John Gould, writing in *The New York Times*, said, "Laura was reduced to a stunning clotheshorse upon whom no discernible thespian demands were made."

Time found that Lee was "only slightly more animated than the portrait of *Laura* that hung over the mantle."

One critic wrote, "She was not *Laura*, she was Lee Radziwill. Another reviewer called the movie, "an exercise in theatrical frustration, and yet another denounced *Laura* as "Truman Capote's folly."

Gore Vidal snidely suggested that Truman would have been better off luring retired First Ladies, Eleanor Roosevelt and Bess Truman, into films. "Eleanor would have been marvelous in those Ethel Barrymore roles, and Bess

ONE OF THOSE HORRIBLE ON-STAGE MOMENTS:

Farley Granger, who's trying to make his attraction to **Lee Radziwill** look convincing, embracing Lee, who's trying to make her acting look convincing

Lee Radziwill taking a cigarette break with her producer, **David Susskind**. He had friendly connections with the Kennedys and did not want to fire his star outright. Instead, he instructed the director to make rehearsals so brutal for her that she'd quit.

Valiantly, she handled the assaults and carried on.

would have made a divine Ma Kettle, replacing Marjorie Main."

All of this bad press infuriated Jackie, because every article included a reference to the younger, "failed," sister of the more famous and successful Jackie Kennedy.

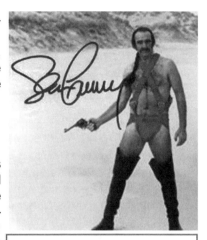

***

Months later, Lee was reportedly furious to read that her performance in *Laura* had destroyed her acting career. "Not at all," she said. Euan Lloyd, a British producer, considered her for a role in *Shalako,* a western set in 1880 New Mexico, although actually scheduled for shooting in a similar landscape environment in Spain. The film was to star Sean Connery. When Lee bowed out, her role went to Brigitte Bardot.

If Lee had been cast in *Shalako*, one wonders what Jackie-Oh would have thought, considering the dress code the directors imposed on **Sean Connery**.

A role in George Kelly's *The Torch Bearers,* with Cornelia Otis Skinner and Maureen Stapleton at the Phoenix Dinner Theater was offered, but Lee turned it down. Roman Polanski also offered her a small role in *Rosemary's Baby* (1968), but Lee rejected that, too.

Lee was embarrassed that Jackie had read her bad reviews, and called her sister every time she received another film offer. Much to Jackie's reported relief, Lee didn't appear in any of the roles she was offered.

When Liz Smith heard that Capote had agreed to write the screenplay for *Laura,* only if Lee had been cast, the columnist called it "old fashioned Hollywood-writer blackmail at its best."

She sought out Capote for an interview, on the pretense of asking about Lee. Of course, what Smith really wanted was "the dirt" on Jackie.

"Truman didn't really give me much dirt on Jackie, other than saying that compared to Lee, Jackie was just a cow," Smith was quoted as saying. "He had nothing but praise for Lee, however.

"She is fragile, ethereal, lovely, smart, beautiful, and witty," he said.

Later, his raves degenerated into blistering attacks.

When Capote appeared on Susskind's TV talk show, he spoke of Lee and her performance in *Laura.* "Lee got much tougher scrutiny than she would have otherwise because she was the whipping post for the underside of the public's feelings toward Jackie. We've got to admit that we had not foreseen the extent to which no matter what Lee did, the press was going to come down on her like hell because they really wanted to say nasty things about Jackie and never could at that time because Jackie was still the widow lady, a little saint. Frankly, I told Lee, 'the dogs bark, but the caravan moves on.'"

"How Could Jackie Betray Me Like This?
I Was Going to Marry Aristotle Onassis."

—Lee Radziwill

Over the years, Capote had learned some of Lee's most personal secrets, and in a prolonged series of small, gossipy betrayals, he entertained his beautiful "swans" with stories of her love affairs and her humiliations. He literally dined out claiming she'd had an affair with her sister's husband when JFK was president. Truman told the story in such detail it sounded as if he had actually been a spy within her bedroom.

He also claimed that Lee had "set her hat" for Aristotle Onassis, and was hoping that he'd marry her. "You see, Lee has this thing for oil tankers," he told Babe Paley.

Lee had sailed the Aegean Sea with Onassis, and they were reported to have had an affair.

Capote always liked to appear to be "in" on all the darkest secrets, and he was one of the first to report that Jackie was also having an affair with Onassis. At the time, no one in his social circle seemed to believe that. "Truman, I love your stories," Babe Paley told him, "but this one needs work."

One night, according to Capote, Lee called him in hysterics. "How could Jackie do this to me?" she reportedly asked. "How could she betray me like this?"

He had more news to tell his gossipy swans. He claimed, "Lee thought she had Ari nailed down, and that a marriage proposal was imminent. But when Jackie signaled she might marry Ari, he dropped Lee. After all, the former First Lady of America, the most famous woman on earth, had a lot more prestige than either Lee or Maria Callas. I told Lee she had to get over it and move on to other game—perhaps a hound-dog not so rich, but perhaps a man better looking."

Capote said to Cecil Beaton, "I told Lee that she should remain in her marriage to

Lee Radziwill is seen nightclubbing with **Aristotle Onassis**.

As Ari's biographer, Peter Evans, wrote: "At twenty-nine, a high-toned Eastern Seaboard postdebutante (Farmington, three terms at Sarah Lawrence), Lee was a lightning rod for men like Ari. He admitted the way she was at home with wealth, the way she took luxury in her stride. She had been born with a taste for money; there is no higher kind of chic."

Stas because he was very tolerant about her infidelities, including her grand passion for Nureyev. Lee told me, 'In pursuit of my adventures, Stas must understand that I need my freedom.' Well, she got it."

As the years went by, Lee and Truman saw less of each other. She stood by helplessly as he sank deeper and deeper into drugs and liquor. She was also shocked by the "rough trade" he brought to her house in London when she invited him to dinner.

At one point, he showed up with a bartender, Rick Brown, whom he'd picked up at Club 45, a rough sailors' dive on West 45th Street in Manhattan. As one biographer described Capote's latest conquest, "Rick was a West Virginia hillbilly who had grown up in a backwoods near where the Hatfields and McCoys had feuded and fought."

Rick later told an interviewer, "Lee Radziwill was a rude bitch. When Truman brought me to her house, she delicately shook my hand, then turned her back on me and never spoke to me again for the rest of the evening."

Lee's biographer, Diana DuBois, speculated on why Capote's friendship with Lee drifted off. "He just wore out her patience. The Truman Capote of the mid-1970s was not the Truman Capote she'd befriended a decade ago. He was so heavily into a cycle of pills and booze by now, and then detoxing in and out of hospitals, that his personal stock plummeted with a lot of his friends. What made matters much worse were his ruinous sexual escapades, usually with disreputable males his socialite friends did not want to have around."

"He was sick, and there was nothing one could do about it," Lee was quoted as saying.

"Babe Paley, once a loyal Capote friend, encountered Jackie at a party in New York. "Truman is on a self-destructive path."

"I haven't seen him lately," Jackie said, not wanting to press the issue.

But Paley continued. "He had a great gift as a writer, but he was squandering his talent. I think he gave up writing completely, in spite of what he claimed. At least Tennessee Williams keeps writing those dreadful plays in his drugged state. As for the third member of their 'gay triangle,' Gore Vidal is practically a book factory, writing all those horrible historical novels, although his essays are a provocative delight even when you disagree with some of the ridiculous political positions he takes."

Stanislas Radziwill died in 1976, and a lot of world attention focused on Lee at the time. The editors of *Vogue* asked Capote to write a "valentine" to her.

Consequently, in his article for *Vogue*, he proclaimed, "I can't think of a woman more feminine than Lee Radziwill—not even Audrey Hepburn and a great seductress like Gloria Guinness."

Actually, at this point his relationship with Lee had traveled south, but he put up a great pretense that they were still the intimate friends they used to be. By writing this flattering "valentine," as published in *Vogue,* he was, in a sense, making a peace offering.

Lee Radziwill Gets Pulled Into a Libel Suit
Between Vidal and Capote

In 1979, Gore Vidal filed a libel suit against Truman Capote for an interview that was published in *Playgirl.*

People magazine wrote, "Not since Oscar Wilde dropped his famous slander suit against the Marquess of Queensberry has a literary lawsuit caused so much excitement. Two best-selling authors, Gore Vidal and Truman Capote, are deadly enemies, a pair of razor-tongued saloon fighters aboil with malice."

Ever since 1961, the tale had been told a thousand times. The allegation was that in 1961, a drunken Vidal was kicked out of a White House party by Bobby Kennedy, with whom he'd had an altercation. That night had led to Vidal's break with Camelot. Unlike what had been falsely reported (and amplified to the world at large by Capote), Gore was not ejected, bodily, out onto Pennsylvania Avenue ("like a drunken cowpoke from a western saloon," as was bruited around afterward by Capote), but he was, after an altercation with Bobby, escorted home by a White House security detail and never invited back.

Because of her love and devotion to Bobby, Jackie sided with her brother-in-law against Vidal. The way she described it, "Gore had squatted down beside my armchair. He'd been drinking heavily. When he went to rise to his feet, he placed his hand on my shoulder."

"Bobby saw that and resented Gore using me as a prop to get up. He told Gore, 'Don't you ever do that again.' The two men had words as I retreated."

"I really blamed myself for the incident because of the heavy drinking. The very next day, as hostess for the White House, I ordered Anne Lincoln, the housekeeper, to have the butlers serve only one alcoholic drink to our guests. She asked about Lyndon Johnson, who was known for ordering eight bourbons before dinner. I told Miss Lincoln that Lyndon could drink in his own quarters and that the one-drink minimum would apply to him as well."

In another "executive order," Jackie instructed Lincoln to inform the White House butlers to refill ("freshen") any guest's unfinished drinks rather than replacing it with entirely new one. "Of course, if they have lipstick traces on the glasses, discard them. But if they don't, recycle the drinks even if you give our guests hepatitis."

***

To bolster his defense in the libel case, Capote wanted to drag Lee Radziwill into the fray, as he cited her as the original source of the story.

Capote had not been invited to the White House, but Lee did attend. It appeared that in a gossipy call she placed to Capote the following morning, she gave him her version of the scandal because she knew how much he detested Vidal. Since he'd heard the story directly from Lee, Capote wanted her to declare herself as an official eyewitness to Vidal's expulsion from the White House, stating to witnesses what she had previously relayed, privately, to him.

To Capote's rage, Lee denied that she had been the source of the story, and made it clear that she didn't want to become involved. When Jackie heard of the lawsuit, and Lee's possible involvement, she pronounced that "this whole mess is just too damn ridiculous." She saw it as a "frivolous squabble" between two authors she'd once befriended, but from whom she had since then distanced herself. "Both Gore and Truman have become too hot for me to handle."

When **Newton Cope** met Lee Radziwill at a dinner party in San Francisco, he asserted that it was "love at first sight."

He got the romance rolling by inviting her to redecorate The Huntington, a charming hotel on Nob Hill left to him by his late wife, the real estate heiress, Dorothy (Dolly) MacMasters.

Lee's lawyers warned that if she admitted to being the source of Capote's version of the story, that Vidal might instruct his lawyers to amend their complaint, naming her as a co-defendant. If Vidal, subsequently, won the case, Lee would be liable for untold damages, whatever the court decided, plus legal fees. The case had already cost Capote $80,000, money he could ill afford.

In 1979, desperately wanting her help, Capote called Lee repeatedly. His desperate calls were not returned.

Behind the scenes, Jackie took a strong stand: "You'll have to forget your previous friendship with Truman. You can't afford to get involved. Because you're my sister, and he was my former friend, I'd suffer at lot of bad publicity as well."

Capote then called columnist Liz Smith and asked her to intervene. Somewhat reluctantly, Smith phoned Lee, a woman she had met but didn't know too well. Lee was dismissive of Truman. Reportedly, Lee told Smith, "All this notoriety is too much for me. I am tired of Truman riding on my coattails. Liz, what difference does the suit make? Truman and Vidal are just a couple of fags."

When Jackie heard this, she said, "Perhaps Lee could have said that more diplomatically…"

When Smith relayed to Capote what Lee had said, he went ballistic. "Riding on her coattails!" he said mockingly. "Who in the fuck is she kidding? She rode on *my* coattails. I even talked David Susskind into casting her in *Laura*. And you know how that turned out. Gene Tierney, Lee was not."

"If the lovely, divine, and sensitive Princess Radziwill has such a low opinion of homosexuals, then why did she have me for a *confidant* for the last twenty years?" he asked.

To her frequent escort at the time, Newton Cope, a middle-aged widower who had married the late heiress, Dolly MacMasters, Lee said, "Now I'm in hot water. The little worm *[a reference to Truman]* is threatening to sue me."

Cope responded, "What can you expect from a has-been writer who is all washed up and fighting for any kind of publicity on the way down?"

Forced to respond, Lee gave Gore's lawyers a sworn statement: "I do not recall ever discussing with Truman Capote the incident of that evening, which I understand is the subject of a lawsuit." When he heard that Lee had been in touch with Vidal's lawyers, Capote said, "She's a treacherous lady, and that's the truth of it. She's treacherous to absolutely everyone."

He told his remaining friends, "I feel betrayed by her. How could she do this to me, after all I've done for her, even trying to make her an actress? Now she's taking Gore's side and giving a deposition. She was the source of my story."

After Lee's dialogue with Liz Smith, during which Lee had labeled Capote a fag, he swore revenge, "as only a Southern fag knows how to do it by twisting a dagger inside a human heart. When I finish with this bitch, she'll be shitting razor blades."

One night at Studio 54, he told his friend, Andy Warhol, "You should just hear some of the things she says about you. She views you as the ultimate social climber."

"I don't really care," Warhol said. "I've always been aware of what kind of woman she is. I'd call her a talent climber."

"I'll tell you one thing. If she is boozing now, can you imagine what she'll be belting down when I'm through attacking her?" Capote asked.

Warhol urged him to back off. "Lee is already weak and vulnerable. You don't want to push her over the edge."

A chance to expose Lee occurred when Capote was invited, on June 5, 1979, to appear on the Stanley Siegel television talk show.

Sally Quinn of *The Washington Post* met Capote at his apartment and escorted him to the television studio in a chauffeured limou-

Lee Radziwill "erotically" dances with her beau, **Peter Tufo.** The prominent Manhattan attorney found Lee "beautiful, intelligent, artistic, creative, and radiant. Did I also add wonderful?"

In time, his opinion changed.

Lee Radziwill defined **Peter Beard,** her new beau, as "half Tarzan, half Byron." He was an author, a photographer, a heartthrob, a party boy, and a wildlife conservationist.

After reading *Out of Africa* by Isak Dinesen (aka Karen Blixen), he headed for the Dark Continent, landing in Kenya.

sine. She could tell how drugged he was.

In the back seat of the limo, he told her, "A cassette of this show is going to be one of the great comic classics of all time."

"Before I'm finished with them, Lee and her beloved sister, Jackie, will need to have an ambulance waiting to take them to Payne Whitney, where they'll need to check in for a very long stay. Before I go off the air, the average subway rider in the New York system will know what a little cunt Lee Radziwill is."

In the waiting room at the studio, Capote told Quinn, "She called me a fag. Well, this fag happens to be alive and well in New York City."

Jackie had been alerted to Capote's appearance, and she tuned in, dreading what she was likely to see and hear.

Siegel announced Capote as one of his guests in advance of his entrance onto the set. Audiences were shocked when Capote,

More Bouvier embarrassments
foisted on Lee and Jackie

Publicity for *Grey Gardens*

drunk and drugged, staggered out into view. After seating himself, he announced, "I'll tell you something about fags, especially Southern fags. We is mean. A Southern fag is meaner than the meanest rattler you ever met. I know that Lee Radziwill wouldn't want me to be tellin' you none of this. But you know us Southern fags—we just can't keep our mouths shut."

Then he launched into an attack on Lee's affairs with various men, some of them conducted during her marriage to Stanislas. "The Principesa tried to seduce William Buckley, Jr. When he didn't respond to her advances, she accused him of being queer."

For a while, Peter Tufo was her beau," he claimed. "She told me that Peter has a face like a ferret and is publicity crazy, riding on her coattails. In this case, I didn't think he was good enough for her.

[Actually, Peter Tofu was a politically connected and prominent lawyer who became the U.S. ambassador to Hungary.]

"La Principesa also went after Peter Beard," Truman claimed. "She told me herself that he was no great catch except perhaps in some provincial town. He eventually dumped her for a chick with less mileage on her."

[Peter Beard was a well-known photographer, artist, diarist, and writer. His photos of Africa and its wildlife had made him a celebrity. He was also a photographer of supermodels and rock stars like Mick Jagger and David Bowie. His friends included Jackie Kennedy, Bianca Jagger, and Andy Warhol.

Jackie was furious that Capote was gossiping about Beard on TV. When she was on the Greek island of Skorpios, Beard had been a frequent visitor. He'd also been a kind of playmate and babysitter for Caroline and John Jr. He taught Caroline how to use a camera, and he climbed Mt. Kenya with John. The Kennedys also visited Beard at his plantation in Kenya.

When Beard was in Greece, Onassis bet Beard that he could not hold his breath under water for more than four minutes. The photographer managed to do that, and the Greek tycoon paid him $10,000. He used part of that money to finance his documentary, Grey Gardens, *a film that exposed the lives and financial straits of Jackie's poor and very eccentric relatives, Edith and Edie Beale.]*

The audience didn't really know a lot about Lee's lovers. They were more intrigued to learn that Lee was "insanely jealous of her sister, Jackie," according to Capote.

Acutely aware of Capote's condition, Siegel asked him if he wanted to continue with the show, or whether he preferred to leave the studio. Capote answered that he wanted to keep talking.

Siegel then asked him if he thought he could "lick" his habits.

"The obvious answer is that eventually I'll kill myself." Capote said.

Back in his apartment at the United Nations Plaza, Capote continued his revelations, with Quinn taking notes.

He spoke more about Newton Cope, who was a particularly prominent figure at the time in San Francisco—in fact, he was called "The Nabob of Nob Hill," because of his vast real estate holdings.

"At the last minute, Lee called off her wedding," Capote claimed. "She didn't like the pre-nup agreement he wanted her to sign. Although the wedding fizzled, the couple still went on their honeymoon to the Caribbean."

Jackie later asserted, "This was not very discreet, to say the least."

Capote reveled to Quinn details of Lee's affair with Roy Jenkins, a rising Labour Party politician in Britain, who, among other posts, had served as Harold Wilson's Chancellor of the Exchequer from 1967 to 1970.

"Jackie urged Lee to go after Jenkins because she believed he was going to become Prime Minister. Lee told me that Jackie said, 'Just think, you'll become the First Lady of the United Kingdom.'"

"I didn't like most of Lee's beaux, but at least Jenkins was a man I respected," Capote said. "When in power, he urged the abolishment of censorship in the British theater and the decriminalization of homosexuality."

"But when Jenkins failed in his bid to become prime minister, Lee dropped him like a hot potato—forgive the cliché," Capote said.

In California, Vidal watched the Siegel show. When it was over, he said, "This is pathology, real nut-house stuff."

In its immediate aftermath, Capote generated a headline: "DRUNK AND DOPED, CAPOTE VISITS TV TALK SHOW," shouted the *New York Post*.

The Post also published a savage cartoon, depicting him with droopy eyes enveloped by piles of discarded liquor bottles and used hypodermic needles, along with a book entitled *Breakfast at the Bowery*. John Cashman, in *Newsday*, wrote, "A talented man of considerable literary stature was making a fool of himself in front of 250,000 viewers."

To recover from his embarrassment, Capote spent that night at Studio 54 with owner Steve Rubell and Liza Minnelli, who was not in great shape herself. In the next few days, Capote announced to friends, "I'm going to kill myself as soon as I work up the courage. I'll hire someone to kill me *In Cold Blood.*"

***

By October of 1983, Capote sent word to Vidal's lawyers that he had no money to pay him even if Vidal won the judgment. He agreed to settle the case by writing Vidal a letter of apology and an admission that he had lied.

Privately, Capote was quoted as saying, "I'm always sad about Gore—very sad that he has to breathe every day."

Vidal retorted, "Truman has made lying an art form—a minor art form."

To the very end, Capote continued to maintain that "Princess Radziwill betrayed me. She was very hurtful to me, and I loved her. Love is blind. I have been in love before with people who were just ghastly. Lee was my number one confidant until I went through that long period when I was in and out of hospitals. I wasn't talking to anybody. Of all my friends, she never wrote me once to say she hoped I was getting well and wished me luck. There has never been any reason for her unbelievable behavior."

After Capote's death, Lee seemed to become more mellow in her opinion of her long-ago friend. She said, "I miss Truman—yes, I do. I had wonderful times with him, really good times. There is nobody like him—nobody who even reminds me of him at all."

Jackie never spoke of Capote ever again.

Media Marketing and the Origins of a *Provocateur*

In 1948, looking like Tadzio, the devilish adolescent from *Death in Venice,* the young author, **Truman Capote**, scandalized the world when he posed for the back cover of his first novel, *Other Voices, Other Rooms.*

Photographed by Harold Halma, who emphasized Capote's self-image as a male Lolito and an *enfant terrible*, the budding writer was depicted as a seductive, sloe-eyed youth, lying supine on a sofa, facing the camera with an emphasis on his petulant mouth, baby bangs, and seductive, come-hither gaze.

One reviewer advised American housewives to keep their husbands away from this tantalizing boy. Another warned, "Something evil and awful this way comes."

Chapter Twenty-Three

"A Fairyland
Inhabited by Vampires"
With Horror, Jackie Follows the Widely Televised Feud Between Gore Vidal and William Buckley

---

Buckley Slams Vidal as a Sexual Deviant; Vidal Labels Buckley "A Closeted Old Queen"
Behind the Scenes, Jackie Gets Involved

Left photo: In 1968, during the Democratic Presidential nominating convention in riot-plagued Chicago, ABC hired right-wing commentator **William F. Buckley, Jr.** *(left)* to face off with **Gore Vidal** *(right, with only the back of his head showing)*, for a nationally televised debate. The moderator was ABC-TV's **Howard Smith** *(right photo)*.

In front of millions of TV viewers, "Mr. Cool" (a reference to Buckley) lost it and threatened Vidal with physical violence, calling him a "queer" in response to charges of Nazism.

Despite her role as the uncrowned Queen of Democratic Party politics in America, and her status as the widow of its assassinated torch-bearer, Jackie refused to attend the 1968 Democratic Convention in Chicago.

517

But her absence resulted from years of soul-searching dialogues with her late husband. As early as 1960, she and JFK, when he was running for president, often talked about where their lives would be in 1968.

According to their plan, he would be retiring from the White House, assuming he'd be re-elected in 1964. They discussed what they might do during retirement, where they might live. Jackie suggesting they might travel frequently. She recommended that they might maintain apartments in New York, London, and Paris, while keeping residences in Palm Beach and Hyannis Port.

Her plans changed drastically when 1968 actually came, and Robert Kennedy was assassinated in Los Angeles after winning the California primary.

Originally, and until she changed her mind, Jackie had agreed to be "showcased," with fanfare and klieg lights, at the Democratic Convention, which she hoped would lead to a nomination of Robert Kennedy (Bobby) as the party's candidate in the upcoming challenge from the Republican right. That challenge would be in the form of Richard Nixon, whom—although she masked her contempt—she had grown to despise.

Jackie had no enthusiasm for Lyndon B. Johnson's choice—Hubert Humphrey—as head of the Democratic ticket and its candidate for president.

At a party, **William Buckley, Jr.,** confronted Jackie, describing his plan to write a book exploding Camelot as a myth of her own making. He wanted to entitle it *The Dark Side of Camelot*. Ironically, in 1997, three years after Jackie's death, investigative reporter Seymour M. Hersh wrote just such a book, with that title.

"I have met some despicable excuses for a man in my life," Jackie told Gore Vidal. "The Buckley thing is at the top of my hate list."

He'd run against her husband in the West Virginia and Wisconsin primaries in 1960, and she had developed an intense dislike for him and his "down-home" approach to campaigning. "The man has no class," she told friends. She cited a "cornpone" picture of the Humphreys holding hands with their "dull-looking children" in front of an extremely modest shingle-sided cabin.

As the convention opened, Jackie had so little interest that she didn't plan to follow the proceedings. But she changed her mind when she read that ABC-TV had hired both Gore Vidal and William Buckley, Jr., to cover the convention

"I'll Sock You in Your Goddamn Face"

On Nationwide TV,
A "Porno-writing Queer" Dukes It Out With a "Crypto-Nazi"

in Dallas. She later admitted, "I watched the proceedings like a cobra about to strike."

Because of Bobby Kennedy's feud with Vidal, her friendship with him had been put into storage. But she despised Buckley—"I loathe him," were her exact words.

Her disdain for this right-wing commentator was not entirely political, but personal.

At least some of it derived from their encounter, in 1965, at a party in Manhattan, to which she was escorted by Ted Sorensen. There, he confronted her to tell her, provocatively, that he was contemplating writing a book entitled *The Dark Side of Camelot*.

Buckley was very frank with her, informing her that the book would revolve around the theme that her husband had been one of the worst presidents in U.S. history.

Buckley sued **Vidal** *(photo above)* for his response to an attack Buckley had written about him in *Esquire*. "Finally, the right-wing creep backed down and dropped the suit," Gore said. "But I had to pay my lawyers for his crazed madness. One never forgives that. Hopefully, the fanatical Buckleys of America will be stopped one day before they destroy the country."

"I want to write about how Kennedy used his old man's bootleg millions and his Mafia links to gain power," Buckley told an astonished Jackie. "I'll write about his charm—your charm, too—but reveal how both of you used it like a weapon."

"I will charge that Kennedy followed only his own moral code, which is actually immoral. He virtually did what he wanted. He was completely reckless, a womanizer from hell. You know that better than anyone. I also want to reveal how he lied to the American people about his health. I plan to suggest that Kennedy's very recklessness had gotten out of control, and that he was on the dawn of being publicly disgraced, which would have cost him the presidency in 1964."

"I plan to suggest that he, with your help, masked personal weaknesses which cast a dark shadow over the House of Camelot."

"He seduced the public and used you as a kind of star magnet to avert attention from his private life."

"I am sorry to do this to you, Mrs. Kennedy, but I am far more interested in history getting it right than in offending one lady, who I understand has had her own detours down the primrose path."

Having listened to him with jaw-dropping astonishment, Jackie withdrew. In a quiet rage, she said, "Please, Mr. Buckley, try not to appear in the same city with me. Your stench is overpowering, worse than the poison gas used on Allied soldiers in the trench warfare of World War I." Then she turned and walked away, leaving the party.

Sorensen later reported to former White House aides and Kennedy loyalists, "Never in my life had I ever heard Jackie take such a forceful stand against anyone. But it was understandable. Here was this obnoxious right-winger not

519

only insulting her to her face at a party, but threatening to explode the so-called Myth of Camelot, which she'd worked so hard to create. He was threatening to reveal all the dark secrets of the Kennedy administration, which she had strived to keep from the public. I had never seen her so enraged."

Vidal, a spokesman from the American left, and Buckley, the darling of the far right, had long been ideological enemies. Buckley even suggested that Vidal was not really an American. "He lives as an expatriate far from these shores, and once applied for citizenship in Switzerland, which would have required a revocation of his American passport."

Executives at ABC decided that they would make "good television" their priority during their coverage of the 1968 Democratic Convention in Chicago, an event that ultimately nominated Hubert Humphrey as the Democratic candidate for U.S. president, a man who had previously functioned as Lyndon Johnson's vice president.

[During the 1968 presidential elections, Humphrey would eventually lose to Richard Nixon.]

In utter astonishment, Jackie watched the convention and the TV commentaries it catalyzed, including the joint appearance of Vidal with Buckley. She was motivated not just with Buckley's vow to tarnish her late husband's reputation, but Vidal's increasingly cynical viewpoint about the Kennedy "Dynasty" as well. He'd become rather hostile about issues associated with Camelot, and had written devastating critiques of Bobby too.

In spite of that, Jackie was willing to root for him. As she told Sorensen, "In spite of some past difficulties I've had with Gore, he's still on our side. At this convention, he's become the holder of the flame against this horrible man, Buckley. I have never wanted to slap someone's face as much as I wanted to slap his at that party. How dare he talk to me that way? I hope Gore makes mince pie out of this man who opposed everything Jack ever did."

She was watching a televised broadcast of the Convention on the evening of Wednesday, August 28 at 9:30 EST, and would never forget what she saw.

ABC anchorman Howard K. Smith, who was stuck in the middle as a moderator, would never forget it either, even though his anchor desk was in another room, separate from the two commentators.

Gore and Buckley were not strangers to each other, having debated twice before—first in September of 1962 and again in July of 1964, with TV host David Susskind functioning as moderator in both of those instances.

What was happening outside the convention hall was more intriguing than the speeches being made inside. Chicago Mayor Richard Daley, later denounced as "a Gestapo leader," had mobilized a massive police force to control violent protests against the Vietnam War. Most of that war had unfolded during Lyndon Johnson's administration, but it had been launched—although on a much smaller scale—by JFK, or so his critics claimed.

On the streets of Chicago, the battle between the police and the mostly young protesters, as described by one reporter, "involved gross police brutality as Mayor Daley's cops beat the shit out of the yippies and hippies assembled to witness the Democratic Party's coronation of miserable old Humphrey."

TV cameras focused on young, presumably American-born men waving the Viet Cong's flag.

That night, some ten million Americans, along with Jackie, had tuned in to ABC to watch the Vidal/Buckley debates, sandwiched into the barely controlled chaos unfolding both inside and outside the Convention Hall.

Vidal defended the protesters. He even claimed that the waving of the Viet Cong flag fell under the U.S. Constitution's guarantee of Free Speech.

In contrast, Buckley, "was hissing like a cobra," *[Vidal's words]* during the attacks he was spewing on the young people rioting in Grant Park. He accused them of "begging the Viet Cong to kill American marines."

Before that infamous television broadcast, Jackie had watched Vidal and Buckley engage in mutual bickering. One Chicago newsman defined it as "hysterical combat."

As their altercation intensified, Buckley defined the protesters as "pro-Nazi."

In immediate response, Vidal charged, "As far as I am concerned, the only sort of pro-crypto Nazi I can think of is yourself."

Buckley exploded in anger. A notorious homophobe, he shot back. "Now listen, you queer! Stop calling me a crypto-Nazi or I'll sock you in your goddamn face and you'll stay plastered!"

TV audiences across the country were stunned. So was Jackie.

She had been watching the debates with her friends Ben and Toni Bradlee. Of all members of the Washington press corps, Bradlee at *The Washington Post* had been the closest to her husband. However, in 1975, after he published his book, *Conversations with Kennedy,* Jackie

The Chicago riots of August of 1968 may have cost the Democratic Party the presidential elections. Using their batons like clubs, the Chicago police, under **Mayor Richard Daley** *(upper photo),* were violently beating Vietnam protesters, their actions projected on hourly newscasts into the horrified consciousness of viewers everywhere

For Buckley, the revolt of the left-wingers represented heinous anarchy. Vidal interpreted it differently, alleging that "The police state and the American empire were murdering free speech." Both men were, in the words of one writer, becoming "angry, defensive, and aggressive," their moods within the Chicago TV studio reflecting opposing sides in the pitched battles outside on the streets.

As early as 1962, Buckley had been referring to Vidal, in public, as "a pinko queer." He threatened that if Vidal wanted to sue him, "I shall fight by the laws of the Marquess of Queensberry."

dropped him from her list of friends.

"Jackie jumped up and glared at the TV set as if she could not believe what had transpired," Bradlee later said.

Howard Smith, the debate's anchorman later said, "Mr. Cool *[a reference to Buckley]* lost it that night. The ice cube turned into a ball of fire. Perhaps this was the first time in his life that Buckley threatened physical violence against those who didn't agree with his position."

"I would expect physical violence from Norman Mailer, not from Buckley," Vidal later said. "I must have really crawled under his skin. Perhaps I labeled him correctly after all. He's a representative of the lunatic right, where Goebbels would have felt at home."

"Actually, he was the first to use the word 'Nazi,'" Vidal later said. "My repeating it was a slip of the tongue. I had meant to say 'fascist' instead."

Buckley later said he should not have used the word "queer." But he couldn't resist a dig, "Gore Vidal, however, is the Evangelist for bisexuality."

Ben Bradlee later reported that watching the Vidal/Buckley broadcast had "ravaged" her *[Jackie's]* mind. She ordered a strong drink from her maid—and later, a lot more. She feared the fallout from that broadcast had only begun—and she was right!"

Bemused and jovial, **Ben Bradlee** *(above)* and his wife, Toni, had long been friends to both Jack and Jackie. Often, they went out as a foursome.

Ben's friendship with Jackie continued during the post-assassination era—that is, until 1975, when, in Jackie's eyes, he committed an unpardonable sin. He wrote a book about his conversations with JFK.

"Buckley is a Homophobe, Anti-Black, Anti-Semitic Warmonger"

—Gore Vidal

As the new year of 1969 dawned, Vidal seemed willing to put the notorious Chicago TV incident behind him.

Buckley, however, was not. Still fuming, he called Harold Hayes, a high-placed editor at *Esquire,* for permission to submit an article attacking Vidal. He wanted it to appear in the magazine's August issue. But he had one condition: "Will I be allowed to charge Vidal with homosexuality?"

Hayes thought Esquire's lawyers might agree to that. "Permission granted, unless I call you and tell you otherwise."

That afternoon, in his role as a provocative editor with a scandal to publicize, Hayes reached Vidal at his home in Ravello along the Amalfi coast in Italy.

He told him about Buckley's plans and offered him space in *Esquire* for a rebuttal, with the understanding that he'd be able to evaluate and/or attack Buckley in an articles that would run in the magazine's September issue."

Vidal agreed, but protested. "Why are you giving space to this dimwit? He's mad. He exists in the mind of the public only because of his attacks on me."

Hayes personally liked Buckley but hated his politics: Hayes didn't particularly like Vidal, but endorsed many of his political views. The editor saw the obvious: Mutually aggressive articles by Vidal and Buckley, each attacking the other, would be good for circulation.

More and more of Jackie's former friends and confidants were, in her words, "betraying me." She was horrified when someone brought her the March, 1963, issue of *Esquire* in which Vidal attacked **Bobby Kennedy** as unfit to ever become President.

After Vidal's attack on Bobby Kennedy, circulation had soared. The cover of *Esquire*'s issue that contained it featured a replica of Bobby sitting in President Kennedy's White House rocking chair. The headline read—WHEN BOBBY TAKES OVER.

Jackie interpreted Vidal's article as a "revenge piece," compiled in retaliation for Bobby kicking Gore out of the White House in 1961. In it, Vidal had labeled the Attorney General as a McCarthy clone—"a graceless, illiberal, and puritanical politician, unqualified by temperament or judgment to be President."

Bobby and Jackie were furious at Vidal.

When she heard of Buckley's upcoming attack on Vidal in the same issue, Sorensen said that Jackie was almost forced to take Vidal's side and forget about his attack on Bobby. She told Sorensen, "Gore is just the advance soldier in the field that Buckley wants to slay. As you know, his ultimate aim is to ridicule and mock Jack's accomplishments in the White House."

***

According to the lawyers at *Esquire*, the first draft of Buckley's article on Vidal was libelous. Even if it were cut and rigorously edited, publishing it would still represent a bit of a risk for the magazine, they said.

Fred Kaplan, Vidal's biographer, wrote: "Buckley's article seemed not only inaccurate, in fact, but whiningly self-serving and viciously homophobic. It was a theocracy of sorts, a justification not of God but of Buckley, an egomaniacal self-projection so vast that it seemed Satanic, the devil in the guise of an infinite self-righteous rectitude."

As stated by Buckley, Vidal was a "money-grabbing pornographer—Myra Breckinridge is pure pornography—whose immorality was purposeful, self-conscious, and serving—and that is a sin. He is also a sexual deviant, and that is an illness. Unlike most sick people, Vidal does not want to be cured."

Before publication, Hayes sent Vidal a copy of Buckley's article, tacitly seeking his permission to publish it. He feared Vidal might sue.

As evidence of their sense of editorial "fair play," *Esquire* planned to provide Vidal with a chance to respond to Buckley's attacks within its subsequent issue. By now, however, Buckley was demanding that only his attack on Vidal be run, and that *Esquire* refrain from publishing Vidal's rejoinder.

When *Esquire*'s August issue appeared on newsstands nationwide, it managed to enrage not only Vidal, but also millions of homosexuals and their sympathizers, Jackie among them.

In his article, Buckley labeled Vidal as an apologist for homosexuality. "The man in his essays proclaims the normalcy of his affliction—that is, homosexuality—and in his art, the desirability of it. Vidal is not the man who bears his sorrow quietly. The addict is to be pitied, and even respected, not the pusher."

In his own defense, Vidal composed and submitted his response, as requested by Hayes, for *Esquire's* September issue. He cited damaging evidence that Buckley was not only a "homophobe, but anti-black, anti-Semitic, and a warmonger."

He also came up with some damaging evidence, claiming that in 1944, Buckley, along with "unnamed siblings," vandalized a Protestant church in their hometown of Sharron, Connecticut, after its pastor's wife sold a house to a Jewish family.

Surprisingly, the actress/entertainer, Jayne Meadows, who was privy to some of the more sordid details associated with the Buckley family, provided "a lot of juice to Gore," although she requested that her name not be cited.

[Jayne Meadows (born 1920) was the wife and business partner of talk show host/comedian Steve Allen, and the sister of Audrey Meadows, famous for her character of Alice Kramden in The Honeymooners.*]*

Some of Vidal's material had to be excised by *Esquire,* particularly the charges that Buckley was a closeted homosexual himself. Vidal did accuse him of having "faggot logic," even suggesting that "where there is smoke, there is a fire."

He claimed that many TV viewers had cited Buckley's "effeminate manners and speech, behavior that made him sound queenlike."

Jackie, too, had heard rumors about Buckley, particularly when she dated one of his classmates from Yale. Her beau at the time told her that Buckley had been known on campus as a homosexual.

Maneuvering behind the scenes, Jackie asked Onassis to intervene. Onassis' lawyer, Roy Cohn, a homosexual himself, was one of J. Edgar Hoover's closest

Actress **Jayne Meadows**, of all people, came to the aid of Gore Vidal by supplying "incriminating evidence" against the Buckleys.

friends. She knew that Hoover, who had files on everyone, would obviously have investigated Buckley.

Onassis agreed to ask Cohn to find out "the dirt" in Buckley's file, and the ever-diligent Cohn did just that, reporting his findings the following week.

The most damaging evidence about Buckley's homosexuality came from a former classmate *[name withheld]* at Yale. At the time the file was made available to Jackie, the Yale man was a successful stockbroker in New York with a wife and three children.

He had told the FBI that to stay on the football team, he had to maintain a certain grade average, and that whereas he had been a poor student, Buckley was considered a scholar and an intellectual.

"I needed help, and I couldn't afford to pay for extra tutoring," the former Yale man said. "I caught Buckley checking me out in the shower room. He seemed fascinated by my cock. I figured out what to do. In exchange for his private tutoring, I would let him perform fellatio on me—nothing else. When I presented the offer to him, he willingly agreed. Our special relationship went on for the rest of the semester. I graduated from Yale, and Buckley took care of me, because I was perpetually horny."

Secretly, Jackie had the file copied. A member of Onassis' staff had it delivered anonymously to Gore's residence to use in any way he saw fit.

***

Buckley did not remain idle while Vidal was digging up a homosexual scandal from his past. He, too, had a detective agency investigating his adversary.

It was learned that Vidal, throughout his life, had often had sex with underage hustlers. Buckley had eyewitness accounts from some of the teenage boys Vidal had picked up on Santa Monica Boulevard who claimed that at the time of their encounters with him, they were under sixteen, maybe in one instance a well-developed thirteen.

Like Michael Jackson in a TV special, Vidal admitted in his memoirs, *Palimpsest,* that he was "attracted to adolescent males—like most men."

The agency discovered that Vidal had taken several "Golden Cock Tours" to Thailand as they were la-

In February of 1964, *Town and Country* published a cover story on **Aristotle Onassis**. There was a certain irony in the headline: WHAT ONASSIS WANTS ONASSIS GETS. At the time, the editors didn't know that Ari wanted Jackie.

In February of 1968, *Esquire* devoted a cover issue to the notorious homosexual lawyer, **Roy Cohn**, who often handled legal matters for Aristotle Onassis.

In a murky payback, Jackie asked Ari to pay Cohn for blackmail evidence that Cohn's closest friend, FBI Director J. Edgar Hoover, had accumulated on William Buckley, Jr.

beled. These tours were often booked by pedophiles, the majority of the participants coming from German cities, especially Berlin. But the detectives had no way of gathering information about Vidal from Bangkok.

Vidal repeatedly denied that he was a member of NAMBLA, the North American Man/Boy Love Association. He did, or so it was once reported, endorse NAMBLA's goal of legalizing "intergenerational sex." Privately, Vidal, a sexual sophisticate, said, "Sometimes, it takes a nubile twelve-year-old boy to get a rise out of an 84-year-old man."

Vidal did make an appearance at a NAMBLA fund-raising in 1978, although he claimed it was to take a stand against Salem-like witch hunts aimed at persecuting gay people. Viewed harshly, his presence was later criticized. He was falsely charged with favoring the rape of young boys, which he had never endorsed.

From afar, Jackie observed how Buckley vs. Vidal lawsuits, threats of exposure, and counter-suits were mushrooming everywhere. Her ultimate conclusion, as told to Sorensen, was that Vidal and Buckley "found so much homosexual scandal about each other that they had to declare a Mexican stand-off before seriously damaging each of their reputations."

"I knew enough, though, to keep my son John away from both of them," Jackie said.

***

After Vidal delivered the draft of his article to *Esquire*, Buckley, in advance of its publication, announced his lawsuit.

Pre-emptively, and not without touches of paranoia and personal vanity, Buckley sent the following telegrams to twenty American magazine publishers:

"Last August, I was defamed on network television by Mr. Gore Vidal. Mr. Vidal has not retracted his libel or apologized to me. On the contrary, he has sought to give renewed currency to that libel and to launch others, to which end he submitted a manuscript to Esquire which Esquire declined to publish because it was defamatory and untrue. Mr. Vidal's activities have left me with no other recourse than a lawsuit, and accordingly, I have filed suit against Mr. Vidal for $500,000 in damage."

By sending these telegrams, Buckley hoped to prevent *Esquire* from publishing Vidal's rejoinder in their September issue.

This began a legal waltz between Vidal and Buckley—with the horrified involvement of *Esquire*— that would drag on for three years. Jackie had closely watched developments before and after the publication of both articles. Aware of the legal heat generated by the affair, Hayes demanded that only facts that could be reasonably proved be allowed in his magazine, or else free speech about political stances which seemed libel-proof. Even after their cuts and edits, both articles still seemed explosive.

Endless meetings with lawyers and precautions preceded publication, but finally each of the two articles was printed. Buckley as promised sued in the

United States District Court, although at this point, he'd upped his claim for damages to $1 million.

Buckley told the press, "I have been defamed. Vidal has accused me of being a Nazi, a homosexual, a war lover, and an anti-Semite."

Buckley's attorney requested the court for a summary judgment, at which time the judge dismissed Vidal's countersuit, virtually labeling it as a "nuisance suit."

Buckley's suit never made it to court. *Esquire* admitted no culpability, but it did agree to pay Buckley's legal fees up to $115,000. However, Vidal was left dangling to pay his own lawyers, with no comparable offer of reimbursement from *Esquire*.

In the immediate aftermath, Buckley summoned a press conference in which he lied, falsely claiming that he had won the case against both *Esquire* and Vidal. He said *Esquire* had "disavowed Vidal's charges against me and in its November issue would publish a retraction."

No such agreement had been reached, and no such retraction ever appeared.

"Let Vidal pay his own unreimbursed legal expenses, which will teach him to observe the laws of libel," Buckley crowed.

Throughout the rest of his life, Buckley would maintain the fiction, at parties and to his friends, that the court had interpreted Vidal's article as defamatory and that *Esquire* "had to pay up" for having published it.

Privately, Vidal said, "The closeted old queen is just deluding herself until the end. She lives in a fairyland peopled by the lunatic fringe and at night, dances with vampires in KKK drag."

It is not known, but Onassis, through Cohn, might have blackmailed Buckley into abandoning his plans for a book that would have exposed Jackie, JFK, and the myth of Camelot. Jackie personally did not want to "leave my fingerprints on any of this maneuvering. Let Cohn do his job. Let's face it: Ari pays him enough!"

"Let Us Speak Ill of the Dead"

—Gore Vidal

The feud and charges of libel continued into the 21st Century. Buckley died in 2008, Vidal outliving him, dying in 2012.

However, in 2003, *Esquire* republished Vidal's attack on Buckley, in a book entitled *Esquire's Big Book of Great Writing*. Apparently, the editor of the anthology was not familiar with the long-ago lawsuit, much to the horror of *Esquire's* administration.

Buckley once again filed suit for libel, and *Esquire* agreed to settle for $55,000 in attorney fees and $10,000 in personal damages to Buckley.

When documents associated with the Vidal/Buckley debate became available on the internet, viewers weighed in with strong opinions. "Sarah Heart-burn" claiming, "I will make my hands bleed applauding for Vidal." She attacked Buckley's suggestion that "HIV-sufferers be tattooed—on the ass.' How the holy fuck can the man be touted in the press as an erudite, wise, political spokesman?"

Upon hearing of Buckley's death, Vidal said, "Although one is not supposed to speak ill of the dead, Buckley was often drunk and out of control. He was always a spontaneous liar on any subject that his dizzy brain might extrude."

He concluded that Buckley was a "most hysterical right-wing queen, much admired by the fascist press in America that merely published Buckley's own delusional evaluation of himself."

In 2008, in the wake of Buckley's death, Deborah Solomon of *The New York Times* asked Vidal, "How did you feel when you heard that Buckley had died?"

"I thought hell is bound to be a livelier place with him in it," he said. "Buckley joins forever those whom he served in life, applauding their prejudices and fanning their hatred."

As for Jackie, she went to her grave in 1994 detesting Buckley. Whenever he appeared on TV, she switched channels.

In October of 1972, **Jackie** threw a surprise party at Manhattan's El Morocco, celebrating the fourth anniversary of her marriage to Aristotle Onassis—not that that marriage had anything to celebrate. Her guest list included Doris Duke, Rose Kennedy, Oleg Cassini, and such New Frontiersmen warriors of yesterday as Pierre Salinger.

Surprise of surprise, she invited William Buckley, Jr. He was shocked, knowing how much she despised him, but he attended anyway. He wished he hadn't.

Years before, he had infuriated her at a party, when he had cheerfully informed her that he was about the expose the myth of Camelot in a book. She waited for almost a decade before confronting him privately at her El Morocco party to inform him of the incriminating data that the Kennedys had amassed on him. "Back off!" she threatened him, "or we'll destroy you."

He got the message.

Chapter Twenty-Four

Rudolf Nureyev—From Russia With Love
"Tales of Tatar Tail"

The Kennedys Confront "Rudi in the Nudi"
Jackie and Lee Vie for the Reincarnation of Nijinski

At first, Jackie was hesitant to introduce **Bobby Kennedy** *(left)* to her new friend, **Rudolf Nureyev** *(right)*. But once the two met, she was shocked at how intimately the ballet dancer and the Attorney General bonded.

RFK's biographer, C. David Heymann, put it this way: "The sexual revolution of the 1960s had little to teach the Kennedy men, who had been enjoying the benefits of free love for decades. But in the try-anything spirit of the time, Bobby may have indulged in an experiment that, even for his lusty family, broke new ground."

Heymann was referring to the secret affair between Bobby and Rudi.

Bundled up not for Siberia, but for the English countryside, **Jackie Kennedy** and **Rudolf Nureyev** were the house guests of Lee Radziwill at her country home.

The Russian ballet dancer, Rudolf Nureyev, captivated

not only the hearts of balletomanes around the world, but lured Jackie Kennedy, her sister, Lee Radziwill, and even Bobby Kennedy and John F. Kennedy Jr. into his web of intrigue.

"When it came to seducing, it was hard to say no to Rudi," said ballerina Margot Fonteyn, who became his frequent partner. "He usually got what he wanted, man or woman. Even otherwise straight men, or at least some of them, couldn't resist that bundle of Tatar charm. Rudi never kept his affairs with the Kennedys a secret, and often relayed boastful tales about his conquests."

The love of his life was Erik Bruhn, the Danish-born *danseur noble.* "A totally reciprocal deep passion existed between the two men," claimed Rudi's biographer, Julie Kavanaugh. Rudi was never faithful to Bruhn, however.

One night at Maxim's in Paris, he told Bruhn: "I was just in New York. I fuck Jackie Kennedy. Now I take you back to hotel and fuck you—all night!"

***

Rudolf Nureyev was the greatest male ballet dancer of his generation. Along with Nijinski, he was one of the most spectacular ballet dancers of all time.

He had a stunning Slavic physical beauty, an extraordinarily athletic and sexual persona, a prodigious endowment that he liked to exhibit, and oodles of Russian charm.

As a stellar member of the *glitterati,* he attracted the attention of international café society—specifically Lee Radziwill, Jackie Kennedy, Bobby Kennedy, and John F. Kennedy Jr. In time, he would seduce all four of them.

In 1961, during the darkest days of the Cold War, Rudi was touring Western Europe with the Kirov Ballet Troupe. At Paris's Le Bourget airport, he had been scheduled to board a flight for London. But shortly before takeoff, KGB officials

Rudolf Nureyev appears above with a smirk.

He had a right to be conceited. He changed the expectations of the ballet world forever. As a dancer who was showcased on every continent except Antarctica, he captivated the media..

Nureyev *(left)* and the Danish ballet dancer, **Erik Bruhn,** were involved in an enduring love affair in spite of their complicated schedules and occasional jealousies. From the moment Rudolf first met Bruhn, he said, "I had to possess him. I had to move inside his body and take over his soul. I had to work it so that he would become obsessed with me. And he did."

"I don't care what the magazines say. I am the sexiest man alive. Just ask Lee Radziwill. Just ask Jackie Kennedy. And if you still don't believe me, ask Bobby and John-John. Nobody in the world can resist me. Everyone who has ever gone to bed with me has fallen madly in love with me." —Rudolf Nureyev

ordered him to board the next plane to Moscow because his mother was dying.

Sensing a trap, the 23-year-old dancer fled into the arms of two French policemen. "Save me! I want to stay."

Later he told friends that he was carrying a pair of scissors with him. "Had anything gone wrong," he said, "I was prepared to plunge the scissors into my heart."

Rudi knew that if he returned to Moscow, he'd never dance again. The KGB had accumulated an extensive file on him, detailing his homosexual encounters.

He was "born wild" in 1938 on a train chugging beside Lake Baikaal in Siberia. In 1945, at the age of seven, he fell in love with the world of dance when he saw his first ballet. He would dance for the rest of his life.

His father nicknamed him "Ballerina." He despised his son and the world of ballet and frequently beat Rudi.

In spite of his father, Rudi stubbornly insisted on taking ballet lessons. He was an amazing pupil and by 1958, he'd evolved into a sensation within the Soviet dance world. His performances, so the critics claimed, were "erotically charged."

Two weeks after his defection, Rudi was performing at the Thêátre des Champs-Elysées in Paris, to shouts of "traitor" coming from Russians or their sympathizers.

A telephone call from the English ballet diva, Margot Fonteyn, changed his life. She was the aging *prima ballerina* of Britain's Royal Ballet. At a charity event, the offstage and onstage liaison of the 42-year-old ballerina and the young Russian exile began.

Prince and Princess Stanislas Radziwill saw Rudi perform in London's Covent Garden and were mesmerized by him. While he was trying to find some permanent residence, the Polish aristocrat, married at the time to Jackie's sister, Lee, invited the ballet dancer to stay with them at what was called "the two prettiest houses in England," their townhouse in London and their country home.

In either house, Lee led a privileged life. Her friend, the French actress/dancer Leslie Caron, claimed that Lee was "overprotected, a child-wife evocative of Nora in Ibsen's *A Doll's House*."

After **Nureyev's** famous leap to freedom, with the KGB in hot pursuit, he was seen dancing with **Margot Fonteyn**, the most celebrated ballerina of the second half of the 20th Century. Late in her career, thanks partly to the dramatic flair of her younger partner, Fonteyn began what she defined as her career's "wonderful Indian summer."

Thanks to their shared execution of *Giselle*, a scene from which is depicted above, they became known as "the Dream Duo" to ballet fans worldwide.

531

At first, Rudi was suspicious of the Prince and Princess. He told Fonteyn that he thought he was being set up for a "three-way."

"We also have those arrangements in Moscow," he said. As it turned out, Rudi's sexual suspicion was only half founded. Lee was powerfully attracted to him. He would be their guest for seven months, as "Rudimania" swept across London. Arguably, Rudi became the first pop icon of the 1960s.

Fonteyn and Rudi were the hottest cultural ticket in the West, creating a sensation in the United States when they performed there in 1960s. His first American review defined Rudi as "a cheetah behind bars."

Truman Capote said, "Everybody, man or woman, wanted to fuck with Rudi, and most of them did, even the Kennedys. Whether he was dancing *Swan Lake* or *Romeo and Juliet*, all eyes were glued to Rudi's ample crotch. I sampled it myself. All nine and a half inches of thick Slavic meat."

Lee called Rudi "my eternal flame," and photographers liked to capture them in intimate situations as they danced together. She was caught on film clinging suggestively to him.

Friends reported that Lee was deeply in love with Rudi and "continued her campaign to make him straight." But as Capote warned her, "It was a hopeless undertaking. Once you've enjoyed the taste of cock, you can't keep them down on the farm."

A free-lance journalist, Diana DuBois, claimed: "Lee was put off by Rudi's homosexuality. That was always a bone of contention. He would tell her that he wanted a 'big cock,' and she would react with disgust."

In the early days, Lee was so taken with this ballet dancer that she purchased for him a Russian double-headed eagle of solid gold studded with diamonds and rubies.

Lee allegedly admitted to Capote (at least he claimed so) that she did have sex with Rudi one time. "It was the most athletic experience

Rudolf Nureyev, the dancer who flew through the air with the greatest of ease. His *grands jetées* were better and higher than those of any other ballet dancer in memory.

Here, he demonstrates that power during a performance of *Don Quixote* with **Lucette Aldous** and the Australian Ballet.

Prince and Princess Stanislaw ("Stas") Albrecht Radziwill enjoy balmy weather at the very posh Half Moon Resort in Montego Bay, Jamaica, during a holiday there in March of 1961.

Her brother-in-law, JFK, had only recently become President of the United States. Lee was beginning to enjoy worldwide attention as the sister of the more illustrious Jackie Kennedy.

I've ever known in bed," Capote quoted her as telling him.

Lee visited Rudi on the French Riviera where he'd rented a villa, "Arcadie," in La Turbie, high in the hills above Monte Carlo. In the guest bedroom, she came across pictures of men engaged in sex.

She came to realize that her sexual pursuit of the young dancer was a losing proposition. Yet their friendship survived, and would endure over the course of almost three decades. It began on a note of intense animal passion and developed into an enduring friendship.

When Rudi arrived in America and was introduced to Jackie, Lee found herself competing against her own sister for Rudi's affection. It would not be the first time the two sisters pursued the same man.

Although she was smart, talented, and charming in her own right, Lee often suffered unfavorable comparisons with her more formidable sibling. The press constantly compared them: Which of the sisters was better-looking? Which could more easily attract men? Which was the better-dressed?

With his special charm, Rudi was adept at "dividing myself into two parts"— shopping on Manhattan's Fifth Avenue with Jackie one week, dancing intimately with Lee in Monte Carlo the next. In time, he drew much closer to Lee. Jackie told some friends, "I envy Lee with Rudi. Perhaps I'm a little jealous. Of course, I would never dare admit that."

Lee was still in love with Rudi, and maybe the problem was that he was much more in love with Jackie than he was with Lee. He thought Jackie had the more alluring personality.

Capote claimed that Jackie fell in love with Rudi on the day she invited him and his dance partner, Margot Fonteyn, to the White House for tea.

Unlike her husband, "Rudi," as Jackie came to call him, admired her passion for the arts and even her choice of antiques. Sitting in the president's old North Carolina porch rocker in the Cabinet Room, he ordered his favorite drink, port with ginger ale, from a White House waiter.

Lee had warned Jackie that Rudi was "ninety-nine and a half percent homosexual," but Jackie wasn't so sure. Rudi was flirting outrageously with her, and she was a notorious flirt herself.

When the room emptied, he impulsively rose from the rocker, grabbed her, and passionately kissed her. "Unlike your beautiful husband, I do not have a bad back," he said. "A strong Russian back made for leaping through the air."

From that point on, according to Capote, Jackie was mesmerized.

After George Balanchine arranged for Rudi and Fonteyn to perform at a state dinner at the White House, journalist May Craig attacked Jackie in print, citing her "fawning devotion to the famous. She won't meet with student reporters, but she'll invite Greta Garbo to dinner."

Rudi complained to Jackie about some of his voracious female fans, including Marlene Dietrich, who called him, "The Boy."

At one time, she had four autographed pictures of Rudi wearing revealing tights in her bedroom. At first, he didn't know who she was, having seen none of her films. He told Jackie, "I thought she was an old show girl."

One night, Dietrich, after having dined with Rudi at Sean Connery's party at the Caprice in London, asked Rudi to drive her home. He whispered to James Bond, "If I'm not back in half an hour, come looking for me. I fear she's thinking about chaining me to her bed and making me her sex slave."

Over dinner one night with Jackie, Rudi told her, "I hate being pursued by aggressive women."

"Does that include me?" she asked.

"You Americans have a great response for that," he said. "Present company excepted." Then he sighed. "Instead of roses from Dietrich, I'd rather receive them from Baryshnikov. The first time I saw him in a pair of white tights, I wanted to devour him."

"I would love to get roses from Baryshnikov," she said. "Please don't try to convert him and destroy my hopes."

After her husband's death, Rudi, on many a night, "warmed the sheets" *[his words]* of the former First Lady's bed.

Capote claimed that Jackie "stole" Rudi from her sister, Lee, with whom the dancer was temporarily feuding. "She destroyed my baby," he charged to Jackie. "Had it cut in little pieces from her body. But with you, I will make nine beautiful children—five boys, four girls."

"Mother wants me to become President of the United States, but I'd rather be an actor," **John F. Kennedy, Jr.**, told Nureyev, who encouraged him.

Here, JFK's son is seen on March 14, 1980, during his first year at Brown University, playing Bonario, a soldier in *Volpone*, the 1606 play by Ben Jonson.

"I'm not a breeding factory," she warned him. "Better call Ethel for that."

"But I've already told my friends about the babies we're going to make."

"Don't you dare!" she shouted at him. "Stop this talk about our private relationship! It'll be fodder for the tabloids. Those friends of yours are malicious gossips!"

"But every part of your life has been in print already, although that is not good for the soul," he said.

Rudi not only admired Jackie for her beauty, but for her financial advice. "The first real money Rudi made was under Jackie's influence," said one of his associates. "She's the one who got him to buy gold just before gold shot up to the sky."

Jackie was hesitant to introduce Rudi to either her son or to Bobby Kennedy. At times Rudi could be flamboyantly homosexual. She feared Bobby might be put off by his exhibitionism. Even so, she arranged a dinner between Bobby and Rudi. "I've never seen two men bond in such a way," she told Lee when their relationship resumed. "Bobby seemed fascinated by Rudi." Jackie later admitted that she had no idea at first that Bobby and Rudi were seeing each other outside her home.

She became aware of that when the phone by her bedside rang one night. She was in bed with Rudi at the time. She picked up the phone. "Bobby," she said, her face lighting up.

A sudden look of distress crossed her brow. She muffled the phone. "He wants to speak to you. I must warn you, he's dangerously jealous of any man who gets near me. He must have had you trailed here."

Rudi eagerly took the phone from her. "Bobby, Bobby, you are the greatest American of them all. Fonteyn has taught me a new word for us—*peccadillo*."

As she made her way to the bathroom, she heard Rudi giggling into the phone like a young teenage girl with her first crush on the star football captain.

One of the first persons to spread rumors of Bobby's bisexuality was the notorious gay attorney, Roy Cohn. Both he and Bobby in the early 1950s had worked for Senator Joseph McCarthy during his notorious witch hunt, trying to round up suspected communists in government and in the movie business. Ironically, Cohn represented Aristotle Onassis later in life.

Cohn sent his boss some incriminating data about Bobby—Onassis' rival for Jackie's affection. In Cohn's dossier, he charged that RFK was a bisexual, indulging in homosexual relations with Nureyev. Enclosed were three photographs snapped at around three or four o'clock in the morning, showing Bobby leaving Nureyev's apartment after an assignation.

Cohn also told Onassis that Bobby had so many enemies that he suspected he would be shot if he ever ran for President of the United States, as he intended doing in 1968.

***

Two weeks later, over cocktails with Capote, Jackie said, "I think Rudi systematically plans to seduce every member of my family, even my son when he grows up. Or before he grows up. He's already talking about teaching John ballet at an early age."

Bolstered and supported by Peter Lawford, Rudi urged John F. Kennedy, Jr. to become a Hollywood movie star. "You already look like one," Rudi told JFK's impressionable young son. "Why not be one?"

One night, Rudi persuaded JFK Jr. to wear a pair of his purple ballet tights. When he saw how JFK looked, Rudi said, "The way you wear those tights, you'd be a sensation, if you could only dance."

"Watch out for that Cossack," Capote warned Jackie. "Rudi has enough charm to seduce Richard Nixon. Forgive me for prying—how unlike me—but I must ask. Is it true what they say about Rudi in bed?"

"Afraid so," she said. "On stage, his movements are the most graceful of any man on earth. But in bed I have a nickname for him: Mr. Jack Rabbit."

There were many sightings of Bobby and Rudi together at New York City night spots, especially at Arthur's. At the time, the celebrity-haunted joint was the most exclusive disco in New York. It was operated by Sybil Burton, the Welsh actress who'd lost her husband, Richard Burton, to Elizabeth Taylor, that "Serpent of the Nile."

Janet Villeha, a *prima ballerina* with the New York City Ballet in the 1960s, spotted "an arrival" at the club one night. "I saw Bobby come in with both Jackie and Rudi. Later on, as I went to make a phone call, I saw Bobby and Rudi in a telephone booth. They were kissing passionately."

All of his lovers knew that Rudi was a devotee of "deep throat" kissing. As one of his boys put it, "He went for your tonsils."

In his famous memoir, *Palimpsest*, Gore Vidal wrote of a revelation Rudi made to him:

"Between Bobby's primitive religion and his family's ardent struggle ever upward from the Irish bog, he was more than usually skewed, not least by his own homosexual impulses, which, Nureyev once told me, were very much in the air. 'We did share young soldier once. American soldier. Boy not lie . . . maybe.' Rudi gave his famous grin, very much aware, firsthand, of the swirls of gossip that envelop the conspicuous. Yet anyone who has eleven children must be trying to prove-disprove? Something other than the ability to surpass his father as incontinent breeder."

***

No one encouraged JFK Jr. to pursue a theatrical career more than Rudi. "John-John" shared his dreams with the Russian ballet dancer, who was falling in love with him.

A bit of a mama's boy, JFK Jr. told Rudi that Jackie was "dead set" against his going into the theater.

"Have some balls," Rudi said. "I know you've got a pair on you. We can't always do what mommy says."

Celebrity psychic John Cohan wrote a tell-all book in 2008, revealing relatively unknown secrets of the stars. No revelation was more shocking than the romantic link between John F. Kennedy, Jr. and Rudolf Nureyev.

As a psychic, Cohan warned JFK Jr. about his possible early death by advising him to avoid racecars, airplanes, and scuba diving.

John patted him on the back. "I'll start calling you my brother, an older brother, who worries a bit too much about me."

Once, when Cohan suffered from a sore shoulder, JFK Jr. offered to massage it. To JFK Jr., Cohan said, "I'm glad I'm straight, because this kind of feely stuff from an attractive, sexy man could certainly tempt the best of them."

JFK Jr. replied with a knowing smile. "I take the Fifth."

One night at New York's infamous Studio 54, Cohan encountered John F. Kennedy, Jr. in the company of family friend, Rudi, and New York's "hottest" male prostitute who advertised his services for $1,000 a night.

"This was a threesome I saw with my own eyes," Cohan wrote. "I think John wanted a new experience. He had confessed to me that he became bored with people and things quickly."

"He always talked about an acting career, which his mother adamantly refused to permit," Cohan said. "I used to caution him on many occasions—no race cars, no airplanes, and no scuba diving. I didn't feel good about these adrenaline rushes he got."

At the club, Cohan also warned Rudi, "Leave John-John alone, because this scene isn't his first preference."

"I love the challenge of seducing a straight man," Rudi told Cohan.

"That night he did just that," Cohan said.

The male prostitute later tried to sell an *exposé* article about the experiences he'd shared with Rudi and John Jr. But there were no takers—the allegation at the time was too controversial.

In his unpublished *exposé*, the male hustler claimed, "John fucked me, really hard, but when I tried to return the favor, he told me that that part of him was 'off limits.' Rudi went down on John, too. John-John played it strictly 'rough trade,'...but what an evening."

Perhaps no picture ever taken of America's prince, **John F. Kennedy, Jr.**, better demonstrates his athletic vigor than this shot taken in September of 1996 at Hyannis Port, two years after the death of his mother. In it, John Jr. is enjoying the dying days of summer in the Northeast.

JFK Jr.'s straight life, frat boy style, was best chronicled by his former roommate Robert T. Littell in 2005 in his memoir, *The Men We Became*. JFK Jr. and Littell first met as freshmen during orientation week at Brown University.

"Going out with John at night was like having a key to the city," Littell asserted. "Doormen bowed and velvet ropes fell when he stepped out of a cab. Sometimes, I felt as though I was with Moses at the parting of the Red Sea."

Littell claimed that their shared apartment was the venue for some strange sexual adventures. One night, one of their friends returned with a female flight attendant and took her to the spare bedroom. Later, Littell and JFK Jr. peeked in on their friend. The door was open a crack.

Inside, they saw their lusty friend rubbing the sheepskin collar of President Kennedy's official commander-in-chief leather jacket across the woman's bare breasts.

Her seducer was getting her excited by informing her that it was "The First Coat" actually worn many times by the assassinated president.

Other than Erik Bruhn, Rudi's most enduring relationship was with ballet dancer Robert Tracy. Meeting in 1979, and except for a separation of eight months, Rudi and Tracy were together until Rudi's death from AIDS at the age of 53 on January 6, 1993.

"When I met Rudi, he said I reminded him of Mars, the young god of vigor and war," Tracy said. "We were never faithful to each other, our sexual link lasting two and a half years. Rudi always told me you have to get the sex thing out of the way before a true friendship can begin."

"There were always guys around who were younger, with better bodies than mine," Tracy claimed, "but our relationship endured. Let there be no doubt about it. I caught Rudi in his years of physical decline—he called it 'the downside of ecstasy.'"

Rudi and Tracy shared a ranch house in Virginia, where a whole room was devoted to an organ so that Rudi could play Bach. Tracy remembered that Jackie was a frequent visitor. "She loved to go horseback riding at our ranch. Rudi always served her caviar. That was the life in those days—helicopters flying in, private jets to London, Paris, or Rome."

"Jackie also visited at our apartment in the Dakota building, opposite Central Park in New York," Tracy said. "We lived in the apartment above Lauren Bacall. Since Jackie knew we were discreet, she arrived with her beau of the moment."

"I think Jackie was a true balletomane," Tracy said. "There were rumors about her and John Kriza. She often asked us many, many questions about Mikhail Baryshnikov. I think she had a crush on him."

When his doctors informed Rudi of his HIV-positive status, he reacted defiantly, indulging in "phallocentric" rhetoric. "I am Tatar. AIDS is not going to fuck me, I'm going to fuck AIDS."

***

Although Rudi could have seduced some of the most famous men and women on the planet, and did on occasion, he much preferred anonymous encounters in public toilets, New York bathhouses, and other gay cruising venues.

In his dressing room, he often received celebrities in the nude. One night Arnold Schwarzenegger came backstage to congratulate him. Rudi sucked on the muscleman's index finger. "I want to know how you taste," he allegedly said. "I've seen pictures of you nude. I want you to put your cock in my mouth."

"You're the sixth person today who has requested that," Arnold reportedly said, retrieving his finger before it was devoured.

Monique Van Vooren, who wrote about Rudi in her 1981 book, *Night Sanctuary*, claimed he "was tortured, and tormented by his sexuality. He was ashamed of being homosexual. And I think he wanted to be degraded." In Diane Solway's *Nureyev: His Life* (1998), she wrote that he preferred "rough-trade, pickups, sailors, lorry drivers, and the like."

One night at one of Rudi's openings (the exact performance unknown), Jackie was in the audience and the stage manager urgently summoned her to come backstage to Rudi's dressing room.

There she found him completely nude. He told her that he was tired of his fans shouting, "*We want Rudi in the Nudi!,*" and that he was going to dance his next performance completely naked.

Using the force of her personality, she urged him to put on some purple tights. After holding the curtain fifteen minutes, Rudi agreed to go on, but his tights were so thin they were almost see-through. Jackie later told friends, "His fans got to see him almost naked, but he was covered enough so that the policemen weren't called."

She later became miffed at Rudi. In her working capacity as an editor at Doubleday, she went to him in 1986 and asked him to write his memoirs.

He turned her down. "Jackie darling," he said, "you know I can't write story of life. Story of life must tell what happened . . . I mean, really happened, not pack of lies. It should not be a cover-up, no truth in it. My not writing book will protect you and Bobby. Even your son."

Jackie's face flashed anger. "And what about my son? What did you do to John?"

"Nothing, not so excited. I encouraged him to be an actor. That's all. Nothing else. I swear it!"

Her upset with Rudi didn't last long. He charmed his way back into her good graces.

She was greatly concerned in 1987 when Rudi announced he was returning to Russia to see his ailing mother. She asked Ted Kennedy as a Senator to write to the Soviet ambassador in Washington, requesting protection for Rudi.

Before leaving New York, Rudi telephoned Jackie: "If I'm not back in Paris in three days, sound the alarm."

"God speed," she wished for him.

For twelve years Rudi carried the AIDS virus. His final artistic statement involved the choreography of a production of *La Bayadère*, which opened in February of 1992 at the Palais Garnier in Paris. During the ten-minute ovation that followed, he needed help to walk across the stage. He is quoted as saying, "The main thing is dancing. Before it withers away from my body, I will keep dancing till the last moment, the last drop."

Rudi died on January 6, 1993 at the age of 54. He was buried at a Russian cemetery in Sainte-Geneviève-des-Bois near Paris, a pilgrimage site even today for his still loyal fans.

Jackie did not make a pilgrimage to Rudi's tomb, but Lee did and wrote about it. She recalled attending his funeral with "all the attendants in black descending the imperial staircase of the Paris Opera *[Palais Garnier]* to surround the coffin. She compared his tomb to "that of a Turkish *kilim*, heavily draped, with thick gold tassels that rest on a black marble plinth."

"He introduced me to so much of what to this day gives me pleasure," Lee continued. "The music of Scriabin, the writings of Lermontov. His tomb is a memorable and theatrical vision befitting an exceptional dancer, an incredible person, and my closest friend."

What befits a legend most?
A State Funeral at the Palais Garnier in Paris.
Nureyev's death sent France into a period of national mourning.

Rudolf Nureyev, pre-defection, in rehearsal at the Kirov.

As flashbulbs snapped, **Nureyev** ("The Tatar Nomad") was forever traveling across the continents of the world.

"I am am a Tatar, not Russian," he said. "Traveling is in my blood. I was, in fact, born aboard a moving train in Siberia."

Chapter Twenty-Five

Jackie, Grace, & The Bullfighter

Jackie Tangles With the Princess of Monaco

On May 4, 1961, when President John F. Kennedy and Jacqueline entertained Prince Rainier and Princess Grace at a White House luncheon, the two combatants pictured above (**Grace**, of course, is the one in the silly hat), were later forced to have a cup of tea together when **JFK** excused himself to talk to Prince Rainier. Jackie at this point had heard about Grace's affair with her husband.

When they were seated, according to a White House staff member, Jackie provocatively asked, "Of the Seven Graces, which one are you?"

"I try to have the qualities of all of them," Grace shot back.

Continuing her provocation, Jackie asked, "Jack and I heard that when Prince Rainier was shopping for a bride, he first considered Marilyn Monroe. At least that was the plan that Aristotle Onassis said he proposed to your prince."

"Yes, I know," Grace shot back. "He found the idea disgusting. We're not promoting Monaco as a destination for Las Vegas style whorehouses."

Jackie wanted the last word, "Oh, I forgot to tell you how much I adore your hat. Did Oleg Cassini design it for you?"

One afternoon, Grace Kelly told Cary Grant, her co-star

in *To Catch a Thief,* "I fell in love with Jack Kennedy when I was a model in New York. I never got over it. He's the man I should have married."

Their fathers, Joe Kennedy and Jack Kelly, were two rich Irishmen who decided that their children should meet. Soon, JFK was seen escorting Grace in and out of the Barbizon Hotel for Women in Manhattan. Their affair was in full bloom.

When the subject of a possible marriage came up, Joe nixed it for his son. His father had learned from Jack Kelly that Grace planned to be a Hollywood star.

"Have you ever heard of a President of the United States bringing an actress to the White House as his First Lady?" Joe asked.

[At that time, Ronald Reagan hadn't married the former B-actress, Nancy Davis.]

Although marriage was out of the question, JFK and Grace got together at certain intervals.

Until Grace married Prince Rainier of Monaco in April of 1956, Jackie had been only vaguely aware that the future princess and her husband had had an affair be-

In *Mogambo (1953)*, shot in Africa, **Clark Gable** was cast as the crusty hero, Vic Marswell, the same role he'd played in *Red Dust* (1932), with Jean Harlow. **Ava Gardner** *(left)* played the whorish Honey Bear, and **Grace Kelly** *(right)* the part of the more demure Linda Nordley.
Gable had long before seduced Ava when they'd filmed *The Hucksters* in 1947. Now, he found Grace willing to succumb to his aging charms too.

All of her Hollywood beaux, including William Holden and Frank Sinatra, were but memories when **Grace Kelly** married **Prince Rainier** of Monaco in 1956.

fore her string of seductions from Marlon Brando, Ray Milland, Gary Cooper, Bing Crosby, William Holden, Frank Sinatra, Cary Grant, James Stewart, Clark Gable, David Niven, Spencer Tracy, Jean-Pierre Aumont, Oleg Cassini, Prince Aly Khan, *et al.*

Gore Vidal was present when JFK was looking at photos and news reports of Grace's wedding in Monaco to Prince Rainier. "I think Jackie's real distaste for Grace began on that afternoon. After looking at pictures of her Royal Highness, Jack announced, right in front of Jackie, 'I could have married her myself.'"

Denouncing him, Jackie ran from the room in tears.

"Their marriage seemed to go on hold after that, at least temporarily," Vidal said. "For sexual favors, Jack turned elsewhere."

Even though aide David Powers had tried to cover it up, Jackie learned that her husband, right before Grace's marriage to Rainier, had spent the night in Washington's Mayflower Hotel with the future princess.

At Hyannis Port, Jackie had confronted him with what she'd learned. Right in front of some members of the Kennedy clan, she told him that she was leaving him.

"Then get the fuck out of here!" he shouted at her. "I should never have married you in the first place. I really wanted to marry Grace Kelly. What a First Lady she would have made, not some Bouvier trash like you."

It took three weeks and constant apologies for Jackie to forgive him for that. She left Hyannis Port that night and headed for New York. Somehow, with the passage of time, she managed to turn her hatred of Jack for what he'd said into anger at Grace.

Jackie's loathing of Princess Grace spilled over into the White House after Jack was elected president in 1960. JFK asked Jackie to organize an official White House visit for Prince and Princess Rainier during the royal couple's visit to Washington.

Biographer Wendy Leigh quoted Letitia ("Tish") Baldrige, Jackie's social secretary, about what happened next. "Grace had a relationship with the President before his marriage to Jackie, and Jackie knew about it. That, in my opinion, is why Jackie changed the White House meal in their honor from a four-hour black-tie dinner dance to a small luncheon. A bit of jealousy perhaps. Jackie never said anything, but you could tell. She didn't really want to talk about the arrangements and was very offhand about how they were made. A luncheon meant that Princess Grace wouldn't look as gorgeous as she usually did at night."

Tish later revealed that Grace "looked dowdy—exactly like an Esther Williams Aquacade in a flowered rubber bathing cap." The President sat on one side of the oval-shaped table with Grace, whereas Jackie occupied the other side with Prince Rainier. Nervous about facing Jack again, and with a jealous Jackie hawk-eyeing her every move, she'd quickly downed two double Bloody Marys before arriving by limousine at the White

The Look of Love:
Grace Kelly was still enamored with **Jack Kennedy**, her former lover, when this picture was snapped the afternoon of their lunch at the White House. Even though he rarely saw Grace after he became president, JFK was always eager for gossip about her. Truman Capote had told him that Grace had had an abortion right before her marriage to Rainier.

House. "She was bombed," Franklin D. Roosevelt, Jr., another guest, claimed.

Roosevelt Jr. had already been privy to many of Jack's secret affairs before his marriage to Jackie, and had once gone out on a double date with Jack and Grace before she abandoned New York for Hollywood.

Tish remembered that Grace "behaved like a schoolgirl around Jack," perhaps recalling that if she'd made the right moves she'd now be First Lady of the ruling country of the Free World and not the princess of a small strip of land on the French Riviera. "She batted her eyelashes at Jack throughout the luncheon," Tish claimed.

She later told Roosevelt Jr. that Jack's rise in politics had been almost unbelievable, recalling that she'd warned him about how hard it would be for a Catholic to be elected. "But he was always such a handsome Irish boy, so full of life, so filled with charm, a real fighter just like his father."

Vidal had warned Jackie, "Don't let Grace be alone for one minute with Jack. In Hollywood, she always laid her leading men—she was notorious for that."

Grace and Jackie were often compared in the press, and both women were considered valuable assets to their husbands. President Kennedy claimed he was the man who accompanied Jackie to Paris, and Prince Rainier called Grace "the best ambassador I have."

Actually it was Grace who had charmed Charles de Gaulle years before Jackie won his heart. Jackie enchanted the French in 1961, Grace having done so in a French/Monegasque state visit two years before, in 1959.

In the days following the 1963 assassination of her former lover in Dallas, Grace came in for an attack when a photograph of her cheerfully holding an air rifle was published around the world. John Cummings, writing in the *Philadelphia Inquirer*, accused Grace "of being selfish and imbued with a heartless *insouciance* at the time of JFK's assassination. While her native land was in deep mourning for the slain President, Princess Grace was on an outing in a Monaco park. A photograph shows her in a shooting gallery on that tragic weekend."

Always sensitive to criticism, and very thin-skinned, Grace shot back, claiming that the photograph was actually taken hours before the tragedy in Dallas.

She was right about that, of course, since Monaco is hours ahead of Dallas. The photo of Grace with the rifle was taken at least nine hours before JFK was assassinated.

As recompense for her trouble and embarrassment at the carnival shooting gallery, Princess Grace made off with a Kewpie doll.

Actually Prince Rainier and Princess Grace were preparing to attend the President's funeral. However, the day they were scheduled to depart, a confidential message came in. A French diplomat had heard Jackie quoted as saying, "I don't want that whoring bitch to show up at Jack's funeral." The Rainiers immediately cancelled their flight.

In spite of that rejection, Princess Grace, because of her love for Jack, flew to Washington about two weeks after the assassination, on December 3, 1963. She was spotted standing by the President's grave with tears streaming down her cheeks. Before leaving France, she'd purchased very special, unique toys for John Jr. and Caroline, each object meticulously crafted by French artisans.

When she telephoned the White House for permission to visit with Jackie, who was still in residence, the former First Lady refused to see her.

In contrast, Her Royal Highness found Bobby only too willing to entertain her. Like his brother, Bobby had also seduced Grace. It was the continuation of an affair that lasted on and off until the end of his life, but only during very rare occurrences when they could secretly come together. At one point, Grace was fantasizing that she might have a chance to become America's First Lady—"but only after Bobby was elected in 1968."

"Our joint divorces would screw his political future, and he'd be a one-time President unless we were so charismatic that the American public forgave us for deserting our spouses," Grace said. "By the time Bobby sought a second term, the public might adore us, even more than they did Jack and Jackie—strange things like that happen." She confided this to David Niven, her intimate friend and former lover.

Before Jackie married Ari in 1968, he'd told her that had she married him in 1966, "You and I would be the Prince and Princess of Monaco." He revealed that he'd owned fifty-two percent interest in Monte Carlo's Société des Bains de Mer, which controlled the casino, the Hotel de Paris, the Yacht Club, and about thirty-four percent of the principality itself. In a move to usurp Onassis' power and to thwart any takeover attempts, Prince Rainier had issued 600,000 shares of new non-transferable shares in the name of the principality.

That effectively reduced Ari's ownership to less than a third. "Beaten and defeated by the prissy Grimaldi faggot, I was forced to sell out, and I departed from Monaco."

***

One of the most highly publicized trips that Jackie ever took was when the Duke and Duchess of Alba, along with Angier Biddle Duke, America's new ambassador to Spain, invited Jackie to Spain in 1966. After a night in Madrid, she flew to Seville where the Duke and Duchess installed her in the Palacio de Las Dueñas.

Also present was Princess Grace of Monaco. The stage was set for a catfight.

In the early 1960s, the most written-about women in the world included Jackie and Grace, who shared honors with Marilyn Monroe,

Dressed for the part, **Jackie**, an expert horsewoman, awed the people of Seville at the April *Feria*, especially when she downed a glass of sherry from nearby Jerez de la Frontera.

"To visit Seville and not ride horseback is equal to not coming at all," she said. Then she mounted a white stallion and made a leisurely *paseo* of the gaily decorated fair grounds, to the delight of 259 paparazzi.

545

Brigitte Bardot, Elizabeth Taylor, Princess Margaret, and, of course, Queen Elizabeth II.

From the very beginning of *Feria de Abril*, the Spring Fair in Seville, held in April of 1966, the press viewed the reunion of Princess Grace and Jackie as a "duel." Their clothing was the first to be communally scrutinized.

Grace opened the festivities clad in a ruffled, pink lace, Andalusian dress presented to her by local flamenco dancers. In contrast, the president's widow was dark and svelte in a black-and-white Andalusian riding costume.

Jackie "completely stole Princess Grace's thunder," wrote a journalist "when America's former First Lady agreed to ride a horse in the *Feria*."

Looking spectacular, Jackie had dressed for the occasion in the traditional *traje corio*, a black trimmed red jacket, a black flat-brimmed hat, and flowing chaps. On the back of a white stallion, she looked spectacular.

Perhaps Grace never got to read a review in a Seville paper of Jackie's appearance. "America's former First Lady revealed to all the world that she should not only have been made a princess like Prince Rainier's wife, but Jacqueline should be anointed Queen of the World." Grace's name wasn't even mentioned, except for the reference to her as "wife."

As part of the festivities, Princess Grace and Jackie encountered each other at Seville's splendid bullring. At that time, the celebrated, handsome, and well-built *El Cordobés* (actually Manuel Benítez Pérez) was the leading matador of Spain.

When **El Cordobés**, Spain's leading matador, spotted Jackie in the stands, he was mesmerized by her, dedicating his bullfight to her, and ignoring Grace Kelly.

He also told her that if the scars on his body were laid end to end, "they would stretch three times around my waist."

Jackie, who had a reputation for being flirtatious, was overheard telling him, "I prefer to do my own inspection instead of taking your word for it."

The paparazzi stumbled over each other to photograph him in his "suit of lights," paying particular attention to the bulging crotch in his matador suit. There was even speculation that he padded himself, although his "dressers" throughout Spain claimed his endowment was real.

Bypassing Grace—actually, ignoring her completely—*El Cordobés* passed his matador hat to Jackie, who placed a Kennedy half-dollar into it before returning it. He then dedicated "the first bull" to Jackie.

Adding insult to injury, two other famous matadors were fighting bulls that day, Paco Camino and *El Viti*. Both of these bullfighters also bypassed Grace and extended their hats to Jackie for a Kennedy half-dollar. Each of them also dedicated their first bull to Jackie.

In front of Jackie, *El Cordobés* performed his most dangerous stunt, as she watched in horror. He broke his *banderillas* down to the size of a pencil, then stood with his back to the bull as it rampaged toward him. A moment before impact, he deftly moved his right leg out of the way of the bull's path. As the bull swerved, he thrust in the *banderillas* at a crippling point just behind its left horn. The audience went wild.

Social critic, Cleveland Amory, had long been a critic of Jackie's. As a spokesperson for the Humane Society of America, he had criticized her in print for being a devotee of fox-hunting. He was horrified when he saw pictures of her at the bullfight. He wrote: "It is a sad and singularly ironic footnote to our modern age of violence that Mrs. Jacqueline Kennedy, of all people, who has seen the barbarism of the present era at such tragic firsthand, should now see fit to condone and even compliment one of the last relics of the barbarism of the past era."

The crossdressing, transgendered son of Ernest Hemingway, Gregory, was so impressed with the "package," on ample display, above, of bullfighter **El Cordobés**, that he made a special journey to Spain to see him dressed in his suit of lights. Here, the bullfighter displays his trophies, including a bull's severed ear and tail, to Jackie, who was sitting ringside in Seville.

***

A "scoop artist" for a Madrid newspaper was in Seville just to record juicy tidbits about Jackie. When the results of his investigation appeared, it caused a sensation. He claimed that *El Cordobés* was seen entering the palace of the Duke and Duchess of Alba where Jackie awaited him. Ostensibly it was for drinks and dinner.

The reporter said he waited outside the palace until three o'clock that morning when *El Cordobés* was seen leaving the palace and getting into a limousine. In print, he claimed, "It is all but certain that *El Cordobés* and the widow of President John F. Kennedy had an affair that night. In seducing her matador, Mrs. Kennedy was blazing a trail originally taken by the movie star, Ava Gardner, who had a particular fascination for Spanish bullfighters, especially Luís Miguel Dominguin. What is it with this fascination celebrated American women have for Spanish bullfighters? I think it has something to do with the bull."

Jackie allegedly found Manuel Benítez Pérez, commonly known as *El Cordobés* (The Cordoban), fascinating, though he was barely literate.

She met him during his heyday in the 1960s when he was the most famous matador of Spain, renowned for his unorthodox, acrobatic, and theatrical style in the ring.

She felt his story would not only make a great book, but an intriguing movie.

In Spain, he became a symbol of hope for poor boys around the country. He had risen fast within the celebrity circuit of Spain, driving a Rolls-Royce, flying his own airplane, and dating stunning women. Orphaned during the wrenching agonies of Spain's Civil War, young Manuel stole chickens to bring home for his mother to put into the pot, and worked as a ditchdigger, a pickpocket, a bricklayer, and a field worker as a means of earning a few pesetas.

Reportedly, *El Cordobés* showed Jackie his wounds as "badges of courage." Only two years before meeting her, he had experienced a near-fatal goring at the Plaza de Toros in Madrid on the horns of an enraged, half blind bull named "Impulsivo."

Because of his ability to draw so many fans, the press dubbed him "The Beatle of the Bullring." Receiving $50,000 per fight, he was one of the highest paid entertainers in the world.

When he met Jackie, he was known for having seduced some of the most celebrated women in the world. As Gregory Hemingway, son of *Ernesto*, said, "If these women weren't attracted to his bullfighting skills, they were to that package he encased in his tight-fitting suit of lights."

El Cordobés was heavily criticized for partying with Francisco Franco, Spain's brutal dictator. Franco liked to go hunting with him.

Jackie commented on the young man's theatricality in the ring. "He was a great showman, exhibiting a kind of razzle-dazzle. He would crouch, then leap away from the onrushing horns in just the nick of time. Talk about Hemingway's *Death in the Afternoon.* Or else he'd rest his head against the bull's hindquarters one moment and mock-box the beast the next moment. Of course, he flashed a smile suited for toothpaste commercials. At one point, I screamed when he flicked his red *muleta.* The beast was charging at him, and he wasn't moving until the last second."

Not all of *El Cordobés'* observers were as kind to him as Jackie. He had dozens of critics, especially classicists. They found "his passes crude and his swordsmanship fit only for the slaughterhouse." Vicente Zabala, one of Spain's leading taurine authorities, claimed, "*El Cordobés* has always been bad for bullfighting—he made underage, inadequate bulls the norm; his style corrupted other fighters, and he encouraged an ignorant public."

To Jackie, El Cordobés said, "I fight for the masses. Those smart guys who think they know so much write great stuff on how to fight bulls. But there's just one trouble: The bulls can't read."

***

[Jackie was prophetic in seeing a book emerging from the life experiences of El Cordobés. In 1968, journalists Larry Collins and Dominique Lapierre released a biography entitled Or I'll Dress You in Mourning." *The bullfighter's story also became the basis for a musical*, Matador, *by Michael Leander and Edward Seago, which opened in London's West End in 1991.*

Jackie, a faithful reader of Kirkus Reviews, *read a description of the biography of El Cordobés before buying a copy.*

"In the small Andalusian town of Palma del Rio, ruled by an autocratic

landowner, Don Felix Moreno, a ragged boy, saw a stereotyped film on bull-fighting that changed his life. He fought Moreno's bulls by moonlight until he killed his seed bull and was exiled."

"There followed years of struggle. Finally, his manager, Rafael Sánchez, known as 'El Pipo,' pawned his family's jewels to bring the young El Cordobés into the bullfight arena of Palma. Before heading into the ring, El Cordobés told his sister, Angelita 'I'll either buy you a house or dress you in mourning.'" The latter promise became the title of the biography.

As part of his training, instead of bulls, El Pipo provided cows on which El Cordobés would practice his maneuvers, helping the young matador fashion his gimmicks for presentation in the ring. El Pipo also bribed journalists to overlook the young man's stylish flaws, and the fact that at least at the beginning of his career, he used weak and rather timid bulls for his bouts in the ring. Rival matadors were not fooled, of course, but his ever-growing public was.

Based on the time he spent in Seville with Jackie, El Cordobés later claimed that he was going to transform Jackie into a motion picture star. As Jackie biographer Freda Kramer wrote: "El Cordobés told everyone that Jackie was going to appear in a picture he was making. He swore on it." The claim merited some space in newspapers. It was even said that Jackie was going to donate her salary to charity.

This was not the only time the press speculated that Jackie was going to star in a movie. For a time, her dear friend, director Mike Nichols, was said to have cast her in a romantic comedy opposite Rock Hudson.

When asked about that rumor, Jackie said, "I'm leaving the acting in the family to my sister Lee."

Her sister's acting had been a disaster. In 1967, Lee would appear in Chicago in the stage production of The Philadelphia Story, and a year later, in a nationally televised remake of Laura, adapted by Truman Capote and produced by David Susskind. both performances were demolished by critics.

Dressed for the part, Jackie, an expert horsewoman, awed the people of Seville at the April *Feria*, especially when she downed a glass of sherry from nearby Jerez de la Frontera.

"To visit Seville and not ride horseback is equal to not coming at all," she said.

Then she mounted a white stallion and made a

Their hapless host, the **Duke of Medinaceli** *(center)*, was caught between two battling divas—**Jackie** *(left)* and **Princess Grace** *(right)*— at a gala party in Seville.

After the exchange of limp handshakes, Jackie and Grace ignored each other throughout the remainder of the evening. In the meantime, El Cordobés was spreading word to the press that he and Jackie would star in a movie together.

leisurely *paseo* of the gaily decorated fair grounds, to the delight of 259 paparazzi.

***

The highlight of the *Feria* was the International Red Cross Ball, a charity debutante party for 2,500 guests hosted by the Duke of Medinaceli.

As usual, Princess Grace expected to be the belle of the ball. She went all out and appeared wrapped in white mink. Her hair was upswept and she was wearing a prince's ransom in diamonds. But she was virtually ignored as the guests rushed to get a glimpse of Jackie when she entered the courtyard bare shouldered and wearing a blue gown designed by Oleg Cassini. Jackie had fashionably arrived an hour late.

Grace was also jealous that the designer, Cassini, her former lover who'd once passionately wanted to marry her, was now showering his attention on the creation of chic *couture* for Jackie.

After battling through the hordes of reporters and photographers, Jackie finally made it to the table of their host, the Duke de Medinaceli. Grace extended a limp handshake to Jackie, then turned her head to avoid her throughout the rest of the evening.

With the poor Duke sandwiched in between them, he tried to make conversation to no avail. The next morning the *New York Herald Tribune* captioned a picture of them, headlining, "Cool Conversation," and noting that Grace and Jackie had little to say to each other. In response, Grace wrote a letter to the newspaper, claiming "I have great respect and admiration for Mrs. Kennedy."

Prince Rainier seemed dazzled by Jackie, but Princess Grace remained frosty, and Jackie turned an Arctic shoulder to Her Serene Highness. Jackie had long ago learned the details of Grace's romantic involvement with Jack as well as her seduction of Bobby, who was Jackie's lover at the time. "Jackie had reasons to detest Grace," Truman Capote later said, "especially when eagle-eyed Grace detected a gleam in the eyes of her prince."

In a huff, the Princess departed for an hour to the powder room. During her absence, Prince Rainier was seen in a secluded area of a patio smoking a cigarette with Jackie, away from the prying eyes of the paparazzi.

At the time of this flirtation between Jackie and Prince Rainier, international rumors were swirling that she was all but engaged to Antonio Garrigues, a widower with eight children. At the age of 62, he'd been appointed Spain's Ambassador to the Vatican. He and Jackie were later spotted together in Rome.

Unknown except to many of her friends, Jackie was a great mimic. After leaving Seville, she headed for some R&R at the swank Marbella Club on Spain's Costa del Sol. Once there, she delivered a devastating satire of Grace as she'd appeared in *Rear Window* (1954) opposite James Stewart, another of Grace's sexual conquests.

"It should have been taped," said Antonio Cordova, a member of the chic clique who had gathered at the Marbella Club. "Jackie appeared with long white gloves and imitated Grace's speech pattern to perfection. Slowly those gloves were removed, and Jackie did the world's most amusing rendition of Grace Kelly imitating Rita Hayworth in her 'Put the Blame on Mame' number. What an evening!"

***

After the *Feria* in Seville, Jackie and Grace virtually ended whatever meager relationship they had, but Grace continued to place calls to Bobby in Washington.

Whatever the nature of Grace's relationship with Bobby, the bond became so strong between them that, in an unprecedented move, Grace volunteered to return to America and campaign for him in his quest for the presidency in 1968. In volunteering, she defied the wishes of her husband, who did not want her to get involved.

RFK called Grace and thanked her, eagerly looking forward to her appearance in America. No doubt, he wanted to continue their affair. Even though he'd already opted to end a high-profile romance with Jackie as a condition of running for the presidency, "he suddenly had become as sexually insatiable as Jack had been," Langdon Marvin claimed. A former aide to JFK, Marvin had provided numerous women available for affairs with the President. "Almost no one refused," he recalled.

Suddenly, from the heat of the campaign trail, Marvin found himself procuring a "gaggle of women for Bobby—airline hostesses, starlets, secretaries, whomever. Bobby was sexually insatiable. He had a penchant for nymphettes."

Marvin admitted that one time at the Carlyle Hotel, he sent Bobby a trio of girls "no more than fifteen. They were attending a private high school in New York. Bobby later thanked me, claiming 'That was the best present I ever got from anybody,' admitting that he'd also enjoyed watching the schoolgirls engage in lesbian sex."

Bobby went out in a blaze of glory, moving ahead toward the presidency and adored by millions, with beautiful women making themselves available to him for the asking—and sometimes he didn't even have to ask.

But then, on June 6, 1968, an assassin's bullet hit its mark, and the party was over.

Apparently, Bobby's assassination affected Grace far more than Jack's. She went into a period of deep mourning.

Jackie shunned any overture for future meetings with Princess Grace. In 1974, less than a year before Ari's death in March of 1975, Jackie was invited to participate in Ari's last extended cruise through the Eastern Mediterranean, with its conclusion scheduled for Monaco.

Jackie had recently had a fight with Ari, ostensibly because he refused to buy her a luxurious villa in Acapulco. Christina, his daughter, agreed to accompany her father instead.

Jackie had told her husband, "You're a fucking ingrate—I don't want your money."

"So be it, my dear," he told her, "Then you won't be disappointed." The next day he drew up a new will.

When the *Christina* arrived in Monte Carlo, Ari called Jackie in Paris and asked her to fly to Nice where a limousine would be waiting for her. He wanted her to host a dinner for Prince Rainier and Princess Grace. She refused, which turned out to be a wise choice.

The dinner aboard the yacht evolved into a disaster, as Ari attacked the prince, who had forced him to sell his shares in the Société des Bains de Mer.

After that dinner, Ari flew to Paris where Paul Mathias, a French journalist, saw Jackie and him dancing the night away in a Left Bank *boîte*. Jackie was demonstrating her new skill with castanets, which she'd learned from a fla-menco dancer in Seville. She even lured a dying Onassis onto the dance floor where he loped about like a wounded antelope.

The last romantic link between the Kennedy family and the House of Grimaldi came when Ted Kennedy, Jr. started to date Princess Stephanie. Be-fore that, Stephanie was rumored to have had an affair with John F. Kennedy, Jr.

Edward (Ted) M. Kennedy Jr. was born in 1961 when his uncle was still president. The twelve-year-old earned international press when he was diag-nosed with osteosarcoma in his right leg, a form of bone cancer. The leg was surgically amputated.

After the death of Princess Grace in 1982, *Ici Paris*, a popular French tabloid, suggested that Prince Rainier was considering marrying Jackie Onas-sis. Later, this rumor was dismissed, one reporter claiming that whatever at-tention Jackie was lavishing on Rainier was merely part of her attempt to persuade His Serene Highness to write his autobiography for Doubleday.

But there was far more to it than that. Jackie and the Prince were spotted together at certain discreet restaurants in Paris, and once cozily sharing drinks in a remote corner of a bar at Paris' Ritz Hotel.

Aides to Rainier said he did seriously consider proposing to America's for-mer First Lady after Grace died. "Marrying Jackie would be an even bigger coup for Monaco than marrying Grace," Rainier told his close friend, actor David Niven. "Princess Jacqueline could bring worldwide publicity to Monaco—new investments and first-class tourism. It would be a sensation far greater than marrying a mere movie star."

It is not known if the Prince actually proposed to Jackie.

Ted Sorensen, former JFK aide, said, "After marrying Jack Kennedy and Ar-istotle Onassis, Prince Rainier was about the only eligible male left in that class for her to marry. In passing, I once mentioned this prospect to Jackie. She hes-itated and said nothing at first. Then she claimed, 'I would have to give such an offer serious consideration.'"

Chapter Twenty-Six

Jackie vs. Elizabeth Taylor

Rival American Divas Battle for Love, Glory, and Men

The Queen of Ancient Egypt Slugs It Out
With the Queen of the Potomac

When her husband was running for president of the United States, **Jackie Kennedy** had not only to face the competition of blonde bombshell Marilyn Monroe, she also learned that her philandering husband was engaged in a torrid affair with **Elizabeth Taylor.**

Revelations about the affair came to light after the death of Dame Elizabeth in 2011. Details were leaked to the press from her private diaries which may, in time, be edited and published.

But long before the world found out about the ET/JFK affair, Jackie knew about it. Her informant in such matters was Peter Lawford himself, who often functioned as a "double agent," feeding Jack information about Jackie and vice versa.

Reportedly, Elizabeth was mesmerized by JFK, whom she was supporting in his presidential bid. During his 1960 campaign, she had several private evenings within his bungalow at the Beverly Hills Hotel. Her marriage to Eddie Fisher (her fourth husband) didn't stop her from sleeping with America's future president.

Being married to Jackie never prevented JFK, of course, from having affairs on the side. Except for Marilyn Monroe, none of his paramours was quite as famous as Elizabeth. Naturally, the tabloids played them off against each other, trumpeting their respective embarrassments and defeats.

During her marriage *[1957-1958]* to Mike Todd, Elizabeth Taylor found herself at the center of a media circus. From 1957 until the end of the 60s, she'd be the most written-about woman in the world, challenged only by Jackie Kennedy after she became First Lady. Images of Elizabeth or Jackie vied for shelf space and sales from magazine racks throughout America.

Although constantly linked together, contrasted, and compared in the press, Jackie and Elizabeth only met one time in their lives. Yet, in spite of that, they were intimately linked at times with the same four men—John and Bobbie Kennedy, Richard Burton, and Aristotle Onassis. Elizabeth didn't endear herself to Jackie when she indiscreetly relayed to friends, "I got Jack long before Jackie sunk her claws into him."

Jackie became the first First Lady that the press treated like a movie star instead of as the wife of a political figure. For the first time, a former occupant of the White House appeared on the covers of *Modern Screen, Photoplay, Screen Stories,* and *Movie Life* even more frequently than on the covers of "mainstream news" publications such as *Time, Life,* and *Look.*

Elizabeth Taylor, "The Queen of the Nile," *(subject of both photos, above)* emoted with Marc Antony (**Richard Burton**) both on and off the screen. For almost a quarter of a century, Jackie avidly followed their fiery romance.

For a while, however, Jackie's marriage to Aristotle Onassis generated more headlines.

Between 1963 and 1973, *Photoplay* featured Jackie more than virtually any other celebrity on its covers. Her picture almost guaranteed a bump in circulation. Many newspaper editorials denounced this "trashing" of Jackie. As one writer asserted, "She's treated just like Liz Taylor or Marilyn Monroe."

Every month Jackie found herself written about in articles which appeared adjacent to features about such flamboyant personalities as Liberace. Many of the stars she was featured next to were merely fast-fading figures in the pub-

What Did JFK and Richard Burton Have in Common?

Each Managed to Seduce "La Liz" (The Vatican's "Erotic Vagrant") and Jackie (the "Demure, Fashion-Crazed Enigma")

lic eye. In one case, a story appeared under the head—JACKIE: MY SUMMER LOVE. It ran next to another story: DAVID McCULLUM'S 60 SWINGING SECRETS.

Tabloid saga:
the Battling Brunettes.

As Wayne Koestenbaum wrote in *Jackie Under My Skin:* "Jackie's adjacency to fly-by-nights proves that stardom has no absolute ground, and that even Jackie was subject to laws of fade-out and fall. She might last no longer than Dolores Hart. That Jackie lingered, in the twilight of *Photoplay*, does not mean she acquired substance or wholeness. Rather, she lasted as ephemera; she lasted as someone we could not pin down or understand. The passion for Jackie ceased to be shallow. She persisted, season after season, in magazines, without any songs or films or TV shows to back her up. Jackie's longevity was a consequence of how little could be proved about her."

Magazine after magazine featured Elizabeth and Jackie in the same issue under such headlines as: *JACKIE WILL MARRY! LIZ WILL DIVORCE! JINX PLAGUES JACKIE & LIZ! JACKIE & LIZ: SOUL SISTERS IN TRAGEDY.*

In November of 1963, shortly before JFK's assassination, both Jackie and Elizabeth appeared on the cover of one issue of *Photoplay* that also featured a story about Paul Newman's two-day visit to a nudist colony. It was   Photoplay that ran a photo of Jackie with the President on their cover alongside Elizabeth and Burton. Jackie's marriage stood for "Taste." Elizabeth's marriage (according to Hedda Hopper, incidentally) stood for "Passion and Waste."

After her marriage to Onassis, Jackie, too, joined Elizabeth in the trash can of journalism. The headlines trumpeted her "shame:" *GOLD-DIGGING JACKIE, JACKIE GREEDY SHOPPER IN PARIS; JACKIE BUYS SEE-THROUGH BLOUSE FOR HER HUSBAND.*

Headlines associated with Liz were even worse: *LIZ AND BURTON ATTACKED FOR THROWING NUDE BEACH PARTY.*

Even when Elizabeth made *Cleopatra* in Rome with Burton playing Marc Antony, one reviewer accused her of "looking like a plump, audacious version of Jackie Kennedy." At least Jackie didn't have to endure being called an "erotic vagrant" by the Vatican.

The Vatican was not only enraged by the adulterous affair of Burton and Elizabeth, but she had also adopted a nine-month-old girl in Bavaria. Originally named Petra Heisis, she was renamed Maria Taylor after her adoption.

She had been born with a crippling hip defect, and Elizabeth felt compelled to provide her with all the expensive medical treatments she needed. Even so, Pope John XXIII denounced the star as an unfit mother.

Whereas the Cuban Missile Crisis *[October 14–28, 1962]* brought the United States to the brink of nuclear disaster, the illicit love affair between Burton and Elizabeth seemingly generated more headlines. "Liz & Dick," as they were called, were accused of (or credited with) sparking the sexual revolution that blossomed during the decades (the 1960s and 70s) of "free love."

Elizabeth had her own private reaction to this massive press coverage. She told Roddy McDowall, "The most famous man on the planet, John F. Kennedy, is fucking the second-most famous woman on earth, Marilyn Monroe, and not a word gets into the press. But let me screw around with some Welsh actor and the media goes apeshit."

Jackie-Oh! Vs. La Liz: How Did It All Begin?

In 1948, Elizabeth starred with the handsome actor, Robert Stack, in *A Date With Judy* for MGM. Stack was considerably older than Elizabeth, but their parents were good friends, so he was evaluated as a suitable escort for Elizabeth.

They'd dated for only a short while before he informed her that "my best pal," John F. Kennedy, newly elected to Congress from Massachusetts, would be at his house at around noon on Saturday. "You might like to meet him. He's charming," Stack said to Elizabeth.

Stack had first met JFK in 1939 when a mutual friend, Alfred de la Vega, had introduced them in Hollywood.

She told Stack she'd already met JFK in 1937 in England when she was "just a little girl," and he was the 20-year-old son of Joseph P. Kennedy, the U.S. ambassador to the Court of St. James's.

Elizabeth had already heard about JFK's first introduction to Hollywood. Stack and the young Jack had shared a secret "bachelor pad" hideaway at the end of a cul-de-sac on Whitley Terrace, high in the Hollywood Hills. "We learned about the birds, the bees, the barracuda, and other forms of Hollywood wildlife there," Stack told her.

What he didn't tell Elizabeth was that JFK had called him before his arrival on the West Coast. He'd said, "I want to fuck every woman in Hollywood. I want to specialize in celebrity

In the early 1940s, **Robert Stack** *(left)* and **John F. Kennedy** were two of the most desirable males "chasing tail" in Hollywood.

According to Judy Garland, "Both men and women, including Howard Hughes, pursued them. The women, who included myself, won out."

poontang—like Dad did."

In the studio's makeup department, very early one Friday morning before a day's shooting at MGM, Elizabeth sat next to June Allyson. She learned that Allyson and JFK had had an affair, and that Allyson was already scheduled for a rendezvous with the young congressman during his upcoming visit. Allyson even suggested, "Perhaps you, Robert, Jack, and me can go out on a double date."

Elizabeth did not tell her about her own upcoming plans to meet Jack.

"That guy can literally charm the pants off a girl," Allyson said. "He calls his penis 'the implement.' He wants a girl at both the front and back doors. But he's a sort of '*Slam, Bam, Thank You, Ma'am*' type of lover. When the dirty deed is done, he wants to rush off to his next conquest."

The following night, when Elizabeth arrived at Stack's house, he directed Elizabeth to his pool, where JFK was waiting. Looking rail-thin, he wore only a pair of white shorts and was resting on a *chaise longue* in the sun. He did not get up to greet her, but put out his hand, capturing hers and holding it for a long time. "Hi, Elizabeth, you are living proof that little girls grow up in delightful ways. You've changed. For the better, I'd say."

"You have, too," she responded.

"In what way," he asked.

"Better looking. More manly. I guess it was the war and the years. I hear you're a big time naval hero."

"Fuck!" he said. "I don't care what you've heard. I won the war single-handedly. Don't let anyone tell you differently." The twinkle in his eyes revealed that he was satirizing his own exploits.

"And now, you're a Congressman!" she said.

"If Dad has anything to say about it, I'll be sitting in the White House at least by 1964."

"I hope you'll issue me a presidential pardon," she said.

"Not likely," he smiled. "I'll summon you to the White House for a command performance."

At that point, Stack came out onto the patio, calling them to lunch.

As they ate, JFK told Elizabeth and Stack that he'd flown to the West Coast to escape "the post-election blues" and because he couldn't attend any more chicken à la king dinners.

"And you're out here to get your jollies!" Stack interjected.

"There's nothing wrong with that!" JFK said. "Right, Elizabeth?"

"There's nothing wrong if you get them with me!" She shocked even herself at how forward she had become.

JFK laughed. "A promise I'll make you keep."

Even though they indulged in mostly small talk, there was sexual tension in the air. She would later confess to Roddy McDowall that she was waiting for one of them, especially JFK, to make the first move.

After lunch, JFK got up and pulled off his white shorts in front of them. He was completely casual about his nudity, as his future wife, Jackie Kennedy, would eventually claim.

"Let's all go for a nude swim," he proposed, jumping into the pool.

In front of her, Stack pulled off his shorts and jumped into the water to swim after JFK. As Elizabeth would later relay to Dick Hanley, "I knew it was show time, and I didn't want to disappoint. I pulled off my dress, bra, and panties, and swam in after them."

At that point, the screen goes black. Elizabeth refused to relay all of the juicy details to Dick, even though he wanted a blow-by-blow description. "I can live vicariously, can't I?"

All she'd confess to was a three-way. "It was my first such experience, but I don't think it will be my last. Bob is the better lover, but Jack has more charm. All I'll tell you is that he's mainly concerned with getting himself off—and not the girl who's lying under him. Bob has better staying power. Jack went first. But he shot off rather quickly. Would you believe that Bob and I were still going at it, and Jack was up beside the bed making a phone call? Then Bob and I finished the dirty deed."

"Are you going to pursue Jack?" Dick asked, "or was that it?"

"No, I'll keep after him," she said. "Not so much because of his love-making, but because of his charm. He has this amazing ability to look at you while you're talking and make you feel that you're saying something so vital that the fate of the whole world depends on it."

***

JACKIE: "I hate Elizabeth Taylor."
ELIZABETH: "Jackie Kennedy is a gold-digging bitch."

When her husband was running for President, and even when he occupied the Oval Office, Jackie Kennedy had to face competition not only from Marilyn Monroe and so many others, but from Elizabeth Taylor, too.

Revelations about the Taylor/JFK affair came to light after the death of Dame Elizabeth in 2011. Details were leaked to the press from her private diaries which may, in time, be edited and published.

It appears that Robert Kennedy himself arranged several liaisons between Elizabeth and the President in 1961, as well as enjoying her considerable charms himself.

But long before the affair with JFK came to light, Jackie knew about it. Her informant was Peter Lawford, who often functioned as a "double agent," feeding Jack information about Jackie, and supplying Jackie with secret data about her husband.

Reportedly, Elizabeth was mesmerized by both the Kennedy brothers. *[Apparently, Teddy never got around to her.]*

During JFK's 1960 campaign for president, she had visited him on occasion in a bungalow at the Beverly Hilton Hotel. She also had perhaps three sexual trysts with him in Beverly Hills during the summer of 1961, when she'd had her first fling with Bobby.

Except for Marilyn Monroe, none of the affairs JFK had were with women as famous as Elizabeth.

"Kennedy did more than fundraising when he came to California," Eddie Fisher later said. "Kennedy was widely known for fucking Elizabeth look-alikes like Judith Campbell Exner. I guess on occasion he wanted the real thing—not merely the mock. I had Judy myself. She made herself up to look as much like Elizabeth as she could."

"Elizabeth swore to me that her relationship with Jack never went beyond friendship," Fisher said. "But I never believed her. I'm sure she never believed me when I told her that I was 'just friends' with some of the women I was bedding. When Jackie heard of the affair, she said some really vicious things about Elizabeth, so I was told. And you should have heard what my potty-mouthed wife said about Jackie. It was a real catfight waged on two different coasts."

Both Burton and Roddy McDowall, his co-star in *Camelot* and his sometimes lover, were emphatically aware of their presence on the night then-Senator from Massachusetts John F. Kennedy and his beautiful and elegant wife, Jackie, came to see *Camelot*. Backstage, the Kennedys greeted Burton and congratulated him, although he later heard that the future president found the music boring. Jackie, however, found the legend of Camelot fascinating. The world would realize the degree to which she was intrigued after the assassination of her husband in Dallas in 1963.

After the performance, whereas Senator Kennedy planned an immediate return to Washington, Jackie planned to remain in New York for two days of shopping.

"I asked her if I could call on her at the Carlyle and discuss the legend of Camelot with her," Burton later confided to Roddy. "To my amazement, she agreed."

The following night, Roddy was eager to learn all the details of Burton's visit to the suite of the future First Lady. "Over drinks, we spent an hour talking about *Camelot*," Burton said. "We had more than one drink. She's a fabulous dame, really fabulous. If I had a dame like Jackie full time, I swear I'd never have to cheat on her."

Julie Andrews as Guinivere with **Richard Burton** as King Arthur as they appeared on Broadway in the musical, *Camelot*.

It became Jackie's favorite musical and led to her creation of the myth of Camelot as a metaphor for the Kennedy administration in the White House.

"I know, I know," said an impatient Roddy. "The question is, did you score?"

"A bull's eye," Burton bragged. "She's prim and proper, but once you get her panties off, she's a tigress."

Was Burton merely bragging to his gay friend and fellow actor, or was he telling the truth? No one knows for sure, although some authors of Taylor/Burton biographies maintain that he did have a brief fling with Jackie, which was one of the reasons the image of Camelot was so imbedded in her brain.

Burton also told Peter O'Toole and Peter Lawford about his affair with Jackie. Burton had already bedded a long line of famous women, and he really didn't have to invent affairs he never had.

Since Jackie was known even during the 1950s for an occasional extra-marital affair *[unlike her husband, who was virtually having a daily extramarital affair]*, it is entirely possible that Burton seduced her.

As Elizabeth herself maintained, "The sound of his voice could probably give a woman an orgasm."

What was important was that Elizabeth came to believe that Burton had seduced Jackie, or in Elizabeth's words, "I bet she seduced him. She's just getting back at me for having had a fling with Jack Kennedy. That bitch!"

Roddy later admitted to his close friends that Elizabeth tried "to pry the truth from me. She told me I had never lied to her before, and she didn't want me to start telling her lies now. I told her, 'I can't talk about it...I just can't.'"

"Thank you," she said. "You've told me just what I wanted to know. Richard fucked Jackie Kennedy!"

Burton confessed to others that Elizabeth did not consider herself particularly attractive. "She has a wonderful bosom, though. But she has the shape of a Welsh village girl. Her legs are really quite stumpy, far too short. Elizabeth feels her feet and arms are too large. But she considers Jackie Kennedy beautiful."

During the filming of *Cleopatra* in Rome, Burton received his friend, Dick Hanley *[Elizabeth's secretary]* in his dressing room one hot afternoon. He was sitting nude in front of his vanity mirror, and had been drinking heavily. At one point, he talked about women he'd seduced.

"The woman who brings out the best in a man—and who is good in bed—is very rare. In my entire life, I've enjoyed only four such women—Elizabeth Taylor, Marilyn Monroe, Jackie Kennedy, and an almost toothless middle aged hag in Jamaica."

***

Gore Vidal later wrote that one night in Paris, Maria Callas told him that Burton, while aboard Ari's yacht, had once confessed to Onassis that he'd seduced Jackie.

According to Callas, "Ari also had a sexual confession to make."

"Remember that night you made up some excuse to leave ship and head for Athens?" Onassis asked Burton. "I think that Elizabeth knew you were actually visiting the brothels there. Well, that's the only night in my life I lured Elizabeth into my stateroom. So, pal, are we even now?"

During the 1960-61 run of the play, *Camelot,* on Broadway, Robert F. Kennedy became a fan of both the musical and, even more, of the character

(King Arthur) portrayed by Richard Burton. Over a period of two months, he attended the musical three times. After each performance, he joined Burton in his dressing room, inviting him for a late night dinner and drinks.

These two unlikely candidates for friendship formed a close bond. Among other interests, they discovered their mutual love of poetry.

Gossip among the rich and famous aboard the *Christina*.

From left to right, **Elizabeth Taylor, Aristotle Onassis, Merope Onassis Konialidis** (Ari's half-sister), and **Richard Burton.**

Although Jackie is credited with creating the myth of Camelot as a metaphor for the Kennedy years in the White House, the concept may have originated with Bobby. After seeing the play for the first time, Bobby later told Jackie, "I came backstage to greet Burton, and I was ushered into his dressing room. I found him sitting in front of his vanity mirror removing his makeup. He was wearing only a jock strap."

In the bowels of the Majestic Theater in Manhattan, RFK told Burton how much he'd liked the cadenced, dignified lyrics of Alan Jay Lerner.

Each evening from December to December,
Before you drift to sleep upon your cot
Think back on all the tales that you remember
Of Camelot.

Ask every person if he's heard the story
And say it loud and clear if he has not
That once there was a fleeting wisp of glory
Called Camelot.

Burton was very flattered by Bobby's assessment of the pleasure he'd given the Kennedys through his depiction of the noble King Arthur in *Camelot*. JFK and Jackie had already expressed their appreciation of the musical.

After JFK saw the play, after his return to Washington, he frequently called Burton. "I like the sound of your voice, especially when you're quoting Shakespeare," Both men had hectic schedules, but made phone contact whenever they could.

On November 22, 1962, Burton was in Puerto Vallarta, Mexico, shooting Tennessee Williams' *The Night of the Iguana*. Word reached them that JFK had been assassinated in Dallas.

Dick Hanley, Elizabeth's secretary, said that "Richard cried on Elizabeth's shoulder and was morbidly destroyed for two weeks. He had difficulty emoting on camera."

Burton sat down and wrote Jackie a long letter, expressing his grief. Because she was overwhelmed with relocation problems, and had received an avalanche of mail, it was two months before she could reply. She invited him to come and see her when he flew East, but warned him to call in advance so they would be able to meet somewhere privately without the paparazzi and nosy reporters.

Apparently, they did have a rendezvous somewhere in Virginia at the secluded private home of a friend of RFK's. In secrecy, these two famous figures managed to slip in a romantic weekend together.

***

Although Burton was sexually attracted to Jackie, and she to him, the real friendship that emerged from all this was between Burton and RFK. When the actor appeared on Broadway in Shakespeare's *Hamlet,* RFK made a special trip to New York to see him. He later told the press that Burton's *Hamlet* was far superior to any he'd ever seen, including the performances of Laurence Olivier.

After the performance, RFK retired with Burton to his hotel suite for a late night supper. As Burton told Michael Wilding, "Bobby and I got pissed, really pissed, and we ended up reciting Shakespeare to each other. At some point, we decided to strip down jaybird naked—not for sex, but as a form of bonding. 'That's what asshole buddies do,' I told Bobby, and he agreed."

"We've become really close, but I fear he'll one day be the recipient of an assassin's bullet." Burton said to Wilding, "He told me that every day, he gets death threats, but he still plans to run for president in '68. I fear for him."

Burton's fear, of course, came true. "Because he was much closer to Bobby than he had been to JFK, Burton was far more devastated by the news of his death. As Bobby lay dying in an L.A. hospital after the shooting, he told Dick Hanley, "I hope he doesn't survive the night. If he does, he will be a complete vegetable, and Bobby would have hated that. He was so bright, so alive."

Once again, Burton sent a deeply moving personal letter to Jackie, promising to meet with her "after the dust has settled over the cities of the plain."

"Jackie was in love with Bobby, and he was in love with her," Burton told Hanley. "I was in love with Bobby, too, although in a very different way from Jackie," Burton claimed. "He put up such a brave macho front to the world, but he lived in fear and insecurities. Somehow, he found comfort with me. Although he had many enemies, he dared show me that he had the sensitive soul of a poet."

***

In a very different way, and under different circumstances, Elizabeth, too, bonded with Robert Kennedy.

On July 9, 1961, Elizabeth, in plunging *décolletáge*, sat next to Attorney General Robert F. Kennedy at a fund-raising dinner for the Cedars of Lebanon Hospital in Los Angeles. Behind them sat Rat Packers Joey Bishop, Dean Martin, Frank Sinatra, and Peter Lawford. A view of RFK was snapped by photographers gazing down at Elizabeth's amply displayed breasts.

When the attorney general finally diverted his gaze, as the focal point of the fundraising dinner, Elizabeth delivered a short, poignant speech written by Joseph Mankiewicz:

"Dying, as I remember, is many things. But most of all, it is wanting to live. Throughout many critical hours in the operating theater, it was as if every nerve, every muscle, as if my whole physical being were being strained to the last ounce of my strength, to the last gasp of breath. I remember I had focused desperately on the hospital light hanging directly above me. It had become the vision of life itself. Slowly, it faded and dimmed like a well-done theatrical effect to blackness.

I died.

It was like being in a long dark tunnel with no light at the end. I kept looking for the light. I heard voices urging me to come back into life, to live. The experience was both painful and beautiful, like child birth itself."

Elizabeth donated $100,000 to the charity, and her fellow guests, including RFK, contributed a massive total of $7 million that night. After the dinner, Bobby invited her for a drive with him along the coast. She suggested that they stop at her cottage in Malibu for a midnight swim. No one knows where her husband at the time, Eddie Fisher, was that night.

As she was to tell Dick Hanley. "It was one of the most memorable nights of my life."

She also recorded the events of that night in her diary, and would allow both Dick and Roddy Mc-Dowall to read it. She had described her experience in such graphic detail that Roddy was a bit shocked. He said, "Elizabeth, my dear, you should have been a pornographer."

As the actress's two memoirs revealed, no one could write more boringly about her own life that Elizabeth. In each of her autobiographical memoirs, she gave almost no details of some of the most infamous events of her life.

In her diary's description of her

At a fund-raiser, **Bobby Kennedy** showed an inordinate interest in **Elizabeth Taylor**'s breasts.

He often followed his older brother in seducing some of the same women—Marilyn Monroe, Jackie Kennedy, and Elizabeth herself.

encounter with Robert Kennedy, she may have been more explicit because Peter Lawford had told her that Marilyn Monroe had recorded "steamy passages" in her red diary about her sexual encounters with both President Kennedy and his brother, Robert. "Elizabeth obviously did not want to be bested by Monroe," Roddy said.

"I can write with passion, too," she told Roddy. "After all, I read *Forever Amber*." She was referring to the pulpy best selling romance written by Kathleen Winsor, who at one time was married to bandleader Artie Shaw after his divorce from Ava Gardner.

"Bobby and I spent about two hours on the beach in the moonlight," Elizabeth told her gay friends. "Our bathing suits became too restraining. Bobby finally got to enjoy those breasts he'd been staring at all night."

"You've got it bad, girl," Roddy said.

"When it was over, he kissed me several times and told me I was a goddess," she relayed, as reported by Roddy and Dick. "Other men have told me that, but coming from Bobby, I really could delude myself into believing it. That night, with Bobby on the beach, I was a goddess. But when I drove home, I found Eddie there and we got into a big brawl. The goddess, I fear, became a harridan."

Later, in her diary, she wrote: "It is a shame that when a man and a woman want to be together, they often have to leave each other while they pay homage to people in their lives they'd rather not deal with. Men and women should be free. Even though I've been married four times, it was four times too many. I will never marry again—and that's a promise I've made to myself that I will never break."

In the months leading up to his assassination, RFK, at least according to Dick Hanley, seduced Elizabeth on three different occasions. On one of these occasions, he left the bed of Jackie Kennedy in New York in 1966, flew to Los Angeles, and woke up in Elizabeth's bed in Beverly Hills the following morning."

As she told Dick, "I have known more perfect bodies, but Bobby's physique thrilled me. He was long and lean, no bulging beefcake. But he moved with such grace...undeniable masculinity. A strong chest, a thin waist, and a cock that was not the biggest I'd ever seen, but one that was gorgeous and knew all the right strokes."

It seemed inevitable that Jackie would hear of Elizabeth's rendezvous with RFK. Jackie often became furious when she heard of Bobby's affairs with other women, such as actress Lee Remick.

A member of Ari's staff informed Jackie that when Elizabeth was considering ending her marriage to Burton, Ari had proposed to her. Elizabeth had rejected his proposal, and within a week had reconciled with Burton.

In spite of her rejection of his proposal, Ari continued his role in her life as a friend. He invited Elizabeth to the 1967 Annual Ball at the Palazzo Ca'Rezzonico in Venice. The paparazzi snapped them together, Elizabeth wearing an elaborate gown and a Kabuki headdress.

Onassis maintained his friendship with Elizabeth, but did not pursue her when he received word from Johnny Meyer, who was more or less his pimp, having previously occupied that dubious post during his employment by Howard Hughes. Meyer managed to be both blunt and mysterious. "Don't ask me how I found this out, but I've learned that Mrs. Kennedy might be available to marry you."

"I will go after her like a hungry lion after a zebra," Onassis vowed.

When Elizabeth heard about the upcoming marriage of Jackie and Onassis, she told a reporter for *Modern Screen*, "It will be the strangest marriage of the century. Mrs. Kennedy is now reduced to taking my rejects."

Her comment was never printed.

Later, Jackie turned down an invitation to sail on another cruise aboard the *Christina* before her marriage. Word reached her that Elizabeth, who went on the voyage, flirted with Onassis every night over dinner.

When Jackie confronted the shipping magnate about it, she told him, "It's either the Taylor bitch or me. Your friendship with this international tramp has to end—NOW!"

Movie Mirror picked up on this feud, crafting headlines that yelled: WHAT REALLY HAPPENED THE NIGHT LIZ TRIED TO CUT JACKIE OUT!

Kiki Feroudi Moutsatsos, who was Ari's private secretary, in a memoir, recalled the cruise that Ari took without Jackie, but with Elizabeth and Burton. Greta Garbo was on board. In the bar, Ari told her that the bar stools were upholstered with the skin of a whale's penis.

Moutsatsos claimed that one night at dinner, she dropped her napkin and ducked down to retrieve it. She saw that the leg of her boss was entwined with Garbo's.

On yet another cruise, Moutsatsos recalled Elizabeth Taylor and Burton sailing with Maria Callas, Ari's longtime mistress. "Miss Taylor was small and delicate and her purple eyes were ravishing and exquisite, almost as if they were a precious gift she graciously and temporarily bestowed on her viewer. Miss Callas' elegant face was dark and piercing. She seemed to view Miss Taylor as a potential rival, even though Burton was aboard. He had had far too much to drink that night; otherwise, the cruise was idyllic."

After his marriage to Jackie, Elizabeth praised Jackie for "making a wise choice" in marrying Ari.

During the first year of their marriage, Jackie and Ari knocked Richard Burton and Elizabeth Taylor off their throne as the world's most famous and most publicized couple.

One night aboard his yacht, Ari told Jackie that he numbered, among his closest friends, Elizabeth Taylor, Richard Burton, Greta Garbo, Eva Perón, and Sir Winston Churchill. For his worst enemies, he cited Richard Nixon, Bobby Kennedy, J. Edgar Hoover, and the entire CIA.

In his diaries, which were published in 2012, Burton made several references to Jackie, but did not admit to an affair. As was rumored at the time, some of the more explosive or embarrassing entries in his diary were not included in the final (published) manuscript.

In October of 1968, Burton wrote, "Ari is 69, claims 62, and she is 39. The youngish 'Queen of the USA' and the aging Greek bandit. He is pretty vulgar and one suspects him of orgies and other dubious things, whereas the Kennedy woman seems, though I've never met her, to be a lady."

Of course, he'd met her in public view on more than one occasion. When Jackie had been First Lady, she'd invited both Burton and his then-wife, Sybil, to the White House to celebrate his success on Broadway in *Camelot*. But as Burton himself once said, "Name me one bloke living, now or long underground, who ever wrote a truthful diary. Some secrets were not meant to be shared."

Nevertheless, that same month, Burton gave his very candid assessment of Jackie. "She has several lovers, and her husband knows it. He has a mistress and she knows it. The Onassises have disappeared completely from the front pages, and for the most part from the papers altogether. I told Elizabeth that they didn't have our stamina."

[Despite Burton's assessment, Jackie Kennedy, wed to Aristotle Onassis, had not disappeared from the newspapers. She had evolved into a media event to be rivaled only by the Second Coming.]

Also, in October of that year, Burton compared Jackie's cache of jewelry to that of Elizabeth's. "I read in the papers that Ari has given Jackie half a million pounds worth of rubies surrounded by diamonds. Now Missey already has, as a result of former battles against Yours Truly, one of the greatest diamonds in the world, and probably the most breathtaking collections of emeralds surrounded by diamonds. Now the Battle of the Rubies is on. I wonder who will win?"

On November 6, 1968, Burton met with Maria Callas. In his diary, he made this notation: "She has massive legs and what seems a slender body from the waist up. She has bags under her eyes, and wears dark glasses most of the time. Perhaps she cries a lot. She is obviously lonely after Ari's marriage to Jackie. If I had a choice between Maria and Jackie, I'm afraid I'd elect Jackie. She sounds more fun, and in snaps, anyway, looks prettier."

On August 9, 1969, while staying at London's Dorchester Hotel, Burton was in a flippant mood, anticipating a possible success for his latest film, *Staircase,* in which he and Rex Harrison appeared as two flamboyant homosexuals.

Wishfully, in his diary, Burton mused that "when the millions pour in, I can probably employ J. Paul Getty as a butler and Onassis as a Greek chef. Elizabeth, topless and mini-skirted, will serve me food and call me 'sir.' That will be the day. Jackie Onassis can be the tweeny and get her orders from Elizabeth. Noël Coward will be brought in every night to be witty and to sing songs. We'll get a defecting Russian pianist, one of the great ones, to play every night. In chains, of course. We'll pour white confetti on his hair and tell him it's Siberia."

***

Secretly, Jackie had wanted to own the notorious Krupp diamond, the world's most perfect specimen of a diamond. Elizabeth Taylor was the proud owner. In 1968, Burton had purchased the 33.19 carat bauble for only $307,000, in spite of its associations with the Krupps, a German family based in the industrial Ruhr valley whose munitions factories had been associated during World War II with the forced labor of Jews. "How ironic," Elizabeth said. "A nice Jewish girl like me owning the Krupp diamond."

She referred to it as "the ice cube," and at parties, she liked to play ball with it, throwing it at other guests, male or female, and asking them to catch it. She freely invited both men and women to "try it on for size."

When Jackie heard these stories, she said, "I'm appalled at the behavior of this vulgar woman! Such ostentation!"

Jackie wanted to outdo Elizabeth and become the owner of the even larger (69.42 carat) Annenberg diamond, evaluated at the time as the most valuable stone available for resale [i.e., not belonging to a museum, such as the Hope Diamond at the Smithsonian] in the world. When it went on sale in 1969, Jackie was hoping that Ari would buy it for her as a token of his love. Privately, she stationed a spy at the Parke-Bernet Galleries on Madison Avenue in Manhattan when it went on sale. She seemed to believe that Ari owed her such a staggering gift for having married him the year before.

Rather brazenly, Elizabeth had told Burton, "I want that pear-shaped rock." He had a dealer place his bids, warning him not to exceed a bid of $1 million. Unknown to Burton, Ari had entered the bidding, but retreated when the price soared to $780,000. Finally, Robert Kenmore, the owner of Cartier's, placed the auction's highest bid—$1,050,000.

Elizabeth was furious, launching into a violent assault on Burton, who finally relented. He arranged to buy the stone from Kenmore for $1.2 million. Once it was in her possession, Elizabeth said, "I don't like it, but I'm keeping it so Jackie won't get it."

"She tells people she doesn't like it," Jackie said, "How outrageous. Well, I like it. It should have been mine."

"The diamond should be on the finger of the most beautiful woman in the world," Burton later said. "I would have had a fit if went to Jackie Kennedy or Sophia Loren, or, even worse, 'Mrs. Huntington Misfit' of Dallas, Texas."

In 1978, Jackie learned that Elizabeth—realizing a tidy profit—had sold the diamond to Henry Lambert, a New York dealer, for $5 million.

[In 2009, at an auction at Christie's in Manhattan, an unidentified buyer paid $7.7 million for the stone.]

***

As part of one of their most frenzied and widely publicized projects, Richard Burton and Elizabeth Taylor flew to Budapest, where he was scheduled to star in what he called "my turkey," a reference to the 1972 release of Bluebeard. Although he had Elizabeth waiting not so patiently in their hotel suite, he was spending time with actress Nathalie Delon.

Elizabeth had planted a spy on the set to report back to her.

Fed up with her husband's womanizing, she accepted an invitation to fly to Rome on May 5, 1972 for dinner with Onassis. He'd sent his private jet to fetch her. Without telling Burton where she was going, she flew out of Budapest, heading southwest to Rome.

Before vacating her hotel, she instructed her staff, "If Richard wants to know where I am, tell the bastard he can read about it in the newspapers."

For her first night in Rome, scene of her *Cleopatra (1963)* debacle of nearly a decade before, Elizabeth accompanied Ari to the very chic Hostaria dell'Orso, whose premises dated from 1300. During the course of its existence, it had been patronized by St. Francis of Assisi, Dante, Goethe, and Rabelais.

In the 1920s, Mary Pickford and Douglas Fairbanks, Sr., had dined there.

Ari and Elizabeth would add their names to the distinguished roster of guests. Regrettably, the *paparazzi* learned of their presence. Outside the restaurant, a mob gathered.

Inside the restaurant, a persistent fan kept annoying Elizabeth, asking for her autograph. Finally, very angered, Ari tossed a glass of champagne in the face of the male fan.

A reporter was dining that evening in the restaurant, and he made sure that the next morning's headlines carried news of the incident.

Burton telephoned Elizabeth the next morning and promised to drop Delon if she'd come back to him. Lured by the sound of his voice, she relented, and flew back to Budapest.

As soon as news of this reached Jackie in New York, she called Ari in Rome. "I thought some harridan, a fishwife perhaps, was on the phone," Ari later told his friends.

She shouted at him, "I'm ashamed of you, making a spectacle of yourself with this harlot. When you fly back to New York, let me know. I can time it so that I'm on a plane to Paris. Perhaps we'll wave to each other somewhere over the Atlantic."

***

The only face-to-face meeting between Jackie and Elizabeth occurred on June 20, 1976, when both of them attended a performance by the legendary British ballerina Margot Fonteyn at Manhattan's Uris Theater. Backstage, Elizabeth and Jackie awkwardly encountered one another on the way to Fonteyn's dressing room. Each woman smiled politely at the other. What did the two fabled divas say to each other? Someone who stood behind them revealed, "They said absolutely nothing—not a word."

After that, coverage of the two divas in the tabloids became less shrill and less frequent. In the November, 1976 issue of Photoplay, reportage on the exploits of Elizabeth vs. Jackie had been reduced to the last words on the cover, without even a picture, and even that ran beneath the larger headline: *THE SALLY STRUTHERS NOBODY KNOWS.*

568

Chapter Twenty-Seven

Teddy Kennedy, Lion of the Senate
Coveting His Brother's Wife

Discovered: Teddy's Declarations of his Enduring Love for Jackie

In these cozy *tête-à-têtes*, **Jackie** and **Teddy Kennedy** share intimate moments. Then and in years to come, they would share many of them, although their love affair largely escaped press attention. But not always.

On Teddy's wedding day, JFK had told him, "Just because you're getting married doesn't mean you have to be faithful." Teddy heeded his brother's advice.

He stood by Jackie though one crisis after another, becoming the one man in her life she could depend on.

When he had a car accident on the island of Chappaquiddick, drowning Mary Jo Kopechne, Jackie was his most steadfast supporter. Kennedy loyalists, including "the Boiler Room Girls" (his secretarial pool) spread rumors about the drowned young woman. One of the secretaries claimed, "She was nothing but a whore. She'd go to bed with any man who had Kennedy written on his zipper."

The most observant of Kennedy-watchers claimed that Teddy Kennedy, the younger brother of JFK and Bobby, fell in love with Jackie Bouvier when JFK first brought her to Hyannis Port in the early 1950s.

Teddy became enchanted with Jackie when he was still an undergraduate at Harvard. She agreed to help him write a paper on art history, a subject he didn't know much about and about which she knew a lot.

After she finished virtually writing the paper for him, he gave her a big, passionate kiss on the mouth. Observers noted that throughout the 1950s, Jackie usually received not perfunctory pecks on the cheek from either Bobby or Teddy, but "real wet kisses," in the words of Kennedy friend Chuck Spalding. "Once I went boating with all three brothers and Jackie, three years after her marriage to JFK. He was sleeping down below. She came on deck and greeted both brothers with a big kiss. They were in their bathing suits. I couldn't help but notice she got a rise out of both of them."

"I never discussed such a subject with the man himself," Spalding said. "He was the biggest

Teddy liked to play football, and he was better built for it than his older brothers. He is seen here in 1955, when Harvard played its traditional rival, Yale. Teddy caught a touchdown pass from his tight end slot, chalking up Harvard's only score in the game's 21-7 loss to Yale.

womanizer of them all, followed by his little brother, Teddy. Bobby had his share of affairs, too. When he was Attorney General, he made use of that bedroom he maintained at the Justice Department, upstairs, above his office, He always found plenty of nooky."

Teddy compulsively recorded both his good deeds and his bad ones in his private diaries. Some of what these diaries contained was first revealed in 1961. In August of that year, before he became a Senator, during the first year of his brother's presidency, Teddy had flown to South America on a fact-finding trip.

At the end of the trip, during his homebound flight aboard a flight operated by Pan American World Airways, he inadvertently left his diary on board after exiting from the plane. Airline officials turned the diary over to the F.B.I., where it was delivered directly to J. Edgar Hoover. In his diary, Teddy had recorded testimonials about his passion for Jackie and his intention to seduce her one

"I Will Love Her Forever"

—Teddy, About Jackie

570

day.

Some of the most salacious comments in Teddy's diary were leaked, and became cocktail party chatter throughout Washington and Georgetown.

Hoover made a copy of the diary, and returned the original to Teddy. The contents were never made public, but Hoover told his lover and chief assistant, Clyde Tolson, among others, about some of the salacious comments it contained.

The hottest revelations included Teddy's descriptions of his longtime love for Jackie. He described his desire—thwarted only by his loyalty to JFK—to consummate their relationship. He admitted, however, that when she had worked on his term paper, that Jackie had allowed him to kiss her. He also claimed that she once told him that he had become the "most beautiful of the Kennedys."

"I think she is physically attracted to me," he wrote. "I sure know that I have it big for her. My day will come. I must be patient."

Before his death, Hoover may have destroyed his copy of Teddy's diary.

Perhaps the F.B.I. chief was prompted to destroy it based on his loyalty to Joseph P. Kennedy. When the elderly Kennedy had heard that Hoover might be considering a run for the presidency, he'd written him, informing him that whether he opted to appear on either the Republican or the Democratic ticket, that he'd become his largest political contributor. Apparently, according to his aides, Hoover was very flattered with such an endorsement. Joseph had also written, "If you decide to run, I will be not only your heaviest contributor, but your hardest campaign worker."

On his deathbed, Teddy left specific instructions that his diaries not be made public until 2034.

A magazine once voted this the "sexiest picture ever taken of **Teddy Kennedy**." Jackie kept it on a table beside her bed except when Bobby came to call. There was always a picture of JFK in her living room on public display.

Three fraternal bathing beauties lined up on the beach *(left to right)*: **Bobby Kennedy**, the bantam weight; **JFK**, the middleweight; and **Teddy**, the heavyweight.

Rose once evaluated her sons, defining Bobby as the best looking. "I believe all of them will grow up to be heterosexuals. If anything, from their father, they've inherited too great an interest in women. I wish each of my boys would be faithful to his wife. But my dreams rarely come true."

The existence of these very private diaries was revealed in the summer of 2010, when the FBI released previously sealed files.

In 2010, after Teddy's death and after much legal wrangling about releasing them, his F.B.I. files were made public. They included a total of 2,352 pages covering, for the most part, the period from 1961 to 1985. The files contained information about the many death threats Teddy had received during the course of his controversial career. Most of the crazies had threatened to merely shoot Teddy, although one man said he was going to kill him with a crossbow.

One tantalizing detail contained within the F.B.I. files revealed that when Frank Sinatra had been more or less shunned by the Kennedys because of his mob associations, he plotted revenge. As stated in the F.B.I. file, "Sinatra wanted to attack the character of Edward and Bobby Kennedy and that of his former brother-in-law, Peter Lawford, by putting them in compromising positions with women." Presumably, during these "set-ups," they would be secretly photographed and subsequently blackmailed.

"During the heyday of Camelot, Teddy joined his brothers at nude sex parties around the White House pool, or in some instances, at Jack Nicholson's home in Los Angeles," said David Powers, a member of JFK's "Irish Mafia" at the White House.

"But Teddy was devoted to Jackie until the day he died...and beyond," Powers said. "He was always there for her, and she was always there for him—a plane accident, the drowning of Mary Jo Kopechne, his aborted dream of becoming president. She was his confidante and lover."

When JFK died, Teddy stood by Jackie, although at the time, most of her world gravitated around Bobby. "He was my rock," she later recalled. "But I'll never forget Teddy's loyalty and concern as well. I knew I had lost one Kennedy brother, but I also knew that I would always have the love of Bobby and Teddy as well."

For business advice after JFK's death, she turned more to Teddy than to Bobby, because she felt Bobby did not have a good sense for business.

JFK had left an estate of $15 million, but most of it was in trust for Caroline and John Jr. He had not updated his will since 1954. Jackie complained to Teddy, "Jack did not adequately provide for me."

She had purchased her Fifth Avenue apartment from funds derived from the sale of their home in Georgetown.

JFK wanted her to receive only $150,000 a year, with the understanding that if she remarried, that annual stipend would be automatically diverted to Caroline and John Jr. Recognizing that she'd need more, Teddy was instrumental in getting Bobby to promise to supplement that income with an additional allowance of $50,000 every year.

Teddy later complained to Rose Kennedy and others, "I love Jackie dearly, but she doesn't know how to live on a budget. She'd spend $100,000 on a flower pot that belonged to Catherine the Great, or else be willing to pay $60,000 on this 18th-century Russian decanter."

Jackie may not have realized how much Teddy meant to her until his life almost ended on June 19, 1964. Fighting for the passage of the Civil Rights Act in Congress, he exited from the Senate Chamber to fly to Springfield, Massachusetts, where the Democrats were holding their State Nominating Convention. As a candidate for re-election as Senator, he was running unopposed and had been scheduled to speak there.

At 8:45PM, a twin-engine Aero Commander 680 became airborne, flying out of Washington's National Airport in the direction of Springfield, carrying Teddy, Senator Birch Bayh of Indiana and his wife, Marvella, and Teddy's legislative aide, Edward Moss.

Another Edward (Edward Zimny) piloted the plane, which encountered thunderstorms all the way to western Massachusetts.

Seeking shelter from the violent storm, Zimny wanted to land, but impatiently, Teddy demanded that he continue. "I'm already late, god damn it," he shouted.

Bayh later claimed that moments after Teddy said that, the plane just seemed to fall to the ground.

Teddy had unfastened his safety belt at the time and was standing in a half-crouched position under the low ceiling. The plane crashed into an apple orchard three miles from the Barnes Municipal Airport *[aka the Westfield-Barnes Regional Airport],* near Springfield. Edward Moss and Edward Zimny were each killed instantly.

When Teddy regained consciousness, he found himself in the Cooley-Dickenson Hospital in Northampton, Massachusetts. Bobby was at his bedside. Teddy's doctor did not expect that he would live through the night. The outlook was dismal: Three vertebrae in his lower spine were fractured (one of them crushed), two ribs were broken, and one of his lungs had been punctured.

Bayh was hailed as a hero. He'd crawled back into the burning plane to pull the injured Teddy from the wreckage.

According to Nancy Tuckerman, when Jackie heard the news, she almost fainted. She dropped all her engagements and flew at once to Northampton.

When he saw her, tears welled in his eyes as he looked up into hers. "Jackie, oh, Jackie," he said in the presence of a nurse. "I fear I'll never walk again."

She met with doctors and then flew in two specialists from Boston, who assured her that with the proper care, Teddy would recover satisfactorily.

As if she were his loyal wife, Jackie stayed by his side, administering to his needs and comforting him.

In January of 1965, Jackie claimed, "It was one of the proudest moments of my life when both Teddy and Bobby were sworn in together as U.S. Senators.

[Teddy reclaimed his seat that year as Senator from Massachusetts. In the meantime, Bobby had established residence in New York and had beaten Re-

publican challengers to become one of New York State's Senators, fighting down charges that he was "a carpetbagger from Massachusetts."]

In July of 1965, Jackie celebrated her 36th birthday at the house within the Hyannis Port compound which she'd inherited from JFK. Both Bobby and Teddy flew to her side to honor her.

Seemingly without the knowledge of other members of the Kennedy clan, except for Teddy, Bobby slipped into the widow's home to spend nights with Jackie, usually not leaving until four in the morning.

Near the end of her visit to Hyannis Port, when Bobby was occupied with business. Jackie wanted to be driven to the end of the Cape, having a late lunch in Provincetown. Teddy agreed to spend the day with her. The Secret Service observed what happened during their excursion.

When Jackie came to stay in her house within the Kennedy compound, **Bobby Kennedy** was "the midnight kissing bandit."

Jackie and Teddy never made it to P-Town. They did get as far as Bunny Mellon's home on Cape Cod, where reportedly they spent eight hours together before driving back to Hyannis Port to face an angry Bobby.

Gore Vidal, then a confidant of Jackie's, later claimed, "To my knowledge, this was the first time Jackie got physical with Teddy. She was in love with Bobby, if she were ever in love with anyone, but she also believed in the revenge fuck—for example, Jackie and William Holden. She'd heard rumors of Bobby's other affairs, and she was jealous. Also, Teddy, before he got old, fat, and jowly, was a real good-looking guy back then. He was seductive to Jackie, and I think she went for the former football player big time."

David Powers witnessed the beginning of Teddy's romantic interest in Jackie that developed and became more passionate shortly after JFK's death, and then continued until up to and after her marriage to Aristotle Onassis.

"Let's face it," Powers once told his cronies, "Teddy has always had the hots for Jackie ever since he first laid eyes on her. In fact, he told me that the reason he married Joan was that she had some of Jackie's qualities. I think he was always determined to get her, but he knew he'd have to wait for the opportune moment—and that would be a hell of a long wait. If Jackie went for both Jack and Bobby, why not Teddy? It's known to happen in families. One brother, two brothers, a trio of brothers. Women have been known for 'brother love' since time began. I knew a case in Boston where a woman lost her husband and then turned around and married his brother—you figure."

One night in Boston, Teddy told Powers, "I've always been in love with Jackie, right from the beginning. She's always been special to me. When Jack died, I knew she was seeing Bobby, too, but that didn't stop me. Bobby couldn't always be with her."

Teddy revealed that he continued his affair with Jackie long after she and

Bobby had ended their sexual liaisons, based on fear that a public revelation would damage his hopes for the Presidency.

The staff at Hyannis Port were among the first to spread rumors about Jackie and Teddy, based on their many late night sightings of Teddy leaving her home at Hyannis Port, often at three or four in the morning.

Powers said that he once, in 1966, went sailing with Teddy and Jackie and that he went below to the galley for a cold beer.

"I guess Teddy and Jackie didn't hear me. I saw something I wish to this day that I had never seen. All three of us were beyond embarrassed. But we got over it."

"I think that Jackie was feeling very vulnerable. She was still in love with Bobby, but she'd heard—whether it was true or not— that he was involved in a torrid affair with Candice Bergen. I mean, she was genuinely attracted to Teddy, but I also suspect that there was an element of payback to Bobby for his cheating heart."

The Beltway crowd, always the first to know, was familiar with Jackie's affair with Bobby in the wake of the President's death. But news of her sexual liaison with the family's youngest brother resonated like a bombshell.

Some biographers have dismissed Teddy's affair with Jackie as "another one of those newspaper romances." But his diaries revealed otherwise, and close personal friends claimed that it was "an affair of the heart."

Although in the beginning, Teddy slipped under the radar screen of the press, the tabloids picked up on the rumors buzzing about Bobby and Jackie. Ted Sorensen said, "The public had a difficult enough time accepting the fact that Bobby and Jackie might be lovers. That Teddy also came in for Jackie's loving care was just too much at the time. But as the years went by, and as she called on him more and more to be the so-called 'man in her life,' the rumors gained traction."

In the late 1960s and 70s, Jackie and Teddy shared many intimate moments together in Washington, Hyannis Port, New York, on a Greek island, or in Palm Beach. Away from the prying eyes of the paparazzi and inquiring reporters, they indulged their long-simmering passion.

Journalist Leon Wagener may have been the first to break the story of a romance between Jackie and Teddy. The reporter wrote, "When Ted finally made love to Jackie, he fulfilled the dream he'd had to possess his brother's beautiful wife. Obviously, he knew it was a grievous sin and an insult to his late brother, but he couldn't control himself."

Wagener quoted a family insider who asserted "Ted in his diaries wrote about his romance with Jackie in great detail. He didn't want his family, especially Rose, to learn of his dalliances with her."

Powers said, "The Kennedy family eventually became aware that Teddy, not just Bobby, was more than a brother-in-law to Jackie, but it was a subject that dare not speak its name. No one wanted to talk about it. The revelations about Bobby and Jackie were already too much for this overburdened family. The thing between Jackie and Teddy was just too much to handle. Another disgrace."

In 1958, with JFK as his best man, Teddy had married Joan Bennett, who had the same name as the celebrated screen beauty. She was a cloistered debutante from a Catholic college, participating as the bride in what was described as "the Wedding of the Year."

Joan told Jackie, "The only reason Ted married me was that he couldn't get me any other way. Believe it or not, I went to my honeymoon bed a virgin."

"How quaint!" Jackie said.

Months later, Joan told Jackie, "I had no idea of what I was getting into by becoming a Kennedy."

Jackie went to great care not to let Joan know about her illicit affair with her husband.

Jackie and Joan had bonded on many issues, especially those associated with the Kennedy family, and the clan had dubbed them the two "outlaw-in-laws." Joan considered Jackie "the most sophisticated woman in the world," and often turned to her for help in solving her marriage problems.

Joan Bennett, a beautiful, cloistered debutante from a Catholic college, married Teddy Kennedy.

Although her marriage began like something from a storybook, it turned—for her at least—into a private hell.

Joan had repeatedly been shocked whenever she was confronted with evidence of Teddy's infidelity, but Jackie, on the other hand, had hardened into a veteran of the serial adulteries of JFK and his brothers. "Kennedy men are like that," Jackie told Joan. "They'll go after anything in skirts. But it doesn't mean anything. Jack always came home to me."

Jackie was disturbed that Joan did not seem to have her resilience and strength, and saddened when she drifted into alcoholism.

It appeared that Ethel, perhaps innocent at the beginning, later came to realize that her husband was carrying on with Jackie. Once at Hickory Hill, Teddy arrived for dinner and came up behind Ethel, grabbing her and embracing her tightly. "Cut it out," she scolded him. "We'll have no more of this Bobby-Jackie stuff."

Chuck Spalding also noted that at one party at Hickory Hill, a band was hired for the night, "Ethel and Bobby were inside the house, Jackie and Teddy were high on daiquiris. With the band playing, she was seen dancing close to Teddy, pressing her crotch against his."

Jackie was aware of Teddy's womanizing and drug and alcohol abuse. Richard E. Burke, who worked on Teddy's staff for ten years, noted that in his autobiography, *The Senator.* One night, in search of something Teddy needed, he opened a drawer in his office. There, Burke found a box of poppers and an old wooden cigar box. In that box, he discovered a plastic via filled with cocaine, as well as a "bullet" *[in this case, an aluminum cocaine dispenser]*.

Burke observed, first-hand, the senator's womanizing. "Teddy owned the proverbial little black book of names and phone numbers, and it was crammed with his entries: Amber, Annie, Bonnie, Carla, Cindy, Claudia, Debbie, Felicia, Florence, Greta, Hillary *[no, not that one]*, Janice, Ellen, Kathy, Laura, Libby, Margaret, Mary Ann, Maureen, Nancy, Nicole, Norma, Patti, Peggy, and Stephanie, to name a *few.* The women were a scattered assortment of types, mostly blonde, some quite smart, others simply bimbos who liked the high times and fast life."

Jackie later told Bunny Mellon, Tuckerman, and others, that her greatest moment experienced with herself, Bobby, and Teddy as a trio came in May of 1965. Queen Elizabeth invited her to the ceremonial inauguration of a monument to JFK at Runnymede, the site in southern England where in 1215, King John *[the dissolute, half-crazed youngest son of Henry II and his wife, Eleanor of Aquitaine]* had signed the Magna Carta. The British government had designated a small plot of land in an English field, a monument in perpetuity to JFK, that would forever belong to the United States.

President Johnson made an airplane available to Jackie, and she asked both Teddy and Bobby to fly with her, along with Dean Rusk, the U.S. Secretary of State. She also took Caroline and John Jr. along on the flight.

Queen Elizabeth herself attended, noting that Jackie shed tears as she heard various speakers laud her husband's deeds and character.

When she returned to America, she wrote to Johnson, thanking him for the use of the airplane. "It was such an emotional and difficult day for me—so many thoughts of all my loss surged in me again."

Teddy Kennedy made a lot of mistakes. One was living an adulterous life, and the other involved recording details about his passion for other women, notably Jackie, in a diary.

His private, innermost musings were later discovered in the seat pocket of a commercial airline and leaked to the media.

The photo, above, shows Teddy's wife, **Joan**, furious and pregnant, after her return from the funeral of Mary Jo Kopechne after she drowned in Teddy's car at Chappaquidick. According to Joan, "It was the beginning of the end for Ted and me."

***

When Bobby decided to run for the presidency in 1968, he knew he would not be able to conceal his affair with Jackie. Both of them knew that they had to bring closure to their romance.

After Bobby's exit as a romantic figure in her life, Jackie turned more and more to Teddy, even though she was also secretly dating Aristotle Onassis.

Just before Bobby's announcement of his candidacy for President, Jackie met with her friend, Truman Capote. He later gossiped about what she revealed.

"I'm in love with two men at the same time, both Bobby and Teddy," she allegedly confessed. "They appeal to me in very different ways. With Bobby, it's a sex thing. We're equals. But with Teddy, it's an incestuous mother/son relationship. Sometimes I hold his head on my breast and cuddle it like a Madonna with her child."

When Teddy and Jackie heard the news of that dreadful event in the kitchens of the Ambassador Hotel in Los Angeles, they turned to each other as never before. At first, neither could believe that Bobby, only a few minutes after winning the California Primary, and like JFK before him, had been assassinated. Jackie told Chuck Spalding, "When Jack died, Bobby was my rock. When Bobby died, Teddy was my rock. I don't know what I would have done without him. He helped me get through the darkest nights."

"After Bobby's death, Teddy and Jackie made a bond sealed not with blood, but with something even more personal...sex," Vidal claimed. "I call it the Devil's Pact. It involved the ongoing promotion of the Legend of Camelot, not the reality of the Kennedy administration. As he proved, based on his reputation as Warhorse (or Lion) of the Senate, Teddy was a far more dedicated liberal than either of his older brothers had ever been. JFK never went too far to the left of public opinion, but Teddy, aided by Jackie, plotted to make himself the Senate's symbol for a new kind of Kennedy liberalism."

Jackie celebrated her 39th birthday on July 28, 1968, at Hyannis Port. Teddy was by her side. Later, they watched *The Thomas Crown Affair,* starring Steve McQueen.

Before midnight, she shocked Teddy by announcing that she planned to marry Aristotle Onassis. "You are the last surviving brother and the head of the family. I am included in that family, and you need to fly with me to Skorpios to look out for my interest in the formulation of a prenuptial agreement."

After Bobby's death, Jackie asked Teddy if he would become Caroline's godfather. "She would like it very much if you, her Uncle Teddy, would take over."

Neither Teddy nor Bobby had wanted Jackie to marry Onassis. But when Teddy saw that she was determined to go through with it, he agreed to fly with her to Greece and organize financial matters with her new groom. He didn't welcome the task "but for you, Jackie, I'll do it. Someone has to see that your interests are protected."

Of the many powerful men she knew, Jackie wanted Teddy to negotiate the details of a pre-nuptial agreement with Onassis. During the most intense of the negotiations, Jackie flew to Athens on a shopping expedition, leaving her husband-to-be alone with her brother-in-law and lover.

During their subsequent negotiations, Onassis likened Teddy's role "to a priestly hustler peddling indulgences."

Onassis, known as "the world's toughest negotiator," assured him that he would replace Jackie's annuity and also ensure that she was protected. He invited Teddy to inspect his kennel of well-trained German shepherd police dogs, always on site to patrol Skorpios.

Teddy was able to persuade him to agree to give Jackie only $1.5 million up front. Back in New York, Teddy turned to financial wizard André Meyer, who at first demanded $20 million up front for Jackie, but finally settled for $3 million.

When Jackie returned from her shopping trip to Athens to reconvene her role in the premarital negotiations, Onassis invited her and Teddy to a celebration aboard the *Christina*. Knowing Teddy's fondness for beautiful young women, he arranged for eight of them to be flown in from Athens.

As a means of concealing his affair with Jackie, Teddy deliberately made a play for one of the blonde bimbos. For whatever reason, Onassis had invited Nico Mastorakis, a professional journalist and photographer, aboard as one of his guests.

When Mastorakis snapped a photo of Teddy, soaked in ouzo and holding a blonde in his arms, the senator became furious. He grabbed the camera from Mastorakis and tossed it overboard. "If you report any of this," Teddy shouted at him, "I'll have your ass."

The next day Jackie and Teddy told Onassis they had to discuss private Kennedy business, and he turned over the *Christina* and its crew to them to sail to an uninhabited offshore island. He assigned two of his security guards to accompany them. Suspicious of their motivations, Onassis ordered one of his guards to discreetly spy on them.

Once they arrived at the island, Teddy asked one of the guards to direct them to its most secluded cove. The guard found a beauty spot for them with warm water and white sands. Teddy instructed the guard to stand at a lookout point and signal if anyone was coming, and he also asked the guard to turn his eyes away to allow them some privacy.

Of course, the guard didn't do as instructed and spied relentlessly on his two charges. He later reported to Onassis that he'd seen them nude and lying together on a blanket, kissing each other passionately. And whereas the Greek tycoon had long ago learned about

Teddy Kennedy *(top left photo)* was blamed for the drowning death, on July 18, 1969, of **Mary Jo Kopechne** *(top right)*. He had been a top contender for the Presidential bid of 1972 until he abandoned the scene of the accident and didn't report it until many hours later.

Teddy later recalled, "I have no memory of how I escaped from the car *(depicted in lower photo)*. I repeatedly swam down, underwater, to see if the passenger was still inside. I was unsuccessful in that attempt."

Jackie's affair with Bobby, it was the first time that Onassis learned that Teddy was also sexually involved with his sister-in-law

Although Onassis decided not to confront Jackie with this indiscretion, he vowed to get "revenge" on Teddy. He did not specify what that revenge would be.

Somehow, Teddy learned that Onassis had uncovered details of his affair with Jackie. "Onassis is powerful and he's ruthless," Teddy told Powers. "He could easily put out a contract on me. He's killed others, maybe Bobby himself."

The Massachusetts senator had long been suspicious that Onassis had been behind the assassination of his beloved brother, Bobby. Reportedly, his diaries revealed that Teddy lived in "constant terror" that Onassis might have him murdered. "I'd wake up in a cold sweat, fearing a killer was in the house."

***

Astronauts were setting foot on the surface of the moon at 11:15PM on that fateful evening of July 18, 1969. Viewers around the world were absorbed with the implications of that event until something occurred that evening that knocked stories about the moon landing off the front pages.

Kennedy associates Joe Gargan and Paul Markham had arranged a weekend party for the "Boiler Room Girls" on Chappaquiddick, a tiny islet off the coast of Martha's Vineyard. These secretaries had previously worked as aides to Robert F. Kennedy, who had been assassinated about 13 months previous to the night in question.

Based on events that transpired on that long ago July evening, one of the secretaries, a blonde, blue-eyed beauty from Pennsylvania, Mary Jo Kopechne, would have her picture plastered during the week that followed on the front page of virtually every newspaper in the world.

Early in 1968, Bobby Kennedy had been forced to abandon his love affair with Jackie to make a run for the U.S. presidency, and at that point he had more or less "surrendered" Jackie to Aristotle Onassis. But he still needed a sexual tryst here and there, as he flew from city to city across the vast American continent.

Bobby's eyes fell on a campaign worker, Mary Jo Kopechne, who was pert and pretty. She'd taught school in Alabama before migrating to Washington in 1963, where she got a job as a secretary to the hard-partying Senator George Smathers of Florida, one of Jack Kennedy's best friends.

At a staff party in Washington, Smathers introduced Mary Jo to both Bobby and Teddy Kennedy. It was rumored—never proven—that Bobby flipped a coin with Teddy to determine who got to her first. "You know the rules, Teddy," Bobby is alleged to have said. "One of your older brothers always gets there first, if Dad hasn't already beaten us to her."

Mary Jo and Bobby launched an affair that was still going on at the time of his assassination in 1968. After Bobby's death, Mary Jo mourned him for a while, but not for long. Soon she was secretly dating another married Kennedy brother, Teddy.

Smathers later asserted that "The call from Mary Jo that I had been anticipating finally came in. She told me she was pregnant with Teddy's child. If word of her condition ever leaked out, the Republicans would take over the White House."

Eventually, Teddy's most trusted advisors learned that on the night of Mary Jo's last automobile ride, he had planned to discuss the delicate subject involving her having an abortion. For Teddy it was the only way, although apparently she did not believe in abortions and actually wanted to have Teddy's baby.

At the party, he announced to the guests that he was driving Mary Jo to the departure point for the ferry departing for Edgartown, the last boat scheduled to leave that evening.

What happened next is still disputed today. Mary Jo got into Teddy's "scraped up knockaround," as he called it, a 1967 Oldsmobile 88. She would never be seen alive again.

At 12:40AM on that fatal night, Christopher Look, Martha's Vineyard's part-time deputy sheriff, spotted a parked car near Dike Road. This was more than an hour after the Senator asserted that the accident had occurred. Teddy stated that he had returned to the cottage, site of the party, on foot.

When Look saw the couple, a man and a woman, parked in the car, he approached the vehicle, assuming that the driver might be lost. But before he reached the Oldsmobile, the vehicle suddenly accelerated, heading for Dike Road and toward the bridge. The deputy sheriff opted not to follow the car, but noticed the license plate, noting only that it began with the letter L. Teddy's license plate was L78207.

Traveling at about twenty miles an hour, Teddy's car headed toward Dike Bridge, a wood-timbered span angled obliquely to the road. It was unlit, with no guardrail. Even though he applied the brakes, to his horror, he drove over the side of the bridge, plunging into tide-swept Poucha Pond. After crashing into the murky waters, the vehicle came to rest upside down.

Battling great odds, he managed to free himself from the car and swim to the surface. He later claimed that he tried to swim down and free Mary Jo, but failed—"maybe seven or eight times."

Teddy walked to the departure point for the Edgartown ferry, which had long ago shut down for the night. Amazingly, in his weakened condition, he swam across the 500-foot channel, although he later claimed he almost drowned.

Back in his room, he took off his clothes and collapsed, but still made no calls. He later said, "I had not given up hope all night long that, by some miracle, Mary Jo would have escaped from the car."

After a sleepless night, he began to call friends for advice. Surprisingly, his first call was to Jackie in New York City. They were engaged in an affair at the time, even though she was married to Onassis.

Jackie, according to unconfirmed reports, advised Teddy to call the police at once and to assert that when he left the scene of the accident, he was in a state of shock and did not realize a passenger was left inside the submerged car. "Plead temporary amnesia," she advised, but he did not heed her warning.

Before he finally turned himself over to the police later that morning, he phoned at least two dozen Kennedy advisors. Long before the crime was officially reported to local authorities, the cover-up had begun. Only when Teddy learned that the police had discovered Mary Jo's body did he cross back and head for the station in Edgartown.

He showed up in person at police headquarters to report the accident. It was widely assumed at the time that he had been drunk and needed time to sober up. If it had been proven that he was driving while drunk, the charges would have been far more serious.

***

A week later, on July 25, Teddy pleaded guilty to a charge of leaving the scene of an accident and causing injury. Judge James Boyle sentenced him to two months in jail but suspended the sentence because of the Senator's "unblemished record." Teddy strenuously denied press speculation that he and Mary Jo had "any romantic relationship whatsoever."

No autopsy was ordered which, of course, would have produced the devastating news that Mary Jo had been pregnant. Dr. Donald Mills, the medical examiner, signed the death certificate, claiming that the cause of death was accidental drowning.

In theory, at least, the District Attorney's office in Massachusetts did investigate the fatal accident, but their data was never made public. A year later when there was a call for retrieval of the file on the accident, the entire dossier had mysteriously disappeared. It has never been recovered.

***

In spite of the scandal, Teddy was so popular with the voters of Massachusetts that when he ran for his Senate seat again in 1970, he won.

He sat out the presidential race of 1972, refusing to run as George McGovern's vice presidential running mate. Four years later, because of renewed interest by the media in Chappaquiddick, he also chose not to run for President in 1976.

In 1980, in his pursuit of an impossible dream, Teddy foolishly sought the Democratic nomination for president against Jimmy Carter. He would lose the nomination and Carter himself, as the Democratic Party candidate, of course, then lost the election to Ronald Reagan.

Jackie called Ted and bluntly told him, "Even if you had won the presidency, you'd be the fourth Kennedy brother to be killed. Let's face it: you get dozens of death threats every week, and all you need is for one of them to be valid."

In his biography, *The Deeds of My Fathers*, author Paul David Pope wrote about how his grandfather and father founded the *National Enquirer* and then expanded it into the best-selling tabloid in America. Maxine Cheshire, a gossip columnist for the *Washington Post*, had stumbled across the facts associated with Mary Jo's pregnancy. In 1980, on the eve of the election, she was willing to sell her information, just as Teddy was challenging Jimmy Carter.

"Once people read it, there'd be no way that Ted Kennedy could ever run for president, maybe not even for dog catcher in Massachusetts," Pope wrote.

Pope said, "the story named names, none of them lacking attribution, and included no anonymous quotes. There were dates, times, places, and supporting documents."

Peggy Dattilo, an *Enquirer* reporter, interpreted the details associated with the assertions that Mary Jo had been pregnant by Teddy as "airtight—good, solid reporting." She told her editors that when the story hit, it would "be huge, bigger than anything since Watergate." In all likelihood, she believed, Teddy would have to resign from the Senate.

But against everyone's expectations, the paper's founder, Generoso Pope Sr., never ran the story. He bought the story simply as a means to kill it, in effect suppressing this scandalous revelation by trading it in a murky back-room deal for an innocuous vanilla-flavored feature article dictated directly by Ted Kennedy himself.

For Pope and his *Enquirer*, for reasons never fully understood, the benefits involved a personal behind-the-scenes interview about how Teddy had become a father figure to his late brother's children. Pope ran the story under the headline: *THE HEARTACHES & HAPPINESS OF RAISING 16 KENNEDY CHILDREN.*

A fair trade? Nearly all newspeople today think not.

"What people cared about was Jackie Kennedy and her two teenagers, Caroline and John Jr.," Pope maintained. "They cared about them a whole lot. JFK's three direct survivors were the Holy Grail of the tabloid world."

***

During the worst scandal of his life, the drowning of Mary Jo, Teddy spent many long evenings being consoled and comforted by Jackie.

He returned the favor in 1975 when Onassis died in Paris. Once again, Jackie called on him to serve as her negotiator, facing an iron-willed adversary, Christina Onassis.

He even flew with her to Paris, arriving the day after Onassis' death. Teddy accompanied Jackie to the small chapel in the hospital where his body was on display in an open bier. On his chest was a Greek Orthodox icon.

Later, an embarrassing incident occurred. As Jackie was leaving the chapel, the paparazzi snapped a picture of her. "Her wide grin stretched from Montana to Texas," said journalist James Brady, visiting Paris at the time.

Later that day, Valentino *[aka Valentino Clemente Ludovico Garavani, best known simply as Valentino, the Italian fashion designer]* visited Jackie in her hotel suite after she'd phoned him in Italy, asking him to fly to her side at once. She demanded a new black dress specifically designed and crafted for Onassis' funeral. "I've got to look right," she told him.

A maid walked in on Jackie as she was being fitted by Valentino.

The maid later reported that when she went to clean up the bedroom and bathroom, she found a nude Teddy shaving in front of the mirror.

Valentino later recalled, "First, I was amazed that Jackie, no stranger to funerals, didn't already have an array of black dresses. Also, it appeared rather shallow of her, even frivolous, that she was more concerned with her image at the funeral than her dead husband. She didn't look like a widow in mourning."

Jackie, Christina ("weeping all the way"), and Teddy flew together from Paris to Greece, the plane leaving from Orly Airport outside Paris.

In Athens, the paparazzi awaited them. Jackie had demanded that Teddy accompany her to the funeral. Privately, aides heard her instructing Teddy, "I want you to bleed that bitch for millions." She was, of course, referring to Christina.

***

The romance of Jackie and Teddy didn't entirely escape the radar screen. Word spread in the London tabloids about a possible romance between them when in January of 1985 they each attended the funeral of Lord Harlech, less formally known as David Ormsby-Gore, in North Wales.

During the course of their involvement in that event, Teddy was seen on several occasions entering Jackie's quarters after eleven at night and not departing until dawn.

After Teddy's failed presidential bid in 1980, he and his soon-to-be ex-wife, Joan, entered a bitter two-year struggle over a financial settlement.

In the 1980s and early 90s, Jackie and Teddy saw less and less of each other, although they talked frequently over the phone. They occasionally got together for a romantic tryst and came together for any type of emergency. She often talked with him about the future of her children.

Teddy and Jackie had long talks about John Jr. running for President of the United States. By this time, the Senator had decided that he would never consider running again for president.

Jackie shared with him her reservations that "some lunatic will try to shoot my son, wanting to be as famous as Lee Harvey Oswald."

"She knew the sacrifices that her son would have to make, but I think Jackie was willing to back him," Teddy said. "By the time John ran, Jackie would by then be the *grande dame* of the Democratic Party. I'm sure she'd campaign for him."

Teddy showed Jackie a letter he'd received from Senator George Smathers of Florida:

[John would make a marvelous candidate. Imagine having another John F. Kennedy in the White House. Even if he's only a 'junior,' he's far and away the

best looking of all the Kennedy kids—he has more Jackie's look than Jack's—and he has all the other attributes that can take him a long, long way—even to the White House.

He is not a political animal like some of his cousins, but if he ever got into the game of politics, he'd be damn successful.

John Jr. would probably come as close to making it to the White House as anyone I've seen of the Kennedys. The question is, how badly does he want it? There are lots of sacrifices ahead. Is he willing to make them?"

***

When Jackie was diagnosed with cancer and was dying in 1994, she talked to Teddy every day and saw him when she could. In her final hours, he was one of her last visitors, offering her what comfort he could and telling her that he loved her.

His devotion was very evident when he delivered, in front of the assembled mourners, a loving eulogy to her memory.

***

In August of 2009, Edward (Teddy) Kennedy, the long-standing senator from Massachusetts, affectionately known as "the Lion of the Senate" for his defense of the middle class and working poor, died at the age of 77 of brain cancer

He was deeply mourned by his devotees. But despite their adulation, he was an object of scorn from his conservative enemies, who objected to, among other things, his scandalous past.

Seen here with long hair, **John F. Kennedy, Jr.**, was photographed on June 7, 1979, at his graduation from Phillips Academy. His girlfriend at the time was Jeanne Christian.

Already, Teddy Kennedy and Jackie were plotting his future, and a role for him as President of the United States.

Brothers who survived JFK's assassination: **Bobby** *(left)*, **the Grieving Widow,** and **Teddy Kennedy**	**Edward M. Kennedy** (1932-2009) RIP, Lion of the Senate

Chapter Twenty-Eight

Jackie Marries Onassis

("A Grizzled Satrap")

And Enrages Half of America

Jackie O and Daddy O Mesmerize the World
A Bizarre Marriage Pact / Jackie's Bottomless Closets

In 1968, it was the marriage that shocked the world. **Jacqueline Kennedy**, the beloved widow of the slain U.S. president, John F. Kennedy, at the age of 39, married the Greek shipping tycoon, **Aristotle Onassis**. At the age of 62, he was old enough to be her father.

Not only was he assailed as an "international pirate," but he was a non-Catholic, which shocked the devout Rose Kennedy. The marriage would become the high point of his life; for her, it would lead at long last to her financial independence.

In one of the lighter moments of their married life, **Jackie** helps a shirtless **Ari Onassis** decorate his bandana-covered head with flowers. Before their marriage turned to ashes, they had many peaceful moments aboard his luxury yacht, the *Christina*. She even sketched portraits of him. He gave her diamonds, and she purchased modish neckties for him in Paris.

In London, she bought him a cigar cutter for his long Cuban cigars.

Jackie was not the first of the Bouvier sisters to be seduced by Aristotle Onassis, the fabulously wealthy Greek shipping tycoon. His

longtime mistress, the opera diva Maria Callas, often entertained Prince and Princess Stanislas Radziwill. Jackie's sister *[Lee Bouvier Canfield Radziwill]* had married the Polish aristocrat after her ill-fated marriage to Michael Canfield. Her marriage to Stanislas was heading for rocky shores when they accepted an invitation from Ari and Maria to sail with them aboard his luxurious yacht, the *Christina,* named after the Greek's daughter.

Reportedly, somewhere during the friendship of this quartet of international jet-setters, Lee and Ari became secret lovers. Their affair was conducted almost in front of Maria and Prince Stanislas, but for months, neither of the cuckolded lovers knew what Ari and Lee were up to.

When Lee made a play for Ari, he

There were quiet moments together, far from the madding frenzy.

"I thought I was buying a prize cow when I married Jackie. How could I know the cow would cost me $50 million?"

—Aristotle Onassis

"I don't dislike Mrs. Kennedy, you know. I hate her!"

—Christina Onassis

"As Jackie became the world's greediest woman, this need for financial independence dominated her life. She would never feel secure or be happy until she could control her own fate. Her only means would be unlimited wealth. Jackie knew she could not depend on anyone else. So many people had let her down early in life. She was a prisoner of her own need to possess great wealth. It would not be easy. But Jackie was prepared to do whatever it took to achieve her dream. Unlimited wealth was her goal. It was essential to her very being, and no one would keep her from her destiny."

—January Jones in *Oh, No...Jackie O!*

"Everybody knows three things about Aristotle Onassis. "I'm fucking Maria Callas. I'm fucking Jackie Kennedy. And I'm fucking rich!"

—Onassis to his aide, Johnny Meyer

had reasons other than her charm and beauty to become involved with her.

After all, her brother-in-law was President of the United States, and Ari had suffered through many unresolved problems and legal issues with his shipping interests there.

When Dwight D. Eisenhower was president of the U.S. in the 1950s, Ari had been hit with criminal charges, claiming he had conspired to defraud the U.S. government through his use of surplus American ships on which he failed to pay taxes. Instead of going to court, he settled for $7 million.

Maria followed Ari around the world, usually aboard his yacht. For a decade or so, they conducted an flamboyant international and tempestuous relationship. Maria referred to themselves as "the two most famous Greeks on earth."

Her first suicide attempt came not over Ari's eventual marriage to Jackie, but when she learned that her lover was having an affair with Lee. Maria had discovered an empty Cartier box with a love note to Lee.

Maria's close companion, Mary Carter, claimed, "When Maria found out in 1963 that Onassis was having an affair with Princess Radziwill, she was so upset she overdosed. It was Onassis who discovered her on the floor of her apartment in Paris. He walked her around, fed her black coffee, and, of course, called a doctor. Onassis saved her life."

In the golden days before the arrival of "The Widow," the tempestuous opera diva, **Maria Callas**, and **Ari Onassis** *(seen together in the upper photo)* were fodder for tabloid gossip for more than a decade. Here, they share a tense moment, contemplating their future.

Below, **Maria** entertains **Sir Winston Churchill** aboard the *Christina*. The former British prime minister was one of Ari's best friends and spent nearly all of his holidays aboard the opulent yacht.

The world first learned of Ari's romance with Lee when Drew Pearson in his *Washington Post* column wrote, "Does the ambitious Greek tycoon hope to become the brother-in-law of the American President?"

Once freed of their respective spouses, Maria always begged Ari to marry her, but he kept postponing it. He told confidants, "Marriage is not on my mind. The reason I won't marry Maria is because I can't stand the thought of sitting through an entire opera and staying awake."

***

589

Collapsing in pain on August 7, 1963, Jackie had been rushed to a hospital. A four-pound son was born six weeks early. Patrick Bouvier Kennedy experienced difficulty breathing. After struggling for life for forty hours, he lost the battle on August 9.

When Lee told Ari that her sister had been depressed after little Patrick's death, he invited her for an R&R cruise aboard the *Christina*. He turned over the yacht to her "without my presence."

Unknown to Lee, Ari had always been far more entranced by the image of Jackie than he was by her younger sister.

Worried about the cruise adversely affecting his 1964 presidential election campaign, JFK told her, "Christ, Jackie, Onassis is an international pirate." But he finally relented and let her go on the cruise.

The President was relieved to learn that Ari was turning over his yacht to Jackie and her friends, but she went behind his back and insisted on Ari's presence during the cruise aboard the *Christina*.

Knowing how well publicized the cruise would be, Jack wanted to shape the guest list. Lee Radziwill and her husband were totally acceptable, even though Prince Stanislas often referred to Ari as "a moral leper." JFK also asked Franklin D. Roosevelt, Jr. and his wife, Suzanne, to go on the cruise as chaperones. The son of FDR didn't really want to go, but he acquiesced to his President's request.

Maria wanted to go on the cruise, but Ari told her no. Later, she said, "Aristo kicked me out. He told me he couldn't have his concubine on board with the First Lady of America."

Sometime during the cruise, even with Lee aboard, Jackie began her affair with Ari. The source for that was FDR Jr., who saw Ari leaving Jackie's onboard suite at three o'clock one morning. When he returned to Washington, he reported the news to both Senator George Smathers and to then Vice-President Lyndon B. Johnson.

Hoping to discredit a President he loathed, LBJ, who liked gossip, spread the news.

No doubt, the Secret Service agent who had been assigned to Jackie during the cruise also transmitted the news to JFK. The President was devastated, even though during Jackie's absence he was conducting perhaps at least five or six illicit sexual trysts a week, usually from within the White House.

JFK called Jackie aboard the *Christina*, demanding that she leave the cruise and return to Washington at once. She refused and slammed down the phone on him.

She had another motivation for defying her husband: During the course of the cruise, she was confronted with the most damaging rumor she'd ever faced in her marriage. Somehow, Ari had heard the accusation that JFK had slept with Jackie's sister, Lee, once back in 1957, when Jackie was in the hospital giving birth to Caroline.

Author January Jones printed this accusation as fact in her biography,

Jackie, Ari & Jack: The Tragic Love Triangle. She wrote: "Another reason for Jackie's erratic moods was the fact that her husband, Jack, had slept with her sister, Lee, while she was in the hospital having Caroline. This was revealed by her step-sibling, Nini Gore Auchincloss. Now who wouldn't be depressed? Can you blame her? As you can see, none of this could ever be revealed without doing irrevocable damage to the Kennedy image."

That Jack slept with Lee is one of the most notorious scandals of the Kennedy era. Another source of the rumor was the gossipy Truman Capote, a confidant of both Jackie and Lee. Although he was often loose with his facts, he never let that stop him from telling a good yarn.

Jackie apparently believed the many stories and rumors. Capote later claimed that Jackie slept with Ari aboard that cruise, shortly before the president's death, "as an act of revenge."

This romantic triangle may be too murky ever to be straightened out, but the alleged Lee/JFK liaison remains one of the most painful rumors Jackie had to confront. Later, thanks to the Internet, the rumor spread around the world.

During the cruise, Ari took Jackie to his dream island of Skorpios, which he had purchased six months previously for $100,000. It was shaped like a scorpion. "Lovely, lovely," Jackie said, little knowing that it would one day become her home. He falsely told her that he was going to build a copy, with 180 rooms, of the Cretan Palace of Knossos on one of the island's hilltops. He never did. It went the way of so many of his promises of yesterday.

At the end of the cruise, Ari presented Jackie with a stunning diamond-and-ruby necklace worth about $50,000 in 1963 dollars.

It is believed that Lee wrote to the President, informing him of this lavish gift to his wife. She may also have claimed that Ari had been showering Jackie with gifts throughout the cruise. "All I got from our Greek tycoon was three little bracelets that even Caroline wouldn't wear," Lee claimed.

Publicly, FDR Jr. denied that there was anything romantic between Ari and Jackie during the cruise. JFK's personal secretary, Evelyn Lincoln, later challenged that statement. "I felt they did have an affair. I think so, yes. Jackie loved money. Onassis had money."

That debate about a possible JFK/Lee affair continues to this day. What is known is that the cruise marked the end of Ari's affair with Lee. "He fell in love with Jackie on that cruise," said Ari's aide, Johnny Meyer.

Christina was one of the first to learn of her father's new attachment to Jackie, referring to it as "my father's unfortunate obsession."

Jackie, in the words of one of the Secret Service agents, returned to the White House "with stars in her eyes—Greek stars."

After the cruise, the White House staff noted a stronger and more independent woman. Jackie had successfully beguiled one of the richest and most powerful men in the world, and she was married to the leader of the Free World.

Back in Washington, Jackie was willing to acquiesce to her husband's latest demands. He wanted her to help him counter the negative publicity of her Onassis cruise. Spurred on by a sense of guilt, she was eventually persuaded to accompany him on a political trip.

"Where are we going?" she asked. "What God-forsaken place in the American wastelands?"

"Dallas," he answered.

***

Aristotle Onassis spun an orbit of dizzying riches, twisted intrigue, and questionable mores. Yet with all the revelations about him, during his lifetime, much of the world never learned some of his darker secrets. His true story revealed a deeply complicated man who was much more complex in his desires and obsessions than the public ever realized.

A young **Ari Onassis**, hot, ambitious, ruthless, and handsome

As Ari once confessed to Richard Burton in the presence of others, "I've been known to walk on the wild side. And I just know that you have, too. We are larger-than-life figures with passions no single woman can satisfy, not even a series of women. For the ultimate satisfaction, and I may be speaking just for myself, I have to go outside the boundaries of usual morality. I visit clubs, particularly in Paris, where unspeakable acts are performed and strange trysts are arranged. I know what it is to be raped—that is, being on the receiving end—and I know what it is to rape others. Sex is one thing and can quickly become routine. But when you're raping a virgin ass and causing great pain, you feel like the ruler of the universe."

When Johnny Meyer worked for the aviator and mogul, Howard Hughes, he was defined as Hughes's "public relations consultant"—read that "pimp"—catering to Hughes' bisexual proclivities, arranging dates for him with the likes of Errol Flynn.

Later, when Meyer was employed by Ari Onassis, he was referred to as "an *aide-de-camp*," an elegant name for a cover-up man. And just as he had done for Hughes, he also arranged sexual trysts for Ari.

Meyer wasn't at all surprised when Ari requested for him to arrange rendezvous, often aboard his yacht, with some of the most beautiful boys in Europe.

"He had a thing for Swedish or Danish boys," Meyer later confessed. "He was real rough on them. At some point they were left bleeding. I think Ari didn't consider it really good sex unless he drew blood from somewhere on the boy."

"It's sick, I know, but I got well paid. And I never lost one night's sleep over the morality—or lack thereof—of my clients."

***

So just who was this mysterious tycoon of bizarre sexual tastes?

Named after the two most famous philosophers of ancient Greece, Aristotle Socrates Onassis (1906-1975), the second husband of Jacqueline Kennedy, was broke at twenty-one and a millionaire at twenty-three. In later life, his ever-present sunglasses evoked memories of Al Capone, the Chicago gangster. Critics claimed that Ari's business practices also evoked Capone's.

By the age of eleven, when growing up as a member of the prosperous Greek minority in Smyrna (a Turkish city known today as Izmir), Ari showed a lusty interest in women, but was forbidden to date. His sexual introduction came in the basement of the Onassis home in Smyrna's suburb of Karatass with the family laundress, who was only about twelve years old herself. His stepmother, Helen, came home unexpectedly and caught her stepson seducing the young girl on a pile of dirty laundry. It was *coitus interruptus.*

Socrates, his father, found out about it. He was rather proud that his son had discovered sex at such an early age, but he advised him, "Never do it with some peasant girl. Sleep up."

Throughout his life, Ari would follow that advice. As his future mistress, opera diva Maria Callas, recalled, "Aristo was obsessed with famous women. He was obsessed with me because I was famous."

As he traveled the globe in later life, he seduced everybody from silent screen vamp Gloria Swanson to tobacco heiress Doris Duke.

Like other Greeks living in Smyrna at the turn of the 20th century, the Onassis family had survived under Turkish rule, their lives controlled by the Ottoman sultan.

In 1919, at the conclusion of World War I, Greek troops, backed up by Allied war ships, occupied Smyrna. But after three politically inconclusive years, during the summer of 1922, the Turks mounted a massive and particularly brutal invasion as a means of reconquering Smyrna. Seeking revenge on the Greeks, the Turkish soldiers slaughtered Greeks by the hundreds. Greeks were hung from lampposts and trees. The smell of burning flesh filled the air.

When the subsequent Turkish occupation of their city, Ari's father, Socrates Onassis, was arrested and tossed into a Turkish prison. His wife, Helen, along with his three daughters, fled to an evacuation center, waiting transport to Greece.

Only sixteen years old at the time, Ari remained in Smyrna with his fiercely courageous grandmother. A Turkish general, accompanied by a very handsome lieutenant, requisitioned the Onassis house, kicking out the old grandmother, who went to live with relatives.

But the general and his lieutenant ordered Ari to stay, especially when they learned that he spoke perfect Turkish. He was a reasonably attractive boy back then, not the 62-year-old who married Jackie and was frequently ridiculed as "the toad." The general and the lieutenant needed a servant boy, someone to cook for them and bathe them at night after heating the water. Before the dawn of the next morning, Ari had been introduced to sodomy.

One would have to see a picture of young Ari to understand why two Turkish officers were interested in his sexual favors. In 1922, George Sevdayan was selling newspapers on the street when he first met Ari, who was hawking cigarettes. "I saw a very handsome young boy peddling those newspapers. Though not very tall, he had particularly penetrating eyes. In spite of his shabby clothes, he was totally different from the other poor kids in the streets. He already had an outstanding personality, and I knew he was going far and didn't give a fuck how he got there, just so long as it was on the way to the top."

In the 1960s, British journalist Peter Evans was summoned to Paris for an interview with Ari about the possibility of writing his autobiography. During their discourse, Ari talked about his homosexual relationship with the Turkish lieutenant, apparently not mentioning the general. But he claimed that he cooperated as a means of securing his father's freedom, since he was in a Turkish prison at the time.

Ari never quite recovered from the trauma of the Turkish rape of his native city of Smyrna in 1922. Three of his uncles were executed. His aunt, Maria, and her husband, Chrysostomos Konialidis, and their daughter perished when the Turks set fire to a church in Thyatire in which hundreds of Christians had sought refuge.

When Ari was allowed to visit his father, Socrates, in prison, he found him sharing a cage with twenty other prisoners. Unshaven and unwashed, he was suffering from dysentery and wracked with nightmares.

Ari told Socrates, "I will do anything—and I mean anything—to obtain your release." After saying that, he returned to their former home where a Turkish general and a lieutenant were waiting for him.

He was smart enough not to resist the sexual advances of the older Turkish officers, who brought food home for him to cook. In time he managed to find bootleg liquor for them. According to reports, Ari became very fond of the general and especially that young lieutenant. Even when they didn't want to have sex with him, he nonetheless made himself available.

His first heartbreak came when he heard that his benefactors had been reassigned and were leaving Smyrna.

Abandoned by his newly acquired friends, Ari made a clever move. He distracted some Turkish border guards and fled to the safety of the U.S. Marine compound. He was a very persuasive teenager and within a day was allowed to board an American destroyer steaming for Lesbos, relative safety, and freedom.

The first chapter of Ari's life had ended. Fame and fortune, and far more adventures than his young mind could have conjured up at the time, awaited him.

After reuniting with his relatives, he decided that Greece could not contain his ambitions. He felt that the New World offered far greater opportunities, and in 1923, he sailed to Argentina, landing in Buenos Aires.

As a newly impoverished young man fleeing from the Turkish/Greek/Armenian conflicts of the early 20th century, Ari became a dishwasher, a laundry man, a night clerk, and a telephone operator. It was in the latter job that he began to make money by eavesdropping on business deals being transacted, many of them illegal. He made notes, studied the financial pages, and thanks partly to his eavesdropping, stayed several steps ahead of his rivals. Suddenly, he was making $1,000 on a linseed oil deal. He speculated on animal hides and furs and made a whopping $10,000. He was on his way. In time, he managed to seduce Evita Perón, who made him an omelet after their night of lovemaking.

"The rest of my story," as Ari so often recalled, "is history."

Or, as his enemies put it, he was a "poor boy who became a rich boy, smuggler, thief, liar, lover, family man, international playboy, and the most glamorous tycoon of the 20th century, wallowing in fabulous wealth and fabled extravagance." He combined famous mistresses and kept boys with infamous, often corrupt deals and unholy alliances.

Evita with **Juan Perón** in 1951. Here, too sick to stand, she relies on him to support her as crowds adore her.

Throughout his life, Ari, according to friends and enemies, always seemed to have a handsome boy or young man stashed somewhere—Athens, Monaco, New York, Paris.

The best reporting on this subject was done by Christopher Andersen, a *New York Times* bestselling author, known for works which include *Jack and Jackie* and *Jackie After Jack*.

When Ari sailed with famous friends (they included Sir Winston Churchill) aboard his luxurious yacht, the *Christina*, he often amused them with stories of ancient Greece and spoke openly about homosexuality. One night he told Franklin D. Roosevelt, Jr., that "every Greek man worth his salt has a wife, a mistress, and a beautiful young boy on the side. It is our custom."

He had read everything he could about Alexander the Great (356-323 B.C.), the King of Macedonia who overthrew the Persian Empire and went on to conquer the known world. He could talk endlessly about Alexander's love for his boyhood friend, Hephaestion. Both boys had been tutored by Aristotle, Ari's namesake.

Ari regaled his guests with stories of Alexander's great love for his companion, Hephaestion. When the youth died in 326 BC, Alexander had the attending doctor arrested and crucified. As an homage to their male-male love affair—the most famous in the ancient world—he also ordered the tails and manes of "all the king's horses" be clipped. He also erected a memorial to his lover—the Lion of Hamadan, which stands in northern Iran to this day, awarding Hephaestion the status of a minor deity.

Ari had the walls of his bathroom on his private island of Skorpios decorated with Grecian homoerotic art printed on specially commissioned wall paper he had made in Athens.

Aboard his yacht, Ari would explain that homosexuality, like hunting, was thought to foster masculine, especially martial, bravery.

"Alexander sacked cities, tortured his captors, killed his rivals, and even

595

sold hordes of people into slavery," Ari claimed. "But he was really a great guy, and that's why I named my son after him."

For years, Ari had kept two boys, one in an apartment near his residence on the Avenue Foch in Paris and another in Athens. His bodyguards claimed that when he first met these boys they were either twelve or thirteen years old.

He also kept two Italian boys in Rome. In Andersen's biography, he quotes Frank Monte, Ari's bodyguard, as saying, "One lived in Ari's apartment, and the other was always on call when Ari wanted him. One

Jackie Kennedy Onassis pictured herself a world class decorator of taste and style. She found the Grecian homoerotic art that her new husband used to decorate certain walls of his yacht, the *Christina*, "a bit much."

was dark, the other was blonde haired but deeply tan. They were handsome in their early twenties. Ari would play around with them, making lewd jokes in front of me and other bodyguards. He mistreated them, even beat them for pleasure."

"Onassis would talk quite openly about his two regular boys and other occasional boys," according to Monte. "He'd say, 'There's nothing wrong with it, I just like to do it with boys.' He'd often take one or the other to his bedroom and after a while there would be the sounds of punches and screams. Then we'd get a call from Ari to fetch the poor kid and throw him out. Sometimes a boy would be yelling, '*No, no, I love you!*'"

As if the homosexual link wasn't shocking enough for some of his friends, over the years there have been revelations from his staff that Ari was also cross-dresser, a trait he shared with J. Edgar Hoover of the F.B.I.

"When he didn't have important guests—or when Jackie wasn't aboard the *Christina*—he often liked to dress up in women's clothing late in the evening," claimed party planner Stratis Kopoulos, who once catered all-male parties for Ari aboard the *Christina*. "When Mrs. Kennedy was aboard, he never wore women's clothing. But he used to with Maria Callas. She was much more tolerant and understanding of such things. In fact, I think he dressed in her gowns. It was bizarre. But during my employment with Onassis, before he fired me for some silly reason, I saw plenty. I could write a book, but he'd probably have me murdered."

His penchant for wearing women's gowns dates back to the 1930s.

Ari liked to dress up in the gowns of his mistresses, including those of Ingebord Dedichen, a socialite whose toes he liked to lick. He'd met this woman—a tall, blonde Norwegian—in the summer of 1934. "He found my feet as smooth as a baby's bottom," Ingebord claimed.

She also noted that he enjoyed anal humor, which she did not. One night he complained that he was suffering from piles and wanted her to investigate before he was scheduled to visit a doctor the following morning. He asked her to check that part of his anatomy. When she did, she was rewarded with a fart in the face.

This tawdry incident was revealed in an incendiary biography, *Aristotle Onassis*, compiled by the London Sunday Times team.

***

It is a little known fact, and one that the Kennedy clan in later years didn't want publicized. But Bobby and Ethel announced that their first choice for their firstborn's godfather was none other than the infamous Red-baiting Senator, Joseph McCarthy.

Bobby was involved with McCarthy's eradication of Communists during one of the most extraordinary episodes of political theater in the history of the American Republic. That involved the dispute between the U.S. Army and McCarthy over the draft status of G. David Schine, the boyfriend of Roy Cohn. J. Edgar Hoover watched the hearings in fascination.

In New York in the 1960s and 1970s, Ari befriended Cohn, the lawyer who became notorious in the 1950s as the chief honcho for McCarthy during the nationwide witch hunt for "pinko commies."

Much of the early animosity between Bobby and Ari stemmed from Cohn's friendship with Onassis, whom Bobby resented. Long before Ari became intimately involved with Jackie, Bobby had intensely disliked the Greek shipping tycoon.

The tension between Cohn and Bobby grew so viperish that Bobby left the Subcommittee in July of 1953 after only five months of service.

Meanwhile, F.B.I. director J. Edgar Hoover also began to cool on McCarthy, fearing that the Senator was overplaying his hand.

Joseph Kennedy, Sr. stayed in touch with the FBI director and, at one point in the 1950s, urged him to resign from the F.B.I. to become his own personal director of security, but Hoover was determined to stay on at the F.B.I.

Both Bobby and Hoover learned that Cohn was supplying beautiful young hustlers to Ari every time he visited New York.

"Ari worshipped physical beauty in men, the Grecian ideal," Cohn told his best pal, New York literary agent Jay Garon and others one night at a gay bar in Manhattan called Country Cousin. "Ari wanted only the best and was willing to pay for it."

"He often preferred blonde boys, but occasionally made special requests," Cohn confided to Garon, who himself had been Hollywood director George Cukor's kept boy when he was young.

"One time he requested a hustler who looked like Sal Mineo, and I came up with a dead ringer,"

Washington did not tolerate Roy Cohn in silence. Here, *TIME* showcases **Cohn** *(left)* and **David Schine** on the cover of an edition from 1954.

597

Cohn said. "Ari paid very well, at least five-hundred dollars back in the days he could have gotten the boy for fifty bucks. He did like to manhandle guys, though. In the old days, he paddled their butts until they were scarlet red, then sodomized them. In later life, he mauled them viciously, and word got out to the hustler community. It got so bad that at one point only masochists would do his bidding."

A young French-Canadian, who danced professionally at a male strip joint, The Gaiety Theater in midtown Manhattan under the name of "Spike Jones," recalled a weekend he spent with Ari in the late 1960s at an estate in Greenwich, Connecticut, which Cohn had rented.

"I was taken there in a Rolls Royce painted money green. The chauffeur's uniform matched the color of the car. Once there, I was ushered into Cohn's private bedroom. The room was dimly lit but I knew at once it was Onassis waiting for me. He was lying completely nude on the bed. He had a large, thick, uncut prick, and I feared he'd cause me some damage."

"The room itself was a bit bizarre," Jones claimed. "A big oak four-poster bed, like something from *Gone With the Wind*, dominated the room, with a mirror overhead so the client could see the action. The walls contained

Top photo: Red-baiting **Senator Joseph McCarthy** *(left)* of Wisconsin and his chief legal honcho, the horrendous **Roy Cohn,** hunted so-called communists in the government, and destroyed careers throughout Hollywood.

In the lower photo, **Cohn,** a notorious homosexual, looked like a cadaver as he entered the final throes of AIDS.

dozens of toy soldiers and a lot of stuffed animals, including Teddy Bears in all colors. There were a lot of statues of oversize devils, showing very large cocks painted pink with scarlet red tips. When I went into the bathroom, it was covered in tiles depicting pink and chartreuse frogs fucking. It was really weird."

"I knew that Onassis would want to screw me," Jones said. "And he did. He turned me over on my stomach. He wasn't interested in the front part of my anatomy. Before penetration, he paddled my ass until it blistered . . . I mean really hard. Then with no preparation, he entered me forcefully, and I screamed. That turned him on. He piled on top of me and pounded me without mercy. He was an older man, and it took him a long time to get off. All the while he was fucking me, he bit into my neck like a vampire. I was bleeding. I think he actually got off drinking my blood. I was told later that he was a Satanist, just like Sammy Davis, Jr., who was also one of my clients one dark night. But that's another story."

"Onassis gave me a thousand dollars that night and told me to keep my mouth shut," Jones claimed. "I usually had to take on ten clients for that kind of money. I couldn't believe that Jacqueline Kennedy was married to that sicko. I bet he didn't pull that shit on her. For the money he paid, I was willing to take him on again, but he never requested me after that one night. He did use other guys from our agency but they were sent to the townhouse where Cohn lived in Manhattan. Cohn was definitely the pimp for Onassis."

"Two weeks later, Cohn called me back to the same estate," Jones said. "My neck had healed somewhat. He thanked me for taking care of his friend Onassis, but warned me he could pay only one hundred dollars. He wanted me to penetrate him but when I took a look, I just couldn't. His entire anus was covered with venereal warts. My hard-on became a softie, and Cohn kicked me out of the house."

In the late 1950s, Ari became a frequent visitor at Le Carrousel in Paris, a club that featured a stage with female impersonators. Partly because of regular injections of female hormones, many of the young men were "incredibly beautiful, feminine, and sexy," as critics claimed.

A "Doctor Burou" performed sex-change surgery on many of them. After the genital surgery, some of them returned to Le Carrousel. In the words of Ari, "they were more beautiful than ever."

The club owner once told the underground press that Ari and "some other very wealthy men" often sponsored the sex-change surgeries so that these "newly liberated bodies could be turned into women."

According to the mistress of ceremonies, "Onassis paid for more surgeries and took more girls as his mistress than any other patron."

***

It was November of 1963. Ari hadn't seen Jackie in months.

Sailing aboard the *Christina*, Aristotle Onassis heard a bulletin on his radio. It was out of Dallas. John F. Kennedy, President of the United States, had been assassinated.

Without alerting anyone, even his closest aides and especially Maria Callas, Ari launched into what he'd later call "my change of plans. My new strategy."

Ari joined Maria in Paris and spent his days watching the coverage of the President's death on television. Noting how brave and courageous Jackie was, Ari told Maria: "There's something Greek about Jackie." The diva was not impressed. "She's just putting on a grand show for the media."

Maria Callas, the greatest opera diva of the 20th century, and Aristotle Onassis, the promethean tycoon who revolutionized the international shipping industry, had begun a tumultuous courtship in 1959 that scandalized and fascinated the world.

"Maria Callas was the greatest artist we in Greece have produced since the age of Pericles," said Manuel Kulukundis, a spokesman for the Greek shipping industry.

Both Ari and Maria were Greeks, although the soprano was raised above a drugstore in Brooklyn. In later life, she sang only when she wanted to—one night she walked out on a performance for the president of Italy.

Callas changed opera forever, and her recordings became legendary.

All her life she fought "The Battle of the Bulge." After seeing sylphlike Audrey Hepburn in *Roman Holiday* in 1953, she went on a rigid diet—no liquor, no pasta, no bread, only one lean meal a day. Transforming herself, she took off nearly 70 pounds. In 1965, she showcased her new look in landmark performances of *Tosca* at the Metropolitan Opera in New York.

Jackie, in mink and diamonds, attended one of her performances and came backstage to congratulate Maria. In a white satin Dior gown, Jackie looked stunning, "Madame Callas, this was one of the most thrilling nights I have ever had at the opera," Jackie said. "You were magnificent."

The prima donna replied, "You are magnificent."

Never again would the two divas have anything good to say about each other.

The world's couturiers, especially Dior and Givenchy, made Callas a symbol of Parisian and Milanese high chic. But in spite of all that, she faced an adversary more glamorous than she could ever be.

"How can I compete against this international prostitute and gold-digger?" she asked.

She was obviously referring to Jackie, who in just three years would become Jacqueline Kennedy Onassis.

***

Callas, of course, was one of the first to realize that Ari had become serious about an attachment of some sort to Jackie. It took the rest of the world longer to catch on.

Even when members of the press learned that Ari had been seen with Jackie, they did not immediately connect a romance between "The Beauty and the Beast." Over the years, Ari had been seen with some of the most famous and beautiful women in the world, paying homage to the likes of Greta Garbo and Elizabeth Taylor.

Maria learned that Ari had been secretly seeing Jackie at her Fifth Avenue duplex apartment in New York throughout 1966 and into 1967. Even as late as January of 1968, Maria and most of the American public did not know how serious the relationship between Jackie and Ari had become. Jackie, it was learned later, had been entertained by Ari on the island of Skorpios and at his plush apartment on the Avenue Foch in Paris.

As Bobby started to run for the presidency in 1968, Ari and Jackie popped up everywhere. They were seen in New York at the exclusive "21" or at El Morocco, even at Ari's two favorite Greek restaurants in New York, Mykonos and Dionysus. Both of them were photographed entering Maxim's in Paris.

Jackie began to confide in him, complaining bitterly that she was "emotionally shackled" by the Kennedys, who held tight purse strings.

In August of 1968, Doris Lilly, a columnist for The *New York Post*, went on *The Merv Griffin Show* and proclaimed that Jackie Kennedy was preparing to marry Aristotle Onassis. The shocked audience vigorously booed her for such an outlandish suggestion. As she left the studio, a hostile crowd had gathered to denounce her, and one member jabbed a pointed metal nail file into her face, dangerously close to her eye. She made her way to a taxi, and en route, she was spat upon. But despite the horrified reaction of the American public, as represented by the audience that day at *The Merv Griffin Show,* the gossip columnist was right.

When columnist **Doris Lilly** *(right)* appeared on **The Merv Griffin Show** and announced that Jackie Kennedy was going to marry Aristotle Onassis, she was booed because of her "outrageous" claim.

After the show, as she was leaving the studio, an angry mob attacked her.

When Callas heard what Lilly had said, she claimed, "My God. Ari has gotten Jackie pregnant. What an ugly little bastard that one will be!"

Lilly, a former lover of Ronald Reagan, was highly critical of Jackie. She said, "She's a hypocrite and, in truth, is a darker, more complicated person than the saintly widow the public saw. She assiduously protects her own privacy, but is herself an incorrigible snoop and gossip. When she moved into her Fifth Avenue apartment, she put a telescope in her living room and used it to try to spy on her neighbors. She is also a narcissist. During her White House days, the walls of her bedroom were lined with magazine covers of herself."

After the assassination of Bobby Kennedy on June 5, 1968, the relationship between Jackie and Ari became intense. "If they're killing Kennedys my kids are Number One targets," she said. "I want to get out of the country."

"Marry me and I will protect you and your children," he promised. "I have the means to do so."

He later admitted to Johnny Meyer, his chief aide, "It was an impulsive thing to do. I was shocked when she said 'yes.'"

Before flying to Greece, Ari had to pay a farewell visit to Callas, in Paris, to face her and break the news. He was blunt. "I'm going to marry Jackie. I still love you, but I need Jackie in my life. It will not be a marriage of love. I need Bobby to win the presidency and look favorably upon my use of U.S. docks. Jackie needs me to buy privacy that she can't find in America. She fears she'll be murdered in the States or that her children will be kidnapped. She needs the armed security guards I can provide. Those Secret Service agents assigned to her are a pack of faggots."

"I could never influence you to do anything," Maria responded. "Go, then, to your woman who sounds like Marilyn Monroe playing Ophelia."

At the door, he told her, "You know I will always love you."

"My pain is too deep to speak anymore," she told him. "Please leave. You will not be the first man to marry a woman you do not love, and Jackie will not be the first woman to marry a man she does not love."

On the day of Onassis' wedding to Jacqueline Bouvier Kennedy, Maria went into seclusion in her apartment in Paris. To protect herself from the paparazzi, she ordered her heavy draperies to be drawn.

When she finally faced the press in Paris, Maria said, "Mrs. Kennedy did well to give a grandfather to her children. Onassis is as beautiful as Croesus." *[It was a reference, of course, to the ancient King of Lydia (ruled 560 BC-546 BC), famed for his wealth. According to legend and myth, he was hideously ugly, but so powerful that his subjects who did not bow and call him the handsomest man in the world were beheaded.]*

in 1969, the Marxist film director, Pier Paolo Pasolini, invited **Maria Callas** *(above)* to interpret the (non-singing) role of the vengeful protagonist in his avant-garde film, *Medea.*

Drawing, chillingly, on her training as an operatic diva and as a deeply betrayed Greek, she didn't have to sing a note.

At least in public, Maria seemed to interpret the announcement of Ari's marriage with a stoic but painful calm. But Lee Radziwill became hysterical during a call to Truman Capote. He later reported, "She was screaming and crying and carrying on."

"How could Jackie do this to me?" Lee sobbed into the phone to Capote. "How could this happen?"

Capote later said, "Lee really thought she had Onassis nailed down. She wasn't in love with him, but she loved all those tankers."

There was a great irony in Jackie's marrying Ari. Years previously, Jackie had rather prudishly warned her that Lee would damage JFK's presidency if she married the Greek tycoon. "Obviously Jackie could give advice, but not take her own advice," Capote said.

***

On October 20, 1968, it seemed that the eyes of the world were focused on the private island of Skorpios, where Jackie married Ari. Some three dozen photographers invaded the island, ignoring signals and warnings from the *Christina.* As one reporter said, "They hit the beach amid the whirr of movie cameras and the rapid-fire clicks of Nikons and Leicas."

A journalist from London wrote: "Jackie looked drawn and concerned. She wore a long-sleeved, two-piece ivory chiffon lace dress with a pleated skirt. Her hair was secured with an ivory ribbon. The groom looked slightly off key in a blue suit."

Jackie's wedding dress was by Valentino.

On the day of their wedding, the press gave them new names—"*Daddy O*" and "*Jackie O*." Ari also presented Jackie with gifts priced at more than $1 million. Reporters dubbed it "the $20 million dollar honeymoon." Within the year he'd present her with another $4 million in jewelry, practically using a shopping cart at Tiffany's and at Van Cleef & Arpels.

She wore her $1.2 million wedding ring topped with a huge, heart-shaped ruby surrounded by diamonds.

Less than two dozen guests gathered on Skorpios in the chapel of the Little Mother of God.

The Vatican announced that Jackie would be living with Ari in "mortal sin," because of his previous marriage, in 1946, to Tina Livanos, the then-17 year-old daughter of another shipping magnate, Stavros Livanos. Tina had sued for divorce in 1960, charging adultery. Jackie was barred from receiving sacraments from the Catholic church, but was not excommunicated.

Guests at the wedding included not only Jackie's children, but Janet Auchincloss and the Kennedy sisters, Patricia and Jean Smith. Rose Kennedy refused to attend.

Ancient rites from the Greek Orthodox Church were included in the ceremony. Father Archimandrite Polykarpos Athanassiou took Ari's hand as he clasped Jackie's, and made three counterclockwise processions around the altar as part of the symbolic "Dance of Isaiah."

At the end of the ceremony, the newly married couple was showered with rice, flowers, and sugared almonds. A golf cart hauled them from the chapel to the pier, where the *Christina* waited to spirit them away on their honeymoon voyage.

Ari also showered Caroline and John Jr. with expensive gifts, but Caroline reminded her little brother of Homer's ancient warning from the *Iliad*, "Beware of Greeks bringing gifts."

A *Washington Post* reporter at the wedding claimed that Alexander and Christina "looked like they were attending a wake."

"My father may need a wife, but I sure as hell don't need a god damn self-enchanted stepmother," Alexander told Christina. "It's a perfect match. Father loves celebrities and Jackie loves gold."

World opinion right after the marriage was almost unanimous, summed up by one comment: "As far as husbands go, Mrs. Kennedy went from a Greek God to a god damn Greek."

In Rome, the magazine *L'Espresso*, wrote that Jackie's marriage to "this grizzled satrap, with his liver-colored skin, thick hair, fleshy nose, and wide horsey grin, who buys an island and then has it removed from all the maps to prevent the landing of castaways; and, on the other hand, an ethereal-looking beauty of 39, renowned for her sophistication and her interest in the fine arts, and a former First Lady at that."

The marriage found two supporters, Elizabeth Taylor, who had been frequently entertained by Onassis, and Jackie's distant relative, Gore Vidal. "He is charming, kind, and considerate," said Taylor. "Jackie made an excellent choice."

Vidal noted that the match was "highly suitable. They have something in

603

common. Both are heavy smokers."

Rose Kennedy said, "Jackie is one of the world's most expensive women to maintain, and Onassis has one of the world's greatest fortunes."

In Paris, when Coco Chanel heard about the upcoming marriage, she said, "Everyone knew she was not cut out for dignity. You mustn't ask a woman with a touch of vulgarity to spend the rest of her life over a corpse."

Chanel's was just one of thousands, even millions of opinions heard around the world. Comedian Joan Rivers mocked the marriage. "Come on, tell the truth. Would you sleep with Onassis? Do you believe she does? Well, she has to do something—you can't stay at Bergdorf's shopping all day."

Headlines around the world denounced Jackie for marrying Ari. One tabloid in London claimed "JACKIE WEDS BLANK CHECK." *Bild-Zeitung* in Germany headlined their overview with "JACK KENNEDY DIES TODAY FOR A SECOND TIME." Even the staid *New York Times* claimed "AMERICA HAS LOST A SAINT."

In her defense, Richard Cardinal Cushing came forward, asking, "Why can't she marry whomever she wants to marry?"

In the weeks to follow, Cushing's defense of Jackie brought him an avalanche of hate mail, "some of which is in the language of the gutter." He decided to retire as archbishop on August 24, 1970, two years before the date he'd previously announced. "I could no longer stand being the victim of such hatred and such violent attacks for expressing an honest and true opinion."

Dorothy Schiff was the long-time publisher of the *New York Post*. During the course of 1968, she sometimes dined with Jackie.

In her autobiography, *Men, Money, and Magic*, she wrote: "Jackie wanted to marry Onassis more than Onassis wanted to marry Jackie." Johnny Meyer, Ari's chief aide, later confirmed that that was true.

When Jackie did marry Ari, the Greek mogul boasted of his sexual prowess to Pierre Salinger, who had been JFK's press secretary,

"Five times a night," Ari claimed. "She surpasses any woman I've ever known. She really goes for my Greek pole."

Salinger later asserted, "Onassis could get very graphic in describing his physical relations with Jackie. Poor Jack must be turning over in his grave."

Much of the world tried to imagine in horrified detail what it was like for Jackie to sleep with Onassis. Ruth Francisco, in her fictional *The Secret Memoirs of Jacqueline Kennedy Onassis,* did it one better—she crafted a loose interpretation of how she imagined the wedding night:

"He sits back and shows me his fat clublike penis, wagging it at me, an old man with a young man's penis, a fat, blood sausage penis. A drop of semen sparkles at the tip. Grinning, he dips his finger in the semen and rubs it on my lips—it tastes of fish and burnt leather. My body itches with disgust. Something squirmy with razor talons scratches to get out of my groin. I want to be punished by this ugly old toad, who puffs and grinds against me, his belly flapping against my body. The black-winged thing ejaculates with my orgasm, grunting, lurching pumping like an old farm machine, then, herky-jerky, wheezing, squealing like a pig. He collapses on me, crushing me with his potato-sack weight."

***

Until his marriage to Jackie, Ari had never faced such publicity. "The worst thing that can happen to a man is to become a celebrity," he said. "It's as if there were a law that you have to walk naked in public—no matter how well built you are, they make you look ridiculous."

Like Marilyn Monroe, Jackie was always late for every appointment. Once, at her Fifth Avenue apartment, she staged a dinner party at 6PM that included Frank Sinatra, Peter Duchin, Leonard Bernstein, Bill and Babe Paley, and Mayor and Mrs. John Lindsay. Ari had to entertain them until Jackie made her appearance at 8:30PM. She made no excuses.

Only three months after their wedding, Ari developed an interest in a young Greek singer, known only as "Marinella." Reportedly, she was the same age as his daughter, Christina. He seemed to like women with large bosoms, a kind of sexual pleasure and body aesthetic he did not get from Jackie,

Consequently, Jackie was left alone on Skorpios, with only fifty servants to keep her company.

But she wasn't alone for long.

She began dating a handsome Greek architect, Alex Hadzimichailis. She was often seen coming and going from his apartment in Athens, or else they were spotted together on the beaches of Skorpios.

She was interested in Greek ruins. Ari, on the other hand, believed that if you'd seen one ruin, you'd seen them all.

Alex served as a kind of tour guide, among other things, as the two of them explored other Greek islands. They showed up for the "Spring of Fertility" ceremony on the island of Kefkada; at an ancient fort on Corfu; and at the Chapel of the Virgin on Rhodes, where an icon is believed by locals to have miraculous powers. At one seaside café, a reporter observed Jackie and Alex enjoying a freshly caught lobster lunch. Alex cracked the claws of the lobster with his strong white teeth. She was heard to exclaim, "What a man!"

Many reporters became aware of this new beau in her life. *France-Dimanche* claimed as fact that Jackie planned to divorce Ari and marry Alex.

Freda Kramer wrote about a day in the life

Seen leaving the Plaza Hotel in Manhattan, **Aristotle Onassis** relates to his stepson, **John F. Kennedy, Jr.**

Initially, he won the boy's heart by giving him hundred dollar bills and purchasing expensive gifts for him. Although Caroline remained sullen and reserved around her new stepfather, John Jr., accepted him as less a paternal figure and as more of a kindly grandfather or else a rich, generous uncle.

of Jackie O: "From a flash of cooling water or chilled martinis in a parched desert, to rubies big as pigeon eggs and diamonds dropping in hands as casually as clusters from a box of Crackerjacks, Jackie received the attentions and gifts due a fairytale Princess."

When Ari was off island, Jackie liked him to remember her by sending little gifts presented in a charming little basket on her breakfast tray. Her gifts of choice were either gold or diamonds. The exclusive Zolotas Jewelry Store in Athens said that in less than a year, they sent her three dozen gold bracelets.

When Apollo landed on the moon, it was also the occasion of Jackie's birthday. He gave her a pair of gold earrings shaped like the moon and set with dangling diamonds as big as ping-pong balls.

Jackie soon took over directing the staff aboard the yacht. She demanded that eight varieties of caviar be on hand at all times, and she wanted in any season the most exotic fruits from around the world flown in on Olympic Airlines.

Jackie in 1967, during her courtship with Onassis.

She was constantly airborne aboard Ari's Olympic Airlines and she received at least eight bomb threats a year. Fortunately, all of these turned out to be crank calls.

As time went by, the couple grew farther and farther apart. In one year alone, they went eight months without ever seeing each other. They also had different friends, moving in widely varied social circles. As Ari said in an interview, "Jackie is a little bird that needs its freedom, and her security, and she gets them both from me. Our agreement is to spend a total of four months a year together." One Christmas, Jackie spent in London with Lee Radziwill; Onassis celebrating in Paris with Maria Callas.

Throughout her marriage to Ari, Jackie suffered a series of nervous breakdowns, some more serious than others. Many of her friends wondered if she were cracking up.

An unidentified member of the yacht crew aboard the *Christina* reported to a newspaper in Athens that Jackie one night attempted suicide by taking an overdose of sleeping pills. She was discovered by a Greek seaman who called a doctor in time to save her life. For his heroic move, Ari gave the seaman a $10,000 reward.

Other rumors surfaced, including one that claimed that in Greece, Jackie dipped into the occult and was seeing some mysterious guru in Athens. It was reported that she was hearing the voice of John F. Kennedy late at night.

One tabloid at the time ran the headline—JACKIE MAKES CONTACT WITH KENNEDY'S SPIRIT.

Each day began with Jackie spending a lot of time looking in the mirror, searching for some new wrinkle.

As she grew older, there were the rumors of face-lifts. On one occasion, she was said to have arranged for a celebrated plastic surgeon to give her a facelife in her apartment in super secrecy, with nurses and operating room equipment brought in. She was also said to have flown to Rio de Janeiro to have cosmetic surgery performed by the famous Dr. Ivo Pitanguy. The brilliant Brazilian surgeon had previously performed face-lifts for such clients as the Duchess of Windsor.

***

During the first year of her marriage, Jackie spent $1.25 million on clothing, though she hardly wore many of the items she purchased. If she liked a blouse, she'd order it in all colors available. Most of her money was spent on Manhattan's Madison Avenue, causing *Women's Wear Daily* to label her as "the retailer's best friend."

"What does she do with all those clothes?" Ari asked. "All I ever see her in is a pair of blue jeans."

Jackie became a world class shopper, often spending $100,000 within ten minutes in a store. She never asked the price. "Charge it to Olympic Airlines," became her refrain.

Sometimes at Parisian fashion shows, featuring the latest designs of Molyneux, Lanvin, and Valentino, she'd buy the entire collection. Of course, she didn't have occasion to wear so many clothes, so she often sold them to resale fashion houses, pocketing the difference to add to her spending money.

Her secretary would deliver the expensive (unused) garments to Encore Consignment on Manhattan's Madison Avenue, Jackie's favorite resale house. She'd often arrive with a stock of garments from such designers as Halsted, Yves Saint Laurent, and Christian Dior. The only item the buyer at Encore ever turned down was Jackie's red maternity dress.

Like Imelda Marcos of the Philippines, Jackie had a shoe fetish—Gucci's for walking shoes, Veneziano's for loafers, and Rome's Casimir's for low-heeled pumps.

In each of her individual closets, scattered at various sites across the globe, she had a different pair of shoes to wear for every day of the year.

In addition to her Fifth Avenue apartment, she had closets to fill on Skorpios, in Athens, and on the Avenue Foch in Paris, as well as a luxurious suite at Claridge's, the most expensive hotel in London. There were other locations in Hyannis Port and New Jersey, as well as in Montevideo *[Uruguay],* where Ari maintained a full-time staff of forty servants at his villa there, even though he and Jackie rarely visited. Not only that, but Ari had purchased the former Barclay Estate in Newport, immediately adjacent to the Auchincloss family's Hammersmith Farm. She also kept a full wardrobe aboard Ari's yacht, the *Christina.*

She also maintained a deluxe apartment in Monte Carlo, where she tried to avoid her dreaded nemesis, Princess Grace.

As *Women's Wear Daily* asserted, "Jackie continues to fill her bottomless closets. She is making Daddy O's bills bigger than ever with her latest shopping spree. She is buying in car-load lots."

In October of 1971, **Jackie and Ari,** while vacationing in the Mediterranean, docked on the island of Capri. Jackie wanted to go shopping.

One day in March, she went into a Saint Laurent ready-to-wear boutique on Madison Avenue and "bought the place out."

London's *Sunday Times* claimed, "It is difficult to resist the conclusion that Jackie's passion for collecting—clothes, objects, ambiences, and people—was a substitute for some deeper emotional need. Most chroniclers of Jackie's life and times have either sedulously ignored her profligacy or else treated it as a tic of personality. It was, however, central to her character and her class."

Jackie seems to rush ahead, as if fleeing from **Ari** and **John Jr.** in front of Manhattan's Plaza Hotel.

***

Although the Greek tycoon had once compared Jackie to a diamond—"cool and sharp at the edges, fiery and hot beneath the surface," his opinion of her had long ago changed to "coldhearted and shallow."

One night in 1971, Jackie and Ari drank and dined at New York's El Morocco. She told him she had no room for him at her 1040 Fifth Avenue apartment. "The decorators have everything torn up," she falsely claimed. "You'll have to check into a hotel."

Ari actually maintained a permanent suite at New York's Pierre Hotel. He rightly suspected that Jackie was privately having intercourse with Teddy Kennedy. His plan involved entrapping the lovers by wiring her phone. That way he could sue her for divorce, charging adultery.

But Jackie's Secret Service agents kept too close a watch on her Fifth Avenue apart-

At the chic Manhattan nightclub, El Morocco, despite of her status as a seasoned forty-something, **Jackie** evokes a Vassar schoolgirl.

Ari evokes some aging "sugar daddy."

ment for him to have men successfully bug her phones.

In fewer than five months after marrying Jackie, Ari was calling Callas, wanting her to take him back, including letting him sleep in her bed again. He said he no longer had sex with Jackie.

His marriage, as he reported, had been a disaster. Jackie had spent nearly $8 million to redecorate the *Christina*. "She spends her $30,000 monthly allowance in ten days," Ari claimed. "She runs up astronomical bills. She charges every piece of designer clothing in Paris and New York. And she makes sure she is somewhere else whenever I fly into town."

Eventually, Ari was drawn back to the bed of the women he really loved. His affair with Maria began anew within her apartment at 36 Avenue Georges Mandel in Paris. As the weeks went by, she was seen with Ari at nightclubs and within high-profile restaurants such as Maxim's.

When Jackie saw a picture of Ari and Callas at Maxim's, she booked a flight to Paris. On her first night in their apartment on Avenue Foch, she demanded that he take her to Maxim's. Once there, within the restaurant's *Belle Époque* surroundings, she asked to be seated at the same table where he and Callas had recently dined. She even ordered the same menu that Ari and the opera diva had consumed.

The next morning, when Callas learned that Ari had accompanied Jackie to Maxim's, the diva flew into a titanic rage, accusing Ari of cheating on her with his own wife.

That afternoon, with its red dome light flashing, Callas, in an ambulance, was rushed to the American Hospital in Neuilly-sur-Seine, just outside Paris.

A bulletin was released by the hospital that evening: The news first came over RTL Radio. "Maria Callas has been admitted to the hospital following a suicide attempt. She is known to have swallowed a quantity of barbiturates, but her condition is not thought to be serious."

The press gathered outside the hospital noted that Ari did not rush to the side of his mistress. After having her stomach pumped, Callas was released within ten hours.

Even though Maria had agreed to become "the other woman," her renewed relationship with Ari was just as turbulent as before. There were good weeks and then violent explosions between these two lovers.

Involved with two of the most famous [and temperamental] women on the planet, Ari began to wind down, losing his stamina. As the months went by, he was frequently dizzy and he tired easily.

In New York, Ari began to meet frequently with the notorious lawyer, Roy Cohn. [Anecdotes abounded about the ferocity of Cohn as a litigating antagonist. It was said that whenever a husband learned that Cohn was representing his wife in their divorce case, he became instantly fearful for his assets.]

After only a few months of marriage, Onassis told Cohn that he had come to believe that Jackie "is playing me for a sucker. Her spending is out of control. She's never where I want her to be. The marriage has gotten down to a monthly presentation of outrageous bills...She is a beautiful woman, but 'millions beautiful' she isn't."

He instructed Cohn to entrap Jackie. "We've got to fix it so she doesn't take me to court demanding a queen's ransom."

"I'm your man, sweetheart," Cohn responded.

When asked about divorce, during one of the few times she actually answered a question from the press, Jackie said, "I will stick to Mr. Onassis until the bitter end."

After he met with Cohn, Ari flew to Paris, where he spent three days with Maria. He told her that he'd hired a private detective to trail Jackie. He was aware that she'd indulged in a number of affairs since marrying him. "She's been far more discreet than I have," he told the diva. "I'll be commencing divorce proceedings."

But by early 1975, all divorce proceedings came to an abrupt halt. Ari had far more pressing problems, as his empire was beginning to crumble. He failed in his attempt to dump his oil tankers as a means of consolidating his holdings. He also had to put his beloved Skorpios on the market.

Faced with dwindling revenues, he was also forced to sell Olympic Airlines. At one point, he grounded all of the carrier's planes and froze the salaries of his employees. The Greek government put into place its own management team and announced that henceforth, it would be running the airline itself.

***

A sick and dying Onassis arrived at Orly Airport in Paris for his final visit. En route to France, his mind had been consumed, after years of "incompatibility," with his divorce from Jackie and with the painful loss of Olympic Airlines to the Greek government.

In a final display of his macho persona, he insisted on walking off the airplane unaided. After clearing Customs, he hobbled weakly to a waiting limousine, which hauled him to his apartment at 88 Avenue Foch.

Once there and in bed, he called Maria at her apartment, telling her that "The Widow," as he called Jackie, was in Paris. He promised Callas that he'd arrange to slip her into the American Hospital where he planned to check in the following morning. He admitted that both Christina and Jackie were opposed to her visiting him in the hospital.

Before going to sleep that night, he told his aide, Johnny Meyer, "You know, I'll soon be joining Alexander."

In the hospital, Ari had his gall bladder removed. Every forty-eight hours, doctors replaced his blood. He faded in and out of consciousness.

His daughter checked out of the Avenue Foch apartment and into the Plaza Athenée Hotel so as not to have to share lodgings with Jackie, whom she loathed even more than she had on the day she had married her father.

Miraculously his condition improved, and Jackie returned to New York.

But back in Paris, Ari took a turn for the worse and entered a rapid decline. The Onassis staff could not reach Jackie. Maria was called secretly by a member of the Onassis staff, who told her she could come to the hospital for a final goodbye.

Wearing a blonde wig, Maria arrived at the back entrance of the hospital and was directed to the service elevator, which still contained a cart of smelly waste products. She crossed her heart before entering Ari's darkened bedroom. He was under an oxygen tent and appeared unconscious, barely alive.

At one point he opened an eye and seemed to recognize her. "It's Maria, your canary," she called out to him. "I will love you forever." Those were her farewell words to her longtime lover.

After that, she flew at once to Palm Beach to hide out and avoid "the attack of the paparazzi."

Christina was in the hospital room with her father one hour before he died. Although he was unconscious at the time, she bent over his body and, in a soft voice, whispered to him, "God is punishing you for your sins."

On March 15, 1975, Ari, under a morphine-induced sleep, with tubes attached to every part of his body, departed from the world. It had rained all day and night in Paris.

Jackie was in bed in New York and asleep when a call came in for her, telling her that her husband was dead. On hearing the news, she called the airlines and began packing at once to go to the funeral.

For her arrival in Paris the day after Ari died, Jackie was greeted with a sea of reporters and *paparazzi.*

In a black Valentino dress and a black leather coat, she read a statement:

"Aristotle Onassis rescued me at a moment when my life was engulfed in shadows. He meant a lot to me. He brought me into a world where one could find both happiness and love. We lived through many beautiful experiences together which cannot be forgotten, and for which I will be eternally grateful."

When Christina heard that, she told her aunts, "It's all bullshit! Jackie is at the funeral with her lover boy, Teddy, trying to bleed every cent from the estate. I've got to pay the whore off."

***

Maria was still awake in her rented Palm Beach villa. She'd been unable to sleep that night. A bulletin came over the radio that Aristotle Onassis had died in Paris. On hearing that news, she went into seclusion, although reporters and the paparazzi began to converge around her villa, hoping for a statement.

Maria opted not to attend Ari's funeral, figuring that her appearance would make the solemn ceremony "a battle to the death for *paparazzi* hoping to catch Mrs. Kennedy and me in a catfight, or Christina pulling the hair of Mrs. Kennedy."

"Let Christina and Jackie fight it out over Aristo's estate," Maria said. When the Onassis will was read, his attorney called her in Paris. "I am so sorry," he said, "Mr. Onassis left you nothing. If you wish, I can return the letters you wrote him."

After the death of Ari, and after the loss of her once golden voice, Maria told friends in Paris, "I have now entered the Norma Desmond period of my life." She was referring, of course, to the tragic heroine of the movie, *Sunset Blvd.*, which had starred Gloria Swanson, a former mistress of Joseph Kennedy.

Maria Callas died of a broken heart on September 16, 1977. She'd told a friend, "Life is no longer worth living after Aristo is gone."

Thousands of letters from fans around the world poured in. One ardent admirer in Milan wrote: "Maria Callas will live forever." An opera fan in New York sent a card, "Maria Callas, *prima donna assoluta* forever."

Author Nicholas Cage wrote the most romantic epitaph to Maria and Ari:

"In the end, happiness evaded Onassis and Callas. But it is not impossible to imagine that after Maria's remains were consigned to the sea, the tides of the Aegean carried those ashes in a southerly direction, around Cape Sounion, below the cliff crowned by the temple to Poseidon, through the Corinth Canal, where the yacht *Christina* passed so often to the Gulf of Corinth and into the Ionian Sea. In a world where the winds and tides brought Odysseus home to Ithaca after ten years of wandering, it's not hard to envision the last relics of Maria Callas finally coming to rest on the green shores of Skorpios, still flowering with the oleander and jasmine that she and Aristo brought there from the Caribbean."

***

On the occasion of Onassis' funeral. On March 15, 1975, Jackie called upon Teddy Kennedy once again to fly to Skorpios to negotiate her share of the estate, this time with Ari's daughter, Christina.

Having flown in from Paris, Teddy showed a lack of sensitivity from the moment he sat in the limousine with Jackie and Christina en route to the church service.

After the limousine pulled away from the curbside, Teddy immediately turned to Christina, telling her, "Now it's time to take care of Jackie."

Christina burst into tears and escaped from the limousine, joining her bereaved aunts in the limousine behind. She later spoke of that moment to friends and business associates. Some of her comments reached the press and were published in biographies.

She said, "I was in a limousine with a pair of hungry vultures waiting to feed off the corpse of my dead father. Ted Kennedy was absolutely ruthless trying to protect his mistress. But it was her smile that drove me from the vehicle. Have you ever seen a carnivorous hyena come to feed as a scavenger? That was Jackie Kennedy. I never called her Jackie Onassis, because she was not a real wife to my father."

Almost deranged out of her mind, Christina had arrived on Skorpios to bury her father. She didn't want "The Professional Widow," as she called Jackie, to attend. "The golddigger has arrived for more gold," Christina told her aunts.

Christina, along with her father's sisters, Artemis and Mirope, bitterly resented Jackie's presence at the funeral. "She looks like she's going to a movie premiere, not a funeral," Artemis later said. The village priest, Apostolos Zavitsianos, said, "I was shocked by the widow's ear-to-ear grin as I was delivering the service. In all my years, I'd never seen that smile on the face of a widow."

On the way to the burial, Jackie tried to take her place behind the funeral cortege. Ari was to be buried next to the grave of his son, Alexander. But Christina and the sisters elbowed Jackie out of the way, forcing her to the rear of the procession.

A reporter from the Athens *Acropolis* crafted the blaring headline, "ONLY CHRISTINA CRIED—JACKIE WAS COLD."

Throughout Greece, people denounced Jackie's behavior at the funeral, angrily criticizing her light-hearted attitude.

It made matters worse when the front pages the next day ran a picture of Jackie, laughing as she had her hair styled at one of the most exclusive hairdressers in Paris.

***

Onassis left an estate of $1 billion, the major share going to Christina. After his funeral, Jackie and Christina engaged in an 18-month legal battle over Jackie's share.

Jackie's attorneys threatened to have a court invalidate Ari's will. Greek law required that a precondition of a will's validity demanded that it had to be composed "in a single sitting in a single location." Ari's final will had been composed during a flight with Jackie from Acapulco to New York. During its composition, in a fit of anger, Ari had interrupted the process for lunch in a Florida coffee shop while his plane was being refueled.

Technically, therefore, the will had not been prepared in one sitting, but at various times in various countries. Jackie's main attorney, Simon Rifkind, argued that if the will were invalidated, Jackie, as Ari's wife and according to the estate laws of Greece, would receive 12.5 percent of Ari's estimated billion-dollar estate. In U.S. dollars, that would total $125 million.

Christina Onassis *(depicted above)* was considered an ugly duckling by her slim and stylish mother, who warned her that she would never attract a husband.

Abandoning a protracted battle in the courts, Jackie agreed to accept Christina's offer of a flat sum of $20 million. Jackie would agree to abandon all future claims to the estate, including her share of the yacht *Christina*, and her one-quarter share of the island of Skorpios. Rufkind successfully negotiated for another $6 million, which would cover estate taxes. Jackie insisted that all of her personal letters to Ari be returned. Both she and Christina agreed not to publicly discuss the terms of the final set-

"How wrong she was," said Christina. "When you're one of the richest women on the planet, the line forms on the right."

tlement.

It is estimated that during the time Jackie was married to Ari, her allowances, jewelry, clothes, and living expenses, including travel, came to some $42 million. That averaged about $7 million annually for every year they were married.

Jackie later regretted the amount of the settlement, telling Teddy and others, "I came away with peanuts. Ari's will was not properly drawn up and, according to Greek law, as his widow I should have received $125 million of his billion dollar estate."

It's hard to imagine that the toady looking **Aristotle Onassis** and **Jackie**, who's having a bad hair day, were two of the world's most written about people.

Here, they look like a nondescript, middle-aged couple on their way to the supermarket.

Chapter Twenty-Nine

Jackie's Nude Photos
"The Billion Dollar Bush"

Playboy and Penthouse Reject the Jackie Nudes, But Hustler and Screw Each Score Publishing Bonanzas

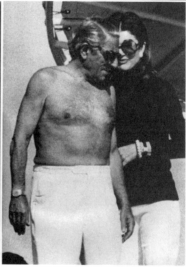

Thanks to Larry Flynt's **Hustler magazine**, nude pictures of Jackie, taken illegally on the Greek island of Skorpios, became the most celebrated nude photographs of all time, rivaled only by those of Marilyn Monroe. MM and Jackie had something in common. They were both familiar with what John F. Kennedy called "my implement."

Admittedly, Jackie's rail-thin body didn't stack up favorably when compared to the voluptuousness of the blonde film goddess. But that didn't prevent the magazine from selling out of multiple printings.

Even though aging, **Aristotle Onassis** was never ashamed to show off his body, even indulging in exhibitionism on occasion. Here, he is depicted aboard his luxury yacht, the *Christina*, sailing the Mediterranean with Jackie.

On his private island of Skorpios, he came up with a diabolical scheme to "take Jackie down a peg or two." He told his chief aide, Johnny Meyer, "She's always running up massive bills suing photographers. I want to set her up with something she can really sue about."

After her marriage to Aristotle Onassis in 1968, Jackie went to live for a few months every year on Skorpios, his private Greek island. She told Rose Kennedy and others that it was a safe haven not only for herself, but for John Jr. and Caroline. But she was soon to discover that even on this remote hideaway, she could not escape the *paparazzi*, a coven of voracious photographers who plagued her in whatever city she visited, especially New York.

Long after the assassination of JFK, **Jackie** *(left)* is seen with her former mother-in-law, **Rose Kennedy**. The Kennedy matriarch was very upset when nude pictures of Jackie surfaced.

She never thought of herself as a nudist. But she did go in for nude swimming in the sea, or else lay nude, from time to time, on a beach. She was also fond of receiving nude massages in the garden.

On several occasions, photographers, using long-range telescopic lenses, managed to snap embarrassing pictures of the former First Lady. Kiki Feroudi Moutsatsos, Ari's personal secretary, later admitted in her book, *The Onassis Women* that she often arranged for the payment of large sums of money to purchase these candid shots, along with their negatives, which she then destroyed.

The aging duenna was no stranger to nudity herself. Once, when author Truman Capote was staying as a guest of a neighbor in a house adjacent to the Kennedy compound in Palm Beach, Rose asked to use the pool, because her own was under repair.

According to Capote, "Here I was with four gay men, enjoying a libation or two, and we look up and there is Rose Kennedy, jaybird naked, walking across the lawn toward the pool."

Kiki warned Jackie about this invasion of her privacy and told her to cover up whenever she left the villa. "Mrs. Onassis just shrugged at the suggestion," Kiki recalled. "She told me 'I have my life to live. If I think about photographers all the time, I will not be able to get out of bed in the morning."

In New York, paparazzo Ron Galella had been Jackie's stalker. To her horror, she discovered she had an equivalent stalker stationed in Greece. Even on Skorpios, Nikos Koulouris was a threat to her privacy. If anything, he was even more aggressive in pursuing embarrassing shots of her than Galella himself.

Koulouris had used stealth techniques to capture Jackie off guard. From his boat anchored offshore, he would swim to the shoreline of Skorpios at night and hide in a clump of bushes until Jackie, in the late morning, came down to the beach. He'd then jump out from behind the bushes and photograph her before fleeing back to his own boat.

Sometimes, he'd rent a speedboat and steer it directly to the shoreline where he'd photograph her with telephoto lenses before speeding away into the day.

He would often yell insults at her, calling her a slut or an international whore, hoping to get a violent (and subsequently photographed) reaction. "I was always searching for what the Americans call 'the money shot,'" he once told a reporter in Athens.

Once, when Jackie was returning with her son to Skorpios aboard a boat from Athens, her own craft was in the process of landing on Skorpios when a boat piloted by a friend of Koulouris almost crashed into the vessel owned by Onassis. The paparazzi had thrown stones at John Jr., who had picked up the stones and tossed them back at the smaller craft carrying Koulouris. Jackie later urged Onassis "to do something about this menace. He's making my life miserable and well as the lives of my children."

One sunny afternoon, Jackie, Ari, and Kiki were having a meal together on the terrace of a restaurant overlooking the port at Nydri, on Levkas, the island adjacent to Skorpios. Suddenly, in the middle of their lunch, Koulouris leaped down from a tree and began to snap pictures of the guests at the table, with a special focus on Jackie.

Ari went into a rage, tossing a chair at the *paparazzo*. "Stupid man! Leave us alone! You're crazy! Get the hell out of here!"

When Koulouris refused to obey the command and continued the assault with his camera, Ari impulsively lifted Jackie's skirt. "Is that what you want to photograph?" he shouted. "Well, shoot away, then get the fuck out of here."

Kiki later claimed that Jackie looked embarrassed and humiliated at what Ari had done to her.

The next day, Koulouris came to Kiki's office in Athens, showing her the candid shot he'd taken of Jackie, which revealed her panties. He demanded—and received—$3,000 for the photograph and its negative.

"I also paid a lot of money to buy back pictures of Mrs. Onassis swimming in the nude with her sister, Lee Radziwill," Kiki said. "Koulouris also took nudes of Mr. Onassis."

[Onassis was really an exhibitionist himself, and often emerged from his quarters in the nude, walking toward the sea.

At the Crazy Horse Saloon, a strip club in Paris, a reporter once asked him the secret of his success with women. He invited the reporter to the men's room, where he dropped his trousers and pulled down his underwear. He then hoisted baseball-sized testicles and an ample uncut penis that measured a very thick five inches flaccid. "As you can plainly see, I've got balls."

On yet another occasion, Onassis directed the crew of his yacht, Christina, to the Italian island of Sardinia, where all the chic people gathered in August. He noticed paparazzi taking photographs of his passengers. He ordered his captain to have two of his men row him ashore to a nearby beach. Once on the beach, he dropped his bathing trunks and shouted to the photographer."Now it's my turn!"

The paparazzi *snapped away, capturing the shipping tycoon's "full monty." The French language tabloid,* France-Dimanche, *ran the pictures of the aging tycoon's crotch.]*

Koulouris also tried to take pictures of celebrities who came to visit Mr. and Mrs. Onassis. He wanted to get candid shots of them—Frank Sinatra, Liza Minnelli, the Forbes family, the Rothschilds, even Prince Rainier and Princess Grace. Rose Kennedy also visited, as did Ted Kennedy.

Richard Burton showed up on Skorpios one weekend, leaving Elizabeth in Athens. Apparently, Jackie did not want to receive her.

Kiki revealed that Ari did not want to entertain Rudolf Nureyev on the island. In lieu of that, he pre-arranged his (complimentary) fare on Olympic Airlines and had booked him into an elegant hotel suite in Athens, where Jackie traveled for a reunion with the dancer.

Rudi, however, did show up for a weekend on Skorpios when Ari had flown away from the island to Paris. Rudi was even more uninhibited about nudity than Jackie was. Proud of his sexual equipment, he'd even posed for nude photographs in New York.

On Skorpios, he and Jackie went swimming in the nude and were secretly photographed. *Paparazzi* blackmailers later demanded $50,000 for these photographs and their negatives, for which Jackie paid $50,000 out of her pocket, not wanting Ari to see them.

She'd actually gone swimming, nude, with Burton, but no pictures ever surfaced of the two of them. Kiki must have known that nude pictures of Burton and Jackie would have been tabloid fodder around the world.

At one point, Koulouris arrived in Kiki's office bearing sexually explicit photographs of Alexander, Aristotle Onassis' son, and Fiona [née Campbell Walter] Thyssen, a woman sixteen years his senior, and with whom Alexander was involved in an affair. At age forty, this New Zealand-born fashion model had previously been married to one of the richest men in Europe Baron Hans Heinrich Thyssen Bornemisza. [In 1986, when his massive art collection grew too large for the villa in Switzerland that housed it, he agreed to display it in Spain in an annex of the Prado. Before that location was chosen, he'd been "wooed" by Margaret Thatcher, Prince Charles, the Getty Museum in L.A., and investors associated with Disney World in Orlando. Rumor had it at the time that his fifth and final wife, Carmen ("Tita") Cervera, a former Miss Spain, was the deciding factor in his final choice.]

The photographs of Alexander with Fiona, for which the paparazzo demanded $10,000, had been snapped when the romantic couple visited Porto-Heli, an island near Piraeus.

When Jackie was shown these photographs, she found the pictures beautiful, even though she detested Fiona. She was particularly impressed with the nudes of Alexander. "Like father, like son," she said. "Lucky Fiona."

In January of 1972, when Ari and Jackie could take it no more, they sued Koulouris in an Athens court. He was convicted on four counts of invasion of privacy and sentenced to six months in prison.

***

Jackie's luck eventually ran out. To her amazement, she learned that ten *paparazzi* dressed in diving outfits, using underwater cameras and telephoto lenses, invaded the waters around Skorpios. They were able to shoot full-frontal nude pictures of Jackie, as well as views of her still-shapely *derrière*. She was forty-one at the time, but still in good shape.

These pictures were not offered by blackmailers to Kiki. Someone had already paid these photographers to execute this stunt, and Jackie didn't know who it was. She suspected that a shipping tycoon in Athens, one of her husband's rivals, had financed the operation.

To her dismay, she received a call from Rome a few days later. The magazine *Playmen* was preparing a nine-page feature article revealing

619

her nudity for all the world to see. She called lawyers in Rome, but it was too late. The magazine was already on newsstands and was being avidly purchased and collected by voyeurs, both male and female.

Even though privately outraged, she put up a brave front in public, telling the press, "This invasion of my privacy really doesn't touch my life. All I'm concerned with is my devotion to my children and to my husband. I'm not a nudist," she asserted. "I sometimes take off my pants to put on a bathing suit. That's how I was caught."

In New York, she got tired of friends such as John Kenneth Galbraith teasing her, "I didn't recognize you with your clothes on."

The only comfort Jackie had was in the knowledge that her nude pictures had been published in Italy, but not in America. But that situation was about to change.

Al Goldstein of Screw Magazine Fantasizes About "Muff-Diving with Jackie Onassis"

Like her paparazzo nemesis, Ron Galella, Jackie came to loathe two publishers—Larry Flynt of *Hustler* magazine and Al Goldstein of *Screw.*

For a woman who cherished her dignity, Goldstein and Flynt violated her ultimate privacy by running full frontal nudes of Jackie.

"If it had been a different world, I could have gotten through life without even knowing who those two sleazeballs were," she told Onassis and others. "But it's a far from perfect world ever since the camera was invented."

In 1968, the cigar-chomping, bearded, Brooklyn-born Al Goldstein launched *Screw* magazine, which was circulated mainly in New York City on Manhattan's Lower East Side and in Greenwich Village. The magazine's first issue featured a pretty brunette in the briefest of bikinis fondling a giant kosher salami.

Goldstein's initial investment of $175 made him a multi-millionaire. At its peak, he sold 140,000 copies of *Screw* every week, until he published the nude pictures of Jackie. Then, his presses ran around the clock, printing 550,000 copies, maybe a lot more.

He paid only $10,000 to *Playmen,* the Italian magazine that had initially published the nudes of Jackie.

From the days of the first issue of *Screw,* the scabrous publisher was an aggressive advocate of hard-core porn. He stated his premise at the beginning. "We will never ink out a pubic hair or chalk out an organ."

Journalist Andy Newman wrote: "Goldstein's most notorious creation was Al Goldstein himself, a cartoonishly vituperative amalgam of borscht belt comic, free-range social critic, and sex-obsessed loser who seemed to embody a moment in New York city's cultural history: The sleaze and decay of Times Square in the 1960s and 70s."

Al Goldstein *(above, right)* and his *Screw* blazed paths across the sexual freedom of the 1960s. Through it all, he survived constant arrests, four ex-wives who graphically described his seven inches, Mafia hit contracts, thousands of death threats, and what could have been a crippling lawsuit from a former First Lady for having published photographs of her wearing only her birthday suit.

The 1973 issue No. 206, of *Screw* screamed in Second Coming headlines—JACKIE O NAKED! Inside was the nude spread of Jackie under the head—JACKIE KENNEDY'S BILLION DOLLAR BUSH. Later, Goldstein issued a nude calendar of Jackie. "Why should a celebrity like Marilyn Monroe monopolize the nude calendar business?" Goldstein asked. "Of course, MM had bigger tits."

In spite of attacks, the *Screw* edition found its devotees, reportedly numbering actor Jack Nicholson among them. In an interview, he admitted that, "I jerked off to *Screw.* However, around that same time, he was not enthralled when Goldstein advocated attendance at the showing of Linda Lovelace's censorship-busting porn film, *Deep Throat.* Jackie was known to have slipped in for a screening of this hardcorn porn that social commentators have

Jackie may not have deliberately contributed to the sexual revolution of the early 70s, but she did discreetly sneak in—like many other prominent personalities of that era—for a screening of the landmark film, *Deep Throat*, the highest grossing adult entertainment film of all time.

It transformed its star, "the sword-swallower," **Linda Lovelace** *(shown above with her co-star,* **Harry Reems***),* into an overnight celebrity.

defined as a film that profoundly changed the sexual morality of the nation.

[After sitting through Deep Throat, Nicholson said, "After you've had your orgasm, your next impulse is not to bend down and look over and watch someone's scrotum pounding against someone's shaved beaver."]

In March of 1962, during the golden years of the Kennedy Presidency, Goldstein had accompanied Jackie and her sister, Lee Radziwill, on a goodwill visit to India and Pakistan as a member of the press corps.

He later claimed, "No woman seemed so revered, protected, innocent, saintly, pure. I was sweaty and hot, but she remained immaculate. She never had diarrhea, she only drank water flown in from the United States. I wanted to patriotically quaff her bush at the Khyber Pass, but these feelings remained deep down and far removed from my professional demeanor."

Perverts from Jackie's Past
(Thank God for the Secret Service)

Al Goldstein, publisher of *Screw*, was part of the press corps assigned to follow **Jackie** *(left)* and her sister, **Lee Radziwill** *(right)* on their state visit to India and Pakistan during her stint as First Lady.

In his autobiography, *I, Goldstein,* he confessed, graphically and erotically, to wanting to inhale the air emanating from her rear.

To alleviate his sexual frustration, and the libidos of the visiting journalists, the Pakistani government supplied hookers to whichever member of the press corps wanted one.

Goldstein later complained, "My favorite thing is eating pussy, and these Islamic bitches didn't go in for that form of sexual expression at all, even when they were hookers."

He later referred to the publication of the Jackie nudes as "the high point of my publishing career."

Goldstein's sexual obsession with Jackie didn't end with the publication of her nudes. For decades to come, he admitted that he continued his fantasies about her. When she entered the field of publishing herself, he asserted, "I wish she'd come to work for *Screw* in our editorial offices. I would have her attend our meetings and take dictation. When she farted, I'd levitate in rapturous ecstasy, the aroma wafting into my nostrils."

In Hustler, Jackie Appears in All Her Glory

The Jackie nudes that Al Goldstein published in *Screw* were a bit fuzzy. From a publisher in Italy, Hugh Hefner at *Playboy* was offered higher-resolution, more technically adroit photos of Jackie snapped on the island of Skorpios. Hefner seemed like an ideal candidate to publish these illicit photographs. He had launched *Playboy* in November of 1953. The first issue of his magazine featured nudes of the blonde goddess Marilyn Monroe, the hottest star in Hollywood at the time.

To everyone's surprise, Hefner rejected the proposal of publishing nudes of Jackie in all her glory.

He may have rejected them because he'd been an early supporter of JFK back when he was a Senator from Massachusetts. As Hefner's biographer, Steven Watts, put it, "The *Playboy* publisher in the 1950s was attracted to the young Senator's sympathy for civil rights, a special cause for Hefner. He saw

Hugh Hefner of *Playboy* launched his skin magazine in 1953 with a nude centerfold of Marilyn Monroe, who at the time was just emerging into her stardom. Years later, he rejected the idea of distributing nude pictures of the former First Lady.

Hefner had backed JFK for president and had interpreted him as a new type of male politician—bold, irreverent, hip, and successful. Based on respect for the slain president's memory—and perhaps to some degree because of fear of reprisals—he said no to the Italian paparazzi hawking the Jackie nudes.

Like Hugh Hefner of Playboy, the cinematically ambitious **Bob Guccione** of *Penthouse* also rejected the Jackie nudes for publication in his controversial magazine.

He had no such discretion, however, when he adapted Gore Vidal's script for *Caligula* into the first major motion picture to feature prominent international stars such as Peter O'Toole, John Gielgud, and Helen Mirren, in a pornographic movie studded with ultra-debauched, XXX-rated scenes.

him as a progressive figure, eager to overturn the stodgy traditionalism of the Eisenhower era. He perceived JFK as a 'Mr. Smith Goes to Washington' politician. Kennedy's vigorous masculine aura also appealed to Hefner. He found the young Senator as being a handsome swinger. He had personal charm and sex appeal that was appealing. Hefner said the joke at the time was that Kennedy, as president, would do for sex for Eisenhower had done for golf."

"JFK was one of us," Hefner proclaimed.

After Hefner rejected publishing the Jackie nudes within *Playboy*, they were offered to Bob Guccione at *Penthouse*. Guccione was known for pushing skin magazines to new frontiers. The Brooklyn-born native, the priest of porn, never revealed why he refused to publish the Jackie photos, because he must have realized their sales potential.

Over the years, he'd run many unauthorized pictures of celebrities, including Madonna and Vanessa Williams, causing the latter to lose her Miss America Crown in 1984.

Among men's magazines, *Penthouse* (under Guccione's direction) was the first to show female public hair, then full frontal nudity, and then the exposed vulva and anus.

Years later, when Guccione hired Gore Vidal to work on a script for the notorious film, *Caligula,* starring John Gielgud, Peter O'Toole, and Malcolm McDowell. Vidal asked him why he had opted not to buy and distribute the Jackie nudes.

"I respected the First Lady too much to turn her into another *Penthouse* pet," he told Vidal. "I was never that heartless."

Flynt, the publisher of *Hustler,* was far more daring (or ruthless) than either Guccione or Hefner. He viewed himself as a "pornographer, pundit, and social outcast." His magazine was attacked as "tasteless, crude, scatological, and gynecologically explicit," and Flynt himself was called "a 20th Century, blue collar Rabelais who mocked religious hypocrisy with an acid tongue and a biting wit."

He seemed the perfect choice of a pub-

Born in the hills of Kentucky, in the poorest county in America, **Larry Flynt** became a teenage runaway, a bootlegger, a scam artist, the owner of string of go-go clubs, an evangelical Christian, and an atheist.

Eventually, thanks to the founding of *Hustler*, he became a millionaire pornographer and publisher, plus a prodigious sexual athlete until shot down, in his prime, by an assailant's bullet. It left him paralyzed from his waist down.

His greatest commercial triumph involved publishing nude pictures of Jackie.

lisher to reveal Jackie's nude anatomy to consumers throughout America. "I snapped up the pictures in a second," he claimed.

By the winter of 1975, *Hustler* magazine was selling out, grossing half a million dollars per issue. But his biggest, most profitable, and most notorious edition was on the way.

When Flynt learned that both Hefner and Guccione had turned down the Jackie nudes, he was able to negotiate the price down to $18,000. He selected five of the best photos taken in 1971.

After *Hustler* hit the streets, it had to keep reprinting 24 hours a day. Before the presses came to a halt, a million copies had been sold.

Men were not the sole customers. Actually, 60 percent of the sales were made to women, often grandmotherly types, who wanted "to get a look at Jackie."

Politicians, including Ohio governor James Rhodes, were seen purchasing the "Jackie edition" of *Hustler.* Rhodes, at least, could claim a scholarly interest, as he'd written books on First Ladies Mary Todd Lincoln and Rachel Jackson.

"Jackie's nude pictures made me a millionaire," Flynt later claimed. "Poor Jackie didn't even get the standard model's fee for showing her bush and tits to the world."

Tabloids and magazines around the world, from Toronto to Tokyo, from Rio de Janeiro to Moscow, ran the photos. It's estimated that a nude Jackie was featured in at least 201 publications.

***

Jackie was sorely tempted to launch a vast flotilla of lawsuits around the world, suing every newspaper and magazine which ran nudes of her, beginning with *Playmen* in Italy and moving on, for starters, to Flynt and Goldstein.

It was Onassis who talked her out of it. "You don't want to get into a pissing contest with a lot of skunks. You'll disgrace yourself all the more, and this scandal will rage on for a decade."

It was with a certain glee that Jackie heard, in reference to the embarassment he had caused her, that Goldstein eventually admitted, "Much of public sentiment turned against me. I was considered more contemptible than bed lice."

When Rose Kennedy saw the pictures, she was enraged. She immediately called Jackie, blaming her for her indiscretion for appearing nude in the garden of her island home. "What an example to set for your children," Rose charged. "You said you married Ari because he had a powerful security team to protect you. What kind of security was that?" Then she slammed down the phone.

Janet Auchincloss was equally enraged. "It's dreadful to think that photographer slime has to go underwater to spy on you. And Ari was supposed to provide protection and privacy for you!"

What these mothers didn't know was that it was Onassis himself who had set up the event, "Hoping to take Jackie down a peg or two."

At some point, Onassis confessed to his notorious gay lawyer, Roy Cohn, that he was the culprit who had discreetly hired the *paparazzi* to take the nude pictures of Jackie. "I got tired of hearing her complain all the time about Ron Galella. I felt that once those pictures were published, her complaints about Galella and others would look like minor shit."

"I organized the whole thing with these frogmen paparazzi," Onassis confessed. "The way I looked at it, if Jackie had nude photographs of herself circulating throughout the world, she could never complain again about any picture being taken of her with her clothes on. Of course, she wanted me to file various lawsuits, but I refused to give her the money. She denounced me as a cheap bastard."

The Price of Fame: Fit, athletic, and a hardy swimmer, **Jackie** kept her figure with frequent exercise that included swimming whenever possible. This is a scene equivalent to what many tourists and paparazzi might have seen from passing boats. What the world's most famous woman never expected was that telescopic photos would be taken when she wasn't dressed.

Alexander and Christina

Onassis' Children Vs. "Our Evil, Gold-Digging Stepmother"

Greek Drama-Rape, Early Deaths, and a Hired Assassin Ari's Doomed Children

Aristotle Onassis and his offspring, **Christina and Alexander**, had a few happy moments together when they posed for this picture. Although he would later be horrified at his daughter's choice of men, Ari called his daughter *"Chryso mou,"* meaning "my golden one." But to him, his real golden boy was his son, Alexander, whom he wanted to take over his empire.

Both his son and daughter blamed Maria Callas for breaking up Ari's marriage to their mother, Tina.

With Jackie Kennedy, Ari's new bride, only a few feet away, **Alexander** and **Christina** discuss their father's marriage to the widow of the slain American president. Her reputation as the most famous woman in the world did not impress either of them. Sarcastically, Alexander said, "Father has made the perfect match. He loves big names, and Jackie has one of the most recognizable names on the planet. She loves money, and Ari has hordes of it. They should be very happy."

Christina's point of view was consistent and expressed to anyone who'd listen: "She's a gold-digging witch who will drive him to an early grave."

627

"Alone at 24, Christina became the sole heir to the Onassis fortune and one of the richest young women in the world. She had a reported tax-free income of $1 million a week, but she was beset with problems. She suffered from a chronic weight problem and violent mood swings, and was unwise in her choice of men. All four of her marriages failed. Death came early for the Queen of Skorpios."*

—William Wright

As Bobby Kennedy pursued the presidency, and after having broken off his romantic entanglements from Jackie, he became increasingly worried that her dating Onassis would seriously harm his candidacy. He and Ethel contemptuously referred to Ari as "the Greek."

In calls to Jackie, Bobby pleaded with her not to marry Onassis. "It will cost me five states," he reportedly told her.

After RFK announced his run for the White House, Ari spoke rather candidly to reporters in Paris. "Mrs. Kennedy is being held up as a model of propriety, constancy, and of so many other of those boring American female virtues. She's now utterly devoid of mystery. She needs a small scandal to bring her alive. A peccadillo, an indiscretion. Something should happen to her to win our fresh compassion. The world lives to pity fallen grandeur."

Ari had hired Johnny Meyer as his chief aide. He'd come to Ari's attention when he'd had a similar position with America's most famed bisexual billionaire, the aviator and film producer, Howard Hughes. Before introducing Jackie to Meyer, Ari told her, "Regardless of how black the deed, Johnny is the man to turn to in your hour of need."

What he failed to tell her was that he had already assigned Meyer the job of spying on her before the marriage took place.

Ari discussed at length a major problem with Jackie. How would his son, Alexander, and his daughter, Christina, get along with Jackie's two young children, Caroline and John, Jr.?

Both of them were soon to find out.

***

Christina and **Aristotle Onassis** were photographed arriving in Paris. Both of them knew he was dying, having trouble with his eyes as a result of *myasthenia gravis*.

Later, in their residence on the Avenue Foch, when she realized that his eyelids were too weak to stay open, she cut strips of adhesive tape to prevent them from closing.

"Gold can't buy happiness for the Queen of Skorpios."

—Christina Onassis

James Auchincloss, the son of Jackie's mother, Janet Auchincloss, remembered the day Aristotle Onassis brought Christina to Newport to visit Jackie at Hammersmith Farm.

"Ari was charming, and Christina was the opposite," Jamie recalled. "She was Daddy's spoiled brat, and she detested everything American. It was obvious that she held Jackie in contempt. I was her tour guide around Newport, and it was a disaster. She was clearly bored."

In vivid contrast, Ari ingratiated himself with both Caroline and John Jr. He secretly slipped five one-hundred dollar bills to the young boy.

Christina shared her impression of Jackie with Alexander. "Mrs. Kennedy has this permanent smile plastered on her face in a sort of silly grin. I looked deeply into her eyes. There was an adding machine there, counting up the millions she expects to get from our father."

Jackie also shared her own impressions of Christina, especially her physical appearance, with Janet. "She's fat and hairy, definitely in need of electrolysis. I suggested to her that she go on a diet. I was astonished to learn that she drinks thirty bottles of Coca-Cola every day."

When Ari returned to Greece, he told Meyer, "Frankly, if Zeus would grant my wish, I'd be able to marry Queen Elizabeth. I date from the A-list, baby. But since Her Majesty is not available, I think I'll settle for Jackie."

Later, both Christina and Alexander were horrified when they learned of their father's plan to marry Jackie. Christina had read that Gore Vidal had called Jackie an "American Geisha," who would do almost anything in exchange for gold. From then on, Christina referred to Jackie as "The Geisha," or as "The Widow," echoing Ethel Kennedy's derisive remark about Jackie.

When Ari's children realized that they could not prevent the wedding, Christina threw a fit, running around the villa on Skorpios, screaming, ranting, and breaking objects, including three ancient Greek vases.

Unlike Christina, Alexander bolted from Skorpios, racing his sports car up and down the streets of Athens, almost killing two pedestrians.

After the wedding, Jackie faced Christina. "I hate you," Christina told her.

Later, Jackie said, "Christina is a spoiled monster with fat legs and chunky ankles, who dresses like a Greek peasant."

Ari told his daughter, "Jackie has no illusions about the Camelot myth she helped perpetuate."

Christina's response was, "I don't like the bitch. Don't trust her. She'll bring you only grief."

***

[Born on December 11, 1950, Christina Onassis was the daughter of Aristotle Onassis and Athina Livanos, known as "Tina." Christina was born in New York City and, as such, automatically became an American citizen at birth.

When she was 3 ½ years old, Ari took her aboard his $6 million yacht, *named after her, telling her, "This is your new home."*

She grew up in a privileged childhood, with murals in her nursery by the then-most-famous illustrator of children's books in the world, Ludwig Bemelsmans. She was thrilled to watch her father empty, raise, and convert the yacht's swimming pool into a ballroom floor. Even though he personally cooked Greek food for her, she preferred American cheeseburgers.

Aboard the yacht, she was fussed over by the likes of Greta Garbo and Sir Winston Churchill. When not sailing, she lived in elegance in Paris, London, and New York, or else at the Château de la Croë on France's Côte d'Azur.]

Although he initially dismissed the complaints of his children, Ari, within three months of his marriage to Jackie, told Johnny Meyer, "The kids were right. I should never have married 'The Widow.' I was on an ego trip."

"Jackie Kennedy made the same mistake that Maria Callas did," claimed Professor Ioannides Georgakis, a close friend of Ari. "For the most part, she ignored Alexander and Christina. Unlike a Greek, she didn't view the family as a horizontal entity, but a vertical one, as an American would view it. She didn't realize that as a stepmother, she was expected to develop deep and close relations with the boy and girl. She didn't attempt to. That, and not the millions she spent, was her greatest error. The children hadn't liked Callas, and they didn't like Jackie. The diva was wrapped up in herself and her opera career. Jackie was devoted to shopping and accumulating worldly goods."

In the beginning, Jackie actually did try to formulate a relationship with her new daughter-in-law. She hosted dinner parties for her in her apartment in New York, and took her shopping for better clothes along Fifth Avenue. But it soon became obvious that they were just not compatible. Jackie told friends that Christina was "spoiled, indulgent, and pampered."

Right from the start, Jackie had urged Christina to improve her physical appearance and to lose some weight. Finally, after three weeks, Christina told her, "Why don't you go fuck yourself? It's not my aim to look like some damn vapid model who stepped out of the pages of *Vogue.*"

Christina turned to Ari's sisters to air her complaints about her new stepmother.

"My proud father is forced to live in the shadow of President Kennedy," she said. "It's not fair to him. She belittles him. On Skorpios, he likes to walk around without his shirt. She's always urging him to cover himself up. 'You look disgusting,' she'll say to him in front of guests. 'Like some hairy ape.'"

After only a month on the island, Jackie no longer took her meals with the Onassis family. "She told us that she was appalled by our table manners." Christina said. "She claims we slurp our soup and put our elbows on the table. She criticizes us for how fast we eat our food."

When he'd married Jackie, Ari had hoped that she could be a role model for his daughter. But it didn't take long for him to realize that was not going to happen. Weight-prone Christina resented Jackie's slender figure. "I always feel like a cow beside her," Christina told her father.

In contrast, she liked Jackie's children, especially John Jr. Years later, she would form a romantic attachment to him.

Jackie also criticized Christina's romantic impulses, accusing her of going from one playboy to another. "Don't you know they are just after your money?" Jackie asked Christina.

"You mean, the reason you married my father?" Christina shot back before storming out of the room.

Christina became infatuated with Mick Flick, the tall, handsome Daimler-Benz heir who was also adored by other women. After only a month, he dropped her, finally telling her that he preferred tall blondes with shapely legs. At one point, she dyed her hair blonde, but the radical change in her appearance didn't work. Flick dumped her anyway.

When Jackie heard that, she said, "I warned you that no man will stay with you unless you lose weight."

Twice divorced, California realtor **Joseph Bolker** was almost thirty years older than Christina at the time of their marriage.

Ari bitterly opposed the union, fearing that the Jewish heritage of his son-in-law would damage his oil-tanker business with the Saudis.

On Skorpios, Ari was hosting a party for Jackie's forty-second birthday when news reached him that Christina, in a three-minute civil ceremony in Las Vegas, had married Joseph Bolker, a twice divorced California realtor nearly three decades older than herself.

Ari was not prepared for the news. Only two weeks before, Christina had referred to Bolker as "a dinky millionaire in real estate."

Ari had pinned his hopes on his daughter marrying Peter Goulandris, scion of a Greek shipping family, and her friend since childhood. He had planned to give Christina a coming-of-age present of twenty-one ships, but after learning about her impulsive marriage, he canceled his bequest and threatened to cut off her $75 million trust fund.

During his first phone conversation with Christina, and overheard by Jackie, he told his daughter, "I cannot forgive you."

"On hearing the news of Christina's marriage, Ari went apeshit," Meyer claimed. "I've seen him fly off the handle many times, but nothing like that night. He was rampant, mad enough to chew nails. Ari was also afraid that having Bolker for a son-in-law would damage his business relations with the Saudis. After all, Bolker was Jewish."

Distraught, Christina flew to London, where Jackie heard she'd overdosed on sleeping pills, but was recovering in a local hospital.

Christina later reconciled with her father, and in May of 1972, she divorced Bolker. He told the press, "Listen, when a billion dollars leans on you, you can feel it."

More tragedy awaited the doomed heiress. Her brother, Alexander, died in

1973 in a plane crash; her mother, Tina Livanos Niarchos, died in 1974 of a drug overdose in Paris; and her father died, as described later, in 1975.

***

In the wake of Ari's own death, the fight between Jackie and Christina reached epic proportions. Jackie didn't want to confront Christina herself, preferring to stay above the fray. She summoned her ever-faithful Teddy Kennedy to Skorpios to defend her interests—and he did.

After her estate fight with Jackie, Christina's life would take many disastrous turns before its tragic conclusion.

It was said that the only two people **Christina** ever loved were her father, Aristotle Onassis, and her daughter, **Athina Roussel**, depicted above. She spent as many of her waking hours as she could with her. It was as if she wanted to lavish onto her all the affection denied her by her own parents when she was growing up.

The deaths of her closest relatives had made Christina one of the world's richest women, perhaps the richest. Her brother's trust fund had reverted to her, as had her mother's estate. She had also inherited the bulk of Ari's estate, which at the time hovered at around $800 million.

She would take three more husbands, including Alexander Andreadis, the Greek shipping and banking heir, whom she married shortly after Ari's death. They divorced within fourteen months.

In 1978, she married a Russian shipping agent, Sergei Kauzov, another disaster, divorcing him in 1978.

Finally, she married a French businessman, Thierry Roussel, with whom she produced a daughter, Athina Onassis Roussel, born in 1985, the only surviving descendant of Ari. They divorced after Christina discovered that Roussel had had a child with his longtime mistress, the Swedish model Marianne Landhage, during the course of his marriage to Christina.

On November 19, 1988, a bulletin was announced from Buenos Aires, asserting that Christina Onassis, after multiple episodes of drug and alcohol abuse, had suffered a pulmonary edema and was DOA at a local hospital. Her remains would be laid to rest on the island of Skorpios beside the bodies of her father and brother.

The press hounded Jackie for a statement. None was forthcoming. Finally, a spokesperson for Jackie said, "Mrs. Onassis will not be attending the funeral."

***

In the wake of Christina's death, three-year-old Athina became one of the richest people on the planet, with a fortune estimated at anywhere from $600 million to $2 billion.

In December of 2005, at the age of twenty, Athina married the Brazilian Olympic showjumper Álvaro de Miranda Neto, nicknamed "Doda," a two-time Olympic medalist.

Twelve years her senior, Doda was exceedingly handsome, standing six feet two with dark hair and a muscular body. From the beginning, Athina was mesmerized by his beauty and charm, but her father, Roussel, objected to the marriage, claiming that the athlete was marrying her for her money.

The battle lines were drawn between the young Brazilian husband and the French father, each fighting for control of his wife's (or his daughter's) vast millions. The inevitable court battle followed, and in the end, Athina and Doda prevailed for control of her empire. Roussel, however, was said to have recieved a settlement of $100 million.

Athina said, "My mother had to buy off Jackie Kennedy; I had to buy off my father."

Today, the globe-trotting Athina and Doda live in São Paulo, in luxurious surroundings. The so-called "richest girl in the world" also own homes throughout Europe, a stable of expensive horses, investments worldwide, and conflicting feelings about her Greek heritage. During the course of her adult life, she sold her grandfather's island of Skorpios to a Russian billionaire, after expressing an aversion to anything Greek. In her words, "I must have been an expensive little girl. My father charged $150 million for my care and feeding between the ages of three and ten."

Alexander Onassis: In Praise of Older Women

"I had Callas, and I had Jackie," Alexander Boasts to Johnny Meyer

Born on April 30, 1948 at the Harkness Pavilion, a clinic in New York City, Alexander Onassis automatically became an American citizen at the moment of his birth. His father, like all Greek fathers, welcomed a male heir. His mother, Athina Livanos, nicknamed "Tina, was the daughter of the Greek shipping magnate Stavros Livanos. She had married Aristotle in 1946, divorcing him in 1960, charging him with adultery.

A neglected child, Alexander grew up in Paris and paid little attention to his education. After a "dirty weekend" in St-Tropez, he flunked his exams at his *lycée [a French secondary school that prepares students for a university]*.

Since bad grades and truancy characterized his early school years, Ari told Johnny Meyer, "What's bred in the bone comes out in the flesh. I refuse to piddle away any more good money on the kid's education."

Consequently, Alexander dropped out of school with only the most elementary education. Actually, he suspected that his father didn't want him to become better educated than he was.

Beginning in 1954, Ari lived only sporadically in his Paris apartment on the *[very posh]* Avenue Foch. His main residence seemed to be his yacht, the *Christina.*

Ari never seemed to be around to give his son much supervision, and he grew up living mostly with his Livanos grandparents at the fabled Château de la Croë.

[The classically inspired building, built in 1867 by Charles Garnier, designer of Paris' iconic Opera house, stood on the peninsula of Cap d'Antibes on France's Côte d'Azur. After King Edward VIII abdicated the throne of England, he took a lease on this building to live with his divorced (American) wife, who had, because of her marriage to him, become the Duchess of Windsor. It was here that Winston and Clementine Churchill celebrated their fortieth wedding anniversary in 1948.]

Alexander became very independent-minded. He had a terrible temper. Once, when angered, he broke all the windows on the ground floor of the château, costing Ari many thousands of dollars.

At the age of fourteen, Alexander began to live the life of an adult. By the time he'd turned sixteen, he had his own deluxe apartment in Paris.

As Ari would later tell Jackie, "I wanted the boy, when he was fourteen, to lose his virginity, so I took him to this bordello in Athens. Not one staffed with women, but with beautiful young boys from all over Europe, each with a round butt."

Alexander Onassis and Christina agreed on one thing: "The Widow" (a reference to Jackie Kennedy) was a horrible marriage candidate for their father.

Otherwise, **Alexander** was jealous of his sister, referring to her as "a spoiled brat who gets everything she wants."

Ari spent $200,000 annually on his daughter, lavishing her with clothes, travel, and jewelry. But to teach his son the value of money, he monitored his expenses and gave him only $12,000 a year, as an employee of Olympic Airlines.

His father told him, "A rich, handsome boy like you can have any girl he wants. But, first, I want you to have sex by subduing a male. Exerting your power and manhood over another male will show that you're dominant. Women will be only too eager to do your bidding, but men are objects to conquer and subjugate."

When Alexander began dating women, Ari bragged about his son's conquests, telling Meyer and others, "The boy has inherited my penis."

His teenage years were spent seducing married women who were part of international society. Most of these women were old enough to be his mother. He never wanted to date women his own age.

Weekends in summer were spent at St-Tropez, where he bragged to his friends that he'd "bagged" Brigitte Bardot. This appears to be a young man's fantasy, although British journalist Peter Evans reported that he did seduce Odile Rodin, the wife of the Dominican playboy, Porfirio Rubirosa.

When he first started driving, Alexander became a speed demon in his Maserati. Pedestrians had to flee for their lives. Sometimes he was stopped by the police. Alexander would ask them, "Do you know who I am?" When he showed the police his driving license, he had the equivalent of fifty U.S. dollars in French francs attached to the license. "I never got a ticket," he later bragged.

Not content with driving a car, he eventually obtained a pilot license at the age of eighteen, when he was once allowed to take the controls of a Boeing 707. Ari opposed his flying, fearing he might have an accident. He constantly reminded Alexander, "You are my only son and heir."

Occasionally, Alexander dined in Paris with his father's mistress, the opera diva, Maria Callas. He sneeringly referred to her as "the Singer."

Ari sent his son to work at his office in Monte Carlo, paying him a shoestring salary of $12,000 a year, plus expenses. He spent little time in the office, but raced cars dangerously along the winding *Corniches* of the Côte d'Azur, once having a serious accident.

"He seemed to have a death wish," his companions concluded.

When not being reckless on the highway, he spent his nights in various boudoirs, mainly when the husbands of his various mistresses were away.

Although two world class seductions lay in his future, Ari's life changed at the age of sixteen when he got the nerve to telephone Baroness Fiona Campbell-Walter Thyssen-Bornemisza, the divorced wife of Heinrich Thyssen, one of the world's richest men.

Alexander had first spotted Fiona when he was twelve and on a holiday at the chic Swiss resort of St. Moritz. She had emerged from a Rolls-Royce during a snowstorm, wearing a full-length black leather coat, her long auburn hair cascading from a black chinchilla hood. "Her face was like a piece of porcelain," Alexander recalled. "She was not only a stunning beauty, but the most fascinating woman I'd ever seen."

She was accompanied, on a leash, with a sleek black panther.

Born in New Zealand, Fiona Campbell was the daughter of a rear admiral in the British Royal Navy. As she grew up, she became one of the top high-fashion models of London. By Baron Heinrich, she'd had two children.

On making his first date with Fiona, the teenager said, "I'll come and pick you up in my Ferrari."

Haute mode: **Fiona Campbell** as a high-fashion model in 1954.

Marrying a Baron was not what it was cracked up to be.

She replied, "Listen, my dear boy, you'll have to do more than that to impress me. I had ten houses, two yachts and a jet plane when you were in diapers. You'll have to impress me as a human being."

Apparently, on their first date, he did more than that. He became her lover.

According to Fiona's friends, she viewed her seduction of the young boy as a one-night stand—"a guilty pleasure," so to speak. In contrast, he seemed to view their coupling as a lifetime commitment.

Fiona was thirty-five, although she looked much younger. When Onassis learned of his son's new mistress, he became enraged. So did his mother, Tina. "I want you to marry a virgin, not a gold-digging international whore," Ari screamed at his son.

Ari later made Alexander a promise: "I will give you anything you want in the world except Fiona."

But Alexander was defiant in refusing to give up his mistress.

Fiona later recalled, "It took me a long time to stop fighting and accept that Alexander and I had become indispensable to each other, and should just try to survive together."

***

Alexander always had a difficult relationship with Maria Callas, erroneously blaming her for the breakup of his father's marriage to Tina. Alexander was only ten when he first met the diva aboard the *Christina,* which had been named after his sister. She was only eight years old when Callas came aboard.

The children avoided the star and refused to dine with her. Fortunately, the yacht was large enough for them to stay out of each other's way. By the end of the voyage, when Callas departed, Alexander made it clear to Ari, "I will never accept her as my new stepmother."

Callas remembered Christmas of 1960 aboard the *Christina* as one of the worst of her life. By that time, Alexander was twelve years old. This time, Callas made a valiant attempt to ingratiate herself to both of Ari's children, even bringing them expensive presents. Both Alexander and Christina not only didn't open them, but tossed them overboard to Greek fishermen.

After lunch Callas always took a beauty nap, and Ari left instructions for the staff and his children to be quiet. Ari had purchased a motorboat for his son, and as Callas tried to sleep, he kept encircling the yacht, revving the engine of his boat, shouting, and screaming.

Not only that, but he came into her stateroom later that day, stuck his fingers down his throat, and vomited on her carpet.

When she returned to Paris, Callas told her confidant, the film director Franco Zeffirelli, "The boy is obnoxious, an evil little demon. I wanted to wring his neck, Ari needs to beat the shit out of him."

***

Eight years later, it was obvious to Alexander that Ari would never marry Callas. He had bigger game in mind—Jackie Kennedy, the most famous widow in the world. If anything, he hated Jackie even more than Callas.

He objected violently to the upcoming marriage of Ari "to this gold-digging American geisha." He was still fuming over all the many attempts Ari had made over the years to break up his love affair with Fiona.

In Paris one night, Alexander plotted a diabolical revenge. Although he had continued to dislike Callas, he did admit to Johnny Meyer, "That doesn't mean I wouldn't fuck her. I hate her with so much passion it's almost sexual."

Impulsively, he telephoned her. It was growing late, but he told her that he had to see her. "It's an emergency. We must talk."

Intrigued, Callas invited him over.

"I was lucky," he later told Meyer. "I caught her when she, too, wanted revenge on Ari for planning to marry Jackie. Before midnight, I was in the saddle, riding high. That divine voice of hers was screaming passion. My only disappointment came at the time of my orgasm—and hers, too, I presume—when she shouted, 'ARISTO! ARISTO! ARISTO!'"

Two weeks later, when Callas met Franco Zeffirelli for dinner, she said, "I should not have given in

For all the years he spent being "crushed under my father's thumb, I got my revenge," **Alexander** *(depicted above against a backdrop of his deathtrap, the Piaggio)* confided to his father's aide, Johnny Meyer.

"I seduced his mistress, Maria Callas, and raped his second wife, 'The Widow Kennedy.' Without sounding conceited, I think both of them truly enjoyed having a young man's dick doing what an old man's dick used to do in the far and distant past."

to him, but he overwhelmed me. In my fantasy, it was a young Aristo seducing me. I never had the pleasure of getting to know his body when it was young and vigorous, the way Alexander's is today. That pleasure, of course, was always denied me, though, I often speculated about what it would have been like. It was everything I'd ever dreamed about and more. Their penises are remarkably similar, although Alexander's is still young and vigorous, and Ari's has grown old and withered. The difference is that Alexander is insatiable. He doesn't want to end our night together until dawn breaks."

***

In spite of his hostility to Jackie, Alexander doted on John Jr. His affection was returned. John was at that impressionable age of burgeoning sexuality when young boys are often sexually confused. Meyer felt that Jackie's son was developing a crush on Alexander, who treated him like an emerging young man and not as a child, almost like Ari had handled his son.

When Alexander agreed to fly Jackie, Caroline, and John Jr. from Skorpios to Athens on a shopping trip, he allowed the boy to sit up front with him at the control panel of his Piaggio P136, an Italian-made twin-engine amphibian flying boat, with an all-metal hull, pusher propellers, a gull wing, and retractable landing gear. En route to Athens, he gave John his first flying lesson.

In subsequent trips, Alexander and John flew to various Greek islands for sunbathing and adventure.

Alexander told Meyer, "I was fourteen when I was introduced to one of the ultimate pleasures of life. I'm going to see that John-John—he hates that name—grows up early to be a man like I did. I think Jackie wants to keep him retarded as a boy."

Jackie objected to Alexander taking her son off alone with no set itinerary, but Ari encouraged it. Unlike Caroline, John and his new stepfather got along fabulously. He told Jackie that Alexander and John were developing a "big-brother/little brother relationship."

In the spring of 1969, when Alexander wanted to marry Fiona, Jackie, in his eyes, committed an unpardonable sin. At the urging of Ari, Jackie met privately with Fiona and convinced her not to marry Alexander. When he heard about this, he was furious and sought revenge.

Johnny Meyer, depicted immediately above, looked like a gangster from "between the wars." He was the ultimate fixer, troubleshooter, and a 24-hour pimp available at any time of the day or night, either for his first employer, Howard Hughes, or for his second one, Aristotle Onassis.

"I know where the bodies are buried," he claimed. "I know secrets on Ari that would get him roasted in the electric chair."

Alexander, like his father, believed that if someone caused him harm, he wanted to inflict even more damage on the enemy.

One hot afternoon on Skorpios, Meyer was in his bungalow when Jackie and Alexander were the only family members on the island. Jackie's children were away, as were Christina and Ari.

From his front window, Meyer spied on Jackie sunbathing in the nude in what she thought was the privacy of her garden. Even though nude pictures had already been snapped of her on Skorpios by concealed paparazzi, she still had not abandoned her habit of nude sunbaths.

He didn't have a clear view, but he heard Alexander's voice as he approached Jackie, who apparently tried to conceal her nudity.

From what he gathered, Meyer assumed that Jackie's stepson had approached her "with all his Greek jewels dangling."

There was a struggle, and he heard Jackie protesting. But her furor soon died down. It appeared from Meyer's perspective that she was either getting raped or else being willingly seduced by Alexander.

Later that night, Meyer invited Alexander to his bungalow for a drink. After assuring the young man that he would report none of what had happened to Ari, Meyer asked for more details. Before that afternoon, Meyer had always suspected that "the boy had the hots for Jackie. She was the kind of older woman he was always attracted to. I think he has a mother complex when it comes to women. Perhaps his real dream is to seduce his mother, Tina."

"The bitch didn't put up much of a fight," Alexander bragged. She got a taste of a young, hard, Onassis Greek dick, not a flabby one attached to an old man. I think I gave her multiple orgasms. If I know her, she'll probably be back tonight knocking on my door and begging for more."

***

For months, Alexander had begged his father to purchase a four-blade, French-made Puma helicopter to replace his aging amphibian, the Piaggio P136, which his son described, with deadly accuracy, as "a death trap."

Finally, Ari gave in and ordered a new Puma for Alexander.

[Although it was clearly understood that Alexander was a licensed pilot in his own right, his complicated roster of homes and hangouts demanded a "backup pilot" who'd navigate the Piaggio and presumably, the Puma, to and from a hangar on Skorpios whenever Alexander wasn't available.]

But first, the Piaggio needed a new pilot, since Donald McCusker had been grounded because of an eye operation. Consequently, Alexander hired another Donald *[Donald McGregor],* who had flown in from Ohio as a replacement for McCusker. Although he had never flown a Piaggio, he was an experienced amphibian pilot.

At 3:15PM, on the afternoon of January 22, 1973, McCusker sat in the pilot's seat with Alexander on his right and McGregor sitting behind them in the rear seat. To introduce the newly arrived American to the aircraft, Alexander has ordered some water landings and takeoffs between the island of Poros and Aegina.

Arriving at the airport in Athens, Alexander announced that he'd forgotten to bring the preflight checklist, which was quite elaborate—fifteen "before starting engines" checks, a dozen "before takeoff" checks, and seven "after-takeoff" checks. But instead of going back to retrieve it, Alexander insisted that he could remember all of them.

Six minutes after boarding, McCusker received clearance for takeoff from a runway that became available after an Air France Boeing 727 had lifted off for a flight to Paris.

After just four seconds, the right wing of the Piaggio dropped sharply and stayed down, which caused the aircraft to lose its balance. The right wing's pontoon struck the ground, then the wing itself. The plane cartwheeled nearly 500 feet along the tarmac before coming to a thunderous crash.

Both of the pilots were seriously injured, but Alexander's head was smashed. The only way the emergency rescue team at the airport could identify him was by means of a blood-soaked handkerchief in his breast pocket. It bore the initials "A.O."

The twenty-four-year-old heir to a vast fortune was gravely injured. Suffering from major internal injuries, including a "squashed' brain, he was rushed to the Red Cross Hospital in the center of Athens. There, doctors placed him on life support.

The word went out to Ari and Jackie, who were in New York at the time. Tina, with her latest husband, Ari's bitter rival, Stavros Niarchos, was vacationing in St. Moritz. Fiona was in London. Christina was in Brazil, where she heard the news over an international radio bulletin.

All these concerned associates made emergency plans to wing their way to Athens as soon as humanly possible.

Before frantically embarking on his flight from New York, Ari had arranged for an English neurosurgeon, Alan Richardson, to be flown from London to Athens aboard a British Airways Trident that normally holds about 150 passengers. On that flight, Richardson was the sole passenger.

At the hospital, after an examination, Richardson confirmed the report of the surgeons in Athens. Alexander was suffering "irrecoverable brain damage."

Rushed to the hospital, with screaming police sirens clearing the way, Ari faced he

A grief-stricken **Christina** *(left photo)* walks with her heart-broken father, **Aristotle Onassis**, to the funeral of her brother and his son.

Shielded under an umbrella and carrying flowers, the ex-Baroness **Fiona Campbell-Walter Thyssen-Bornemisza** *(right)*, arrived at Alexander's funeral escorted by two unknown young men.

She later said, "The brain defends itself to a degree. You drink a lot of wine and take sleeping tablets, but it's the little things that break you in the end."

awesome fact: Alexander was neurologically dead. He agreed not to "pull the plug" until Christina had flown in from Rio de Janeiro.

Dr. Richardson had given Ari the bad news. Alexander had suffered a contusion and edema of his brain matter. The right frontal fossa had been severely fractured. Not only that, but the right temporal lobe had been reduced to pulp. "Mr. Onassis, there is no hope for your son," Richardson said. "He's in God's hand tonight. We can't save him."

When Fiona arrived at the hospital, Ari let her spend fifteen minutes alone with her young longtime lover. She saw that his head was completely bandaged except for his eyes, which were closed, and his nose. She later said, "At times like that, you remember the strangest little things. Plastic surgeons had worked on his nose to make it not so sharp, and he was proud of his new look. His brain was smashed, I was told, but I thanked God his nose was intact. Later,

I was told by Ari himself that there was no hope. My beloved Alexander would not make it through the night."

Instead of shunning her after their last tense meeting, Jackie came up to her. "I thought she was going to extend sympathy. I was shocked. She said nothing about Alexander's dying. My worst suspicion about her was confirmed."

Jackie had heard that Alexander had recently dined with his father in Paris at Fouquet's on the Champs-Elysées," Fiona said. "They had talked about Ari's divorcing her."

"Was there talk of a settlement?" Jackie asked. "I need to know the amount agreed upon."

"Mrs. Onassis," Fiona said, "they did talk about a settlement, and Alexander confided in me what it was. But I'm not getting involved. You must talk to Ari yourself, or else have your lawyers do it for you."

With that refusal, Jackie turned her back on Fiona and walked away to stare blankly out of a hospital window.

The screams of Christina pierced the hospital corridors as two nurses escorted her into her older brother's "death chamber," as she called it.

She threw herself on his bed and cried and screamed until a doctor was summoned to sedate her. Nurses carried her away to another room.

After she was gone, Ari kissed his son's bandaged face. With tears streaming down, he turned to the chief surgeon, "Please remove life support. Let us not torture my poor son any more."

When Fiona was informed of Alexander's death, she screamed in anguish and fainted.

Although both Fiona and Christina had been reduced to hysterics, Ari seemed stoic as he escorted Jackie out of the hospital. Her eyes hidden behind large sunglasses, observers could not detect her composure. She seemed rigid and stone-faced.

***

In the immediate aftermath of his son's death, Ari became outraged, as if his fury had been slowly bubbling before bursting out. He was convinced that the plane had been sabotaged, and he announced that he was offering a $5 million reward for the arrest, trial, and conviction of the saboteurs. He blamed everyone from the Greek military junta to the CIA. He even blamed members of the rival shipping families, especially the houses of Livanos and Niarchos.

Not only that, but he asked the Greek police to pursue a manslaughter case against McCusker, the "official" and unfortunate pilot, when he recovered.

Nothing came of that.

Finally, he blamed God, with the belief that He was seeking retribution for his arrogance and pride in marrying Jackie, a woman he didn't really love.

Before departing from Athens, Ari asked Meyer to investigate the possibility of having Alexander frozen with the Life Extension Society in Washington, He considered having his son's body kept in a cryonic state until medical science advanced to the point that surgeons could bring Alexander back to life and restore his brain capacity.

Ari's close friend, Yanni Georgakis *[one of the few academics that Ari respected, and with whom he had discussed theological issues]* in the meantime, had flown to Athens to convince him to abandon the frozen body idea. "As Alexander's father, you have no right to interfere with the journey of his soul to Heaven."

Ari finally agreed that his son's body would be buried on Skorpios.

He also hired Jacques Harvey, a Parisian investigative reporter, who studied the case for weeks before concluding that Alexander's death had, indeed, been the result of an accident, not a conspiracy, and not sabotage. "God is responsible," Harvey told Ari.

Before Alexander's burial on Skorpios, Jackie and John Jr. had a fierce argument when she refused to allow him to attend. "He was like a brother to me," John protested. "I loved him, and I want to pay my respects. I should be allowed." He called Alexander "My co-pilot in the sky."

"That is all well and good," Jackie said. "But you're not going."

"I am going, and you can't stop me!" he said, defiantly.

"In that case, I'll call security," she said. "You won't go!"

"I hate you, you bitch!" John shouted at her. He had never condemned her that harshly before.

Stunned by his words, she looked at him in disbelief.

She later told Ari and Meyer, "John is growing up. He's becoming a man. I know you planned for Alexander to take over all your business interests one day. I think from this day forth, you should start training John to take over your enterprises one day. He is your son, too."

***

Ari's fun-loving personality, according to friends and staff, underwent a significant change when he faced what he called "the greatest tragedy of my life."

Although he had been critical and demanding of his son, he also loved him "more than life itself."

Friends and servants reported that Ari never recovered from the loss of his son. He didn't want to see anybody, even though Jackie tried to console him.

"When Alexander died," claimed author Nicholas Cage, "Onassis' *raison d'être* may have died with him."

Usually a man of charm and wit, Ari grew testy and even cruel to his staff. He cut off most of his friends and would not take their calls. His close friend, Peter Duchin, the bandleader, claimed that Ari "became morose, snapping, nit-picking, critical—just extremely difficult to even be in the same room with. All the spark he had was gone. Jackie got the worst of it."

Finally, tired of his denunciations, Jackie fought back. He punched her in the face, blacking her eye, which she concealed the next day by wearing large dark sunglasses, even at night. He would hit her again on several occasions. When questioned about this, he said, "All Greek husbands, I tell you, all Greek men, without exception, beat their wives. It's good for them."

In his bitterness and in his suffering over the loss of his son, the sadistic side of Ari surfaced as never before. Jackie found him insufferable and tried to keep an ocean between herself and her husband. If anybody suffered, according to Ari's bodyguards, it was his kept boys.

"He seemed to take out all his frustrations on them," claimed former bodyguard Tony Harvey. "He beat them with violence. One kid I had to take to a hospital in Athens. Legal action was threatened, and Onassis paid him off handsomely, at least enough to set the boy up for life."

***

Before Alexander's body had turned cold, Johnny Meyer was on a flight from Athens to Nice. He had been told to search thoroughly Alexander's apartment in Monte Carlo and remove "the family jewels." That was Ari's code for any incriminating evidence that his son might have accumulated.

Before Meyer boarded that plane to southern France, Ari had instructed him, "Don't leave anything behind that my enemies could use against me. I don't want the slightest scrap of evidence linking me with the assassination of Bobby Kennedy."

When he'd learned that Bobby might stand in the way of his marriage to Jackie, Ari had become enraged.

One of Ari's best friends, Yanni Georgakis, a loyal confidant, could also maintain a certain objectivity about the tycoon. He once was overheard claiming, "Ari is a charming psychopath with no moral imperatives at all. When he pursues a goal, he doesn't let anything stand in his way, and will stop at nothing."

Meyer had been sailing with Ari in the middle of the Atlantic Ocean when news reached him that Bobby had died in the wake of his shooting at the Ambassador Hotel in Los Angeles, following his successful win of the California Primary. Kennedy was finally dead. It was Jackie herself who had ordered that the slain Presidential candidate be taken off life support.

Ari had told Meyer, "Sooner or later some hit

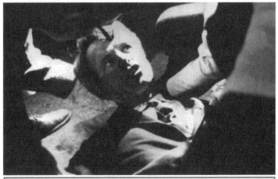

Of the many conspiracy theories whirling around the assassination of **Robert F. Kennedy** in Los Angeles in 1968, the most tantalizing concerned what role, if any, Aristotle Onassis played in the gunning down of his nemesis. Very few men ever knew the full story. One of them was Johnny Meyer, who was mysteriously killed.

man was going to shoot the little bastard. At least Jackie is free of the Kennedys. The last link has been broken."

Ari was forgetting the influence of Teddy Kennedy over Jackie.

During her last sail aboard the *Christina*, Jackie had told Meyer, "I've warned Bobby to drop out of the campaign. I told him that he would be killed. I said *would* be killed, not *could* be killed."

[It had been election day, June 4, 1968, in California. At 12:41AM, Bobby Kennedy had concluded his victory speech after winning that state's primary.

He exited the convention area of the Ambassador Hotel through the kitchen, where a small crowd of supporters had gathered, mingling with employees of the hotel.

Suddenly, Sirhan Bishara Sirhan—a 24-year-old Palestinian immigrant, a Christian Arab born in Jerusalem, with strong anti-Zionist beliefs—bolted forward from behind a tray stacker beside an ice machine. He began firing wildly from a .22 caliber Iver-Johnson Cadet revolver.

Bobby was shot three times before some of his supporters wrestled Sirhan to the ground. Amazingly, he broke free and grabbed the revolver again . But when he tried to fire again, he discovered he'd used up all the bullets.

Three of the shots had hit Bobby, one fired at a range of about an inch, entering behind his right ear and dispersing fragments throughout his brain. Two other bullets entered at the rear of his right armpit, one of them lodging in the back of his neck, and the other exiting from his chest.

Ethel was rushed to his side, and he seemed to recognize her. Minutes later, medical attendants arrived to cart him to the hospital on a stretcher. His last words before he lost consciously were, "Don't lift me!"

All efforts at surgery at Good Samaritan hospital were in vain.

Robert F. Kennedy was pronounced dead at 1:44AM.

The announcement was sent out around the world. Radio and TV stations throughout America, Europe, South America, the Middle East, China, Japan, and Australia, interrupted their broadcasting to bring the news of the assassination of another Kennedy brother.

Earlier at the White House, President Lyndon B. Johnson (then at the end of his second term and himself no longer a candidate) was preparing a major attack on Bobby's candidacy, favoring his own choice for Democratic contender, Hubert Humphrey. When news about the shooting reached him, Johnson kept demanding, "Is he dead? Is he dead yet?"

When it was confirmed that RFK was indeed dead, Johnson got into an argument with his aides. He didn't want Bobby buried at Arlington, claiming, "He is not entitled to a grave there."

Finally, his aides convinced him that it would be political suicide for him if he resisted an Arlington burial for the former New York Senator and Attorney General.

In jail today, serving a life sentence at the Richard J. Donovan Correctional Facility in San Diego County, California, Sirhan claims that he does not know why he shot Kennedy—"or even if I did."

At the Nice airport, Meyer rented a car and drove it eastward to Monaco. He had the keys to Alexander's apartment and entered it for a thorough search. With a hired safecracker, he broke into Alexander's vault and removed all the documents, packing them into a leather suitcase. He not only made off with "the family jewels," as Ari had called them, but he found several bugs, evidence of wiretapping. Fiona had previously warned her young lover that aides to Stavros Niarchos, Ari's longtime competitor, might well be eavesdropping on their private conversations.

Alexander had once told Meyer that he believed that his father was behind the plot to kill Bobby.

Ari claimed that Alexander was accumulating incriminating evidence to link him with the assassination.

His father suspected that he was going to use the evidence he was gathering to blackmail Ari and free himself from "financial bondage."

"The boy wants his independence, but I keep him on a tight purse string," Ari said. "I hold money over the boy's head like a deadly club."

Before leaving the Côte d'Azur, Meyer destroyed all evidence linking Ari to financing the assassination of Bobby. In reviewing the data, Ari was linked to an anti-American Palestinian named Mohmojud Hamshari, who, according to published reports, had long wanted to "kill a high-profile American on U.S. soil."

Hamshari had flown to Los Angeles, where the young fanatic, Sirhan Sirhan, was recruited, since he already possessed a strong desire to assassinate Bobby.

These charges were aired in 2004 when Peter Evans published his book, *Nemesis*, which caused massive speculation. A respected journalist, Evans had been a foreign correspondent for the *London Daily Express.*

He spent years investigating "the love triangle" of Jackie, Bobby, and Ari. The two men were deadly enemies, bitter competitors spinning around the favors of one woman, Jacqueline Kennedy

After unearthing the Greek tycoon's plethora of shady dealings during his tenure as Attorney General, Bobby had barred Onassis from trading with the United States, enraging Onassis and provoking his undying hatred.

In his book, Evans boldly stated that "Aristotle Onassis was at the heart of the plot to kill Bobby Kennedy."

The revelations were stunning and controversial. Both *Newsday* and *The London Financial Times* praised Evans' exhaustive research and revelations.

His book was also filled with unattractive revelations about Jackie herself, defining her rather aptly as "an acquisitive iconic bride."

In the wake of its publication, condemnations came in from all quarters, including from Kennedy biographer C. David Heymann, who labeled Evans' revelations as "unconfirmed and seemingly ludicrous."

Bobby's death provoked nowhere near the 2,000 books that were generated by JFK's assassination in 1963. One of the books that addressed it included *Who Killed Bobby?* by Shane O'Sullivan. Unlike Evans, he mentioned Ari only in a passing reference.

***

Long after Ari died in 1975, Meyer returned to America and lived in Florida. He realized that with both of his former employers—Howard Hughes and Aristotle Onassis—dead, he might make some serious money by selling, with the help of a ghost writer, some of this most explosive revelations to the tabloids. He made some calls, suggesting $100,000 should be paid for his documentation on Ari's financing of Bobby's assassination. Such a massive scandal, Meyer reasoned, would generate headlines around the world.

But before he began serious negotiations with the media, he was killed mysteriously in an accident. After leaving a party, he was said to have parked his car on an incline and got out to relieve himself, a common enough occurrence in the world. But instead of urinating by the side of his car, he was said to have stood in front of the car. Somehow, the brake was released and the car rolled over him, crushing him. Death was instant.

The speculation was that someone, perhaps a person riding beside him, or hiding in the back seat, had stepped on the gas, with or without assaulting him before setting the car in motion. No evidence was ever found to bring a murder charge against an alleged assailant.

***

What Jackie knew, if anything, about Ari's link to the murder of Bobby is not known. Not even a rumor has surfaced. No one close to her ever came forth to claim she ever discussed a conspiracy.

Shortly after Ari died, a letter from her to her then-new husband was discovered. In it, she wrote, "When death ends one dear relationship, as it did for me in 1963, it often creates another sweeter still."

It might be assumed that she was referring to her marriage to Ari, but she wasn't. In the subsequent line, she wrote: "There was a time when Bobby meant more to me than life itself."

Chapter Thirty-One

John-John & The Material Girl

Plugging Madonna

Blonde Ambition Encounters the Handsome Hunk

The romance of **Madonna** with **John F. Kennedy, Jr**. was as unlikely a mating as the sexual link between President John F. Kennedy and Marilyn Monroe.

Madonna and John came from such different worlds. He was born the son of the President-elect of the United States, becoming the most famous baby in the world. He followed in his father's footsteps, seducing some of the most exciting women anywhere, notably Madonna and Princess Di. As a seducer, he was called "His father's son in more ways than one."

Madonna in the 1980s became the planet's top female pop star, a self-made icon who rose from obscurity to shock the world.

The son of the late president was just one in a long string of conquests that reportedly included Warren Beatty (her *Dick Tracy* co-star), Mick Jagger, Jack Nicholson, and Prince, plus lots of Latin men and light-skinned black males.

A former friend claimed, "It's no joke, size counts to her. She's not interested in somebody who's not above average." The men she seduced, from all reports, met her measurement standards.

Madonna's role model,

a virtual icon for her, was Marilyn Monroe. Marilyn had had an affair with John F. Kennedy, Sr. It seemed almost logical that Madonna should follow in her footsteps. The president wasn't around to seduce any more, but his son, John F. Kennedy, Jr., was around—and in her words, "hot."

The unlikely pair met when JFK Jr. launched his glossy political lifestyle magazine, *George*, named after the nation's first president.

As a novel idea, he contacted Madonna, asking if she would write an essay for the inaugural issue, to be entitled, "If I Were President."

She sent him the draft of an essay which more or less outlined her case of why she did not want to become President of the United States. As if to back up her point, she enclosed a picture of herself (for publication) in a sexy blue bikini straddling a diving board.

"I like the idea of being an inspiration to the downtrodden, of educating the masses. I like the idea of fighting for equal rights for women and gays and all minorities. I like the

Pictured above *(left)* **Marilyn Monroe** performed her most celebrated dance number, singing "Diamonds Are a Girl's Best Friend" in the film *Gentlemen Prefer Blondes* (1953), in which she co-starred with another busty star, Jane Russell.

Above *(right)*, **Madonna** imitates Monroe, wearing an equivalent gown in the same shocking pink. Madonna always wanted to be a comedienne in the movies like MM.

In her video, Madonna, in the words of Christopher Andersen, was "Gowned and coiffed like Monroe, dripping with diamond bracelets. She prances over a platoon of panting tuxedo-clad suits while she sings her unrepentant paean to greed."

"I will be a symbol of something," Madonna predicted. "Like Marilyn Monroe stands for something. It's not always something you can put a name on, but she became an adjective."

idea of embracing other countries and other cultures and promoting world peace. Fighting the good fight, as it were. But I think I'd rather do it as an artist. Because artists are allowed to make mistakes and artists are allowed to have unconventional ideas and artists are allowed to be overweight and dress badly and have an opinion. Artists are allowed to have a past. In short, artists are allowed to be human. And presidents are not. So the question is: How can someone be a good leader if he or she isn't allowed to be human? I'd rather eat glass."

When she did meet with JFK Jr., she told him what she'd do as president: "Send Rush Limbaugh, Bob Dole, and Jesse Helms to a hard-labor camp; welcome Roman Polanski back into the country; deport Howard Stern; and invite the entire armed forces of America to come out of the closet."

When the magazine was first published, it had the largest circulation of any political magazine in the nation because of the celebrity status of JFK Jr. But it soon began to lose money in both advertising and circulation.

JFK Jr. went backstage to greet Madonna after her "Who's That Girl?" performance in Madison Square Garden. Don Johnson, then at the peak of his *Miami Vice* fame on TV, was also there with flowers, but Madonna rejected him before walking away with the prize hunk of the night, JFK Jr. himself.

The JFK Jr./Madonna sightings began in New York during the weeks leading up to Christmas of 1987. "Could it really be true?" the public asked, "that Madonna was actually dating the son of Marilyn Monroe's former lover, his father, President John F. Kennedy?"

The symbolism that MM, the blonde bombshell of the 50s had been replaced by another bombshell in the 80s, Madonna, wasn't lost on the tabloids.

JFK Jr.'s biographer, Wendy Leigh, claimed, "In her own mind, Madonna wasn't just Marilyn emulated but Marilyn reincarnated, sent here to fulfill her psychic destiny. At every step, Madonna continued her consumption of the Marilyn mystique, but she craved something more. John F. Kennedy, Jr. was just the dish to finish off the meal—the ultimate Monroesque experience."

At a newsstand, John purchased the latest edition of *Vanity Fair* with a provocatively posed Madonna on the cover. Inside she had posed for two nude pictures as part of an "Homage to Norma Jean" pinup layout.

JFK Jr. and Madonna were seen working out together at a private gym, Plus One, in Manhattan's Soho district, after which they were also spotted jogging together in Central Park. Here was America's Prince Charming, its most eligible bachelor, dating the world's "most glamorous and exciting woman."

Madonna, a woman who doesn't shock easily, was surprised when she saw the latest issue of *George*. It featured Drew Barrymore on the cover, and she was dressed as Marilyn in a replica of the gown MM had arranged to have sewn on her before singing "Happy Birthday, Mr. President" to a startled President Kennedy at Madison Square Garden in 1962.

"I just couldn't believe that John would pay homage to such a woman," said Ted Sorensen, "especially considering all the pain MM had caused Jackie."

Ever since the 1940s, Jackie had read *Life* magazine. One issue shocked her, the one featuring Madonna imitating the physicality of Marilyn Monroe. Sorensen said, "It was like Marilyn coming back from the grave to haunt Jackie. Marilyn stole her husband. Now Madonna was trying to take her son away."

During her son's affair with Madonna, Jackie could be seen purchasing the tabloids in the lobby of Doubleday's offices on Fifth Avenue where she was employed as an editor. John didn't keep her abreast of developments, so she had to read about her son in the papers.

"Madonna realized that adding John F. Kennedy, Jr.'s scalp to her sexual belt would be another publicity coup," said author Leigh.

In his biography of Madonna, Andrew Morton wrote: "Although JFK Jr. and Madonna were lovers for a brief period, the affair was not a success. John Junior was intimidated by Madonna's reputation as he was by his mother (he was a mother's boy). For all her outward aggression, explained one of her former lovers, Madonna is a woman who expects her man to take control, more of a kitten than a tigress in the bedroom. Rather rue- fully, she explained to friends after the end of her affair with Kennedy that he was just too nervous for them to click sexually. The chemistry certainly wasn't there. 'Some guys can handle the fame, others can't,' said a former lover. "He couldn't.'"

Madonna's boudoir escapades were de- scribed differently by Stephen Spignesi in his slim volume *J.F.K. Jr.*: "As anyone who has seen Madonna's photo book, *Sex*, can attest, the Mate- rial Girl is a sexual virtuoso. If sex were a high school, she'd be in the advanced class. She ap- parently is familiar with S and M, lesbianism, inter- racial sex, and multiple partners; and she is also an uninhibited exhibitionist who reportedly prefers sex partners as wild and experienced as herself."

Madonna has been quoted as saying, "I don't like to give blow-jobs, but I do like getting head— for a day and a half."

Even though JFK Jr. may not have been the greatest lay of Madonna's life, their intimacy con- tinued for a few weeks. He gave her the keys to his apartment. One afternoon when he came in from the office, he found her lying on his couch clad in nothing but sheets of transparent plastic wrap. "Dinner's ready, John," she allegedly called out to him.

Stories began to run in the tabloids that as part of his lovemaking John would apply creamy peanut butter to her legs and would then lick it off like a puppy. Madonna denied such rumors. "What the fuck! Do you know how many calories there are in peanut butter? Yes, to low fat whipped cream. No, to that fucking peanut butter story."

She told a friend, "I'm dating someone re- spectable, not some rent boy picked up on a street corner. For all we know, John might even become President of the United States one day."

Christopher Andersen's book, *Madonna: Unauthorized* had a certain shock value in 1992 when it more or less predicted that Madonna "was almost bound to die an untimely death."

Actually, he had associated that idea with the wrong party in the Madonna/JFK Jr. love affair. It was the son of the former pres- ident who would die an untimely death several years later in an airplane crash.

The book maintains that Madonna had read every Mon- roe biography ever written and felt she "was the undisputed heiress to the Monroe *Persona*." She confided that she "felt fated to consummate a sexual rela- tionship with JFK's only son." When Jackie heard of her son's new main squeeze, she asked friends, "What designs does this volatile creature have on my son?"

Even if mad-dog passion wasn't there, Madonna knew a hunk when she bedded one. She became particularly intrigued by a color photograph of John without his shirt. "His body is chiseled, raw-boned, lean, and muscular," she told a gay pal. "He is extraordinarily handsome, and when he's on top of you and looks down at you with those bedroom eyes, you melt."

If Madonna began to collect male beauty photographs of him, he returned the compliment by plastering provocative posters of her on the walls of his bachelor apartment.

Even his clothing style changed. Madonna lured him into a more punk look, and he was photographed in leather jackets and ripped jeans. He even grew a goatee resting under his mop of spiked hair. According to Andrew Morton, Thomas Lift, a friend from college, claimed that John told him, "It's like she put a spell over me. I'm obsessed with her."

According to reports, Madonna wanted to hurry up and divorce Sean Penn so she could marry John and "become part of the Kennedy clan. I want to have a little boy with John. He, too, I predict will grow up to be a president some time in the 21st century."

Author J. Randy Taraborrelli quotes a friend of Madonna who claimed, "I heard from good sources that Madonna did what she could to interest John in having a baby, but he didn't take the bait and wanted to wear protection."

In his biography of Madonna, Morton quoted a good friend of John's, Steven Styles, who had gone to Brown University with John.

According to Styles:

"He telephoned me one day and sounded uncharacteristically depressed. He eventually confessed that he had fallen in love with a married woman who was a very celebrated personality. Conflicted, he said he didn't know what to do. He was torn by his desire for this woman and his need to conform to societal pressure that he find the so-called 'right girl,' someone whom his mother and the other Kennedys would approve. And he said, 'Believe me when I tell you that this is not the right girl.' I asked him who she was. When he told me, you could have knocked me over with a feather. It was Madonna."

At one point after their lovemaking, Madonna told John that he should let a gay man make love to him. "That way you'll understand more what a woman feels from a man."

"Been there, done that," John reportedly said.

During her affair with John, Madonna was still married to Penn, an estranged husband prone to jealousy.

Penn had an arsenal of rifles and handguns in the basement of his Malibu villa. He would go down there on occasion to practice his marksmanship. At one point he put up a poster of John and fired with bullets from his .357 magnum. He got John right between the eyes.

John attended a party that was a tribute to Robert De Niro sponsored by New York's Museum of the Moving Image. Penn showed up with Liza Minnelli, Jeremy Irons, and Matt Dillon.

After about fifteen minutes John walked up to Penn and extended his hand.

Sex, Madonna's coffee table book, became notorious, as it featured strong adult content and softcore pornographic photos depicting simulations of sexual acts which included sadomasochism and analingus. Featured in the book were Isabella Rossellini, Vanilla Ice, Naomi Campbell, and gay porn star Joey Stefano.

Jackie was horrified.

The handshake was not intercepted. "I know who you are," Penn said in a voice cold as an Arctic night. "You owe me a god damn apology." Fearing a scene, John turned and walked away.

The next morning a funeral wreath of white roses with a black-and-gold ribbon was sent to John. The inscription read, "My Deepest Sympathy," and a personal card read, "Johnny, I heard about last night. M."

Of course, all of Madonna's plans to snare John could be dashed if she did not win favor with "The Queen of America," the formidable Jackie herself. Madonna realized early in her dating with John that he was very much influenced by his mother. "Jackie ultimately was the decider," Madonna said.

Madonna not only wanted to screw around with John, but meet his mother. To her, Jackie Onassis was a far greater American icon than Marilyn. "Her style, her grace, her beauty, there's no one like Jackie O," Madonna told a friend.

It took a lot of persuading on John's part to get Jackie to agree to entertain Madonna at her elegant Fifth Avenue apartment.

Reportedly, the meeting was stilted. Jackie was stiff and formal with Madonna and made it clear that she did not welcome intimacy. It was doubly clear that the former First Lady also didn't want her son dating a "notorious" figure like Madonna. As if to remind Jackie that she was a married woman at the time, Madonna provocatively signed her name in Jackie's guest book as "Mrs. Sean Penn."

After Madonna left the apartment, Jackie angrily called John from her office at Doubleday the next morning. "What in hell's name are you doing dating such a tramp?" she demanded to know. "You know she's just using the Kennedy name for publicity. She's just a social climber. At least you don't have to worry about her being after your money. She can buy and sell you any day."

Steven Styles, John's friend from Brown, claimed that John told him, "My mother wants the best for me. But sometimes, that means I have to keep secrets from her. Otherwise, I'd never be able to date. Let's face facts: No woman will ever be good enough for her. Unless she's royalty....but even then."

Madonna was a Roman Catholic, at least technically, but she was hardly as devout as Jackie. In fact, Jackie's priest called her when he heard that John was dating Madonna. "She's a heretic and should be excommunicated from the church," the priest said. "She uses crucifixes and other of our sacred images in her music videos. To mock us. She's immoral and sacrilegious. Nothing good will come out of John's involvement with a woman like that."

At Jackie's powerful urging, John eventually withdrew from Madonna. Both of them moved on to other partners. But they parted with that famous line, "Let's be friends."

When Cher heard of the JFK Jr./Madonna affair, she summed up her feelings on the subject: "Madonna could afford to be a little more magnanimous and a little less of a cunt."

Chapter Thirty-Two

Farewell, Jackie

The Final Curtain of a Life Beyond Her Wildest Dreams

"I Refuse to Believe I'm Going to Die"

Maurice Tempelsman, The Diamond Merchant and Father Figure

Diamond merchant **Maurice Tempelsman** was an unlikely beau for **Jackie** in her declining years, but he won her over with his financial savvy and his loving support of her. "Other husbands and lovers have betrayed me," she told Ted Sorensen. "But Maurice will always be there for me." Caroline and John Jr. were at first suspicious of him, but he won them over, too, by showing his love and devotion to their mother.

Maurice recalled that one of his most painful experiences involved the compilation of Jackie's final will and testament, a long, complex document that left most of her estate to her son and daughter. After Jackie's funeral, John Jr. told Maurice that he'd like to have his mother's apartment for himself to live in during the renovation of his loft in Tri-Be-Ca. The older man moved into the Sherry Netherland.

Later, with Caroline, John sold Jackie's apartment at 1040 Fifth Avenue to oil tycoon David Koch for $9.5 million, and John and Caroline, over Maurice's protests, auctioned off their mother's possessions at Sotheby's.

Deep into midlife *ennui,* Jackie, in

July of 1975, resumed a life of second widowhood in Manhattan, focusing on her teenage children. She seemed bored, agreeing with Norman Mailer's assessment of her as "A Prisoner of Celebrity."

She needed a purpose in life, and didn't think she'd find it as the wife of yet another powerful man. In August, she'd traveled to the ruins of the ancient amphitheater at Epidaurus *[on Greece's Peloponnese peninsula, south of Athens]*, where she was met with hostile Greek women, yelling insults at her for abandonment of her late husband, Aristotle Onassis, during the final hours of his life.

After her return to America, several career opportunities were presented to her. It seemed that dozens of people or corporations wanted to link their name with hers. Along with those offers came weekly, sometimes daily, proposals of marriage, including several from lesbians.

Some members of the Democratic Party in New York wanted her to run for the U.S. Senate, representing the Empire State as her former brother-in-law, Robert Kennedy, had done. Mayor Edward Koch wanted to make her the city's Commissioner of Cultural Affairs at a salary of $62,000 a year.

At least ten fashion houses in the United States, London, and Paris wanted her to be their spokesperson, hoping she'd also create a signature collection, "The Jackie Look." Her most enticing offer was to become the U.S. Ambassador to France. Gracefully, she rejected all proposals.

By summer's end, she decided she wanted to do something in publishing. She had lunch with Thomas Guinzburg, the president and publisher of Viking Press *[an American publishing company owned by the Penguin Group, which acquired the company in 1975]*. It eventually led to her being hired as a consulting editor at a salary of $200 a

Michael Jackson had always been fascinated by other celebrities. For years, he defined Diana Ross as a role model. As an adolescent, during the period he lived with her, he tried on her gowns when she was away. At Neverland, he sometimes insisted that his staff address him as "Miss Ross."

After meeting **Jackie Kennedy**, however, he dumped Diana as a role model and replaced her with the former First Lady.

Despite multiple screwups and setbacks, Jackie worked long and hard, during her latter-day career as an editor at Doubleday, to get him to produce an candid and authorized version of his memoirs.

She was less than enchanted with the results. Nevertheless, *Moonwalk* emerged as the most commercially successful book she ever helped produce during her publishing gig.

Jacqueline Kennedy Onassis, "The Prisoner of Celebrity"
Moonwalks with Michael Jackson

week. Her last paying editorial job had earned her $42.50 a week when she was an inquiring camera girl for the *Washington Times-Herald.*

On the first Monday morning she was to report to work, she arose early and boiled an egg in her luxurious apartment overlooking Central Park, and then took a taxi to Viking's offices in Manhattan at Madison Avenue at 58th Street. Screams of JACKIE! JACKIE! echoed through the canyons of Manhattan that early morning when she arrived.

Whenever possible, she tried to avoid appearing in "the river of sludge," *[her name for tabloid journalism]* and the paparazzi, especially in anything associated with her nemesis, Ron Gallela.

One editor, Helen Marrkel, likened her arrival at Viking to a Hollywood premiere.

Viking, noted for its top drawer editors, was a prestigious house that had released works by John Steinbeck, Saul Bellow, Dorothy Parker, D.H. Lawrence, Thomas Pynchon, Sherwood Anderson, Arthur Miller, and James Joyce.

Although the office staff showed only good manners to her when she was nearby, they gossiped about her, relentlessly, behind her back. Many seasoned editors who had spent long, hard years rising within their career ranks, resented how, with no real experience, she'd breezed into her post. One editor claimed, "Mrs. Onassis' presence was resented as an insult to other editors."

Some of these editors seemed to take delight at board meetings in rejecting her proposals for new books. One such incident occurred when Jackie pushed Viking to publish the memoirs of Lord Snowden *[aka Antony Armstrong-Jones]*, former husband of England's Princess Margaret. After Jackie invited him to lunch with the Viking elite, she later claimed that "the editors were rude to him. They didn't find the idea of his memoirs high brow enough for them."

Jackie viewed her new position as a chance to nurture writers and to champion pet projects. She did not easily make friends, and was often seen eating lunch alone, enjoying a juicy burger in Manhattan's stylishly crowded, two-fisted bar and grill, P.J. Clarkes.

She did not play the regal princess, but became a hard-working, though inexperienced, editor, doing her own photocopying, and making her own coffee and phone calls.

There was a problem, however: The Viking switchboard was flooded with crank calls, and the building that contained it received an occasional bomb threat from a Kennedy hater. Reporters disguised themselves as messenger boys and tried to slip in to get at her for

More to Jackie's liking was fashion maven **Diana Vreeland,** "The Empress of Fashion."

For her work as one of the guiding lights behind *Harper's Bazaar* and *Vogue,* Vreeland was hailed by Jackie as "totally imaginative, totally futuristic, and totally *in toto.*"

a story.

The first book on which she worked was *Remembering the Ladies: Women in America (1750-1815).* This tome included the tantalizing information that women in colonial America ingested the root of a certain plant as a means of inducing abortions.

Guinzburg later praised her social networking skills in luring a number of big-name writers into the Viking orbit.

Her next book, *In the Russian Style,* was devoted to the lavish aesthetic of 18th and 19th Century Imperial Russia. Although favorably reviewed in most quarters, it also had its critics, one of them labeling it "glitter and gold with little substance."

Other achievements included collaborating with Diana Vreeland *[priestess of high fashion and long-term duenna at Vogue magazine]* on a coffee table book, *Inventing Paris Clothes (1909-1939).* She also encouraged a Chicago ecclesiastic, Eugene Kennedy, to write an award-winning biography, *Himself: The Life and Times of Richard J. Daley.*

Jackie's most contentious relationship was with Barbara Chase-Riboud, an African-American sculptor and poet, who signed to write *Sally Hemings,* a biography of the slave mistress of Thomas Jefferson.

Before the science of DNA proved that Chase-Riboud's conclusions were correct, the 1979 publication of her novel was denounced by some Jeffersonian scholars who seemed to want to protect the reputation of America's third president.

The poet-sculptor had met Jackie during her marriage to Onassis, and had admired her self-deprecating humor, her style, and charm. The original novel ran 800 pages, and Viking wanted it cut.

There were also problems of historical inaccuracies. Chase-Riboud was hostile to making changes, even though some of them were relatively minor. A fight ensued. Guinzburg later pronounced her as "one of the most difficult authors in our experience." There were charges of racism. Jackie left Viking just as the book was in production. Chase-Riboud charged that "Viking embarked on a series of perversities" but finally an agreement was reached, changes were made, the book was finally published and distributed, becoming one of the most talked about of the year.

Jackie might have stayed at Viking were it not for an unfortunate incident. In 1977, against her wishes, Viking published a novel, *Shall We Tell the President?,* by bestselling author Jeffrey Archer. It centered on a plot to assassinate a fictional president inspired by the life and persona of Teddy Kennedy.

Its publication had nothing to do with Jackie—in fact, she never read it—but she suffered a backlash. John Leonard, writing in *The New York Times,* reviewed the novel, calling it trash. "Anybody associated with its publication should be ashamed of herself."

That "herself" was an obvious but unfair reference to Jackie.

Under pressure from the Kennedy clan, and horrified at the bad publicity she was getting, Jackie resigned from Viking.

She issued a public statement: "I tried to separate my lives as a Viking employee and a Kennedy relative. But this fall, when it was suggested that I had something to do with acquiring this book and that I was not distressed, I felt I had to resign."

***

Nancy Tuckerman, Jackie's former secretary at the White House, was working at the time for Doubleday *[since 2009, an imprint that's part of the Knopf Doubleday Publishing Group]*, and she suggested that Jackie should join that publishing house, one of the most prestigious in the world. After meeting with executives, Jackie signed on as an associate editor in 1978, at an annual salary of $50,000.

One of the senior editors, who did not want to be named, claimed that Jackie was hired mainly to bring in books by other celebrities and as Doubleday's "secret weapon," generating massive publicity for the firm and attracting high-profile authors.

There was another reason, too: The publisher wished that one day, Jackie would write her own tell-all autobiography which, it was predicted would become one of the bestsellers of the 20th Century.

In an interview with *Publishers Weekly,* she said, "I'm drawn to books that are out of the regular experience—other cultures, ancient histories. One of the things I like about publishing is that you don't promote the editor—you promote the book and the author."

Once they got used to her, the editors at Doubleday treated her better than those at Viking. She showed up with her lunch from home, often only a yogurt and a piece of fruit. She attended office parties and

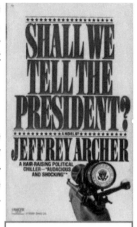

Against her objections, Viking published this book by **Jeffrey Archer,** the former British MP who had served two years in prison for a perjury conviction. It was a fictional account of an attempt to assassinate an American president clearly inspired by Teddy Kennedy.

Jackie was attacked for her insensitivity at not preventing its publication, forcing her to resign. Publishing insiders have since referred to this title as "the book that ended Jackie Onassis' career at Viking."

even an office picnic. Of course, she was hounded by the press. And unlike the other editors, she had to shred her memos to keep them from appearing in the tabloids.

In spite of her millions, her fame, and her power, "she often looked more like a frightened little chicken than a former First Lady who ruled the world, so to speak," claimed an editor.

The same editor revealed that Jackie was "not without her petty jealousy. I was on the elevator with her one morning when Sophia Loren got on. We were going to publish an Italian cookbook by the star. Loren had been one of JFK's former lovers, or so it was rumored. All attention focused on Loren, not on Jackie. The former First Lady stormed off the elevator. She always com-

Jackie defined **Gelsey Kirkland** as the greatest ballerina of her generation, but didn't fully anticipate how controversial her memoirs, *Dancing on My Grave,* would be. The dancer wrote candidly about her health issues, her addictions, and her tempestuous offstage romance with Mikhail Baryshnikov.

Jackie's promotion and work on *Call the Darkness Light* caused the author, **Nancy Zaroulis**, to earn a million dollars.

A reporter asked Zaroulis if it would be a challenge to spin Jackie's life into a novel. She replied, "It would take a genius to turn Jackie's life story into a novel that anyone could believe was true."

Jackie collaborated with **Diane Vreeland** on two books, including *In the Russian Style,* which was associated with exhibitions that the fashion editor had organized at the Costume Institute. "Knowing you has taught me more than you could ever know," Jackie wrote.

Jackie worked closely with the French-American historian **Olivier Bernier** in his edited publication of the memoirs of the Duchess d'Abrantès, who became France's first gossip columnist, writing about the peccadilloes and scandals *At the Court of Napoléon.*

plained about being gawked at. But when she wasn't, she got mad."

The first novel she acquired, *Call the Darkness Light,* by Nancy Zaroulis, became a best-seller when it was published in August of 1979. Jackie talked to Gloria Steinem of *Ms.* magazine about the novel.

"The manuscript seemed to weigh about twenty pounds, and I thought it was going to be just too depressing. It's the story of a girl working in the mills in Lowell, Massachusetts, in the 19th century. Once I started to read it, I couldn't put it down."

When news reached Jackie about the assassination attempts on the lives of Ronald Reagan and Pope John Paul II, she was deeply disturbed. She was even more horrified at the murder of John Lennon. Working with Jonathon Cott and Christine Doudna, long-time associates of *Rolling Stone* magazine, Jackie released *The Ballad of John and Yoko,* a compilation of *Rolling Stone's* coverage of the Beatles over the years. The tribute was published in 1982.

Cott later said, "She had an incredible sense of literary style and structure. She was intelligent and passionate about the material. She was an ideal reader and an ideal editor."

Some of her favorite books were by Olivier Bernier, a brilliant Franco-American historian and scholar. His books included *The Secrets of Marie Antoinette* (1985); and *At the Court of Napoléon* (1989).

Carly Simon, Jackie's close friend, was lured into writing successful upmarket children's books, beginning with *Amy the Dancing Bear* (1989).

Dance literature was enriched when Jackie enticed Martha Graham, the doyenne of modern dance, to write *Blood Memory,* published in 1993, one of Jackie's last books as an editor. Francis Mason also wrote *I Remember Balanchine* about George Balanchine, the great Russian *émigré* choreographer.

Jackie's greatest dance memoir, however, was Gelsey Kirkland's bestselling *Dancing on My Grave* (1986), written with her husband, Greg Lawrence. Jackie considered Kirkland the greatest ballerina of her generation, and urged her to write a tell-all, even delving into what was called her "self-destructive spiral," once cited as "sliding down the razor blade of life," all about eating disorders, cocaine snorts, bulimia, anorexia, and prescription drug abuse.

Kirkland later said, "When Jackie offered me a chance to write my autobiography, she helped rescue not only my life, but my career as a ballerina. She was both friend and editor. When we had conflicts, including a drastic trimming down of my book with my husband, Greg, I remembered she was my friend and supporter and that super topped her role as editor."

The book occupied a prolonged perch on *The New York Times* bestseller list. Reviews were mixed, ranging from "hot stuff" in the words of one writer to smears and attacks on both the dancer and her editor.

Writing in *Vanity Fair,* James Wolcott was critical of Kirkland's nightmarish cycle of drug addiction and seizures. He wrote: "Is this the place to note that the book's editor is Jacqueline Kennedy Onassis? I guess not."

One of Jackie's great publishing coups at Doubleday was Naguib Mahfouz's celebrated *The Cairo Trilogy—Palace Walks* (1990), *Palace of Desire* (1991), and *Sugar Street* (1992).

[*Born to a lower middle-class strictly Islamic family in Egypt, Naguib Mahfouz (1911–2006), was one of the first contemporary writers of Arabic literature to explore themes associated with*

Jackie first read the works of the Egyptian Nobel Prize winner, **Naguib Mahfouz**, in French. A devotee of Mediterranean culture herself, she lobbied Doubleday to acquire and publish his classic **Cairo Trilogy**.

Although she never met Mahfouz, she mailed him "love letters," claiming "I'm your big fan." Deaf and diabetic at the time, he was quite old when he gracefully responded to her praise.

existentialism. In 1988, he won the Nobel Prize for Literature. His most famous work, The Cairo Trilogy, depicts three generations of different families in Cairo from the debut of World War I until after the 1952 military coup that overthrew the Egyptian government's British-backed puppet, King Farouk. Before the Nobel Prize he was largely unknown to western readers.]

Jackie also persuaded Joseph Campbell *[an acclaimed authority on comparative mythology and comparative religion]* and Bill Moyers to adapt their televised mini-series into a book, *The Power of Myth* (1988).

In 1993, near the end of Jackie's life, she was rumored to have offered $2 million to Camilla Parker-Bowles to write a tell-all about her long affair with Prince Charles. That came in the wake of the release of secretly taped phone conversations in which the Prince of Wales told his mistress that he wanted to return to life "as a tampon and live forever in your knickers."

Of course, that offer was never accepted. Camilla was holding out for bigger game, a proposal of marriage from His Royal Highness.

Editors and authors at Doubleday, as well as half the world, were shocked when Nancy Tuckerman announced in February of 1964 that Jackie had developed cancer.

Up until the very end of her life, she was in negotiation with various authors about possible books. An example was John Loring, the design director at Tiffany's. With the cooperation and sanction of Tiffany's, he had already published six books with her. *The Tiffany Wedding*, the style manual he released for brides-to-be, with Jackie as editor, is still in use today throughout America.

"With her gone, I couldn't continue to work with another editor at Doubleday," he said. Many other authors working with her also took their manuscripts to other houses.

Shortly before her death, Jackie sent a number of memos to "my authors." It read: "I can beat this! All will be well!"

***

As an editor, Jackie was alert to the irony of her greatest publishing coup being the so-called memoirs of Michael Jackson. "Of all the wonderful books I edited, it was *Moonwalk* that the masses wanted to read, not, say, Jakob Walter's *Diary of a Napoleonic Foot Soldier* (1991)."

Jackie and Michael Jackson were an unlikely combination to form any sort of relationship, much less a friendship, but such strange occurrences happen in the world of celebrities.

One night at the Rainbow Grill, Jackson was introduced to Jackie, who would play an important role in his future. "All memories of his goddess, Diana Ross, were forgotten when he encountered Jackie O," said the gossipy Truman Capote to Lee Radziwill. "He developed a fixation on her. All he could talk about was her voice, which sounded a bit like Michael's own whispers. Her clothing. Her hair styling. Her manner. Her polite manners. Her sophistication. Until that meeting, I think Michael had wanted to transform himself into Miss

Diana. But after meeting Jackie, I think then and there that he raised the bar on his transgendered dreams. Instead of a black diva like Ross, he apparently decided that he wanted to transform himself into a white woman like Jackie. After all, she was the most famous and most admired woman in the world at the time. Who wouldn't want to walk, act, talk, and look like Jackie? Even *moi*. Michael truly believed the American Dream—in his case, that you could be born a poor black ghetto boy and grow up to become a rich white woman."

Michael's interest in Jackie was first piqued weeks before he actually met her. Bob Weiner, a reporter for the *New York Daily News*, invited Michael to his apartment for an interview and a home-cooked meal. While Weiner was in his kitchen preparing a chicken and rice dish, Michael amused himself by "grazing" through the wealth of books and photographs that were scattered across the apartment.

At one point, Weiner heard Michael let out a yelp. Rushing in from the kitchen, he spotted Michael staring at a celebrity nude calendar. One of the snapshots was of a nude Jackie. "I can't believe what I'm seeing!" Michael said. "Why would a woman like Mrs. Kennedy pose nude for the *paparazzi*?"

Weiner patiently explained that the picture had been taken on Skorpios with a hidden, long-range camera. Jackie had no idea that she was being photographed and that her privacy had been invaded.

Weiner later expressed surprise that he had "encountered an eighteen-year-old millionaire with his innocence intact."

After their first meeting, Michael virtually "stalked" Jackie, if the not-always-reliable Capote can be believed. "He showered her with invitations. If she had agreed, Michael would have taken her out every night. I don't know what she saw in this inexperienced black boy from somewhere in the Middle West, but Jackie told me that she was intrigued with Michael and his sheer audacity."

Jackie had never heard of **Michael Jackson** until her son, John Jr., told her about his growing fame.

During her awful experience convincing Michael to compose his memoirs, and supervising their contents, Jackie urged Michael to tell his story more candidly, and in more intimate detail, but her pleas went unheeded. Jackie complained frequently about the book's lack of depth, and about his lack of cooperation to Doubleday.

The editors there concluded that she didn't like him, and that she regarded him as some kind of freak.

She was aware that she'd become his new role model.

"As of yet, I have no opinion of Michael," Jackie told Capote. "I am just formulating one. I can't figure him out. It seems he's stalled on the bridge between boyhood and manhood. He also seems strangely asexual. I honestly believe that even though Michael is an adult, he hasn't completely figured out for himself yet if he wants to be gay or straight. I, naturally, have my own ideas about where he's going, which road he'll take. I think his future sex life—that is, if he has a future sex life—is going to be very difficult for him. Fraught with hazards."

If Jackie did say that, and Capote maintained to Lee that she did, it was a perceptive observation.

***

At his family's compound in Encino, California, Jackson was leaving for the afternoon. He was accompanied by an unknown blonde-haired boy of great beauty, a Tadzio, perhaps no more than twelve. Michael was going on a shopping expedition to buy the child as many toys as he wanted.

La Toya ran after him. She had an urgent message. "The First Lady of the World is on the phone, and she wants to speak to you," La Toya said.

"You mean, Nancy? I've already been to the White House, accepted that award."

"More famous than Nancy," La Toya said.

"That could be only one person," Michael replied.

Racing back into the house, he nervously picked up the receiver. In a whispery voice, he said, "Hi, this is Michael."

On the other end of the phone, an even more famous whispery voice greeted him. "Michael, you dear. It's been far too long. As they say in the Garment District, have I got a deal for you. This is Jackie Onassis!"

When Michael accepted the call from Jackie, she was working for Doubleday in New York and was at the time the most celebrated editor in publishing. Her boss had given her a budget of $300,000 to offer Michael for his memoirs, even though—in his mid-twenties—he was still a bit young to be penning an autobiography. One editor at Doubleday told Jackie, "If Michael agrees to this, we should call his memoirs *An Unfinished Life*."

After exchanging pleasantries about their few previous meetings, she got down to business and pitched the offer of a memoir.

"But my life has only begun," he protested.

"There's such a great interest in you—millions of fans around the world—that we at Doubleday wanted to hear your story as you saw your life. The early years. The struggles. The incredible success. What it's done to you."

"If memoirs are such a great idea, then why haven't you written one?" he asked provocatively.

"Doubleday has a standing offer with me of $5 million for my autobiography, but I have too many secrets. A memoir from me couldn't be honest, and therefore I'll never write one."

"I know you must have many secrets—not only your own but the intimate details of so many other famous lives. But what secrets do I have? I'm still a virgin. Never been kissed. At least not on the mouth."

"That's a unique story in itself," she said with a slight sense of mischief. "Imagine a man living for a quarter of a century and still a virgin. You and my late husband, Jack, had a lot in common."

"Now you're pulling my leg," he said. "I'm told that when you let your hair

662

down, you have a wicked sense of humor."

"If you only knew," she said. "One time at the White House, I was doing this really horrendous impersonation of Lady Bird Johnson. Guess what? In flies Lady Bird herself."

"I'm also told you like gossip."

"I don't deny that."

"Then I think you'd be very disappointed in any memoir I wrote," he said. "I have no gossip to share."

"Perhaps I would be disappointed," she admitted candidly. "But I don't really expect you to tell everything. But because you're the biggest star in the world, we at Doubleday want your story."

"I don't know . . ."

She'd later recall that he seemed so hesitant, yet wavering. "Let me fly to the Coast and pitch this idea to you in person. As you know from having met me, I'm very persuasive."

"That you are." He hesitated again, leading her to conclude that he was one of the least articulate men she'd ever encountered.

"I'm not going to debase myself in any book," he warned. "The tabloids already do that for me. Do you know a good libel lawyer?"

"I never sue for libel," she said. "Let the jackals write what they wish. Just tell your story from your heart. Just be Peter Pan. That's all you have to do."

"I'd like that!" He agreed to a meeting in Los Angeles.

"I'm packing my bags," she promised.

After putting down the phone, he was eager to tell family and friends of this remarkable offer he'd just had from Jackie. "I remember every word of the dialogue," he claimed.

Privately he confessed that he had little or no interest in writing a memoir. "As for that $300,000 advance, that's peanuts in the music business," he said. "We count in the millions." He confided to his family that if he agreed to do the memoir, he would have a chance to solidify his friendship with Jackie. "Imagine me, Michael Jackson, born in a bungalow in Gary, Indiana, and growing up one day to be friends with Jackie Kennedy Onassis. She gave me her private phone number in New York. Imagine that!"

Jackie, along with her assistant, Shaye Areheart, flew to Los Angeles in the autumn of 1983 to convince Michael to write his autobiography. Their initial meeting had been pre-arranged as a luncheon at Chasen's, a posh Los Angeles restaurant. Jackie and Areheart arrived on time and were kept busy as well-wishers came to their table. In a city known for famous movie stars, Jackie outdazzled all of them—all except Michael. Their meeting had been scheduled at one o'clock. By two-thirty, Michael still hadn't shown up, and Jackie and Areheart went ahead and ordered lunch.

Jackie Onassis, hailed as the world's most desirable woman, wasn't used to being stood up. Initially embarrassed, she decided to forgive Michael. "He's very shy," she told her colleagues. Privately she was enraged.

The woman who'd charmed Charles de Gaulle and Nikita Khrushchev didn't give up that easily. She called Michael the following morning, using her most seductive voice. At first, he seemed intimidated and didn't want to take her call. Finally, he relented. He came to the phone and pleaded for her to forgive him for his rudeness. "The idea of writing an actual book devoted to my personal life paralyzed me," he said. "I changed costumes three times that morning and was ready to go. Then at the last minute I got cold feet."

Before the end of their conversation, he invited her to tea that afternoon at Hayvenhurst. When a chicly dressed Jackie arrived at Encino, she found only two staff members. Michael had ordered the rest of the household to leave, including photographer Steve Howell, who wanted to capture the historic union of this famous pair on film. "He kicked us out. We didn't get to see her. All of us were horribly disappointed and mad at Michael for his insensitivity."

He was awed by Jackie, considering her the epitome of grace, style, and charm. Once he'd held Diana Ross in such awe, but seemingly had graduated from that, moving on to bigger game. "And what bigger game could there have been than Jackie Onassis?" Howell asked. "My God, she was the most famous person on Earth meeting the second most famous person on Earth."

"It was a lovefest," said a staff member who was allowed to remain behind to serve tea. "Jackie and Michael were practically cooing at each other. I couldn't tell where Jackie's whispery voice ended and Michael's whispery voice began."

As Jackie would later reveal, "I didn't end up interviewing Michael. He ended up interviewing me."

"How do you live with the dread that every time you walk out your door, fans or the paparazzi are waiting to take your picture?" he asked her.

"I consider the alternative," she said. "Life as a recluse. A Georgetown widow peering out through the draperies at throngs gathered on the street in front of my house. That wasn't an option for me, so I moved to New York. Of course, I can't take the rush of people at times. Perhaps that's why I married Ari. He could almost guarantee my privacy when he wasn't invading it himself."

"How do you handle being a celebrity?" he asked.

"I don't know anything else," she said. "It comes easy for me. I couldn't imagine being unknown. Almost from the beginning of my life, I was on stage or being exhibited somewhere. Of course, not the kind of notoriety that came later. Actually, I've often pondered your question myself. Maybe I would miss the fame. At first anonymity sounds wonderful, at least the freedom it would give you. Imagine going shopping on Fifth Avenue without the gawkers and the paparazzi. I've asked a few movie stars what it was like to have known world adulation, then neglect. Gloria Swanson once told me, 'It's like the parade has passed me by.' She said she missed the adoring fans and the hysteria they once generated for her."

At the end of the afternoon, Michael still hadn't agreed to write his memoirs. Instead, he proposed *The Michael Jackson Scrapbook*. "You know, a picture of my boa constrictor, Muscles. My first report card. The first song the Jackson 5 ever recorded. Stuff like that."

"I once compiled a book devoted to memorabilia of an early trip to Europe with Lee," she said, referring to Lee Radziwill, and obviously turned off by the idea of a Jackson scrapbook.

The next day, Michael invited Jackie on a tour of Disneyland, with him as her personal guide. "He knew all the hidden corners, the names of all the animals, the thrill of every attraction," she said. "I found it boring, but he was mesmerized. I think he has the heart of an eight-year-old."

After that day at Disneyland, Jackie seemed fascinated by the topic of Michael's sexual orientation. For such a worldly woman, this was out of character. Among others, she discussed it with J.C. Suares, who would become the book designer for *Moonwalk*. According to Suares, "She repeatedly asked me if I thought Michael liked girls."

She even discussed it with Peter Lawford, thinking that as a Hollywood insider he might know something. "I have never known Jackie to be so intrigued with someone's sexual orientation," Lawford later said. "She was one of the most sophisticated women in the world. Both she and Lee included many homosexuals, especially those in the arts, among their best friends. Truman Capote, Rudolf Nureyev. Jackie even had a distant kinship with gay author Gore Vidal."

She confided to Lawford, who was to die the following year, that, "When I first met Michael in New York in the late 70s, I just assumed he was gay, but hadn't admitted that to himself yet. After seeing him so many years later on his home turf in Encino, I think he's figured out he's gay. But his gayness, I suspect, has a strange twist to it."

"What do you mean exactly?" Lawford asked her.

"I mean, it's not gay like two handsome men who look like Paul Newman and Rock Hudson getting together. I have great intuition about these matters. Michael is gay, but his gayness is different. There's something fishy going on here. Something he's hiding from the world, something that will never be revealed in *Moonwalk*. The book will hardly be a candid confession, but a glossy, glitzy thing. Michael's mythology of himself. But in spite of what I've said, I predict it'll be a bestseller."

The staff at Doubleday was eager to hear Jackie's impressions of Michael even before she eventually landed the deal to publish a memoir, not a scrapbook.

"He seems to have no perspective on his life" she claimed. "That's understandable. He's only twenty-five. Of course, I've met men his age who ruled kingdoms. I think he's more interested in projecting an image of himself than he is in telling any truth. Maybe his truth would completely destroy his image."

It took Michael two weeks to make up his mind to accept Jackie's offer. "Of course, I'll need a ghostwriter," he told her.

"I can arrange that," she promised. She confessed that she'd been less successful in pursuing other celebrities. "I even went to your rival, *[the artist formerly known as]* Prince, and tried to get him to write a memoir. He turned me down. There have been other rejections. Katharine Hepburn, Bette Davis,

Greta Garbo, Ted Turner, Brigitte Bardot, Barbra Streisand, Barbara Walters, Rudolf Nureyev."

"I've heard of some of these people, but some of those celebs are too obscure," he said. "Their biographies won't sell."

She concealed her astonishment.

Later, she amused friends with her description of Hayvenhurst. "It's La La Land," she claimed, "with a damn chimpanzee running amuck. Jack would have hated it, and Ari would have called in moving vans to cart off every tasteless stick. I haven't seen such *kitsch* since I saw photographs of Mrs. Khrushchev's home. Animals in cages. Tacky awards and trophies. Jackson family pictures. Furniture that only a demented queen could have purchased. It wasn't even *nouveau riche*, not even 'Jewish Renaissance,' but artifacts from the Land of Oz. Let me put it this way: Michael decorates like he selects his wardrobe."

In the months ahead, Jackie, from her publishing base in New York City, listened to Michael's endless demands and insecurities about the project. She

Celebrities Who Escaped

Throughout the many chapters of her life, Jackie rigorously objected to the authorization of her memoirs for publication.

Ironically, however, her editorial duties included persuading other celebrities to publish their frank and candid biographies through Doubleday. With the exception of Michael Jackson, who didn't really reveal much, most of them, including all the persons noted below, resisted her formidable persuasive powers.

Rudolf Nureyev, Brigitte Bardot, Camilla Parker-Bowles, Bette Davis, Elizabeth Taylor

Greta Garbo, Princess Diana, Barbra Streisand, Barbara Walters

also read one disappointing chapter after another. Finally, in despair, she told her staff, "Dealing with the mercurial Mr. Jackson is like being in a train wreck—worse, an airplane crash."

***

As Michael Jackson's editor, Jackie was disappointed in the editorial content of *Moonwalk*. But she was eventually delighted that it sold half a million copies in 14 countries.

She had urged Michael to include many incidents he'd related to her, including the disastrous filming of *The Wiz* with Diana Ross.

She wanted to capture some of the dynamic tension that had existed between Michael and Ross in his bio, but he said, "I don't want to hurt her feelings. It's always difficult when a new star rises to replace an old star—take Betty Grable getting replaced by Marilyn Monroe."

Jackie was frankly bored with the details of Michael's life, even though she'd commissioned his so-called autobiography.

She spent much of her time with him seeking juicy details about Elizabeth Taylor. Her interest in Taylor began at the time of her affair with Richard Burton. The Taylor/Burton scandal during JFK's administration competed with the public's hunger for news about Nikita Khrushchev and the Cuban missile crisis.

Michael did share some gossipy tidbits with Jackie. "Elizabeth complains to me about her stumpy legs and double chin," he said. "She considers you one of the three most beautiful women in America, right up there with Ava Gardner and Lena Horne. Elizabeth told me that you are exquisite, your dignity enhancing your beauty."

"She also told me that she and Burton consoled Maria Callas when Onassis tossed her under the bus to marry you."

In her role as the book's editor, the usually articulate Jackie penned the forward to *Moonwalk*. It was one of her less than elegant public statements:

"What can one say about Michael Jackson? To many people, Michael Jackson seems an elusive personality, but to those who work with him he is not. This talented artist is a sensitive man, warm, funny, and full of insight. Michael's book, *Moonwalk,* provides a startling glimpse of the artist at work and the artist in reflection."

She later told members of her staff at Doubleday, "I didn't believe a word I wrote."

***

By the 1980s and beyond, "Jackie O" was no more. If the press had any nickname at all for her, it was "Granny O."

She was often spotted strolling in Manhattan's Central Park with her grandkids.

She had become the dowager First Lady, the last Queen of America. No one had been crowned since she left the throne.

Had she lived into her eighties, she would have become America's sensational *grande dame*, its "Queen Mum," but with a lot more style and a little less gin and tonic than Queen Elizabeth's mother.

After roaming the world, Jackie had made Manhattan her permanent home, her image as a New Yorker as iconic as that of Woody Allen or Brooke Astor.

In her lifetime, she'd gone from "Saint Jackie" to "the Scarlet Woman" and back again to a more pristine image, known as a loving mother and a hardworking editor of books.

Reggie Nadelson, writing in *The Independent,* claimed, "In the end, she liberated herself from the Kennedys and became the last real Kennedy—glamorous, desirable, mythic."

Surprisingly, in a more liberated age, virtually no one criticized Jackie for taking a married man as her lover.

He was Maurice Tempelsman, one of the world's leading diamond merchants.

She had met him in the 1950s. During her reign over Camelot, he and his wife, Lily Bucholz, had been heavy contributors to the Democratic Party, and frequent visitors to the White House.

Born in 1929, the same year as Jackie, Maurice was a Belgian-American entrepreneur known for his diamond trading in American business circles, in Russia, and throughout Africa.

He came into the world as the son of a Yiddish-speaking Orthodox Jewish family in Antwerp, Belgium. The young man and his family fled from Belgium in 1940 after the Nazi takeover, emigrating to the United States. At the age of sixteen, Maurice was working with his diamond broker father.

During his marriage to Lily, he had three children.

His lawyer, former presidential candidate Adlai Stevenson, had helped him form relationships with the powerful Oppenheimer diamond mining family and also with various heads of African states. He was also one of a select few who were allowed to purchase diamonds directly from the famous DeBeers diamond cartel.

He played a key role in the diamond industries of such countries as Gabon, Angola, Botswana, Namibia, and Sierra Leone.

His first date with Jackie was on August 20, 1975, the year Onassis died. Lily had refused to grant him a divorce. He escorted Jackie to the Broadway musical, *Chicago,* and later, they were seen dining at the chic *La Côte Basque.*

As New York society noted, Maurice was as unprepossessing as Jackie was captivating. He was balding, pudgy, urbane, and a diamond tycoon worth some $300 million. As such, he was called "the poor man's Aristotle Onassis."

In the beginning, he was not seen as a beau because of his unattractive appearance. He was viewed as her financial adviser, which he was. He did take the $20 million she'd acquired in the aftermath of the death of Onassis, based on the settlement worked out with Christina and her lawyers, and over a period of time, expanded it into $200 million, a tenfold increase.

After a life of triumph and tragedy, she wanted understanding, emotional support, stability, and serenity, and apparently, she found all of those qualities in Maurice.

As Gabrielle Rotello wrote in *Newsday:* "The odd couple were unsanctified by religion, unnotarized by the law, and the press and public hardly knew what to call him. Adviser? Friend? Escort? Or what to call them. Companions? Partners?"

As *People* magazine so blatantly and accurately maintained, Maurice was Jackie's last love. What he didn't have in looks, he made up for in financial savvy.

"After having me, Jack and Bobby Kennedy, Peter Lawford, William Holden, Gianni Agnelli, and even that thing, Marlon Brando, Jackie is settling for this?"

In the statement above, Frank Sinatra was talking about Jackie' final romantic involvement, this time with a married man, Maurice.

She said, "I truly hope my notoriety doesn't force him out of my life." It didn't. This Orthodox Jew was with her to the end, tending to her needs on her final day.

Sinatra finally declared that he understood the relationship. "I just heard that Tempelsman has turned Jackie's $20 million into $200 million."

By 1982, he'd moved into her Fifth Avenue apartment, conversing with her in French and presiding over her dinner parties that usually consisted of twelve guests, everybody from Candice Bergen to Henry Kissinger. Maurice would jump to his feet, rushing to the kitchen to supervise the making of French sauces.

Back at table, he could converse on a wide range of subjects—art, politics, the theater, and music.

A friend, Yvonne Clerque, who traveled with Jackie and Maurice to Provence, in France, claimed, "She was radiant in his presence. They were truly affectionate with each other, truly in love."

But inevitably, such peace was not meant to last.

***

In January of 1994, Jackie had been suffering from swollen lymph nodes. She was referred to Dr. Carolyn Agresti at the New York Hospital-Cornell Medical Center. There, she underwent a CAT scan and biopsies. The results confirmed that she had non-Hodgkin's lymphoma, a form of cancer.

"I can't believe it," she said. "I've always taken such good care of myself." She seemed to have overlooked that she'd been chain-smoking throughout most of her adult life.

During the weeks ahead, as she began chemotherapy, her face lost its once radiant glow. When brushing her hair one morning, "large, frightening clumps fell out." The first time that happened, she screamed.

"Each day I seem to grow weaker," she told Nancy Tuckerman.

When she next visited the Cornell Medical Center, cancer specialist Dr. Anne Moore delivered what amounted to a death blow.

"Your most recent MRI shows that the cancer has spread to the membranes that cover your brain and your spinal cord. In other words, the cancer has metastasized."

"I can't believe this is happening," Jackie said. "Not to me."

In the April days that followed, she often could not get out of bed. She began to experience splitting migraine headaches, stabbing back pain, and a weakening of her muscles.

In the way she'd planned JFK's funeral, she began to orchestrate her own. She told John Jr., "I want my death to be nothing less than a small masterpiece."

During her final visit to Cornell, she was delivered a final piece of devastating news: "I am so sorry, Mrs. Onassis, but your cancer has spread to your liver," Dr. Moore said.

At her side, Caroline cried out, "Oh, my God, no!" Then she burst into uncontrollable sobbing.

For the last time, Jackie left the hospital. She had signed a living will, expressing her desire not to be hooked up to a life support machine. As she returned to her apartment, she realized that she'd entered her tomb. But nonetheless, she wanted to die at home.

She took her last walk through Central Park on Sunday, May 15, 1994, on the arm of Maurice. Wearing a brown wig and a large scarf, she held on tightly. She looked at the winding paths, the mowed grass, and the trees that she'd known since she was a toddler, trying to implant their images on her fading mind.

Only three days before she'd called Teddy. "I don't think I can take it anymore," she told him. "The pain is unbearable."

In the remaining hours of her life, John Jr. read her two poems by Colette and kissed her goodbye for a final time.

Teddy flew to New York to be at her deathbed. He spent thirty minutes alone with her in her bedroom with the door shut. He never discussed those final minutes with her.

At 10:15PM on May 19, 1994, Jackie's heart stopped beating in the presence of John Jr., Maurice, and Caroline.

That following morning, John appeared outside her apartment building to address the assembled crowd of reporters, photographers, tourists, and onlookers. "My mother died surrounded by her friends and her family and her books," he said. "And the people and the things that she loved. She did it in her own way and on her own terms, and we felt lucky for that. Now she's in God's hands."

She was just two and a half months shy of her 65th birthday.

***

On May 23, as the world watched, her funeral was conducted at the Saint Ignatius Loyola Church, at 53 East 83rd Street in Manhattan, the same church where she'd been baptized in 1929 and later confirmed as a teenager.

At the service, Maurice rose to read lines written by the Greek poet, Constantine Cavafy.

[Cavafy's poem, "Ithika," replicated in the pages that follow and reminiscent of her deep exposure to Greece through her marriage to Onassis, had always been one of her favorites.

The very cosmopolitan Cavafy (1863-1933) was born in Alexandria of a family that emigrated, based on the civil unrest and bloodshed of their times, between Egypt, the U.K., and Turkey. A modernist who excelled at ancient references interspersed with nihilism and a frequent references to homoerotica, he is considered the most important Greek poet of the 20th century. Some of the archives associated with his life and work are supported by the Onassis Foundation.]

> "And now the journey is over,
> Too short, alas, too short.
> It was filled with adventure and wisdom,
> Laughter and love
> Gallantry and grace,
> So farewell, farewell."

After kissing Lady Bird Johnson and Hillary Clinton on the cheeks, Teddy Kennedy delivered the eulogy:

"No one else looked like her, spoke like her, wrote like her, or was so original in the way she did things. No one we knew ever had a better sense of self. During those four endless days in 1963, she held us together as a family and as a country. In large part because of her, we could grieve and then go on. She lifted us up, and in the doubt and darkness, she gave her fellow citizens back their pride as Americans. She was then thirty-four years old. Jackie was too young to be a widow in 1963, and too young to be a widow now."

***

Back in her apartment, John opened a letter that she'd asked him not to read until after her burial.

"My dear, beloved son,
You are going to take your place in history. I want to be looking down on you as you assume a future position of power, like your father. He attempted to make the world a better place. Bobby was going to carry on in his footsteps. Now the bur-

671

den will be on you.

In my heart, I know you will succeed beyond your greatest dreams. It is with eternal love and pride in you that I send you on your way, which I know will be the road to glory.

When your battles are over, and the burden passes from you, I know one thing that is good and true. you will be the greatest Kennedy of them all.

Your mother, Jacqueline."

Author Norman Mailer, who had been both her friend and foe, delivered his assessment:

"Jackie Kennedy Onassis was not merely a celebrity, but a legend; not a legend, but a myth—no, more than a myth: She is now a historic archetype, virtually a demiurge."

Tributes

"Her presence was evident in the warmth of every room and the charm of every hall [of the White House]. Clearly, her beautification efforts will be one of her enduring legacies."

—Ronald Reagan

"She was very kind to me when my husband was shot and when we didn't know whether he was going to live or not…She wrote me a very sweet, sensitive note and called me…she couldn't have been nice to me at that time when I really needed it."

—Nancy Reagan

"She showed us how one could approach tragedy with courage."

—Jimmy Carter

"Jimmy and I were touched by the delightful and gracious atmosphere that Jacqueline Kennedy Onassis created in the White House. The charm of each room has been permanently enhanced as a result of her contributions."

—Rosalynn Carter

"Jacqueline Kennedy Onassis was a model of courage and dignity for all Americans and all the world. Even in the face of impossible tragedy, she carried the grief of her family and our entire nation with a calm power that somehow reas-

sured all of us who mourned. More than any other woman of her time, she cap-
tivated our nation and the world with her intelligence, elegance, and grace."
—Bill Clinton

I"f she taught us anything, it was to know the meaning of responsibility—to
one's family and to one's community. Her great gift of grace and style and dig-
nity and heroism is an example that will live through the ages."
—Hillary Clinton

"It leaves an empty place in the world as I have known it. We shared a unique
time and I always thought of her as my friend."
—Lady Bird Johnson

"Jackie Onassis brought great dignity and grace to the White House and was
indeed a charming and wonderful First lady."
—George W. Bush

ITHIKA

by Constantine Cavafy

When you set sail for Ithaca,
wish for the road to be long,
full of adventures, full of knowledge.
The Lestrygonians and the Cyclopes,
an angry Poseidon—do not fear.
You will never find such on your path,
if your thoughts remain lofty, and your spirit
and body are touched by a fine emotion.
The Lestrygonians and the Cyclopes,
a savage Poseidon you will not encounter,
if you do not carry them within your spirit,
if your spirit does not place them before you.
Wish for the road to be long.
Many the summer mornings to be when
with what pleasure, what joy
you will enter ports seen for the first time.
Stop at Phoenician markets,
and purchase the fine goods,
nacre and coral, amber and ebony,
and exquisite perfumes of all sorts,
the most delicate fragrances you can find.
To many Egyptian cities you must go,
to learn and learn from the cultivated.
Always keep Ithaca in your mind.
To arrive there is your final destination.
But do not hurry the voyage at all.
It is better for it to last many years,
and when old to rest in the island,
rich with all you have gained on the way,
not expecting Ithaca to offer you wealth.
Ithaca has given you the beautiful journey.
Without her you would not have set out on the road.
Nothing more does she have to give you.
And if you find her poor, Ithaca has not deceived you.
Wise as you have become, with so much experience,
you must already have understood what Ithacas mean.

With admiration, affection, and respect
Rest in Peace

Jacqueline Bouvier Kennedy Onassis
1929-1994

ITS AUTHORS

DARWIN PORTER

As an intense and precocious nine-year-old, **Darwin Porter** began meeting movie stars, TV personalities, politicians, and singers through his vivacious and attractive mother, Hazel, a somewhat eccentric Southern girl who had lost her husband in World War II. Migrating from the depression-ravaged valleys of western North Carolina to Miami Beach during its most ebullient heyday, Hazel became a stylist, wardrobe mistress, and personal assistant to the vaudeville comedienne Sophie Tucker, the bawdy and irrepressible "Last of the Red Hot Mamas."

Virtually every show-biz celebrity who visited Miami Beach paid a call on "Miss Sophie," and Darwin as a pre-teen loosely and indulgently supervised by his mother, was regularly dazzled by the likes of Judy Garland, Dinah Shore, Veronica Lake, Linda Darnell, Martha Raye, and Ronald Reagan, who arrived to pay his respects to Miss Sophie with a young blonde starlet on the rise—Marilyn Monroe.

Hazel's work for Sophie Tucker did not preclude an active dating life: Her *beaux* included Richard Widmark, Victor Mature, Frank Sinatra (who "tipped" teenaged Darwin the then-astronomical sum of ten dollars for getting out of the way), and that alltime "second lead," Wendell Corey, when he wasn't emoting with Barbara Stanwyck and Joan Crawford.

As a late teenager, Darwin edited *The Miami Hurricane* at the University of Miami, where he interviewed Eleanor Roosevelt, Tab Hunter, Lucille Ball, and Adlai Stevenson. He also worked for Florida's then-Senator George Smathers, one of John F. Kennedy's best friends, establishing an ongoing pattern of picking up "Jack and Jackie" lore while still a student.

After graduation, as a journalist, he was commissioned with the opening of a bureau of *The Miami Herald* in Key West (Florida), where he took frequent morning walks with retired U.S. president Harry S Truman during his vacations in what had functioned as his "Winter White House." He also got to know, sometimes very well, various celebrities "slumming" their way through off-the-record holidays in the orbit of then-resident Tennessee Williams. Celebrities hanging out in the permissive arts environment of Key West during those days included Tallulah Bankhead, Cary Grant, Tony Curtis, the stepfather of Richard Burton, a gaggle of show-biz and publishing moguls, and the once-notorious stripper, Bettie Page.

For about a decade in New York, Darwin worked in television journalism and advertising with his long-time partner, the journalist, art director, and distinguished arts-industry socialite Stanley Mills Haggart. Jointly, they produced TV commercials starring such high-powered stars as Joan Crawford (then feverishly promoting Pepsi-Cola), Ronald Reagan (General Electric), and Debbie Reynolds (selling Singer Sewing Machines), along with such other entertainers as Louis Armstrong, Lena Horne, Arlene Dahl, and countless other show-biz personalities hawking commercial products.

During his youth, Stanley had flourished as an insider in early Hollywood as a "leg man" and source of information for Hedda Hopper, the fabled gossip columnist. When Stanley wasn't dishing newsy revelations with Hedda, he had worked as a Powers model; a romantic lead opposite Silent-era film star Mae Murray; the intimate companion of superstar Randolph Scott before Scott became emotionally involved with Cary Grant; and a man-about-town who archived gossip from everybody who mattered back when the movie colony was small, accessible, and confident that details about their tribal rites would absolutely never be reported in the press. Over the years, Stanley's vast cornucopia of inside Hollywood information was passed on to Darwin, who amplified it with copious interviews and research of his own.

After Stanley's death in 1980, Darwin inherited a treasure trove of memoirs, notes, and interviews detailing Stanley's early adventures in Hollywood, including in-depth recitations of scandals that even Hopper during her heyday was afraid to publish. Most legal and journalistic standards back then interpreted those oral histories as "unprintable." Times, of course, changed.

Beginning in the early 1960s, Darwin joined forces with the then-fledgling Arthur Frommer organization, playing a key role in researching and writing more than 50 titles and defining the style and values that later emerged as the world's leading travel accessories, *The Frommer Guides,* with particular emphasis on Europe, California, New England, and the Caribbean. Between the creation and updating of hundreds of editions of detailed travel guides to England, France, Italy, Spain, Portugal, Austria, Germany, California, and Switzerland, he continued to interview and discuss the triumphs, feuds, and frustrations of celebrities, many by then reclusive, whom he either sought out or encountered randomly as part of his extensive travels. Ava Gardner and Lana Turner were particularly insightful.

One day when Darwin lived in Tangier, he walked into an opium den to discover Marlene Dietrich sitting alone in a corner.

Darwin has also ghost written books for celebrities (who shall go nameless!) as well as a series of novels. His first, *Butterflies in Heat,* became a cult classic and was adapted into a film, *Tropic of Desire,* starring Eartha Kitt, among others. Other books included *Razzle-Dazzle,* about an errant female movie star of questionable morals; and an erotic thriller, *Blood Moon,* hailed as "pure novelistic Viagra, an American interpretation of Arthur Schnitzler's *La Ronde."*

Darwin's novel, *Marika,* published by Arbor House, evoked Marlene Dietrich for many readers.

His controversial novel, *Venus,* was suggested by the life of the fabled eroticist and diarist, Anaïs Nin. His novel, *Midnight in Savannah,* was a brutal saga of corruption, greed, and sexual tension exploring the eccentricities of Georgia's most notorious city.

His novel, *Rhinestone Country,* catalyzed a guessing game. Which male star was the inspiration for its lovable rogue, Pete Riddle? Mississippi Pearl praised it as "like a scalding gulp of rotgut whiskey on a snowy night in a bowjacks honky-tonk."

Darwin also transformed into literary format the details which he and Stanley Haggart had compiled about the relatively underpublicized scandals of the Silent Screen, releasing them in 2001 as *Hollywood's Silent Closet,* "an uncensored, underground history of Pre-Code Hollywood, loaded with facts and rumors from generations past."

Since then, Darwin has penned more than eighteen uncensored Hollywood biographies, many of them award-winners, on subjects who have included Marlon Brando; Merv Griffin; Katharine Hepburn; Howard Hughes; Humphrey Bogart; Michael Jackson; Paul Newman; Steve McQueen; Marilyn Monroe; Elizabeth Taylor; Frank Sinatra; John F. Kennedy; Vivien Leigh; Laurence Olivier; the well known porn star, Linda Lovelace; all three of the fabulous Gabor sisters, plus Tennessee Williams, Gore Vidal, and Truman Capote.

As a departure from his usual repertoire, Darwin also wrote the controversial *J. Edgar Hoover & Clyde Tolson: Investigating the Sexual Secrets of America's Most Famous Men and Women,* a book about celebrity, voyeurism, political and sexual repression, and blackmail within the highest circles of the U.S. government.

He has also co-authored, in league with Danforth Prince, four *Hollywood Babylon* anthologies, plus four separate volumes of film critiques, reviews, and commentary.

His biographies, over the years, have won more than 30 First Prize or runner-up awards at literary festivals in cities which include Boston, New York, Los Angeles, Hollywood, San Francisco, and Paris.

Darwin can be heard at regular intervals as a radio commentator (and occasionally on television), "dishing" celebrities, pop culture, politics, and scandal.

A resident of New York City, Darwin is currently at work on his latest biography: *Love Triangle—Ronald Reagan, Jane Wyman, & Nancy Davis.*

DANFORTH PRINCE

The publisher and co-author of *Pink Triangle*, **Danforth Prince** is one of the "Young Turks" of the post-millennium publishing industry. He's president and founder of Blood Moon Productions, a firm devoted to researching, salvaging, compiling, and marketing the oral histories of America's entertainment industry.

One of Prince's famous predecessors, the late Lyle Stuart (self-described as "the last publisher in America with guts") once defined Prince as "one of my natural successors." In 1956, that then-novice maverick launched himself with $8,000 he'd won in a libel judgment against gossip columnist Walter Winchell. It was Stuart who published Linda Lovelace's two authentic memoirs—*Ordeal* and *Out of Bondage.*

"I like to see someone following in my footsteps in the 21st Century," Stuart told Prince. "You publish scandalous biographies. I did, too. My books on J. Edgar Hoover, Jacqueline Kennedy Onassis, and Barbara Hutton stirred up the natives. You do, too."

Prince launched his career in journalism in the 1970s at the Paris Bureau of *The New York Times.* In the early '80s, he resigned to join Darwin Porter in researching, developing and publishing various titles within *The Frommer Guides*, jointly reviewing the travel scenes of more than 50 nations for Simon & Schuster. Authoritative and comprehensive, they were perceived as best-selling "travel bibles" for millions of readers, with recommendations and travel advice about the major nations of Western Europe, the Caribbean, Bermuda, The Bahamas, Georgia and the Carolinas, and California.

Prince, along with Porter, is also the co-author of several award-winning celebrity biographies, each configured as a title within Blood Moon's Babylon series. These have included *Hollywood Babylon—It's Back!; Hollywood Babylon Strikes Again; The Kennedys: All the Gossip Unfit to Print;* and *Frank Sinatra, The Boudoir Singer.*

Prince, with Porter, has co-authored four books on film criticism, along iwth such provocative biographies as *Elizabeth Taylor: There is Nothing Like a Dame.* He and Porter also co-authored *Pink Triangle: The Feuds and Private Lives of Tennessee Williams, Gore Vidal, Truman Capote, and Members of their Entourages.*

Prince, a graduate of Hamilton College and a native of Easton and Bethlehem, Pennsylvania, is the president and founder (in 1996) of the Georgia Literary Association, and of the Porter and Prince Corporation, founded in 1983, which has produced dozens of titles for both Prentice Hall and John Wiley & Sons. In 2011, he was named "Publisher of the Year" by a consortium of literary critics and marketers spearheaded by the J.M. Northern Media Group.

According to Prince, "Blood Moon provides the luxurious illusion that a reader is a perpetual guest at some gossippy dinner party populated with brilliant but occasionally self-delusional figures from bygone eras of The American Experience. Blood Moon's success at salvaging, documenting, and articulating the (till now) orally transmitted histories of the Entertainment Industry, in ways that have never been seen before, is one of the most distinctive aspects of our backlist."

Publishing in collaboration with the National Book Network (www.NBN-Books.com), he has electronically documented some of the controversies associated with his stewardship of Blood Moon in more than 50 videotaped documentaries, book trailers, public speeches, and TV or radio interviews. Any of these can be watched, without charge, by performing a search for "Danforth Prince" on **YouTube.com**, checking him out on **Facebook** (either "Danforth Prince" or "Blood Moon Productions"), on **Twitter** (#BloodyandLunar) or by clicking on **BloodMoonProductions.com**.

During the rare moments when he isn't writing, editing, neurosing about, or promoting Blood Moon, he works out at a New York City gym, rescues stray animals, talks to strangers, and regularly attends Episcopal Mass every Sunday.

INDEX

684

685

689

697

700

BLOOD MOON PRODUCTIONS
Entertainment About How America Interprets Its Celebrities

Blood Moon Productions is a feisty and independent New York based publishing enterprise dedicated to researching, salvaging, and indexing the oral histories of America's entertainment industry. As described by *The Huffington Post*, "Blood Moon, in case you don't know, is a small publishing house on Staten Island that cranks out Hollywood gossip books, about two or three a year, usually of five-, six-, or 700-page length, chocked with stories and pictures about people who used to consume the imaginations of the American public, back when we actually had a public imagination. That is, when people were really interested in each other, rather than in Apple 'devices.' In other words, back when we had vices, not devices."

Reorganized with its present name in 2004, Blood Moon originated in 1997 as the Georgia Literary Association, a vehicle for the promotion of obscure writers from America's Deep South. For several decades, Blood Moon and its key players (Darwin Porter and Danforth Prince) spearheaded the research, writing, and editorial functions of dozens of titles, and hundreds of editions, of THE FROMMER GUIDES, the most respected name in travel publishing.

Blood Moon maintains a back list of at least 30 critically acclaimed biographies, film guides, and novels. Its titles are distributed by the National Book Network (www.NBNBooks.com), and through secondary wholesalers and online retailers everywhere.

Since 2004, Blood Moon has been awarded dozens of nationally recognized literary prizes. They've included both silver and bronze medals from the IPPY (Independent Publishers Association) Awards; four nominations and two Honorable Mentions for BOOK OF THE YEAR from Foreword Reviews; nominations from The Ben Franklin Awards; and Awards and Honorable Mentions from the New England, the Los Angeles, the Paris, the Hollywood, the New York, and the San Francisco Book Festivals. Two of its titles have been Grand Prize Winners for Best Summer Reading, as defined by The Beach Book Awards, and in 2013, its triple-play overview of the Gabor sisters was designated as Biography of the Year by the Hollywood Book Festival.

For more about us, including access to a growing number of videotaped book trailers, TV and radio interviews, and public addresses, each accessible via **YouTube.com,** search for key words "Danforth Prince" or "Blood Moon Productions."

Or click on **WWW.BLOODMOONPRODUCTIONS.COM;** visit our page on Facebook; subscribe to us on Twitter (#BloodyandLunar); or refer to the pages which immediately follow.

Thanks for your interest, best wishes, and happy reading. Literacy matters! Read a book!

Danforth Prince, President
Blood Moon Productions, Ltd.

PINK TRIANGLE

The Feuds and Private Lives of Tennessee Williams, Gore Vidal, Truman Capote, and Famous Members of their Entourages

Darwin Porter & Danforth Prince

Softcover, 700 pages, with photos   ISBN 978-1-936003-37-2

Also available for e-readers

The *enfants terribles* of America at mid-20th century challenged the sexual censors of their day while indulging in "bitchfests" for love, glory, and boyfriends.

This book exposes their literary slugfests and offers an intimate look at their relationships with the *glitterati*—MM, Brando, the Oliviers, the Paleys, U.S. Presidents, a gaggle of other movie stars, millionaires, and dozens of others.

This is for anyone who's interested in the formerly concealed scandals of Hollywood and Broadway, and the values and pretentions of both the literary world and the entertainment industry.

***

"A banquet... If *PINK TRIANGLE* had not been written for us, we would have had to research and type it all up for ourselves...Pink Triangle is nearly seven hundred pages of the most entertaining histrionics ever sliced, spiced, heated, and serviced up to the reading public. Everything that Blood Moon has done before pales in comparison.

"Given the fact that the subjects of the book themselves were nearly delusional on the subject of themselves (to say nothing of each other) it is hard to find fault. Add to this the intertwined jungle that was the relationship among Williams, Capote, and Vidal, of the times they vied for things they loved most—especially attention—and the times they enthralled each other and the world, [*Pink Triangle* is] the perfect antidote to the Polar Vortex."

—Vinton McCabe in the NY JOURNAL OF BOOKS

"Blood Moon prides itself on mixing tabloid journalism, going to the source of gossip itself—okay, hearsay, or the quickly deteriorating minds of aging witnesses—with genuine moments of hard-work research (and there always is some of that in Blood Moon Productions' books) to come up with their titles.

"Full disclosure: I have been a friend and follower of Blood Moon Productions' tomes for years, and always marveled at the amount of information in their books—it's staggering. The index alone to *Pink Triangle* runs to 21 pages—and the scale of names in it runs like a *Who's Who* of American social, cultural and political life through much of the 20th century...The only remedy is for you to run out this February, in time for Valentine's Day, and buy *Pink Triangle*."

—Perry Brass in THE HUFFINGTON POST

"We Brits are not spared the Porter/Prince silken lash either. PINK TRIANGLE's research is, quite frankly, breathtaking. PINK TRIANGLE will fascinate you for many weeks to come. Once you have made the initial titillating dip, the day will seem dull without it."

—Jeffery Tayor in THE SUNDAY EXPRESS (UK)

ABOUT THE AUTHORS: Darwin Porter, himself an unrepentant *enfant terrible*, moved through the entourages of this Pink Triangle with impunity for several decades of their heyday. Early in 2014, he wrote a book about it.

"Every literate person in America has strong ideas about The Pink Triangle. This *exposé* of its members' feuds, vanities, and idiosyncracies will be required reading if you're interested in the literary climate of 'The American Century.'"   **—Danforth Prince**

THOSE GLAMOROUS GABORS
Bombshells from Budapest
Darwin Porter

Zsa Zsa, Eva, and Magda Gabor transferred their glittery dreams and gold-digging ambitions from the twilight of the Austro-Hungarian Empire to Hollywood. There, more effectively than any army, these Bombshells from Budapest broke hearts, amassed fortunes, lovers, and A-list husbands, and amused millions of *voyeurs* through the medium of television, movies, and the social registers. In this astonishing "triple-play" biography, designated "Best Biography of the Year" by the Hollywood Book Festival, Blood Moon lifts the "mink-and-diamond" curtain on this amazing trio of blood-related sisters, whose complicated intrigues have never been fully explored before.

From *the New York Review of Books*: "You will never be Ga-bored...this book gives new meaning to the term compelling.

"Be warned, *Those Glamorous Gabors* is both an epic and a pip. Not since *Gone with the Wind* have so many characters on the printed page been forced to run for their lives for one reason or another. And Scarlett making a dress out of the curtains is nothing compared to what a Gabor will do when she needs to scrap together an outfit for a movie premiere or late-night outing.

"For those not up to speed, Jolie Tilleman came from a family of jewelers and therefore came by her love for the shiny stones honestly, perhaps genetically. She married Vilmos Gabor somewhere around World War 1 (exact dates, especially birth dates, are always somewhat vague in order to establish plausible deniability later on) and they were soon blessed with three daughters: **Magda**, the oldest, whose hair, sadly, was naturally brown, although it would turn quite red in America; **Zsa Zsa** (born 'Sari') a natural blond who at a very young age exhibited the desire for fame with none of the talents usually associated with achievement, excepting beauty and a natural wit; and **Eva**, the youngest and blondest of the girls, who after seeing Grace Moore perform at the National Theater, decided that she wanted to be an actress and that she would one day move to Hollywood to become a star.

"Given that the Gabor family at that time lived in Budapest, Hungary, at the period of time between the World Wars, that Hollywood dream seemed a distant one indeed. The story—the riches to rags to riches to rags to riches again myth of survival against all odds as the four women, because of their Jewish heritage, flee Europe with only the minks on their backs and what jewels they could smuggle along with them in their *decolletage*, only to have to battle afresh for their places in the vicious Hollywood pecking order—gives new meaning to the term 'compelling.' The reader, as if he were witnessing a particularly gore-drenched traffic accident, is incapable of looking away."

—New York Review of Books

About the Author:

Darwin Porter spent more than a half-century collecting anecdotes and interviews with virtually everyone ever associated with the Gabors, including a gaggle of Hungarian and Viennese eyewitnesses who remembered the Gabors before their American debuts. **Jolie Gabor**, the trio's mother, was a frequent guest within Porter's home in New York City, and for a period of three years, the Austrian-born cabaret singer, **Greta Keller** (Jolie Gabor's best friend and each of the three sisters' godmother) was a semi-permanent resident there. Jolie and Greta, "two shrewd and hard-nosed battleaxes from the mine fields of Old Europa," are included among the many sources which contributed to the hundreds of never-before-published revelations which permeate this astonishing triple biography.

Softcover, 730 pages, with hundreds of photos, ISBN 978-1-936003-35-8
ALSO AVAILABLE FOR E-READERS

INSIDE LINDA LOVELACE'S DEEP THROAT

DEGRADATION, PORNO CHIC, AND THE RISE OF FEMINISM

DARWIN PORTER

"THIS BOOK IS A WINNER!" An insider's view of the unlikely heroine who changed the world's perceptions about pornography, censorship, and sexual behavior patterns forever

The Beach Book Festival's Grand Prize Winner: "Best Summer Reading of 2013"
Runner-Up to "Best Biography of 2013" *The Los Angeles Book Festival*
Winner of a Sybarite Award from HedoOnline.com

"This book drew me in..How could it not?" Coco Papy, *Bookslut.*

A Bronx-born brunette, the notorious Linda Lovelace was the starry-eyed Catholic daughter in the 1950s of a police officer who nicknamed her "Miss Holy Holy." Twenty years later, she became the most notorious actress of the 20th century.

She'd fallen in love with a tough ex-Marine, Chuck Traynor, and eventually married him, only to learn that she had become his meal ticket. He forced her at gunpoint into a role as a player within hardcore porn, including a 1971 bestiality film entitled *Dogarama.*

Her next film, shot for $20,000, was released in 1972 as *Deep Throat.* It became the largest grossing XXX-rated flick of all time, earning an estimated $750 million and still being screened all over the world. The fee she was paid was $1,200, which her husband confiscated. The sexy 70s went wild for the film. Porno chic was born, with Linda as its centerpiece.

Traynor, a sadist, pimped his wife to celebrities, charging them $2,000 per session, It became a status symbol to commission an "individualized" film clip of Linda performing her specialty. Clients included Elvis Presley, Frank Sinatra, Milton Berle, Desi Arnaz, Marlon Brando, William Holden, Peter Lawford, and Burt Lancaster. The Mafia had found its most lucrative business—pornography—since Prohibition.

After a decade of being assaulted, beaten, and humiliated, Linda, in 1980, underwent a "Born Again" transformation. She launched her own feminist anti-pornography movement, attracting such activists as Gloria Steinem, and scores of other sex industry professionals who refuted their earlier careers.

Critics claimed that Linda's *Deep Throat* changed America's sexual attitudes more than anything since the first Kinsey report in 1948, that she super-charged the feminist movement, and that to some degree, she re-defined the nation's views on obscenity.

The tragic saga of Linda Lovelace changed beliefs about entertainment, morality, and feminism in America. This book tells you what the movie doesn't.

Darwin Porter, author of some twenty critically acclaimed celebrity exposés of behind-the-scenes intrigue in the entertainment industry, was deeply involved in the Linda Lovelace saga as it unfolded in the 70s, interviewing many of the players, and raising money for the legal defense of the film's co-star, Harry Reems. In this book, emphasizing her role as a celebrity interacting with other celebrities, he brings inside information and a never-before-published revelation to almost every page.

INSIDE LINDA LOVELACE'S DEEP THROAT
The Most Comprehensive Biography Ever Written of an Adult Entertainment Star
and Her Relationship with the Underbelly of Hollywood
Softcover, 640 pages, 6"x9", with hundreds of photos. ISBN 978-1-936003-33-4

PAUL NEWMAN
The Man Behind the Baby Blues, His Secret Life Exposed

Darwin Porter

Drawn from firsthand interviews with insiders who knew Paul Newman intimately, and compiled over a period of nearly a half-century, this is the world's most honest and most revelatory biography about Hollywood's pre-eminent male sex symbol.

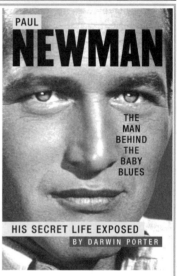

If you're a fan of Newman *(and who do you know who isn't)* you really should look at this book. It's a respectful but candid cornucopia of once-concealed information about the sexual and emotional adventures of an affable, impossibly good-looking workaday actor, a former sailor from Shaker Heights, Ohio, who parlayed his ambisexual charm and extraordinatily good looks into one of the most successful careers in Hollywood.

Whereas the situations it exposes were widely known within Hollywood's inner circles, they've never before been revealed to the general public.

But now, the full story has been published, as recorded by celebrity chronicler Darwin Porter—the giddy heights and agonizing crashes of a great American star, with revelations and insights never before published in any other biography.

ABOUT THE AUTHOR: "There are guilty pleasures. Then there is the master of guilty pleasures, Darwin Porter. There is nothing like reading him for passing the hours. He is the Nietzsche of Naughtiness, the Goethe of Gossip, the Proust of Pop Culture. Porter knows all the nasty buzz anyone has ever heard whispered in dark bars, dim alleys, and confessional booths. And lovingly, precisely, and in as straightforward a manner as an oncoming train, his prose whacks you between the eyes with the greatest gossip since Kenneth Anger. Some would say better than Anger."

—**Alan W. Petrucelli,** *The Entertainment Report*
Stage and Screen Examiner, Examiner.com

Paul Newman, The Man Behind the Baby Blues
His Secret Life Exposed

Recipient of an Honorable Mention from the New England Book Festival, this is the most compelling and unvarnished biography of Paul Newman ever written.

Hardcover, 520 pages, with dozens of photos. **ISBN 978-0-9786465-1-6.** Also available for E-readers

LOVE TRIANGLE
RONALD REAGAN, JANE WYMAN, & NANCY DAVIS
All the Gossip Unfit to Print / Available in November 2014

Most of the world remembers Ronald Reagan and Nancy (Davis) Reagan as geriatric figures in the White House in the 1980s. And it remembers Jane Wyman as the fierce empress, Angela Channing, in the decade's hit TV series, *Falcon Crest*.

But long before that, two young wannabee stars, Ronald Reagan and Jane Wyman, had arrived in Holly-hwood as untested hopefuls. Separately, they stormed Warner Brothers, looking for movie stardom and love— and finding both beyond their wildest dreams. They were followed, in time, by Nancy Davis, who began her career posing for cheesecake in a failed attempt by the studio to turn her into a sex symbol.

In their memoirs, Ronald and Nancy (Jane didn't write one) paid scant attention to their "wild and wonderful years" in Hollywood. To provide that missing link in their lives, Blood Moon's *Love Triangle* explores in depth the trio's passions, furies, betrayals, loves won and lost, and the conflicts and rivalries they generated.

A liberal New Deal Democrat, Reagan quickly became a handsome leading man in "B" pictures and a "babe magnet." Reagan himself admitted he developed *"Leading Lady-itis"* even for stars he didn't appear with. He launched a bevy of affairs with such glamorous icons as Lana Turner, Betty Grable and Susan Hayward, even a "too young" Elizabeth Taylor.

He eventually married Jane, but he was not faithful to her, enjoying back alley affairs with the likes of "The Oomph Girl," Ann Sheridan. Jane, too, had her affairs on the side, notably with Lew Ayres (Ginger Rogers' ex) while filming her Oscar-winning *Johnny Belinda*.

After dumping Reagan, Jane launched a series of affairs herself, battling Joan Crawford (for Hollywood's most studly and newsworthy attorney, Greg Bautzer); and Marilyn Monroe (for bandleader Fred Karger, marrying him, divorcing him, marrying him again, and finally divorcing him for good.)

Reagan's oldest son, Michael (adopted), later said, "If Nancy knew that one day she would be First Lady, she would have cleaned up her act." He was referring to her notorious days as a starlet in the late 1940s and early 50s, when the grapevine had it: "her phone number was passed around a lot." The list of her intimate involvements is long, including Clark Gable, whom she wanted to marry; Spencer Tracy; Yul Brynner; Frank Sinatra; Marlon Brando; Milton Berle; Peter Lawford; Robert Walker; and others.

Love Triangle, a proud and presidential addition to **Blood Moon's Babylon series**, digs deep into what these three young movie stars were up to decades before two of them took over the Free World.

LOVE TRIANGLE: Ronald Reagan, Jane Wyman, & Nancy Davis
All the Gossip Unfit to Print. Darwin Porter and Danforth Prince
A hot, scandalous paperback available in November, 2014. Biography/Entertainment 6" x 9" 500 pages with hundreds of photos   ISBN 978-1-936003-41-9

BLOOD
MOON
Productions, Ltd.